THE
SPANISH
CIVIL
WAR

HUGH THOMAS

THE SPANISH CIVIL WAR

HARPER COLOPHON BOOKS Harper & Row, Publishers
New York, Evanston, and London

FIRST HARPER COLOPHON EDITION *published* 1963 *by Harper &
Row, Publishers, Incorporated, New York, Evanston, and London*

LIBRARY OF CONGRESS CATALOG CARD NUMBER: 61-6177

CONTENTS

Book I – The Origins of the War

Book II – Rising and Revolution

Book III – European Embroilment

viii   CONTENTS

Book IV – The Siege of Madrid

Book V – The War in the North

Book VI – The War of Attrition
December 1937 – November 1938

Book VII – The End of the War

ILLUSTRATIONS

*These illustrations will be found
in a group following page 130*

Manuel Azaña, Prime Minister, later President of the Republic

Generals Franco and Mola at Burgos

One of Madrid's sacked churches

Manuel Azaña talks with Luis Companys, the Catalan leader

Indalecio Prieto, Socialist leader

Santiago Casares Quiroga, Prime Minister at the outbreak of
the Civil War

José Antonio Aguirre, President of the Basque Republic

The Foreign Legion advances

José Antonio Primo de Rivera, founder of the Falange

Ramón Serrano Suñer, Nationalist Minister

General Queipo de Llano, 'the Radio General', in old age

The People's Army on their way to the Front

Largo Caballero, Socialist Prime Minister of the Republic
1936–7

Juan Negrín, Republican Minister of Finance and Prime
Minister from 1937

Nationalist troops cross a bridge half destroyed by the Republicans

MAPS

PREFACE

The time has come when a study can usefully be made of the Spanish Civil War. In addition to the vast amount of reporting and pamphleteering produced at the time, much valuable material has been published which should cause a revision of many of the preconceptions once held about the war. Many of the leading actors have written their accounts of what happened. Others, mellowed by time, are willing to speak in the language of history to the dispassionate observer. A new and more objective general picture can now be formed, in place of that prevalent at the time. Of course, like all history, this picture is incomplete, shadowy, inadequate. New material will become available which may alter some of the judgements formed here. Yet even if every official paper bearing on the war in every country had been available to me, I do not know that I would gain a totally accurate impression of the subtle minds of, say, General Franco, and the Republican Prime Minister, Dr Negrín. And would a ton of military and other papers enable one to form a complete picture of what the war meant to the Spaniards?

A bibliography of the books and other matter which I have consulted in the preparation of this work is given at its conclusion. I must nevertheless here record my chief debts, both to books and to persons. In discussing the origins of the Civil War, I have relied heavily upon Señor Salvador de Madariaga's *Spain* (London 1942), Gerald Brenan's *The Spanish Labyrinth* (Cambridge 1943), a book of genius which illuminates the whole of twentieth-century Spanish history, Professor Alison Peers' *The Spanish Tragedy* (London 1936) and the *Historia de la Cruzada Española*, edited by Joaquín Arrarás (Madrid 1940–3, 35 volumes). For my account of the rising of 1936, *La Cruzada* has been once again invaluable. For the revolution which followed, on the Republican side, Frank Jellinek's *The Civil War in Spain* (London 1938) and Franz Borkenau's *The Spanish Cockpit* (London 1937) were of profound assistance to me. My account of the war itself would have been far more difficult had it not been for the following

general works: *Historia de la Guerra en España* by Julián Zugazagoitia (Buenos Aires 1940); the volumes in the *Survey of
International Affairs for 1936–39*, the joint work of Professor
Arnold Toynbee and Miss Katherine Duff (Oxford 1938 and
1948); *La Guerra de Liberación* by General José Díaz de Villegas
(Barcelona 1957); *Operaciones Militares de la Guerra de España*
by Luis María de Lojendio (Madrid 1940) and *Historia Militar
de la Guerra de España* by Manuel Aznar (Madrid 1940); the
last two of these books are, as their titles suggest, chiefly military
works. Mr Henry Buckley's *Life and Death of the Spanish Republic*
(London 1940) was an essential source of information. On
special aspects of the war, I was greatly assisted by Mr G. L.
Steer's *The Tree of Gernika* (London 1938) and by the careful
research of three American scholars: Mr D. C. Cattell, who
assembles a vast amount of material in his two works *Communism
and the Spanish Civil War* (Berkeley 1955) and *Soviet Diplomacy and
the Spanish Civil War* (Berkeley 1957); Mr F. J. Taylor, who
analyses the American interest in the war in *The United States
and the Spanish Civil War* (New York 1956); and Mr R. G. Colodny,
whose *Struggle for Madrid* (New York 1958) was of great help to
me in the construction of Book V of my own work.

I must also acknowledge the help of the following persons:
especially, in planning, Señor Adolfo Martín Gamero, Director-
General of the Office of Diplomatic Information in Madrid,
and his staff; Señor Ramón Serrano Suñer; Lieutenant-General
Martínez Campos y Serrano, Duque de la Torre; Mgr Angel
Herrera y Oria, Bishop of Málaga; Señor Manuel Fal Conde,
sometime head of the Traditionalist Communion; Señor Melchor
Ferrer, the distinguished historian of Carlism; Señor Pablo de
Azcárate, previously Ambassador in London of the Spanish
Republic, who has allowed me to use his own memoirs and
archives and has answered many questions which I have put to
him; Señor Jesús María de Leizaola, President of the Basque
Government in exile, who has also answered several of my
questions; Señor Manuel de Irujo, sometime Minister of Justice in
the Republican Government; General Emilio Herrera and
Señor Fernando Valera, respectively Prime Minister and Minister
of State of the Republican Government in exile, who have
also made available to me certain interesting documents; Señor
Julián Gorkin, sometime editor of the POUM newspaper *La
Batalla*; Señor Julio Álvarez del Vayo, Republican Foreign

Minister; Fr Alberto Onaindía, sometime Canon of Valladolid, who is such a mine of information on the history of the Spanish Church; Mr Luis de Ortúzar, sometime head of the Basque police; Señor Salvador de Madariaga; Mr Frank Jellinek, once correspondent of the *Manchester Guardian* in Spain, with whom I have enjoyed many conversations, and who has made available to me his own invaluable collection of primary material of the time; Dr and Mrs Kenneth Sinclair Loutitt; Mr Stephen Spender; Mr Peter Kemp; Mr Claud Cockburn; Mr Humphrey Hare; Mr Peter Kerrigan; Mrs Frances Cornford; Miss Margot Heinemann; Mr Arthur Koestler; Mr Miles Tomalin, who has shown me his diary of the period when he was a member of the International Brigade; Mr George Aitken, who has given me invaluable information on the time when he was Commissar of the XV International Brigade; Mr Fred Copeman; Mr Malcolm Dunbar; Mrs Thora Craig; Mr Bernard Malley; Mr Henry Buckley, Reuter's Correspondent in Madrid, who has allowed me to pick his brains remorselessly during my stays in the Spanish capital; The Viscount Dunrossil; Mr Giles Romilly; Mr Philip Toynbee; Lord St Oswald, who as Rowland Winn acted as Reuter's Correspondent on both sides during the Civil War; Mr George Palaczi-Horvath; Mrs Kitty Wintringham; Captain Noel Fitzpatrick, who has shown me his own memoir of the period when he was serving with the Spanish Foreign Legion; Mr Alec Digges, Secretary of the British International Brigades Association; L'Amicale des Voluntaires de l'Espagne Républicaine; Mr Richard Bennett; Mr Philip Noel-Baker; Mr Gerald Brenan; Señor José García Pradas, sometime editor of the Anarchist paper *CNT*; Señorita Federica Montseny, sometime Minister of Health in the Government of the Republic; and Mr V. S. Pritchett.

I must acknowledge in addition the help given to me by a large number of Spanish men and women during visits to Spain, especially during my tour of the principal battlefields of the war in 1959.

I am also most grateful to Mr James Joll and Mr Raymond Carr, of St Antony's College and New College, Oxford, respectively, who kindly read through this book at a primitive stage, and made many valuable criticisms and suggestions; to Mr Tom Burns, Mr Eric Hobsbawm and Dr Batista i Roca who have kindly read and commented on parts, or all, of the MSS in proof; to Mr I. J. McIntyre, for his assistance with certain works in Russian; to Mrs William Phipps, for her help with the pictures;

to the Hon. Vanessa Jebb for making the Index; to my publishers for a great deal of excellent advice, and for their patience and their incessant labour on the text; and to Mr James MacGibbon, who first suggested the project to me and who has at all times given me encouragement during its lengthy preparation.

AUTHOR'S NOTES

1] *Spanish place names:* The following Spanish place names have been anglicised:

Andalucía – Andalusia	Menorca – Minorca
Cataluña – Catalonia	Navarra – Navarre
La Coruña – Corunna	Sevilla -- Seville
Extremadura – Estremadura	Zaragoza – Saragossa
Mallorca – Majorca	

All other Spanish place names have been left in their original forms.

2] *References in footnotes:* Where only one work by an author is referred to as a source, the name only of the author is given. The full title of the work can be found in the Bibliography. Where two or more works by the same author are referred to, a short title of the work is given as well as the name of the author. Where more than one book by the same author is cited in the Bibliography but only one is referred to in the footnotes, that one is marked in the Bibliography with an asterisk. In the case of an edited book by several authors a short title only is given after the first mention: e.g. *Cruzada, Les Evénements Survenus.*

Acknowledgements

The following acknowledgements are due for the illustrations: To Wide World Photo Service of America for the portrait of Manuel Azaña; for 'Moscardó, Varela and Franco after the relief of the Alcázar'; 'General Yagüe entering Barcelona'; and 'Largo Caballero at the Front'. To Associated Press for 'Generals Franco and Mola at Burgos'; 'Nationalist troops crossing a bridge'; and 'The Foreign Legion advances'. To the Exclusive News Agency for the portraits of José Antonio Primo de Rivera, Ramón Serrano Suñer, General Queipo de Llano, La Pasionaria, André Malraux, Indalecio Prieto, and Santiago Casares Quiroga; for 'Manuel Azaña talking with Luis Companys'; and 'One of Madrid's sacked churches'. To the late Robert Cappa-Magnum for 'The People's Army on their way to the Front'; 'Death in Action'; 'A mountain bivouac of militiamen in the Sierra'; and 'Republican refugees on their way into France'. To the Keystone Press for the portraits of José Àntonio Aguirre, Juan Negrín, General Miaja with Major Attlee, General Mario Roatta, General Hugo Sperrle, and Ernö Gerö. To Miss Margot Heinemann for the portrait of John Cornford.

Acknowledgements are due to Mr W. H. Auden and Messrs Faber and Faber for permission to quote from his poem 'Spain'; to Mr. Edgell Rickword for permission to quote from his poem 'To the Wife of a Non-Intervention Statesman'; to Mr A. L. Lloyd for his translation of a poem by Miguel Hernández; to Librairie Gallimard for permission to quote from Claudel's *Aux Martyrs Espagnols*; to Mr C. Day Lewis and the Bodley Head for permission to quote from his poem 'Nabarra'.

Miaja, General José, *Republican General*

Mola, General Emilio, *Military Governor of Pamplona, Nationalist General*

Montseny, Federica, *Anarchist*

Negrín, Dr Juan, *Socialist*

Nin, Andrés, *member of the POUM*

Orgaz, General Luis, *Monarchist General*

La Pasionaria (Dolores Ibarruri), *Communist*

Prieto, Indalecio, *Socialist*

Primo de Rivera, José Antonio, *Falangist*

Queipo de Llano, General Gonzalo, *chief of* Carabineros *(customs guards), Nationalist General*

Redondo, Onésimo, *Falangist*

Rodezno, Count of, *Carlist*

Rojo, General Vicente, *Republican General*

Sanjurjo, General José, *Nationalist General*

Serrano Suñer, Ramón, *Falangist*

Varela, General José, *Nationalist General*

Yagüe, General Juan, *Nationalist General*

Some groups and political parties with their abbreviations and approximate English equivalents

CEDA (*Confederación Española de Derechas Autónomas*) – Catholic Party

CNT (*Confederación Nacional del Trabajo*) – Anarcho-Syndicalist Trades Union

FAI (*Federación Anarquista Ibérica*) – Anarchist Secret Society

JONS (*Juntas de Ofensiva Nacional-Sindicalista*) – Fascists

POUM (*Partido Obrero de Unificación Marxista*) – Trotskyists

PSUC (*Partido Socialista Unificado de Cataluña*) – The United Catalan Socialist-Communist Party

UGT (*Unión General de Trabajadores*) – Socialist Trade Union

UME (*Unión Militar Española*) – right-wing officers group

UMR (*Unión Militar Republicana*) – Republican officers group

PSOE   Partido Socialista Obero Español

BOOK I
THE ORIGINS OF THE WAR

I

PROLOGUE

The Cortes on June 16, 1936 – the Government of Casares Quiroga – Gil Robles speaks – the threats to democratic life – Calvo Sotelo – La Pasionaria – Calvo Sotelo's dispute with the Prime Minister

The Cortes, the parliament of Spain, stands halfway up the hill leading from the Prado to the Puerta del Sol.[1] Bronze lions cast from guns captured in the Moroccan Wars guard its doors. At the summit of its Corinthian columns, Justice hopefully embraces Labour on a granite pediment. Today, the gilded corridors and saloons of the Cortes are used only occasionally, when a few honorific dignitaries give formal assent to decrees issued by the Head of State. On June 16, 1936, however, this classical building was the centre of attention of all Spain.

Over five years had then passed since Alfonso XIII, last of the Bourbon kings, had abandoned the Spanish throne – to avoid, as he put it (somewhat exaggerating his own importance in the minds of his people) the disaster of a civil war. These had been five years of incessant parliamentary activity. Before the King left, there had been eight years, from 1923 till 1931, when, most of the time under the genial military dictator General Primo de Rivera, the Cortes had been as deserted as it is today. Now, in June 1936, parliamentary life in Spain seemed again likely to be destroyed.

An anxious group of middle-aged, middle-class liberals were gathered on the blue Government bench at the front of the semicircular debating chamber in the Cortes. Honest and intelligent men, they and their followers hated violence. They admired the pleasing, democratic ways of Britain, France and America. In both this hatred and this admiration, they were, however, alone among Spaniards of their time, solitary even among the four hundred other deputies sitting or standing around and above them, as best they could, in the crowded debating chamber.[2] Yet the men of this Government had a fanaticism of their own hardly

---

[1] The animated central square of Madrid where many revolutions have begun.
[2] The Cortes of the Second Republic had 473 members.

typical of the materially minded countries which they desired to
reproduce in Spain.

Observe, for example, the Prime Minister, Santiago Casares
Quiroga.[1] A rich man from Galicia, he had spent much of his life
calling for home rule for his own poor province, although the only
advantage the Gallegans could have gained from this would have
been a better rail service.[2] Although Casares seemed to act according to liberal, Wilsonian, principles formulated beyond the
Pyrenees, no one could have been more Spanish. He was a passionate liberal when the rise of organised labour caused liberalism
to seem as anachronistic as the liberals' foe of feudalism. Yet since
there had not been in Spain a middle-class revolution on the
model of that in France in 1789, one can hardly blame Casares
and his friends for their attitude. In the early years of the Republic,
in 1931 and 1932, the eyes of Casares Quiroga (then Minister of
the Interior) had appeared, to both friends and enemies, to burn
in his small head like those of St Just. Now they were marked by a
strange, ironic optimism, only explicable as a symptom of the
tuberculosis from which he was already suffering. How rightly did
Thomas Mann contend in *The Magic Mountain* that this disease
expresses the predicament of the liberal civilisation of which
Casares was the Spanish representative!

The nature of the crisis in Spain was laid publicly bare on June
16, 1936 by Gil Robles, the sleek young leader of the Spanish
Catholic Party, the CEDA (*Confederación Española de Derechas
Autónomas*). He recalled that the Government had had, since the
elections in February, exceptional powers, including press censorship and the suspension of all constitutional guarantees. Nevertheless, during those four months, 160 churches, he said, had been
burned to the ground, there had been 269 mainly political murders
and 1,287 assaults of varying seriousness. 69 political centres
had been wrecked, there had been 113 general strikes and 228
partial strikes, while 10 newspaper offices had been sacked. 'Let
us not deceive ourselves!' concluded Gil Robles, 'A country can
live under a Monarchy or a Republic, with a parliamentary or a

---

[1] A Spaniard's full name consists of his Christian name (or names), his father's
surname (also his own) and his mother's surname, placed in that order. Spaniards often
call themselves by all these names. They may drop their last name (that of their mother).
They will naturally never drop their father's surname. Casares Quiroga, for example,
might be referred to as 'Casares' but never as 'Quiroga'.
[2] This was admittedly necessary. It is a commentary on Spain rather than on
Galicia that autonomy seemed the only way to achieve it.

presidential system, under Communism or Fascism! But it cannot live in anarchy. Now, alas, Spain is in anarchy. And we are to-day present at the funeral service of democracy!' Angry cries broke out from all over the chamber, some in agreement, some in dissent.[1]

The conditions of the country and the *régime* were as grave as Gil Robles described them. In addition to the incessant crimes of violence, men at both extremes of the political spectrum were being drilled for actual fighting as military formations. 'All out on Sunday' was an instruction by a score of Spanish political leaders. Both Casares Quiroga and Gil Robles, representing the two groups which had dominated the history of the Second Republic, could themselves no longer control events. Both indeed were sustained in the Cortes by the votes of deputies whose aims were mainly different from their own. The elections of the preceding February had been contested by two alliances: the Popular Front and the National Front. The former had consisted, besides the middle-class liberals like Casares, of the large but internally divided Spanish Socialist party, of the small but cohesive Spanish Communist party, and of several other working-class groups. Behind the Socialist party itself, there was the powerful Socialist trade union, the UGT (*Unión General de Trabajadores*),[2] one of the best organised workers' movements in Europe. The National Front consisted not only of the CEDA, but also of the Spanish Monarchists, the Fascists of the Falange, and other middle-class parties. It could be regarded as the political front for all the forces of old Spain, the largest landowners of the south, the Army, as well as of the Church and the *bourgeoisie*. Some other middle-class parties who described themselves as the Centre also ran in those elections. Their near extinction showed how little the middle path appealed to Spaniards.

The Popular Front had gained the day in February 1936 though, by the quirks of the Spanish electoral law, their majority of seats in the Cortes was much greater than their total of votes cast would have strictly entitled them. But afterwards not all the parties which had shared in the electoral alliance took part in the Govern-

---

[1] This and succeeding speeches are taken from the *Diario de Sesiones de las Cortes Españolas*, 16.6.36. The translation of Calvo Sotelo's speech is that in *The General Cause*, 15 fl. The other translations are by the author. The figures in Gil Robles's speech were never contested by the Government and may be accepted as roughly, though not precisely, accurate. Many of these crimes had been committed by Gil Robles's late allies in the preceding elections, the Spanish Fascists of the Falange. See below, page 68.

[2] General Union of Workers.

ment. Indeed, the Government was composed exclusively of the liberal Republicans,[1] while it depended for its majority upon the working-class groups. This would never be a recipe for strong government. It was peculiarly unhappy in Spain in 1936, when the working-class parties themselves were in a perpetual state of revolutionary effervescence. And, apart from those groups who at least co-operated with the democratic system so far as to contest seats in the Cortes, there remained, outside, the great army of nearly two million Anarchist workers, chiefly in Andalusia or Barcelona, roughly organised in the CNT (*Confederación Nacional del Trabajo*), and directed by a secret society, the FAI (*Federación Anarquista Ibérica*). This huge, self-absorbed and passionate movement, already throbbing with anonymous violence like a great city at war, behaved as hostilely against the progressive Government of Casares Quiroga as it had done in the past against the Governments of the Right. And then there was the Army. Who in that early summer in Madrid had not heard rumours of plots by leading Generals, to establish 'order' or more simply a military dictatorship? Indeed, after Gil Robles had finished speaking in the Cortes, a Socialist deputy firmly declared that most of the churches had been burned by *agents provocateurs* to intensify the crisis, bring down the Government and justify just such a military rebellion.

The Socialists were bitterly divided among themselves. Some were liberal reformists. Some were intellectual Fabians. Some were passionate revolutionaries. Some were dazzled by the flattery of Communists, and some were aghast at the recent rise of Communist influence. But all could agree vociferously with the simple accusations levelled at the Right by their spokesman.

When their cheering had died down, the Monarchist leader, Calvo Sotelo, at last proudly rose. Like Casares Quiroga, he was a native of Galicia; but also, like Casares, he lacked the quiet dispassion for which that rainy region is celebrated. Had he gypsy blood? Was he as strong a man as his superbly handsome face suggested? All one knew for certain was that he was violent, eloquent and very able. On leaving the University of Saragossa in 1915, he was named private secretary to Maura,[2] the most high-

---

[1] The two purely Republican parties, the Republican Left and the Republican Union, were in fact joined by representatives of the Separatist parties of Galicia and Catalonia, which were, however, of much the same social origins as themselves.

[2] It was he who went into an election with the simple programme, '*¡Nosotros somos nosotros!*' (We are us.) The leading slogan of the opposition was equally laconic at that time, consisting merely of the exclamation '*¡Maura No!*'

minded and unbending Prime Minister of Alfonso XIII. Shortly afterwards, Maura made him Civil Governor[1] of Valencia at twenty-five. General Primo de Rivera gave him the Ministry of Finance at thirty-two. Prudently spending the first years of the Republic in Paris to escape the consequences of condemnation as an ally of tyranny, he returned to Spain only when the Republic had begun to founder. Elected to the Cortes as a Monarchist, he was in truth without doctrine, save a justified belief in his own administrative powers. The eclipse of Gil Robles was his gain. Already experienced and at the height of his powers, he acted as if he thought the future of Spain was inevitably in his hands.

The disorder in Spain, he said, in a speech punctuated by interruptions, was the result of the democratic Constitution of 1931. A viable State, he believed, could not be built upon that Constitution. 'Against this sterile State,' he went on, 'I am proposing the integrated State, which will bring economic justice, and which will say with due authority: "no more strikes, no more lock-outs, no more usury, no more capitalist abuses, no more starvation wages, no more political salaries gained by a happy accident,[2] no more anarchic liberty, no more criminal conspiracies against full production." The national production will be for the benefit of all classes, all parties, all interests. This State many may call Fascist; if this be indeed the Fascist State, then I, who believe in it, proudly declare myself a Fascist!'

When the ensuing storm of derision and applause had died down, he went on: 'When I hear talk of the danger from Monarchist Generals, I smile a little, for I do not believe (and you will grant me a certain' – he paused – '*moral* authority for this assertion), that there is, in the Spanish Army, a single soldier disposed to rise on behalf of a Monarchy and against the Republic. If there were such a person, he would be mad – I speak with all sincerity, mad indeed, as would be any soldier who, before eternity, would not be ready to rise on behalf of Spain, and against anarchy – if *that* should be necessary.'

The Speaker of the Cortes, the swarthy and square jowled Diego Martínez Barrio, requested Calvo Sotelo not to make such announcements, since his intentions could be so easily misunder-

---

[1] The provinces of Spain are administered by Civil Governors established in the various provincial 'capitals'. These are political appointments, under the Ministry of the Interior. The authority of the Civil Governor is shared by the commander of the garrison of the city in question, who is styled the Military Governor.

[2] All Ministers of the Republic were entitled to a pension.

stood. The Speaker was an experienced politician of obscure birth from Seville, who had been once briefly Prime Minister. Now he was leader of the so-called Republican Union party. He had hither-to represented in his political life with considerable success the idea of compromise. This was so rare in Spanish affairs that his enemies attributed his rise to his occult power as a Mason of the thirty-third grade.

With deliberation, the Prime Minister answered Calvo Sotelo: 'After Your Excellency's words, the responsibility for whatever happens will be yours. You come here today with two aims only: to condemn Parliament as impotent, and to inflame the Army, trying to detach units from their loyalty to the Republic. But I give my assurance. Parliament *will* work. The Army *will* do its duty.'

The most notable Spanish Communist, Dolores Ibarruri, known as 'La Pasionaria' (the passion flower), spoke next. Always dressed in black, with a grave but fanatical face which caused the masses who listened to her platform speeches to suppose her a kind of revolutionary saint, she was now about thirty-five. Years before, as a girl, she had been a devout Catholic. In those days, she had wandered from village to village in the Basque provinces, selling sardines from a great tray which she bore on her head. But Dolores la Sardinera married a miner from Asturias, one of the obscure founders of the Communist party in northern Spain. She transferred her devotion from Our Lady of Begoña to the prophet of the British Museum Reading Room. She became celebrated for her appeals to Spanish womanhood to bear sons without the encum-brance of husbands. The Right spread rumours that she had once cut a priest's throat with her own teeth. She was to become a great orator, and was already an artist in words and timing. But her personality was less strong than it publicly appeared since she was unrebellious in her adherence to the party instructions from Moscow. In the Cortes nevertheless she stood out as the only striking leader possessed by the Spanish Communist party, which was anyway very small. There were only sixteen Communist deputies, and outside in the country, the party possessed 30,000 members at the most.[1]

When she spoke in the Cortes on June 16, she dismissed the Fascists of Spain as mere gangsters. But was there not a 'Fascist International', directed from Berlin and Rome, which had already named a day of reckoning in Spain?

[1] See below, page 71.

A Catalan businessman, Ventosa, next expressed his alarm at the apparent optimism of the Prime Minister. Ventosa was the political lieutenant of Francisco Cambó, the greatest industrialist of Barcelona and probably the richest man in Spain. One heard it said that Cambó's wealth had already been transferred abroad. And the question was, was it wiser, from the point of view of the flight of capital, to seem hopeful or concerned? The Government could never decide. Meantime, Joaquín Maurín, leader of the semi-Trotskyist Marxist party known as the POUM,[1] announced that there existed already a 'pre-Fascist situation' in the country. Then Calvo Sotelo rose once more to answer the Prime Minister. 'My shoulders are broad,' he said, 'I do not shun, indeed I accept with pleasure, the responsibility for what I do . . . I recall the answer given by St Dominic of Silos[2] to a Spanish king: "Sire, my life you may take from me, but more you cannot take." Is it not, indeed, better to perish gloriously, than to live in contempt? But I, in turn, bid the Prime Minister to reckon up his responsibilities; if not before God, since he is an atheist, at least before his conscience, inasmuch as he is a man of honour.' He spoke then of the *rôles* of Kerensky and Karolyi, in delivering Russia and Hungary over to Communist Revolution. 'My honourable friend will not be a Kerensky, since he is not unconscious of what he is doing. He possesses full knowledge of what he conceals, and of what he thinks. God grant that he will never be compared with Karolyi, the conscious betrayer of a thousand-year civilisation!' Calvo Sotelo sat down. As he did so, the expected shouts and applause rang through the chamber.

The reverberations of this debate, with its threats and warnings, echoed all over Spain. They found their way to the President, Don Manuel Azaña, the embodiment of the Republic, gloomily watching the collapse of all his hopes from the rich loneliness of the National Palace.[3] They found their way to those Generals who for so long had been employing their ample leisure with tactical schemes for a military rising against the Government. They reached, too, to José Antonio Primo de Rivera, son of the old dictator and leader of the Spanish Fascists, the Falange, in his prison in the port of Alicante, whither he had been vainly sent as a hostage for the good behaviour of his followers. They reached to

[1] *Partido Obrero de Unificación Marxista.* See below, page 71.
[2] A local saint from near Burgos.
[3] Previously (and later) the Royal Palace.

that other group of Spaniards whose activities and aspirations lay
outside the Cortes, the Anarchists. They found their way indeed
to most of the twenty-four and a half million people who then
formed the population of Spain. The question implicit in all
minds, as the summer mounted, as the bull-fight season attained
its meridian, was: 'Will it be war?'

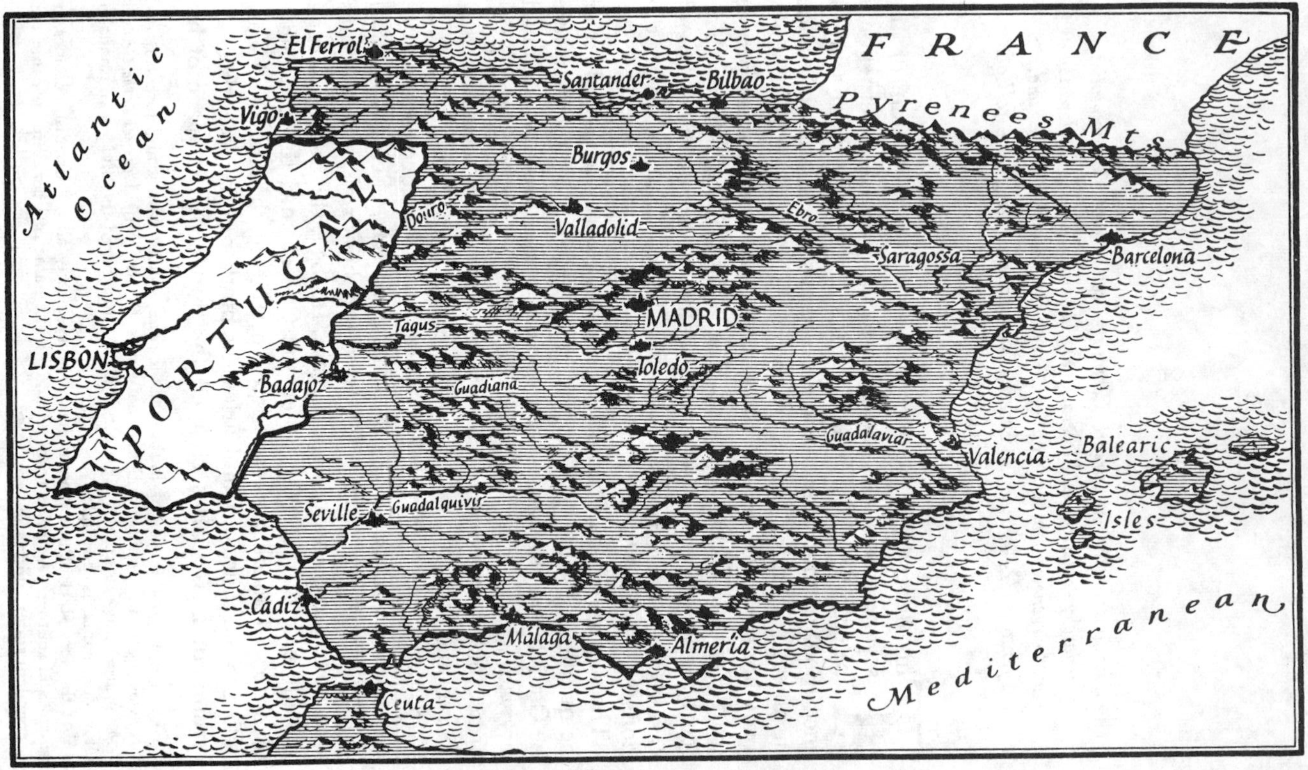

MAP I. THE PHYSICAL FEATURES OF SPAIN

2

Divisions of the Nineteenth Century – collapse of the absolutist Monarchy – clerical and liberal quarrels and wars – the Restoration and Regency – breakdown of the parliamentary régime under Alfonso XIII – Primo de Rivera's dictatorship – his fall – fall of the Monarchy (1931)

This debate in the Cortes was the culmination of the several passionate quarrels as to how Spanish society should be organised which had continued almost without a break since 1808. In that year, the enfeebled absolute monarchy made an abject surrender before Napoleon. The help of the British Army under the Duke of Wellington enabled the Spanish people to drive out the French in the ensuing War of Independence.[1] The Bourbons were brought back in the loathsome person of Ferdinand VII, briefly known as *El Deseado* (the Desired). But thereafter the Monarchy was no longer sacrosanct.

The succeeding half century was dominated by a struggle over the question of a liberal Constitution. The chief contestants were the Church and the Army, the two Spanish institutions which had survived with some credit from the War of Independence, the former being implacably conservative, the latter being mainly liberal and honeycombed with free-thinking Masonic lodges. Throughout, this quarrel was almost war.[2] In 1820, a group of liberal officers forced a Constitution upon King Ferdinand, who in 1823 brought in a French Army, the 'hundred thousand sons of St Louis', to do away with it again. In 1834, the quarrel turned into the first Carlist War, when the Church and the passionate advocates of local regional rights in the north and north-east rallied to the cause of Don Carlos, the brother of the recently dead Ferdinand. Don Carlos claimed the throne in the place of his

---

[1] There is no good reason to doubt that the rising against Murat and Joseph Bonaparte was a genuine popular and national rising. Fichte in his *Addresses to the German People* praised this example of 'a people in arms' and adjured the divided Germans to follow the Spaniards' example.

[2] At the very start of this gloomy half century, nearly all the Spanish colonies in central and southern America revolted and, in the name of liberalism, became the independent states which they are today.

infant niece, Isabella II, Ferdinand's eldest daughter. Isabella was championed by the liberals and the Army, both representing the claims of Castile to dominate the Peninsula. This conflict, which was part war of religion, part war of secession, was only ended in 1839, when the liberals won, though they did not gain an outright victory. All the rebel Carlist officers, for instance, were permitted to join the regular Spanish Army. Partly as a result (and partly because the confiscation of the Church lands in 1837[1] greatly reduced its immediate political power), the quarrel between liberals and clerical conservatives took the form thereafter of an incessant series of *coups d'état* (*pronunciamientos*) by one General after another, at one moment in the liberal interest, at the next in that of the conservatives. The *pronunciamiento*, usually causing a few deaths at least, became the customary way of changing Governments in the mid-nineteenth century.

This curious era ended in 1868, when Queen Isabella II, a nymphomaniac, was herself expelled by the greatest of Spain's liberal Generals, General Prim. If the occasion of her expulsion was her excessive reliance on her ultra-right-wing confessor, Father Claret, the real cause was a protest against the whole system of government over which Isabella had vaguely presided. However, the succeeding seven years were very confused. First, a brother of the King of Italy, the Duke of Aosta, was brought in as king as Amadeo I. He found Spain far too difficult to rule and therefore abdicated after a year. So the first Spanish Republic was proclaimed. Since all the regions of Spain were becoming not unnaturally restive under the misrule from Madrid, this was intended as a Federal Republic, in which all the provinces would have certain local rights. However, the group of enlightened intellectuals who had planned this arrangement in Madrid were powerless to prevent a general decline into chaos. In the north of Spain, the Carlists rose again under a grandson of the Old Pretender, and were generally supported by the Church throughout the Peninsula. In the south and south-east, many of the coastal towns proclaimed themselves totally independent societies. Once again, the Army took over power. While restoring order, the Generals decided that there was no alternative save to bring back the late Queen Isabella's young son, then a cadet at Sandhurst, as King Alfonso XII.

---

[1] The Church was compensated in cash – and in wages. For example, thereafter the village priests were paid by the state. See below, page 34.

There followed the thirty years of Spanish history known as the Restoration and the Regency. Alfonso XII died in 1885 at the age of twenty-eight, leaving a posthumous son Alfonso XIII for whom his mother, María Cristina, acted as Regent till 1902.[1] A nominally liberal Constitution had been promulgated in 1875 but this was incessantly abused by all politicians, whether liberal or conservative. Universal male franchise was nominally introduced in 1890. But the results of the elections were always faked through the agency of the local political bosses, the *caciques*. The mass of the people of Spain therefore came to look upon the parliamentary system as a means of excluding them from all political articulation.

This was one reason for the spread of syndical ideas throughout the working classes. By the time of the first World War, there existed in Spain two very powerful general trade unions, the first the CNT (*Confederación Nacional del Trabajo*),[2] dominated by the Anarchist ideas of Bakunin; the second, the UGT (*Unión General de Trabajadores*),[3] was Marxist, though reformist and Fabian rather than Bolshevist. The Socialists of the UGT collaborated with the *régime* so far as to seek election to the Cortes and, in the cities, where the *caciques'* manipulation of votes became increasingly difficult, they succeeded in gaining election. But for the Anarchists of the CNT, the *régime* was something unclean; and the violence, the murders and lightning strikes undertaken by the Anarchist militants from the 1890s onwards caused the Governments of the day to be in a state of permanent anxiety and turmoil.

Two main problems, however, caused the collapse of the Constitution established at the Restoration. The first was the question of Catalonia. The Catalans had always aspired to a certain recognition of their undoubtedly separate character from the rest of Spain. This had been one of the questions at stake in the Carlist wars. The 'Catalan question' would nevertheless not have become acute once more had it not been for the development of Barcelona as the centre of Spanish industrialism. Irritation with the incompetence of the central Government at Madrid, as well as with the high tariffs demanded by Castilian landowners to protect their wheat and olives, led the new rich of Barcelona at the turn of the

---

[1] It was during this period that nearly all the main actors of the Civil War between 1936 and 1939 were born. An old man of seventy in 1936 would have remembered the Carlist Wars of the '70s from his childhood. One of eighty might have taken part.

[2] National Confederation of Labour. See below, page 42.

[3] General Union of Workers. See below, page 25.

nineteenth and twentieth centuries to become Catalan Nationalists. The Catalan language, customs and artistic traditions were feverishly revived. This, together with the Anarchist faith of the workers and the demagogic atmosphere inculcated by the Radicals[1] made Barcelona at the turn of the century the wildest city in Europe. The ornate architecture favoured by the prosperous *bourgeoisie* was the lavish backcloth to a mounting series of Anarchist crimes. These years culminated in 'The Tragic Week of Barcelona' of 1909.

The Spanish Army had suffered an ignominious and crushing defeat at the hands of the Riffs, near Melilla. The Government ordered the Catalan reservists to Morocco in reinforcement. There ensued a week of rioting, in protest, at Barcelona. The riots had apparently no leadership and no aim, though it would seem probable that the Radical but anti-Catalan demagogue, Lerroux, did his best to stimulate the violence. Forty-eight churches and other religious institutions were burned. Drunken workers danced maniacally in the streets with the disinterred bodies of nuns. When the riots were quelled, the Catalan business men were generally ready to compromise with the central Government in the face of the new threat now presented by the working class. But the workers of Barcelona continued to lead their comrades in the rest of Spain in protests against the *régime* of King Alfonso. In 1917, a general strike, in which the Socialist and Anarchist trade unions co-operated, spread from Barcelona to the rest of the country. To the surprise of the strike leaders, the Army (which had itself been susceptible to syndicalist ideas and had seemed to be likely to align itself with the working class) was loyal to the King, and shot down the strikers. Despite incessant street fighting and indiscriminate murders by Anarchists and by *agents provocateurs*, Barcelona was ruled by martial law.

The second crisis for the *régime* derived from the Moroccan Wars in which the Spanish Army was tied down until 1925. A long, slow campaign culminated in the defeat of Anual in 1921, when King Alfonso XIII encouraged one of his field commanders, General Silvestre, to a rash action. A parliamentary enquiry was set on foot which, it was believed, would condemn both Monarch and Army.

By 1923, the Spanish parliamentary system was bruised almost to death. The Catalan and Moroccan questions, and the permanent

---

[1] See below, page 21.

threat presented by the Anarchist CNT (whose membership
already amounted to over one million, chiefly among the workers
of Barcelona and of Andalusia) were too much for the politicians of
the King. It was hardly to be expected that Alfonso should refuse
an ultimatum, presented in the nineteenth century style of *pronunciamiento*, by General Miguel Primo de Rivera, Captain-
General of Catalonia: 'We have reason on our side and therefore
force, though so far we have used force with moderation. If an
attempt is made to trick us into a compromise which our conscience
considers dishonourable, we shall demand greater penalties and
impose them with greater severity. Neither I, nor the garrisons
of Aragón from whom I have just received a telegram in support,
will agree to anything but a military dictatorship. If the politicians
make an attempt to defend themselves, we shall do the same,
relying on the help of the people, whose reserves of energy are
great. Today we are resolved on moderation, but on the other
hand we shall not shrink from bloodshed.'[1]

The dictatorship of General Primo de Rivera followed. It lasted
until January 1930. It was a curious period. 'My Mussolini', as
King Alfonso was alleged to have presented Primo to King Victor
Emmanuel of Italy. But the General was no Fascist. He possessed
neither a mass following nor an expansionist foreign policy.
Although he imprisoned those who protested against his rule (and
banned all political parties), there were no actual political executions during his seven years' power. An ambitious programme of
public works (roads and railways in particular) gave the *régime* an
air of prosperity. These were, after all, the boom years of the late
1920s. The financial policy of young Calvo Sotelo, the Minister
of Finance, gained for Primo the support of Spanish capital. With
the help of the French, the dictator brought to an end the running
sore of the Moroccan War, whose scandalous character (in both
direction and cost) had been the chief reason why he had come to
power in the first place.[2] Yet the dictatorship can only be measured
by the personality of Primo de Rivera himself. He was very patriotic, comparatively magnaminous and personally brave. Once he
entered a theatre and began to smoke, while notices everywhere

[1] From the document made public by Count Romanones in the Cortes during King
Alfonso's 'trial', December 1931.
[2] See below, page 59, for the effect of the Moroccan War on the Spanish Army. Mr
Brenan describes how in the year 1895 in one campaign against the Riff there had
been but one casualty among the Spanish Expeditionary Force: the Commander-in-
Chief. He had been killed by Primo de Rivera himself for trading arms with the enemy.

proclaimed that smoking was forbidden; on being informed of this prohibition, he rose and announced, cigar in hand, 'Tonight, everyone may smoke!' He would work enormously hard for weeks on end and then disappear for a *juerga* of dancing, drinking and love-making with gypsies. He would be observed almost alone in the streets of Madrid, swathed in an opera cloak, making his way from one café to another, and on returning home would issue a garrulous and sometimes even intoxicated *communiqué* – which he might have to cancel in the morning.

Primo de Rivera fell partly because of his contempt for the liberal and professional middle class of Spain, partly because of the slump of 1929 which caused the collapse of all those grandiose financial schemes which he had introduced. When even his finance minister, Calvo Sotelo, deserted him, he took the extraordinary step of addressing a telegram to all the garrisons of Spain announcing that he would retire if his brother officers declared against him. They did so, and he did retire. 'And now,' he remarked in the last of his famous *communiqués*, 'and now for a little rest, after 2,326 days of continuous uneasiness, responsibility and labour.' He left Spain and died a few months later in a second class hotel in the Rue du Bac in Paris, his last hours divided between brothel and confessional.

He left behind him no basis for any future *régime*. For a while the King attempted to govern as Primo had governed, through a directory of Ministers led by a General. However, there was no powerful section of Spanish society which now supported the throne. Many of the Army officers thought that the King had behaved dishonourably in accepting Primo's resignation. The Church was equivocal, with many of its most influential figures concerned (following the still Wilsonian mood of Pope Pius XI) to establish a democractic system if at all possible. Neither *bourgeoisie* nor lower classes had anything to hope for from a continuance of the Monarchy. In the autumn of 1930, a pact was signed at San Sebastián between certain Republican politicians and intellectuals, the Socialists (who had earlier collaborated with the dictatorship of General Primo de Rivera) and the advocates of Catalan regional rights. Three eminent intellectuals, Dr Marañón, Don José Ortega y Gasset and the novelist Pérez de Ayala, formed themselves into a 'Movement for the Service of the Republic'. Ortega wrote a famous article announcing, 'Spaniards! Your state is no more! *Delenda est monarquía!*' In December, a *coup d'état* on the old lines of the nineteenth century was prepared. The plotters issued the following statement: 'A passionate demand for Justice surges upwards from the bowels of the Nation. Placing their hopes in a Republic, the people are already in the streets. We would have wished to communicate the people's desires through the due process of Law. But this path has been barred to us. When we have demanded Justice, we have been denied Liberty. When we have demanded Liberty, we have been offered a rump parliament like those of the past, based on fraudulent elections, convoked by a dictatorship, the instrument of a King who has already broken the Constitution. We do not covet the culminating drama of a revolution. But the misery of the people of Spain moves us greatly. Revolution will always be a crime or an act of insanity when Law and Justice exist. But it is always just when Tyranny prevails.'

The sequel was swift. First, the garrison at Jaca, led by two zealous young Captains, rose against the King before the conspirators in the rest of Spain gave the word. Captured while marching their men in the direction of Saragossa, the two officers, Fermín Galán and García Hernández, were shot for rebellion. It was said that the King himself had interfered specially to prevent a reprieve. The indignation was great. When the civilian plotters were tried, they defended themselves by saying that the King had broken the Constitution in accepting Primo de Rivera as dictator. They were released after only a token term of imprisonment. Given the prevailing mood of opinion, the King found it impossible to refuse elections. Municipal elections were arranged therefore for April 12, 1931.

When the results of these elections began to come in, it became clear that in all the large towns of Spain the candidates who supported the Monarchy had been heavily defeated. The size of the Republicans' vote in cities such as Madrid and Barcelona was enormous. In the country districts the Monarchy gained enough seats to secure for them a majority in the nation as a whole. But it was well known that in the country the *caciques* were still powerful enough to prevent a fair vote.[1] By the evening of the day following the elections, great crowds were gathering in the streets of Madrid. The King's most trusted friends advised him to leave the capital without delay, to prevent bloodshed. After some hesitation Alfonso issued a dignified announcement: 'Sunday's elections

[1] The final figures of these elections were never published and were probably never even counted. At 2 p.m. on April 13, 22,150 Monarchists had been elected and 5,875 members of Republican parties.

have shown me that I no longer enjoy the love of my people. I could very easily find means to support my royal powers against all-comers, but I am determined to have nothing to do with setting one of my countrymen against another in a fratricidal civil war. Thus until the nation speaks, I shall deliberately suspend the use of my Royal Prerogatives.' With these grave and somewhat cryptic words, the last of the Bourbons drove away from Madrid to the coast and to exile.

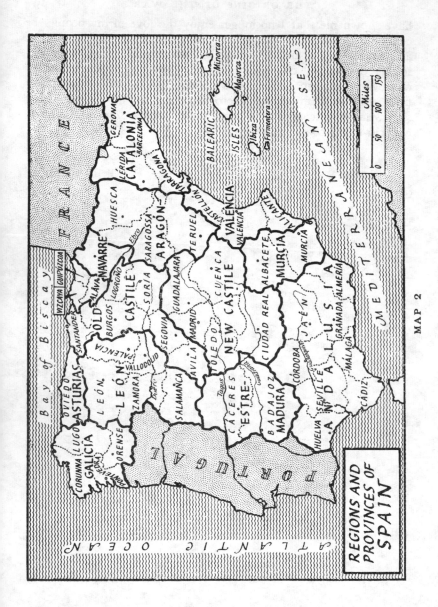

REGIONS AND
PROVINCES OF
SPAIN

MAP 2

3

The coming of the Second Republic – composition of its first Government – Alcalá Zamora – the Radicals – the pure Republicans – Azaña – the Institución Libre de Enseñanza *– Largo Caballero, Indalecio Prieto and the Spanish Socialists – the Esquerra and Catalan Nationalists – Cardinal Segura*

'This young and eager Spain has at last arrived at its majority,' exclaimed the happy Republicans rapturously in 1931. And after all, the Monarchy had been overthrown without bloodshed. A new Government had taken over the Ministries in Madrid with remarkable ease. The first Prime Minister of the Republic was Don Niceto Alcalá Zamora, a barrister from Andalusia with the flowery and nineteenth-century style of eloquence typical of that region. Once a Minister of the King before Primo de Rivera's dictatorship, he and others of his Cabinet were mobbed by wildly cheering crowds as they drove slowly through Madrid towards the Ministry of the Interior. Both Don Niceto and Miguel Maura,[1] who became Minister of the Interior and was therefore immediately responsible for the maintenance of order in the country, were Catholics. They could therefore be regarded as expressing the acceptance by at least a moderate section of the Spanish Church of the end of the Monarchy. Was it not rumoured after all that 'the village priests had voted for the Republic' in the famous municipal elections?

However, the other members of the first Cabinet of the Republic were all anti-clerical if not atheist. There were two members of the Radical party, which had risen to notoriety in Barcelona in the early years of the century. Alejandro Lerroux, ex-sacristan and ex-croupier, son of an Andalusian cavalry vet, the Radicals' founder and known in his youth as 'the Emperor of the Paralelo'

---

[1] A son of Don Antonio Maura, the leading conservative statesman of King Alfonso's reign, and brother of the Duke of Maura who had been a member of the King's last Cabinet until April 14. Miguel was regarded as the black sheep of this remarkable Jewish family until one of his nieces, Constancia de la Mora y Maura, married the Republican air chief Hidalgo de Cisneros, and became a Communist.

(the brothel district of Barcelona), was Foreign Minister of the Republic. Age, however, had cooled the passions of this corrupt demagogue. He was no longer the man who had called in 1905 on his followers from the slums of Barcelona to rise against their employers and the Church: 'Young barbarians of today! Enter and sack the decadent civilisation of this unhappy country! Destroy its temples, finish off its gods, tear the veil from its novices and raise them up to be mothers! Fight, kill and die!'[1] Yet the Church could not know that Lerroux would become almost respectable once he had gained power. His inclusion in the Cabinet, together with his moderate lieutenant, Diego Martínez Barrio, the arch-Mason from Seville,[2] caused the greatest anxiety in the Spanish hierarchy.

There were, however, a more formidable group of anticlerical politicians than these two Radicals in the first Ministry of the Second Republic. These were those middle-class or professional men who, representing thousands like them, were the direct heirs of all the nineteenth-century liberal reformers of Spain. They were the men of the Constitution of Cádiz of 1812 who had sought to destroy all the religious orders, all the great estates, all the bureaucratic restraints on mercantile or industrial freedom. They were also and especially men whose intellectual outlook had been formed by the *Institución Libre de Enseñanza* (Free Institute of Education), founded under the Restoration by a group of university teachers who had refused to take an oath of loyalty to 'Church, Crown and Dynasty' and were therefore deprived of their teaching posts. The state of mind inculcated by the *Institución* derived from the idealistic pantheism of the German Krause, whose lectures the first leader of the dissident teachers, Sanz del Río, had attended in Berlin. The *Institución* was thus at first antipolitical. But there has not yet been a period in Spanish history when the advocacy of free thought has been politically neutral. Reluctantly, therefore, through their love of intellectual truth, the men of the *Institución*, led by Professor Francisco Giner de los Ríos, were drawn into politics. They were also chiefly responsible for that limited renaissance of Spanish culture which had followed the loss of the last American colonies in the Spanish American

War of 1898.[1] Later, the spirit of the *Institución* moved those who were the most formidable intellectual opponents of the dictatorship of General Primo de Rivera.

These Republicans were represented in the new Cabinet of 1931 by several men. There was Fernando de los Ríos, a nephew of the founder of the *Institución*, himself an ex-professor at the University of Granada, technically a Socialist but, with his flowing and beautiful Castilian speech, above all a humanist and far too individual to be a very reliable member of any Marxist party.[2] There was Casares Quiroga, the Gallegan lawyer who was to be Prime Minister at the start of the Civil War.[3] He had been charged to tell the garrison of Jaca to delay their rising in 1930, but had arrived too late. There was the Jacobin Álvaro de Albornoz. There was the schoolmaster and educationalist Marcelino Domingo. And there was the new Minister of War, Manuel Azaña, who, though himself not actually an old pupil of the *Institución*, curiously completely reflects its effect. For had he lived in a happier country he might have given his life to literature. As it was, his brilliant translations from George Borrow, Bertrand Russell and Stendhal, an autobiographical novel about his schooldays, and a number of critical and polemical works are all that he left behind – save for a pile of speeches. For he was drawn into politics – in the tradition of the *Institución* – by the condition of his country. He was born in 1880 in a house between two convents in Alcalá de Henares, the crumbling ex-university and cathedral city twenty miles from Madrid, where Cervantes was born, and where the great Cardinal Ximénez de Cisneros was buried.[4] He lost his religious faith at the Augustinian college at the gaunt monastery of El Escorial. He then took a law degree and studied in Paris. He passed into the Civil Service, becoming chief clerk at the Registration Office (the Spanish equivalent of Somerset

[1] This was the celebrated 'Generation of '98' associated with men such as Miguel de Unamuno, Ortega y Gasset, Joaquín Costa the economist, Salvador de Madariaga, Antonio Machado, the publicist Ramiro de Maeztu, the novelist Pío Baroja, the essayist Azorín, the playwright Benavente who were the leading intellectuals in Spanish universities about the year 1898. Signor Garosci (in his remarkable essay in bibliography, *Gli Intellettuali e la Guerra di Spagna*, Rome 1959, p. 7) suggests an analogy between this group of intelligent Spaniards and the Russian liberals of Belinsky's generation described by Sir Isaiah Berlin.

[2] He left the Socialist party in 1934 to become incorporated in a smaller party of his own.

[3] See above, page 4.

[4] And where the Russian secret police would in the Civil War establish its headquarters.

House). Living alone either at Alcalá or in Madrid, carrying on literary work, translating here, reviewing there, Azaña seemed typical of many other middle-class intellectuals of the period – and not only in Spain. Typical also was his foundation of a Republican party which was (as typically) swiftly suppressed by General Primo de Rivera. Several things, however, marked out Azaña from others. First, he was ugly. His face seemed likely to burst open with its spots, and its heavy jowls of fat. His consequent self-consciousness led him to keep very much to himself, to subject himself to constant self-analysis in his writings and even in his speeches, to shun society (especially that of women), even to be scorned by his fellow-intellectuals – and, in consequence, to lay up within himself intellectual reserves which were to bring him to the leadership of Spain and which help to explain his lonely arrogance, shown in times both of victory and of defeat. Fastidious and sensitive to a degree, he was accused of being a homosexual.[1] This is a somewhat rare condition in Spain, and would explain the sometimes baffling secretiveness of Azaña's behaviour.[2] Yet one other point of difference in Azaña was that he was eloquent. He showed this first in many speeches at the Ateneo, the club in Madrid which had been the centre of liberal activity in Spain since the early nineteenth century. As a result, Azaña became connected with, and respected by, the other Republican leaders. He became the Ateneo's secretary and then founded a new Republican party of his own. Azaña became Minister of War in 1931 – mainly because no one else among the unmilitarily-minded liberals had troubled to inform themselves about the Army. Immediately Azaña sought in his speeches and conduct to imbue the new Republic with a dignity which only time could really have given it but which it needed immediately to be able to survive at all. An admirer of Cromwell and Washington, Azaña cultivated a superhuman detachment and an intellectual purity which led him to overlook the existing facts of Spanish life. Utterly unself-seeking, the enemies who quickly gathered were forced to personal insult in order to attack him. He was known to readers of right-wing papers as 'The Monster', because of his ugly face. Yet at times thousands were to regard him as the 'strong man of the

---

[1] There is a possibly apocryphal story which well illustrates his character. It was said that a journalist once asked Don Manuel how he had come to embark upon this sexual eccentricity. 'Just like you,' replied Azaña, 'asking questions.'

[2] He did, however, eventually marry, at the age of forty-six, the sister of Cipriano Rivas Cherif, his one-time collaborator on his literary magazine.

Republic'. Always marvellously eloquent, master of every subject on which he spoke, vacillating at critical moments, ironic in the face of disaster, given to bouts of dictatorial intransigence and optimism tempered by despair, he exactly reflects, like Léon Blum, the difficulties of an intellectual in politics.[1]

Apart from Fernando de los Ríos, there were two Socialists in the first Cabinet of the Republic. These were Indalecio Prieto and Francisco Largo Caballero. They represented in effect both the Socialist party and the Socialist general trade union, the UGT,[2] of which Largo Caballero was the Secretary-General. Founded by those Spaniards who supported Marx in his quarrel against the Anarchists,[3] the growth of both party and union had, until just before the first World War, been very slow. Neither could gain any foothold in the great industrial centre of Barcelona where the Anarchists were so powerful. Hence the Socialists found their chief strength among the typographers and iron-workers of Madrid, among the miners of Asturias, and in the industrial areas growing up in the Basque provinces around Bilbao.

In 1908 the UGT, a small ascetic union organised on the English model with paid officials and strike funds, still numbered only 3,000. Two developments stimulated membership. The first was the establishment throughout Spain of the *casas del pueblo*, Socialist club houses comprising the committee rooms of the local trade union branch, a free lending library and a café. The barracks of the Civil Guard, the church and the town hall were now accompanied in most of the whitewashed *pueblos* of Spain by a fourth building, also like them the outpost of a centralising idea but one combining revolutionary ideas with education. The second favourable development for the UGT was the Great War of 1914–18, which brought both greater prosperity to Spain, greater political consciousness and greater interest in the affairs of the rest of Europe. In 1920, the UGT numbered 200,000. Already by this time, the Socialists had sent a few members to the Cortes of the Monarchy and had abandoned their previous boycott of the *régime*. The next year the Spanish Socialist party formally severed

[1] There is as yet no biography of Azaña. There are valuable studies by the Socialist Julián Zuzazagoitia in his *Historia de la Guerra de España* (Buenos Aires 1940), 125–34, in Ramos Oliveira's *Politics, Economics and Men of Modern Spain*, 300, and also in Garosci, 89–109. A very hostile study is given by Arrarás in his introduction to Azaña's Memoirs.

[2] See above, page 5.

[3] See below, page 41.

all connections with the Russian Bolsheviks.¹ A small number of
Socialists left to found, with certain discontented Anarchists, the
Spanish Communist party, which remained, however, for a long
time, isolated and insignificant.²

In 1925, the venerable and incorruptible founder of the Spanish
Socialists, Pablo Iglesias, died. As a young man he had helped to
achieve the break with Bakunin in 1871 and ever since had shrewdly
and honourably led the party through innumerable vicissitudes.
His successor as leader of the party and Secretary-General of the
UGT was his chief lieutenant, Largo Caballero, an ex-plasterer
who had spent his life as a union official and as a conscientious and
hard-working member of the Madrid Municipal Council.³ He
was a man without great passion or talent for ordinary parliamentary procedure and was no public speaker. Nevertheless, it
was startling when he chose to collaborate (even if briefly) with the
dictatorship of Primo de Rivera as 'counsellor of state'. The
explanation was to be found in his morbid fear of losing ground to
his rivals in the working class, the Anarchists, who were still four
times more numerous than the Socialists. Certainly, this move was
not unsuccessful. The UGT had for a long time been respected
by the *bourgeoisie* for its discipline, its reasonable behaviour in
strikes (in contrast with the Anarchists) and its centralist flavour.⁴
As a result of its experience under Primo, there seemed a strong
possibility that it would develop into the type of official union that
exists in Scandinavia. It was certainly not surprising that Largo
Caballero should become the first Minister of Labour under the
Republic.

Indalecio Prieto, his colleague in the Republican Cabinet, was
a very different sort of Socialist. Born in Oviedo, he removed as a
child with his widowed mother to Bilbao, where he worked as a
newsboy. His quick brain attracted the attention of a Basque

¹ At first, the Socialists were, however, in favour of affiliation to the Comintern.
Before committing themselves finally they despatched Fernando de los Ríos to Russia
as a *rapporteur*. 'But where is liberty?' asked that bearded individualist from Andalusia.
'Liberty,' replied Lenin, 'what for?' (*La liberté? Pour quoi faire?*) Finally (though only
by 8,809 votes to 6,025) the Socialist party pronounced themselves against the Russian
connection.

² See below, page 71.

³ In 1905 Iglesias and Largo Caballero succeeded in being elected to the Madrid
Municipal Council for the first time by emulating the electoral frauds perfected by their
opponents. Iglesias entered the Cortes in 1911, and Largo Caballero and several other
Socialists followed in 1917.

⁴ The UGT continued to have a following of little more than 10,000 in Barcelona
until 1936.

millionaire, Horacio Echevarrieta, who made him first his private
secretary and later editor of his newspaper, *El Liberal de Bilbao*.
In 1918, Prieto was elected as a Socialist to the Cortes where his
easy eloquence attracted general attention – and the jealousy of
Largo Caballero. Thereafter, the antagonism between the two
was almost the chief characteristic of the Spanish Socialist party.
Prieto had become a rich man. Bald, fat, with a double chin and
small eyes, he seemed, and behaved, more as an enlightened
member of the upper classes than as a labour leader. He was a
member of the liberal club, the Ateneo. As a successful parlia-
mentarian, he opposed the Socialist collaboration in the Government of Primo de Rivera. Prieto was popular with the middle
class. But among the workers the sterner, more ascetic figure of
Largo Caballero always commanded more affection.

The only other member of the Republican Cabinet of 1931 was
a Catalan scholar (a distinguished classical historian), Nicoláu
d'Olwer. He was less of a professional politician than anyone
else in the Cabinet and his inclusion in it was intended to satisfy
the Catalan Nationalists that their interests would be considered.

Five of the members of this Government had one further
attribute in common: they were Freemasons and therefore suspected of anti-Spanish loyalties.[1]

In the nineteenth century, nearly all the Spanish liberals had
been members of one or other of the Masonic lodges which, though
first introduced into Spain in the eighteenth century, greatly
spread during the Napoleonic Wars. In the present century, progressive persons seem, in Spain and elsewhere on the Continent,
to have felt obliged to join a lodge largely as an act of protest.
Although they subscribed to the French revolutionary principles
of Liberty, Equality and Fraternity on their induction, Masons,
however, formed a club without any strong political policy, whose
members would help each other when it seemed appropriate. Yet
though without overt political purposes, Spanish Masonry was
actively antireligious as well as merely anticlerical.[2] Since to
disbelieve in God in Spain was an act with political consequences,

---

[1] Arrarás, *Historia de la Segunda República*, 53. The five were De los Ríos, Martínez
Barrio, Álvaro de Albornoz, Casares Quiroga and Marcelino Domingo. Azaña
apparently became a Mason early in 1932.

[2] It seems that there was a breach between English and Continental Masons in the
1880s, when the Continental brothers decided that they could no longer stomach any
reference to God, even under the name of the 'Supreme Architect', in the statutes of
their order.

churchmen and the Right Wing in general believed Masonry to be
a devilish international plot, organised in the City of London, and
designed to establish atheistic Communism. To the Jesuits,
Masonry seemed especially vile since its secret ways and rites
appeared a profane parody of their own order.[1] Such hostility, of
course, would be likely to increase the secretiveness of the Masons.
However, the Freemasons of Spain were unable even so to maintain any clear political front. The lodges were useful meeting
places for plotting against Primo de Rivera. But later, there were
certainly deep divisions within them. Some Generals such as Sanjurjo, Goded, Queipo de Llano, Fanjul and Cabanellas, who later
took prominent rôles against the Republic, were believed to belong
to a military lodge, many of whose members were, however, fervent
Republicans. The relation of Masonry to Marxism was also hotly
debated in the lodges throughout the period of the Republic. The
political rôle of the Freemasons cannot therefore be regarded as of
major political importance at this time in the history of Spain,
though some politicians such as Martínez Barrio obviously owed
much of their influence to their rank in the Masonic order.[2]

The problem of Catalonia was the first with which the new
Republic had to deal. The triumph of the anti-Monarchists in the
municipal elections in Barcelona had been even greater than
elsewhere. To be precise, furthermore, the victory there had
been gained by the Esquerra, a party whose name was the
Catalan word for 'Left'. Its leader was a very honourable and
personally delightful old Colonel named Francisco Macía, who
had spent the years of Primo's dictatorship plotting in France.
Its leader apart, the Esquerra was a party of small businessmen and of the lower middle class of Barcelona generally. It
was a political body very different, that is, from the Lliga,
the party of large businessmen who had revived Catalan
Nationalism in the late nineteenth century. By 1930, however,
the great Catalan industrialists had been frightened by the
Anarchist faith of most of the workers in their factories into
a tacit alliance with the right wing in Spain, and even with the
central governments in Madrid. Though not forsaking their

---

[1] Since many distinguished people became Masons who could not be accused of
being secret Communists, the clerical publicists are obliged to distinguish between those
who were blind instruments in the hands of 'the terrible brother' and those who knew
his dark purposes.

[2] There is a useful account of Spanish Freemasonry in La Révolution Espagnole vue par
une Républicaine, an account by a woman deputy of the Radical Party, Clara Campoamor.

advocacy of limited home rule for Catalonia, they had begun
hesitantly to see the rest of Spain as the best market for their goods
(as well as a source of raw materials) rather than as a hated drag
on their labour. Few economic motives entered into the reasons
of the followers of Colonel Macía and the Esquerra. They wished
to carry on their own affairs as much as they could. And when the
Esquerra municipal councillors who had been elected on April
13 in Barcelona came out on to a balcony in the great Plaza de
San Jorge, there were heard not only the *Marseillaise* and *Els
Segadors*, the Catalan national song, but also cries for an independent
Catalan Republic. And when Luis Companys, Macía's lieutenant, a subtle, dapper young lawyer (who had gained a considerable reputation in the early 1920s for defending Anarchists
for nugatory or non-existent fees) proclaimed the Republic in
Barcelona, he proclaimed it as 'the Catalan Republic'. For a day
or two it seemed indeed that Catalonia might become an independent State. So Nicoláu d'Olwer, de los Ríos and Marcelino
Domingo made a hasty visit to Barcelona to persuade Colonel
Macía and the Esquerra to await the passage of a Catalan
statute of home rule by the new Cortes (which would shortly be
elected). And Colonel Macía reluctantly agreed, although the
city of Barcelona was in his hands.

The honeymoon period of the new Republic lasted under a
month. During this time, the Republic was caricatured in the
Press as *la niña bonita*, the pretty girl, in the style of the apparently
happy Marianne north of the Pyrenees. The Government made
plans for an election in June which would establish a provisional
Cortes. This would approve a Constitution and pass the laws
necessary to implement the Constitution. Meanwhile, the Royal
flag of red and gold was changed for a tricolour, the National
Anthem was altered from the Royal March to the Hymn of
Riego, and many streets were rechristened with Republican-
sounding names.

The enemies of the Republic were, however, already gathering.
The first shot in the contest which was to continue until the Civil
War was the grave but violent pastoral letter of Cardinal Segura,
Archbishop of Toledo and Primate of the Spanish Church, made
public at the beginning of May. This proud and uncompromising
prelate combined intelligence with intense fanaticism. A bishop
at 35, he had been translated from his wild Estremaduran diocese
by the special intervention of the King. He was a scholar who

boasted of three doctorates, and when he undertook social
work once a year he worked as hard as a parish priest. In 1931
he was still under fifty and at the height of his powers. His pastoral
letter began with a eulogy of Alfonso XIII and ended with these
threatening words: 'If we remain "quiet and idle", if we allow
ourselves to give way to "apathy and timidity"; if we leave open
the way to those who are attempting to destroy religion or if we expect the benevolence of our enemies to secure the triumph of our
ideals, we shall have no right to lament when bitter reality shows
us that we had victory in our hands, yet knew not how to fight like
intrepid warriors prepared to succumb gloriously.'[1]

[1] *El Sol*, 7.5.31. Quoted Peers, *The Spanish Tragedy*. 'Quiet and idle'; 'apathy and
timidity' were phrases used in an encyclical of Leo XIII.

4

*The Church in Spain in 1931 – its rôle in Spanish history – the
Church and education – relations with the Vatican – El Debate*

The Church in Spain in the 1930s numbered 20,000 monks,
60,000 nuns and 31,000 priests. There were nearly 5,000
religious communities, of which about 1,000 were male,
the rest female.[1] It was estimated by moderate Catholics that
two-thirds of the Spaniards in the 1930s were not practising
Catholics – that is, that though they might use churches for
baptisms, weddings and funerals, they never confessed or went
to Mass. According to the Dominican Fr Francisco Peiró, only
5% of the rural population of New Castile carried out their Easter
duties in 1931. In some villages of Andalusia, only 1% of men
attended church.[2] In some villages the priest said mass alone. In
the rich parish of San Ramón, in Madrid's suburb of Vallecas,
90% of those educated in religious schools did not confess or
attend mass after leaving school.[3] Though figures cannot easily be
found for the whole of Spain, these quoted give statistical support
to the unwise remark of Manuel Azaña that Spain had 'ceased
to be Catholic'.[4]

In fact (as one can see from reading his whole speech), Azaña
meant that Spain was no longer totally Catholic, as she had been,
for instance, in the golden sixteenth century.[5] At that time the
Church alone had linked the various provinces, which otherwise

[1] Spanish Geographical Institute 1930. Quoted by Jellinek, 46–7.
[2] Spanish women are certainly more religious than their husbands.
[3] Quoted Brenan, *Spanish Labyrinth*, 53.
[4] *Diario de Sesiones*, 13.10.31. If Azaña had said that Spain had ceased to be clerical
he would have been more accurate.
[5] Before 1500, the position of the Church was hardly very different from that elsewhere in Europe. Though Spain's mediaeval history is often represented as a continuous
crusade, religious intolerance was exceptional before the fifteenth century. Moors,
Christians and Jews lived together in conditions of mutual respect. The great mediaeval
hero El Cid was an opportunist who allied with Islam against his Christian king in
Castile.

maintained separate parliaments, courts and civil services. The Spanish Inquisition, instituted as the tribunal of religious orthodoxy, was the only legal body to be respected throughout the land. At the same time, there was a great outburst of religious enthusiasm. This partly derived from the final triumph of the *Reconquista* with the conquest of Granada in 1492. Partly it was the fruit of the conquests beginning to be made by Spaniards, in the name of the Church, in America in the same extraordinary year. Partly it was caused, as it was sustained, by the clerical reforms carried out by Cardinal Ximénez de Cisneros in time to avoid in Spain the possibility of a Protestant Reformation. This religious enthusiasm itself gave support to the plans of the new Habsburg kings who succeeded to the Spanish throne by marriage. Financed by the wealth brought by the American colonies, these princes sought to realise a Catholic cultural and political unity in Europe never achieved anywhere, even at the height of the Middle Ages. The powerful Spanish armies were used in a new attempted *Reconquista* – that of Europe from the Protestants and the Mediterranean from the Turks. The Spanish king proudly buckled on the temporal sword of the Counter Reformation, while the Society Jesus, founded by the Basque Ignatius and always retaining Spanish characteristics, became its theological leaders.

The golden century of Spain, therefore, when that country joined forever the ranks of those which have been once, however briefly, the greatest on earth, was also the apogee of the Spanish Church. And, while the Church was the link binding the nation together geographically, it also did so socially. Others attributed the prowess of Spanish arms to the easy relationship between officers and men, who customarily dined together in the same mess. At this time noblemen would often serve as privates in the Army. Like the development of good relations between the Spanish colonists and the natives in America, this democratic spirit must be ascribed to the Church, whose egalitarian teaching was then sincerely observed in Spain. Spanish theologians were freed by the absence of a Reformation from the endless arguments about forms of service which then wearied the north of Europe. They therefore could discuss, in notably modern terms, the relations between citizen and society, and even argue as to the desirability of a more equal distribution of land. The sense of national purpose and social unity, for which the Church was mainly responsible, was finally demonstrated in the great flowering of Spanish literature and painting which lasted until the middle of the seventeenth century.

All nations, however, are forever scarred by the epoch when they have been great. Great nations customarily decline for the same reasons which earlier raised them above others. The bastard-mediaeval aspirations of the Habsburgs exhausted the treasury. The Spanish Church's hostility to commerce, in addition to the ease with which gold and silver could be imported from America, completed the extinction of the economic vitality of Spain noticeable until the 1550s. Cervantes, writing when the economic consequences of the Spanish furious pursuit of grandeur were being already felt, made Don Quixote, the greatest character in Spanish literature, the archetype of the knight errant in search of vain and archaic glory; and the quixotic maintenance of a mediaeval set of standards and judgments in the new world of post-Renaissance Europe swiftly became the mark of the country which had been the first to reveal the real New World beyond the Atlantic.[1]

The very ideas of social justice preached by the theologians reinforced a pre-commercial outlook more reminiscent of scholasticism than anticipatory of Socialism. The intellectual decline of the Church continued, so that learned men in the greatest university of Spain, at Salamanca, were solemnly discussing, in the late eighteenth century, what language the angels spoke and whether the sky was made of winelike fluid or bell metal.[2] During these years there was hardly a single Protestant in Spain and hardly a single critic of the Church's hold over the mind of the nation.

In the middle of the eighteenth century, the ideas of the French *philosophes* began to be popular at the court of the Spanish Bourbons. The liberal reformers opposed all feudal survivals as much as the Church. But, after the collapse of the Bourbons in the Napoleonic Wars, the Church, gaining popularity from its championship of the opposition to Napoleon, became the centre of resistance to liberal ideas. Its most violent protagonists grouped themselves into the Society of the Exterminating Angel. The Carlist War

---

[1] Spain possessed, until the eighteenth century, the largest empire in the world. But Spanish culture became, like the customs of the court, over-formal, and vanished altogether after the death of Velázquez in 1660. The free institutions of the provinces, once the most living of Spanish things, decayed under the dead hand of the bureaucracy of the Habsburgs and their Bourbon descendants.

[2] Quoted by Brenan, *Spanish Labyrinth*, 55.

followed. During this period the low level of clerical intellect persisted: hardly a single work of theology was published in Spain in the first thirty years of the century.[1]

The liberals' greatest success was to disentail the Church lands in 1837. Though the Church later received compensation, this was in cash and capital. The land could not be repurchased from the middle-class speculators who had bought it up. Henceforth, though the Church maintained an implacable opposition to liberal ideas, its hold over the working classes in the country was much reduced.

The development of the ideas of the *Institución Libre de Enseñanza* in the late nineteenth century coincided with a new expansion of the power of the Roman Church. The losing battle which Rome had fought in France, Germany and Italy in the last quarter of the nineteenth century caused the elaboration of a policy to keep at least one country – Spain – 'safe from liberal atheism'. A great burst of religious building followed, with the consolidation of the Church's wealth in Spanish capital. The Jesuits in particular were believed to hold vast fiefs in the gradually increasing wealth of the country, in all sorts of concerns, from antique-furnishing businesses to, later, dance halls and cinemas. The interpretation put by the Spanish Church upon the modernising encyclicals of Popes Leo XIII and Pius XI was, indeed, that they permitted the accumulation of clerical capital. The saying 'money is very Catholic'[2] became almost a proverb. In the Church Catechism published in 1927, the question, 'What kind of sin is committed by one who votes for a liberal candidate?' elicited the answer, 'Generally a mortal sin.' But the answer to 'Is it a sin for a Catholic to read a liberal newspaper?' was, 'He may read the Stock Exchange News.'[3] Meantime, while the liberals in the nineteenth century had freed the universities from the control of the Church, certain orders, especially the Jesuits and the Augustinians, had retaliated by establishing secondary schools of a public school type (such as that at El Escorial, where Azaña was educated). There the humanities were badly taught but there was a high standard of technical education. The State might claim to provide primary education free to all (theoretically) from 1901 onwards. But the schoolmasters were mainly Catholics and children spent much time saying the rosary. These schools were far too few – in

[1] Menéndez Pidal, *The Spaniards in their History*, 261 fl. Brenan, *The Spanish Labyrinth*, 44 fl.   [2] *El dinero es muy católico*.   [3] Quoted Trend, 61.

1930 in Madrid alone there were 80,000 children who did not go to school. But through its influence over the schools which did exist, the Church was able to maintain its power over the young Spaniards.

Yet Cardinal Segura, when he made his unmistakable attack on the Republic in May 1931, did not speak for all his flock. The political feelings of the Spanish Church were too subtle and too contradictory to be summed up in one strong letter. Many members of the hierarchy and the orders might be as actively Monarchist as the Primate, though through fear of what was to come rather than from loyalty to what had passed away. But the group of intellectual Catholics who wrote for the Madrid newspaper *El Debate* (owned by the Society of Jesus) clearly favoured a liberal Catholicism which would perhaps capture the urban proletariat for the Church, or at least make some concession towards democracy. Cardinal Segura had denounced *El Debate* as a 'liberal sheet'. Thus no clear statement could be made of the political attitude of the Church as such. It was true, certainly, that since the confiscation of ecclesiastical lands in 1837 the orders and the hierarchy had been capitalists and friends of capitalists. But many individual monks and most priests (except for those in fashionable quarters of large cities) received as small a stipend as their parishioners.[1] The hierarchy was accurately regarded as the ally of the upper or *bourgeois* classes. But the village priest, and even the priest in a poor part of a big town, was usually regarded as a comparatively amiable counsellor, one who could, sometimes with success, intervene with the authorities on behalf of the oppressed.[2] The Spanish working class, however, were maddened when a priest openly showed himself hypocritical, by flagrantly contradicting Christ's teaching on poverty or showing himself a respecter of well-born persons. Then no fate would be too unpleasant for the priest, and his church would be in danger of fire. Even in their most sacrilegious and blasphemous moments the Spanish workers thus showed themselves passionately concerned about religion.

It was always rare for villagers to wish to kill their own priest or to burn his church unless he was known as a hypocrite or a friend of the *bourgeoisie*. In these circumstances, the act would often be left

---

[1] This, of course, helped to maintain their low intellectual level.

[2] This was specially the case in the Basque provinces of the north of Spain. See below, page 52.

to people who might come in from other *pueblos*. It was certainly uncommon for Spaniards to burn a local Virgin or a local church. In the famous procession in Seville during Holy Week, the escort of a Virgin from a poor parish would glare with ferocity at the Virgin from a rich Church in a fashionable quarter. The Archbishop of Seville himself remarked that 'these people would be ready to die for their local Virgin, but would burn that of their neighbours at the slightest provocation.'[1]

These paradoxes reflect the fact that, despite its decline, its frequent ignorance and its intermittent corruption, the Spanish Church – due to its pre-eminent position when Spain was great – remained until the twentieth century the embodiment of the Spanish nature. When the Church declined, the chief unifying force in the country lost its vitality also. Spain therefore fell apart both geographically and socially. Partly due to the profound penetration of the Roman Catholic religion into the nature of the people, all the inevitable disputes which succeeded were carried on with a peculiar and uncompromising intensity. And all parties to these disputes aspired to that total national and exclusive position which in Spain has only ever been possessed by the Church.[2]

There is no doubt that the Spanish Church in the twentieth century embarrassed the Vatican. Pope Pius XI was still in 1931 in his most enthusiastic Wilsonian mood. He may be supposed to have been at least as realistically liberal as the Madrid writers on *El Debate*. His Secretary of State, Eugenio Pacelli, was already toying with those ideas for Christian democratic parties which he brought to more successful fruition when Pope (as Pius XII) after the second World War. When the new Spanish Republican Government (headed by the progressive Catholics Alcalá Zamora and Miguel Maura) demanded the removal of Cardinal Segura from Toledo, the Vatican went to no trouble to help the Primate, who was accordingly asked to leave the country. He did so, and his reputation was not enhanced when a few months later he returned without passing a customs post. He got as far as Guadalajara before being apprehended. The Government then escorted him once more from the country, under guard. He did not return to

[1] To Father Alberto Onaindía who has reported the remark to me.
[2] Even the Spanish Fascists of the Falange (see below, page 69) looked backwards in Spain to the age of the Catholic kings, whose symbol, the yoke and the arrows, they took as their own.

Spain until after the start of the Civil War. Meantime, Monsignor Gomá, a scholar who had been Bishop of Tarazona, succeeded him as Archbishop of Toledo.[1]

[1] However, the Vatican shortly quarrelled with the Republic by refusing to accept the Ambassador which the Government had named for the Holy See. Cardinals Gomá and Segura met on July 23, 1934 in France and had a curious discussion, in which they agreed Pope Pius XI was a man 'without affection, cold and calculating', who had too much sympathy for Catalonia and was being misled by Angel Herrera and Cardinal Vidal y Barraquer, the Archbishop of Tarragona. Iturralde, I 265. For interesting speculations that Angel Herrera and Mgr. Tedeschini, the papal Nuncio, actually encouraged the expulsion of Segura, see Iturralde, I 344 fl.

5

The riots of May 1931 — the burning of the churches — the Monarchists' plots — character of Spanish Anarchism

Meantime, on Sunday, May 10, 1931, within a few days of the publication of Cardinal Segura's bombshell, a group of army officers and aristocrats thought to be specially loyal to King Alfonso were observed gathering in a house in the Calle Alcalá, one of the main streets in Madrid.[1] Nominally, they were merely founding the Independent Monarchist Club. But the Royal March was played on a gramophone. A crowd gathered. Two Monarchists who arrived late were delighted by the number of people in the street and shouted *!Viva la Monarquía!* Their taxi driver firmly replied by crying *¡Viva la República!* The Monarchists struck the driver, and a rumour immediately spread that they had killed him. The crowd became infuriated and set fire to several motor cars of the Monarchists attending the meeting inside. In a moment, the number of people in the street seemed to increase one hundredfold. An angry crowd set out for the offices of the Monarchist paper *ABC*, which they proceeded to burn. The Civil Guard[2] dispersed the rioters by firing over their heads. The next day, however, the riots took a new lease of life. The Jesuit Church in the Calle de la Flor, in the very centre of Madrid, was razed to the ground, in the middle of the morning. On its brown and burned walls, the words 'The Justice of the People on Thieves' was chalked up in bold letters.[3] Several other churches and convents in Madrid were also burned during the day.[4] Within a few days the fires had spread to Andalusia, especially to Málaga. There was widespread alarm all over Spain. No one had actually

[1] This runs from the Puerta del Sol to merge with the Gran Vía just before the Plaza de la Cibeles. In the 'thirties, this was the main café street of Madrid. There was a bull-fighters' café, a writers' café, an artists' café, an actors' café and so on. In 1960, these cafés have given way to large banks.

[2] See below, page 48.

[3] Fernsworth, 131.

[4] All religious houses in Spain, whether lived in by monks or nuns, are known as *'conventos'*.

died, though several monks escaped only just in time. Even so, the Republic was felt to have stained its record. The Government publicly blamed the Monarchists for provoking the riot and suspended not only *ABC* but also *El Debate*. The new Minister of War, Manuel Azaña, in the first of many rash *obiter dicta*, said that he preferred that all the churches of Spain should burn than that the head of a single Republican should be harmed.[1]

Some of those gathered in the house in the Calle Alcalá were definitely plotting an insurrection against the Republic. They did this without the approval of King Alfonso (then in Paris), who had encouraged his followers (including army officers) to serve the Republic.[2] Some days before he had given a dignified interview to *ABC* in which he had said: 'Monarchists who wish to follow my advice will not only refrain from placing obstacles in the Government's path, but will support it in all patriotic policies. High above the formal idea of the Republic or the Monarchy stands Spain.'[3] Though no doubt he saw this method as the best means of being able to return to the Spanish throne, there is no reason to think that Don Alfonso wished to make matters impossible for the new Government. As a result the vast majority of the officers of the Army, Air Force and Navy had already by early May taken an oath to the new *régime*.[4] But some had no intention of working with the Republic.[5] The leading spirits among the plotters were Generals Orgaz and Ponte. There was also Ramiro de Maeztu, once a member of the Generation of 1898, who had since then been an Anarchist, an Ambassador and a journalist, before becoming a leading theorist among the progenitors of Spanish Fascism. There was the right-wing poet, José María Pemán. There was a Navarrese intellectual, Víctor Pradera. And there were other younger Monarchists such as Sáinz Rodríguez, young, enormously fat ('a latitudium of flesh', he called himself), erudite and bohemian. While angry crowds were gathering outside, these conspirators

---

[1] The Republicans' indifference to what happened to the Monarchists was partly due to the damage caused in the preceding month by the flight of capital.

[2] Ansaldo, 15. This account is confirmed by General Herrera who, as Gentleman of the Bed Chamber, followed King Alfonso to Paris. The King adjured him to return to Spain.

[3] *ABC*, 5.5.31.

[4] See below, page 58. On April 25, Azaña issued a decree allowing all officers who wished to retire on full pay. This over-zealously fair act merely created a number of unemployed officers with means and time to plot against the new *régime*.

[5] None of these very early plotters against the Republic seem actually to have taken the required oath to serve and defend it.

decided on a three-point programme: They would form a new and legal Monarchist party, rather misleadingly named *Renovación Española*; they would found a review *Acción Española* under Ramiro de Maeztu's editorship which would publicly argue in favour of an insurrection against the Republic (this would also form a centre of studies to 'collect texts on the question of the legality of an insurrection'); and they would found an organisation to create 'the ambience of revolution' in the Army. This would be known as the *Unión Militar Española*.[1]

As for those who protested against the meeting outside in the Calle Alcalá, it seems that these were at first, at least, simply idle *madrileños* walking about before lunch on Sunday, who were excited by what seemed a flamboyant affront to the Republic. But the careful burning of the churches on the following day (and probably the burning of the headquarters of *ABC*) was the work of the Anarchists.

The Spanish Anarchists at this time numbered no less than a million and a half men and women.[2] The vast majority of these could more accurately be described as Syndicalists, being organised in the large general union, the CNT (*Confederación Nacional del Trabajo*). This had been founded in 1911 to co-ordinate the large number of trade organisations then existing in Spain which looked generally to the abolition of formal government and its replacement by agreements and pressures of trade groups. But the CNT had always been dominated by more violent and active Anarchist militants. When in the early 'twenties there had seemed a possibility of the CNT agreeing to collaborate with the *régime*, the reformists had been forced out of the union. The active Anarchists then formed a secret society whose numbers were never published, and whose task was to maintain the Anarchist ideals in the CNT in all their purity. This society was the greatly feared FAI (*Federación Anarquista Ibérica*).[3]

---

[1] For all the above see Bertrán Guell, 81 fl, whose account is generally confirmed by the officially sponsored *Historia de la Cruzada*. The plots against the Republic now have an ample literature. For the Carlist side, the works of Lizarza and Maiz are essential, though I have been able to supplement these from unpublished letters in the Carlist Archives. See also Cacho Zabalza's *Unión Militar* (Alicante 1940) which shows that the Unión was from the beginning composed almost exclusively of junior officers. Its leader was Colonel Bartolomé Barba, helped by liaison officers throughout Spain.

[2] Brenan illuminates the literature on the Anarchists in *The Spanish Labyrinth*. But Peirats presents all the most important texts for the period of the Civil War. A useful English introduction is Richards's *Lessons of the Spanish Revolution*.

[3] Peirats gives a figure of 30,000 for the FAI in 1936.

The general aspirations of the Spanish Anarchists in 1931 had hardly been modified since the arrival in Spain of Bakunin's first emissary in 1868. Before that time the whole body of revolutionary Socialist ideas, which had already been so much discussed in northern Europe, had almost no Spanish adherents. Certain small co-operative movements did exist in Seville and in Barcelona. Several intellectuals of the clerical or artisan class had been attracted by the ideas of federalism and devolution suggested by Proudhon and Fourier. But in 1868 there arrived in Madrid Fanelli,[1] an Italian deputy, once a companion-in-arms of Garibaldi, now a passionate admirer of Bakunin, who was still the leading figure in the International. Although Fanelli spoke only Italian and French, and though only one among his audience of ten (mainly printers) understood a little French, his ideas had an extraordinary effect. By 1873, there were 50,000 followers[2] of Bakunin in Spain, at first known as 'Internationals' and later by the more accurate name of Anarchists. To these a great new truth seemed to have been proclaimed. The State, being based upon ideas of obedience and authority, was morally evil. In its place, there should be self-governing bodies – municipalities, professions or other societies – which would make voluntary pacts with each other. Criminals would be punished by the censure of public opinion. Bakunin was no doubt influenced, like Tolstoy, in forming such views, by a nostalgia for the Russian village life which he had himself known in childhood. The Spaniards, among whom his ideas so fruitfully spread, may not fancifully be represented as subconsciously hankering for a similar simplicity of the days before the grasping modern State, of the mediaeval village societies and provincial autonomous units which had flourished in Spain as in the rest of Europe.[3]

In 1871, the dispute between Marx and Bakunin in the International caused a split in its branch in Spain. The mass of the Spanish movement, the Anarchists, continued, almost alone in

[1] His Anarchism took the active form of becoming domiciled on the Italian railway, upon which, as a deputy, he had a free ticket.

[2] *The Times*, 3.9.1873. Quoted Brenan, *Spanish Labyrinth*, 155.

[3] For the conversion of the working class of Spain to revolutionary ideas, the Church, which was to suffer so much in consequence, had paradoxically prepared the way. The Church's communalism, its puritan hostility to the competitive instinct, particularly of its Spanish practitioners and apologists, made the ideas of Fanelli seem merely an honest continuation of the old faith. The religious character of Spain also made the converts to the new collectivism, as it had made the liberals, more passionate, less ready to compromise, more obstinate than any other similar group in Europe.

Europe, to follow Bakunin. (A minority, the Socialists, formed a party of their own, following Marx.) The first Anarchist initiates – mainly printers, schoolmasters and students – began a deliberate policy of education, directed chiefly towards the Andalusian labourers. Revolutionary militants moved about from village to village, living like wandering friars. They organised night schools, where peasants learned to read, to become teetotal, vegetarian, faithful to their wives, and to discuss the moral evil of coffee and tobacco. After trade unions were made legal in 1881, Anarchism began to establish itself in Barcelona, where many Andalusian labourers had gone to seek work.[1] The strike, instantly and ruthlessly carried out, was the weapon which the Anarchists believed could lead to the achievement of the Anarchist society. Hence, even after the formation of the CNT in 1911, there was no strike fund, since the Anarchists put their trust in swift and brutal action, rather than in prolonged bargaining, requiring financial reserves. The Andalusian workers were too poor to make regular contributions. Nor, even in 1936, was there more than one paid official for the whole union.

The CNT was divided into two groups, though the division was never properly noticed even by themselves. First, there were the workers of the cities, above all of Barcelona, who were really Syndicalists, and who were groping for that 'vertical' order of society first suggested in France in the late nineteenth century. The plan was for all the workers in one factory to delegate members to a 'syndicate', which would negotiate with other syndicates questions of lodging, food and entertainment. The second group were the rural Anarchists, notably in Andalusia, whose theory represented an idealisation of their own town, the *pueblo*, all of whose inhabitants would co-operate to form their own self-sufficient government. The significance of the ideal is suggested by the second meaning of the word *pueblo*, which can be translated 'people', as opposed to the upper or middle classes. The inference was that these latter were essentially and inevitably foreigners in their own town.[2]

In Andalusia, Anarchist strikes were frequently successful in securing higher wages or shorter hours (if not the 'Golden Age' foreshadowed by their leaders), for the landowners, or their

[1] The city had increased in population from below 100,000 to over a million in the century.
[2] Pitt-Rivers, 18.

agents, feared the violence of the strikers' tactics. In Barcelona, there were long and bloody struggles between workers and factory owners, who knew that they had an unlimited labour reserve from which to draw. As a result, the Anarchists turned in the 1890s increasingly towards terrorism. This was simultaneously being extensively practised by their Russian co-believers, with whom some of the Spanish Anarchists were then connected by personal friendship.

In the early years of the present century, the Anarchists' hatred of, and increasing separation from, the middle class made them prize in their ranks all who made protests against middle-class society, including common felons. The organisation of the FAI in 1927 meant the development of a whole army of shock troops in a more or less perpetual state of war against the rest of Spain. The FAI retained their fantastically high ideals. But they believed that it was with a pistol as well as with an encyclopedia that freedom could be achieved. They were inclined to believe every word that they read. When they came across a passage in Bakunin suggesting that the new world would be gained when the last King was strangled in the guts of the last priest, they would be likely to wish to test immediately whether this was so. Their passionate concern was to create through 'the propaganda of the deed' an atmosphere of panic among the middle class. They might do this through burning churches – as in May 1931.[1] They might place their faith in the violent, sudden, political and perhaps general strike in one town after another. Or they might murder. They had no relations with any other movement and the notion of becoming a political party in the normal sense of the word was repugnant to them.

The movement had a clever tactical leader in the 1930s in José García Oliver. To Mr Cyril Connolly, the English critic, he described his aim as 'to eliminate the beast in man'.[2] But he had himself spent years in prison for crimes of violence. During the Civil War, after he had become Minister of Justice, one of his attendants stretched out his arm to a quivering archivist and invited him to shake a hand which had killed two hundred and

---

[1] Church-burning is a Spanish and not a specially Anarchist phenomenon. The first recorded outbreak was in 1834, about the time that the Spanish working class decided that the hierarchy at least had deserted their interests for those of the aristocracy or the new *bourgeoisie*.

[2] Connolly, *Condemned Playground*, 195. See his remarkable speech as Minister of Justice in January 1937, page 368.

fifty-three men.[1] The other chief Anarchist leaders were Federica
Montseny, a formidable middle-class intellectual from Barcelona
with remarkable powers of organisation; Juan Peiró, a glass-
maker; and two inseparable men of violence, Durruti and Ascaso.
Durruti, a native of León, had come as a metal-worker to Barcelona
in his childhood. Here he had met Ascaso, a baker and café waiter.
Together these two had committed many crimes of violence before
fleeing from Spain, wandering through South America, and
setting up an Anarchist bookshop in Paris. Their most notorious
crimes had been the murder of the Archbishop of Saragossa,[2] the
attempt on King Alfonso in 1921, the murder of a female lace-
maker of Madrid, and the celebrated assault on the Bank of Spain
at Gijón. These men, however, were not common criminals.
They were dreamers with a violent mission, characters whom
Dostoievsky would have been proud to have created. Can one
blame the Spanish *bourgeoisie* if they trembled when they knew
that an army of nearly two million workers was led, though hardly
controlled, by men such as these?[3]

---

[1] *General Cause*, 371. This work consists of the evidence of mass lawsuit brought by the
Nationalist Government at the end of the war. It is a document which for obvious
reasons must be used warily. Nevertheless, much of the information in it is corroborated
by other sources. This remark, attested by persons still living, does not seem *prima facie*
unlikely.

[2] A life of Durruti published during the Civil War gives this version of this crime:
'Durruti and Ascaso heard that there was a condition of injustice in Saragossa. Accordingly they went up to the city from Barcelona and murdered Cardinal Soldevila, who
was the leading proponent of reaction.'

[3] Throughout the 'thirties, the CNT continued to be divided between the most
extreme opponents of existing society, led by the FAI, and those Syndicalists, the
Treintistas, followers of Angel Pestaña, who favoured a certain degree of co-operation
with society. The controversy continued until the CNT Congress in Saragossa in
1936, when the *Treintistas* re-entered the CNT, though Pestaña remained outside.

6

The plots and burnings of May 1931 gave to the Government a clear warning of the threats which seemed likely to beset it from both Left and Right. But the Ministers naturally knew nothing of the details of the Monarchists' plans. Nor did they take the Anarchists as seriously as they should have done. They attributed the church burnings to the provocation of the Monarchists. And in June an election was held which suggested that the majority of the people were behind the *régime*. These elections were held on the rough understanding that one member would represent about 50,000 male votes. They were undoubtedly the fairest that had been held in Spain. As a result, there were elected 116 Socialists; 60 Radical Socialists and 30 members of Azaña's Republican Action party (both of these could be regarded as liberals of Azaña's persuasion); 90 Radicals following Lerroux; and 22 Progressives, following Alcalá Zamora. In addition, there were elected 43 members of the Catalan Esquerra and 16 of Casares Quiroga's Gallegan Nationalists. All these could be expected to vote generally with the Government. Against these, the Right could muster only 60 members. Of these the majority were members of middle-class parties who seemed ready to give the Republic a chance. Only 19 were members of the *Renovación Española*, the legal Monarchist party formed in accordance with the conspiracy of the previous month. The Government felt itself almost secure. And this feeling of confidence was not diminished by the series of violent strikes organised by the CNT in July and August. Still, three deaths occurred during a general strike in San Sebastián. And the Government had recourse to artillery to crush a general strike in Seville. Thirty people were killed and two hundred wounded. This was a major political action. The Government thus treated a general strike as if it were a definite political attack upon the *régime*, and they were quite justified in so doing. However, since the Socialist Largo Caballero was Minister of Labour and the UGT was entirely behind the Government, violent hatreds within the working class could not be avoided.

By the autumn, a committee of the newly elected Cortes had prepared a draft Constitution. Here the Government committed a major blunder. It would have been too much to hope that the new *régime* could refrain from preparing for itself a written Constitution. But it was a grave mistake to make the Constitution of the Republic a highly controversial political document, full of emotive phraseology and containing many articles repugnant to many influential and powerful Spaniards. The liberals of 1931 were thus repeating the mistake of so many of their nineteenth-century predecessors. They identified the new *régime* only with their own political views. Thus the draft Constitution began by announcing 'Spain is a democratic Republic of workers of all classes, organised in a *régime* of liberty and justice'. Government 'emanated from the people' and all citizens were equal. The country would renounce war as an instrument of national policy. No titles of nobility would be recognised. Both sexes would vote at 23.

If these articles were certain to cause controversy, the religious clauses which followed would clearly bring fury. The payment by the State to priests was to stop in two years – though these salaries had been part of the compensation which the Church had been paid after the confiscation of their lands in 1837. All religious orders were to be registered with the Ministry of Justice. If they were judged a danger to the State, they would have to be dissolved.[1] Orders which required a vow, beyond the three normal canonical vows, would anyway be dissolved. This was merely another way of banishing the Jesuits, from whom (above a certain rank) a special oath of loyalty to the Pope is customarily exacted. No Order was to be permitted to hold more property than it required for its own subsistence, nor was any Order to be allowed to indulge in commerce. All Orders were to submit their annual accounts to the State. All education meanwhile was to be inspired 'by ideals of human solidarity'. Religious education, that is, was to end. Every 'public manifestation of religion' – such as Easter or Christmas processions – would have to be officially sanctioned. And divorce was to be granted as a result of mutual disagreement between the parties or on the petition of either party if just cause could be shown.

[1] An earlier draft of the Constitution had demanded the total dissolution of all orders.

The inclusion of these severely anticlerical clauses in the Constitution of the Spanish Republic was political folly. It might have been that the implementation of such conditions would ultimately have made for a juster and happier Spain. Azaña, for instance (who had secured the modification of certain even more extreme provisions), had undoubtedly suffered when at school under the friars at the bleak Augustinian school at El Escorial. Nevertheless, it would have been wiser to have delayed before the presentation of such total disestablishment. It would have been wiser to have waited until the place of the Augustinian and Jesuit schools could be taken by lay establishments of comparable quality. For with all their shortcomings these orders had created the best secondary schools in the country.[1] Even liberal newspapers denounced these measures. Yet Azaña thundered in the Cortes: 'Do not tell me that this is contrary to freedom. It is a matter of public health.' Afterwards, all Spanish Catholics were forced into the position of having to oppose the very Constitution of the Republic if they wished to criticise its educational or religious policy.

The debates in the Cortes on these clerical clauses brought the first of many Governmental crises in the Second Republic. Alcalá Zamora, the Prime Minister, and Miguel Maura, the Minister of the Interior, both Catholics, resigned. The Speaker of the Cortes, the Socialist reformist Besteiro, assumed the temporary rank of President of Spain and called on Azaña to form another Government. Since he had assumed the leadership of the Government parties in the religious debates, he was the obvious choice. But his promotion greatly angered the Radical Lerroux, who thereupon passed with his 90 followers into Opposition. Thereafter, the Government was strictly anticlerical, being composed of the new liberals of Azaña's way of thinking and of the Socialists. However, Alcalá Zamora agreed to become the first President of the Republic. So it still could not be said that the Catholics were entirely excluded from the *régime*.

The Constitution was finally passed in the Cortes at the end of 1931. It remained for the Government to introduce the large amount of legislation which would enact all its clauses. The Ministers first busied themselves with a law 'for the Defence of the Republic'. The Constitution had provided for the suspension of all guarantees of freedom for thirty days, in the case of an emergency.

---

[1] Every provincial capital had a state secondary school, but their character varied greatly.

This new law empowered the Minister of the Interior to suspend public meetings. It was naturally attacked by the Right as suggesting the way to a dictatorship. On the last day of 1931, however, a specially terrible incident occurred which caught the attention of the whole country.

In the wild and empty region of Estremadura there stands a small *pueblo* of 900 inhabitants named Castilblanco. The conditions here were not notably different from elsewhere in the region. There was no special shortage of food. Violence was unknown. The local branch of the CNT, however, asked permission to hold a meeting. This was refused. The Anarchists determined to go ahead. The Civil Guard then came to the defence of the authorities.

The Civil Guard now numbered about 30,000 in all Spain. It had been established in 1844 in order to keep order in the countryside, which had been agitated for a long time by bandits using guerilla methods successfully employed against the armies of Napoleon. The Civil Guard was organised like an army, and was led by a General and officers with military rank. Many of the rank and file were ex-regular soldiers and non-commissioned officers. With their green uniforms, three-cornered hats and gaunt barracks, this police force conducted itself as if it were an invading army. Members of the Civil Guard never served in the part of Spain from whence they came. They were not encouraged to speak to anyone in the village in which they were quartered. They had a deserved reputation for ruthlessness. 'When one joins the Civil Guard,' remarked Ramón Sender, 'one declares civil war.'[1]

In Castilblanco in 1931 the Civil Guard were as unpopular as elsewhere in Spain. Their fate was terrible. When they tried to prevent the holding of a CNT meeting, the whole population of the village fell upon them. Four were killed. Their heads were beaten in. Their eyes were gouged out. Their bodies were mutilated. On one of the bodies, 37 knife wounds were afterwards discovered. And, as in the village of Fuenteovejuna in Lope de Vega's play of that name, there was no possibility of bringing the killers to trial. The village, and no single person, was responsible.[2] This tragedy

---

[1] Sender, *Seven Red Sundays*.

[2] There is nothing to suggest that this outburst was premeditated on the part of the CNT or the FAI. On the other hand, it could easily have been so. It was certainly an example of 'the propaganda of the deed'.

was followed by several comparable but less dramatic events in other *peublos*. In Arenaldo the Civil Guards were successful and wreaked unnecessarily violent revenge; but in Sallent in the Llobregat valley near Barcelona the CNT took over the whole town for a few hours, raised a red flag on the town hall and declared themselves an independent society.[1]

The alarming frequency of these violent explosions against the *régime* from the working class seems to have encouraged the Government to broach at last a solution of those fundamental social problems which lay at the heart of Spanish working-class unrest, and particularly of the problem of Spanish agriculture.

Of the active population of Spain in 1936 of eleven million, two million might be named middle class, two million might be named lower middle class (tradesmen or small artisans), four and a half million agricultural workers, and about two to three million industrial workers or miners. The last group, thanks to good organisation and the relative recentness of industrial development, had gained at the hands of the first a reasonable standard of living. Among the agricultural regions, the north, north-east, and the coast along the Mediterranean to Valencia, were covered with small holdings large and fertile enough to support a family. Here there were few large estates. These areas, which were irrigated more than elsewhere, were also comparatively close to the industrial centres in Catalonia and the Basque provinces. The rest of agricultural Spain was undeveloped and poor. In the two Castiles, Andalusia and Estremadura, out of 1,026,412 'landowners' paying tax, 847,548 enjoyed an income of less than 1 peseta[2] a day in 1936 money.[3] In the north-west, in Galicia, where a large number of small proprietors cultivated small barren plots, the figures must have been similar. La Mancha and New Castile were chiefly farmed by tenant farmers and small proprietors. Andalusia and Estremadura were provinces of great and mainly neglected estates, from which a multitude of landless labourers (known as *braceros*)

---

[1] The Government took five days to recapture the town. Many Anarchists were deported as a result. Among them were Durruti and Ascaso. The latter wrote from his prison ship: 'Poor *bourgeoisie* which has to have recourse to such action to survive. But of course they are at war with us, and it is natural that they defend themselves by martyrising, murdering and exiling us.' (Peirats, I 51.)

[2] One peseta was equivalent to sixpence.

[3] Report of the Institute of Agrarian Reform quoted by Salvador de Madariaga, 113.

sought to gain a living. Conditions in both areas were in 1936 much the same as they had been since the *Reconquista*, or even the Romans. At the height of summer, labourers might gain as much as 6 pesetas a day – though this was exceptional. From spring to autumn, for four or five months, the average wage for these men was between 3 and 3½ pesetas. For the rest of the year, they would be unemployed.[1] The labourers lived in the large stagnant villages for which the south of Spain is celebrated, never on the land itself due to the mediaeval need to gather the population together in easily defensible clusters. To these *pueblos* the agents of the landowners would repair when labour was required. The *braceros* would assemble, at dawn in the village square, as in a slave market, 'dressed in a loose cotton jacket with sandals of hemp or esparto grass', and those who had nothing, political or industrial, against them would be chosen for work. Those who refused the wage offered were not missed, since the agent could bring in labour from a neighbouring village – or even from Portugal.[2]

The tenant farmers of these areas were in much the same plight as the other two classes. They were at the mercy of their landlords, from whom they held land on short leases. They usually paid rent, in kind or in money, determined by a proportion of the crop and its profits. They were also at the mercy of the money-lenders to whom they had to have recourse to pay for the tools of their employment.

Most landowners in Andalusia and Estremadura had little feeling towards their land and their labourers. If they found it profitable they would cease cultivation altogether. Many regarded their estates as they would distant colonies, and visited them rarely. They left the administration of their property in the hands of a local agent, the *cacique*, who also ensured its political docility. Others, who were as willing to regard their labourers as slaves, were almost as poor or as indebted as their tenants. They might live in large houses surrounded by servants and daughters, but they would be quite unable to afford a rail fare to Madrid, much less the cost of a hotel there.

The problem of Spanish agriculture was the central sore which radiated throughout the country. It was the source of Anarchist strength. For the CNT had always its most active followers among the landless labourers of Andalusia and among those Andalusians,

[1] Brenan, *Spanish Labyrinth*, 120–1.   [2] Ramos Oliveira, 227.

or sons of Andalusians, who emigrated to the factories of Barcelona. If the Republic had embarked upon agrarian reform before attacking the Church, all but a very few rich landowners might have supported the reformers. And indeed, as it was, the Agrarian Law introduced in 1932 met with little opposition in the Cortes. The law only applied to Andalusia, Estremadura, three provinces of Castile (Ciudad Real, Toledo, Salamanca) and Albacete in Murcia. All unworked estates over 56 acres would be taken over by the Institute of Agrarian Reform, who would pay compensation by calculating the total value of the area from tax returns.[1] Land secured would be controlled by the State and distributed either to selected individual peasants or to co-operatives of peasants.[2] In both cases the State would be the new landowner.

This law might be, as Largo Caballero (still Minister of Labour) put it, 'an aspirin to cure an appendicitis'. It did not deal with Galicia or with many parts of Castile, where conditions were almost as bad as in the south. It only touched the edge of the question of agricultural credit. It provided no immediate new plans for irrigation. Only $1\frac{1}{2}$ million hectares[3] (3% of the whole country) were irrigated at this time. Irrigation could probably have brought another 6 million acres under effective cultivation. Yet even so had this law been fully carried out it would have been the start of a solution of the agrarian problem of Spain, and of its attendant miseries. Due to the extraordinarily varied climate and countryside, all the world's greatest crops (except coffee) are grown in Spain. And despite the low rainfall, poor soil and the proximity to the surface of rock in much of the country, Spain could be made into a considerable agricultural country. Gibbon after all termed Roman Spain 'the opulent country'.

Admittedly, such an agricultural revolution would depend on complementary industrial and financial encouragement. In the early 1930s this was impossible, because of the very slump which had been one of the main reasons for the collapse of the Monarchy, and whose continuance in the industrial side of the Spanish economy assisted the fall of the Republic. The background to the disputes in the Cortes on religious education was the closing of mines and factories and the fall of the peseta. However, through-

---

[1] This was clever since tax evasion had been considerable.

[2] This was naturally a matter of dispute between the Socialists and liberal Republicans in the Government. The former favoured collectivisation, the latter individual lots.

[3] One hectare = 2·471 acres.

out the Republic, agricultural (though not industrial) production
continued to rise.[1]

[1] The fall of Spanish industrial production, and the consequent rising unemployment
among industrial (though not agricultural) workers was clearly a grave exacerbation
of the troubles of the Republic. And if Spain's agriculture was wasted, Spain's minerals
and ores, if fully developed, might make her a formidable industrial power. In lead,
silver, copper, mercury, iron and pyrites Spain is among the leading world producers.
These mines are believed to be developed even today to only 10% of their capacity.
Nearly every stone and chemical is found in Spain – particularly salts, potash and
sulphur, together with lignite and bituminous coal. The rapidity of Spanish rivers is a
continuous source of great electric power. There are, of course, many natural enemies
in Spain – especially drought and barren soil. But it is not against these but against
each other that Spaniards have turned the full weight of their energies during the past
four centuries. The picture of the Christian conquerors permitting the irrigation
channels of the Moors in Granada to be filled in should be a perpetual spectre before
the eyes of those who sacrifice all for an ideal. The figures for the main agricultural
and industrial products of Spain for the ten years before the outbreak of war are given
in Appendix I.

7

7

The Catalan Statute – the Basques – the Army – new plots –
General Sanjurjo's rising of 1932

The .Agrarian Law passed the Cortes without much argument. The increasingly vociferous right-wing opposition kept their special anger for the Statute of Catalan Autonomy. The previous year a plebiscite had been held in Catalonia. This had given 592,961 votes for home rule, and only 3,276 votes against. In no free elections anywhere perhaps has so overwhelming a vote been given. The Constitution of the Republic, meanwhile, provided that Spain should be if necessary 'federable'; any number of regions which so wished, that is, should be able to choose some measure of self government. By the summer, the Catalan Statute had become law. The Barcelona Municipal Government would be reorganised as the Catalan Government, with the name of 'Generalitat' – a mediaeval town council. This body would have certain limited powers in education, police and taxes. Catalan and Spanish would both be official languages. (The system somewhat resembled that today existing in Northern Ireland, since Catalonia, like Northern Ireland, continued to send deputies to the central parliament as well as to the new local chamber in Barcelona.) The Catalans had expected rather more considerable powers, especially in respect of control of the Civil Guard. But even so it was a great moment when the moustachioed Colonel Macía appeared with Azaña on a balcony in the Plaza de Cataluña to receive the cheers of the crowds, who had waited for so long for the satisfaction of their desires. 'I have every confidence,' said Macía, 'in the goodwill with which you will receive this Statute. But it is not the Statute for which we voted.' Thus began the short, tumultuous and tragic history of the Catalan Republic.

Meantime, another and comparable bid for home rule was being made by the Basques.

The Basques are a race of some 600,000 people who have lived from the earliest times around the Western end of the Pyrenees.

53

Of these, about 470,000 live in Spain, the rest in France. The origin of this people is unknown. Those anxious to belittle the differences between Basques and Spaniards have identified the traditional Basque dance, the *Espata Danza*, with the *Tripidium* of the Iberians, observed by Strabo. They have therefore argued persuasively though not conclusively that the Basques are Iberians who have preserved, in their remote valleys, their identity. But the Basque language, spoken in the country districts in the Basque provinces has certainly been impossible to link with any other.[1] The only real certainty about the Basques is the fact of the existence of an individual society in the mountainous Spanish provinces of Guipúzcoa, Vizcaya, Álava and Navarre[2] (and to a lesser extent among the Basques in France) since before records began.

The main characteristics of this society have been, from time immemorial, religious devotion, political independence and agricultural self-sufficiency. Since the Church here has remained close to the land, the churches have stayed the centres of civic life in Basque villages. Local councils customarily still meet in verandahs on the side of these normally somewhat squat buildings. Inside, the puritanism of the Basque approach to religion is expressed in the custom of seating men and women in different places, either divided by an aisle or with the men sitting in a gallery and the women below. The Basque priests claimed that, in 1936, 99% of the agricultural population of Guipúzcoa, Álava and Vizcaya and 52% of those in industrial areas (among those who were Basques by blood)[3] were practising Christians.[4]

Politically, from the early Middle Ages at least, assemblies composed of representatives of all men over 21 would meet every two years under an oak tree at Guernica, in Vizcaya. There, the Monarch, or more usually his representative, would swear to respect Basque rights. An executive council would then be elected by lot to rule for the next two years. Both the oak tree and the city of Guernica acquired a sanctity for the Basques, suggesting a transference to political life of an ancient worship of the oak.[5]

[1] Save perhaps with an obscure group in Hungary, who may be quite recent Basque *émigrés* in descent.

[2] Navarre is chiefly inhabited by the Basques, and the Basque tongue is still spoken there. But for reasons which will become clear below (see page 61) their political history has taken a different course.

[3] The figure sank to 15% among non-Basques living in Basque cities.

[4] *Le Clergé Basque*, 15.

[5] This worship existed in primitive times in many places in Europe where oak trees prevailed.

These customs were apparently well developed even before the arrival of the Moors – by whom the Basques were never conquered. Despite these marked separate habits, the Basques remained a regular part of Castile.[1] Much of Castile was indeed colonised by Basque settlers when it was reconquered from the Moors. The first real movement to assert themselves undertaken by the Basques was in the early nineteenth century when, due to their intense Roman Catholicism, as well as the strength of their local feeling, they formed the bulk of the armies of the Carlists in their war against the centralising and anticlerical liberals. As a result, in 1839, the Basques' local rights were abolished.

The anger caused by this measure of the Castillians was, in the late nineteenth century, intensified by the arrival of industrialism in Spain. The Basques had long been known for shipbuilding, because of the numbers of oak trees in Vizcaya. In the late nineteenth century, Bilbao also became a great industrial town, due to the large and easily shipped iron ore deposits around it. By the twentieth century, 45% of the merchant fleet of Spain came from the Basque provinces, as did nearly all Spain's annual production of iron. There grew up in Bilbao a society resembling that of the Basques' chief commercial partners, the British. A comfortable middle-class security was embodied in the great Basque banks, with their branches throughout Spain, and by the bankers' imposing clubs and fine mansions. (The working class of Bilbao remained, however, less anglicised – as was expressed in their habit of eating domestic cats stewed in sherry.) And the Basque businessmen, like the Catalans, added their sober weight to that of the romantics who, led by Sabino Arana-Goiri, began to demand the revival of those local rights abolished, after all, such a short time before. The Basque demands for self-government were always urged in a dignified manner. This, and their Roman Catholicism, caused their failure to reach any quick agreement with the Republican or left-wing parties then disposed, because of their strict Wilsonianism, to support the demand for autonomy of any region which wanted it. Indeed, the Basque deputies walked out of the Cortes during the discussion of the clerical clauses of the Constitution. However, a Basque Statute was eventually brought forward which would have given the Basques much the same degree of

[1] Except for those who lived in Navarre, who were ruled by the semi-independent monarchs of that little kingdom until the sixteenth century.

autonomy as that enjoyed by the Catalans. In June 1932, delegates from the four provinces met in Pamplona. Those from Navarre rejected the Statute by the narrow majority of 123–109. Henceforward, their ways diverged from those of the Basques. For the delegates from the other three provinces approved the Statute by an overwhelming majority. This approval was subsequently approved in a plebiscite of the three provinces.[1] For, by this time, all classes in the Basque provinces, including the Socialists[2] (many of whom were immigrants from Asturias, Andalusia, or Galicia), backed the demand for limited independence. All indeed, gave their support to the ancient Basque slogan, 'For God and our old laws.' Nevertheless, no alliance of any kind existed between the Basque Nationalists and the working-class organisations.

These Basque Separatists were more exclusively Nationalist than the Catalans. Their movement gathered momentum through the anti-clericalism of the Republic. Unlike those of Barcelona, their best markets and their source of raw materials were outside Spain. They half believed that they could live by themselves on their own wood and iron. They were peaceful people who disliked controversy and hated fighting. It is easy to understand, therefore, why they felt that they had had enough of Spain. It is an ironic tragedy that this distaste for the Spanish connection drew them into the Civil War and destroyed them.

The leader of the Basque Nationalists was a young lawyer, José Antonio Aguirre. He was of a middle-class and Carlist family and owed much to his good looks, his youth and his prowess as a games player at the Bilbao Athletic Club.[3]

The comparative success of the two Separatist parties in Catalonia and the Basque provinces had repercussions elsewhere in Spain. The Separatist movement in Galicia had been begun under the dictatorship of Primo de Rivera. A Statute for Gallegan autonomy was being planned by Casares Quiroga, now Minister of the Interior in Azaña's Government. There were similar stirrings among the Valencianos, and even among the Castillians. It did

---

[1] Out of a total electorate of 489,887 in the three provinces, 411,756 had voted in favour of the Statute, 14,196 had voted against, and 63,935 abstained.

[2] The working classes in Bilbao were neither so Catholic nor so independent-minded as the *bourgeoisie*. Their adoption later of the centralising ideas of the Socialist UGT, one of whose chief centres was Bilbao, was also to be a cause of class tension.

[3] Yet the Basques were still so far to the Right that they were approached in 1932 both by the conspirator General Orgaz and by ex-King Alfonso for help in return for some compromise on home rule. The approach was rejected (Aguirre, 342–3).

indeed seem that Spain might be geographically divided up again, and an age of city states be inaugurated. This was yet one more potent cause of fear and hence a disposition to sanction a recourse to force among those who might lose from such a dismemberment.

The Church and many of the respectable middle class had been estranged from the Republic by the religious clauses in the Constitution. The landowners had been angered by the Agrarian Law. It was the Army who were most offended by the Catalan Statute and the apparent developments in the direction of a federal Spanish State.

The days were past when a Frenchman such as Brantôme could feel pride in the human race when he saw the Spaniards riding to their wars in Flanders, 'like princes in their arrogant and insolent grace'. Indeed, in recent times, the Spanish Army had shown few suspicions even of competence. Wellington found the Spaniards fighting by his side brave but extraordinarily ill-disciplined. English observers of the Carlist Wars had noted the same. The first Carlist War was concluded not by a victory in the field, but by a treaty of compromise enabling all the Carlist officers to join the regular army at full pay. This had begun the long era of preponderance of officers to men in the Spanish Army. In the last years of the Monarchy, for example, there were 19,906 officers (including 219 Generals) for 207,000 men[1] – a proportion of one officer for every ten men.[2]

It was a commonplace to say that this large force was maintained not to fight Spain's enemies abroad, but to enforce order within her borders. Ever since the Napoleonic Wars, the officers of the Spanish Army had been accustomed to use their force to direct Spanish political life. Apart from the Carlist Wars, there had been no fewer than forty-three *pronunciamientos*, successful or unsuccessful, between 1814 and 1923. Between 1868 and 1875, the Army had deposed the Monarch, brought in another prince from Italy, established a Republic, restored order and finally restored the Monarchy. Though the defeats in the Spanish-American War of 1898 had lost the Army much prestige, the insults 'made against her honour' by a Catalan newspaper in 1905 had secured the amazing concession that all attacks against the Army should be tried by military law. In 1917, the Army had crushed the nation-

---

[1] Madariaga, 139.
[2] Nineteenth-century figures were far more absurd. In 1898 there was one General for every hundred men.

wide general strike, though itself at that time honeycombed with
Syndicalist ideas. From 1923 until 1930 General Primo de Rivera
had maintained a military dictatorship, and he had only left office
when he had received notice that the garrisons were against him.
Meantime, the militarily disastrous Moroccan wars had from 1909
until 1927 given the Army innumerable opportunities for glory
and grandeur. With this political background, it was inconceivable
that the Army should for long willingly remain out of the limelight
in the history of the Republic.

It was for this reason that Azaña when Minister of War had
determined to reduce the power of the Army. With his usual
fatal facility for creating a phrase which would be remembered, he
announced that he would 'triturate' the military caste. He had
attempted to do this by abolishing the special legal position of the
Army created by the Law of Jurisdictions of 1905. He abolished
the Supreme Council of the Army (and the Navy), thus bringing
the Services under control of the ordinary courts. He abolished the
eight Captains-General who had hitherto held almost vice-regal
powers in the eight old provinces or regions of Spain. He gave all
officers a choice between swearing loyalty to the Republic and
retiring on full pay. Many availed themselves of this generosity
and thereafter employed their time like Generals Ponte and Orgaz
in plotting against the new *régime*. Azaña also carried out various
dismissals intended undoubtedly to make the Army a more
efficient if smaller force. But others of his measures – such as the
annulment of promotions won by gallantry in the field – were
bound to make Azaña and his Government specially unpopular
in orthodox messes. Azaña himself constantly maintained that
he thought that no one could be more loyal to the Republic
than the average officer. And when the Inspector General
of the Army, General Goded, a very political General indeed –
he had helped in Primo de Rivera's *pronunciamiento* and then had
risen abortively against him – arrested a Republican Colonel,
Julio Mangada, for crying *Viva la República* after he had himself
cried *Viva España* at a mess dinner, Azaña supported Goded, and
imprisoned Mangada for insubordination. Yet many of the serving
officers continued to seethe quietly. Those who had retired continued to plot.

Throughout most of the Republic, the Spanish officers numbered
15,000. These commanded 115,000 men who were, except for
the Foreign Legion and the native Moorish troops (these being

known as 'the Army of Africa'), all conscripts doing their national service.[1] The period of conscription was nominally for two years, but it rarely exceeded eighteen months in practice. This army (again excepting the Army of Africa) was divided into eight infantry divisions, one cavalry division, two mountain brigades and two artillery brigades. It was spread about Spain in garrisons established in the capitals of the provinces. The actual size of the Army was undoubtedly even smaller than these figures suggest, for many units were below strength.

Most of the leading officers of the Army had fought in the wars in Morocco,[2] to whose atmosphere of dangerous comradeship they looked back nostalgically. There, though many of their comrades had been killed, there had been opportunities for swift promotion and the unfettered exercise of military rule. Political incompetence at Madrid had caused them to fight this war on a shoestring, without adequate arms or supplies. After Primo de Rivera, with the aid of the French, had finally defeated the Riffs, the officers who had made their name in those hard campaigns were still recalled with affection by the two forces which had chiefly helped them to win. These were the Foreign Legion, composed, despite its name, mainly of Spaniards, together with some Portuguese, French and Germans, which had been founded in 1920 as a shock force; and the Moorish *Regulares*, native troops raised to be half-soldiers, half-policemen, to keep down the conquered areas. The Foreign Legion had a reputation for peculiar violence. Its favourite motto was 'Down with intelligence. Long live Death.' Both forces were staffed by Spanish officers, and in 1936 numbered 34,000 in all.

Many Spanish Army officers saw, in their own traditions, the embodiment of a certain idea of a timeless, supremely Castillian Spain, without politics, creating order and banishing all things non-Spanish (by which they understood Separatism, Socialism, Freemasonry, Communism and Anarchism). They could persuade themselves that their oath, as officers, to 'maintain the independence of the country and defend it from enemies within and without'[3] took precedence over their oath of loyalty to the Republic. The average Spanish officer after all was by middle life dissatisfied,

---

[1] *Enciclopedia Universal Ilustrada*, 1936–9; *Segunda Parte*, 1447.

[2] Spanish Morocco consisted firstly of the four so-called *Presidios* of Ceuta, Melilla, Alhucemas, and Peñon de Vélez de la Gomera, which had been for a long time an integral part of Spain; secondly, of the Spanish protectorate of north-western Morocco.

[3] Article 2 of the Constitutive Law of the Army.

irritable and right wing. In this respect, he was no different from officers in other countries during time of peace. In Spain, as elsewhere, the young officer, when still supported by family money, is generally happy. He is happy too, while his uniforms and handsome figure can still dazzle the marriageable girls of his family's acquaintance. There follows a short engagement, promotion to captain, marriage. There are mounting expenses, appearances have to be kept up, but pay remains low. The military zeal of youth departs. The high-spirited lion of the ballroom becomes an embittered employee of the State. His wife is worn by the exigencies of incessant economising. She points enviously at her husband's once scorned civilian contemporaries. These experiences are part of the lot of officers in all countries. In Spain (though less often elsewhere), there seemed to be a way out. The officer could dream of a *coup d'état*, which would place him in a position superior to his clever liberal and commercial friends.[1]

For all these reasons the plots directed in the first place by the Monarchist General Orgaz were notably successful. The secret organisation which it had been decided should be created to develop 'the ambience of revolution in the Army', the UME (*Unión Militar Española*), made considerable headway. In the summer of 1932, many passions were aroused among officers by the passage of the Catalan Statute. It was not only that the creation of a Catalan State seemed to threaten the integrity of the Spain which the officers had sworn to defend. Catalan home rule seemed a deliberate affront to the Army itself, who between 1917 and 1923 had spent so much time maintaining Barcelona in a condition of martial law. Had not General Primo de Rivera been harder on Catalan Nationalists than on any other of his critics?

At the same time, other anti-Republican schemes were prospering. The meetings which had begun in the Calle Alcalá in May 1931 had continued sporadically, with an ever widening group of participants. At the end of 1931, King Alfonso in exile abandoned his discouragement of his eagerly insurrectionary followers. This followed his own trial and condemnation to life imprisonment *in absentia*, by the Cortes. A pact was even signed between his party, the orthodox Monarchists of *Renovación Española*, and the followers of his distant cousin, the Carlist Pretender Don Jaime, The orthodox Monarchists had few constitutional prejudices to dispute with the Carlists who now called themselves by the more

[1] Ruiz Vilaplana, 207–8.

respectable name of 'Traditionalists'. So the two groups formally agreed to co-operate. Their alliance became known as the TYRE (*Tradicionalistas y Renovación Española*). However, when Don Jaime died shortly afterwards, his successor as Pretender, his aged uncle Don Alfonso Carlos (who had commanded a division in the Second Carlist War) denounced this agreement, and thereafter the Carlists themselves were divided. The uncompromising followers of Don Alfonso Carlos began to attempt to revive the memory of their old and violent 'communion' – for they did not like to think of themselves as a mere political party. As in the nineteenth century, their greatest strength could be expected to be in the north, and especially in Navarre. Though technically a Basque province, and though Basque is still spoken in many Navarrese villages, the political accidents of the past and the economic developments of the present caused Navarre to follow the Carlist rather than the Basque Nationalist path. For the Navarrese were a contented group of peasant proprietors nestling in the foothills of the Pyrenees. The reason for their admittedly narrow majority against the Basque Statute was simply that Navarre had no businessmen, no *bourgeoisie*, anxious to be free to carry on a Western, commercial life. Navarre was zealously Catholic, with nothing to cause its priests to modernise or humanise Christian doctrine. A journey to Navarre was indeed still an expedition into the Middle Ages. Needless to say, the clerical reforms of the Republic caused intense resentment in Navarre, and would probably have been enough by themselves to rekindle the old spirit in those Pyrenean Valleys – and indeed elsewhere, for by mid-1932 there were few large towns which did not have a Carlist branch, usually directed by some exquisitely polite and aristocratic man of violence.

The political ideas of the Carlists were primitive. Some years later, a group of politicians were discussing the idea of a return of the Monarch in the presence of the Count of Rodezno, the tall and cynical aristocrat who led the Traditionalist party in the Cortes. One of the politicians turned to the Count and asked who would be Prime Minister if the King should come back. 'You or one of these gentlemen, it is a matter of secretaries.' 'But what would you do?' 'I!' exclaimed the Count, 'I should stay with the King and we should talk of the chase.'[1] The *politique* of the chase was indeed the essence of the Carlist view of society. The orthodox

[1] Serrano Suñer, 59.

Monarchists were often very rich men, landlords or financiers. The Carlists were often to be found among the poorer aristocrats of undoubted lineage, but who were not able to pay their local debts.

There was nothing fraudulent about the Carlists' deeply religious, semi-mystical hostility towards the modern world (especially liberalism and the French Revolution) and their fervent loyalty towards *Dios*, *Patria* and *Rey*. Yet while the Anarchists thought that a pistol and an encyclopedia would give them a new world, the Carlists put similar faith in a machine-gun and a missal.

All these plots came to a premature head in the unsuccessful *pronunciamiento* of General Sanjurjo in August 1932. This officer was then the most famous soldier in Spain. A veteran of the Spanish-American War, he had been in field command at the end of the Moroccan War. It was he, 'the Lion of the Riff', who had brought back victory to Spain in 1927. Earlier he had taken part in Primo de Rivera's *pronunciamiento* in 1923. He was a brave, hard-drinking philanderer, whose sensuous face indicated a remarkable mixture of indolence and strength. In 1931 he had been commander of the Civil Guard and had told the King that he could not count on that corps to support the Monarchy. In 1932, when filling the post of commander of the *Carabineros* (customs guards), he was easily persuaded by his Monarchist and military friends that it was his duty to rise against the Republic. 'You alone, my General, can save Spain,' they told him.[1] He personally seemed to have had doubts about the matter and hardly gave adequate attention to the plot's organisation. Apparently, however, he had been specially appalled by the village tragedies the previous winter. He had actually visited Castilblanco at the time, and had heard eye-witnesses describe how the women of the village had danced in frenzy round the corpses of the Civil Guard. Several Carlist leaders, such as the Count of Rodezno and the fanatical young Andalusian lawyer, Fal Conde, were closely involved in the plot. A number of aristocratic officers formed the backbone of the conspiracy – including most of those who had been meeting intermittently since May 1931.[2] The aims of the rising seem to have been vague.

---

[1] *Cruzada*, IV 489. Sanjurjo had strong Carlist connections, since his father had been a Brigadier in Don Carlos's army and his mother's brother had been Don Carlos's secretary. He himself had been born in Pamplona in 1876, in the middle of the Carlist War.

[2] A very large number of these plotters were either young officers who had only taken their oath of loyalty to the Monarch in the years immediately before his departure, or were old Generals who had served the Monarchy for a very long time.

It was not a bid for the restoration of the Monarchy, but an attempt simply to overthrow the 'anticlerical dictatorship of Azaña'. In his manifesto, however, Sanjurjo made use of precisely those words which had been employed by the makers of the Republic two years before: 'A passionate demand for justice surges upwards from the bowels of the people, and we are moved to satisfy it. . . . Revolution will always be a crime or an act of insanity when Law and Justice exists. But it is always just when Tyranny prevails.'[1] Before the rising occurred, a young Monarchist airman, Major Ansaldo, was despatched to try and gain the support of the Italian Fascist *régime* for the rising. Ansaldo saw Marshal Balbo, and promises of diplomatic support in the event of victory were forthcoming.[2] Inside Spain, a fledgling Fascist group, the so-called Nationalist party of Burgos led by Dr Albiñana, also gave the rising support.

The affair was a fiasco. Azaña and the Government knew – through the treachery of a prostitute – of what was afoot. Indeed, the matter had been talked about in the cafés for weeks.[3] General Sanjurjo was briefly triumphant at Seville, but in Madrid everything went wrong. Most of the would-be rebels were captured, though only after a certain amount of fighting in the Plaza de la Cibeles. Azaña nonchalantly watched the battle, a cigarette at his lips, from the balcony of the Ministry of War. Sanjurjo was persuaded by his advisers to flee to Portugal. Apprehended on the frontier, he was brought back to be tried with another 150 rebels. The General was at first condemned to death, but his sentence was then commuted to life imprisonment and he was taken off to the penal settlement at Santoña. 144 of the lesser rebels, mostly officers and including two princes of the House of Bourbon, were deported to the foetid Spanish African colony of Villa Cisneros.[4] The first rising against the Republic thus ended in the total discomfiture of the rebels.

---

[1] Arrarás, 464 fn.   [2] Ansaldo, 18–20.

[3] One of the conspirators, José Félix de Lequerica (future Foreign Minister under General Franco) was asked by the judge trying him how he knew the date fixed for the insurrection. 'From my concierge,' was the reply. 'For weeks he has been saying that the date was being postponed. At last, yesterday, he declared solemnly: "It is tonight, Don José Félix".'

[4] Four of these prisoners – the Duke of Seville, Martín Alonso, Serrador, and Tella – later distinguished themselves as Nationalist commanders in the Civil War.

8

Casas Viejas – decline of Azaña's Government – the elections of November 1933 – Gil Robles and the CEDA – José Antonio Primo de Rivera and the origins of the Falange – the beginnings of Spanish Communism

Manuel Azaña and his Government weathered the rest of the year 1932 without great difficulty. For much of the time, the right-wing papers *ABC*, *El Debate* and *Informaciones* were suspended. The Anarchists were comparatively quiet. A purge of the Civil Service was begun to remove those 'incompatible with the *régime*'. The autumn session of the Cortes was occupied with the passage of the Law of Congregations, which developed the religious clauses of the Constitution. The Jesuits had already left Spain, in February. Now laws were prepared naming the dates for the end of religious teaching and the beginning of the other restrictions on the Orders of religion: ecclesiastical elementary schools were to close on December 31, 1933, and secondary schools and universities three months before. This would mean that in a country where there were already too few schools, another 350,000 children would have to be educated. Herculean efforts were, however, already being made by Marcelino Domingo, the Minister of Education, to realise this part of the Republic's ideals. 7,000 schools had been built within one year of the inauguration of the Republic, and another 2,500 in the twelve months from April 1932 till April 1933. The salaries of teachers in elementary schools were raised to the still excessively inadequate annual sum of 3,000 pesetas.[1] Travelling schools were sent into remote provinces. By the end of 1932, 70,000 children were being educated in secondary schools in place of the 20,000 three years before.

The nation was also engaged by the trial of the Majorcan millionaire Juan March, who had obtained a monopoly for the distribution of tobacco in Spain from Primo de Rivera. March was convicted of fraud; but he later bribed his way to sensational

[1] About £70.

escape from Guadalajara prison and thereafter used his considerable wealth (valued at £20 million sterling) to sabotage the currency of the Republic, which, nevertheless, maintained itself in these years at more or less the same rate: 55–56 pesetas to the pound.

The peace of the country was, however, once more broken in January 1933, this time by an almost mortal thrust from the Left. On January 11, an Anarchist rising occurred at the village of Casas Viejas in the province of Cádiz. Some at least of the Anarchists who raised the *pueblo* were strangers to it. Though the Mayor gave in, the Civil Guard did not, and telephoned for help from nearby Medina Sidonia. Reinforcements shortly arrived in the shape of a detachment of *Guardia de Asalto*[1] (Assault Guards). This corps had been founded after the May riots in 1931 as a kind of special constabulary for the defence of the Republic, and was composed of officers and men supposed to be specially loyal to the new *régime*. The *Asaltos* drove out the Anarchists, who established themselves on a small hill outside. Meantime, a detachment of the Civil Guard and *Asaltos* embarked on a house to house search for arms. One veteran old Anarchist named Seisdedos (literally, six fingers) refused to open his door. A siege began. Seisdedos, with his daughter Libertaria acting as gun-loader, and accompanied by five others, refused absolutely to surrender. The infuriated *Asaltos* had already lost several lives. A telegram arrived from the Ministry of the Interior authorising the strictest methods of repression. About a dozen prisoners taken earlier in the day were shot. An aircraft was procured which dropped bombs on the besieged Anarchists. Seisdedos, Libertaria and the other defenders died in the blaze. The next morning the Anarchists outside the village surrendered. A number were arbitrarily shot, Menéndez, Director-General of Security, having authorised the *Asaltos* to make use of the '*Ley*' *de Fugas* – execution while trying to escape.[2]

Azaña and Casares Quiroga, Minister of the Interior at this time, never really recovered from the consequences of this incident. They were immediately accused by the Right, with a certain hypocrisy, of 'murdering the people'. Martínez Barrio denounced the Government for creating a *régime* of 'blood, mud and tears'.

---

[1] Technically *Guardia de Asalto*, but henceforth abbreviated to *Asaltos*.
[2] The Report of the Commission of the Cortes on Casas Viejas is the best source on Casas Viejas, though it should be read in conjunction with Hobsbawm, who has made a careful study from Cádiz newspapers of the time. See also the account in Plá, II 188 fl.

Ortega y Gasset openly proclaimed that the Republic had disappointed him. Azaña's majority sank in the Cortes to a low figure. In April 1933 municipal elections were held in those areas which had returned Monarchists in 1931, and which had been as a result deprived of representation. The Government parties returned 5,000 councillors, the Right 4,900 and the Centre Opposition now led by Lerroux and his Radicals 4,200. It was evident that the popularity of the Ministry was in marked decline.

In the summer of 1933, therefore, Azaña resigned. All the laws complementing the Constitution had been passed. It was clearly time that the nation should once again pronounce on the work of the Government, and elections were prepared for the following November. Martínez Barrio formed a caretaker administration. Azaña and his friends went to the polls in defence of their remarkable flood of legislation: for, in addition to the main laws on education, religious orders, agriculture, the Army and Catalan home rule, the Ministry had introduced a new and most advanced divorce law, a law legalising civil marriage, laws on forced labour, collective rents, mixed arbitration boards, minimum wages, labour contracts, female rights, and Civil Service recruitment. There had been a new penal code. It was as if all the reforms of Sir Robert Peel, Gladstone and Asquith had been crowded into two years' debate. One cannot be surprised that the elections went against Azaña. But the extent of his defeat was unexpected. For his own party *Acción Republicana* only gained eight seats. Altogether, the parties which had supported the late Government gained only 99 seats, of which 58 were Socialists. The Centre, led by Lerroux's Radicals, gained 167 seats (the Radicals returned 104 seats and the Lliga, the Catalan business-men's party, 25). The Right won 207 seats. Of these, 43 were members of the Monarchist-Traditionalist alliance. There were 86 'Agrarians', a party which existed in the main to maintain the interests of the Castillian growers of wheat and olives. But the largest group on the Right, and indeed in the entire new Cortes, was the new Catholic party, the CEDA (*Confederación Española de Derechas Autónomas*).

This party had been created as a political reflection of *Acción Católica*, the large social Catholic movement started in the early 'twenties. The core of the CEDA was, however, *Acción Popular*, begun after the fall of the Monarchy to maintain Catholic interests in the politics of the Republic. The driving force behind the CEDA was Angel Herrera, editor of *El Debate*, whose aim (like, no doubt, the aim of both Pius XI and his Secretary of State, Eugenio Pacelli) was at bottom to attempt to create a Christian Democratic party in Spain on the model of those more successful after 1945 in Germany, Italy and France. However, this task was excessively difficult in Spain in the 1930s. The anticlerical character of the Constitution meant that the CEDA were unable to swear allegiance to the *régime* as it was then organised. The minor measures of anticlericalism (such as the secularisation of cemeteries and the cancellation of church parades in the Army) probably caused as much fury as the more drastic laws. Then the CEDA was inevitably an alliance of many points of view. The leaders did not wish to offend those rich men on the Right upon whom they relied for funds. They genuinely wished to prevent the *bourgeoisie* from veering towards the Monarchists and those who were totally opposed to the new Republic. Finally, José María Gil Robles, the young barrister who was picked as the leader of the CEDA from among the members of the staff of *El Debate*, undoubtedly allowed this position to go to his head. He travelled to Germany and met Hitler. He seems certainly to have played with the idea of establishing a corporative State in Spain on the model of Dolfuss' Austria. He allowed his followers to greet him in the elections as '*Jefe*' (Chief), as it might be 'Duce' or 'Führer'. His studied vagueness about his intentions – no doubt because he was concerned to keep all his followers together – roused suspicions of Fascism on the Left. This was, after all, the year of Hitler's assumption of power in Germany.

There were several reasons why the CEDA led by Gil Robles became the most powerful party in Spain after the elections of 1933. First, the Republic had given the vote to the women of Spain for the first time, and it was notorious that the female sex would vote as their confessors instructed them. And the Church as a whole made no secret about its support for the CEDA. Secondly, there was a natural swing to the Right after the two years of Republican rule, which could have been anticipated. Thirdly, while the parties of both Right and Centre combined in electoral alliances, those of the Left were in disarray. For the great Spanish Socialist party, with all the weight of its prestige and its disciplined trade union was heading Leftwards.

This change in the Socialist party derived primarily from the old fear of Largo Caballero of losing ground to the Anarchists.

Though the UGT had increased in numbers during the years when its leaders had co-operated with the Government, the CNT had also done so. The effective and co-ordinated violence of the Anarchists in recent months caused Largo to decide that it was his duty to attempt to win the Spanish working class for Socialism. This, he believed, could only be done by breaking publicly with the Republican middle-class parties, with whom the Socialists had collaborated in the Government, and by setting out to be the most extreme of all the Spanish proletarian parties. Furthermore, Largo seems to have been convinced by his new intellectual advisers, Luis Araquistain and Julio Álvarez del Vayo, that collaboration with Azaña and the *bourgeoisie* could never be successful.[1] In the elections of 1933, the Socialists polled 1,722,000 votes. But because of their isolation they gained only 58 seats, while the Radicals, with only 700,000 votes, gained 104 seats.

Among the many deputies in the Cortes elected in 1934 on behalf of small parties, there were two men who were the single representatives of their parties. These were José Antonio Primo de Rivera, the young barrister son of the old dictator, who openly proclaimed himself a Fascist; and Cayetano Bolívar, who had been returned as Communist deputy for Málaga.

Spanish Fascism had been inaugurated, while Primo de Rivera was still dictator, by Giménez Caballero. Beginning life, like most European Fascists, as a Socialist, this excitable middle-class part-poet, part-journalist, had come to admire Mussolini through the influence of Curzio Malaparte, whom he had known in Italy in 1928. Returning to Spain, he propagated a curious theory of militant 'latinity'. This attacked every development which had caused the decline of the Mediterranean countries. Germany was viewed at this time by Giménez Caballero with particular hatred, and for a while he regarded Russia as an ally of the Mediterranean. Rome was the centre of Giménez Caballero's world, being the capital of religion, as well as of Fascism. These views were, however, somewhat revised after Hitler's assumption of power in Germany in 1933. Even before that, the Nazis had had their admirers in Spain. In March 1931, a poor ex-student of the University of Madrid, Ramiro Ledesma Ramos, founded an extreme magazine, *La*

---

[1] Madariaga sees these two brothers-in-law of middle-class extraction as the *éminences grises* who drove Largo Caballero, the solid, LCC-type Socialist to revolution. There is something in this theory and certainly their replacement of Fabra Rivas as chief advisers to Largo Caballero assisted in the swing to the Left of this party.

Conquista del Estado (The Conquest of the State). In this he had
proclaimed a policy resembling that of the early German Nazis.
Ledesma even carried his admiration to the extent of copying
Hitler's quiff. He was otherwise a man of remarkable and Puritan
intolerance. In *La Conquista del Estado*, he announced that he did
not seek votes, but 'the *politique* of military feeling, of responsibility
and of struggle.' The centres of the movement were to be 'military-
type teams without hypocrisy before the rifle's barrel'.[1] One man
was immediately drawn to this steely programme. This was
Onésimo Redondo, who, like Giménez Caballero and Ledesma,
was of the middle class, had studied law at Salamanca, and worked
for a while as a treasury official. He became a Reader in Spanish
at the University of Mannheim, where he admired 'the imperturbable ranks of the Nazis'.[2] Returning to his native Valladolid
in 1930, he was responsible, with Ledesma, for the formation of
a movement portentously named *Juntas de Ofensiva Nacional-
Sindicalista* (always known as JONS). The programme of the
movement was contained in the 'sixteen points' of Valladolid of
1931. These included a denunciation of separatism and of
class war, the approval of Spanish expansion to Gibraltar,
Tangier, French Morocco and Algeria and 'the implacable
examination of foreign influences in Spain.'[3] Like comparable
German documents, the programme included penalties for
those 'who speculated with the misery and ignorance of the
people' and demanded the control (the 'disciplining') of profits. Unlike Hitler, Ledesma and Onésimo Redondo gave a
place to the Roman Catholic religion, which they named as
embodying the 'racial' tradition of the Spaniards. Catholicism
meant indeed the same to them as Aryan blood did to Hitler. But
they nevertheless criticised the Church in Spain of the time. They
regarded the CEDA, for instance, as the committed ally of
'reaction'. Here they were still opposed to Giménez Caballero.
Onésimo Redondo succeeded in founding a trade union of 3,000
workers at Valladolid in 1933. But this, for all its proletarian
aspirations was all the mass following that the Fascist movement
in Spain ever gained – save for a number of Anarchists who
had quarrelled, from personal rather than intellectual reasons,
with the CNT. Some of these Anarchist recruits included,
from the beginning, men who were simply gangsters. With
this small foundation, the JONS carried on training on Sun-

[1] *Cruzada*, III 423.   [2] *Loc. cit.*   [3] *Op. cit*, 424–5.

days, while its university representatives carried on open warfare with the FUE (*Federación Universitaria Española*), the students' union controlled by left-wing students. Meantime, other Fascist or National Socialist groups were founded and, in the prevailing political ferment, many newspapers and books, periodicals and pamphlets appeared urging a Fascist 'solution' to Spain's troubles. A vociferous group of young men gathered around José Antonio Primo de Rivera, who gradually emerged as the Leader of all the Spanish Young Fascists, a post which no one else seemed to covet.[1]

José Antonio was a tall, handsome lawyer, then in his early thirties, and filled with an engaging desire to please. Even his 'Marxist' enemies admitted his charm. His speeches and writings leave the impression of a talented undergraduate who has read, but not quite digested, an overlong course of political theory. He had begun his career as a Monarchist. He remained a Catholic. For his paper *El Fascio* (of which only one issue ever appeared) he wrote in 1933: 'The country is a historical totality . . . superior to each of us and to our groups. The State is founded on two principles – service to the united nation and the co-operation of classes.'[2] A year later, he announced: 'Fascism is a European inquietude. It is a way of knowing everything – history, the State, the achievement of the proletarianisation of public life, a new way of knowing the phenomena of our epoch. Fascism has already triumphed in some countries and in some, as in Germany, by the most irreproachable democratic means.'[3] José Antonio was always ready to fight anyone who ventured to criticise his father, and indeed his career was in some ways simply an attempt to vindicate the old dictator. He was in fact a young man genuinely concerned to find a national way of restraining the incoherence of liberalism. His favourite poem was Kipling's 'If'. He would read sections of this to his followers, before Sunday parades or possible street clashes. José Antonio founded his own party, the Falange Española, in 1933, the name being ominously taken from the Macedonian unit of battle responsible for the destruction of democracy in Greece in the fourth century BC. After the murder of one of the members of this party by a member of the FUE, José Antonio and Ledesma Ramos negotiated the amalgamation of

---

[1] Indeed, Giménez Caballero had in 1932 offered the supreme command of the Falange to Prieto. *El Socialista*, 19.5.49.

[2] *Cruzada*, V 594. [3] *Ibid.*, VI 21.

the Falange and the JONS. The new united party had aims approximately the same as the sixteen points of 1931. It adopted the JONS' symbol of the yoke and arrows and its black and red flag (the same as that of the Anarchists) but with José Antonio as the leader.[1]

The Spanish Communist party in 1933 probably did not number more than three thousand members.[2] Their leaders were insignificant. The party had been founded in 1921 by those dissident Socialists who had favoured affiliation to the Comintern, with the help of certain dissident Anarchists. The Communists had seemed so unimportant in the 'twenties that Primo de Rivera did not trouble to ban the party formally. At the start of the Republic a number of Communist exiles returned from abroad. But the leaders, chiefly Catalan, had by this time quarrelled with Stalin, having sided with Trotsky in the controversies in Russia following Lenin's death. These heretics therefore quickly broke with the official Spanish Communist party, to form various small working-class groups of their own – the leading one of these being the Workers and Peasants' Revolutionary Alliance.[3] Although not Trotskyist in the sense of being strict followers of Trotsky (they were not affiliated to the Fourth International), these men could justifiably be regarded as such since they were Marxist opponents of Stalin who shared Trotsky's general views: permanent revolution abroad, working-class collectivism at home. The quarrels between these groups were intense and prolonged. In keeping with the policy of the Soviet Government and of the Comintern, both kept themselves completely aloof at this time from all other parties in Spain, especially from the Socialists who were described by party jargon as 'social fascists'. This boycott led the Marxist groups into an occasional tactical (but not ideological) alliance with the Anarchists.

The Communists' meagre strength at this time lay in Seville, Málaga, Barcelona and Madrid. A large proportion of their members were semi-skilled workers such as café waiters. They

---

[1] The amalgamation of the Falange and the JONS was not final until February 13, 1934.

[2] At the IVth Congress of the Comintern it was said there were 5,000 members of the Spanish Communist party in 1922; at the Vth Congress, the figure remained the same. In 1931, according to figures given at the VIIth Congress, there were only 800 members. By 1934, the Comintern estimated officially that there were 20,223 members. (All these figures in Lazitch, *op. cit.*, p. 246.)

[3] This became the central group in the party which later became known as the POUM (*Partido Obrero de Unificación Marxista*).

were regarded with much more alarm than their numbers would have suggested as necessary. This was partly because of the quantity of Communist propaganda and partly because of the party's known relations with the Soviet Union. But it was also partly because most members of the Spanish *bourgeoisie* did not distinguish carefully between one or other of the proletarian parties. The Anarchists, after all, incessantly announced that they were trying to achieve 'libertarian Communism'.

In common with other Communist parties, the Spanish Communists had attached to them an 'instructor' sent from the Comintern. In Spain, this *rôle* was played by an Argentinian of Italian origin, Vittorio Codovilla (known in Spain as Comrade 'Medina'). He had spent most of his life organising the Communist parties in South America, and apparently arrived in Spain in late 1933. He was a very fat man. Jacques Doriot, when still the bright hope of the French Communist party in the early 'twenties, remarked *à propos* of Codovilla's enormous appetite: 'Louis XIII liked having around him men who ate a lot. Codovilla will do well under Stalin.'[1] Later a Bulgarian, Stepanov, came to assist Codovilla. Other agents from the Comintern also floated purposefully about Spain at this time and there is no doubt that certain Socialists such as Álvarez del Vayo acted as 'fellow travellers' with Communism. But it is not possible to know precisely what effect such persons had on the course of events. Both they themselves and their special enemies overestimated their importance. The Spanish Communists were always specially unruly. During 1934, 1935 and especially in 1936, the Soviet Union was in general attempting to forge an alliance against Hitler with Britain and France.[2] From 1934 onwards the policy of the Comintern was to establish a 'Popular Front' or alliance of all left-wing parties, working class and *bourgeoisie* included, to resist 'Fascism' – that is, any right-wing party whose activities might assist Hitler and (to a lesser extent) Mussolini. From 1934 onwards, therefore, there was emphasis by all Communist parties on the need to preserve 'parliamentary

[1] Gorkin. Throughout the 'thirties, the head of the 'Latin' section of the Comintern was the Italian Communist leader, Palmiro Togliatti, who had escaped from Mussolini's Italy in 1924, and who passed at that time under several *aliases*, notably 'Ercole Ercoli'. Before the arrival of Codovilla, Togliatti's chief representative in Spain was the German Heinz Neumann, veteran of the German and Chinese revolutions.

[2] The best summary of Soviet policy during the time of the Popular Front is given, in my opinion, by Leonard Schapiro (*The Communist Party of the Soviet Union*, London 1960, 482 fl). For reasons given below (p. 263 fn), however, I attach less importance to the evidence of General Krivitsky in *I was Stalin's Agent*.

bourgeois democracy' – admittedly until it could be replaced by 'proletarian democracy'. Yet it was precisely at this time that the Spanish Socialist party, directed by Largo Caballero, chose to head violently leftwards. The Spanish Communists were therefore forced, in order to extend their influence over the now impressionable Socialists, to adopt a position considerably to the Left of the policy favoured by the Comintern and by the Soviet Government.

The Spanish Socialist party in 1934 would have had a profound admiration for the Soviet Union and its achievements since 1917, even if the Spanish Communists had not been there to point to the Russian example. It was a time, after all, when thousands in even the sophisticated quarters of the Western World were ready to believe the American Lincoln Steffens, who returned from Moscow in 1929 to tell those waiting for him at New York airport: 'I've seen the future! And it works!'[1] The Soviet Union indeed had not yet seemed to have betrayed its first ideals. The facts of agricultural collectivisation were not yet known, and the persecution of Trotsky not understood. Stalin's purges of the old Bolsheviks had not started.[2] The Spanish Communist party were to claim that they were responsible for the elaboration of the Popular Front pact in the Spanish general elections of February 1936. But it required little prompting for the Socialists to adopt the salute with the clenched fist and bent arm (originated by the German Communists), the red flag, the revolutionary phraseology, the calls to unite in the face of international Fascism demanded throughout the world by Communist parties.

[1] I am indebted to Mr Maurice Richardson for this quotation. Cf Whittaker Chambers, *Witness*, 195, for a description of these years of 'the great drift' to Communism of middle-class intellectuals in America. Probably more important than any secret agent in Spain for the spread of Communist ideas were the tales told by Spanish workers who after the Asturias Revolution (see below, page 81) went to work on the Moscow underground. They thought this a miracle of engineering and returned to Spain full of enthusiasm for what they had seen.

[2] Kirov was assassinated in December 1934. Kamenev, Zinoviev, and others were tried for treason in January 1935. They were sentenced to imprisonment. Shortly they would be tried again with more drastic consequences.

9

Lerroux in power – the great strike of Saragossa – the Monarchists at
Rome – the Samper Government – the Ley de Cultivos *– the Basque*
mayors – the CEDA enters the Government – the October Revolution
in Madrid, Barcelona and Asturias—the character of Franco

The history of Spain during the two and a half years after
the general elections of November 1933 was marked by a
steady decline into chaos, violence, murder and, finally war.
From time to time during these tumultuous years, individuals
would attempt vainly to halt the terrible and, as it transpired,
irreversible process. They lacked the energy, luck and self-confidence necessary for success. Few can be excused for the part they
now played. For no one, and no group, possessed that greatness
and magnanimity which could alone have prevented disaster. Yet
if one cannot excuse, it is similarly hard to blame. Given the circumstances existing in Spain in the winter of 1933-4, each and everyone now played out their doomed *rôles* with inexorable logic. A
great man, possessed of the habits of compromise, compassion and
understanding might have softened the sharpness of the quarrels
which agitated the country. Such a man was not forthcoming.

The first Governments after the elections were coalitions of the
Centre, and were chiefly composed of Radicals. Lerroux became
Prime Minister. Gil Robles and the CEDA undertook to support
him in the Cortes but did not join the administration itself. This
Catholic party stood – ominously as it seemed – in the wings, waiting for the crucial moment when Gil Robles should give the word
to take over power. The transformation, meanwhile, of Lerroux
into an ally of the Catholic party of the Republic was too much for
his chief lieutenant, Martínez Barrio, who passed into opposition at
the head of his own group of Radicals, renamed the Republican
Union party.

The Government's first difficulties derived from a rash of
especially violent spontaneous strikes, all directed by the Anarchists
who attacked isolated Civil Guard posts and derailed the Barce-
lona-Seville express, killing nineteen people. In Madrid there was

a telephone strike. In both Valencia and Saragossa there were general strikes lasting for weeks. The great general strike at Saragossa of this year lasted indeed for 57 days. The CNT never issued strike pay, but the workers' resilience astonished and alarmed the rest of the country. The strikers decided at one point to send their wives and children away to Barcelona by rail. The Civil Guard fired on the train, and prevented it from reaching its destination. It was hard indeed to consider the country at peace.

In the New Year of 1934, the Government inaugurated a series of measures designed to halt the reforms of their predecessors. The substitution of lay for religious schools was indefinitely postponed. The Jesuits were shortly found teaching again.[1] Priests were paid two-thirds of their salary of 1931. And, though the Agrarian Law remained on the statute book, its application was in most places tacitly abandoned. An amnesty was granted to political prisoners – including General Sanjurjo and all those imprisoned at the time of the rising in 1932. This act of clemency merely stimulated the old plotters to new schemes. The Carlists in particular were very busy. From 1933 onwards, the villages of Navarre (like the cities of the south and centre of Spain, where the Falange, the Anarchists, the Socialist and Communist youth trained in arms) rang again with the noise of drilling. The Carlists' red berets (*boinas rojas*) were weekly seen in the market places. A dashing and ambitious young Colonel, Enrique Varela, who had twice won Spain's highest medal for gallantry in Morocco, was procured to organise training of these new *Requetés* – as the levies had been named in the Carlist wars, from a line of the marching song of their most ferocious battalion. Varela (whom the Carlist leaders Fal Conde and the Count of Rodezno had met in Guadalajara prison after the 1932 rising) travelled about these Pyrenean villages dressed as a priest, known as *Tío Pepe* (Uncle Pepe), acting as a missionary of war. When promoted a General, he was replaced by Colonel Rada.[2]

On March 31, 1934, Antonio Goicoechea, the ageing dandy who was Monarchist leader in the Cortes, together with two Carl-

[1] Though the decree formally banishing them continued to be law.

[2] Neither Rada nor Varela had Carlist or Navarrese connections. Both indeed were Andalusians. Varela was the son of a Sergeant-Major and had from the earliest age been a man of overpowering ambition. His bravery in Morocco was a byword. For this section I have used the Carlist archives in Seville and Antonio Lizarza, in his *Memorias de la Conspiración* (Pamplona 1953), 33 fl. His description of events is borne out generally by the historian of the military rising, the Catalan Felipe Bertrán Güell, in his *Preparación y Desarollo del Alzamiento Nacional* (Valladolid 1939). The diary of Maiz has also been of help.

ists (Rafael Olazabal and Antonio Lizarza) and General Barrera, visited Mussolini. The Spaniards gave an impression of disaccord as to the aim of their projected plots. Mussolini, however, brushed this aside by saying that all that was necessary was that the movement should be 'Monarchist and of a corporative and representative' tendency. He promised 1½ million pesetas, 200 machine guns and 20,000 grenades to the Spanish rebels, and agreed to send more when the rising had started. The money was paid the next day.[1] Thereafter, the *Requetés* developed fast, committees being formed to deal with, for example, recruitment of officers, propaganda, arms purchase and strategy.[2]

Four days after the strange meeting in Rome Lerroux resigned as a protest against the vacillation of the President, Alcalá Zamora, in giving his signature to the Amnesty Law. His successor Samper was also a Radical. He concentrated so far as was possible in doing as little as he could, so as not to exacerbate the situation even further. This policy postulated an entirely static political situation, which did not exist. In June, a serious situation arose in Catalonia. The Catalan Government, the Generalitat, had passed a law, the *Ley de Cultivos*, which set up an arbitration procedure for questions relating to leases of vineyards.[3] The proprietors of the vineyards complained to the supreme legal body of the Republic, the Tribunal of Constitutional Guarantees, which, by a small majority, rejected the *Ley de Cultivos* on the grounds that the Generalitat could not pronounce on such a matter. But Luis Companys, who, on Macía's death, became President of the Generalitat, solemnly ratified the law of his own accord. In taking this step which constituted a challenge to the Government in Madrid, Companys was egged on by his Counsellor for the Interior, Dencás, who was bent on using the strength of Catalan nationalism to further his own semi-Fascist designs. Despite this aspect of the Catalan dispute, Azaña nevertheless emerged from the silence which he had kept since his fall to praise the

[1] Lizarza, 23–5. News of this meeting was first revealed when certain documents were captured in Goicoechea's house during the Civil War. Goicoechea himself admitted the events in 1937.

[2] Carlist Archives. From this time onwards Don Alfonso Carlos' nephew, Xavier of Bourbon Parma, acted in conjunction with Fal Conde as 'national delegate'.

[3] This question had become acute because the vine-growers in general held their land for a period equivalent to half the length of life of the vine. The new vines planted after the phylloxera ravages had, however, a life less long than those that had existed before the epidemic. This meant that a vine grower had far less security in 1930 than in 1880.

Catalan Esquerra (of which Companys was now the leader) as 'the only truly Republican party in Spain'.

This serious constitutional dispute was still simmering when the question of the separatist aspirations of the Basques also came to the fore. The Basques' financial relations with the central Government in Madrid had been dictated by the *Concierto Económico* of 1876. This gave the Basques an autonomous fiscal system, by which they taxed themselves and paid a single sum to the State. The municipal councils of the Basque provinces now decided that certain laws introduced by the Samper Government threatened the *Concierto*. (Of course, after the elections of 1933 there had been no chance of the achievement of a Basque statute on the Catalan model.) The Basque mayors therefore decided to hold a new series of municipal elections in the three provinces of Vizcaya, Guipúzcoa and Álava, wherein the elected representatives would declare themselves publicly in favour of the *Concierto*. The Government forbade the elections. When, despite this prohibition, the elections were nevertheless held, the mayors were arrested. A series of wild demonstrations in favour of Basque home rule followed throughout the three provinces.

While both separatist problems in Spain had thus become simultaneously acute, the nation was further shocked by the sudden rumour that 70 cases of arms had been landed in Asturias by the steamer *Turquesa*.[1] The Government proclaimed a state of alarm. Gil Robles, in a great meeting of the CEDA held at Covadonga, the sanctuary in Asturias commemorating the point where the Visigoth King Pelayo began the *Reconquista* of Spain from the Moors, announced: 'We will no longer suffer this state of affairs to continue.' The CNT and UGT, acting together for the first time since 1917, immediately proclaimed a general strike in Asturias, so making it very difficult for the CEDA delegates to this meeting to return home to Madrid. A week later, Gil Robles declared that, when the Cortes met again in October, he and his party would no longer support the Government of Samper. The clear inference was that he would himself take over power. At this, the UGT issued a statement denouncing Gil Robles, 'the lay Jesuit'. If the CEDA should enter the Government without declar-

[1] These were arms bought from certain Portuguese revolutionaries in Cádiz by leading members of the UGT. The steamer left Cádiz with the destination 'Jibouti' pasted on the cases but was later diverted to the Asturias. See an article of Prieto's in *España Republicana* of Buenos Aires, quoted in Blasco Grandi *Togliatti en España* (Madrid 1954), 9.

ing support for the Republic, the UGT would not answer for their
future action. The inference was that the UGT would regard the
entry of the CEDA into the Government as the first step towards
the establishment of a Fascist state in Spain. Gil Robles's reluctance
to declare his adhesion to the Republic derived from a fear of losing many of his right-wing supporters if he did so, since he would
seem to be accepting the still unrevised anticlerical clauses of the
Constitution. But this was the late summer of 1934. The Spanish
Socialists of the UGT had seen how the German and Austrian
Socialists had been overwhelmed by Hitler and Dolfuss respectively
during the last 18 months. Where lay the difference between
Dolfuss and Gil Robles?

The time for the re-assembly of the Cortes drew near. On
October 4, Gil Robles withdrew the support of the CEDA from
Samper's ineffective Government, which immediately resigned.
Spain held its breath. To everyone's surprise, the President Alcalá
Zamora did not ask Gil Robles to form a Government. Instead,
Lerroux was once more entrusted with this difficult task. But he
included three members of the CEDA in his Cabinet, though not
Gil Robles himself.

The reaction was swift and violent. In Madrid, the UGT proclaimed a general strike and certain Socialist militants advanced
firing towards the Ministry of the Interior in the Puerta del Sol.
However, the Anarchist CNT did not support the strike. The
Alianza Obrera[1] which Largo Caballero had tried to form throughout the country of all working-class parties only extended in
Madrid to the Socialists and some Communists. There was general
confusion. Largo Caballero dithered. By the end of the day, the
Government were masters of the situation, and all the Socialist
leaders had been arrested.

In Barcelona, the entry of the CEDA into the Government
stimulated Companys to a proclamation of 'the Catalan State'
as part of a 'federal Spanish Republic.' Once again Companys
was stimulated to this precipitate action by his adviser, Dencás,
who had by now raised a new militia, the '*Escamots*'. This force was
organised on the model of Fascist militias, although it was nominally Catalan Nationalist. Yet the burden of Companys' public
appeal to Catalonia was an attack on the Fascism of the CEDA:
'The monarchical and Fascist powers which have been for some
time attempting to betray the Republic have attained their object,'

[1] Working-class Alliance.

announced Companys. 'In this solemn hour, in the name of the people and of parliament, the Government over which I preside assumes all the functions of power in Catalonia, proclaims the Catalan State of the Federal Spanish Republic, and, strengthening its relations with those who direct this general protest against Fascism, invites them to establish the provisional Government of the Republic in Catalonia.' This curious speech was at once a proclamation of a quite new relationship between Catalonia and the rest of Spain and also an incitement to the Opposition to declare themselves the Government, if necessary establishing themselves in Barcelona. It was not lost on Lerroux and his Ministers in Madrid that Azaña was actually at this moment in Barcelona.[1]

This Catalan rebellion was, however, crushed nearly as quickly as the general strike had been in Madrid. There was some fighting between Dencás's *Escamots* and the *Mozos de Escuadra* (the special security force established to protect the Generalitat) against the Civil Guard and the regular soldiers. Some twenty people were killed. The Anarchists of the FAI and CNT held aloof. Companys sent for General Batet, commander of the division established in Barcelona, and asked him to transfer his allegiance to the new Federal *régime*. Batet, who was a Catalan, vacillated for a moment, and then answered, 'I am for Spain.' He thereupon arrested Companys and his Government – with the exception of Dencás, who escaped down a sewer to freedom.[2] All resistance was quickly overcome in the rest of Barcelona, and Companys broadcast a dignified appeal to his followers to lay down their arms.

The 'October revolution' was thus overcome in Madrid and in Barcelona. There were other outbursts and strikes in the rest of Spain, but, with one exception, these were also crushed. The exception was Asturias.[3] Here the rising – for such it undoubtedly was – was directed by the tough and highly politically conscious miners of the region. These miners were almost the show working

[1] There is no evidence to suggest that Azaña knew what the Catalans and the Socialists were plotting. On the other hand, I think Professor Peers is right in suggesting that Azaña was perfectly ready to accept the Presidency of a new federal Spain, if such a crown had been offered to him.

[2] His future history is obscure, but there seems little doubt that he later worked as agent for Mussolini.

[3] The Asturias revolution of 1934 awaits its historian. The following account is chiefly based on the narratives in *La Revolution d'Octobre en Espagne*, a pamphlet issued by the Government in Madrid in 1935, Mrs Leah Manning's *What I saw in Spain* (London 1935), Jellinek's account in *The Civil War in Spain* and Manuel Grossi's diary of events, *La Insurrección de Asturias*, written in Cartagena prison in 1935.

class of Spain. Their action was primarily politically rather than economically inspired. And while, elsewhere in Spain, the working-class parties had all been divided about the attempted rising, in Asturias Anarchists, Socialists, Communists and the semi-Trots-kyists of the Workers and Peasants' Alliance co-operated under the rallying cry UHP (*Unión de Hermanos Proletarios*).[1]

The rising in Asturias was carefully prepared throughout the province, with its centres in Oviedo, the capital, and in the nearby mining towns of Mieres and Sama. The signal for the rising as elsewhere was the entry of the CEDA into the Government. But the miners were very well organised for this eventuality. They had supplies of arms. They had dynamite. They already possessed joint workers' committees to direct their activities. And their reaction to the apparent 'Fascist' conquest of power in Madrid was to launch, so far as was possible, a full-scale working-class revolu-tion. 'Towards half past eight in the morning,' recorded Manuel Grossi, 'a crowd of about two thousand persons gathered before the town hall of Mieres, already occupied by the rebel workers (*obreros insurrectos*). I proclaimed, from one of the balconies, the Socialist Republic. The enthusiasm was indescribable. *Vivas* for the revolution were followed by others for the Socialist Republic. When I managed to make myself heard again, I gave instructions to continue the action . . .'[2] This implied attacks on the Civil Guard posts, churches, convents, town halls and other key buildings in the villages and towns of the province.

Within three days of the start of the revolution, much of the Province was in the hands of the miners. Each town or village was controlled by a revolutionary committee which made itself res-ponsible for the feeding and the security of the inhabitants. A radio station installed at Turón maintained excitement and morale. The arms factories at Trubía and La Vega (Oviedo) were taken over by a committee of their workers and were made to work night and day. Elsewhere, factories and mines were deserted (in recent years many of the latter had anyway been partially closed). Recruitment offices demanded the services of all workers between the ages of eighteen and forty for the 'Red Army'. Thirty thousand workers had been mobilised for battle within ten days.[3] The degree of co-

---

[1] Union of Working-class Brothers. UHP is pronounced 'oo-archie-pay'.

[2] Grossi, 25.

[3] *Le Révolution d'Octobre*, 40. Grossi speaks of 50,000 miners being under arms by the end of the revolution; 30,000 is more probable. Of these, some 20,000 may be supposed to have been members of the UGT, 4,000 of the CNT, and 6,000 of other groups.

operation between the different parties surprised even themselves. Even the Anarchists recognised 'the need for temporary dictatorship', though the mere fact that the scale of this activity was limited to a group of *pueblos* prevented questions of State organisation from dividing them from the Communists. The Communists in some *pueblos* showed themselves keener on establishing their own dictatorship than sending men to the front. But as a rule, the cry UHP! was in no way misleading.

While the miners of Asturias had thus successfully established a revolutionary Soviet throughout their province, they were also engaged all the time in fighting. This occurred mostly at first in Oviedo and in Gijón. The regular troops based in Asturias and commanded by General López Ochoa were too few in number to be able to conduct any more than a holding operation in the region of Avilés, to the north-west of Oviedo. In the meantime, there was a certain amount of pillage and unprovoked violence on the part of the revolutionaries. The local committees set out to maintain discipline throughout the area under their control. And to a great extent they were successful in so doing. But there were a number of outrages. Several churches and convents were burned. The bishop's palace and much of the University of Oviedo were destroyed during the attempts to capture the Pelayo barracks, which were held by the Civil Guard. Several priests were shot, especially in Turón. At Sama, 30 Civil Guards and 40 *Asaltos* sustained a siege of a day and a half. When they surrendered they were all shot. Certain women of the middle class were raped and killed. These atrocities were no doubt the consequence of confusion rather than of design; but they inevitably greatly worsened the crisis.

The Government in Madrid now found themselves faced by what no one, either workers or *bourgeoisie*, would have denied was in fact a civil war. Indeed, the committee in control of the mining village of Mieres were contemplating a march on Madrid itself. Though they did not of course know this, Lerroux and his Ministers now took several severe decisions. First they sent for Generals Goded and Francisco Franco to act as joint Chiefs of Staff to direct the suppression of the rebellion. And secondly, they accepted the advice of these two officers when they recommended the despatch of the Foreign Legion, the key corps in the conquest of Morocco, to reduce the miners.

Francisco Franco Bahamonde was just forty when he reached

the War Office under Lerroux.[1] Born in 1892 at El Ferrol in Galicia, the son of a naval paymaster, and of naval ancestry on both sides of his family, he was at first himself intended for the Navy. But there was no room in the Naval Cadet School. Instead he went, in 1907, to the Infantry Academy at Toledo. Then he was posted to Morocco, where he became, in quick succession, the youngest Captain, Major, Colonel and General in the Army – gaining the last rank after the victorious end to the campaign. He had commanded the Foreign Legion from 1923 to 1927 and had suggested, and later led, the landing in Alhucemas Bay in 1925 behind the lines of Abd-el-Krim, which led to victory. Throughout these years Franco was totally dedicated to his profession – he never drank, never went out with women and, at that time (as his pious biographers make haste to interject), never went to Mass.[2] He was known as a strict, even a cruel, disciplinarian. He had a reputation for incomparable bravery and for extraordinary good luck under fire. He was a brilliant organiser and the efficiency of the Foreign Legion was chiefly due to him. He had gained his first experience of fighting revolutions during the General Strike of 1917, when he was temporarily posted to Oviedo. He had married – after many delays due to campaigning – a strongly Catholic girl of good Asturian family, Carmen Polo. Franco was short in height and even in early middle life had developed a plump stomach. His voice had also acquired a high-pitched tone which caused him to give military commands the note of a prayer. He had the patience and caution of the typical native of Galicia, qualities so notably lacking in the characters of Casares Quiroga and Calvo Sotelo. His caution indeed, in the years of the Republic, amounted to vacillation. He had a great reputation as the 'brilliant young General', but he consistently refused to declare himself on any side in politics. When in April 1931 it was rumoured in the Madrid cafés that the Government intended to appoint him High Commissioner of Morocco, Franco announced publicly that he would refuse such a post since to accept would reveal 'a prejudice in favour of the *régime* recently installed and of lukewarm loyalty to those who only yesterday epitomised the nation.'[3]

[1] There is no adequate biography of this clever, harsh, patient and unimaginative General. Hagiographies abound, but these do less than justice to their subject.

[2] His puritanism may be attributed to the indiscretions of his father, the naval paymaster, who lived licentiously until his death, in his nineties, nearly ten years after his son had become Head of State.

[3] *ABC*, 18.4.31.

Yet when Monarchist conspirators were asked, 'Is Franco with you?' they were unable to give a clear answer. He had never been associated with the officers who supported General Sanjurjo in the *Pronunciamiento* of 1932.[1] At the same time, Republicans thought from addresses he had given, when commandant at Saragossa, that he was a friend of authoritarian rule. They knew too that he had for a long time been interested in politics. As early as 1926 he had been demanding books on political theory to be sent to his headquarters.[2] But the General's brother, Ramón, a noted pilot who had been the first man to fly the South Atlantic, was thought to be a Republican. He had certainly been so in 1930, when he had dropped Republican pamphlets (and had been with difficulty restrained from dropping bombs) over the Royal Palace during the abortive Republican rising of that year. On the other hand, Franco's brother-in-law – the two had married sisters – was the CEDA youth leader Ramón Serrano Suñer.

The Government called not only on General Franco to direct the battle against the miners but also upon his old corps, the Foreign Legion, chiefly because they doubted whether any other regular troops would be successful. The Minister of War, the Radical Diego Hidalgo, later explained that he was appalled at the alternative prospect of seeing the young conscripts from the peninsula dying in Asturias because of their inexperience. They would be fighting against past masters of dynamiting and of the technique of the ambush. 'I decided,' he wrote, 'that it was necessary to call on the units which Spain maintains for its defence, whose *métier* is to fight and die in the accomplishment of their duty.'[3] Within a few hours of General Franco's arrival at the Ministry of War, the Foreign Legion was despatched under Colonel Yagüe to relieve the regular garrisons in Asturias.

The legionaries were immediately successful. Accompanied by certain Moorish *Regulares* and by aircraft, they swiftly 'liberated' Oviedo and Gijón. In these towns, the conquerors gave themselves over to a repression which exceeded in horror and number any of the atrocities committed by the miners. After fifteen days of war and revolution which seemed, nevertheless, a lifetime to all

---

[1] Bertrán Güell names him as having been among the conspirators who plotted together earlier in 1932. He was then angered by Azaña's dissolution of the Academy at Saragossa.
[2] Information deriving from Dr Gregorio Marañón.
[3] *La Revolution d'Octobre*, 41.

who took part, the rebels finally surrendered. Belarmino Tomás, the Socialist leader who had been at the centre of all the fighting, spoke in the following terms to a great crowd of miners gathered in the main square of Sama: 'Comrades, red soldiers! Here before you, certain that we have fulfilled the mandate with which you have entrusted us, we come to speak of the melancholy plight into which our glorious insurrectionary movement has fallen. We have to describe our peace conversations with the General of the enemy army. We have been defeated only for the time being. All that we can say is that in the rest of the Provinces of Spain the workers did not do their duty and support us. Because of this failure, the Government has been able to conquer the insurrection in Asturias. Furthermore, though we have rifles, machine guns and cannons, we have no more ammunition. All we can do therefore is to arrange peace. But this does not mean that we abandon the class struggle. Our surrender today is simply a halt on the route, where we make good our mistakes, preparing for our next battle which must end in the final victory of the exploited . . .'[1]

There followed a terrible retribution. One of the conditions for the surrender of the miners had been that the Legion and the *Regulares* should be withdrawn from Asturias. This condition was not kept, and indeed it had only been authorised by General López Ochoa, and not by the Ministry of War. These forces behaved in the conquered territory precisely as if they were a victorious army living off the sufferings of the vanquished. Some 1,300 persons were estimated to have been killed during the campaign (and nominally also during the repression) and nearly 3,000 wounded. But of the dead only 100 had been Civil Guards, 98 soldiers, 86 *Asaltos* and *Carabineros*. Over one thousand were officially listed as civilians – but these must be presumed mostly miners. Such figures are likely to be over modest, though it is doubtful whether they reached the number of 5,000 later named by the victims of the repression. Certainly most of the deaths occurred after the end of the fighting, at the time when the Legion were driving home their victory by terror.[2] Thirty thousand political prisoners were also

[1] Grossi, 218.
[2] A statement by the Ministry of the Interior on January 3, 1935, gave a casualty list for all Spain in October 1934 of 1,335 killed and 2,951 wounded; 730 buildings had been destroyed or seriously damaged. Oviedo was a ruin, though the estimated cost of the rising did not exceed £1 million. No fewer than 90,000 rifles were captured, together with 33,000 pistols, 10,000 cases of dynamite, 30,000 grenades and 330,000 cartridges.

made in Spain during October and November 1934. Of these, the great majority were in Asturias. The *casas del pueblo* of the region were turned into extra prisons, and those held within were subjected to every kind of indignity and many to torture.[1] A journalist, Luis Sirval, who ventured to point out these terrible things, was himself arrested and murdered in prison by three young officers of the Legion. Meantime, in Madrid, Generals Franco and Goded were regarded as the saviours of the nation.

[1] For an entirely *vraisemblable* account of the repression of the Legion in Asturias, see the first chapters of Martín Blázquez.

10

Consequences of Asturias – Lerroux's attempt at a middle way –
straperlo – *the Republic in an* impasse – *the elections of February*
16, 1936

After the revolution of October 1934 and the manner in
which it had been quelled, it would have required a superhuman effort to avoid the culminating disaster of civil
war. But no such effort was forthcoming. All the Socialist leaders
were in prison.[1] They were accompanied there by leaders of the
Catalan Government, by Azaña and by several other left-wing
politicians. In these conditions, the Asturias rising assumed an epic
significance in the minds of the Spanish working class. Some, echo-
ing the last words of Belarmino Tomás in the doomed gathering in
Sama, prophesied darkly that October 1934 would be to Spain
what 1905 had been to Russia. Largo Caballero passed his captivity in reading, apparently for the first time, the works of Marx and
Lenin. Now approaching seventy, after a lifetime of cautious re-
formism, this long respected and moderate Socialist leader became
increasingly dominated by revolutionary images. Meantime, in
Paris, Romain Rolland expressed the feeling which the combatants
certainly felt about the Asturias rising when he announced that the
world had seen nothing so beautiful since the Paris Commune.[2]

Asturias, naturally, caused a thrill of horror to run through the
Spanish middle class. To them it now seemed that almost anything,
even a military dictatorship, was preferable to the continuation of
the present state of political disintegration. Would General Franco
perhaps take over power now that he was Chief of Staff and in the
Ministry of War? Why did not Gil Robles and the CEDA make the
best use of their opportunity? There was surprisingly little talk at
this period of the Falange, chiefly because José Antonio was engaged in a controversy with the old leader of the JONS, Ledesma
Ramos. The latter had always regarded José Antonio as no more

[1] Prieto, however, escaped to France (as he had done in 1930 at the time of the Jaca
rising). He had opposed the scheme of a rising against the Government.
[2] Quoted by Grossi.

THE ORIGINS OF THE WAR 87

than a *señorito*, and bitterly criticised him for his contacts with the Church and the upper class.[1] Eventually, after Ledesma had written a series of articles denouncing José Antonio as the 'tool of reaction', he was expelled from the Falange. These events, and the continuing financial difficulties of these young Spanish Fascists, caused their numbers to remain almost static during the period following the Asturias revolution when one might have expected them to increase their appeal. They continued to parade in their blue shirts on Sundays. But with their working-class enemies cowed or in prison, they seemed to have little to do. Other semi-Fascist groups, such as those centred around Ramiro de Maeztu's *Acción Española*, kept up a vociferous and passionate campaign of polemics. Nor, with General Franco at the Ministry of War and Monarchist or known right-wing officers being given commands, was there much activity among the military conspirators at this time. The Carlists, however, were still active in Navarre. Not content with drilling their prospective rank and file they had even opened a military academy for the training of officers in Pamplona. And, as a development of the agreement of March 1934 with Mussolini, four hundred young Carlists were sent to be trained in Italy for modern warfare.[2]

Lerroux meantime was still Prime Minister of Spain. In the following months he did his best to steer a moderate and middle path through the maelstrom of Spanish politics. Thus when the Monarchists demanded that the Catalan Statute should be abolished altogether after Companys' revolution, Lerroux (here

[1] José Antonio's relations with the Army and other forces of the 'old Spain' which Ledesma denounced derived partly from financial necessity, partly from his liking for the social connections with which, as the son of the dictator, he had been brought up, but also partly because he had no confidence that his party would grow fast enough to defeat Socialism. It was in those words at least that he had put it in a curious letter to General Franco just before the Asturias rising, on September 24, 1934. In this, he intimated to Franco that he would be willing to support a military *coup d'état* to restore the 'lost historical destiny of the country'. Franco did not, apparently, answer the letter. (This information was first published in *Y*, the review of the *Sección Femenina* of the Falange in October 1938. It is quoted in full in Ximénez de Sandoval, 224.)

[2] Lizarza, 42. It is instructive to note that Colonel Rada, who was concerned with the training of the Carlist levies in Navarre, also had close relations with the Falange. For a time he commanded the Falange militia, and, on the morning of October 7, 1934, when the Socialist general strike began in Madrid, he drove about looking for trouble in the same motor car as José Antonio, Ledesma Ramos and the pilot Ruiz de Alda. The last named was José Antonio's closest associate at this time (apparently he thought of the name 'Falange'). He was himself a native of Estella (Navarre). José Antonio also had several discussions in 1934–5 with Colonel Barba of *Unión Militar*. (Cacho Zabalza. 23.)

supported by the CEDA) secured its suspension only, with the Catalan provinces being administered under a Governor General. The most difficult question for the *régime*, however, concerned the punishment of the rebels of 1934. For, by late March 1935, the military tribunals which had been set up to try the offenders had named twenty death penalties. Of these two had already been carried out.[1] By this time, too, Luis Sirval, the journalist who had drawn attention to the horror of the repression of the Legion, had also been murdered. Lerroux and the Radicals, picturing the lasting bitterness which would be caused by the execution of, say, Belarmino Tomás and González Peña (the two Socialist deputies for Asturias) or of Companys, favoured the commutation of all further death sentences. The CEDA, however, and therefore the CEDA Ministers, supported the death penalty. Lerroux was supported by the President, Alcalá Zamora, who recalled how General Sanjurjo and his co-plotters had been reprieved in 1932. The sentences were commuted. The CEDA Ministers resigned. After a prolonged Governmental crisis, Lerroux formed a new Cabinet in which the CEDA now had five representatives, including Gil Robles as Minister for War. But there were no more executions. Companys, Largo Caballero and other leaders convicted of rebellion were sentenced to thirty years' imprisonment – a sentence which no one for a moment believed would be carried out in full. Azaña was released, the charges against him having failed to gain an absolute majority in the Cortes.[2]

The new right-wing and Catholic Government of Spain now proceeded to waste their opportunities. A revision of some clauses of the Constitution was proposed. This might have modified the character of regional autonomy, established a senate, and altered the divorce and marriage laws. An independent financier, Chapaprieta, prepared to introduce a budget – which had not been seen in the Republic since 1932. He desired to prune Civil Service corruption and bureaucratic waste. But these measures, admirable in themselves, would have cut Government spending on education – including the still miserably inadequate teachers' salaries. However, no budget and no constitutional revision were ever agreed. First, the moderate CEDA Minister of Agriculture,

---

[1] These were, firstly, on a bandit of Barcelona whose part in the revolution hardly differed from his normal activities; and secondly, on a Sergeant in the regular army, Vázquez, who had deserted from his unit in Asturias and then joined the miners.

[2] The vote against him was nevertheless 189–68. He was tried in the Cortes, since there was no evidence to bring him before a military tribunal.

Jiménez Fernández, resigned over a proposed alteration of the Agrarian Law. Chapaprieta himself formed a Government, in which Lerroux became Foreign Minister. But next the whole Radical party was suddenly and irretrievably ruined by a financial scandal. A Dutch financial adventurer, Daniel Strauss, persuaded certain of the Radical Ministers to favour a scheme to introduce a new type of roulette wheel, the *straperlo*. Strauss promised that in return for permission to introduce the *straperlo*, he would guarantee vast profits. When the scandal broke, Lerroux's nephew and adopted son was found to be intimately concerned with Strauss. Lerroux himself, whose finances had always been tricky, was also clearly involved. He and the other Radicals resigned amid howls of public execration. To many Spaniards, the *straperlo* – the word passed into the language as signifying a financial scandal affecting public men – symbolised the failure of middle-class democracy to establish proper standards of public conduct. Finally, within a matter of weeks, the Prime Minister Chapaprieta quarrelled with the CEDA over the proposed budget. Gil Robles and his friends resigned.

This was, as the enemies of democracy hastened to point out, the twenty-sixth Governmental crisis of the Republic. Seventy-two Ministers had served in one or other of the Cabinets of the past four and a half years. Each of these drew pensions to maintain themselves in the dignity of ex-Minister. The feeling in the country towards democratic procedure closely resembled that in France in May 1958, after fifteen years of the Fourth Republic. Alcalá Zamora tried every combination of parties to try and achieve an administration. He was unsuccessful. After due deliberation, Alcalá Zamora decided to dissolve the Cortes and to call for new elections. In order that there should be some Government to carry on the business of administration until after the vote, Alcalá Zamora named Portela Valladares, an ex-Minister of the Monarchy and the indefatigable historian of the Priscillian heresy, to form a caretaker Government.

The Cortes was dissolved on January 4. The elections were to be held on February 16. The electoral campaign which intervened between these dates was dominated by Gil Robles. His photograph as the '*Jefe*', with a legend beneath demanding for him 'the Ministry of War and all the power', stared threateningly from the hoardings of the cities. However, as the campaign got under way, it became clear to the leaders of the CEDA that their path to power might not be so easy as they had at first assumed. They therefore began to arrange common lists, with various other right-wing parties. The Falange, the Monarchists and Carlists, together with the 'Agrarians' and 'Independents', eventually stood in alliance in most places with the CEDA in a block which they named 'the National Front'. But delay in deciding to ally un-doubtedly cost the National Front a number of votes.

To the Left of this alliance there were various independent parties of the Centre. These included Lerroux and his Radicals, the Lliga (Catalan businessmen), the Progressives – followers of Alcalá Zamora – and a 'Centre party', hopefully launched at the last minute by the Prime Minister, Portela Valladares. Also classed among the parties of the Centre were the Basque Nationa-list party, who, although ever since 1934 they had been on extremely bad terms with the Right and their Catholic colleagues of the CEDA, still had no intention of making a clear alliance with the Left.[1]

The parties of the Left in the elections of February 1936 had been grouped in a Popular Front pact. The name had been pro-posed by the Communist party. The previous August, the 7th Congress of the Comintern had been held in Moscow. Dimitrov, the Bulgarian Communist then General Secretary of the Comintern (due to his defiant behaviour when accused of setting fire to the Reichstag) had defined the political aims of world Communism in the face of the threat presented to the Soviet Union by the rise of Hitler: 'The formation of a joint People's Front providing for joint action with Social Democratic parties is a necessity. Cannot we endeavour to unite the Communist, Social Democratic, Catholic and other workers? Comrades, you will remember the ancient tale of the capture of Troy. The attacking army was unable to achieve victory until, with the aid of the Trojan Horse, it penetrated to the very heart of the enemy camp. We, revolutionary workers, should not be shy of using the same tactics.'[2] With these words, the policy of the Popular Front was formally launched. Communist parties were blamed for having in the past treated every *bourgeois*

---

[1] Nor with the Right. A group of Basque deputies were unsuccessfully reprimanded for not joining hands with the CEDA by Mgr. Pizzardo, Assistant Papal Secretary of State. (From a diary of one of those present, quoted by Iturralde, I 394.)

[2] Minutes of the 7th meeting of the Comintern, published by the Communist party of Great Britain. The image of the Trojan horse should be regarded as a justifica-tion to foreign Communist parties of the idea of collaboration with the *bourgeoisie* rather than as a specially sinister threat to the *bourgeoisie* itself.

party as Fascist. Now they were adjured to preserve *bourgeois*, parliamentary democracy until it could be replaced by 'proletarian democracy'. This policy of the Popular Front went, of course, even further than that of the so-called United Front in the 1920s. Then (as in Eastern Europe after 1945) Communist parties had been instructed to make common cause with other working-class parties. With the Popular Front, they had to establish relations with middle-class parties also. This policy was for the Soviet Government and for its most trusted followers on the executive committee of the Comintern at best a compromise. It was a compromise dictated by the need to preserve the long term Communist aim of the overthrow of all capitalist and *bourgeois* society at the same time as the recognition that the Soviet Government needed to ally with some at least of the *bourgeois* countries (France and Britain above all) to withstand Hitler's Germany.

The consequences of the Popular Front were to be more important in Spain than anywhere else. But for the time being, the Spanish Communists hardly contributed any more than the name of the Popular Front Pact. For the conditions for collaboration in Spain between working-class parties and the liberal parties, as represented by Azaña (who now called themselves the Left Republican party), and also somewhat surprisingly by Martínez Barrio's ex-Radicals of the Republican Union party, existed without the Communists having to exert themselves. Such conditions had indeed existed throughout most of the Republic. The difference was that in 1936 the middle-class followers of Azaña and Martínez Barrio were prepared to accept alliance with the Socialists even in their revolutionary mood of Asturias, in place of their moderate mood of 1931. By both these large parties, also, the Spanish Communist party was still regarded as too small to be a threat. (In France, on the other hand, the very size of the Communist party rendered its collaboration with Blum more difficult.) The semi-Trotskyists of the Workers and Peasants' Alliance shortly to be rechristened the POUM (*Partido Obrero de Unificación Marxista*) after another shuffle of internal power, also supported the Popular Front in the elections of February 1936. But the Anarchists of the FAI and CNT remained outside. Nevertheless, at the last minute, they did encourage their members in some districts to repeat before the ballot box the unity with other parties first expressed in the Asturias rising. This was because one of the main measures of the Popular Front programme was an amnesty for all political prisoners.[1]

Other measures in the programme of the Popular Front also harked back to Asturias. All those suffering from unemployment for political reasons would be reinstated – a clear warning to those employers who had secured new labour to replace those in prison, or those whom they had sacked after the strikes of October 1934. An indemnity to the victims of 1934 would be paid by the State. The Catalan Statute would be restored. Other regional statutes would be negotiated. The Agrarian Law and other reforms begun in 1933 would be given priority.

The ensuing election campaign was fought comparatively cleanly. Alcalá Zamora had lifted all press censorship and also the 'state of alarm' which had existed in many areas since the time of the Asturias rising. Words, but only words, were violent. 'Vatican Fascism', proclaimed one election leaflet, 'offered you work and brought hunger; it offered you peace and brought five thousand tombs; it offered you order and raised a gallows. The Popular Front offers no more and no less than it will bring: Bread, Peace and Liberty!'[2] Lerroux and the Radicals concentrated their efforts on destroying the Centre party launched by Portela. Calvo Sotelo, ex-Minister of Finance under the dictatorship of Primo de Rivera now appeared for the first time as a national figure as leader of the Monarchist *Renovación Española* in place of Antonio Goioechea (since he had attended several meetings of plotters against the Republic while in exile in Paris during 1931 and 1932, he was no stranger to the general conspiratorial character of the party). On January 19, he warned all patriotic Spaniards that if they did not vote for the National Front, a Red Flag would fly over Spain – 'that Red Flag which is the symbol of the destruction of Spain's past and of her ideals.'

Spain went to the polls on February 16, the Sunday of the Carnival before Lent. Thirty-four thousand Civil Guards and 17,000 *Asaltos* were on duty. *Carabineros* guarded banks and Embassies in Madrid to enable as many police as possible to guard the polling stations. Conditions were generally calm. Three men were

[1] The motives of the Soviet Government and its labyrinthine intrigues throughout the time of the Popular Front are further discussed on pages 214 fl below. I have here only indicated that much of the story which seems essential for the understanding of the elections of February 1936.

[2] *Pan, Paz y Libertad.* From a leaflet in my possession. The five thousand refers to the number of workers allegedly killed in the repression of Asturias.

reported later shot in various villages. There were some disturbances in Granada, where the polling booth was held up by force, while others stuffed votes into the ballot urn. But such instances were rare. *The Times* correspondent, Ernest de Caux, reported that voting had been 'generally exemplary'.[1] The results of the first round of the elections were as follows. (I have given the figures for second round in parentheses.)

Popular Front

Socialists	85		(99)
Republican Left	75	(Azaña's party)	(87)
Republican Union	32	(Martínez Barrio)	(39)
Esquerra	20	(Catalan Separatist Left)	(36)
Communists	14		(17)
Others	30		—
	256		**278**

Right (*National Front*)

CEDA	94	(Gil Robles)	(88)
Agrarians	12	(i.e. landowners)	(11)
Monarchists	11	(Calvo Sotelo)	(13)
Independents	12		(10)
Traditionalists	11	(Carlists)	(9)
Others	3		(3)
	143		**(134)**

Centre

Centre Party	19	(party of Portela Valladares, the outgoing Premier)	(16)
Lliga	11	(Catalan businessmen)	(12)
Radicals	8	(Lerroux)	(4)
Progressives	6	(Alcalá Zamora)	(6)
Basques[2]	5		(10)
Others	5		(7)
	54		**(55)[3]**

[1] *The Times*, 17.2.36.
[2] If the seats obtained by the Basques were included among their future allies of the Popular Front, the seats of that group would be increased to 261, and those of the Centre decreased to 49.
[3] There were 3 seats still vacant after the second ballot.

Since electors voted for alliances and not individual parties, it was not possible to give an aggregate of the votes cast for each party. However, the aggregate votes for each group were:

Popular Front	4,176,156
Basque Nationalists	130,000
Centre	681,047
National Front	3,783,601

Thus the Popular Front had established itself as the leading group in terms of votes cast as well as seats. But if the Centre and the Right had added their votes together they would have had a small numerical majority.[1] This had, of course, nothing to do with the Constitution as then organised. The Left had gained far fewer seats in 1934 than they would have done if these had been in direct proportion to the votes cast in their favour. But later there was much juggling with these figures to prove that the Popular Front had assumed power illegally. Meantime, there were still 20 more seats to fill. These were those where no one had gained 40% of the votes cast.[2]

[1] And if the seats where a second round of voting was necessary under the Constitution were nevertheless reckoned with the general aggregate in the first round, the Right could have had a majority over the Left.

[2] The amount of juggling with the figures is endless since in respect of several persons of the Centre and therefore of the votes cast for them, the distinction as to whether they were really Left or Right was blurred. As to intimidation, if one or two incidents occurred, these stood out because they were exceptional. Further, if some of these incidents could be put down to the Left, there is no doubt that, in country districts, peasants extremely left-wing in aspiration voted Right. They did this, as they had always done, out of fear of the local *cacique*, or landowner's agent. Thus, in August, Dr Franz Borkenau visited the village of Alía in the Tagus valley to find it in a state of the most intense revolutionary excitement which he had seen in all Spain. Yet this village had voted solidly Right in February. Such realities make the incessant chopping about of the number of votes cast and the number of seats somewhat fanciful.

*Franco and Portela Valladares – the prisons are opened – Azaña back
in power – the Falange's murder campaign – Largo Caballero as 'the
Spanish Lenin' – Calvo Sotelo's emergence – Mola at Pamplona –
quarrels of the Left – Alcalá Zamora removed – the April riots –
Azaña President – Communist plots – José Antonio joins the
conspiracy*

While the results of the first round of the elections of
February 16 were coming in, General Franco, still
Chief of Staff at the Ministry of War, called on the
Prime Minister, Portela Valladares. As a result of his and Goded's
pacification of the Asturias, this vacillating but ambitious officer
had gained a reputation as an implacable enemy of the Left. Perhaps he had already seen in the enthusiasm with which the middle
class had hailed his conduct of the repression a glimpse of what
prizes were possible for him if he only kept his head. Asturias may
finally have convinced him that the divisions in Spain were past
healing and that it was time he threw in his lot with the forces of
'order'. Yet he was still an unpolitical General. Unlike most of his
colleagues in the Spanish Army, he had no *cuadrilla* of sycophants
urging him to this or that course of action. People would still be
heard asking: 'Where does Franco stand?' Salvador de Madariaga (then Republican representative at the League of Nations)
and Dr Marañón separately met Franco during the winter of
1935–6. Both believed the Chief of Staff to have been sincere when
he told them that he had no intention of joining any plot against
the Republic.[1] But nevertheless, three weeks later, Franco urged
the caretaker Prime Minister of Spain, Portela Valladares, to

[1] Dr Marañón met Franco at dinner at the Spanish Embassy in Paris. Franco was
returning from the funeral of King George V in London, where he had represented
Spain and walked in procession behind the ill-fated Marshal Tukhachevsky, representing Russia. The intellectual physician and the General of the Legion walked along the
banks of the Seine, and Franco said that everything would calm down in Spain within
a few weeks.

declare a State of War[1] and so prevent the Popular Front from
entering office. Portela replied that such an act would provoke
a revolution. Yes, answered Franco, but with the support of the
Government, there would be force enough to crush it. Portela
prevaricated. He was a rich man, a democrat and a Freemason.
He discussed the matter with Diego Martínez Barrio, leader of the
Republican Union – and also a Mason of the thirty-third grade.
Naturally, thereafter the frenzied enemies of Freemasonry alleged
that Portela's actions were determined by some Masonic instruction transmitted poste-haste by Martínez Barrio from Zurich, or
the Bank of England, or wherever the supreme board of the world's
Grand Masters were at that time gathered. Portela was next
visited by Calvo Sotelo, who spoke in the same vein as Franco had
done. However, the next day, Portela handed over power to Azaña,
as the outstanding politician of the Popular Front.[2] This was, of
course, a perfectly constitutional act. No secret Masonic instructions would have been required to suggest it to the outgoing
Prime Minister. General Franco, together with Generals Fanjul
(lately Under Secretary at the War Office under Gil Robles),
Varela (the ex-trainer of the Carlists) and Emilio Mola, in command in Morocco, Orgaz and Ponte decided to take no immediate counter-revolutionary step. In Alicante, however, a too
hasty Captain, Gilbert, marched his men out into the street,
presumably in an attempt to take over power in that city.
He was later shot by his Corporals, though his death was
described to the Press as suicide.[3] Nearby, the excited pro-Popular
Front crowd attempted to release the lepers of the asylum at
Fontilles. The lepers wisely refused to leave.[4]

Elsewhere, the enthusiasm of the Popular Front knew no
bounds. Great crowds massed before the Ministry of the Interior
in Madrid and cried 'amnistía!' (amnesty). In Oviedo, the Popular
Front militants anticipated the consequences of the election and

---

[1] This was the final emergency situation envisaged under the Law of Public Order
of 1932. The other two conditions envisaged were a 'State of Prevention' and a 'State of
Alarm'.

[2] *Cruzada*, IX 439. Mr Lawrence Fernsworth (*Spain's Struggle for Freedom*) alleges
that Portela told him that Gil Robles contemplated a *coup d'état* at this moment. However, I prefer the story of Mr Henry Buckley, who visited the headquarters of the
CEDA the day after the elections, to find Gil Robles furious that any unconstitutional
action should be demanded of him. Franco also unsuccessfully approached General
Pozas, commander of the Civil Guard, at the Ministry of the Interior. He also refused
to act against the Popular Front.

[3] Jellinek, 219.   [4] *The Times*, 18.2.36.

opened the prisons, where most of the captives taken after the Asturias Revolution were held. Certain common criminals were also released by chance at the same time. And the first act of Azaña as Prime Minister once again was indeed to sign an amnesty decree covering all political prisoners. The Socialist and Catalan leaders of 1934 were freed. Companys and his counsellors left prison to be hailed once again as leaders of their beloved city amid scenes of enthusiasm such as even Barcelona's leafy and flower-laden avenues had never seen. Another decree of Azaña empowered the Catalan deputies to elect their own Government. Companys and his friends were, as expected, triumphantly chosen and returned to the Generalitat. The Tribunal of Constitutional Guarantees then declared illegal the suspension of the Catalan Statute. Azaña meantime formed his Government. It was entirely composed of representatives from his own party, the Republican Left, Martínez Barrio's party, the Republican Union (Martínez Barrio himself became Speaker of the Cortes), of Companys' Esquerra (Catalan Left) and Casares Quiroga's Gallegan Autonomists. Casares Quiroga, as in 1933, was Minister of the Interior. This was, of course, a minority Government dependent for its majority in the Cortes on its late electoral allies of the Popular Front.

Azaña and his Ministers began their new administration with an appeal for calm. They maintained a State of Alarm, with rigid press censorship. New Civil Governors were appointed throughout the country – mainly members of Azaña's own party. Because of their part in the Asturias repression, Generals Franco and Goded were dismissed from their positions in the War Ministry, the former being despatched to command the forces in the Canary Isles, the latter to the similar command in the Balearics. The Government also set to work to carry out the provisions of the Popular Front pact. The Institute of Agrarian Reform set to work once more. Between 50,000 and 75,000 peasants were settled (chiefly in Estremadura) with their own land under these auspices before the end of March.[1] Other measures attendant on the amnesty decrees were introduced. This meant, however, that employers had to take back men whom they had sacked after the strikes of 1934 and also to indemnify them for lost wages. At the same time they had either to retain those engaged in their place or to compensate them. This predicament typified the challenge of

[1] Azaña told Madariaga that the figure reached 75,000. *The Bulletin of Spanish Studies* reported 40–50 thousand. (Madariaga, 345.)

the new Government to Spanish industry. As a result, the peseta fell, leading financiers began to remove their wealth – and even themselves[1] – from the country.

But this difficulty was so small compared with the other threats to law and order in Spain as to seem almost technical. From the moment of the elections onwards, a trail of violence, murder and arson spread across the face of the country. This was partly caused by the spontaneous euphoria of the Left at being released from prison, or at least from the rule of the CEDA and the Radicals. It was also the conscious work of the Falange, determined to exacerbate the disorder in Spain and so justify the establishment of a *régime* of 'order'. José Antonio Primo de Rivera had himself lost his seat in the elections and was accordingly even less favourably inclined towards the idea of democratic institutions. The Falange probably still did not possess as many as 25,000 members in all Spain at the end of February 1936, but this made no difference to their provocatory power. Riding round in motor cars armed with machine guns, the *señoritos* of the Falange did everything they could to increase disorder, from an attempted assassination of the author of the Constitution of the Republic, the Socialist lawyer Jiménez de Asúa, to church-burning – which would be attributed to the Anarchists. The militants of the FAI and CNT still held totally aloof from the *régime*. They continued to believe that with an encyclopedia and a pistol they would be free – free from every political encumbrance. The decline of the Republic filled them with the same ebullient satisfaction as it did the Falange. And the *pistoleros* of the two groups continued to work in common – especially against the Socialists, who were still wont to refer to the Falange with disgust as the 'FAI-lange'.

The quarrel of the two vast trade unions of Spain, the CNT and UGT, reached its climax during the first part of 1936. Differences of views on the character of strike action led to incessant gun warfare between them. But even this was not the main dispute within the Spanish working class. For the old quarrel between Prieto and Largo Caballero, inside the Socialist party, latent ever since 1917, now also came to a head. During the weeks after the election of February, Largo Caballero had become intoxicated by the prospect of revolution. Partly this derived from his own reading of Marx and Engels in prison. Partly he was stimulated

---

[1] Juan March left on February 16, and thereafter was in close touch with the military conspirators.

by what seemed to him real prospects of power. Partly he was in a hurry. Finally, also, he surrendered completely to the flattery of his friends in the Spanish Communist party.[1] They had begun to name him the Spanish Lenin. This experienced municipal councillor and trade union official was entranced by the inappropriate nickname. While the votes of his party kept the Government of Azaña in power, Largo Caballero moved about Spain making declamatory prophesies to wildly cheering crowds that the hour of revolution was near. The real policy of Largo Caballero was no doubt far more moderate than he suggested in these apocalyptic orations. But no one was to know this for sure. From March 1936 onwards, the quarrel between Largo's wing of the Socialist party and that which still looked to the reformist Prieto was open. This was waged daily in the two Socialist newspapers controlled by Largo and Prieto respectively: *Claridad* and *El Socialista*.[2]

If the Left were thus increasingly disunited (while at the same time more confident than ever that the future was theirs), the Right and what remained of the Centre began, during the spring of 1936, to make common cause. Impelled by a common fear that the rising tide of violent Leftism would overwhelm the whole of Spanish society, members of the CEDA, the Army officers, the Carlists, Monarchists, the small and the grand *bourgeoisie*, and even the Radical followers of Lerroux, all came to think of the Government of Azaña as comparable to that of Kerensky before the appearance of the Bolsheviks, in the Russia of 1917. Opposition maintained an alliance of these groups that victory in the elections

[1] But at this time there were still only about 10,000 Communist party members in all Spain, though the party itself claimed to number 35,000. The party was most influential around Madrid and had little following in Catalonia and the Basque provinces. Apart from La Pasionaria the leaders of the party were all comparatively unknown. The secretary was José Díaz, an ex-Anarchist, and also an ex-bootblack from Seville, a man of simplicity and energy. Though in public he invariably followed the Comintern policy, he frequently quarrelled with it in private. His closest intimate was the director of propaganda and editor of *El Mundo Obrero*, Jesús Hernández. This man, in his early thirties, was nevertheless already a veteran Communist having been more or less a professional terrorist from the age of sixteen when he had been found guilty of an attempted murder of Prieto. Afterwards he went to Moscow, and was elected to the Cortes in 1936, where he was known for the wit as well as the violence of his speeches. The other leading Communists were Pedro Checa, Mije and Uribe, the Marxist theorists of the party.

[2] Immediately before the Civil War the UGT numbered 1½ million members. About half of these were rural workers. Rather more than half the remainder were factory workers or miners. The rest were clerks or shopkeepers. Salvador de Madariaga concluded that the quarrel in the Spanish Socialist party made civil war inevitable.

would have made difficult. The decline of the Centre (including the almost total extinction of the Radicals) had been the most remarkable aspect of the late elections. Lerroux had himself lost his seat. After the Popular Front had taken power, few members of the Centre groups delayed their at least tactical support of the Right. The CEDA was in fact still the largest single party in the Cortes.[1] But its failure to secure an outright victory suggested to many of its erstwhile supporters the failure of that particular experiment in Christian democracy. Gil Robles's place as *jefe* of the Spanish middle class, the white hope of the Right, was taken by the more dangerous and unscrupulous Calvo Sotelo, who made himself the chief spokesman of the Opposition when the Cortes met again. But then the Cortes did not seem to most Spaniards in this torrid spring to offer great hope.[2]

Meantime, the Generals' plot, half Monarchist, half purely military, which had its roots so long ago at the start of the Republic, once more took shape. The 'exile' of General Franco to the Canaries and of Goded to the Balearics had been intended to banish to harmless posts those suspected of treason to the Republic. At the same time, General Mola, previously in command in Morocco, had been transferred to be Military Governor of Pamplona. Before these officers left Madrid in late February they held several meetings with General Varela and others present. They agreed they would support a military rising if the President were to give power to Largo Caballero, or if anarchy should overwhelm the country. Varela and Orgaz were anxious for an immediate rising, Mola was more cautious. Franco called on Azaña before he set out for the Canaries, and bluntly warned the Prime Minister against the dangers of Communism. Azaña poohpoohed the idea.[3] Thereafter, Franco seems to have almost finally

[1] Full figures of the CEDA were never given. Its core, *Acción Popular*, probably numbered 12,000.

[2] In the second round of the elections, on March 3, the Popular Front gained 8 seats, the Basques 5, the Right 5 and the Centre 2. Thus the Popular Front emerged with 278 seats, and could count on another 10, from the Basques. The Right had 134 seats. The Centre had 55 seats. One final question disturbed the division of the Cortes. It was alleged that disturbances had prevented a free vote in Cuenca and in Granada. So, in the face of opposition from the Right, new elections were held there in May. Both seats were won by the Left, who thereby increased their number of seats to 266, while the Right dropped to 146.

[3] Even this dialogue was curiously oblique. Franco said: 'You are wrong to send me away. At Madrid, I would be of more use to the Army and to the peace of Spain.' Azaña answered: 'I do not fear developments. I knew about Sanjurjo's rising, and could have prevented it. I preferred to let it fail.'

committed himself to the idea of a military rising 'to save Spain'. But even so he vacillated once or twice more.

For the next few months Mola was the centre of the military conspiracy. He was a devious, somewhat literary-minded General, with a foxy face framed by narrow spectacles. He had been Director-General of Security at the time of the fall of the Monarchy and as such had incurred the particular enmity of the Republican intellectuals. 'Shoot Mola' had been a popular slogan for the rioters of 1930–1. As a result he had been left without employment during Azaña's first Government.[1] Before 1936 he had not associated with the plots against the Republic. But conspiracy was nevertheless peculiarly his *métier*. Messengers were despatched all over Spain from Pamplona, and especially to Lisbon, where General Sanjurjo undertook (as expected) to lend to the plot his prestige and his Carlist connections. Sanjurjo visited Germany in February – ostensibly to attend the Winter Olympic Games. He and Colonel Beigbeder, Military *Attaché* at the Spanish Embassy in Berlin, a lean, ascetic ex-veteran of the Moroccan Wars and of Breton origin, were said to have visited German arms factories with Admiral Canaris, head of German military intelligence. Canaris had old connections in Spain, from whose ports he had, in the First World War, directed submarine attacks upon Allied shipping. While Sanjurjo did not actually make any purchase of arms (since he supposed that his conspiracy would be immediately successful) he presumably assured himself that German military aid, if it should be necessary to secure the success of the rising, would be contemplated by Canaris at least.[2]

Mola's plans were made clear in a circular in April. The planned rising was to be no *pronunciamiento* of the old style. Two branches of the plot, one civil, one military, were to be set up in all the provinces of Spain, the Balearic and Canary Isles, and Spanish Morocco. The aim of the movement, declared Mola, was

[1] Though his memoirs of his period at the Ministry of the Interior had great success.

[2] As it was. See below, page 228. The Carlists had as yet no contact with Mola, but all the same, at St Jean de Luz, Prince François Xavier of Bourbon Parma, nephew (and prospective heir) of the aged Carlist Pretender, Don Alfonso Carlos, presided over a committee of war. This purchased 6,000 rifles, 150 heavy machine guns, 300 light machine guns, 5,000,000 cartridges and 10,000 machine guns. Of these, however, only the machine guns, which were bought in Germany, reached Spain before July 1936. The rest were confiscated at Antwerp and the personal intervention of Prince François Xavier with the King of the Belgians could not free them. (*Cruzada*, XIII 447.)

to establish 'order, peace and justice'. All could take part in the
rising (in some ways the circular reads like a company prospectus)
'except those who receive inspiration from abroad, Socialists,
Masons, Anarchists, Communists, etc.' The provincial branches
were instructed to work out detailed plans for seizing public
buildings in their areas, particularly lines of communication, and
to prepare a declaration announcing a state of war. At this point
Sanjurjo would fly in from Portugal and become president of a
military junta 'which will immediately establish the law of the
land'. In some places – such as Seville – the Falange was allotted
an important part in the rising, but nowhere were the political
aims of that party mentioned. (Franco had talked with José
Antonio in the house of his brother-in-law, Serrano Suñer, before
leaving for the Canaries and had suggested Colonel Yagüe, the
lion-headed and flamboyant Falangist at present in command of
the Foreign Legion, as a useful contact between the Falange and
the Generals. This matter remained undecided, however, for
some weeks yet.) Mola's plan was drawn up on the understanding
that everything should be ready within twenty days – that is, the
end of April. It included the following provision: 'It will be borne
in mind that the action, in order to crush as soon as possible a
strong and well-organised enemy, will have to be very violent.
Hence, all directors of political parties, societies or unions not
pledged to the Movement will be imprisoned: such people will be
administered exemplary punishments so that movements of
rebellion or strikes will be strangled.'[1] The document was signed
'*El Director*' – that is, Mola.

Azaña and his Government were meanwhile doing what they
could to maintain order. On February 27, they closed the headquarters of the Falange in Madrid. On March 15 (when a Falangist had placed a bomb in Largo Caballero's house) José Antonio
was arrested, nominally on a charge of keeping arms without
licence.[2]

Other arrests of Falangists followed. But instructions con-

---

[1] Bertrán Güell, 123.

[2] A possibly apocryphal story describes how, before his arrest, Azaña sent for José
Antonio and asked him to leave the country. 'I cannot,' answered José Antonio, 'my
mother is ill.' 'But your mother died many years ago,' answered Azaña. 'My mother is
Spain,' allegedly replied José Antonio, 'I cannot leave her.' This story appeared in
O Século of Lisbon, November 21, 1936. It is certain that Eduardo Aunós, one of José
Antonio's followers, proposed that he should fly the country about this time. 'Certainly
not,' answered José Antonio, 'the Falange is not an old-fashioned party of plotters with
its leaders abroad.' (Ximénez de Sandoval, 520.)

tinued to reach the *pistoleros* and bomb-throwers, even from inside the walls of the Model Prison. A week later, the Republic received a blow from the Left, in the manner of Casas Viejas. Despite the renewed impetus given to the Agrarian Reform, thousands of landless peasants who had voted for the Popular Front considered the pace of relief too slow. In Estremadura, villagers began to go out on to the large neglected estates, mark out their claim, assume ownership over a particular area, and then hold a meeting in the village square on return, crying *Viva la República*. At the village of Yeste, where the Emperor Charles V had passed his last days in a monastery, there was a violent clash between Civil Guard and villagers. Eighteen villagers and one member of the guard were killed. Despite this apparent victory for the forces of 'law and order', such local invasions by the villagers continued. And thereafter the Government did not dare to interfere.

Shooting between Falangists and members of the FAI, between Socialists and Anarchists, and between the two wings of the Socialist party also continued daily. The FAI and CNT issued a series of threatening announcements, and staged a chain of lightning strikes. All that the Prime Minister, Manuel Azaña, the strong man of the Republic, could do was to reflect that the Spanish working class were 'raw material for an artist'. On April 4, he gave an interview to Louis Fischer, the American journalist. 'Why don't you purge the Army?' asked Fischer. 'Why?' demanded Azaña. 'Because some weeks ago there were tanks in the streets, and you were in the Ministry of the Interior until two o'clock in the morning. You must have feared a revolt.' 'Café gossip,' answered Azaña. 'I heard it in the Cortes,' returned Fischer. 'Ah, that's one big café,' replied Azaña, adding smiling: 'The only Spaniard who is always right is Azaña. If all Spaniards were *Azañistas* all would be well.'[1] But to another journalist he admitted more accurately, '*Sol y sombra!* Light and shade! That is Spain.'[2]

On April 7, even Prieto surrendered to the prevailing panic, by insisting on the deposition of Alcalá Zamora. The Constitution provided that if a President were to dissolve the Cortes twice during his term of office, he could be removed – provided a vote of censure were carried against him in the Cortes. The Popular

---

[1] Fischer, *Men and Politics*, 307.
[2] Fernsworth, 176. Seats in Spanish bull rings are named either *Sol* or *Sombra*, according as to whether they are shaded or not.

Front now took advantage of this provision, even though Alcalá Zamora's dissolution of the Cortes had led to their own elevation to power. They feared that Alcalá Zamora might use his position to assist a right-wing *pronunciamiento*. The Right in the Cortes made no attempt to support the President since they had no love for him either. Alcalá Zamora thus abandoned the National Palace, to spend the rest of his life in exile cursing those who had removed him.

This move altered nothing. On April 13, a judge, Manuel Pedregal, who had condemned a Falangist to thirty years in prison,[1] for the murder of a Socialist newsboy, was himself assassinated. On April 14, a bomb was flung at the presidential tribune during the parade held in the Paseo de la Castellana in honour of the fourth anniversary of the Republic. A Lieutenant of the Civil Guard was shot by the *Asaltos*, apparently because he was thought to have had his own revolver trained on Azaña. The funeral of this officer on the 16th occasioned a general demonstration of strength. The hearse of the dead officer was accompanied on its way to the East Cemetery by most of the Madrid Falangists still at large, all shouting 'Spain! One, Great and Free!' Enthusiastic members of the Socialist youth movement sang the *International*, saluted with their fists and sprayed the *cortège* with bullets. At the cemetery itself, a running battle occurred between the Falangists and *Asaltos*. About a dozen people were killed during the course of the day – among them Andrés Sáenz de Heredia, a first cousin of José Antonio, shot down by a Lieutenant of the *Asaltos*, José Castillo. This death was to have further and more alarming consequences three months later.

All sorts of rumours circulated. The Right alleged that Bela Kun, the Hungarian Communist, and regarded throughout the Western world as a mixture of Robespierre and Lenin, had arrived in Seville, to start a revolution.[2] The accusation that Azaña was playing the *rôle* of Kerensky was repeated daily in the Cortes. Towards the end of the month, a number of Spanish

---

[1] This was a Falangist named Ortega who was also murdered at the start of the Civil War in his prison at Santoña.

[2] This was certainly not true. Bela Kun was at this time an ill and weak man, and was shortly shot. A reliable informant met Bela Kun in Moscow in 1935, and tells me that he was so weak that he could never have reached Spain, and that he would have been no danger if he had. It is possible however that Ernö Gerö, the Hungarian Communist who under the name of 'Singer' had been for a time 'instructor' to the French party, did visit Spain at this time.

Communists who had successfully fled abroad and had reached Moscow after the Asturias rising returned to their native country. Álvarez del Vayo, the journalist adviser of Largo Caballero, also returned from Moscow. Shortly afterwards, it was largely through him that the Socialist Youth merged with the Communist Youth movement – to be thereafter dominated by the latter. Even among Largo's special entourage, this caused alarm. Araquistain, editor of Largo Caballero's newspaper *Claridad* and brother-in-law of Álvarez del Vayo, burst out: 'We have lost our youth. What will happen to the Spanish Socialist party?'[1] Prieto could not contain his anger. Further, precisely at this time a large number of the CEDA youth movement, which had never been very successful under Gil Robles's guidance, also took a step towards extremism, and joined the Falange – even though that body had itself been publicly banned after the riots at the time of the funeral of the Civil Guard Lieutenant. Among those who joined the Falange was the leader of the CEDA Youth, General Franco's brother-in-law, Ramón Serrano Suñer, who now became one of the most important links in the chain of communications between the Generals and the Falange. He had been at the University of Madrid with José Antonio in the early 'twenties and thus old social ties eased the path of ideological alliance.

Mola's military rising could not, after all, take place in April. The plan had all depended on General Rodríguez del Barrio, Inspector General of the Army. He took fright at the last moment and feigned illness. General Orgaz, with a troop of Civil Guard, had planned to await the signal in the friendly Italian Embassy. Now this and other plans had to be cancelled by General Varela, by telephone. Indeed, if the rising had occurred in April, neither the Carlists nor the Falange would have been prepared to act fully with Mola. The political leaders of the Carlists were still busy in Lisbon negotiating with General Sanjurjo the nature of the future Spain after the rising. Fal Conde at first demanded simply the dissolution of all political parties and

---

[1] The remark was made to Mr Henry Buckley, then *The Times* correspondent in Madrid. Araquistain himself, who became a passionate anti-Communist, alleges that he often at this time saw the Comintern agent, Vittorio Codovilla, arriving to call on Álvarez del Vayo (he lived in a flat above). But one must remember that this was a period when the Popular Front was a reality for large numbers of people all over the world. A Comintern agent seemed an ally to be welcomed. The Socialist Youth hardly needed very careful manipulation at this time to get them to merge with the Communists.

the establishment of a government of three men only – Sanjurjo as President and in control of defence, an Education Minister and an Industrial Minister.[1] And, while these political aims were being discussed by means of secret messengers, new details kept on being added to the tactical plan of operations. In Madrid, Calvo Sotelo moved backwards and forwards from the Palace Hotel to the Ritz, to other private houses, making arrangements with financiers. But what of the Falange? Busy with their assassinations and street fighting, the now secret direction of the party warned against joining forces with the military plotters: 'We will be neither the vanguard nor the shock troops nor the invaluable ally of any confused reactionary movement.'[2] Brave words, and they may well have expressed the real views of those old Falangists who had been street fighting ever since Ledesma launched *La Conquista del Estado* in 1931. But, by this time, the die was cast. The Falange could obviously not stand outside the events which would follow the military rising. Nor indeed did they want to.

On May 1, the traditional working-class parades were held throughout Spain. They were accompanied by a general strike called for most cities by the CNT. All along the avenues of the great cities the now united Socialist-Communist Youth paraded as if they were part of an embryo Red Army. The salute of the clenched fist was given to the sound of the *International*, or to one of the splendid songs composed in the course of the fighting in the Asturias – or perhaps to *Primero de Mayo* (First of May), or *The Young Guard*. Enormous portraits of Largo Caballero, Stalin and Lenin were carried like banners down the Castellana in Madrid, from whose elegant balconies the *bourgeoisie*, representing the Spain of Charles V, watched with fascinated horror. Surely this could not go on? Four days later, from his prison, José Antonio (who had always liked Sanjurjo because of his friendship with his father) wrote an open letter to the Spanish soldiers, calling upon them to make an end of all the attacks made upon 'the sacred identity of Spain'. 'In the last resort,' he added, 'as Spengler put it, it has

---

[1] Earlier, the Carlists had wanted a rising by themselves, and Sanjurjo had agreed to head a provisional Government of monarchical restoration (with the Carlist Pretender as King) if such an isolated rising were to occur.

[2] Bravo, *Historia de la Falange*. Between February and July 1936, the Falange's numbers, like those of the Communists, greatly increased, perhaps to as many as 75,000. Apart from Onésimo Redondo's organisation at Valladolid (which had gained some following also among the workers of Seville) these were young middle-class men or undergraduates not yet established in professions.

always been a platoon of soldiers who have saved civilisation.'[1] Gone were the days when José Antonio would say that serving soldiers were useless, that they were all chicken-hearted, and that the most cowardly was Franco.[2] Even so, the Falange was not yet truly part of the military plot. Before the month of May was out, José Antonio was to remark that he could agree with all the sentiments in a speech by Prieto.

On May 10, 1936, Manuel Azaña was elected President of the Spanish Republic in place of Alcalá Zamora, by 238 to 5, in the electoral college assembled in the Retiro Palace. The occasion was quiet, save for a fight in the corridors between Araquistain, still supporting Largo Caballero, and Julián Zugazagoitia, editor of Prieto's *El Socialista*. The CEDA and right-wing parties did not put forward any candidate and abstained from voting. After a few days, Casares Quiroga became Prime Minister, with a Cabinet much the same as Azaña's. Azaña's acceptance of the elevation surprised some of his followers, since it was thought curious that he should choose this moment to abandon the post of head of Government when there was no other statesman of comparable stature to take his place. Yet it became clear that he welcomed the opportunity to exchange the anxious tumult of the Cortes for the isolated grandeur of the National Palace. He apparently persuaded himself that his own presence as Head of State would calm the middle class against fears of revolution. But these fears were not easily appeased. A Socialist woman deputy of German extraction, Margarita Nelken, announced, "We want a revolution but it is not the Russian revolution which can serve us as a model, since we must have huge flames which can be seen all over the world and waves of blood which turn the seas red.' On May 24 Largo Caballero made a great speech at Cádiz: 'When the Popular Front breaks up,' he announced, 'as break up it will, the triumph of the proletariat will be certain. We shall then implant the dictatorship of the proletariat, which does not mean the repression of the proletariat, but of the capitalist and *bourgeois* classes!'[3] All sorts of plots and plans to achieve this were now prepared. Despite the fact that the establishment of a Communist *régime* in Spain would have been contrary to the general lines of Stalin's moderate foreign policy at that time, the Communist party of Spain, intoxicated by their capture of the Socialist Youth, continued to feed

[1] Ximénez de Sandoval, 551.   [2] Ansaldo, 125.
[3] Quoted Aznar, 25.

Largo with flattery and to egg him on to more and more extreme statements.[1] Meantime, in mid-May, the CNT held their annual congress at Saragossa. The controversy between the *Treintistas* and the FAI was successfully solved. The Congress demanded a continuation of the lightning strikes, an intensification of the struggle against the UGT and the *bourgeois* Government, in order to secure a 36-hour week, one month's holiday with pay, higher wages[2] and ultimately, 'libertarian Communism'.

Yet while the working class and the Left in general were still bitterly divided on practically every question, of policy and of tactics, the ranks of the Right were finally closing. On June 1, José Antonio wrote from his prison giving full support to the military conspiracy on behalf of his party in a letter to Mola. He also promised that 4,000 Falangists would help the rising at the start.[3]

In early June, therefore, final (and now strategic) arrangements were made by Mola. General Queipo de Llano, the handsome, tall and tipsy commander of the *Carabineros*, who had joined the plotters late (having been first rebuffed by Mola) would take command in the difficult task of Seville;[4] General Saliquet would raise Valladolid; Mola would be responsible for Burgos and Pamplona; General Villegas would command in Madrid, General

[1] I have come to the conclusion that the three documents alleged to have been found in four separate places after the start of the Civil War, and making plans for a Socialist-Communist *coup d'état* by means of a simulated rising of the Right are not forgeries. They have been often reprinted, and an English version of the texts, with a facsimile of the document allegedly found at Lora del Río, is in Loveday, 176 ff. The three documents were (a) a plan to establish Largo Caballero, his followers and the Communists as a 'Soviet', between May 11 and June 29; (b) general instructions for revolution; (c) a purported record of a meeting of the Communist party in Valencia, on May 16. The first reference I have found to these documents is in the *Diario de Navarra* of August 7, 1936, a date rather early for clever propaganda forgeries. The fact that these documents were probably genuine does not mean that the plans they envisaged were ever likely to be put into effect. They were dreams more than blueprints, or rather plans for hypothetical circumstances which might never arrive. They do not justify the rising of the Generals, because the plans for this were already far advanced before the plans of their enemies could have been prepared. It is instructive to note that the only historian of the military conspiracy who mentions the possibility of a 'Communist' or left-wing rising as having played any part in the motives of the Generals is the most recent, B. Felix Maiz.

[2] This demand caused the interminable building strike which immobilised the industry for the rest of the summer and brought incessant gun-battles between the UGT (who accepted arbitration) and the CNT (who did not).

[3] *Cruzada*, IX 511.

[4] *Ibid.*, XIII 445. He had apparently become disgusted by the Republic due to its failure to make him War Minister in 1931 as he had hoped. He had been deeply implicated in the Republican plot of 1930 and fled the country with Ramón Franco.

THE ORIGINS OF THE WAR

Cabanellas (also generally held to be a staunch Republican) in Saragossa, General González Carrasco in Barcelona; Franco would fly to take command of the Army of Africa, and Goded to lead the garrison at Valencia. Other cities were divided between other trusted officers. Junior officers who helped the rising would be rewarded by immediate promotion 'or, if they prefer, a civil appointment with an equivalent salary.'[1]

On June 5, Mola circulated a political document describing how the success of the rising would be followed by a 'Directory', comprising a President and four others. All would be officers. They would have the power to issue laws. These would later be ratified by a constituent assembly elected 'by suffrage in the manner that shall be deemed most appropriate'. The Cortes and Constitution of 1931 would, of course, be suspended. Those laws not in accord with the 'new organic system' of the State would be abolished and those who received 'inspiration from abroad' would be outlawed. The new system would thus be much as the old dictator Primo de Rivera would have wished, despite certain verbal concessions to the Falange and Carlists. But the Carlists (with whom Mola was now in contact) did not agree to the programme immediately, despite a six-hour interview between Mola and Fal Conde in the Navarrese Monastery of Irache.[2]

This was the mood in which Spain, still celebrated by mediaeval historians as the country where democracy was born several generations before it had been developed in England, approached the debate in the Cortes on June 16.

[1] *Cruzada*, XIII 444.
[2] *Ibid.*, 449. In addition to Mola's difficulties with the Carlists he was also not fully at one with the *Unión Militar*. See the letters in Castillo, *Barcelona: Objetivo Cubierto*, which show that the UME wanted to arraign all the post-1932 Ministers for treason.

12

Revolutions of the past and the eve of disaster

The midsummer of 1936 thus saw the culmination of one hundred and fifty years of passionate quarrels in Spain. 1808, 1834, 1868, 1898, 1909, 1917, 1923, 1931, 1932, 1934, and February 1936; these were the critical dates, becoming more and more frequent, in the inflammation of the Spanish tragedy. Recall how in 1808 the old Monarchy collapsed for ever and how from 1834 open war was waged, over the question of a liberal Constitution, for five years. Recollect how in 1868 a corrupt Monarchy was expelled by the Army, and how the country dissolved into a war which was at once religious and regional while the working-class organisations were founded by the representative of Bakunin. Remember how in 1898 the Spanish-American War brought back the over-large army from the last colonies to unemployed frustration in Spain surrounded by innumerable reminders of past glory, and how a valiant group of middle-class young men sought to prepare the intellectual and economic renaissance of the country by 'placing a padlock on the Cid's tomb'.[1] Note how in 1909 class hatreds, exacerbated by Catalan Nationalism, brought a week of bloody rioting in Barcelona which vented itself in particular against the Church. Recall how in 1917 a revolutionary general strike was crushed by an itself insurrectionary army and how the military dictatorship of Primo de Rivera, established in 1923, was the only Spanish Government of the century to give the country any rest from political murders, strikes and sterile political intrigue. Consider how the liberals whose protests brought the expulsion of both the Dictator in 1930 and the King in 1931 had been unable to create a democratic habit powerful enough to satisfy the aspirations of either the working or the old governing classes and how the liberals had themselves mortally angered the latter when not strong enough to secure the implementation of their reforms. See how in 1932 a section of the Right had attempted to overcome their electoral

[1] The phrase was the inspiration of the economist Joaquín Costa.

defeat by a *pronunciamiento* in the old style, and how in 1934 a part of the Left, after their own electoral defeat and impelled by continent-wide fears of Fascism, had also staged a revolt, which in Asturias had temporarily established a working-class dictatorship. Observe how, in February 1936, the two sides which by then had taken shape in Spain and which referred to themselves by the military word 'front' put their quarrels finally to the test of the polls and how the narrow victory of the Popular Front had brought in a weak but progressive Ministry, regarded by its own Socialist and Communist supporters as a curtain raiser to far-reaching social and regional change. Note finally that most of the leading men of Spain in 1936 had lived through a generation of turbulence, and that many of them like Largo Caballero, Calvo Sotelo, Sanjurjo, had played important if equivocal *rôles* throughout. Here were ranged the masters of economic power in the country, led by the Army, and supported by the Church, that embodiment of Spain's past glory. All these believed that they were about to be overwhelmed. Opposed to them were 'the professors' – many of the enlightened middle class – and almost the entire labour force of the country, maddened by years of insult, misery and neglect, intoxicated by the knowledge of the better conditions enjoyed by their class comrades in France and Britain and by the actual mastery which they supposed that the working class had gained in Russia. Tragedy could not now have been avoided.

The Second Spanish Republic failed because it was from the start not accepted by powerful forces politically both to the Left and to the Right. Furthermore, in attempting to solve the most pressing problems which then faced Spain (and whose existence had led to the collapse of previous *régimes*) it estranged many who had at first contemplated collaboration with it. The five and a half years of the Republic was thus a time when, by the passion caused by crises both before and during the Republic, two sides were taking shape powerful enough to prevent each other from winning immediately if war should come. There had been three main quarrels in Spain since the collapse of the Monarchy in 1808: that between Church and liberals; that between land-owners and, later, *bourgeoisie* on the one hand and working class on the other; and that between those who demanded local rights of one kind or another (notably in Catalonia and in the Basque provinces) and the advocates of strict central control by Castile.

Each of these three disputes had fed, and been superimposed on top of, each other,[1] so that any desire for moderation on the part of one group of contestants was extinguished by a renewed violence on the part of the other.

It was upon these searing quarrels that the country was constructed. There were no habits of organisation, compromise or even articulation respected, or even sought by all Spaniards. Insofar as there were traditions common to all Spain, these were of violent disputes. As the years went by, all of these increasingly partook at the same time of religious, class and regional characteristics. Yet all Spaniards were nevertheless, consciously or unconsciously, aware that Spain had once been the greatest nation in the world, that at that time the country had at least seemed to be united, and that these continual disputes were unworthy of so great a history. This partly at least caused Spaniards to think that there was something undignified in any compromise of their ideals (even if this meant that they could never become practical political programmes). At the same time, also, a very large number of people wanted a 'new Spain' – (which might mean a hundred different things) which would be worthy of Spain's great past and indeed of the continuing qualities of her superb people. Such motives moved at bottom those *señoritos* who sang the Falangist hymn *Cara al Sol* (Face to the Sun):

> *Face to the sun, wearing the tunic*
> *Which yesterday you embroidered,*
> *Death will find me, if it calls me*
> *And I do not see you again . . .*
> *Arise* (Arriba!) *battalions and conquer –*
> *For Spain has begun to awaken.*
> *Spain – United! Spain – Great!*
> *Spain – Free! Spain – Arise!*

The same thoughts moved those passionate revolutionaries who sang the Anarchist *Hijos del pueblo* (Sons of the People):

> *Son of the people, your chains oppress you*
> *This injustice cannot go on!*
> *If your life is a world of grief,*

---

[1] Though not in the same order as they had always been in the past. For example, in the first Carlist War the Liberals stood as the advocates of control by Castile against the regional claims of the Basques and Catalans, while in 1936 the heirs of the Liberals stood for some kind of federation of provinces.

Instead of being a slave, it is better to die!
Workers,
You shall suffer no longer!
The oppressor
Must succumb!
Arise
Loyal people
At the cry
Of social revolution!

BOOK II
RISING AND REVOLUTION

13

Franco's letter of June 23 – the Carlists disputes with General Mola –
the date of the rising fixed for July 15 – the journey of the Dragon
Rapide – *manoeuvres in Morocco – the murder of Lieutenant*
Castillo – the murder of Calvo Sotelo

On June 23, General Francisco Franco wrote from his semi-banishment in the Canaries to the Prime Minister of the Republic, Casares Quiroga. He protested against the recent removals of right-wing officers from their commands. These events, said the General, were causing such serious unrest that he felt bound to warn the Prime Minister (who was also War Minister) of the peril 'involved for the discipline of the Army'.[1] This letter was a final statement by Franco 'before history', as he might himself have put it later, that he had done his best to secure a peaceful settlement, though he must really have known that nothing could be done at this late hour.[2] The Prime Minister did not, however, reply to the letter. And it was Franco's last vacillation. At the end of June all that was needed for a final date to be given for the rising was an agreement with the Carlists.

Yet on July 1, 1936, General Mola was forced to circulate a document to his co-plotters counselling patience. In Morocco, the Army of Africa began its summer manoeuvres. In Tenerife, Franco fretted in his enforced inactivity, and occupied himself with rumoured plots of assassination. The cities of the mainland were in the grip of a building strike, which the UGT wished to abandon because of the general disorder and which the CNT wished to continue—apparently for the same reason. In Madrid there were strikes by lift-workers, waiters, and bull-fighters – all called by the left wing of the UGT. Rumours abounded. On one occasion panic spread because of a tale that a group of monks had poisoned the children's chocolates in a lower-class suburb.

---

[1] *Cruzada*, IX 523.
[2] The Monarchist pilot Ansaldo, however, writes that well on into this summer of 1936 (and despite his activities immediately after the elections) Franco was vacillating. 'With Franquito or without Franquito,' expostulated Sanjurjo, 'we shall save Spain.' (Ansaldo, 42.)

Murders for political reasons were reported almost daily at the start of July. On July 2, for example, two Falangists sitting at a café table in Madrid were killed by shots from a passing motor-car. Later the same day, two men leaving the Madrid *casa del pueblo* were killed by a gang of men armed with sub-machine guns. Such minor warfare had continued unchecked since the elections of February. On almost none of these occasions had the killers been apprehended – though, of course, political murderers are less easily detected than their private counterparts. On July 8, seventy Falangists were arrested in Madrid, and several hundred in the provinces, for allegedly planning disorders. These included Fernández Cuesta, chief of the Madrid Falange. In the Ministry of War, meanwhile, the loyal Republican officers observed excited conferences among those whom they knew to be enemies of the Republic. García Escámez, a subtle and charming Andalusian, who had led part of the Legion in Asturias, and was now Mola's lieutenant at Pamplona, appeared with news and plans. And the loyal Republican officers themselves began to take counsel together.[1] These last days before the Civil War later acquired a peculiar poignancy for these men, for it was the last time when they would speak with colleagues later to be on the other side of the battle-line.

Yet Mola had still not reached agreement on policy with the Carlists. The outstanding points were in respect of the latter's insistence that the rising should take place under the Monarchist flag and that its success should be followed by the dissolution of all political parties. On July 7, Mola wrote to Fal Conde (with the other leading Carlists, in St Jean de Luz) promising to bring up the question of the flag as soon as possible after the rising and affirming that he had no relations with any political party. 'You must realise,' he added, 'that everything is paralysed by your attitude. *Certain things* have so far advanced that it would be impossible now to withdraw. I beg of you for the sake of Spain an urgent reply.'[2] On July 7, Fal Conde wrote back demanding guarantees that the future *régime* should be anti-democratic and insisting that the question of the flag would have to be decided immediately. Mola, by now beside himself with anger, refused these conditions. 'The

[1] Martín Blázquez, 72.
[2] Carlist Archives Seville. The 'certain things' seem to have been firstly an assurance to the Falange that the rising would occur on July 15, and secondly the hiring of an aircraft to take Franco to Morocco.

traditionalist movement,' he wrote, 'is ruining Spain by its intransigence as surely as is the Popular Front.'[1] However, on July 9 General Sanjurjo from Lisbon wrote a conciliatory letter which both Fal Conde and Mola seemed able to accept. Meanwhile the streets of Pamplona were prepared for the annual festival of San Fermín. Now, as in other years, young bulls were let loose in the town on their way to the bull ring and were contested indiscriminately by the young men, watched by their women folk in carnival dress from balconies. Among the young men were many who, within a week, would be enrolled among the Carlist forces. Among the spectators could be seen the sly, bespectacled face of Mola, accompanied by General Fanjul, a leading plotter from Madrid, and Colonel Carrasco, who was to lead the rising of San Sebastián.

In London Luis Bolín, correspondent of the Monarchist daily paper *ABC*, now chartered a *Dragon Rapide*, from the Olley Airways Company of Croydon, to transport Franco from the Canaries to Morocco, where he would seize command of the Army of Africa.[2] There were, apparently, no aircraft in Spain fast enough for so delicate a journey. The Spanish plotters also considered an English pilot more likely to be trustworthy than one of their own compatriots.[3]

Two days later, on July 11, the English aeroplane left Croydon, piloted by a Captain Bebb, who had no idea of the nature of the enterprise in which he was engaged. Accompanying him were Bolín, a retired major, Hugh Pollard, and two fair-headed young women, one of them Pollard's daughter, the other a friend. These passengers, likewise in ignorance of the purpose of the journey, had been procured by the English publisher and Catholic historian, Douglas Jerrold, to give the flight the air of an ordinary, rather than an extraordinary, intrigue.[4] That night in Valencia, the radio station was seized by a group of Falangists who announced, mysteriously, that 'the National Syndicalist revolution' would soon break out, and then vanished before the police arrived. The same

---

[1] Carlist Archives.

[2] Bolín had received his instructions from his editor, Luca de Tena, who had himself been passed the order by Colonel Alfredo Kindelán, of the Spanish Air Force, and one of the communication channels of the conspiracy.

[3] The *News Chronicle* (7.11.36) published an account of these events by the pilot Captain Bebb.

[4] *Cruzada*, XIII 62–3. Pollard, however, had had, as Mr Jerrold put it, 'experience of revolutions'. (Jerrold, 371.)

day in Madrid, Casares Quiroga had been once again warned of what was to occur. 'So there is to be a *rising*?' he enquired with absurd joviality. 'Very well, I, for my part, shall take a *lie-down*!'[1] The following day, July 12, was a Sunday. In Morocco, the manoeuvres of the Foreign Legion and *Regulares* reached their conclusion with a parade taken by Generals Romerales and Gómez Morato, respectively Commander of the East Zone of Morocco and Commander of the Army of Africa. Álvarez Buylla, High Commissioner in Morocco, proudly dressed himself in the uniform of Captain of artillery which had been his twenty years before. Neither of the two Generals, nor the High Commissioner, were privy to the plot in which so many of the other officers at the parade were to take leading parts. Gómez Morato was the object of special dislike in orthodox military circles since he had organised the changes in command ordered by Azaña and Casares to secure loyal officers in important positions. The night of the parade, these two Generals telegraphed to Madrid that all was well with the Army of Africa. But, at the manoeuvres, the conspirators held last minute meetings. At a conference of young officers, Colonel Yagüe, Commander of the Foreign Legion, had even used the word 'crusade' (afterwards to become conventional usage in Nationalist speeches) to describe the movement behind the rising. And the cry of CAFE! – which, to initiates, signified *¡Camaradas! ¡Arriba Falange Española!* – was heard at the official banquet at the end of the parade. Álvarez Buylla asked why people were demanding coffee, while the fish was still on the table. He was informed that the cry came from a group of young men, who were, it was to be feared, a little drunk.[2] The same day, meanwhile, the *Dragon Rapide* had reached Lisbon, where Bolín conferred with Sanjurjo.

That evening at nine o'clock, Lieutenant José Castillo of the *Asaltos* was returning to his home in the centre of Madrid after his day's duty. Earlier in the year, he had killed the Marquis of Heredia, a Falangist and first cousin of José Antonio, in the riot at the funeral of the member of the Civil Guard who had himself been shot on the fifth anniversary of the start of the Republic. From that time, Castillo had been marked out for revenge by the Falange. In June, he had married; and his bride had received an anonymous letter on her wedding eve demanding why she should marry a man who would so 'soon be a corpse'. As he reached home on

[1] Peirats, I 136.   [2] *Cruzada*, IX 557.

July 12, a hot Sunday of the Madrid summer – officials and foreign diplomats had already begun to leave the capital for San Sebastián – Castillo was shot dead by four men with revolvers, who swiftly escaped into the narrow and crowded streets.[1]

This was the second of the officers of the *Asaltos* who had been murdered in recent months – Captain Faraudo, an instructor, had been killed by Falangists while walking with his wife in the Gran Vía a month before. So the news of the death of Castillo caused a great fury when it reached the *Asalto* headquarters at Pontejos barracks, next to the Ministry of the Interior in the Puerta del Sol. And the news was quickly followed by the body, accompanied by a gesticulating and angry crowd of people, including many from the *casa del pueblo*, situated in the same street as Castillo's apartment. Passions were running high, and vengeance was demanded. Someone suggested that a street fight should be provoked against random groups of Falangists or *señoritos*, and certain colleagues of the dead man did drive out into the streets in a generally threatening manner. At this point, however, the comparatively sophisticated suggestion was made that revenge should be taken upon the leaders of the Right rather than upon the rank and file.[2]

Now this suggestion came not from any member of the corps of *Asaltos*, but from Captain Condés of the Civil Guard, a convinced adherent of the Left. He had been dismissed for his complicity in the rebellion of 1934 and had been recently reinstated by the Government of Casares Quiroga – who, it is said, personally retained Condés as a special agent. Nationalist historians allege that Casares Quiroga, his chief of police and Condés had been plotting the death of Calvo Sotelo ever since the famous debate of June 16, when the Monarchist leader had chosen to interpret the Prime Minister as having threatened his life. On July 11 La Pasionaria was alleged to have openly threatened his death.[3] One of the two police escorts attached to Calvo Sotelo as a member of the Cortes was reported to have told Calvo Sotelo's friend, the

---

[1] The murderers of Castillo were Falangists. One of them, having fought with distinction in the Civil War and served Germany and Japan in the World War, may still be met in Madrid, where he lives in prosperity.

[2] *Cruzada*, IX 532–4; Villegas, 46–8; Acedo Colunga, 316–24.

[3] This was in the Cortes. She was supposed to have cried, 'That is your last speech,' as Calvo Sotelo sat down after another violent oration. But there is no record of the remark in *Diario de Sesiones*, nor was it heard by two such reliable witnesses then present as Mr Henry Buckley and Señor Miguel Maura.

deputy Bau, that his superior officer had given orders not to prevent any murder of Calvo Sotelo, and indeed, if the attempt should occur in the country, he was to aid the murderers. The escort had been then changed for one in whose reliability Calvo Sotelo could trust – though the Minister of the Interior in Casares's Government, Moles, apparently gave no further attention to the matter. It is finally alleged that, on this night of long knives, Casares Quiroga was called to the telephone while attending a sumptuous ball at the Brazilian Embassy and asked for his agreement to the murder of his chief parliamentary opponent. The conflict between these allegations, even between those written many years later, does not make any of them more credible. It seems probable that the truth of what occurred was somewhat as follows: Captain Condés suggested that instead of a general street-battle with the enemy, Calvo Sotelo and perhaps Gil Robles should be arrested. These, like José Antonio, should be regarded as hostages for the general good behaviour of the Right – including the military plotters. The Prime Minister may have given his agreement to this course of action. And of this there is no doubt. Shortly after midnight, a storm-troop car, and a touring car, set out from the Pontejos barracks on a journey of vengeance. In the storm-troop car there were Captain Condés; two members of the Communist-Socialist Youth; a gunman named Victoriano Cuenca, once the bodyguard of General Machado of Cuba; a student of medicine who was at the time treating Cuenca for gonorrhoea and several *Asalto* troopers. In the touring car there were two Captains and three Lieutenants of the *Asaltos*. The storm-troop car left for the home of Calvo Sotelo, the touring car for that of Gil Robles.[1]

Now the leader of at least the first of these expeditions had made the reservation that his quarry, instead of being merely arrested, should be assassinated. This reservation may have been implanted in the mind of Captain Condés – if the idea was not his own – by some member of the Socialist-Communist Youth. Condés was himself associated with that body. And it is possible that this suggestion was made on the specific instruction of the Spanish Communist party, who may have desired now just such an outrage, so as to cause a final break.[2]

---

[1] The following account is based on *The General Cause*, 18 fl, with several modifications, e.g. I do not believe that Casares Quiroga had foreknowledge of the murder, as is there alleged.

[2] See above, page 108.

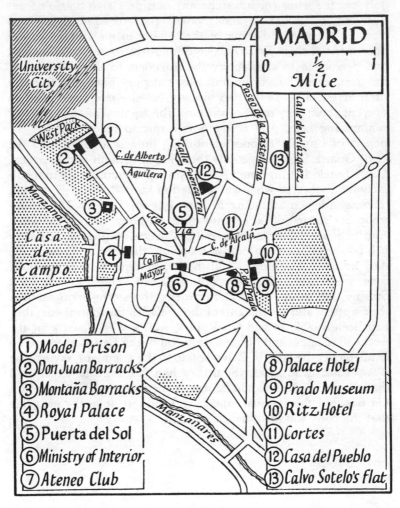

MADRID

0   ½   1
      Mile

University
City

West Park

C. de Alberto
Aguilera

Calle Fuencarral

Paseo de la Castellana

Calle de Velázquez

Manzanares

Casa
de
Campo

Gran
Via

C. de Alcalá

Calle
Mayor

P. del Prado

① Model Prison
② Don Juan Barracks
③ Montaña Barracks
④ Royal Palace
⑤ Puerta del Sol
⑥ Ministry of Interior
⑦ Ateneo Club

⑧ Palace Hotel
⑨ Prado Museum
⑩ Ritz Hotel
⑪ Cortes
⑫ Casa del Pueblo
⑬ Calvo Sotelo's flat

Manzanares

MAP 3

At all events, at about three o'clock in the morning of Monday, July 13, the *sereno* (nightwatchman) outside Calvo Sotelo's front door, in a fashionable and modern part of Madrid, allowed Condés, Cuenca and some of the *Asaltos* to go upstairs to the apartment of their victim. Calvo Sotelo was roused from his bed and persuaded to accompany the intruders to the police head-quarters, even though his status as a deputy gave him freedom from arrest. The *Asaltos* had already cut the telephone wires to prevent their prey from confirming the legality of their visit or summoning help. And Calvo Sotelo saw to his satisfaction the papers of Captain Condés identifying him as a member of the Civil Guard. So, courageously though not without apprehension, Calvo Sotelo left his family, promising to communicate immedi-ately he discovered what was wanted of him – 'unless,' he added, 'these gentlemen are going to blow out my brains.' The storm-troop car started off at seventy miles an hour, no one speaking. After about a quarter of a mile, Cuenca, sitting immediately behind the politician, fired two shots into the back of his neck. He died immediately, although his body remained upright for some time, since two *Asaltos* were sitting closely wedged against him. Still no one spoke. Shortly afterwards, the storm-troop car met the Captains and Lieutenants of the *Asaltos* in the touring car; they had been unable to find Gil Robles, who was in Biarritz for the weekend. Condés and his men drove on to the East Cemetery and handed over the body of Calvo Sotelo to the attendant, saying that it was some dead *sereno* whom they had found in the street, and that the papers for it would be sent in the morning. The attendant did not find this unusual, and it was only at noon the next day that the body was identified.

14

Consequences of the murder of Calvo Sotelo — two funeral services in the East Cemetery — Mola meets General Batet — Franco leaves Tenerife

There were few members of the middle class in Spain who were not aghast at this murder of the leader of the parliamentary opposition by members of the regular police, even though they might suspect that the victim had been concerned in a conspiracy against the State. It was now natural to assume that the Government could not control even its own agents, even if it wished to do so. During the course of July 13, Captain Moreno, who had been in the touring car, was arrested, together with several troopers. But Captain Condés went into hiding, and his political assistants, including Cuenca, disappeared into the massing crowds of Socialist and Communist militants. The corps of *Asaltos* placed difficulties in the way of the police who, at the natural and urgent behest of Calvo Sotelo's family, had begun without enthusiasm to investigate the crime.[1] The Cabinet, meantime, spent July 13 in almost continuous session. They ordered the closing of Monarchist, Carlist and Anarchist headquarters in Madrid. But the members of the two former organisations (though they were now hardly two) and many others, were that day busy calling at Calvo Sotelo's home in memory of the dead man. At eight o'clock in the evening, the UGT and the Communist party declared their full support of the Government. At midnight, Prieto (who had declared in that day's issue of *El Socialista* that war would be preferable to this series of murders) led a delegation of Socialists, Communists, the UGT and the central executive of the *casas del pueblo*, to demand from Casares Quiroga that he should distribute arms to the workers' organisations. Casares refused, acidly adding that, if Prieto continued to come to see him so often, it would be

---

[1] After the start of the Civil War, Condés and Moreno were both killed in the Guadarrama. The documents in the Ministry of the Interior, relating to the investigation, were seized by a group of militiamen on July 25 and have never been seen since.

he who would be governing Spain.[1] Throughout another hot
night, Madrid anxiously waited. The militiamen of the left-wing
parties – those militants, that is, upon whom the parties would
rely if fighting should come, and who had already been provided
with whatever arms there were in the arsenals of their organisations – kept watch, especially around the prisons and the ministerial buildings. Members of right-wing parties wondered whose
would be the next turn to hear a fatal knock at the door.

In the meantime, Mola at last gave a firm date for the rising.
It would now begin in Morocco on July 17, at 17 hours – 5 o'clock
in the afternoon. The Carlists agreed to this in a declaration signed
by Fal Conde and Prince François Xavier of Bourbon Parma at
St Jean de Luz. This assumed Sanjurjo's compromise letter of
July 9 as describing the aims of the rising. But had it not been
for Calvo Sotelo's murder, the clashes between Mola and Fal
Conde would no doubt have continued. The plotters now believed
that it would be hard to win Madrid and, they thought, Seville
(though not, apparently, Barcelona) at the first shot. In these places
the garrisons, together with the Falange and other militant supporters were to maintain themselves in their barracks, and await
relief. For the plan then was that Mola, from the north, Goded,
from the north-east, and Franco, from the south, with the other
Generals in the other garrisons, would march in a central direction
on the capital. Sanjurjo would fly from Portugal to wherever
seemed most appropriate. The old campaigners of the Moroccan
Wars, headed by 'the Lion of the Riff', would thus be at last in
command of their own country, after conquering their own
countrymen.

The next day, July 14, there were two funerals in the East
Cemetery in Madrid. First, that of Lieutenant Castillo, whose
coffin, draped in the red flag, was saluted, with clenched fists, by a
crowd of Republicans, Socialists, Communists and *Asaltos*. Then, a
few hours later, Calvo Sotelo's body, swathed in Capuchin hood
and gown, was lowered into its grave surrounded by vast crowds
saluting with arms outstretched in Fascist style. On behalf of all
present, Goicoechea took an oath, before God and before Spain,
to avenge the murder. The Vice-President and permanent secretary of the Cortes were attacked by middle-class crowds (including
many well-dressed women) shrieking that they wanted nothing to
do with parliamentarians. Some shots were fired between Falan-

[1] Zugazagoitia, 22.

gists and *Asaltos*, and several people were wounded – of whom four died. These two funerals were really the last political meetings in Spain before the Civil War.

The atmosphere in Madrid was very excited all day. The Government suspended the right-wing papers *Ya* and *Época* for publishing sensational accounts of the murder of Calvo Sotelo without submitting their copy first to the censor. They prorogued the Cortes, in an attempt to give passions time to cool. The leaders of the right-wing parties protested, and threatened to withdraw from Parliament altogether. Largo Caballero, returning from a visit to London, left his train near El Escorial at the request of the Government and motored to Madrid to avoid the demonstrations which would have attended his arrival at the North Station.

The left-wing organisations once again maintained their vigil during the night, the eve of the Virgin of Carmen – as Prieto, the anticlerical, romantically reminded his readers next day in *El Socialista*. The dispute between UGT and CNT continued, sporadic firing between the two unions being heard in southern suburbs. During the day, also, the diplomat Sangroniz arrived at Tenerife to inform Franco that an aircraft to take him to Morocco would arrive the next day at Las Palmas.

In the morning of July 15, there was a meeting of the Permanent Committee of the Cortes – a body composed of representatives of all the leading parties in the Cortes in proportion to their numbers. First, the Count of Vallellano, for the Monarchists, made a formal protest at the death of Calvo Sotelo, and announced that his party would take no further part in Parliament, since the country was plainly in anarchy. He left the meeting. Within a few hours, he and Goicoechea, followed during the next two days by many of those leading aristocrats and right-wing persons who knew that their lives would be endangered if there were to be fighting in the capital, left for safer cities, such as Burgos or, in many cases, abroad. Meantime Gil Robles spoke in the Cortes Committee. He paid an eloquent tribute to the memory of Calvo Sotelo, who so lately had been his rival, and whose fate he had so nearly shared. He listed the acts of violence which had occurred in the last month – including sixty-one murders and ten robberies of churches. The responsibility for all these acts he laid upon the Government. He recalled how members of the political parties supporting the Government had openly said that, against Calvo

Sotelo, all violence was legal, and how the threats to his life revealed by Joaquín Bau had been ignored by the Minister of the Interior. He concluded by announcing that the Cabinet had made democracy a farce, and had itself become an administration of blood, mud and shame. He thus publicly declared that he had failed to incorporate the CEDA in the democratic process of parliamentary government, and that he washed his hands of Parliament. He undoubtedly knew of the military rising, though he was not implicated in its development. Afterwards, he left Madrid for Biarritz. The Cortes Committee meanwhile agreed to summon the Cortes for the ensuing Tuesday, July 21 – a request being later issued by the party leaders that all deputies should leave their firearms in the cloakroom. The forthcoming meeting (which never occurred) was therefore immediately nicknamed the disarmament conference. Outside Madrid, on July 15, the *Dragon Rapide* arrived at last, at Las Palmas. In San Sebastián, a memorial service was held for Calvo Sotelo, at which *vivas* were given for Monarchy and one man was killed in the following riot.

July 16 was the last day before the rising. In the morning, Mola went to Logroño to meet General Batet, commander of the 6th Division with its headquarters at Burgos. This was a man known to be loyal to the Government, even though it had been he who, while in command at Barcelona, had coolly crushed the Catalan and left-wing revolt of 1934 in that city. Mola feared an assassination at this *rendezvous* and the officers who went with him were armed with grenades. But Batet merely told Mola that certain *pistoleros* were on their way from Barcelona to kill him, and suggested that he should leave Navarre. Mola smiled at the idea, which was put forward in good faith. Batet then asked Mola for a declaration that he did not intend to rise against the Government. 'I give you my word that I shall not launch myself upon an adventure,' answered Mola, who later boasted of the adroitness of this remark.[1] The meeting ended without further conversation. And later Mola succeeded in passing a message through to José Antonio in Alicante Prison about the final arrangements for the rising.

In Madrid, the day passed comparatively calmly. The Ministry of Labour published its award in respect of the building strike, which the employers refused. They re-opened their works, pending an appeal to the Cortes. Some UGT workers returned

[1] Iribarren, 89.

but the CNT remained out. In Barcelona, hitherto unalarmed during July, the rumours were incessant that the Army was about to rise. Armed members of the various organisations stood on guard at all Republican or left-wing headquarters. Many Falangists were arrested, some admitting that they were on their way to loot a Republican newspaper office. By this time, indeed, there was little more pretence anywhere in Spain that the Right, and all those who later supported the Nationalists in the war, recognised the Government of Casares Quiroga as the legitimate administration. That Government itself now clearly regarded the right-wing parties as its declared enemies, though it did not yet regard the Left as its allies or agents. As for the parties of the Left, there is no doubt that they all were conscious of the imminence not only of the military rising but also of their own greatest opportunity.

The Government then took certain steps designed to limit the extent of a rising if it should occur. General Varela, plotting in Cádiz, was arrested and imprisoned. The destroyer *Churruca* was despatched from Cartagena to Algeciras, and the gunboat *Dato* told to weigh anchor at Ceuta. These measures were intended to prevent the transport of any units of the Legion or the *Regulares* to the mainland. But the Government was naturally itself hampered in its precautions by having no knowledge of the loyalty of the commanders of these ships.

Meanwhile, in the Canaries, Captain Bebb was dissimulating, with success, to the authorities at Las Palmas, as to why he had landed without papers at the airport. At Tenerife, Franco was preparing his journey to Las Palmas. At this point, General Balmes, Las Palmas' Military Governor, accidentally shot himself dead at target practice. This absurd tragedy (which in the excitable atmosphere was rumoured to be either murder or suicide) gave Franco an excuse to go to Las Palmas for the funeral. Otherwise, he had planned to say that he had to make a tour of inspection. The Under-Secretary at the Ministry of War gave Franco permission by telephone to leave Tenerife. Half an hour after midnight on the night of July 16–17, the General boarded the small island boat, accompanied by his wife and daughter, on the first stage of a journey which would lead him to supreme power in Spain but which he would almost certainly not have begun had he known how long it would last. At the same moment, Colonel Valentín Galarza, in the War Ministry at Madrid, passed on a final message from Mola to Goded in Majorca: he should go to take command at Barcelona and not to Valencia, where his place would be taken by General González Carrasco.[1] Meanwhile, Mola's brother, Ramón, came from Barcelona to Pamplona to express his fears lest the rising should fail in the Catalan capital. The General calmed his brother, who therefore returned to Barcelona and, like so many brothers, to his death.

---

[1] *Cruzada*, XXIII 460. Goded's motives in demanding this change. Iturralde, I 86 alleges that he thought Barcelona a suitable place in which to arrange a compromise if the rising should fail. This would explain the frantic declarations to the contrary of Goded's son in *Un Faccioso Cien por Cien*.

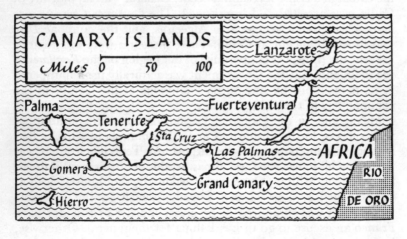

MAP 4

Manuel Azaña, Prime Minister, later President of the Republic

Generals Franco and Mola at Burgos

One of Madrid's sacked churches

Manuel Azaña talks with **Luis Companys**, the Catalan leader

(*below left*) Indalecio Prieto, Socialist leader

(*above right*) Santiago Casares Quiroga, Prime Minister at the outbreak of the Civil War

José Antonio Aguirre, President of the Basque Republic

The Foreign Legion advances

José Antonio Primo de Rivera, founder of the Falange

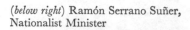

(*below right*) Ramón Serrano Suñer, Nationalist Minister

General Queipo de Llano, 'the Radio General', in old age

The People's
Army on their
way to the Front

Largo Caballero, Socialist
Prime Minister of the Republic
1936-37 (*extreme right*),
at the Front

Juan Negrín,
Republican Minister of
Finance, and Prime
Minister from 1937

Nationalist troops cross a bridge half destroyed by the Republicans

Death in Action

(*above*) The Republican General Miaja with Major Attlee

(*below*) La Pasionaria

A mountain bivouac of militiamen in the Sierra

General Mario Roatta,
leader of Mussolini's
'volunteers' in Spain

General Hugo Sperrle, Commander of the German Condor Legion, at his trial at
Nuremberg

André Malraux, who
led the French fliers
for the Republic

Ernö Gerö, Hungarian Comintern
agent in Catalonia

John Cornford,
the English poet killed
in the Sierra Morena

(*above*) Moscardó, Varela and Franco after the relief of the Alcázar

(*left*) General Yagüe enters Barcelona

Republican refugees on their way into France

15

The rising in Melilla – in Tetuán – in Ceuta – in Larache – the news reaches Madrid – Constitutional Counter-measures – the risings in Andalusia – Queipo de Llano at Seville – events at Granada, Córdoba, and Algeciras

That night in Melilla, General Romerales toured the city in search of suspicious activity. At the *casa del pueblo* he joked with the local Socialist leaders: 'The masses at vigil I see.'[1] He returned home, convinced that all was well. He was the fattest of Spain's two hundred generals, and one of the easiest fooled. The next morning, the officers who were in the plot at Melilla held a meeting in the map department of the headquarters. Colonel Seguí told his confederates the exact hour of the rising – five o'clock. Arrangements were made for the seizure of public buildings. These plans were then revealed to the local leaders of the Falange, one of whom, however, Álvaro González, was a traitor. He immediately informed the local leader of Martínez Barrio's party, the *Unión Republicana*, who told the head of the *casa del pueblo*, who told Romerales. And, immediately after the conspirators returned to the map department after luncheon and when arms had already been distributed, Lieutenant Zaro surrounded the building with troops and police. The Lieutenant then confronted his insurrectionary superior officers. 'What brings you here, Lieutenant?' demanded Colonel Gazapo jovially. 'I have to search the building for arms,' answered Zaro. Gazapo immediately telephoned Romerales: 'Is it true, my General, that you have given orders to search the map department? There are only maps here.' 'Yes, yes, Gazapo,' replied Romerales, 'but it must be done.'[2] The hour of decision had arrived, prematurely but none the less certainly. Gazapo telephoned next to a unit of the Foreign Legion to relieve him and his fellow officers now besieged by

[1] *Cruzada*, X 17.
[2] Aznar, 45–7; Lojendio, 24 give much the same account. There is no left-wing account of the rising in Morocco. Fernández de Castro (*passim*) gives a very detailed account of events in Melilla.

Zaro. The latter vacillated, agreed that his men could not fire on the legionaries, and surrendered. Then Colonel Seguí left for Romerales' office, which he entered with revolver drawn. Inside, a furious altercation was going on between certain of Romerales' officers who were insisting that the General should resign and others who wanted to resist. Casares Quiroga, from Madrid, informed by telephone of the sinister meeting in the map department, had ordered Romerales to arrest Seguí and Gazapo. But who would carry out such an order? Romerales sat in an agony of indecision at his desk. Then Seguí entered and forced his General to resign at the point of his revolver. The revolutionary officers declared a state of war, occupied all the public buildings of Melilla (including the aerodrome), closed the *casa del pueblo* and all left-wing centres, and arrested all the leaders of Republican or left-wing groups. There was violent fighting around the *casa del pueblo* and in the lower-class districts, but the workers were taken by surprise and their arms were few. All those captured who were known to have resisted the rebellion were shot, Romerales included. By the evening, lists had been obtained of members of trade unions, left-wing parties and Masonic lodges. All such persons were also immediately arrested.[1] Anyone known or suspected to have voted for the Popular Front in the elections of February was also in danger of execution. Melilla was henceforth ruled by martial law; and the manner of its insurrection was the model followed throughout the rest of Morocco and Spain.

Colonel Seguí meantime telephoned Colonels Sáenz de Buruaga and Yagüe, respectively entrusted with the organisation of the rising at Tetuán and Ceuta, the other two leading cities on the North African coast. He also telegraphed to Franco (now at Las Palmas attending Balmes's funeral) explaining why the rising at Melilla had had to take place earlier than the hour agreed. In the early evening, telegrams were despatched by Yagüe to the garrisons on the mainland of Spain, giving the simple and long-awaited password – 'As usual (*Sin novedad*)'.[2] From Madrid, meanwhile, Casares Quiroga had tried to find either Romerales or Gómez Morato, the overall commander in Africa. He found the latter at the Casino in Larache: 'General, what is going on at

---

[1] *Documents on German Foreign Policy 1918–45*, Series D Vol III (Germany and the Spanish Civil War 1936–9), 9. This volume of the German Foreign Ministry Documents is hereinafter referred to as *GD*.

[2] *Cruzada*, X 44.

Melilla?' 'In Melilla? Nothing. Why?' 'Because a garrison has risen.'[1] Gómez Morato left the Casino and flew immediately to Melilla, where he was captured the moment he set foot on ground at the airport.[2]

At Tetuán Colonels Asensio, Beigbeder (the ex-Military *Attaché* at Berlin, whom the Republic had transferred) and Sáenz de Buruaga had by this time also risen. The last named telephoned the High Commissioner and, arrogantly referring to him as

MAP 5. SPANISH MOROCCO

Captain of Artillery – in the uniform of which rank he had so proudly appeared at the parade at the end of the manoeuvres – demanded his resignation. Álvarez Buylla telephoned Casares Quiroga, who ordered him to hold out at all costs, telling him that the fleet and the air force would relieve him the following day. But the High Commissioner was now barricaded into his own residence, surrounded by those few officers who remained loyal to him. Outside, Major Castejón and the 5th Bandera of the Foreign Legion[3] were digging trenches in the square. A little later Major Lapuente, a first cousin of General Franco, telephoned from San Ramiel airfield to say that he and his air force squadron would stay

---

[1] Aznar, 48.   [2] *Ibid* 45. These events are also described in *Cruzada*, XI 28.
[3] A Bandera was a self-contained unit of 600 men including maintenance units and mobile artillery.

loyal to the Government. 'Resist, resist,' Álvarez Buylla encouraged, as Casares had encouraged him. But, by this time, with
night falling swiftly, the Residence and the airport were the only
points not in the hands of the rebel Colonels who, like their
colleagues at Melilla, had totally crushed all resistance from all the
trade unionists and left-wing or Republican groups. Beigbeder
went to inform the Caliph and Grand Vizier of Tetuán of what was
afoot, and gained their provisional support. He also took command
of the Department of Native Affairs in the city, the civil servants
accepting the change from the administration of Álvarez Buylla
without a murmur.[1] In Ceuta, at eleven at night, Yagüe, with the
Foreign Legion, took over command of the city more easily, no
shots being fired to resist him at all.[2] In Larache, on the Atlantic
coast, the rising did not occur till two o'clock in the morning on
July 18. Fighting here was bitter, between rebels and officers loyal
to the Republic, supported by trade unions. Two rebel officers
were killed, along with five *Asaltos* on the other side. But by dawn
the town was in the hands of the Nationalists, and all their enemies
arrested or shot.[3] At the same time, General Franco, with General
Orgaz, who had also been despatched by the Republic into
semi-exile to the Canaries, made themselves masters of Las Palmas.
Franco immediately declared martial law throughout the archipelago. While he was dictating a manifesto, the expected telephone
call came from Casares Quiroga. The Prime Minister was told
that Franco was visiting garrisons. No more communications took
place between the General and the Government. At a quarter past
five in the morning of July 18, Franco issued his Manifesto, from
Las Palmas, making special reference to the exceptional relationship that Spanish officers were supposed to feel towards the
country itself, rather than to any particular government, denouncing foreign influences, and promising in emotive terms a new
order after the victory. This Manifesto was immediately broadcast
on all Canary and Spanish Moroccan radio stations.[4] Then, in the
hot dawn of July 18, the rising began on the mainland.

Casares Quiroga and the Government of Spain attempted
throughout July 17 and 18 to crush the revolt against them by
ordinary constitutional means. While repeatedly telephoning
Álvarez Buylla and others loyal to him in Morocco to resist at all

---

[1] *Cruzada*, X 34–40.   [2] *Ibid.*, 44.   [3] *Ibid.*, 44–5.
[4] *Cruzada*, X 67–71. An English translation of Franco's manifesto may be seen in
the sycophantic biography of the General by S. F. Coles, 175-7.

costs, the Prime Minister (who had learnt of the rising at Melilla
from Romerales at midday) ordered certain warships to leave their
bases at El Ferrol and Cartagena for Moroccan waters. On July 17
he acted, that is, as if he supposed that the revolt would be confined to Morocco. This caution naturally infuriated the left-wing
leaders, who anticipated a rising at any moment on the Spanish
mainland and who thought that whatever arms the Government
possessed should be handed over to them. But this revolutionary
action was refused by Casares, who announced that anyone who
gave arms to the workers without his orders would be shot.[1] In
consequence, the streets and cafés of Madrid throughout the night
of July 17 were choked with voluble people, none of them knowing
what was happening, and all of them angry because their lack of
arms prevented them being able to take precautions to save themselves if a rising should occur. However, in the War Ministry, a
group of left-wing officers were in control, and General Pozas head
of the Civil Guard, and General Miaja, in command of the Madrid
division, were known to be loyal. The conspirators in Madrid
meanwhile held hurried and anxious meetings in their own houses.

The first news given by the Government of the rising was in the
morning of July 18 when Madrid Radio announced that 'no one,
absolutely no one on the Spanish mainland, has taken part in this
absurd plot',[2] which would, the Government promised, be quickly
crushed in Morocco. However, while these words were being heard
without belief by the citizens of Madrid, risings were in fact taking
place, as agreed, throughout Andalusia. Nearly everywhere on
July 18 the Civil Governors in the large towns followed the
example of the Government in Madrid, and refused to co-operate
fully with the working-class organisations who were clamouring
for arms. In most cases, this brought the success of the risings and
signed the death warrants of the Civil Governors themselves,
along with the local working-class leaders. Had the rebels risen in
all the provinces in Spain on July 18 they would probably have
been everywhere triumphant by July 22, when they expected to be.
But had the liberal Government of Casares Quiroga distributed
arms, and ordered the Civil Governors to do so too, thus using the
working class to defend the Republic at the earliest opportunity, it
is possible that the rising would have been crushed.[3]

---

[1] Zugazagoitia, 41.   [2] *The Times*, 20.7.36.
[3] The pontifical historian of the Anarchists, Max Nettlau, who arrived shortly in
Barcelona, later tried rather unsuccessfully to rationalise this. 'Where a measure of

For the Republic, the events of July 18 seemed bad enough. The pattern was everywhere the same as at Melilla. From dawn onwards and at various times until mid-afternoon, the garrison would rise, and would be supported immediately by the Falange and, in most cases, by the Civil Guard. Where there was no garrison, the Civil Guard, Falange and local right-wing persons would act by themselves. The appointed leader of the rebels would declare a state of war, thereby formally announcing military law, and this proclamation would be read from the balcony of the town hall in the main square. This seizure of power would be resisted by the Socialist, Communist and Anarchist militias, as best they could, while the Civil Governor would vacillate in his office and attempt to telephone to Madrid. The officers loyal to the Republic, and, in most cases the *Asaltos*, would resist the rising and attempt to rally both the Civil Government and the working-class organisations. A general strike would be called by both UGT and CNT, and barricades, of wood, stone or sandbags, or of whatever was at hand, would immediately be erected. Fighting would follow, with both sides showing extreme disregard of personal safety.

On July 18, the risings all occurred in Andalusia. In Seville, General Queipo de Llano, commander of the *Carabineros* carried out what was by any reckoning an extraordinary *coup de main*. Like Sanjurjo in 1932 he had no connection with the city previous to the rising, and indeed had only arrived there on July 17 in his *Hispano-Suiza* (his official motor-car) in which he later boasted that he had earlier carried out '20,000 miles of conspiracy' under pretence of inspecting customs posts. Accompanied by his ADC and three other officers only, he established himself during the morning of July 18 in an office in the headquarters that had been abandoned because of the heat. Then he went along the passage to see General Villa-Abraille, commander of the Seville garrison. 'I have to tell you,' said Queipo, 'that the time has come to take a decision: either you are with me and your other comrades, or you are with this Government which is leading Spain to ruin.' Villa-Abraille and his staff were unable to make up their minds, apparently because they were afraid that, as in 1932, the rising would fail and they would be sent off to Villa Cisneros if they sup-

autonomy existed,' he wrote in the *CNT-FAI Information Bulletin*, July 25, 'the people could and did get arms at the right time. Where autonomy did not exist little or nothing could be done and the enemy thus – and only thus – gained a temporary advantage.'

ported Queipo. Queipo therefore arrested them, and ordered them all to go into the next room. Since there was no key, he merely ordered a corporal to stand in front of the door and shoot anyone who came out. Next he went, this time accompanied only by his ADC, to the infantry barracks. On arrival he was very surprised to see the troops drawn up under arms on the square. Queipo nevertheless went up to the Colonel, whom he had never seen before, and said: 'I shake your hand, my dear Colonel, and congratulate you on your decision to put yourself on the side of your brothers-in-arms in these hours when the fate of our country is being decided.' 'I have decided to support the Government,' said the Colonel. Queipo expressed astonishment, and said, 'Shall we pursue the interview in your office?' Inside, the Colonel held to his position, and Queipo withdrew from him the command of the regiment. But no other officer would take his place. Queipo then sent away his ADC to fetch one of the three officers who were accompanying him. He was himself left entirely alone in face of these officers who seemed to oppose him. He began to joke with them, and they all said that they were afraid of what had happened after Sanjurjo's rising in 1932. Eventually, Queipo found a Captain to take over the regiment. He thereupon went to the back of the room and shouted to the other officers at the top of his lungs: 'You are my prisoners.' With remarkable docility they allowed themselves to be shut up. But next Queipo discovered that there were only 130 men in the regiment. Fifteen Falangists now appeared, to put themselves at his disposal. But this was a small force to capture a great city with a population of a quarter of a million people. The crucial development, however, was when the artillery barracks agreed to support the rising. Heavy guns were brought into the Plaza San Fernando and the Civil Government was surrounded. At this point, and after only a few exchanges had been fired with a group of *Asaltos* gathered in the solemn Hotel Inglaterra, the Civil Governor telephoned Queipo and meekly surrendered on condition that his life was spared. The Civil Guard of Seville then rallied to the rising. By the end of the morning the whole of the centre of Seville was in Queipo's hands. Meantime, the working-class organisations had tumbled to what was afoot. Radio Seville called for a general strike and for the peasants of nearby villages to come into the city to assist their comrades. Large crowds assembled at union headquarters calling for arms. But of these there were only a small supply. Yet, during the afternoon, the workers were busy building barricades throughout the suburbs. Eleven churches were set ablaze, together with the silk factory belonging to the Monarchist Marquis Luca de Tena. Meantime Queipo captured the radio station. At eight in the evening, he broadcast the first of what were to become a notorious series of harangues. In a voice seasoned by many years' consumption of sherry and valdepeñas, he declared that Spain was saved and that the rabble who resisted the rising would be shot like dogs.[1] But night came with Seville still divided in two.[2]

During the day, Cádiz, Jerez, Algeciras and La Linea also were generally overcome, although in none of them, as in Seville, was resistance finally crushed till the arrival in the following days of the first units of the Army of Africa. In Córdoba, Colonel Cascajo, the Military Governor, battered his civil colleague, Rodríguez de León, into submission by artillery, even although urgent voices on the telephone from the Ministry of the Interior in Madrid promised relief within hours. In Granada, a stalemate existed: General Campins, the Military Governor, lectured his officers on the evil of the rising in Morocco. In the streets, supporters of the Popular Front, with the Anarchists, carried on daylong demonstrations. The conspirators in the city held their hand, although they listened with enthusiasm to the broadcast of Queipo de Llano. At the port of Huelva, near the Portuguese frontier, although isolated from the rest of Republican Spain by the rising at Seville, the town passed immediately into the hands of the Popular Front. General Pozas from the Ministry of the Interior in Madrid telephoned an urgent order to the commander of the Civil Guard to send a column against Queipo in Seville. Major Haro therefore set off with a small force of Civil Guards, but on arrival at that city he immediately rallied to Queipo's side. In Málaga, the rebel General Paxtot dithered, and eventually gave up the attempt to declare a state of war, when threatened by telephone with bombardment by the fleet. But this was the last success of the Government during the day. In the evening, the last Republican resistance in Africa, at Tetuán, came to an end.[3]

---

[1] *Canalla, canaille*, or rabble, remained Queipo's favourite word throughout the war.
[2] *Cruzada*, XI 154–202; *ABC de Seville*, 18.7.37; Bahamonde 26 fl.
[3] Left-wing resistance continued at Santa Cruz de la Palma till July 28. Otherwise the Canaries were also conquered for the rising by July 20. (*Cruzada*, X 76.)

16

Madrid waits – 'the people want arms' – revolt and counter-revolt in the fleet – failure of constitutional means of reducing the revolt – the atrocities – resignation of Casares Quiroga – Martínez Barrio and the effort of compromise – Mola's refusal – Martínez Barrio resigns – the arming of the people

The Government in Madrid discovered its defeats by telephone, as in Morocco; a rebel commander would answer insultingly, crying '¡Arriba España!' in place of the Civil Governor or the loyal Military Governor. News travelled in this way also to the unions and political parties, who would telephone to their comrades in other towns and discover enemies in control, say, of the railway station or the post office. André Malraux has vividly described these exchanges: '*Allo Ávila?*' said Madrid, '*comment ça va chez vous? Ici la gare.*' '*Va te faire voir, salaud. Vive le Christ-Roi!*' '*A bientôt. Salud!*'[1] Throughout the day Casares continued, however, to act as if he were in command of the country, and as if there were no need for emergency measures. He consulted with Generals whom he knew to be loyal to the Republic, such as Núñez de Prado and Riquelme.[2] He also talked with President Azaña, with the Speaker of the Cortes, Martínez Barrio, and with Sánchez Román, a leading Madrid lawyer who had been too far to the Right to commit himself to the Popular Front. This group of leaders of the Republic discussed how a compromise might be arranged which would avoid both the overthrow of the *régime* and a civil war. But, by now, thousands of workers were jostling each other in the streets of Madrid, all demanding arms. A delegation of taxi-drivers called on the Premier to offer him 3,000 taxis to fight the rebels. The UGT possessed 8,000 rifles, but these had already been mainly distributed to the Communist-Socialist Youth and the militant members of the UGT, who were now beginning to abandon their

[1] Malraux, 8. Ávila did not in fact rise till July 19. The telephone exchange itself continued to serve both parties impartially – as it did throughout the Civil War – a feat of which its American management were justly proud.

[2] Careful examination suggests that all the General Officers in the Spanish Army who actively supported the Republic were Freemasons.

jobs and act permanently as political police in the streets. But 8,000 rifles were not enough to resist the garrisons of Madrid and their Falangist supporters, though as yet there was no sign of any movement in any right-wing quarter. Special editions of *Claridad* and *El Socialista* demanded 'Arms for the People' in banner head-lines.[1] 'Arms, arms, arms' was cried all day by great masses of men and women in the streets around the *casa del pueblo*, the Ministry of War and in the Puerta del Sol. But Casares refused. In the late morning he despatched General Núñez de Prado to Saragossa to attempt to reach a compromise with General Cabanellas, in com-mand of the division there, who was believed to be a Republican. 'A forthcoming change of Ministry will satisfy all the General's demands and obviate the necessity for a rising,' Núñez de Prado told Cabanellas. Nevertheless, he was arrested and later shot, together with his ADC. Back in Madrid, the Cabinet sat in con-tinuous if oddly peripatetic session in the Ministry of War, in the Royal Palace, and later still in the Ministry of the Interior in the Puerta del Sol. At twenty past seven in the evening, Madrid Radio announced that the rising had everywhere been crushed, even at Seville. This was the first official admission that anything untoward was taking place on the mainland of Spain. The news was followed by a series of decrees dismissing Franco, Cabanellas, Queipo de Llano and González de Lara (in command at Burgos) from their commands. Thereafter the wirelesses of the hot capital played strident music, partly to soothe, partly to exhort, the expectant crowds.[2] From time to time, the loudspeakers would announce: 'People of Spain! keep tuned in. Do not turn your radios off. Rumours are being circulated by traitors. Keep tuned in.'[3] At ten in the evening, La Pasionaria broadcast the first of many violent speeches in the Civil War demanding resistance throughout the country, urging the women of Spain to fight with knives and burning oil, and ending with the slogan, 'It is better to die on your feet than to live on your knees! *No pasarán!*' (They shall not pass.) And this last cry, an echo of Verdun, repeated syllabically, became immediately the chief rallying cry of the Republic. But still Casares, with Azaña supporting him, refused to hand out arms to the masses. From being regarded as a revolu-

---

[1] The Anarchists in Madrid appeared indifferent to all these events, being still pre-occupied by their building strike (Zugazagoitia, 57).

[2] The most popular song, played incessantly during these hot nights, was 'The Music Goes Round and Round and it Comes Out Here'.

[3] De la Mora, 227.

tionary, the Prime Minister became hated as a reactionary. His nickname, *Civilón* (civilian), after a famous bull who refused to defend himself, was repeated everywhere scornfully. As for the conspirators of Madrid, they continued disunited and indecisive.

During the day the Government had done what it could to reduce the already successful revolution in Morocco. Tetuán and Ceuta were bombed. But this merely caused the Sultan and Grand Vizier to accept more easily the change foisted upon them by Beigbeder. Nor did it inflict any military damage. Then there was the fleet, which Casares Quiroga also tried to use against the rebels in Morocco. Three destroyers arrived at Melilla from Cartagena on the morning of July 18. On their way, the officers had heard Franco's broadcast from Las Palmas. They secretly resolved to join the Nationalists. On arrival at Melilla, they received orders to bombard the town. The captain of the destroyer *Sánchez Barcáiztegui* described the aims of the rising to his men, and then demanded their support for it. He was greeted by a profound silence, which was eventually interrupted by a single cry 'To Cartagena!' And this cry was taken up by the whole ship's company. The officers were overpowered and imprisoned, and the *Sánchez Barcáiztegui* raised its anchor to break out of the rebel town into the open sea. Precisely similar scenes occurred in the other destroyers, the *Lepanto* and the *Almirante Valdés*. The three ships then put themselves at the orders of the Government and each formed a committee of their crews to act in place of the officers.[1]

The constitutional means of opposing the rising thus met with failure. It did so inevitably since the majority of the forces of so-called law and order – the Army and the Civil Guard – were with the rebels, who claimed to represent law and order themselves. The only force capable of resisting the rebels was that of the trade unions and left-wing parties. Yet for the Government to use this force would mean that it accepted the inevitability of a left-wing revolution. It is not surprising that a middle-class liberal such as Casares shrank from this decisive step. But once again, at the stage that Spanish affairs had reached on the night of July 18, such a step was also inevitable. Already in the towns where risings had taken place, in Morocco and in Andalusia, the opposition to them had been that of the revolutionary parties of the Left. It was a Revolution against which Queipo de Llano was fighting in Seville, though one which he had provoked himself.

[1] *Cruzada*, X 46–7.

So now there was to spread over Spain a great cloud of violence, in which all the quarrels and enmities of so many generations would find full outlet. With communications difficult or non-existent, each town would find itself on its own, acting out its own drama apparently in a vacuum. There were now not two Spains but two thousand. The geographical differences within Spain were a prime factor in the social disintegration of the nation. Regional feeling had sown the wind and now reaped the whirlwind. Sovereign power ceased to exist and, in its absence, individuals as well as towns acted without constraint, as if they were outside society and history. Within a month nearly a hundred thousand people[1] perished arbitrarily and without trial. Bishops would be torn to pieces and churches profaned. Educated Christians would spend their evenings murdering illiterate peasants and professional men of sensitivity. The vast majority of these crimes were the work, on both sides, of men convinced that what they were doing was not only right, but noble.[2] Nevertheless these events inevitably caused such hatreds that, when some order was eventually established, it was an order geared solely for the rationalisation of hatred known as war. And it would be quite wrong to think that there was much repugnance at this development. Spaniards of all parties leapt into the war like the cheering, bellicose crowds in the capitals of the rest of Europe in 1914 at the start of that war of which, perhaps subconsciously even in 1936, the people of Spain felt they should have been a party.

Some of these terrible prospects were suspected by Casares Quiroga, as he feverishly paced his office, recently regilded, in the Paseo de la Castellana, on the night of July 18. Exhausted, he concluded that he could do no more than resign. The President, Azaña, also had only too clear a vision of the disasters which lay ahead. He therefore called upon Martínez Barrio, the arch-priest of compromise, to form a Government to attempt to treat with the rebels. The new Ministers were all moderate men. They included the middle-of-the-road barrister, Sánchez Román. This name was greeted by the crowds which heard it from Radio Madrid in the cafés and the streets with cries of 'Treason' and 'Traitors'. A hundred thousand workers pushed their way from the *casa del pueblo* down to the Puerta del Sol. '*Sol, Sol, Sol,*' cried the crowd as they went and then again: 'Arms, arms, arms.' Meantime the

[1] See below, pages 168, 176 for calculation of this figure.
[2] See below, pages 170, 179 for further speculation on the motives of the atrocities.

attempt at compromise was made. General Miaja, in command of the Madrid division, whom Martínez Barrio had named as his Minister of War, and who was known as an easy-going Republican officer (being nicknamed 'Papa' in the Army), telephoned Mola at Pamplona. After an exchange of courtesies, Mola bluntly announced that he was about to rise against the Government. A little later, Martínez Barrio telephoned Mola to offer him a post in the Government. 'The Popular Front cannot keep order,' answered Mola, 'you have your followers and I have mine. If we were to seal a bargain we should be betraying our ideals and our men. We should both deserve to be lynched.'[1] This brave remark by General Mola would cost the country thousands of lives, including, indeed, his own. It was obvious by then in Pamplona that the rising would be neither quickly successful nor quickly defeated. Mola thus bears great responsibility for the course of events. But then, how could he have drawn back at this late stage? And, if he had, would not others have brushed him aside? A similar telephoned appeal by Martínez Barrio to General Cabanellas at Saragossa also failed.[2] So, towards dawn at the end of this *nuit blanche* of July 18–19, new consultations were held between Azaña, Martínez Barrio and the Socialist leaders, Prieto and Largo Caballero. The latter urged that there was now no alternative to an issue of arms to the trade unions. The loudspeakers of Madrid Radio shortly announced that a new Government was being formed which would accept 'Fascism's declaration of war upon the Spanish people'. This administration, like that of Casares Quiroga, was entirely composed of middle-class liberals from Republican parties. But the Socialists, Communists and Anarchists declared themselves behind the new Ministers and formally sank their differences. The Prime Minister was José Giral, a professor of chemistry by profession and a close friend of Azaña; he had previously been Minister of Marine. In addition, General Pozas, head of the Civil Guard and General Castelló, Military Governor of Badajoz, became Ministers of the Interior and of War respectively. Both had emerged as loyal Republicans, and Giral hoped that their presence would persuade members of the middle class to support the Government as well as adding to its military efficiency.

[1] Bertrán Güell, 76. Iribarren, 101–2.
[2] Cabanellas had been presumed a Republican. He was finally persuaded to join the rising by a young officer who put a revolver to his head and told him that he had a minute to decide.

And the new Government immediately took the irrevocable step from which Casares, constitutional to the end, had shrunk. The people would be armed! As the sun was rising on July 19, lorries carrying rifles were driven fast along the streets of Madrid from the Ministry of War to the headquarters of the UGT and the CNT, where they were received by the waiting masses with rapturous excitement, and by cries of '*No Pasarán*' and '*Salud*.' And these orders to distribute what arms there were were given by telephone to all the Civil Governments in the provinces, although in many cases such orders were too late: for this occurred just when, in the summer dawn, the second wave of risings was about to break over Spain. It was at this moment also that Franco at last arrived on African soil, flown by the *Dragon Rapide*, to be greeted by Sáenz de Buruaga on the same San Ramiel airfield at Tetuán where the previous day the last Republicans had been overwhelmed – they had been led by Franco's own cousin, Major Lapuente;[1] and that the *Churruca* was landing at Cádiz the first unit of the Army of Africa to reach the mainland of Spain, 200 Moorish *Regulares*; and that the crews on the warships sailing south to Algeciras were about to rise against their officers. Well might so tough a revolutionary as the Communist El Campesino later express his wonderment that a single day could have held so much 'bloodshed and battle'.[2]

In Madrid, in Barcelona, and elsewhere the bullfights arranged, as usual, for Sunday afternoon were cancelled.[3] The bloody *corrida* of the Spanish nation, so long foretold, had itself begun.

[1] Lapuente was later shot. Franco had left Las Palmas in the *Dragon Rapide* in the morning of July 18. The aircraft stopped at Agadir and Casablanca before reaching Tetuán. It is just possible that the prudent General delayed his arrival in Morocco till it was certain that his friends had won there.

[2] Campesino, 5. The credit for the expression may be more accurately due, one cannot but think, to Señor Julián Gorkin, the indefatigable editor of the works of El Campesino.

[3] No more bull-fights occurred in Spain, except in irregular circumstances, until the end of the Civil War.

July 19 – Battle of Barcelona – Gijón – Oviedo – Galicia – the Basque provinces – Burgos – Saragossa – Pamplona – Valladolid – revolution in the Fleet – the rising in Madrid

In Barcelona, recently so unusually quiet, the greatest battle of July 19 was fought. On the previous night, this magnificent city had run wild with rumours. Crowds had massed all the way from the great central Plaza de Cataluña down the leafy avenue, the Ramblas, with its bars and flowers, to the edge of the harbour at the Plaza Puerta de la Paz where Columbus's statue, on its tall column, surveys the Mediterranean. The General commanding the division based at Barcelona, Llano de la Encomienda, had warned his officers that, if circumstances should oblige him to choose between two extreme movements, he would not hesitate to name Communism rather than Fascism. Among those who heard this were the leaders of the rising planned to begin the next day – including General Fernández Burriel of the cavalry who was to be in command till General Goded's arrival from Majorca. Their plan was for the troops in the various barracks to join up at the Plaza de Cataluña. They supposed that it would be an easy task to reduce the remainder of the city. But the plotters had failed to take adequate account of the hostility towards them of the Civil Guard in the town under General Aranguren and Colonel Escobar,[1] and the sheer numbers of the mainly Anarchist workers. In the late evening of July 18, President Companys of the Generalitat refused to give 'arms to the people'. Nevertheless, the CNT took by assault several arms depôts and were prepared for the now inevitable struggle. Thus in one moment the Anarchist leaders passed from the status of hunted criminals to – what? Certainly not defenders of democracy, but 'leaders of the Anti-Fascist Revolutionary Alliance'. Meantime, Companys received news from Llano de la Encomienda that all was quiet in the garrisons. Nevertheless, the President was unable to sleep. At two in the morning, he and Ventura Gassol, the poet who was his counsellor of culture,

---

[1] He appears as Colonel Ximénez in Malraux's novel *L'Espoir*.

walked out into the Rambla, Companys wearing a soft hat pulled
low over his eyes, his companion with a dishevelled forelock giving
him the air of a nineteenth-century violinist. The brilliant gaiety of
a Saturday night of the Barcelona summer was slowly giving way
to something in that city equally traditional: a revolutionary dawn.
The crowds suddenly appeared to be less holidaymakers than

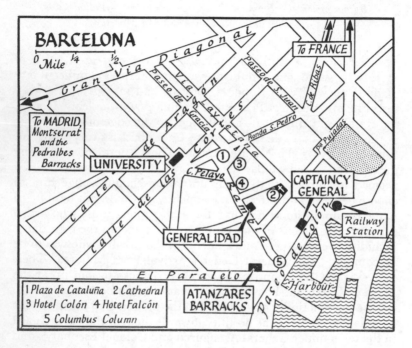

MAP 6

armed workers and, on the loudspeakers, the dance music had
given way to stirring admonitions to proletarian action. From
Radio Madrid, the voice of La Pasionaria could be heard evoking
memories of the rising of Spain of 1808 against the soldiers of
Napoleon. At four in the morning, the news was brought to
Companys that troops under Colonel López-Amor had left the
Pedralbes barracks in the north of the city and were marching
towards the Plaza de Cataluña.

The men in the barracks had been roused early and given a
generous portion of brandy, being variously told that they were

being sent to crush an Anarchist rising or to march round the town
in honour of the so-called Barcelona Olympiad, a left-wing festival
arranged in opposition to the official Olympic Games which were
about to open in Berlin. But the junction between the different
groups of rebels was never effected, since all were met by the
furious resistance of the workers, led by the Anarchists, and supported by the Civil Guard (who at Barcelona, almost alone in
Spain, were completely loyal to the Government)[1] and the *Asaltos*.
An artillery column under Colonel López-Amor succeeded in
reaching the Plaza de Cataluña, and there capturing the telephone
building by a trick, but they got no farther. The officers directing
the rebellion were unable to deal with the revolutionary un-
orthodoxy of their opponents; a second artillery detachment, for
example, was overcome by a column of armed workers who
advanced with rifles in the air, and with 'passionate words' begged
the rebels not to fire. They then successfully urged the troops to
turn their guns on their own officers. Most of the battles of
Barcelona were much less easy, and were only gained by the
workers through extreme disregard of personal safety. Goded
arrived from Majorca (which he had secured with hardly a shot
fired) in mid-morning. He failed either to put enough heart into
his men or to ensure reinforcements from elsewhere. Fighting
continued all day, the Plaza de Cataluña becoming strewn with
dead men and dead horses. In the early evening, the old Captaincy
General where Goded had set up his headquarters, near the
harbour, was stormed. Goded, being himself captured, was
induced to broadcast an appeal in dignified but defeated tones to
his followers to lay down their arms precisely as Companys had
done when defeated in the Revolution of 1934. Goded did this
apparently to restrain his followers in Majorca from sending the
aid which he had earlier begged. The voice of the General was
heard all over Republican Spain, and was everywhere greeted with
enthusiasm. By the evening, there only held out in Barcelona the
Atarazanas Barracks near the harbour, and a pair of machine
gunners on the summit of Columbus's column who had been spray-
ing the foot of the Ramblas and the Plaza Puerta de la Paz all day.[2]
Elsewhere on July 19 the day had been tumultuous and confused.

---

[1] The enthusiasm in Barcelona when a troop of mounted Civil Guard rode slowly
down the Ramblas giving the Red salute knew no bounds.
[2] This account of the battle of Barcelona is based on the narratives in *La Cruzada*, *The
Times*, Jellinek, Francisco Lacruz, Abad de Santillan and Borkenau.

There were many unresolved conflicts. In Asturias the Civil Guards of Gijón held out in the Simancas barracks. In Oviedo, the centre of the revolution of 1934 and since February 1936 in a perpetual state of revolutionary effervescence, a curious situation had arisen. The city was considered lost for the rising. But Colonel Aranda, in command of the garrison, who had gained in Morocco the reputation of being the cleverest strategist in the Army, first posed as 'the sword of the Republic' to both the Civil Governor and the trade unions. He argued that the situation was not serious enough to necessitate the arming of the workers: González Peña, who had led the Asturian rising in 1934, was persuaded together with Belarmino Tomás, another Socialist deputy, to agree with Aranda, whose political affiliations were not known. Four thousand miners, supposing Oviedo securely held, left by train for other parts of Asturias and for Madrid. Then, at nine in the evening and having spoken with Mola on the telephone, Aranda declared himself with the rebels. He was supported by the *Asaltos* as well as the Falange and Civil Guard. The Left in Oviedo panicked. But the remainder of Asturias was hostile to him and by July 20 he was closely besieged by a new force of miners.[1]

In the Basque provinces, the third and southern province of Álava, whose capital is Vitoria, was captured without difficulty for the rebels led by Colonel Alonso Vega.[2] But the two other provinces, Vizcaya and Guipúzcoa, were as easily held for the Government. In the capital of Vizcaya, Bilbao, there was no rising. The regiment quartered there had naturally been implicated in the rising, but was betrayed by the blacksmith.[3] In San Sebastián, the capital of Guipúzcoa, Colonel Carrasco, the Military Governor, was arrested during the morning. Prieto, meanwhile, telephoned incessantly from Madrid to make certain that the far from revolutionary Basque Nationalist Party would support the Government. But he need not have worried. By midday, both Bilbao and San Sebastián, together with all the mountainous and fishing villages of the two provinces, had undergone a kind of universal voluntary mobilisation. Juntas of defence were set up in both cities, and various prominent right-wing persons were arrested and their motor-cars requisitioned. The Basque Nationalist politicians, led by Manuel de Irujo, were the inspiration of these steps.

[1] Zugazagoitia, 33 fl.
[2] The population of Álava is partly Basque, partly Navarrese. See above, page 54.
[3] Zugazagoitia, 94.

Meantime, the military plotters dilly-dallied. At last, a telephone call from Mola encouraged Colonel Vallespín in the Loyola barracks in San Sebastián, to decisive action. Two cannon of these barracks were pointed at the Civil Government building, whose entire staff fled, allowing Colonel Carrasco, who was detained there, to escape. This he did, and established himself with another group of right-wing persons in the María Cristina hotel. Rebel Civil Guards also moved into the Gran Casino Club. This was the moment when the handsome summer capital of Spain could have been won for the rising. Everyone was very nervous in San Sebastián. When a pistol shot was heard over San Sebastián Radio, the announcer had to explain, 'The shot you have just heard was caused by a comrade falling down and loosing off his weapon. There is no victim.'[1] However, Colonel Vallespín delayed till 'mañana', though Colonel Carrasco declared a state of war. And, during the night, a strong Republican column from the arms centre of Eibar began to make for the city.[2]

In Galicia, the rebels' chief opposition was to come from the crews of the warships in the harbours of Corunna, Vigo and El Ferrol. These were not overpowered immediately, however, and indeed the Corunna rising did not start till July 20. At El Ferrol, night fell with the rebels in control of the port, but with the seamen in control of the battleship España and other vessels, and in the act of bombarding the shore. In the other towns of Galicia, the rising was only to be assured after terrible street-fighting, for the grave and poverty-stricken peasants came in from the country in carts and on foot as if to a fiesta, resolved to fight to the death.

The rebels' most outstanding victories on July 19 were at Burgos, Saragossa, Pamplona and Valladolid. At the first of these, the old capital of Castile, a grave, reserved and very conservative city, the rising triumphed without any difficulty and with hardly a shot fired. 'The very stones are Nationalist here,' the Countess of Vallelano remarked proudly to Dr Junod of the Red Cross in August.[3] Colonel Gavilán was the moving spirit of the rebels here (General González de Lara having been arrested and taken away to Guadalaja prison the day before), and it was he who arrested the loyal General Batet, and the equally loyal Colonel Mena, in command of the Civil Guards. The wives of the Civil

[1] The Times, 30.7.36.   [2] Cruzada, XXVI 242 fl; Lizarra, 20 fl, 40.
[3] Junod, 98. It is unlikely that she used the word 'Nationalist', since this was rarely employed at this time.

Guard had earlier prevented the Civil Governor from giving arms
to the people, saying that they would be used to kill their husbands.
In this city there were many prominent right-wing persons such
as Sáinz Rodríguez and Goicoechea to celebrate the victory.[1] In
Saragossa, the troops went out into the streets at dawn, and were
in command of the main points of the town before the trade unions
could organise any resistance.[2] In the rest of Aragón, Huesca and
Jaca were as easily gained, though at Barbastro, near the Catalan
border, the commander of the garrison, Colonel Villalba, eventually decided to support the Republican side. His adhesion to the
rebels had been taken for granted and he may be regarded as the
most prominent officer to defect from the Nationalist conspiracy.
At Teruel, the capital of the southernmost province of Aragón, the
leading rebel declared a state of war before seven soldiers only. The
Civil Governor annulled it but the Civil Guards and *Asaltos* rallied
to the rising. The consequent general strike was not enough to
prevent the bloodless success of the rebels. In Navarre, there was
never any doubt about the Nationalist victory. Mola declared a
State of War at Pamplona with the enthusiastic support of the 6,000
Carlist *Requetés* whom he had been promised, and immediately the
whole province was in his hands. The scenes of religious enthusiasm combined with warlike zeal at least equalled the excitement in
Navarre during the nineteenth-century Carlist wars. In red *boinas*,
old men and young, all singing the old Carlist song 'Oriamendi',
poured into Pamplona from nearby villages, demanding arms.
Here, as in Burgos, the commander of the Civil Guard supported
the Popular Front, and he was shot by his own men.

At Valladolid, that other cathedral city of the Castillian plain,
where Columbus died in poverty, General Saliquet, previously on
the retired list, and General Ponte, the veteran Monarchist conspirator, unexpectedly appeared in the office of the commander of the
division, General Molero, a Freemason, and demanded his adhesion to their cause. The rebels gave their brother-officer a quarter of
an hour to reflect, and retired into an outer room. While the
minutes passed, the noise could be heard of the start of street-
fighting between Falangists and workers. Suddenly, General
Molero flung open the door, cried '*Viva la República*' and one of his
aides opened fire. A short fight ensued, two junior officers being
killed on either side, but the rebels emerged victorious. Molero
was led away, to be later shot for 'rebellion'. In the city, the

[1] *Cruzada*, XII 401–11; Ruiz Villaplana, 30 fl.   [2] *Cruzada*, XV 196 fl.

railway workers fought gallantly all day against their well-armed opponents, who included the Civil Guard, *Asaltos*, and civilians as well as the Falangists. The *casa del pueblo* never surrendered and was razed to the ground. By evening, however, Valladolid had been conquered. Luis Lavín, the Civil Governor, who had been appointed by Casares Quiroga especially to crush the Fascism of the city, found himself deserted by all his staff and friends. He therefore got into his motor-car and attempted to flee to Madrid. He was caught, and brought back a prisoner to his own house, where General Ponte had by then established himself. His only request was that he should be taken away to prison by the servant's entrance, not the front door.

Of the other towns of Old Castile, Segovia was won for the rebels without bloodshed, as was Ávila, where eighteen Falangists, including Onésimo Redondo, were released from prison. Zamora and Palencia were also quickly captured for the rising, though the officers, Civil Guard and right wing remained in both cities on tenterhooks for several days, due to the incessant rumours of the imminence of a train full of miners – who eventually returned to plague Aranda at Oviedo. In León, 2000 miners did arrive, demanding arms. The Military Governor, General Bosch, proposed that some arms should be given on condition that they left the town. In the event 200 rifles and 4 machine guns were handed over. León itself remained unrebellious till the next day, when the miners were well on their way to Madrid.[1] In Estremadura, Cáceres and its province was captured for the rising, but Badajoz, thanks to the loyalty of the garrison under General Castelló, remained Republican. In New Castile and La Mancha there was only one rebel success – at Albacete, captured by the Civil Guard. As for Andalusia during July 19, Queipo de Llano tightened his hand on Seville, but its suburbs remained in working-class hands. In the Andalusian towns where the rising had been generally successful on July 18, sporadic fighting continued, the Nationalists being greatly assisted in Cádiz and Algeciras by the recently arrived units of Moors from the Army of Africa. The stalemate of Granada persisted all day. Castelló, from the Ministry of War, telephoned to General Campins, the Military Governor, to equip a column to march on Córdoba. But the two senior Colonels of the garrison answered that it was doubtful whether the officers would agree to lead such a force. Another Colonel, alluding to the

---

[1] *Cruzada*, XV 134–7.

general strike then beginning, declared that Granada was already in Marxist hands. The idea suggested itself to Campins that the militias of the Popular Front should undertake the expedition demanded by Madrid. So he went to the artillery barracks and to the assembled officers announced: 'Gentlemen, the military rising has failed. I trust you to remain absolutely loyal to the Republic. I have orders from the Ministry of War to take over the arms of this garrison.' A silence greeted his words, and this he took for consent. But by midnight the militiamen still remained unequipped.[1]

There was a similar stalemate at Valencia. In mid-morning, all was ready for the rising, with several thousand civilian supporters assured, when bad news came in from Barcelona. General González Carrasco, who had arrived from Madrid to lead the rebels, suddenly had a moment of uncertainty, and the Military Governor, General Martínez Monje, who was not in the plot, similarly vacillated. The Valencian workers, led by the Anarchist dockers, meanwhile were massing in the streets. The college of St Thomas of Villanueva and the Church of the Two St Thomases were pillaged and set on fire. The Generals continued to dither, while certain left-wing officers of the Civil Guard began to distribute arms to the people. The matter was thus left unsettled by the time night fell. This uncertainty was reflected down the coast at Alicante and at Gandia. But there was no doubt about the Popular Front success farther south still at Almería and throughout all those parts of Andalusia where there had been no rising on July 18. By nightfall, this passionate and poverty-stricken part of Spain was aflame with revolution.

In the Balearics, while Majorca was secured by Goded for the rebels, the NCOs and troops of the garrison at Minorca prevented the success of the rising there by General Bosch.[2] At nightfall that officer had proclaimed a state of war at Port Mahon, but was closely besieged. In Ibiza the rising had nevertheless triumphed, as in the other small islands of the archipelago. Spanish Morocco was perhaps the calmest of all the Spanish dominions on July 19, 1936 – if one excepts those foetid colonies along the West Coast of Africa where news of the rising had not yet been brought. General Franco inspected his old friends in the Legion, established a concentration camp at Tetuán and made plans for the transport of

---

[1] *Cruzada*, XI 275–89.
[2] Not to be confused with General Bosch of León.

the Army of Africa across the straits. There was no fighting – at least on land. In Moroccan waters, matters were different.

On the eventful dawn of July 19, the *Libertad* and the *Cervantes* were sailing south from El Ferrol. They had been despatched by the Government to crush the rising in Morocco. Later, the only seaworthy Spanish battleship, the *Jaime Primero* also left Vigo for the south before the start of the rising in that port. Upon all these ships, upon the *Churruca* which had landed the first cargo of Moors at Cádiz, and upon all the warships at Cartagena, the same revolutionary events occurred as on the three destroyers sent the day before to Melilla: that is, the men, stimulated by radio messages from the Admiralty in Madrid addressed to them and not to their commanders, overwhelmed and imprisoned those of their officers whom they did not kill. The most violent battles occurred on the *Jaime Primero*, where the officers, in mid-ocean, resisted the ship's company to the last man.[1] (To the laconic question as to what should be done with the corpses – asked by the committee of the ship's company which took over command – the Admiralty replied: 'Lower bodies overboard with respectful solemnity.')[2] So, by the evening of July 19, an extraordinary fleet, run by self-appointed committees of their crews, were gathered in Gibraltarian waters, so obstructing access by General Franco to southern Spain. The gunboat *Dato* did, however, run a second cargo of *Regulares* across the straits in the evening of July 19, while part of the 5th Bandera of the Foreign Legion were flown to Seville by three Breguet aircraft.[3]

It was now also that the rising in Madrid occurred at last, and, by this time, the unions and political groups were ready to meet it. (On the urgent demand of the CNT, the prisons were opened and all the Anarchists held there, together with some common criminals, were set free.) The nominal leader of the rebellion in Madrid, General Villegas, had decided that the task was too much for him; and so General Fanjul, the deputy who had once been Under-Secretary for War under Gil Robles, was prevailed upon to take his place. He arrived at the Montaña barracks in the afternoon. To that large rambling edifice on the west of Madrid, overlooking the valley of the sluggish river Manzanares,

---

[1] Those officers who were merely imprisoned were shot at Cartagena during August. It was calculated, by Nationalist writers, that of the officers actually on their ships at the time of the rising 98% were killed (Lojendio, 40).

[2] *El Socialista*, 21.7.36.   [3] Lojendio, 38–9.

there also repaired, during the day, other officers from other barracks in Madrid, and a number of Falangists. Fanjul gave a lecture on the political aims of the rising and on its legality. Then the rebels attempted to sally out into the streets of the capital. But by this time a huge crowd had assembled outside the gates, many of them armed – though, of the 55,000 rifles issued by the Government to the trade unions, the bolts of 50,000 were in the Montaña barracks – an added reason for reducing that fortress. The density of the crowd rendered it physically impossible for the rebels to go out. They therefore resorted to firing with machine guns. The crowd replied; but there was no further development until the morning.

18

During the night of July 19–20, fifty churches in Madrid were set on fire. The working-class parties gained effective control of the capital. On the morning of July 20, a crowd even larger than that which had gathered the previous day assembled in the Plaza de España. All shouted 'Death to Fascism' and 'All to the aid of the Republic' with exultant monotony. The lance of Don Quixote, whose statue stands in the centre of the square, was enthusiastically interpreted as pointing towards the Montaña barracks.[1] Five hours of bombardment of that fortress followed. Aircraft and two pieces of artillery (drawn by a beer lorry) were included among the weapons of assault. Rebellion was encouraged among the soldiers in the barracks by loudspeakers. Inside, Fanjul, though confident, had no plan of concerting measures with the other garrisons in Madrid. Nor did they recognise him as leader. The garrisons could only communicate with each other at this time by signals over the roof tops. Fanjul nevertheless by this means implored General García de la Herrán, at the suburb of Carabanchel, to send a force to relieve him. But there was no possibility of a relief getting through. At half-past ten, Fanjul and Colonel Serra, the previous head of the garrison in the barracks, were wounded. Half an hour later, a white flag appeared at a window of the fortress. The crowd advanced to receive the expected surrender. They were greeted by machine-gun fire. This incident was repeated twice more, maddening the attackers. Confusion among the defenders rather than guile was, however, responsible. Some of the rank and file wanted to yield and were therefore ready to betray their officers. 'Onwards! To the struggle! Onwards!' repeated the assembled masses. Eventually, a few

---

[1] The Nationalists later pointed out that Don Quixote's arm, in this statue, is outstretched in Fascist salute, and not bent, with a clenched fist.

minutes before noon, the great door of the barracks broke beneath repeated assaults. The crowd burst maniacally into the courtyard, where for some moments everything was hysteria and bloodshed. A militiaman appeared suddenly at an outside window and began to throw rifles down to the crowd still in the street. One giant revolutionary conceived it his duty to fling officer after officer, disarmed and yelling, from the highest gallery upon the insensate mass of people in the courtyard beneath. The succeeding massacre beggared description. Most of the officers, including Serra and even some who might have supported the Republic were killed. Those who were saved were flung into the Model Prison, many with wounds undressed. General Fanjul was with difficulty saved from death and carried off to be tried. The precious supplies of bolts (and ammunition) were also saved, from mass distribution, and borne off to the Ministry of War by the *Asaltos*.

The successful attackers now marched to the Puerta del Sol. There, however, their victory parade was interrupted by firing from all sides. A unit of *Asaltos* cleared the houses surrounding the square, while the people lay on their faces. As for the other garrisons in Madrid, the officers of the barracks of the engineers at El Pardo drove off northward towards Valladolid, telling their men that they were on their way to fight General Mola. Among those so tricked was Largo Caballero's son, who was immediately imprisoned. In the suburb of Getafe, the Air Force officers loyal to the Government scotched an attempted rising at the air-base there; in that of Carabanchel, the artillery barracks were also captured by loyal officers, together with units of the militias: here the rebel General García de la Herrán was killed by his own men. And one by one the other garrisons were also captured.[1]

Immediately afterwards, hastily armed militia-forces, with enthusiasm their greatest, and, in many cases, their only, weapon, mounted in taxis, lorries or requisitioned private motor-cars, and streamed out southwards towards Toledo and north-eastwards towards Guadalajara. For in both these nearby towns the rising had been temporarily successful. At Toledo, the over-whelming numerical superiority of the militia drove back the rebels under Colonel Moscardó into a small and easily defendable area centring on the Alcázar, the half-fortress, half-palace set on a height commanding the city and the river Tagus. Moscardó re-

---

[1] The chief sources used in the account of the battles in Madrid were *Cruzada*, XVII 386–481; Borkenau, 127; *The Times*, 5.8.36; Ramos Oliveira, 268; *El Socialista*.

sisted attempts by the War Office and the Government to persuade him to surrender. Eventually, he was barricaded in with a force of about 1,300 of which 800 were members of the Civil Guard, 100 officers, 200 Falangists or other right-wing militants and 190 cadets of the Academy (which was then on its summer vacation). The Colonel also took with him 550 women and 50 children, mostly dependents of the defenders and other Toledans. Finally, he also, in his own words, took with him 'the Civil Governor with his entire family, and a number of persons [i.e. about 100] of left-wing politics as hostages'.[1] The garrison was well supplied with ammunition from the neighbouring arms factory, though food was scarce from the start of its siege. As for the militia making for Guadalajara, both that town and Alcalá de Henares were captured with comparative ease, though the Civil Guard at Guadalajara put up a most valiant resistance under the leadership of General González de Lara.

All this time the Civil Guard in Madrid, whose loyalty to the Government was suspect, were held confined in their barracks; and victory over the rising meant, in Madrid and its surroundings as elsewhere, the start of the Revolution. Large portraits of Lenin henceforth accompanied those of Largo Caballero on the hoardings of the Puerta del Sol. Don Manuel Azaña might still linger, gloomy and aghast, in the Royal Palace; and his friends might still hold the portfolios of government; but, in the streets, the people ruled. The Socialist-led UGT was the real executive body in the capital. With the Communist-Socialist Youth as its agents, it maintained such order as existed. Syndicalism had thus come to Madrid as a result of the great anti-popular rising. For the workers, July 20 was a day of triumph.

In the evening, many assassinations were committed by trigger-happy militiamen. Two strongly Republican officers, Colonel Mangada and Major Barceló, set up summary courts in the Casa de Campo to try officers captured in rebel barracks – men who in many cases they had known, and hated, all their careers. During the evening and the night the first executions began under this inauspicious authority. By this time there were some 10,000 militiamen in Madrid ready for any battle that might follow.

In Barcelona, the rising had been completely subdued by the

---

[1] *General Cause*, 320–1. The question of whether there were hostages or not in the Alcázar was thus at last laid to rest by Moscardó's statement after the war.

evening of July 20. The Atarazanas barracks had surrendered at
half past one, after a prolonged battle. The other points of
resistance were then easily overwhelmed. The Anarchist leader
Ascaso was killed in the assault on the barracks. Here also Mola's
brother, Captain Ramón Mola, was killed in the moment of defeat.
Over 500 persons, of whom about 200 were 'anti-Fascists', had
been killed and 3,000 wounded in the two days' battle.[1] Immediately, President Companys was visited by Anarchist leaders,
headed by García Oliver and Durruti. These formidable men
of violence sat before Companys with their rifles between their
knees, their clothes still dusty from the fight, their hearts heavy
at the death of Ascaso.

Companys then made to them the following skilful speech:
'First of all, I have to say to you that the CNT and FAI have never
been accorded their proper treatment. You have always been
harshly persecuted, and I, who was formerly with you,[2] afterwards
found myself obliged by political exigencies to oppose you. Today
you are masters of the city.' He paused, and then spoke depreca-
tingly of the part played by his own party in defeating the rising.
'If you do not need me, or do not wish me to remain as President of
Catalonia, tell me now, and I shall become one soldier more in the
struggle against Fascism. If, on the other hand, you believe that, in
this position which, only as a dead man, would I have abandoned
if the Fascists had triumphed, if you believe that I, my party, my
name, my prestige, can be of use, then you can count on me and
my loyalty as a man who is convinced that a whole past of shame
is dead, and who desires passionately that Catalonia should henceforth stand among the most progressive countries in the world.'[3]
This oration confirmed an already growing conservatism in the
minds of the leaders of the Anarchists. Although they still supported the idea of libertarian revolution elaborated by Bakunin's
first disciples, their achievement of power as well as the comradeship forged in the battles of the last days, led them to co-operate,
for the first time, with the other parties of the Left. So they accepted
Companys as the leader of the Catalan Government. To co-ordinate their power in the city with the power wielded by the other
organisations, a so-called 'Anti-Fascist Militias Committee' was

---

[1] CNT-FAI. *Información Propaganda*, 22.7.36.
[2] An allusion to Companys' previous practice as a barrister when he would often
defend Anarchists in the courts for nominal fees.
[3] García Oliver in *De Julio a Julio*, 193.

set up. This was to remain in permanent session, and was composed of three representatives each of the UGT, CNT, FAI and Esquerra, one from the POUM and the Rabaissaires[1] and two from all the Republican parties. And this body, dominated by its Anarchist representatives (Durruti, García Oliver and Joaquím Ascaso[2]), was the real Government of Barcelona after the defeat of the rising. Though there were isolated instances of firing at militiamen by concealed rebel sympathisers the main work thereafter of the committee was to prepare militia forces to march against Saragossa and, also, to organise the revolution in Barcelona.

In Granada, the stalemate at last came to an end on July 20. At midday, the streets were full of workers demanding arms, which the officers in the garrisons were still refusing to deliver to them, despite the orders of General Campins. General Pozas telephoned from Madrid to urge upon the Civil Governor 'desperate and bloody resistance' against the least manifestation of military rising. This was now being brewed by Colonels Muñoz and León. Campins, making unwisely a further visit to the artillery barracks, was denounced as a traitor by one of his own Captains. He heard, to his amazement, that the entire officer corps of the garrison, the Civil Guards and the *Asaltos* stood with the rebels. Campins turned to leave, to find his way barred. His ADC suggested that the General should sign the declaration of a state of war. This he did, after a visit to the infantry barracks had proved to him that the officers there also were with the rebels. At this moment, the troops of the garrison of Granada received the order to sally out into the streets of the city. But their commander was not General Campins, who was confined to prison, but Colonel Muñoz. The city was then occupied with extraordinary ease. The crowds, being unarmed, dispersed at the arrival of the military before the town hall, and the Civil Governor and his staff were arrested without resistance. Only one Nationalist soldier was killed in this conquest of the centre of the town. By night, only the working-class quarter of El Albaicín, directly beneath the Alhambra, held out. This was not reduced until July 24. It was accomplished with uncountable casualties suffered by the working classes.[3]

At Valencia, the stalemate continued for some days still, though the balance was tipped firmly on July 20 towards the Republic.

---

[1] The Vine Growers' Party, begun in 1934 to protect their stock against landlords.
[2] Brother of the Ascaso killed on July 20. (See above, page 158.)
[3] *Cruzada*, XI 281-8.

While certain officers of the Civil Guard had begun to distribute arms to the trade unions, Martínez Barrio arrived in the city, having been charged to act as President of a Provincial Junta for the Levante provinces. The President of the Cortes succeeded in persuading General Martínez Monje to support him in this scheme. Since the General was a Mason, it was as usual assumed that the occult powers of the Grand Orient played a significant part in this *volte-face*. Meantime, the garrisons of the city were now besieged by thousands of workers. General González Carrasco, flitting uneasily from refuge to refuge, gave up all for lost, and sought to escape. This he eventually did, *via* North Africa. His followers in the garrisons remained beleaguered, while eleven churches were set ablaze and the Archbishop's palace destroyed.[1]

The similar uncertainty was resolved at Alicante, where General García Aldave allowed himself also to be persuaded by the wiles of Martínez Barrio.[2] (In Alicante prison, meanwhile, José Antonio Primo de Rivera and his brother Miguel continued to languish without hope of release.) In the stalemate at San Sebastián the rebels continued to hold out at the María Cristina Hotel and the Loyola barracks. But the arrival of the armed workers from Eibar caused them to abandon hope of gaining the town. Henceforth, they were besieged as closely as were the Civil Guards at Gijón.

In Seville, the victory of Queipo de Llano was finally confirmed on July 20. The first units of the Legion arrived by air from Morocco, under Major Castejón. This officer led his *tercios* into a final assault on Triana, the working-class district on the other side of the River Guadalquivir. All the districts resisted to the end, with practically no arms. In that named San Julián the slaughter was allegedly horrible. The legionaries apparently forced all the men they found there into the streets and killed them with knives. The lower part of Triana was then shot to pieces by cannon.

In Corunna, on the north-west tip of the Spanish Peninsula, there were two Generals, Salcedo, the General of the division, and Caridad Pita, the Military Governor. The former was cautious and lethargic, the latter a ferocious adherent of the Government and the Popular Front. The leader of the conspiracy in Corunna was Colonel Martín Alonso, who had been imprisoned at Villa Cisneros for his part in the rising of 1932 and who had

---

[1] *Cruzada*, XXIII 460–502; Cerro Jiménez, 18–27; Borkenau, 114–15.

[2] *Cruzada*, XXIII 533–48. The fates of these two Generals were different. Martínez Monje remained as Military Governor, while García Aldave was shot.

escaped from thence in dramatic circumstances. Salcedo delayed deciding whether or not to join the rising until he could see whether it would be successful. At last, at midday on July 20, with the supporters of the Popular Front out in the streets, General Caridad Pita, bringing good news from Barcelona and Madrid, persuaded him to declare for the Government. But both were immediately arrested by Martín Alonso. Within a few hours, the rebels had cleared the centre of the town and had captured the Civil Governor, who, with his wife, was shot, with the two Generals[1] being shot some months after, with other officers.

In the working-class district, the battle continued for two days, the workers being reinforced by a column of miners from Asturias. Eventually, the fight was decided by the superior weapons of the rebels. Their opponents were able nevertheless to withdraw in comparatively good order towards Gijón. The last struggle here took place in the public garden where the grave of Sir John Moore, the Peninsular War hero, is still commemorated.[2]

At El Ferrol the battle between the seamen in the warships and the rebels victorious on land continued all day. Hesitation and division of opinion led to the surrender of the *Almirante Cervera*. This was followed by the raising of a white flag on the *España*. Thereafter, the torpedo boats and coastguard sloops, upon which there had also been revolutions, similarly gave in. Thirty officers had been assassinated, but many more had been imprisoned and went free. All the revolutionary seamen were shot. Thereafter, El Ferrol became the chief and, for some time, the only Nationalist naval base. In León, the rising occurred at two in the afternoon of July 20. The Civil Governor much regretted the absence of the miners who had left for Madrid the previous day. Nevertheless, in a heat such as even that inland suntrap had rarely experienced, the workers fought with great tenacity against the troops who came out into the streets against them under General Bosch. Nevertheless, the rebels won, as they did in all the Province. The only battle of note was fought at Ponteferrada, a centre of communications in the region, where certain of the wandering miners who had left Oviedo thinking it securely in the hands of Aranda, and who had gathered some arms at León, were massacred in the market

[1] There were many rumors about the manner of the death of the Governor's wife, a fellow intellectual. Pregnant, an abortion was first performed upon her, and she was then lowered into a grave on a stretcher where she was there shot. One of the stretcher-bearers went mad.
[2] *Cruzada*, XIV 14–28.

square.[1] At Minorca General Bosch was overwhelmed on July 20 by the combined forces of the Popular Front and of the other ranks in his own garrison. Thus the important naval base of Port Mahon was won for the Republic. The General, with eleven officers, was later shot without trial.[2]

One further event of importance occurred on July 20. Mola had sent to Lisbon an aircraft flown by a young Monarchist pilot, Ansaldo, to carry General Sanjurjo to Burgos. Ansaldo arrived at Sanjurjo's villa to find forty excited people gathered round the General, listening to contradictory news on the wireless, receiving frantic telephone calls, and making incorrect predictions in an *ex cathedra* style. Ansaldo solemnly announced himself 'at the orders of the Head of the Spanish State!' All present burst into singing the Royal March, many wept with emotion, others cried 'Long live Sanjurjo! Long live Spain!' However, the Madrid Government complained of the use of a Portuguese military airfield by a rebel pilot. The Portuguese authorities, though most sympathetic to Sanjurjo, requested Ansaldo to take his plane to a more distant landing ground. He eventually had to take off from a small field, surrounded by pine-trees, at Marinha. Here, to the pilot's alarm, the General insisted on taking with him two heavy suitcases, which contained full-dress uniforms for his use as Head of the new Spanish State. It was probably this excessive luggage that made it hard for the aircraft to rise. The propeller struck the treetops and the machine burst into flames. Ansaldo was thrown out with injuries, but his passenger was burned to death – a victim of his sartorial vanity rather than (as was inevitably alleged at the time) of Republican (or even General Franco's) sabotage.[3] This casualty, following the murder of Calvo Sotelo, the continuing captivity of José Antonio, and the recent capture of Goded, left Franco and Mola as the only two provedly outstanding persons on the Nationalist side; and, while Mola was coping with the consequences of a far from wholly successful revolution in the north of Spain, and was preparing to fight on three fronts, Franco was already firmly in control of Morocco and of the veteran Army of Africa.

By July 21, a rough line might have been drawn dividing the areas where the rising had been generally successful from where it had mostly failed. Running from halfway up the Portuguese-Spanish frontier in a north-easterly direction this line would turn

[1] *Cruzada*, XV 134–47.   [2] *Cruzada*, XVI 300–36.   [3] Ansaldo, 51.

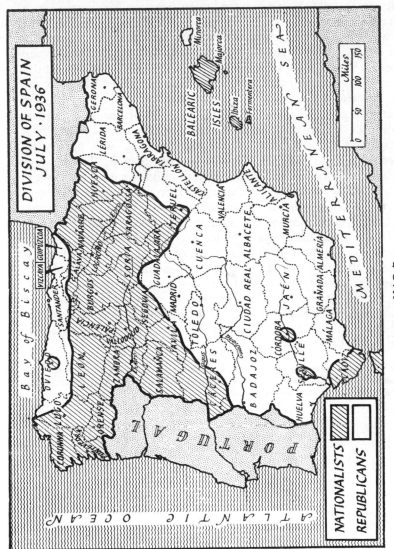

to the south-east at the Guadarrama mountains near Madrid, and then to Teruel (about a hundred miles from the Mediterranean in Aragón). It would then run north to the Pyrenees, meeting the Spanish-French frontier about half-way across its length. Except for the long strip of coastline comprising Asturias, Santander and the two coastal Basque provinces, all to the north and west of this line was Nationalist territory (which also comprised Morocco, the Canaries and the Balearics, except Minorca); to the south and east, except for the main Andalusian cities of Seville, Granada, Córdoba, Cádiz and Algeciras (all of which, save the last two, were isolated from each other) the territory was principally Republican. Within the Republican territory in Toledo, San Sebastián, Valencia and Gijón, certain buildings were held by the rebels. Albacete and Oviedo, though surrounded by enemies, were totally held by them. In many generally Nationalist towns, fighting went on for some days more in working-class suburbs.

In the Andalusian countryside, the situation was particularly confused. Events in the mining town of Pozoblanco were typical. The Civil Guard first carried out a successful rising on July 18. Then the miners surrounded their own town and starved the Civil Guard into surrender. All 170 of the besieged were then shot. This took four weeks. Such events were the final terrible culmination of all those wild risings at Castilblanco, Casas Viejas and Yuste in the past.[1]

[1] As for the few remaining Spanish colonies, events there were delayed, but eventually Guinea, Fernando Po, Ifni and Villa Cisneros were all gained for the Nationalists – though the fighting continued at Guinea for two months.

19

Nationalist Spain – the persecution – numbers of atrocities – death of García Lorca – legal justification for the repression

Behind this uncertain dividing line, two Spains swiftly appeared. In Nationalist Spain the order of life was above all military. Everyone with the smallest military position now had life made easy for him. Civilians were constantly insulted – and even accused of cowardice for the mere fact of being civilian. 'Those who don't wear uniforms should wear skirts' was an incessant jibe. Martial law decrees gradually took over the whole field of justice. All administrative and judicial officers were 'investigated', to prove their security in the new conditions. A judge merely had to be a man of right-wing sympathies and pliant to the military will. Nationalist rule became, as it had set out to be, the opposite of revolution in the usual sense of that word. All political parties which had supported the Popular Front were banned. Even the old right-wing and Centre parties, including the CEDA, vanished. Political life as such ceased. The only groups permitted in Nationalist Spain were the Falange and the Carlists, and these were 'movements' rather than political parties. The *casas del pueblo* and left-wing newspaper offices were closed down. Strikes were made punishable by death. Private rail and road movement was banned. Throughout Nationalist Spain, all Masons, all members of Popular Front parties, all members of trade unions and, in many areas, everyone who had voted for the Popular Front in the elections of February were arrested and many of these were shot. 'That's Red Aranda,' the Monarchist Count of Vallellano remarked to Dr Junod, the astonished Swiss Red Cross representative, while driving past the town in August, 'I am afraid we had to put the whole town in prison and execute very many people.'[1]

The number of executions varied from district to district, accord-

[1] Junod, 89. For the above and the following see Bahamonde, Ruiz Vilaplana, Bernanos, *passim*. At the time, the strict press censorship and limitation of journalists' freedom of movement made news from Nationalist territory hard to come by: even so, a large number of journalists were expelled by Captain Bolín, the Nationalist press chief.

ing to the whim of the local commander or authorities. Civil Governors and officials of the Civil Government, if they had been appointed by the Popular Front Government, were almost always shot. So were those who sought to maintain the general strike declared at the time of the rising. The wives, sisters and daughters of men executed sometimes shared their fate. Often they would have their heads shaved, and their foreheads daubed mockingly with some working class sign such as the letters UHP or UGT. Then they might be raped. These atrocities had a special purpose. Though the rebels were well armed, they were few in number. In a place such as Seville, the large working-class population had to be terrified into acquiescence of the new order before the Nationalist commanders could sleep peaceably in their beds. Hence, not only did the rebels feel bound to act with extraordinary ruthlessness towards their enemies, but also they had to act openly, and expose the bodies of those whom they killed to public gaze. All that the Church officially insisted upon was that those killed should have the opportunity for confession. 'Only 10% of these dear children refused the last sacraments before being despatched by our good officers,' recorded with satisfaction the Venerable Brother at Majorca. Mourning, however, was generally prohibited even to the relations of those who had thus made a good death.[1]

Day after day, from the time of the success of the rising, the arrests continued. Who knew with what crime those taken would be charged, or whether they would ever come back? The French Catholic writer, Georges Bernanos, who was at the time in Majorca, described how men were arrested by the Nationalist armed gangs 'every day from lost villages, at the time when they came in from the fields. They set off on their last journey with their shirts still clinging to their shoulders with sweat, with their arms still full of the day's toil, leaving soup untouched on the table, and a woman, breathless, a minute too late at the garden wall, with a little bundle of belongings hastily twisted into a bright new napkin: *Adiós: Recuerdos.*'[2] In most cases, however, the arrests

---

[1] Bernanos, 68. Mr Lawrence Dundas (*Behind the Spanish Mask*) suggests that the real terror in Majorca did not begin till after the Republican attack on the island in August-September. The Chief Almoner of the Prisons of Nationalist Spain, Fr Martín Torrent, later added a new theological point by saying: 'Happy is the condemned man, for he is the only one who knows when he must die. He has thus the best chance of putting his soul in order before he dies.' Alba, *Histoire des Républiques Espagnoles*, 371.

[2] Bernanos, 72–3. Bernanos was staying at this time in the house of the Falangist family of De Zayas.

were made at night, and the consequent shooting also done in the dark. Sometimes the executions would be single, sometimes collective. Sometimes, the official in charge, out of compassion, would arrange for a generous supply of wine to be at hand, so that the doomed might steep their despair in the wisdom of intoxication before death. The next morning, the bodies would be found. Often these would be of distinguished members of the parties of the Left, or of officers loyal to the Republic. But no one would dare to identify these corpses. For example, the corpse of Colonel Mena, the head of the Civil Guard in Burgos, a loyal Colonel of a cavalry regiment, and five other well-known citizens of that city were condemned to rest for ever beneath a tomb marked 'Seven unidentified bodies. Found on the hill near the 102 km stone on the road to Valladolid'.[1]

After a while (at least in the north), the exposure of corpses to the public gaze was suspended, on the request of General Mola. He declared himself inconvenienced by the bodies on the roadside. Henceforward, the executions occurred discreetly, in the orchards of a remote monastery or among the boulders on some desolate hillside.

Many details of the events of these days remain obscure. It was said, for instance, that many victims were compelled to dig their own graves before being shot in them. Wives of militiamen were said to have been not only raped, but to have had their breasts cut off. Prisoners were alleged to have been drenched in petrol, and then set alight. Many of these stories were invented for propaganda purposes, sometimes by Republican Spaniards, more often abroad. Arthur Koestler, then working with the propaganda department of the Comintern in Paris, later described how such distortions were deliberately written into his book, *The Spanish Testament*, by his superior, the Czech impresario of propaganda, Otto Katz.[2] But some of the most damning allegations of atrocities (including those given above) were prepared by the respectable council of lawyers in Madrid. It is certain that men were shot in the face of their families, and sometimes tortured also. It is also certain that General Franco gave orders that no appeals for clemency should reach him until after the execution of the sentence.[3]

[1] Ruiz Vilaplana, 65.

[2] Koestler, *The Invisible Writing*, 333–5. See below, page 217.

[3] Private information deriving from the daughter of a Nationalist Admiral who was shot at the start of the war. The woman later intervened when she heard that the judge who had condemned her father to death was being tried in Nationalist territory. She did not prevent his execution.

A schoolmaster of Huesca was beaten almost to death by Falangists to make him confess knowledge of 'revolutionary plots'. To try and commit suicide he opened a vein with his teeth.[1] In Navarre, and Álava, Basque Nationalists were shot without confessors. One man was told by certain *Requetés* to extend his arms in the form of a cross and to cry '*Viva* Christ the King!' while each of his limbs were amputated. His wife, forced to watch, went mad as he was finally bayoneted to death.[2]

As for the authors of these atrocities, most of them were members of the old parties of the Right rather than the Falange. The Civil Guard, the military, the remains of the CEDA – these were the real authors of the proscriptions. The Falange seem to have done their best to establish some standards of justice.[3]

It is furthermore impossible to find accurate figures for the number of those killed in the first days of the rising by the Nationalists, either in street battles or by summary execution. Very high figures were given by Republicans. Ramón Sender named a figure of 750,000 executions in Nationalist Spain to mid-1938. The Madrid Council of Lawyers reported that in the first weeks of the war 9,000 workers were killed in Seville[4] (20,000 by late 1937), 2,000 in Saragossa, 5,000 in Granada, 7,000 in all Navarre and 400 in Algeciras. A Catholic deputy and the head of the English Catholic College at Valladolid have separately testified to the deaths of 9,000 persons in that city.[5] According to Bernanos, there were 3,000 assassinations in Majorca from July 1936 till March 1937. A student of the indiscreet Portuguese press, whose reporters in Nationalist Spain appeared genuinely appalled at these atrocities estimated that 200,000 Nationalist executions had occurred by July 1937. Antonio Bahamonde, for a year propaganda chief to Queipo de Llano in Seville (and who fled abroad, sickened by his job), estimated in early 1938 that 150,000

---

[1] Fernsworth, 205.   [2] Aberrigoyen, 115.

[3] On neither side at this time was there any compassion or even thought for the friends of one side or the other caught on the wrong side of the dividing line. Mola, for instance, reacted to a Red Cross suggestion of exchange of political prisoners by saying to Dr Junod: 'How can you expect us to exchange a *caballero* (gentleman) for a Red dog? If I let the prisoners go my own people would regard me as a traitor (an obsession with Mola) . . . You have arrived too late, Monsieur, those dogs have already destroyed the most glorious spiritual values of our country.' (Junod, 98.) For comparable remarks on the Republican side, see below, page 178.

[4] A future Republican ace pilot, Colonel Lacalle, later dropped lilies from the air on Republican graves at Seville.

[5] Private information.

had by then been executed in the military area controlled by his ex-master. All these figures seem certain to be very greatly exaggerated. Republicans who experienced life in Nationalist Spain, in prison or outside, would naturally overestimate the executions, not necessarily from malice but since the recollection of a series of nocturnal executions amounting even to twenty deaths would be magnified by imagination. Whereas the Madrid council of lawyers estimated a figure of 7,000 executions in Navarre in the first month of the war, the Bishop of Vitoria (displaced from his See by the Nationalists) named a figure of 7,000 for all those killed in Navarre, Vizcaya and Álava, in the whole war.[1] The Nationalist authorities themselves have not published any figures for the number of deaths attributable to them away from the battlefield. A careful examination of the meagre evidence[2] suggests that a very approximate figure of 40,000 Nationalist executions during the whole war is likely. This would cover those shot arbitrarily after capture at the start of the war, those shot after trial and many killed in street-fighting in conditions little better than those of a murder-trap. There were also executed, for 'rebellion', many officers loyal to the Government. These included six Generals: Molero of Valladolid, Batet of Burgos, Romerales of Melilla, Salcedo and Caridad Pita of Corunna and Campins of Granada. Admiral Azarolo, in command of the arsenal at El Ferrol, was also executed.[3]

Among these deaths, the most unforgettable was that of Federico García Lorca, the greatest Spanish poet of the day. Though never a member of any political party, his brother-in-law was the Socialist Mayor of Granada and he had many connections with intellectuals of the Left. After the victory of the rising in Granada, his home town (to which he was paying a brief visit), García Lorca took refuge with a fellow poet and friend, Luis Rosales, whose brother was a Falangist. Despite this apparent protection, he was taken out and shot. The exact manner of his death, as of his final resting place, is a matter of doubt. The local Falangists may have been responsible. So may the Civil Guard, whose

---

[1] Basque Government letter to the UN Sub-Committee on Spain, 1946, 76.
[2] See Appendix II.
[3] See below for comparable Republican figures, which I believe to be higher than these. In small towns the Nationalists shot more people, when they captured it, than the Popular Front had done; in a small village in the province of Málaga there were 12 'Red' executions and later 111 Nationalist. But this proportion was reversed in large towns.

souls the poet had once compared to the rude texture of the cloth
of their uniform. He certainly now rests in an unidentified grave in
a remote part of the province of Granada.[1]

The legal justification for all these summary executions was
simply the state of war which had been proclaimed to exist on the
day of the rising. It was assumed that the Government of the
Republic were the rebels and the Nationalists the legitimate
power. In the beginning, no form of trial at all was used. A man
shot was deemed a man judged. A series of emergency military
tribunals were, however, shortly set up, composed of retired
officers and conscripted legally trained persons. The former
acquired legal status and the latter military, so both were pleased.[2]
Yet undoubtedly the paradoxical legal position 'troubled all who
were not blindly sectarian'.[3]

What were the springs of this wash of violence? As among the
working classes, many of the actual killers no doubt truly enjoyed
bloodshed. But the rest, the majority, were men who considered
from the depths of their being that they had a duty to extirpate
the unclean heresies of liberalism, Socialism, Communism and
Anarchism. For they believed, before God, that these ideas were
destroying their own beautiful and timeless Spain.

[1] See Brenan, *The Face of Spain*, 127–47. Mr Brenan went to seek out the poet's
grave in 1950 and believed that he discovered it at Viznar, on the edge of the Duke of
Wellington's Andalusian estate. For ten years, no one alluded to García Lorca in
Nationalist Spain. Then the Falange began to place the blame for his execution on the
Catholics, saying that a false rumour that the Republicans had shot the dramatist
Benavente induced the Catholic deputy for Granada, Ruiz Alonso, to order García
Lorca's death in reprisal. Another theory as to the poet's death is that he was killed,
like Marlowe, in a brawl while looking for the gipsies who gave him such delight.
Brenan's investigation is generally confirmed by other works such as Claude Couffon,
Cómo Murió García Lorca (in *La Nueva Democracia*, New York, July 1953); Jean Chabrol,
J'ai Trouvé les Assassins de Lorca (Paris 1957); Rivas Cherif, *Poesía y Drama del Gran
Federico* (*Excelsior*, Mexico, January 7, 1957); and Vázquez Ocaña, *García Lorca: Vida
Cántico y Muerte* (Mexico, 1957). But according to the latter, the poet was not killed
till August 18. The possibility of García Lorca's murder as a revenge by a lesser poet
of the Falange cannot be entirely ruled out.
[2] Ruiz Vilaplana, 159.
[3] Ansaldo, 83.

20

*The revolution – the churches burn – estimates for the number of
working-class and Republican assassinations – responsibility
of the Government*

Revolution meantime was sweeping through all the towns where the Nationalist rising had been defeated, and in those places where it had not even occurred. Committees of control were everywhere formed, nominally proportionate to the parties of the Popular Front, together with the Anarchists. In fact they reflected the real political strengths in the town concerned.[1] The committees would seek then to change the society of the town and its surroundings in accordance with the views of the strongest party. The first steps, common to all Republican Spain, would be the proscription of right-wing parties, and the requisition of hotels, right-wing newspapers, factories and the houses of the rich. In the latter, the revolutionary parties and unions would find sumptuous new headquarters. Roads would be guarded by patrols of militiamen. Various sub-committees would be set up to deal with all departments of life. Republican Spain thus constituted less a single state than an agglomeration of separate republics. The regional confusion was as it had been in the 1870s or in the Napoleonic Wars, though greatly increased by class and religious passion.

For the revolution began everywhere with a great tide of assassination, destruction and spoilage. Militia units from the political parties and unions formed themselves into gangs with names resembling those of football teams. There were, for instance, the 'Lynxes of the Republic', the 'Red Lions', the 'Furies', 'Spartacus' and 'Strength and Liberty'. Other gangs took the name of political leaders of the Left, in Spain and abroad. Their passions were directed firstly against the Church. Throughout Republican

[1] These committees were formed everywhere save in Madrid, where the Government of Giral was nominally in control, though in fact power had passed to the UGT and Largo Caballero (see below, page 184).

Spain, churches and convents were indiscriminately burned and despoiled. Practically nowhere had the Church taken part in the rising. Nearly all the stories of firing by rebels from church towers were also untrue.[1] But the churches were nevertheless attacked, as the outposts of upper or middle-class morality and manners. Destruction rather than loot was the aim. An Anarchist in Madrid for instance was heard to upbraid a boy for stealing a chair, rather than breaking it.[2] Certain churches and convents in central positions in Madrid were saved from attack by the Government. But in the provinces the assaults were most thorough. In Barcelona, only the cathedral was effectively protected. The greatest works of art, however, were preserved. Although many minor treasures were lost, the only really disastrous act of vandalism was the burning of ten thousand volumes of the library of the cathedral of Cuenca, including the celebrated *Catecismo de Indias*. Such burning was usually watched with unconcern rather than with excitement. But the breaking of images and of sacred objects, or the wearing by militiamen of ecclesiastical robes, was often greeted with laughter. Most of those who watched church-burnings were, not unnaturally, those with houses nearby, and who were afraid lest the flames should spread to their property. Thereafter the churches, whether gutted or still usable as a store or refuge, were as firmly closed in Republican Spain as were right-wing political party offices.[3]

These attacks were accompanied by a colossal and uncontrollable onslaught on the lives of members of the Church and of the *bourgeoisie*. The Nationalists since the war have named a figure

[1] There was some 'provocation' afterwards – though this might be expected. For instance, the CNT-FAI information bulletin reported on July 25: 'In San Pablo Hospital on Saturday a priest entered into a heated argument with a doctor, pulled out a revolver and discharged his whole magazine, not at the doctor but at the wounded around him. Bystanders were so infuriated that they picked out four of the most priestly and Fascist of the brethren and shot them out of hand.'

[2] Protestant churches were not attacked, and remained open. There were, however, only 6,259 protestant communicants in all Spain at this time (Toynbee, A., *Survey 1938*, I 286 note).

[3] Convents were emptied of all their denizens. To some, of course, this was an act of freedom. For there were many Spanish girls who had been forced to take the veil against their own wishes when young. For others it brought a disaster of a different kind. An informant has told me of the following tragedy. One girl, freed from a convent in Barcelona, could only find a dress with sequins to fit her for her return to her village. It was undoubtedly unsafe for her to wear a nun's habit in travelling through Catalonia. So she wore the sequins. On arriving at her village, her family and friends presumed that she had been a prostitute while they had thought her safely behind the doors of the nunnery. They stoned her to death.

of 85,940 for all reputed murdered or executed in Republican
Spain during the war.[1] This calculation is certainly not an under-
estimation, though it compares favourably with the wilder
accusations of three or four hundred thousand made during the
course of the war.[2] Of those killed, 7,937 were religious persons:
12 were bishops,[3] 283 nuns, 5,255 priests, 2,492 monks and 249
novices. (The figure for murdered priests thus compares well with
Paul Claudel's glorification of '*Seize mille prêtres massacrés et pas une
apostasie!*'[4]) The approximate accuracy of these figures is corroborated by such other evidence as is available. If the overall figure
is accepted, about 75,000 persons may be supposed to have been
executed or murdered between July 18 and September 1, 1936 –
for nearly all the illegal killings in the Republic occurred at the
start of the war.

The figures, like those of the Nationalist fury, are cold but
overwhelming. Many of these crimes were accompanied by a
partly frivolous, partly sadistic cruelty. The parish priest of
Navalmoral, for example, told the militiamen who took him
prisoner, 'I want to suffer for Christ.' 'Oh do you,' they answered,
'then you shall die as Christ did.' They stripped him and scourged
him mercilessly. Next, they fastened a beam of wood on their
victim's back, gave him vinegar to drink, and crowned him with
thorns. 'Blaspheme and we will forgive you,' said the leader of the
militia. 'It is I who forgive and bless you,' replied the priest. The
militiamen discussed how they should kill him. Some wished to
nail him to a cross, but in the end they simply shot him. His last
request was to be shot facing his tormentors so that he might die
blessing them.[5]

---

[1] *General Cause*, 402. Of these, about 5,000 were women. 500 women were killed in
Madrid and its provinces. Some children also were shot. A visitor to Madrid's mor-
tuaries at this time has told me of seeing bodies of small boys in pyjamas.

[2] On the other hand, there is just a possibility that the figure was played down to
avoid giving too terrible an impression abroad of Spanish characteristics.

[3] These were the Bishops of Jaén, Lérida, Segorbe, Cuenca, Barcelona, Almería,
Guadix, Cuidad Real and Tarragona (suffragan bishop), the apostolic administrator
of Barbastro who was Titular Bishop of Epirus, and the apostolic administrator of
Orihuela, who ranked as a bishop. The Bishop of Teruel was also murdered in Catalonia in 1939.

[4] *On nous met le ciel et l'enfer dans la main et nous avons quarante secondes pour choisir.*
    Quarante secondes, c'est trop! Soeur Espagne, sainte Espagne, tu as choisi!
    Onze évêques, seize mille prêtres massacrés et pas une apostasie!
    Ah! Puissé-je comme toi un jour à voix haute témoigner dans la splendeur de midi!
                             Claudel ('*Aux Martyr Espagnols*')

[5] Carreras, 104.

The Bishop of Jaén was killed with his sister by a specially invited militiawoman nicknamed *La Pecosa* (the freckled) before a crowd of two thousand tumultuous people near Madrid in a piece of swampy ground known as 'Uncle Raymond's pool'. The Bishops of Guadix and Almería were forced to wash the deck of the prison ship *Astoy Mendi* before being murdered near Málaga. The Bishop of Ciudad Real was murdered while at work on a history of Toledo. After he was shot, his card index of 1,200 cards was destroyed. A nun was killed because she refused the proposition of marriage offered to her by one of the militiamen who stormed her convent of Nuestra Señor del Amparo in Madrid. The 'Blood Committee' of El Pardo (Province of Madrid) became gradually intoxicated on communion wine while they tried the parish priest. One of the militiamen shaved himself using the chalice as a washing bowl. There were isolated instances of the violation of nuns, before their execution.[1] The corpse of a Jesuit was laid in the Calle Maria de Molina, Madrid, with the placard 'I am a Jesuit' fastened about his neck. In Cernera, rosary beads were forced into monks' ears till their tympanum was perforated. Several priests were undoubtedly burned alive. An exhibition of the exhumed bodies of nineteen Salesian nuns attracted great crowds in Barcelona. Don Antonio Díaz del Moral of Ciempozuelos was taken to a corral filled with fighting bulls, where he was gored to unconsciousness. Afterwards, one of his ears was cut off, in imitation of the amputation of the ear of a bull in honour of a matador, following a very successful *faena*. Certain persons were burned, and others buried, alive – the latter after being forced to dig their own graves. At Alcázar de San Juan, a young man distinguished for his piety (and also perhaps his sanctimoniousness) had his eyes dug out. In that province, Ciudad Real, indeed, the crimes were extraordinarly atrocious.[2] A crucifix was forced down the mouth of a mother of two Jesuits. Eight hundred persons were thrown down a mine shaft. And, always, the moment of death would be greeted with applause, as if it were the moment of truth in a *corrida*. Then there would be shouts of 'Liberty! Down with

---

[1] Four nuns were raped and murdered at Pozuelo de Alarcón, near Madrid (*General Cause*, 59). But assaults on women were very rare in Popular Front Spain. Sánchez del Arco, a journalist of *ABC de Sevilla* with the advancing Nationalist armies in southern Spain, notes that none had occurred at all in the villages he visited. (Sánchez del Arco, 55.)

[2] Don Alicio León Descalzo was even castrated and his sexual organs were forced into his mouth.

Fascism'. More than one priest went mad at these events. One Barcelona parish priest wandered crazy for days before being asked for his union card. 'What need have I of cards, I am the priest of St Just,' he unwisely remarked.

No one said 'adios' any more, but always 'salud'. A man named Fernández de Dios even wrote to the Minister of Justice asking if he could change his surname to Bakunin, 'for he did not want to have anything to do with God'.[1] 'Do you still believe in this God who never speaks and who does not defend himself even when his images and temples are burned? Admit that God does not exist and that you priests are all so many hypocrites who deceive the people.' Such burning questions and demands were put in countless towns and villages of Republican Spain. At no time in the history of Europe or even perhaps the world has so passionate a hatred of religion and all its works been shown. Yet one priest who, alongside the death of no fewer than 1,215 monks, nuns and priests (55 were nuns) in the province of Barcelona, managed to escape to France through the help of President Companys, was generous enough to admit that 'the Reds have destroyed our churches, but we first had destroyed the Church.'[2] And after all, not all, not even a majority, of priests in Republican Spain were killed. Those who were not, or did not flee abroad, 'collaborated' with the Republic. They were simply regarded as men who had chosen a certain métier, and were treated in no way different from a dentist, say, or a lawyer – save that they were not allowed to practise or wear the uniform of the cassock. If they had disgraced the métier, and had, say, in the past, never worn a clean collar for the funeral of a poor man, but always had done so for a rich man, they would be killed.[3] This social motive for killing explains the motives of the religious onslaught. The Spanish working class attacked churchmen because they thought them hypocrites and because they seemed to give a false spiritual front to middle-class society or upper-class tyranny.

[1] The Under-Secretary of the Ministry wrote back saying, 'It would seem advisable to abbreviate the long and complicated procedure where the necessity for the change of name appears justified by its notoriety.' (General Cause, 196–7.) Most of the above incidents are described in that work, in Estelrich, or in Carreras. The 'atrocities' have an enormous literature in Nationalist Spain, nearly every province being meticulously covered. The Republicans, having lost the war, have naturally been unable to compile similar analyses for Nationalist territory.
[2] Salvador de Madariaga, 377.
[3] The same was true of doctors. Doctors known to be devoted to their poor patients were left at liberty.

Of course, in terms of numbers killed, the onslaught against laymen was more violent than it was against churchmen. All who could conceivably be suspected of sympathy for the Nationalist rising were in danger. As among the Nationalists, the irrational circumstances of a civil war made it impossible to lay down what was or what was not treason. Membership of the CEDA, or the Falange (as indeed of the Church) was *prima facie* a cause for suspicion of hostility to the revolution. In the country districts, revolution itself consisted primarily of the murder of the upper classes or the *bourgeoisie*. Thus the description, in Ernest Hemingway's novel *For Whom the Bell Tolls*, of how the inhabitants of a small *pueblo* first beat all the male members of the middle class with heavy flails and then flung them over a cliff is near to the reality of what happened in the superb Andalusian town of Ronda. There 512 were murdered in the first month of war.[1]

In the larger towns, where the potential enemy was more numerous, more sophisticated procedures were followed. All the political parties and unions of the Republic set up investigation bodies which were proud to call themselves, on the Russian model, by the name of '*checa*'. Twenty-six of these existed in Madrid alone.[2] A positive maze of different groups, each with supreme power, each responsible to one party or department of state or even individual, characterised these first days of the Civil War in the Republican cities. The different *checas* would sometimes consult with each other before taking their victim 'for a ride' (*dar un paseo*). But this was a formality by no means always followed. The cross-examination of suspects was invariably carried out amid insults and threats. Sometimes, the chief of the *checa* would show a card from a distance to suggest to the accused that this was his own membership card of a party hostile to the Popular Front. Sentences of death by these 'courts' were indicated on the appropriate documents by the letter 'L' for Liberty, but with a full stop added. This was an instruction for the immediate execution of the prisoner. The task would be undertaken by special brigades often composed of ex-criminals.

Perhaps the most feared of all in Madrid was the *checa* known as 'the dawn patrol', from the hour at which it carried out its activities. But there was little to choose between this gang and 'the brigade of criminal investigation' led by an ex-printer, García

---

[1] Pemán, *Un Soldado en la Historia* (*Vida del General Varela*).
[2] *General Cause*, 82.

Atadell.[1] Both these bodies drew on the archives of the Ministry of the Interior to help them in their task of tracking members of right-wing parties. And, indeed, functionaries of these *checas* of the early days later became actual police officials of the Republic.[2]

Most of the murders committed by the *checas* were clean deaths by shooting. However, there were certainly some bestial acts committed also. The Communist *checas* seem to have been specially feared for their tortures.

In the vast majority of cases, these arbitrary murders were of the rank and file of the Right. Often members of the working class would be killed by their own acquaintances for hypocrisy, for having kow-towed too often to their social superiors, even simply for untruthfulness. In Altea, near Alicante, for example, the postmaster was killed with a hatchet by an Anarchist for having overcharged for stamps and for the glass of wine that buyers of stamps were forced to take while waiting.[3] Most of the actual political leaders of the Right, together with Generals and others who had taken part in the rising, were imprisoned. These were numerous, and were far more eminent than any corresponding prisoners held by the Nationalists. Some of them such as General López Ochoa, who had commanded the troops that crushed the Asturian revolt in 1934 (and had shown himself so moderate that he had to be replaced) were dragged out of confinement or even hospital to be killed. Others, such as those sent to the Model Prison in Madrid, were treated well for the time being.

In the chaos there were many settlements of personal scores. A convict released from the common prison broke into the apartment of a judge who had condemned him some months before, killed him in the presence of his family, and escaped with the family silver

[1] This individual was later captured by the Nationalists. Arthur Koestler met him in Seville prison in early 1937. He was killed by the *vile garrotte*, the strangling machine which appears in Goya's *Disasters of War*. The victim, tied to a post in a sitting position is slowly choked to death between an iron collar round his throat and a vice turned through the post against the back of his neck. (Koestler, *The Invisible Writing*, 347.)

[2] For example, Atadell's assistant, Pedrero García, became later head of the SIM (see below, page 492). Tagüeña, head of the dawn patrol, went on to lead an army corps.

[3] Then as now in small Spanish villages the purchase of a stamp is a complicated matter. Individual stamps are wrapped up in tissue paper, and folded neatly. The Altea incident was told me by an informant who lived in Altea. The Anarchist was himself later killed by a Communist, first because he was an Anarchist, secondly because he had secret relations with the Falange. The whole incident illustrates the difficulty of reaching certainty about the motives of the atrocities.

tied up in a sheet.[1] There were also many mistakes. For instance, a great musician of liberal views was arrested by an Anarchist gang in his house in the *bourgeois* part of Barcelona. 'But I am your friend,' he protested when about to be taken out to be shot. The Anarchists refused to believe him. It seemed impossible to them that the great man could live among the *bourgeoisie*. To prove his identity, and save his life, the musician took up his instrument and played to them. The Anarchists listened with tears running down their cheeks, both because they found the music unbearably moving and because they realised how nearly fatal their mistake had been.[2]

But others were not able to prove their innocence so easily. Innocence? What of? In innumerable cases a man of wealth, living in comfort, was inevitably presumed guilty. Throughout this troubled time, the heads of such men as the President of the Republic, Azaña (whose bedroom window in the National Palace faced the Casa de Campo, where so many killings occurred), naturally did not rest easily at night. For though they could not control the killings, they were, as the Government, ultimately responsible for them. Since they did not resign, they could hardly expect to escape blame for such events. Some in official positions in the Republic even showed themselves at least indifferent to the fate of so many of their compatriots. An official of the Generalitat, for example, was reluctant to consider an arrangement which might exchange the political prisoners of Barcelona for those taken by the Nationalists. To save his comrades in south Spain would mean the forgiveness of his enemies in Barcelona.[3] Yet many others, motivated by personal feelings rather than politics (they ranged from Companys to La Pasionaria) went out of their way and risked their reputations to intervene on behalf of likely victims of violence.[4]

Who were the killers? In general they can only be understood as the final explosion of a mood of smouldering resentment and hatred which had lain beneath the surface in Spain for genera-

---

[1] Madariaga, 378.   [2] Private information.

[3] Junod, 95. However, in Madrid, Dr Junod secured for the Red Cross from the Prime Minister Giral a proposal that all women and children should be allowed to leave Republican territory, if they wished. But this was dependent on a *quid pro quo* from the Nationalists – which was never forthcoming (see above, page 168 fn.); nor would Giral have had the power to enforce his proposal.

[4] A general amnesty formally cleared all these assassins in January 1937. The Government could at that time hardly have acted otherwise since a high proportion of those responsible were then in the new Army.

tions. In fact, many of the killers (like García Atadell of Madrid) were butchers of the sort that all revolutions spawn; many actually enjoyed killing and even gained from it a near-sexual pleasure. But most were not of this kind. The Socialists and Communists who formed part of murder gangs seem to have killed members of the *bourgeoisie* as part of a military operation, thinking that the battle was being fought on all fronts all the time and that he who did not strike first would himself be struck. The Anarchists of the FAI and CNT were different once more. They killed as if they were mystics, resolved to crush for ever all the material things of this world, all the outward signs of a corrupt and hypocritical *bourgeois* past. When they cried 'Long live liberty' and 'down with Fascism', while some unjust steward was dying, they voiced deep passions of fearful sincerity. Many of those captured in Barcelona were taken thirty miles down the coast to be shot overlooking the superb Bay of Sitges. Those about to die would pass their last moments on earth looking out to sea in the marvellous Mediterranean dawn. 'See how beautiful life could have been,' their assassins seemed to be saying, 'if only you had not been a *bourgeois*, and had got up early and had seen the dawn more often – as workers have had to do.'[1]

[1] If the Anarchists had not spent so much petrol driving future victims to beautiful places to die, and trying to burn churches to the ground, the task of their armed forces against the Nationalists in Aragón in August would have been a good deal easier.

21

The character of Nationalist Spain

The nominal leadership of the Nationalists was vested from July 24 onwards in a *junta* established at Burgos under the presidency of the bearded General Cabanellas. He had been allotted this post by Mola to pacify rather than to dignify him. Furthermore, Mola needed a more active General in command at Saragossa.[1] Mola consulted the Monarchists[2] Goicoechea and the Count of Vallellano before setting up the *junta* of Burgos but apparently not Franco,[3] nor the Falangists. Mola desired originally that civilians should join, but no names were suggested which commanded general acceptance. The *junta* was composed at first of the leaders of the rising on the peninsula alone – Generals Mola, Saliquet, Ponte and Dávila. Franco became a member in early August. However, on the mainland, Franco remained for a long time something of a myth. He was spoken of incessantly, but no one seemed to know where he was.[4] At the beginning of the rising, the Nationalist *communiqués* were very confident. Franco was said to have already crossed to the mainland. Mola was announced at the gates of Madrid. But then the news became very vague. It was presumed that Franco was organising to such a pitch of perfection that defeat would be impossible.[5]

Mola inaugurated the *junta*. Amid the ringing of all the bells of Burgos in a deafening saraband, the foxy General shouted hoarsely from a balcony in the main square: 'Spaniards! Citizens of Burgos! The Government which was the wretched bastard of liberal and Socialist concubinage is dead, killed by our valiant army. Spain, the true Spain, has laid the dragon low, and now it lies, writhing on its belly and biting the dust. I am now going to take up my position at the head of the troops and it will not be long before two

---

[1] *Cruzada*, XIII 513.

[2] Don Juan arrived in Spain, made for the front, and then offered his services to Mola, but was rebuffed. Other members of the royal family, however, fought or agitated for the Nationalists.

[3] Ruiz Vilaplana, 225.   [4] *Ibid.*, 45.   [5] Dundas, 56.

banners – the sacred emblem of the Cross, and our own glorious flag – are waving together in Madrid.'[1] The *junta* then held its first meeting and, since there was nothing much for it to do, shortly adjourned to an inconspicuous table in the café of the Casino. Cabanellas and two Colonels thereafter formed a kind of secretariat to give such administrative directions to Nationalist Spain as proved necessary. The business of ordinary government was made difficult by the absence both of civil servants and of all records. However, the want of the former was made up for by the voluntary service of members of the middle class anxious to ingratiate themselves with the new *régime*. A simple adherence to the well-tried rules of martial law compensated for the lack of records. In fact, Cabanellas and his *junta* were as much *rois fainéants* as were Giral, Azaña and Companys. Mola ruled north Spain from El Ferrol to Saragossa and from the Pyrenees to Ávila. Franco controlled Morocco and the Canaries. Queipo de Llano ruled Nationalist Andalusia. His nightly broadcasts, full of coarse and inconsequent ribaldries, of threats to kill the families of the 'Reds' on the Republican fleet, and of boasts of the terrible sexual powers of the legionaries and the *Regulares*, made him famous throughout Europe. In the north, Mola spoke incessantly on Radio Navarre, Radio Castile and Radio Saragossa, reserving his special hatred for Azaña, 'a monster who seems more the absurd invention of a doubly insane Frankenstein than the fruit of the love of woman. Azaña must be caged up so that special brain specialists can study perhaps the most interesting case of mental degeneration in history.'[2]

Beneath this military government, the Falange, its numbers swelling with its successes, acted more as a political police than a political party. The German aircraft manufacturer, Willy Messerschmitt, who travelled in Nationalist Spain in August, reported that the Falange appeared to have no real aims or ideas. They seemed 'merely young people for whom it is good sport to play with firearms and round up Communists and Socialists'.[3] And, with most of the leaders, including José.Antonio Primo de Rivera, Fernández Cuesta and Serrano Suñer, in Republican prisons, the Falangists' time was certainly taken up with activity rather than with political theory. Patrols of Falangists prowled the streets of Nationalist Spain incessantly, stopping suspicious persons, demanding papers and shouting *¡Arriba España!* at every opportunity.

---

[1] Ruiz Vilaplana, 219.   [2] *Diario de Navarra*, 16.8.36.   [3] *GD*, 88.

All taxis, private cars and buses were requisitioned. Many buildings were also taken over, and contributions to Nationalist funds forced from persons or institutions of dubious loyalty to the 'movement'. In some places, bank accounts were investigated. Notices everywhere called on citizens to abstain from talking politics. There was a silence in Nationalist cities which strongly contrasted with the babel-like conditions in the Republic. Nevertheless, radio stations played incessantly the old Royal March, the Carlist marching song 'Oriamendi' and, increasingly, the Falangist hymn 'Cara al Sol'.

In Seville, Queipo's dashing portrait was plastered up all over the city. Elsewhere, after a few days, photographs of Franco were seen everywhere. Shops sold patriotic emblems. Falange posters were enormous, covering entire façades of buildings. 'The Falange calls you,' these cried, 'now or never. There is no middle course. With us or against us?' Carlist posters were also large, not only in Navarre. 'Our flag is the only flag,' they announced, 'the flag of Spain! Always the same!' The question of which flag the rebels should use was, in fact, still undecided. It was, indeed, almost the most important political issue. Should it be the flag of the Monarchy or the flag of the Republic?

The working class in most places in Nationalist Spain were greatly cowed, and with reason. Many who had previously been attached to some working-class party rallied to the Falange to try to secure some political protection for themselves and their families. In several cases, such secret political malingerers were discovered and later punished, sometimes by death.[1]

The Nationalists needed, for the establishment of their society, the support of the Church. Except for the Basque church, this in general they obtained. Nevertheless, just as there were some priests and monks who supported the Republic even while so many of their brothers were being killed, so there were churchmen who felt qualms at the series of cold-blooded murders committed, as they well knew, in Nationalist Spain in the name of Christ. For example, two fathers of the Heart of Mary in Seville complained to Queipo de Llano at the execution of so many innocent persons. The priest of the Andalusian village of Carmona was deprived of his living by the Falange for protesting at their executions.[2]

Among the hierarchy, only the Bishop of Vitoria (whose

---

[1] Bahamonde, 20–1.
[2] Bahamonde says he was shot. I can find no confirmation of this.

diocese included the Basque provinces) was reluctant to give the full support of his position and prestige to the 'Movement'. On the day of the Virgin of Kings, in Seville, Cardinal Ilundaín attended Mass in company with Queipo de Llano while a picket of Falangists attended the effigy of the Virgin in the procession afterwards. For no sooner had the war begun than the Falangists began as a party to show a remarkable religious fervour which had not marked their policy or beliefs before. It became obligatory for the rank and file Falangists to attend Mass, confess and take Communion. Propagandists represented the ideal Falangist as half monk and half warrior. The ideal female Falangist was described as a combination of Saint Theresa and Isabella the Catholic.[1] Archbishops, bishops, canons and priests meantime daily implored the protection of the Virgin for the Nationalist troops, begging her to arrange for their swift entry into Madrid. Some priests actually fought with the Nationalist forces. However, it was rare to find a churchman so bloodthirsty as a priest in Estremadura, who caused four militiamen and a wounded girl to be buried alive in graves which they had dug themselves. Later, in Badajoz, the same churchman found a militiaman taking refuge in a confessional in the cathedral. He allegedly pulled out a revolver and killed him.[2] Other priests such as the fanatical Fr Fermín Yzurdiaga, from Pamplona, became members of the Falange. Yzurdiaga was for a time chief of the Propaganda department at Nationalist headquarters.

[1] Dundas, 48. The last image was ascribed to Pilar Primo de Rivera, José Antonio's sister.
[2] Bahamonde, loc. cit.

Republican Spain – the revolution in Madrid – in New Castile – in Barcelona and Catalonia – in Valencia and Andalusia – in the Basque provinces, Santander and Asturias

After the end of the first wild rapture of victory over the rising, Madrid became bellicose rather than revolutionary. The streets were full of militiamen in their blue *monos* – the boiler suit which became adopted as a kind of uniform in the Republican armies on the Madrid front. In this customarily elegant, even dandy-conscious city, to be well dressed risked an accusation of Fascism. Hundreds of working-class girls were seen in the streets collecting money, in particular for the Comintern's International Red Help. All the time, optimistic loudspeakers announced victories on all fronts. Foreign observers noted the apparent absence of a psychological crisis among the Spaniards as a result of war. The sex life of Spain, for example, did not seem to suffer as great an upheaval as that occasioned in all belligerent countries by the World War, or as that which overwhelmed Russia in its civil war.[1] Nevertheless, marriages were celebrated with the greatest ease at militia headquarters, and the partners shortly afterwards with equal facility forgot them. Later, the Government recognised as legal any marriage between militiamen celebrated after July 18 before any war committees or officers. 'Marriage by usage' was also instituted. By this, a woman was considered wedded to any man with whom she had lived ten months, or less if she became with child.[2] Divorces were similarly easy to obtain.

The UGT was the real executive organ of Madrid, since it was responsible for food supply and the essential services. The permanent civil servants were in many cases disloyal to, or unhappy about, the cause for which they found themselves now working, and lessened daily in importance – like, indeed, Giral's Govern-

[1] Borkenau, 134.
[2] *Gaceta de la República*, 13.4.37. Needless to say, this decree caused numerous cases of bigamy, and the decree was reversed – causing even greater confusion. By 1937, there was a great deal of promiscuity in the Republic.

ment itself. There were several measures designed to purge the Civil Service, but many persons disloyal to the Republic remained. The UGT worked in comparative harmony with the CNT, its old enemies, though the building strike, the cause of their most recent enmity, was not settled until early August. A popular poster showed two dead CNT and UGT militiamen with their blood mingling in a pool beneath.

Behind the UGT in Madrid there loomed the Communist party. The propaganda and tactical political skill of its leaders, were the chief reason for Communist predominance, though the hostility between Largo Caballero's and Prieto's wings of the Socialist party played a part.[1] Communist propaganda, directed by Jesús Hernández, was careful to concentrate on two themes – its now moderate, non-revolutionary social policy, and the identity of the present resistance to the rising with the resistance of the Spanish people in 1808 to Napoleon.

The revolution over which the UGT presided did not at first appear very far-reaching. There was expropriation (only) of those concerns or mansions whose owners were known to have sided with the Nationalists. This meant, however, the forcing open of thousands of bank accounts and innumerable confiscations of residences, jewels and articles of private wealth.[2]

The Socialist-Communist Youth established itself in the financier Juan March's palace, and the Palace Hotel became a home for derelict children. Right-wing newspapers were taken over by their left-wing rivals. All industry connected with the supply of war material was also requisitioned, nominally by the Ministry of War, in fact by committees of workers. Managers of other firms later asked for the formation of such committees, to share their responsibilities, and so avoid a worse fate. Such committees increasingly took over Madrid's industry and, since they were responsible to the unions, and the unions to political parties, those concerns became ultimately, if indirectly, politically led. However, by August, only 30% of the industry in Madrid was, even in this way, controlled by the State. Banks were not requisitioned, though they functioned under the close supervision of the

---

[1] The Communists gained greatly in prestige also from their efficient organisation of their so-called Fifth Regiment. See below, page 241.

[2] According to the *General Cause*, 390, the total confiscation of money and securities amounted (in all Spain throughout the war) to 330 million pesetas (£8 million) and of gold and jewels to 100 million pesetas (£2½ million). These figures seem quite probable.

Ministry of Finance. There was a moratorium on debts, and a limitation of withdrawals from current accounts, but otherwise banking continued normally. The only other financial policy followed at this time was a reduction by 50% of all rents.[1] Apart from the nightly assassinations, and the consequent bodies lying about in the Casa de Campo,[2] the most obvious outward signs of revolution in Madrid were indeed the collective restaurants organised by the trade unions. To these was distributed the food which the unions seized on its arrival from the agricultural areas of the Levante. At these restaurants a lavish dish of rice and potatoes, boiled with meat, was served in unlimited quantities.[3] There was no bread, a reflection of the rebel possession of the wheat-growing plains of north Castile. Nationalists at this stage thought that they might even be able to starve the Republic into surrender. At such collective restaurants, and increasingly in stores and other shops, vouchers issued by the unions were exchanged for a meal or an article. After a while, wages in Madrid began increasingly to be paid by these pieces of paper. Money began to die out, and traders only bought what they were certain to sell. This economic chaos was eventually ended by the Madrid municipality, which thereafter controlled the issue of vouchers, and supplied the families of militiamen, the unemployed and the beggars of Madrid with the means to food. However, a large number of merchants lost money by accepting such promissory notes for which the equivalent in cash was never paid. Militiamen themselves began to be paid 10 pesetas a day (raised in some cases from the factories in which they had been employed, in others paid by the Government or the unions),[4] a sum which continued to be paid to their dependents in the event of their deaths.

The towns and countryside of New Castile, Republican Estremadura and La Mancha were, like the capital, dominated by the UGT and by the Socialist-Communist Youth. Anarchists were rare. The revolutions therefore in these areas followed the example of Madrid. The old municipal authorities continued, working alongside the Popular Front committees. Expropriation was exceptional. The shops and businesses of, for example, Talavera de la

---

[1] *The Times*, 21.7.36.
[2] With the incessant wit for which Madrileños was always celebrated, these tragic bodies were nicknamed *besugos* – a kind of fish with glassy eyes and permanently open mouth.
[3] Barea, 124. [4] Sloan, 229.

Reina, in the Tagus valley, might be covered with notices announcing 'here one works collectively'. But this indicated an agreement to distribute profits between owner and workers, not workers' control. In the country, in La Mancha as in New Castile, the large estates had all been confiscated and were run by the local branch of the UGT. No material advantage came to the workers, who were paid at the same wage as previously. To the south, at Ciudad Real, the chief town of La Mancha, only one concern, an electricity plant, had been expropriated. Market, shops and cafés carried on as before. Dr Franz Borkenau, visiting this area in August, noted that, at a new collective farm near Ciudad Real, the cattle seemed in good health, and that the wheat was harvested on time, being stored in the chapel. Before collectivisation, the labourers had lived in Ciudad Real and had come out for harvesting. Now they were settled in the manorial building, where they did their own cooking. Food, though not plentiful, was better than before. Before the war, these same labourers had wrecked machinery brought in by the landowner, since they supposed that he was trying to bring down wages. Now a threshing machine from Bilbao was welcomed and admired.[1]

The revolution which centred upon Barcelona in July 1936 differed from that in the centre of Spain in being Anarchist in direction. The real executive organ in Barcelona, and therefore of Catalonia, was the Anti-Fascist Militias Committee, which had been formed on July 23 and which was led by the FAI and CNT. Barcelona thus became a proletarian town as Madrid never did. Expropriation was the rule – hotels, stores, banks, factories were either requisitioned or closed. Those that were requisitioned were run by managing committees of former technicians and workers.[2] Account books were examined with fascination. What waste, what profits, what corruption they seemed to show! And then (as a workers' committee on the Barcelona *metro* remarked) 'we set out on the great adventure!' Since the great pompous mock-Gothic Chamber of Commerce had been taken over by the FAI and CNT as headquarters, it seemed that nothing could go wrong.

---

[1] Borkenau, 149.
[2] The vast majority of Barcelona factory owners had either been shot or had fled. Those who remained were chiefly those who had a good reputation for labour relations. The Ford and General Motors works were seized in Barcelona in early August. After a protest by the American Government, the Spanish Government undertook compensation. In general the Republic tried not to offend other countries by requisitioning of foreign concerns.

No one was to be seen in middle-class clothes. To wear a tie was to risk arrest.[1] All the 58 churches of Barcelona save the cathedral (preserved by order of the Generalitat) were burned, some more finally than others. Much valuable petrol was wasted in an attempt to burn Gaudi's Sagrada Familia, which was alas made of cement. A few churches and convents remained to be dealt with by early August. By then, whatever excitement there had been earlier at such scenes had died, and the area of destruction was carefully limited by the fire brigade.

Power had by then given to the Anarchists of Barcelona a sense of responsibility which amazed those members of the middle classes still in the city. The CNT ordered all its members to return to work. Yet the CNT's power itself was now considerable. It possessed its own radio station, eight daily newspapers, innumerable weeklies, and periodicals dealing with every aspect of society. Meetings were frequently held, addressed by the best orators in the Anarchist movement. In this expansion of activity, certain Anarchists saw the decay of the purity of their ideals: their leaders, they felt, were becoming politicians, men interested in power. This was the only occasion in history that an Anarchist movement has controlled a great city. It is remarkable what little use the Anarchists made of this opportunity.

After the murder of Trillas, president of the UGT dockers – presumably by Anarchists – the FAI and CNT joined with other parties in denouncing the crime. Together they threatened death to any who took upon themselves the task of carrying out shootings or looting: 'the Barcelona underworld is disgracing the Revolution'. The FAI ordered all its members to exercise the utmost vigilance to prevent such abominable activity. 'Smash the riff raff! If we do not, the crooks will smash the revolution by dishonouring it.'[2] The Anarchist policy remained officially restraint – at least till after 'the fall of Saragossa'. But at night, on the road out of Barcelona towards the Tibidado mountain, shots continued to be heard. 'Fascists' continued to be arrested. What would happen after victory? Certainly not the petty *bourgeois* democracy of the Esquerra. Instead, the UGT and CNT could surely 'administer the whole economic life of Spain without outside aid'.[3] But on

[1] The Anarchist paper *Solidariad Obrera* denounced the Russian Foreign Minister Litvinov as a *bourgeois* because he wore a hat. The Anarchist Hatters Union immediately registered a protest.
[2] *CNT-FAI Information Bulletin*, July 25.   [3] *Ibid.*, August 10.

July 26 the CNT of Catalonia formally instructed its followers to 'look no further' than the victory over Fascism.

An extraordinary consequence of the Anarchist domination in Catalonia was the beginning of the development of the Catalan Separatist movement (still the nominal rulers of Catalonia) into a party which customarily supported the Government of Madrid.[1] The advance of the Barcelona militias, Anarchists at their head, far into Aragón, might be represented as a responsible defence of the central Government. However, on August 9, a mass Anarchist meeting was held at the Olympia theatre in Barcelona to protest against the conscription by the Madrid Government of certain classes of reserves to serve under regular officers. 'We cannot be uniformed soldiers. We want to be militiamen of Liberty. To the Front, certainly. But to the barracks as soldiers not subject to the Popular Forces, certainly not!'[2] In protesting against the central Government, they were thus apparently joining hands with traditional Catalan Separatism. But the Generalitat, fearing the consequences of political armies, agreed with the Government of Madrid, and argued for a regular army, with officers named from above, and their political faith obscured. Now the Generalitat was supported, on this all-important point, by the new united Socialist party of Catalonia (PSUC),[3] composed of four left-wing groups which had come together after the rising. Though a veteran Socialist (and anti-Anarchist), Comorera, became Secretary-General of this party, the Communists (as in the amalgamation of the national Socialist and Communist youth movements in April) by their superior efficiency, ruthlessness and skill, dominated the united party. The PSUC even affiliated to the Comintern. The Barcelona UGT (which of course followed the political lead of the Socialists) also came under Communist control. That trade union in Barcelona had increased its membership from about 12,000 on July 19 to about 35,000 at the end of the month, partly because of the help afforded by a party or union card to gain food, partly because of the urge towards association common to all revolutionary circumstances. Though it remained a diminutive body

---

[1] This was not noticed for a long time. In August, with the taking over of the Bank of Spain in Barcelona, and the break between the University of Barcelona with that of Madrid, the apparent tendency was quite the contrary.

[2] *CNT-FAI Information Bulletin*, August 10. The document continues by recalling that the people in the French Revolution defied the world; but Napoleon's uniformed army led to Waterloo.

[3] *Partido Socialista Unificado de Cataluña*.

beside the CNT (whose membership in Barcelona alone amounted to 350,000) it was a valuable prize for the Communists.

The PSUC naturally favoured the 'army system' rather than that of the militia, since its Communist leaders did not command mass support, and since their chief hope of dominance was by infiltration into the officially recognised Government. No party was in truth more interested in bringing their political interests into the Army, but they planned to do this through persuasion of officers and a regular system. Formally, however, Communist policy in Barcelona as in Madrid was that nothing should be done to jeopardise the winning of the war and that 'political adjustment between comrades' should await victory. The PSUC nevertheless did quarrel with the Anarchists over certain minor reforms instituted by the Generalitat – a 15% rise in wages, return by the pawnshops of all articles pledged for less than 200 pesetas, and a forty-hour week. The PSUC also made economic claims on behalf of the widows of dead fighters on the first day after the defeat of the rising. But García Oliver, on behalf of the CNT, declared that the working hours needed were those 'necessary for the defeat of the revolution'. The Communists, though planning to leave social reform until after the victory, were glad that the immediate demands of the very poor should be appeased, so preventing them, out of nihilism, from joining the Anarchists.

The flickering quarrel between Anarchists and Communists, the direct reflection of the disputes so many years before between Bakunin and Marx, became acute over the suggested entry of the PSUC into the Generalitat. On July 31, Companys elevated himself from being merely President of the Generalitat to be President of Catalonia. This was a new step towards Catalan sovereignty and one upon which he did not consult the Government in Madrid. Three members of the PSUC joined the reconstituted Generalitat. The Anarchists threatened to leave the anti-Fascist Militias Committee unless the PSUC resigned from the Generalitat. And this they did. Their time to strike back would come later. Already they tried to disarm Anarchist militiamen in quarters which they controlled – acts which were furiously and successfully resisted by the CNT who denounced this as treachery. 'Comrades,' the FAI appealed on August 5 to the PSUC, 'together we have beaten the bloody beasts of Fascist militarism. Let us be worthy of our victory by maintaining our unity of action until the final triumph. Long live the Revolutionary and anti-Fascist Alliance.'

Standing apart from both Anarchists and PSUC, was the POUM, the semi-Trotskyist group, chiefly ex-Catalan Communists, which grew greatly in membership at the start of the war. Many joined this party believing that it represented a mean between the indiscipline of the Anarchists and the strictness of the PSUC. Foreigners in Barcelona joined the POUM in the romantic supposition that it indeed embodied a magnificent Utopian aspiration. Dr Borkenau noted the atmosphere of political enthusiasm among these *émigrés*, who clearly enjoyed the adventure of war, felt relief that the sordid years of exile were past, and had complete faith in 'absolute success'. And the POUM, with new headquarters in the Hotel Falcón in the Ramblas, concentrated on pushing its unfamiliar name before the public, by painting its initials in large letters on motor-cars and buses, and by agitating for 'a government of workers only'.

The organisation of Catalonia and of Republican Aragón reflected the events in Barcelona. A political committee was formed in all *pueblos*. Power, as elsewhere, lay in the hands of the strongest party, regardless of formal representation. Thus the POUM predominated in the province of Lérida; the CNT elsewhere.[1] Usually, a red flag, decorated with a hammer and sickle, would be hung outside the town hall indicating the magnetic attraction of the USSR to all the proletarian parties, not only to the Communists. The railways and public services were run by committees of the UGT and CNT alone. In all the *pueblos* the churches were burned. In some places, where the burning did not occur till August, and especially in the middle-class resorts along the Costa Brava, regret was marked. Dr Borkenau observed sad women carrying to the pyres prayer-books, images, statues, and other talismans, which had been less an object of religious value than of family pride, a part of familiar daily life. Only the children were pleased, as they cut off the noses of statues before throwing them to the flames. In general, all the *bourgeoisie*, including priests, lawyers and doctors, were shot, and their houses and land appropriated by the municipality. As elsewhere in Catalonia, the ruthlessness of the revolutionaries was tempered by mad streaks of generosity. For example, the French poet of the air Antoine de Saint Exupéry, then a correspondent for *L'Intransigeant*, succeeded

---

[1] Sometimes, as in the village of L'Hospitalet, the CNT would take their antagonism against Catalan Separatism to the point of placing notices banning Catalan. (Jaime Miravitlles in *La Fleche*, 24.2.39.)

with some others in persuading a village revolutionary committee to spare the life of a monk who had been hunted in the
woods. This secured, the Anarchists shook hands excitedly with
each other and also with the monk, congratulating him on his
escape.[1]

There were no large estates in Catalonia, and there was indecision as to what should be done about those lands which had
been taken over. The eventual solution – not reached in most of
Catalonia until the autumn – gave half the expropriated land to
be run by the committee, while the other half would be divided
among the poorer peasants. The committee of the *pueblo* would also
receive half the rents, while half would be remitted. Throughout
Catalonia, there was a lack of foresight in the peasants' treatment
of *bourgeois* property. In Seriñena, where some members of the
middle class (including the vet) had been spared, Dr Borkenau,
with the English Communist John Cornford,[2] watched the destruction of all the documents relating to rural property. A huge bonfire
was set ablaze in the middle of the main square, the flames rising
higher than the roof of the church, young Anarchists throwing on
new material with triumphant gestures.[3]

Down the coast at Valencia, Martínez Barrio's *junta*, sent by
Giral to control the five provinces of the Levante, was even more
ineffective before the committee in control than was the Generalitat before the Anti-Fascists Militias Committee. Martínez Barrio
was forced to live in the country, not in Valencia at all. Yet
though the CNT was the strongest group, dominating the port
and the transport and building workers, Valencia was more
bourgeois than Barcelona, with fewer expropriations. The UGT
controlled the white-collar workers, and these closely followed
Largo Caballero's position. The Republicans, with considerable
following among the lower middle classes and the richer peasants
of the Valencian *huerta*, were divided between those who saw in
present circumstances a chance for the development of a Valencian
Separatist movement and the strict supporters of Azaña and Giral.
The Communist party in Valencia was small and disliked, and it
had constant quarrels with the Anarchists. Its policy in Valencia
was as moderate as that of the Republicans, and it alone gave support to Martínez Barrio. The Communist party later gained
support among the rich Valencian peasants, through its championship of the distribution to individual peasants of expropriated

land against the Anarchist plan of collectivisation and the abolition of private commerce in farming.

In Andalusia, the revolution was chiefly Anarchist in inspiration, without even the limited central authority which Barcelona provided for the Anarchist revolution of Catalonia. In most *pueblos* the old municipalities had merged with the new committees. Control of roads and public services was shared by old officials and militiamen appointed by the committee. Each town acted entirely on its own responsibility. The comparative proximity of the Nationalists in Seville, Granada, Córdoba and the ports of Cádiz and Algeciras gave a brutal urgency to what was done. There was also some hostility between the Anarchist leaders of cities such as Málaga and those of small *pueblos*. The former desired to intervene in the *pueblos*, and were resisted by the local leaders who regarded this as an attack on their own rights.[1] The nature of the revolution was everywhere more extreme than elsewhere in Spain. In several places, private property was entirely abolished, along with the payment of debts to shopkeepers. Often money itself was declared illegal. In Castro del Rio, near Córdoba, a *régime* was set up comparable to that of the Baptists of Munster of 1530, all private exchange of goods being banned, the village bar closed, the inhabitants realising the long-desired abolition of coffee. 'They did not want to get the good living of those they had expropriated,' noted Dr Borkenau, 'but to get rid of their luxuries.'[2] The great estates in this region were still worked by their former labourers, who received no pay at all but were fed from the village store according to their needs. In between the *pueblos*, an uncertain and wild condition prevailed. The land was dotted with places where the rebel Civil Guard had abandoned their garrisons and, retreating to hilltops, monasteries and other easily defensible points, held out almost indefinitely, living as highwaymen by robbing from the neighbourhood. The longest surviving encampment of this kind was established by Captain Cortés of the Civil Guard in the monastery of Santa María de la Cabeza in the north of the mountains of Córdoba.

The generally Anarchist pattern of revolution in Andalusia was varied in the province of Jaén, which had had a strong UGT following for several years, and in Málaga and Almería, where the dock workers were chiefly Communists. In the province of Jaén there was little social change. In the straggling, stagnant town of

[1] Pitt-Rivers, 18–19.　　　　[2] Borkenau, 167.

Andújar, for example, though five of the *bourgeoisie* had been killed, their land had been left unexpropriated. The UGT left to the municipality the administration of the large estates nearby, with the result that the labourers worked the same hours as before for the same starvation wage. The revolution in Málaga, though led by the Communists, was distinguished for its arbitrary inefficiency. Partially isolated from the rest of Republican Spain (because of the Nationalist hold on Granada, to the north-east), living under daily threat of aerial attack, with constant rumours that land attacks were about to be made upon it, Málaga lacked the enthusiasm which distinguished the revolutions in the north.

The Republican territory lying along the north coast of Spain was cut off from the remainder of the Republic by the central plain of North Castile and by the mountains of Navarre, controlled by General Mola. Here there were three societies, centring on Bilbao and San Sebastián; on Santander; and on Gijón. In the former towns, and throughout the provinces of Vizcaya and Guipúzcoa, the predominance of the Basque Nationalists permitted the continuance of a markedly middle-class social order.[1] Both Bilbao and San Sebastián, and the territory around them, were controlled by committees of defence, but upon these the Basque Nationalists held a majority over the UGT, the Communists and the Anarchists. Of the last three groups only the Anarchists (with strength among the fishermen and builders) were really inclined to make a stand against the Basques, who themselves regarded all the working-class parties with distrust. Hence in the new Basque motorised police corps and disciplinary battalions (for the militiamen) no members of the left-wing revolutionary parties were permitted, though there were many persons of dubious loyalty to the Republic itself.

About five hundred persons were shot in the Basque provinces by militiamen, apart from Colonel Carrasco and some officers and Falangists who actually took part in the rising. The Anarchists were mainly responsible. But, after the start of August, there was little persecution of the upper and middle class.[2] Priests went free and church services continued. Only two churches were burned, these being at the very start of the war in San Sebastián. Expropriation of capitalists occurred only when they had taken part

[1] The following derives from Steer and Lizarra.
[2] Though some three thousand political prisoners were nevertheless held in prison-ships and fortresses, among them many women and children.

in the rebellion. The goods of such persons were handed over to a state board on which employees were represented but which they did not control.

The only measures of social change in the Basque provinces were a decree forbidding anyone to be a director of more than one company (a blow at the Basque millionaires, though not at the *bourgeoisie*), the cut in rents by 50% which obtained elsewhere in Republican Spain, and the institution of a Public Assistance Board for those in need. At the same time, the Vizcaya arms industry – the Eibar gun plants, the small arms factories at Guernica and Durango, the Bilbao grenade and mortar factories – were taken over by the Bilbao Defence Committee. The Basque Nationalists also gained control of the financial structure of their provinces. New boards were formed to control the great Basque banks. There were four members of the old board, two shareholders, two depositors and four employees elected by their colleagues. The Basque Ministry of Finance, however, chose the shareholders and depositors, and had to approve the members of the old board and the employees' representatives.

Despite this comparative moderation, the Basques came inevitably into conflict with the Roman Church.[1] After the failure of an attempt by a Roman Catholic friend of José Antonio Aguirre, the Basque leader, to persuade him and his party to join the Nationalists, the Bishops of Vitoria and Pamplona, in a pastoral letter broadcast on August 6, publicly condemned the adhesion of the Basque Catholics to the Republican side. The Basque priests, under the Vicar-General of Bilbao, consulted together and advised the Basque political leaders to continue to support the Republic. The reasons for this advice were given as firstly, that there were no proofs that the pastoral letter was authentic, since no copies of it had arrived; secondly, that the pastoral letter had not been promulgated with due formality; thirdly, that there were suggestions that the Bishop of Vitoria did not have full freedom of action (this was correct: the Bishop was almost a prisoner in his palace); fourthly, that the Bishops could not know the truth of what was going on in the provinces of Guipúzcoa and Vizcaya; finally, that a change of attitude by the Basque Nationalists would bring untold miseries upon many people and upon the Church. Thereafter the Basque priests continued in their defiance, remaining with their flocks, whose spiritual needs they continued to

[1] *Le Clergé Basque*, 25 fl.

serve. They frequently intervened on behalf of persons in danger
from left-wing violence, especially their brethren in Asturias and
Santander. The Basque Catholic leaders continued in their support of the Republic and afterwards shared in its Government.
They justified this ideologically by arguing that the four conditions named by St Thomas Aquinas as justifying a rebellion against
the State did not exist, and that recent papal encyclicals had
denied that rebellion could ever be legal.[1]

Along the coast in Asturias, the situation in Gijón was complicated by the continued resistance of the Civil Guard in the
Simancas barracks under Colonel Pinilla. During the siege,
however, relations between the UGT, CNT and Communist
party in Gijón became closer even than those which had been
achieved during the 1934 rebellion. Belarmino Tomás, a Socialist
deputy, was Governor of the province of Asturias with governmental powers delegated to him. Due to the cut in land communications with Madrid, he had to act in almost as independent a way
as his Basque and Catalan colleagues. He presided over a committee of two Communists, two members of the CNT, two of the
UGT, two of the FAI, two of the United Socialist Youth and two
of the Republican Left, together with one of the Libertarian
(Anarchist) Youth. The mines of Asturias were controlled by
a council composed of a director, representing the State, certain
technicians, a deputy director and secretary chosen by the
Asturias mines councillor, and three workers. The director could
not act without the workers' agreement, and this administration
can be therefore regarded as a unique mixture of nationalisation
and workers' control.

The houses of Gijón were ruined by the incessant attacks of the
Nationalist Cruiser *Almirante Cervera*. Its people were poor, puritan
and confident of the future. A huge poster on the hoardings displayed a red Spain and, in the centre, a lighthouse giving a beam

---

[1] The conditions named by St Thomas were:

(i) The common good (religion, justice and peace) must be gravely compromised.

(ii) The rebellion must be regarded as necessary by the social authorities as a whole
and by prudent men who represent the people in its national organisation.

(iii) There must be a strong probability of success and the probable harm done by
the revolt must not be greater than the probable harm done by the absence of the revolt.

(iv) There must be no other remedy for the elimination of the danger to the common
good.

See the interview between Manuel Irujo, the Basque who later joined the Republican Government, and Prince von Löwenstein. (Löwenstein, 90–104.)

stretching over Europe. The legend read: 'Spain will be a light to the world. *Viva* the Popular Front of Asturias.' At night loud-speakers would bellow to empty streets false good news from far-away battlefields. Gijón, perched on the edge of the unfriendly Atlantic, gave the impression of being a lonely Soviet all of its own.[1]

As for Santander, that city was a rigid outpost of the UGT, as its ancient position as Castile's only port might have suggested. Its defence committee also acted with a great degree of independence from the central Government in Madrid.

From the start of the Civil War, the military tactics of all these three provinces remaining faithful to the Republic in the north were greatly hampered by separate political direction. The only thing they had in common was, after a few weeks of war, a similar lack of food. There was sometimes beer, cigarettes, cheese and some fish, but there was very little else to eat. The symbolic figure of north Spain in late 1936 was the native of Gijón known as 'the man the cats are afraid of'. He could pounce on a cat from a distance of twenty yards. And that night there would be chicken on the menu for dinner.

[1] Jellinck, 415. Though written from an extreme point of view, this publication of the Left Book Club is invaluable for its detailed social and economic analysis of life in the Republic.

23

The first campaigns – the battles of the Sierra – the Alcázar incident –
composition of the two sides – arms from abroad

By July 22, there was true war in Spain rather than mere
rebellion and resistance to it. Everywhere in Republican
cities, the feeling of *fiesta* which had followed the defeat of
the rising gave way to a fear that Nationalist armies were on the
march towards them. The militias of the unions and parties, even
in the smallest towns, began to think of themselves as soldiers as
well as streetfighters and revolutionaries. Indeed, they had to do so.
For as early as July 19 Mola sent his adjutant, the Andalusian
Colonel, García Escámez, south with 1,600 men, mainly regulars,
but with two companies of *Requetés* and one of Falangists, to relieve
Guadalajara. This he might have accomplished if he had not
halted to secure the victory of the rising at Logroño where the
Military Governor had been somewhat unwilling to commit himself. As it was, this first real striking force of the war reached a point
twenty miles from Guadalajara before finding it had fallen to the
militias of Madrid. So García Escámez withdrew to the north side of
the Somosierra Pass across the Guadarrama, the most easterly of
the northern gates to Madrid.[1] Here, the railway tunnel had been
held for the Nationalists by a group of Madrid Monarchists under
the brothers Miralles, since July 19. Against them the militia forces
which had earlier taken Guadalajara were now advancing.

To the north-west of Madrid, at midnight on July 21, a mixed
force of regular soldiers and Falangists under Colonel Serrador
(another ex-plotter of 1932) set out from Valladolid, also for
Madrid *via* the Guadarrama, amid scenes of wild enthusiasm. It
was making for the pass known as the Alto de León. This force
was accompanied by Onésimo Redondo, the founder of the JONS
at Valladolid, who had recently been freed from gaol at Ávila. The
Alto de León had been occupied by a large militia force from
Madrid. The Nationalists swiftly realised the importance of holding

[1] Aznar, 113–14.

their enemy beyond that point. Otherwise, all Old Castile would be menaced. At the same time, Mola despatched two forces under Colonels Beorlegui and Cayuela, both partly *Requetés*, *Carabineros* and Falangists, in the direction of the Basque provinces, the first to relieve the beleaguered garrison in the Loyola Barracks at San

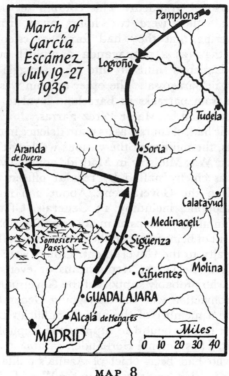

March of García Escámez July 19-27 1936

Pamplona

Logroño

Tudela

Soria

Aranda de Duero

Calatayud

Medinaceli

Somosierra Pass

Sigüenza

Cifuentes

Molina

•GUADALÁJARA

Alcalá de Henares

MADRID

Miles
0 10 20 30 40

MAP 8

Sebastián, the second to march upon the old Basque town of Tolosa.[1]

In Barcelona, meanwhile, it was continually rumoured that a Nationalist army was about to march on the city from Saragossa. In fact, 1,200 *Requetés* had arrived at Saragossa from Pamplona. This force merely enabled the Nationalists to undertake several punitive expeditions to conquer those surrounding Aragonese towns where the Popular Front was in temporary

[1] Aznar, 128.

control. No general offensive against Barcelona was contemplated. Nevertheless, on the urgent demand of the Government of Madrid, on July 23, two columns set out from Barcelona to 'liberate' Saragossa. The first column was composed chiefly of Anarchist militiamen led by Buenaventura Durruti, to whom the success of the revolution had brought enormous self-confidence and wild dreams of personal grandeur. This column set out with such excitement that they were two hours away from Barcelona before discovering that they had forgotten essential supplies. Thus it was that (as a propaganda pamphlet put it) ' "The Free Man" launched himself into the struggle against the Fascist Hyena in Saragossa'. The other column was chiefly composed of men from barracks in Barcelona loyal to the Republic and was commanded by Major Pérez Farras.

The Republic had, of course, as its main defence in these developing campaigns, the militias of the various working-class organisations. True, the War Ministry in Madrid, nominally in control of operations, was chiefly staffed by regular officers who had remained loyal to the Government. About 200 regular officers served the Republic, including 13 Generals. Of these officers, an uncertain number, perhaps as many as half, probably rationalised the accident of being in Republican territory at the time of the rising into loyalty to the Government. Others were undoubtedly men of the Left, Socialists, Republicans or even Communists. Among those who probably supported the Government by chance rather than conviction was the easy-going General Miaja, who had been once a member of the anti-Republican *Unión Militar*.[1] Others still felt merely bound to support the Republic because of their oath to it. Thus Colonel Hernández Sarabia, a long-standing Republican who had been chief of Azaña's military household in 1932, worked as Under-Secretary to the War Minister, General Castelló, with Major Menéndez as his Adjutant. Due to Castelló's increasing melancholy at the development of events,[2] Hernández Sarabia became in effect the War Minister. General Riquelme who had taken part in a famous conspiracy against Primo de Rivera in 1926,[3] was in general field command at Madrid. The

---

[1] *General Cause*, 282. Miaja, when commander-in-chief on the Madrid front in 1937, went to some trouble to have his membership card destroyed.

[2] He soon actually went mad, and Hernández Sarabia succeeded him. His madness was probably impelled by the death of his brother José at the hands of the Anarchists in Estremadura.

[3] *Cruzada*, II 164.

militias sent against the Nationalists, with the battle cry 'A la Sierra', were also led, at the start, by regular army officers. Captain Galán, a regular officer though a member of the Communist party, brother of the 'hero of Jaca', led the militia at Somosierra; and Colonel Castillo led the forces which first mounted and later abandoned the pass at the Alto de León.

A further force advanced in the direction of Ávila, to cut off that town from the Alto de León. This was led by Colonel Mangada – the poet-officer who had been arrested, and later imprisoned by Azaña (then bent on gaining the confidence of the officers) for crying 'Viva la República' at a dinner in 1932 at which Goded, then Inspector-General of the Army, had cried merely 'Viva España'. Though he captured several pueblos where the Civil Guard had declared for the Nationalists, he did not march any farther than Navalperal, twenty kilometres short of his objective, since, though amazingly popular, he was cautious and feared to lose communication with Madrid. His failure to advance upon the then poorly defended city of St Theresa was, however, explained by the Nationalists as being due to the appearance of the Saint herself who allegedly (but surely untypically) lied to Mangada that Ávila was 'full of armed men'. Nevertheless, the advance which he did make was enough to cause his men to carry him in triumphal procession to the Puerta del Sol in Madrid, and to elect him to the rank of General.[1]

In the meantime, the battles of the Alto de León and Somosierra, the first real conflicts of the Civil War, were fought with extraordinary ferocity, both sides using their limited but approximately equal number of aircraft to bomb the other and most prisoners being killed.[2] The Government forces, though superior in numbers, suffered heavy losses, due both to the Nationalist artillery – which was considerably superior to their own – and to the naïve courage of the inexperienced militiamen. On July 22, the Alto de León and, on July 25, the Somosierra Pass were both gained by the Nationalists. But the remainder of the heights of the Guadarrama were held by the Republic. The Falangist Onésimo Redondo died in action at the Alto de León. On the Republican side, Colonel Castillo and his son were shot by their own men for

[1] Mangada's column was accompanied by a group of Madrid whores who infected the militiamen with gonorrhea to such an extent that their fighting power was greatly diminished. When they refused to go home, Mangada had several of them shot.

[2] Doctors on both sides had to fight to secure even wounded men from being shot in their beds.

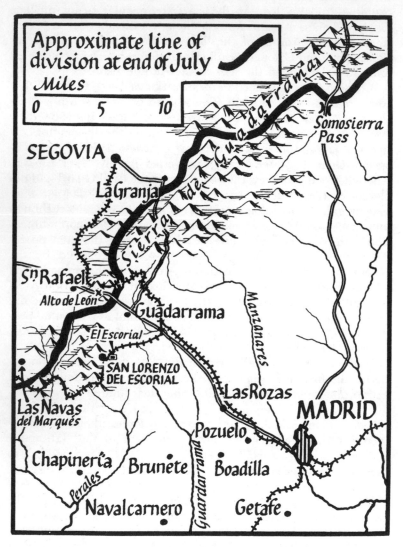

Approximate line of
division at end of July

Miles

0   5   10

SEGOVIA

La Granja

Sierra de Guadarrama

Somosierra
Pass

Sⁿ Rafael

Alto de León

Guadarrama

El Escorial

SAN LORENZO
DEL ESCORIAL

Manzanares

Las Rozas

MADRID

Las Navas
del Marqués

Pozuelo

Chapinería

Perales

Brunete

Guadarrama

Boadilla

Navalcarnero

Getafe

MAP 9

'treason'. But his only treasonable act was that of failing to lead the militias to the victory which they felt they deserved. It was not easy for an officer of the Spanish Army to lead a body of men who sometimes insisted on a show of hands before an attack.

The most celebrated incident of this period in the Spanish War occurred, however, at Toledo. From Madrid the Minister of Education, the Minister of War, and General Riquelme had been furiously telephoning Colonel Moscardó, commander of the Nationalist garrison still holding out in the Alcázar, in an attempt to persuade him to surrender. Finally, on July 23, Candido Cabello, a leader of the militia in Toledo, telephoned Colonel Moscardó to say that if Moscardó did not surrender the Alcázar within ten minutes he would shoot Luis Moscardó, the Colonel's son, whom he had captured that morning. 'So that you can see that's true, he will speak to you,' added Candido Cabello. Luis Moscardó then uttered the single word 'Papa' over the line. 'What is happening, my boy?' asked the Colonel. 'Nothing,' answered the son, 'they say they will shoot me if the Alcázar does not surrender.' 'If it be true,' replied Colonel Moscardó, 'commend your soul to God, shout *Viva España* and die like a hero. Goodbye my son, a last kiss.' 'Goodbye father,' answered Luis, 'a very big kiss.' Candido Cabello came back on to the telephone, and Colonel Moscardó announced that the period of grace was unnecessary. 'The Alcázar will never surrender,' he remarked before replacing the receiver. Luis Moscardó was in fact killed on August 23.[1] The Alcázar

[1] Doubt has recently been thrown on the validity of this celebrated story by two exiled Republicans in New York, General Asensio Torrado and Luis Quintanilla, a Socialist painter. The doubts were propagated on p. 173 of *The Yoke and the Arrows* by Herbert Matthews, at the time *New York Times* correspondent in Madrid. This version of the story alleges that the son had been killed in the Montaña barracks, that the telephone between Toledo and the Alcázar had been cut on July 22 and that the whole story did not appear in any newspapers until some months after the relief of Toledo – not until, indeed, the Nationalists needed counter-propaganda to counter the rumours which had then reached Miguel de Unamuno of the ill-treatment of the hostages in the Alcázar. After the appearance of the American edition of this book in 1957, a convincing pamphlet was written by the Nationalist historian, Manuel Aznar (*The Alcázar will not Surrender*, New York 1957). As a result, in the English version of his book (London 1958), Mr Matthews dropped his first reason for supposing the story an invention, though he maintained the other two. Aznar had answered these by pointing out that the wires were not physically cut but merely controlled by the Toledo Exchange on July 22 and that news of the incident appeared immediately after the relief of the Alcázar, even indeed in the *New York Times* of September 30. In addition a number of affidavits as to the truth of the occurrence have been obtained from eye-witnesses on both sides of the line. I have no doubt that the Nationalist account is correct. (See Moscardó's statement in the *General Cause* 329.) Another son of Moscardó was shot in Barcelona.

remained besieged. Though food supplies were low, there was plenty of water and ammunition. The provisions were shortly supplemented by a daring raid on a nearby granary, which brought back two thousand sacks of wheat. Horsemeat (there had been 177 horses in the Alcázar at the start of the siege) and bread were the basic diet in the Alcázar.

While the Alcázar at Toledo continued to hold out, the Loyola barracks in San Sebastián surrendered to the Basques on July 27, and the Civil Guards of Albacete were overwhelmed on July 25. The officers in Valencia were also stormed in their barracks. Those who were not killed in the assault were tried and in most cases executed. The remaining points of Nationalist resistance within Republican territory were therefore Oviedo, the Simancas Barracks at Gijón, the Alcázar and several isolated spots in Andalusia.

At the same time, the dividing line in Spain itself was being altered, in the south and in the north and north-east. The as yet few members of the Army of Africa, legionaries and *Regulares*, who had been transported across the Straits of Gibraltar, were enough to enlarge substantially the area dominated by General Queipo de Llano from Seville. Huelva, the whole of the southern coast from that port up to the Portuguese border, the once rich though now neglected land between Seville, Cádiz and Algeciras, and that between Seville and Córdoba, passed into Nationalist hands, after a series of rapid marches by officers and men trained in Moroccan wars.[1] Instead, therefore, of merely controlling in Andalusia a few cities where the rising had been successful, the Nationalists now held a compact territory striking a deep wound into the heart of the Revolutionary south. As yet Granada and several towns on the way to it were still beleaguered. But their relief did not seem distant. In all such towns or villages as were captured, the expected and bloody reprisals were immediately enacted as atonement for the revolutionary atrocities of the preceding days.

In the north, in the Basque province of Guipúzcoa, the line was also sensibly altered in favour of the Nationalists. Colonel Beorlegui advanced from Navarre, with 700 Carlists to take the village of Oyarzun, two miles south of the halfway point along the road from San Sebastián to the border town of Irún. The skill with which this Colonel altered the direction of fire of his small group gave the

---

[1] Huelva had fallen to the Nationalists after a delayed rising by the Civil Guard whose officers had first refused to lead an expedition against Seville.

impression to the Basques that they were being threatened by a large army. And so Oyarzun was not assaulted, being only occasionally bombarded by old 155 millimetre guns from the seaside fortress of Nuestra Señor de Guadalupe.

In Aragón, the revolutionary armies of Barcelona, Durruti and his Anarchist column in the lead, and Major Pérez Farras[1] in command, were still bursting westwards bringing fire and death to the villages and towns on the way to Saragossa and Huesca. In some of these, such as Caspe, the rising had at first been triumphant. But the fervour of the masses from Barcelona immediately brought revolution, varying according to the political complexion of the column, to the places they entered, whether or not they had to fight for them. Except at Caspe, where the Civil Guard under Captain Negrete held out for some hours against overwhelming odds, using the wives and children of members of the local trade unions as human barricades, the columns from Barcelona had not yet met any serious resistance.

Neither side in this unfolding conflict felt equipped to fight it successfully. On the Nationalist side, the Army of Africa constituted about 32,000 men, but of these half had to remain in Morocco to keep order.[2] The Nationalists could also rely on about two-thirds of the Civil Guard – about 22,000 in all – but only about 1,000 *Asaltos*. About two-thirds or approximately 40,000 of the rest of the Army were with the Nationalists, but of these the rank and file were unreliable conscripts, and they were therefore mostly used as garrison troops. Although only about 200 regular officers remained with the Republic out of 14,000, approximately 5,000 potentially rebel officers were captured on Republican territory.[3] The Carlist *Requetés* numbered 14,000 at the start of the Civil War. The Falangists probably disposed of about 50,000. Thousands of volunteers shortly rallied, however, to the *Requeté* and Falangist banner. Moroccan tribesmen were recruited, with the connivance of their Sultan, to reinforce the *Regulares*. On the Spanish mainland, recruiting bases were established in every town, promising pay at 3 pesetas a day. At these points, there were many working-class volunteers. Yet,

[1] This officer was known for his left-wing and separatist views. He had been named by Companys in command of the Catalan forces in 1934 for the abortive revolution of that year.

[2] *Enciclopedia Universal Ilustrada*, 1447.

[3] Serving Spanish officers in 1936 were 10,698. The remainder were officers retired by Azaña. The 8,000 NCOs rallied to the rebels almost to a man.

for the time being, the only strong units in the Nationalist Army were the Legion and the Moroccan troops. These were still nearly all in Africa, although three groups had got across to the mainland by sea and air. Further transportation by sea was dangerous, because of the revolution in the fleet. Aircraft were necessary – to carry the Army of Africa across the straits themselves and to protect any ships which might venture across. But Franco had only three old Breguets and one Fokker taken in Tetuán, some hydroplanes from Ceuta, a Dornier captured in Cádiz, and a Lufthansa Junkers commandeered in the Canaries.[1] Mola was similarly badly off. The Nationalist fleet only consisted of the old battleship *España*, the cruiser *Almirante Cervera*, the destroyer *Velasco* (all in El Ferrol), the gunboat *Dato* and some coastguard sloops.[2] Conscious of these deficiencies, as early as the evening of July 19, General Franco had decided to seek aid from abroad.[3]

The Government of the Republic, meantime, controlled the industrial regions around Bilbao and Barcelona, and – what Prieto at this time regarded as being proof of their ultimate victory – the Bank of Spain, with its sixth largest gold reserve in the world. They, also, however, suffered from an acute shortage of arms, as of trained men to use them. Aeroplanes, in particular, seemed to be the key to victory, and although the Government retained almost all the aircraft in the Spanish airforce, and over half its staff, this hardly constituted a fighting force. The Republican fleet, consisting of the battleship *Jaime Primero*, three cruisers, fifteen destroyers, and about ten submarines, was ill-managed and almost without officers.

Hence, the Republic also decided, independently of General Franco, though almost at the same moment, to seek arms abroad.

[1] To these were added in the next few days another Dornier and two small Savoia hydroplanes, from private sources (*Cruzada*, X 116).

[2] The *República*, a large cruiser renamed the *Navarra*, was too badly damaged in the fighting at Cádiz to be used again. The *Canarias* and *Baleares*, two new 20,000 ton cruisers, were still in construction at El Ferrol.

[3] *Cruzada*, X 118.

BOOK III
EUROPEAN EMBROILMENT

24

Reflections on Spain's relations with the rest of Europe

For many generations Spain had neither been feared as an enemy nor valued as a friend. The Spanish Army had required the aid of the French to finish the fifteen years war with the Riffs. The Spanish Air Force was not suspected of existence. As for the Navy, Sheridan's jest 'The Spanish fleet, thou canst not see, because – it is not yet in sight' was on the tip of the tongue of the British Permanent Under-Secretary at the Foreign Office, Sir Robert Vansittart.[1] If the Spanish Civil War became an international crisis, if both sides accused the other of causing a foreign invasion, if cries of 'we don't want foreigners here' were to ring out as battle slogans in the lonely valleys of Aragón, and if nearly every foreigner who has written of the war records some Spaniard on one side or the other wishing that the 'foreigners' would leave the Spaniards to fight their own battles, it should be clearly understood that it was Spaniards themselves who sought, even implored, aid from outside, and not the Powers of Europe who insisted on intervening.

Most of the political groups in Spain were more strongly attracted, because of their own country's weakness, towards other countries, than were comparable groups in other countries. This was true not only of persons on the Left, who admitted that their aims were to draw Spain closer to France, England, or Russia: but also on the Right, even those whose loudest cry was that they wished to preserve, or intensify, Spain's isolation from the rest of Europe. If Catholics saw an international plot in Freemasonry, Masons were equally justified in believing that those loyal to the Church of Rome were involved in as great a conspiracy directed by the true, as well as the black, Pope. The middle classes of Spain had strong commercial and financial connections with

---

[1] He quoted the line in his memoirs (p. 438) when mocking the promise given by Salvador de Madariaga, Spanish representative at the League of Nations (of which Spain had been throughout a conscientious member), to support collective security in the Abyssinian crisis of 1935.

other countries. An American company owned the Spanish telephone system. The British Rio Tinto Company owned almost all of Spain's large copper deposits. The Armstrong Company owned a third of Spanish cork. The waterworks of Seville were also British-owned.[1] The French controlled the silver mines at Peñarroya and the copper mines of San Plato. The Belgians had large holdings in Spanish timber, tramways and railways, and in the coal mines of Asturias. A Canadian company controlled the electricity of Catalonia.[2] These, the most important of many foreign investments, were extensive interests in a country as little developed as Spain. Then there was the Falange which, for all its nationalism, was certainly no more representative of the Spanish tradition than, say, the Anarchists. And, while there was undoubtedly a great increase in Russian literature and propaganda in Spain before the Civil War, there was also a comparable increase in information about Nazi Germany. The Nazi party had a strong following among the German colony in Spain, which numbered between 12,000 and 15,000.[3] The Spanish section of the German Labour Front had over 50 branches. German tourist offices and bookshops proliferated during the months before the Civil War, and close relations were reached between the Falangists and the local Nazi leaders. When so many ideas and 'solutions' to Spain's troubles were being canvassed, the example of Nazi Germany, the efficient and disciplined enemy of decadent, democratic France, exercised a powerful influence over the imaginations of young Spanish middle-class people.

Spain is in truth no more unique, biologically or intellectually, than any other country. Her differences from other nations have derived from her slow development as a nation. Spanish troubles have always been European troubles. All the Spanish civil wars have indeed been engagements in that general European civil war which has lasted since the Renaissance. Those Spaniards who seek to turn their national pride into a political ideology are idealising the preservation in Spain of certain aspects of pre-industrial European society, including a greater sense of personal dignity and an absence of material self-concern, but also a greater willingness to undertake violence, than exists elsewhere. The permanent

[1] In 1935, the United Kingdom took nearly 50% of Spanish exports (£11 million out of £23 million) and provided 17% of her imports.
[2] Ramos Oliveira, 258–61.
[3] GD, 483.

fossilation of such a society, even if possible, can only preserve the form, and not the vitality, of the society concerned.

In a broad sense the Spanish Civil War was primarily the result of general European ideas and movements upon Spain. After all, from the sixteenth century onwards, each of the leading political ideas of Europe has been received with enthusiasm by one group of Spaniards and opposed ferociously by another, without any desire to compromise being shown by either side: the universal Roman Catholicism of the Habsburgs, the absolutism of the Bourbons, French revolutionary liberalism, romantic and then commercial separatism, Socialism, Anarchism, Communism and Fascism: with the exception of the last-named, these concepts have all been imbued in Spain with the sharp contrast of light and shade which is the most remarkable attribute of the Spanish landscape and which is so marvellously reflected in the paintings of Ribera. The very sharpness with which these political ideas stand out from each other in Spain is peculiarly Spanish. No one has ever been more absolutist than the Spanish absolutists. The virtues and shortcomings of liberalism are nowhere better demonstrated than by the Spanish liberals. The Spanish Anarchists are the only Anarchists in European history to have made any mark upon events. Even in 1936, there were proponents of all the ideas named above in the Cortes (except the Anarchists, who boycotted the elections), and not excluding the first of them – although that point of view was four hundred years old. Spain has thus been a litmus paper by which the political ideas of Europe have been tested. And the advocates of each idea have desired to impose their own views exclusively, and to expel all others as brutally and as finally as the Moors and Jews were expelled in the sixteenth century. Each group has wished to emulate the nineteenth-century Spanish General Narváez, who, when asked on his deathbed if he forgave his enemies, replied: 'My enemies? I have none. I have had them all shot.'

It was perhaps inevitable, therefore, that the Spanish Civil War which began in 1936 should become a European crisis. As in the War of the Spanish Succession, the War of Independence and during the first Carlist War, the prestige, the wealth and, in some instances, the people of the rest of Europe became, during 1936 to 1939, intimately connected with the Spanish conflict. General European ideas had brought Spaniards to the pitch of war. European Great Powers became entangled in the war at the

Spaniards' request. The same Great Powers were then responsible for much of its course, above all for assisting one side or the other in the conflict when they seemed to be losing. Throughout the Civil War the alternate repugnance and attraction which the rest of Europe has always had for Spain, and Spain for the rest of Europe, was reflected in the diplomatic and other international implications of the fighting. The last campaign of the war, finally, was made possible by external assistance at the crucial moment.[1] This interpretation of the war may not be accepted by Spaniards, even of the losing side. But that is to be expected. Even a liberal Spaniard like Professor Altamira can write a history of Spain without mentioning the Duke of Wellington. Yet without the Duke of Wellington a Bonaparte might still be king in Madrid.[2]

[1] See below, page 566. A more detailed consideration of the total effect of the foreign intervention in the Civil War will be found on pages 611 fl and in Appendix III.

[2] The 3rd Duke of Wellington is alleged to have said that on a visit to Spain in 1912 to attend the centenary celebrations of the Peninsular War, he met no Spaniard who knew his grandfather had been in Spain at the time.

25

The Republic asks aid from France – Blum agrees – Franco sends for
help from Mussolini – the reactions to the war in Moscow – the re-
flections of Stalin – Togliatti, Duclos, Vidali, Gerö go to Spain –
Franco appeals to Hitler – Blum and Delbos go to London – Eden's
advice – the condition of England

On the night of July 19, Giral, the new Prime Minister of
the Republic, sent a telegram, *en clair*, to the Prime
Minister of France: 'Are surprised by a dangerous military *coup*. Beg of you to help us immediately with arms and
aeroplanes. Fraternally yours Giral.'[1] The extraordinary fact that
the Spanish Premier sought to communicate direct with his
French colleague is explained by the manner of signature. For
Giral, now leader of the Spanish Popular Front, it seemed probable that Léon Blum, head of a French Popular Front Government, was likely to be more sympathetic than the Spanish Ambassador in Paris, Cárdenas, a diplomat of the old school.[2]

Léon Blum, that passionate and sensitive Frenchman, had
been Prime Minister of France only since June 5, at the head of a
Ministry of Socialists and Radicals, which enjoyed the support of
the Communists. Like the Republican Government, it had been
formed as a result of a Popular Front electoral alliance. Though
pacifist in inclination and anxious to proceed with the redress of
social problems at home, Blum and his colleagues felt immediately
that the predicament of the Spanish Republic was supremely

---

[1] *Les Evénements Survenus*, 215. This was the account given of their tenure of office in
France by the politicians of the 'thirties to a parliamentary commission of enquiry in
1946. Vol 3 refers to Spain, and all future references to this work refer to that volume.
(The full title and description of this work are given in the Bibliography.) The relations of the French Popular Front with Spain were discussed by Blum and Cot,
his Air Minister. Their account was confirmed to Mr James Joll, by Oreste Rosenfeld,
one of Blum's secretaries, and present throughout these discussions.

[2] A later calculation suggested that only 3% of the diplomatic corps of Spain supported the Government. This brought semi-civil war to many Spanish Embassies and
legations abroad. In Rome the local Ambassador Zulueta was barricaded in by his
rebel Chancery. In the end, however, all countries respected diplomatic practice and
left diplomatic premises in Republican hands till they changed recognition.

important to them. For at this time in Paris, Lyons, and in all the cities of France there were incessant street clashes between Left and Right, between the Socialists or Communists and Fascist groups such as *La Croix du Feu* and *L'Action Française*. A Fascist *coup* often seemed near, even in France. This sympathy for the Republic was supported by strategic calculations, since a Nationalist Spain would probably be hostile to the French Popular Front, if not to France as such. When, therefore, Blum received Giral's telegram, on the morning of Tuesday July 20, he hastily summoned his Foreign Secretary, Yvon Delbos, and Edouard Daladier, his War Minister. Both these Ministers were Radicals. Yet although they might have been supposed likely to sympathise less with the Spanish Republic than the Socialist members of the Cabinet, the three men immediately agreed to send aid to Giral.[1]

The same day, July 20, General Franco sent Luis Bolín, in the *Dragon Rapide*, still piloted by Captain Bebb, to Biarritz, where he took aboard Luca de Tena, editor of the Monarchist paper *ABC*. He consulted the millionaire Juan March, whose financial support was especially important now that the rising had clearly turned into Civil War. Luca de Tena and Bolín flew on to Rome to approach the Italian Government for the supply of war material.[2] At the same time a Nationalist *communiqué* proudly announced that 'the interests of Spain are not alone at stake as our trumpet call sounds across the straits of Gibraltar'.[3]

The following day, Tuesday July 21, the first reaction to the Spanish crisis occurred in Moscow. A joint meeting was held of the Comintern and Profintern (the body set up to co-ordinate Communist activity in trade unions). There was strong support for the idea of aid to the Republic, and a new meeting was arranged for July 26 at Prague.[4]

The reaction of Stalin and the Soviet Government towards the outbreak of Spanish War (whatever part the Spanish Communists had played before) was dictated above all by the question of how it affected the current needs of Soviet foreign policy. If, as

---

[1] *Loc. cit.*   [2] *Cruzada*, X 126.
[3] *New York Times*, 21.7.36.
[4] This derives from *prima facie* probable Nationalist sources, deriving from documents allegedly discovered in Madrid after the end of the war. It may be seen in *Cruzada*, XXVIII 99. In addition, the information appeared in 1937 in *I accuse France*, a pamphlet published in London, by 'A Barrister'. The meeting has been confirmed by Albert Vassar, the German who was then a representative of the Comintern with the French Communist party.

in the case of China in 1926 (and perhaps in that of the Greek Communists in 1947), Communist opportunities would have to be sacrificed, then sacrificed they would be – with the long-time casuistical justification of the action that the aims of Communism could not be different from those of Russia. In Europe, the Soviet Government undoubtedly had a genuine fear of Nazi Germany. The Soviet *régime* was born out of three years of civil war, from 1917 to 1920, which had greatly marked the feelings of all Russians towards the prospect of war. Fears of a new conflict caused Russia to emerge from her isolation of the late 1920s to enter the League of Nations in 1934 and to conclude the pact with France in 1935. Litvinov, the Foreign Minister, had spoken eloquently in the League for collective security, including economic sanctions and military action, against breaches of the covenant – that is, against Germany, Italy and Japan.[1] A Nationalist victory in the Civil War in Spain would mean that France would be surrounded on three sides by potentially hostile countries. This would make it easier for Germany to attack Russia without being afraid of French attacks in her rear. For this tortuous reason, the Soviet Government had a strong interest in the prevention of a Nationalist victory.

The Spanish War also afforded to the Spanish Communist party, with its discipline, its skill at propaganda, and its prestige deriving from its connection with Russia, a great chance to secure in Spain the establishment of the second Communist State.[2] But such a Communist victory would have alarmed Britain and France, the two powers to whom, for diplomatic reasons, Russia wished to draw closer. It might even make a general war more likely. It might waste Russian war material. For these reasons, Stalin probably did not send orders to the Spanish Communist party, and his chief agents there, Codovilla and Stepanov, to make full use of their opportunity to gain control of the Spanish Republic. Nor did he send arms to Spain.

[1] The interpretation that the whole aim of the Soviet Popular Front policy was to enable the Communist parties to move from the extreme Left of the political spectrum to the Centre and then to conclude an alliance with the Right and the Fascists, the process being completed by the Nazi-Soviet pact of 1939, has been rejected. Stalin no doubt kept the idea of an arrangement with Germany in the back of his mind if Litvinov failed to secure an effective alliance with Britain and France. See below, page 342 for proof of this.

[2] This assumes that the Communists' *rôle* in bringing war was small – i.e. a clever word at an appropriate moment on the night Calvo Sotelo died, a word of encouragement to Largo Caballero on the path of revolution.

Yet the fact that he was about to embark upon a new stage of the purge of the old Bolsheviks must have caused the Russian dictator to listen with unusual attention to the leaders of the Comintern at this time. And they must have had their own feelings as to what should be the Communist reaction to the war in Spain. At the very least, they could hardly help seeing in Spanish events an opportunity to reassert themselves. They could point out to Stalin how, while he dithered, the followers of Trotsky were already naming him 'liquidator and traitor of the Spanish Revolution, abettor of Hitler and Mussolini'. With crablike caution, therefore, Stalin seems to have reached one conclusion, and one conclusion only, about Spain: he would not permit the Republic to lose, even though he would not help it to win. The mere continuance of the war would keep him free to act in any way. It might even make possible a world war in which France, Britain, Germany and Italy would destroy themselves, with Russia, the arbiter, staying outside.[1] Thus the Soviet Government would support the agitation for aid to Spain, for the time being only in food and raw materials, and ensure that Russian factory workers made a 'contribution' from their wages for Spanish relief. At the same time, the Comintern representatives in Spain would be reinforced. The able and ruthless leader of the Italian Communist party in exile, Togliatti, thus went to Spain using the names 'Alfredo' and 'Ercoli' as the director of the tactics of the Spanish Communist party.[2] He was for a while accompanied by the French Communist, Jacques Duclos. Vittorio Vidali, another Italian Communist, who had known years of revolutionary activity in the United States, arrived in Spain to act (under the *nom-de-guerre* 'Carlos Contreras') as military adviser of the Spanish Communist militiamen. One more Communist

[1] This motive would certainly explain why Russia, and French Communists, were so anxious that France would be drawn into the war on the side of the Republic. Some support is given to this interpretation of Stalin's policy by Litvinov's reply to a question put by the French Government (about the end of July, presumably) as to what the Russian reaction would be to a general war arising from French intervention. While he admitted that the Franco-Soviet pact would impel Russian help to France if the latter were attacked by a third power, 'it would be quite a different matter if war were to come as a result of the intervention of one of our countries in the affairs of a third'. (Statement made by Jules Moch, then Sub-Secretary of State to Blum, to Señor Julián Gorkin.)

[2] Togliatti's biographers, Marcella and Maurice Ferrara, say that Togliatti did not reach Spain until June 1937. Hernández, on the other hand, speaks of him as well established by August 1936. It is probable that in fact he was merely a visitor to Spain (possibly at times for long stretches) during 1936 and the first half of 1937.

international leader who shortly went to Spain was the sinister Hungarian, Ernö Gerö, who had worked for many years in Paris under the name of 'Singer' and who now appeared as 'Pedro' or 'Gueré'. He was responsible for the guidance of the Communists in Catalonia. Stepanov and Codovilla, the two Comintern representatives who had been in Spain for some time, remained. Thus, henceforward, Stalin was most ably represented in Spain. And the Spanish Communist party was guided not by José Díaz or La Pasionaria but by the far more skilful political tactician, Togliatti.[1] Meantime, the Propaganda Department of the Western European section of the Comintern, under its brilliant German Communist chief, Willi Muenzenberg, was ferociously active from its headquarters in Paris in linking the cause of the Spanish Republic with the general anti-Fascist crusade, which had been begun when the Soviet Government had adopted the twin policies of the Popular Front and Collective Security.[2] Although from the outside, the policy enshrined in these powerful personalities seems monolithic and overwhelming, it should be understood that many of the minor cogs in the great Communist organisation of this time had ideas and views of their own, which they personally pursued. Men like Gerö, however, were Stalinist bureaucrats. For this reason, it would be an unjustifiable simplification to speak *tout court* of a Communist policy in Spain.

While these matters were being haltingly mooted in Moscow, Franco's agents, Bolín and Luca de Tena reached Rome, in the evening of July 22. They immediately saw Count Ciano, the Italian Foreign Minister. Four years later, Ciano told Hitler that Franco had said that twelve transport aircraft would enable him to win the war in a few days .[3] To Franco's first emissaries Ciano showed interest and asked about the nature of the Nationalist movement, but did no more. It was not clear to the Italian

[1] Jesús Hernández, *Yo, Ministro de Stalin en España*, 33 fl. This unpleasant work of the leading Communist renegade from Spain is the best source of Communist policy in Spain. See also, for Togliatti in Spain, Einaudi, 192.

[2] Koestler, *Invisible Writing*, 313, 198. Muenzenberg previously known as the 'Red Hearst' of Germany, was a journalistic genius. Son of a carpenter, he would have allied himself with the devil to gain money or support. With his gift for gathering duchesses, bankers and Generals, as well as intellectuals, in support of one or other of his causes, he really invented the fellow-traveller. His assistant in Paris was Otto Katz, *alias* Simone, a Czech who was also his guard. By July 1936, Muenzenberg was already beginning to quarrel with his bosses in Moscow, who found him too independent. When he broke with the party in the winter of 1936–7, much of the vitality went out of the Comintern propaganda department.

[3] Hitler's interview with Ciano at Brenner, September 1940. *GD*, 993.

Government what connection Franco had with the Monarchist plotters to whom Mussolini had pledged, and already given, help in 1934.[1] Apparently also Franco did not know of the details of that arrangement. It was not until Mola sent Goicoechea, the central figure in the events of 1934, to Rome on July 24, that the Italians agreed to furnish aid to the Spanish rebels.[2] But, also on July 22, Franco made his first approach to Germany for help. On his behalf, Colonel Beigbeder, who had installed himself in the Department of Native Affairs at Tetuán, sent a 'very urgent request' to General Kuhlenthal, German Military *Attaché* in Paris, for 'ten transport aircraft with maximum seating capacity' to be purchased through German private firms and brought by German pilots to Spanish Morocco.[3] In the evening of the same day, a Nationalist Air Force officer, Captain Francisco Arranz, accompanied by Adolf Langenheim, head of the Nazi party in Tetuán, and Johannes Bernhardt, a German businessman in Tetuán and director in Morocco of the economic branch of the *Auslandorganisation* (the foreign department of the Nazi party) set off with a private letter to Hitler to support Beigbeder's request. They travelled in a Junkers requisitioned from the *Lufthansa* at Las Palmas.[4] Bernhardt was an ex-sugar merchant from Hamburg who had left that city under a financial cloud. In Tetuán he was employed in a company which sold kitchen stoves to the Spanish garrison. He had in this way made friends in the officers' mess. Both he and Langenheim saw possibilities of personal advantage in the sale of German raw materials to the rebels.

Meantime in Paris, the Spanish Ambassador, Cárdenas, visited Léon Blum and on behalf of Giral made a request for 20 Potez bombers, 8 light machine-guns, 8 Schneider cannons, 250,000 machine gun bullets, 4 million cartridges, and 20,000 bombs. The export to Spain of these items would require licences from the French Government, and, since the French arms industries had been nationalised, the purchase itself, though technically private, would in effect need the approval of the French Cabinet. Now, almost at the same time as this was agreed, a telephone call was received in the Quai d'Orsay from Corbin, the French

---

[1] See above, page 76.   [2] *Cruzada*, X 126.   [3] *GD*, 4.
[4] *Cruzada*, X 127. Cf footnote to *GD*, 1. Mola also apparently sent an agent to Berlin. The Germans could not believe that Franco's and Mola's emissaries did not know each other and later instructed Arranz to repair to a particular café where Mola's man was also sitting. Only when the two Spaniards showed no sign of recognising each other did they believe the lack of co-ordination between North and South in Spain.

Ambassador in London. Personally of the extreme Right, Corbin was so faithful an interpreter of English wishes (especially to the Government of the Popular Front) that he was known as 'English Ambassador in London'. The British Government, as a result of telegrams received from their Ambassador in Paris, was alarmed about the French reaction to the Spanish crisis. A meeting had previously been arranged in London for July 23 and 24 between the British, French and Belgian Foreign Ministers to discuss a possible approach to Hitler and Mussolini for a new five-power treaty of collective security. Baldwin, through Corbin, urged Blum to accompany his Foreign Secretary, Delbos, to discuss Spain with Baldwin and Eden. On the advice of Alexis Léger, the Martiniquais Secretary-General of the Quai d'Orsay (now known as the Nobel prize-winning poet St Jean Perse, author of *Anabasis*), Blum agreed.[1] For Léger's *cauchemar* (a favourite diplomatic word of the time) was that Baldwin's Britain might turn away from a left-wing France to join Germany.[2] At the same time, Cárdenas, the Spanish Ambassador resigned (because of his Nationalist sympathies) leaving two Spanish Air Force officers to conduct the details of the arms transaction, until Fernando de los Ríos, a Republican ex-Minister, arrived from Geneva the next day to take charge from them.

On July 23, the conference in London began in the morning. Blum arrived in time for luncheon. In the hall of Claridge's hotel, Eden asked: 'Are you going to send arms to the Spanish Republic?' 'Yes,' said Blum. 'It is your affair,' Eden replied, 'but I ask you one thing. Be prudent.'[3]

Now this advice by Eden reflected accurately the profound desire for peace felt by the British Cabinet and the British people at this time. The leader of the Opposition, Major Attlee, might already have voiced the sympathies of the Labour party and the English working class for their Spanish comrades, in a resolution on July 20 pledging 'all practicable support'; and large sections of the English middle and upper classes might openly favour the Nationalists; nevertheless, there was no politician in England pre-pared to argue that the country should actually involve itself on one side or another in the conflict. The question was, what kind of

[1] United States Foreign Policy (*State Department Papers*, henceforward referred to as *USD*), 1936 Vol 2 447–9. The same story appears in Cordell Hull's *Memoirs*, 476.
[2] See *The Diplomats*, a symposium edited by Gordon Craig and Felix Gilbert. Here, there is an interesting essay on the diplomacy of Léger, 38.
[3] *Les Evénements Survenus*, 216–17.

neutrality should be observed. The Labour party at first believed that neutrality signified that the Republic should be allowed to purchase arms, from Britain as from elsewhere. Here they were in disagreement with the Conservative critics of the Government, such as Winston Churchill, who, though opposed to Germany and Italy as much as the Opposition (for traditional not ideological reasons), did not believe that the Spanish conflict had any significance (not even strategic) for Britain. Churchill himself was alarmed by the revolutionary character of the Republic, and personally wrote a few days later to Corbin, the French Ambassador, to protest against French aid to the Republic, and to urge 'an absolutely rigid neutrality'.[1] Eden at the Foreign Office also attempted to secure this policy, both for Britain and for France. The supposition of the British Government was that the German re-militarisation of the Rhineland in February and the Italian conquest of Abyssinia had satiated the dictators, who could now be induced to help create a new European order.[2] In this design, the outbreak of 'the Spanish crisis' was, above all, an unwelcome interruption for Baldwin's Government.

Meanwhile, the British Ambassador to Spain, Sir Henry Chilton, had set up the British Embassy to Spain in a grocer's shop at Hendaye, on the French side of the International Bridge.[3] He was an unimaginative type of diplomat, very much of the old school: his American colleague, Claude Bowers, who was admittedly very Republican in his sympathies, reported to Washington that everything Chilton did was 'intended to cripple the Government and serve the insurgents'.[4]

English public opinion meantime was as inflamed by the

---

[1] Churchill, *The Gathering Storm*, 168. Churchill made his attitude very clear to the Republican Ambassador in London, Azcárate, in October. On being presented to Azcárate by Lord Robert Cecil, Churchill turned red with anger, muttered 'Blood, blood, blood', and refused the Spaniard's outstretched hand. In 1938 Churchill's attitude to the Republic entirely changed. (Azcárate, 4.) See below, page 531.

[2] As for the staffing of the Western and League of Nations Department in the Foreign Office, the official at the Spanish desk was Mr (now Sir) Evelyn Shuckburgh. The other members of that department included at that time, Mr (now Sir Roger) Makins, and Mr Donald MacLean.

[3] The chief member of the diplomatic corps had already left Madrid for the summer capital of San Sebastián before the rising. By July 22 they were all established, safe and sound (after several adventures), in St Jean de Luz, the other side of the French frontier. The Embassies in Madrid were in the hands of junior members of the diplomatic staff, or of Consuls, while the Ambassadors were out of harm's way. There was, at this time, no German Ambassador to Spain – none being appointed since Count Welczeck had left for Paris in April.

[4] *USD*, 1937 Vol 1 224.

Spanish War as it had once been by the French Revolution. This was, of course, a time of high political consciousness. In the early spring, the first issue of *New Writing* had appeared. This publication announced that it did not 'intend to open its pages to writers of reactionary or Fascist sentiments'.[1] The Left Book Club, which set out to publish a book each month against Fascism and War, had begun in May. This had been followed by the Right Book Club. Such literary commitment to politics was the reflection of the heavy social problems as well as of general moral or international alarms caused by the lure of Russia, the decline of religion, 'the breakdown of standards', the rise of Hitler. The hunger march, the means test, the unemployed, were the characteristics of the age as much as the Peace Ballot, to which over eleven million had already subscribed. The official Labour opposition to Mr Baldwin's Government seemed ineffective. Able leaders such as Churchill and Lloyd George glowered in the political wilderness. The time was to be perfectly expressed by W. H. Auden in his poem 'Spain 1937':

> *Tomorrow for the young the poets exploding like bombs,*
> *The walks by the lake, the weeks of perfect communion;*
> > *Tomorrow the bicycle races*
> *Through the suburbs on summer evenings. But today the*
> *struggle.*

Another verse of the same poem now became apposite:

> *'What's your proposal? To build the just city? I will.*
> *I agree. Or is it the suicide pact, the romantic*
> > *Death? Very well, I accept, for,*
> *I am your choice, your decision. Yes, I am Spain.'*

Among intellectuals of the Left, Spain became immediately the central point of life, work and artistic inspiration. Stephen Spender wrote that Spain 'offered the twentieth century an 1848'.[2] Philip Toynbee, an undergraduate member of the Communist party, recalled how the news of the Spanish War caused him to think that at last 'the gloves were off in the struggle against Fascism'.[3] Rex Warner, also a Republican sympathiser, wrote 'Spain has torn the veil of Europe'. Among intellectuals, there

---

[1] Lehmann, 236.   [2] Spender, *World within World*, 187.
[3] Toynbee, *Friends Apart*, 85.

was no difficulty whatever in deciding which side in the war was 'right'.[1]

But society in general was divided: the *Morning Post, Daily Mail, Daily Sketch* and *Observer* supported the Nationalists and the *News Chronicle, Daily Herald, Manchester Guardian, Daily Express* and *Daily Mirror* were generally Republican. *The Times* and *Daily Telegraph* tried to be impartial.[2]

[1] In 1937 the periodical *Left Wing* took a reasonably fair poll of English writers and asked them which side they 'backed'. Only five – among them Evelyn Waugh, Eleanor Smith and Edmund Blunden – were for the Nationalists. Ruby Ayres, Norman Douglas, T. S. Eliot ('I still feel convinced that it is best that at least a few men of letters should remain isolated and take no part in these collective activities'), Charles Morgan, Ezra Pound, Alec Waugh, Sean O'Faolain, H. G. Wells and Vita Sackville-West were among the 16 who were neutral. The remaining hundred writers committed themselves, many in passionate terms, in favour of the Republic. These included Lascelles Abercrombie, W. H. Auden ('The struggle in Spain has X-rayed the lies upon which our civilisation is built'), George Barker, Samuel Beckett (who commented simply, in capitals, in the well-loved style of *Godot*, 'UPTHEREPUBLIC!'), Norman Collins, Cyril Connolly ('Intellectuals come first, almost before women and children') Alastair Crowley, Havelock Ellis, Ford Madox Ford, David Garnett, Louis Golding, Lancelot Hogben, Laurence Housman, Brian Howard, Aldous Huxley, Storm Jameson, Dr C. E. M. Joad, Professor Laski, John and Rosamond Lehmann, C. Day Lewis, Eric Linklater, F. L. Lucas, Rose Macaulay, A. G. Macdonnel, Louis MacNeice, Ethel Mannin, Francis Meynell, Naomi Mitchison, Raymond Mortimer, John Middleton Murry, Sean O'Casey, V. S. Pritchett, Herbert Read, Edward Sackville-West, Stephen Spender, James Stephens, Sylvia Townsend Warner, Rebecca West and Antonia White.

[2] *Punch* hailed the Civil War on July 29 with one of Sir Bernard Partridge's inimitable cartoons: a guitarist named 'Revolution' appears at the window of a sad woman in a Seville-like street. 'What, you again?' says she. The assumption was clearly that the Left had begun the war. On August 12, Sir Bernard appeared rather less partisan. Against a background of burning cities, the damsel 'Spain' is fought over by two bandits, Communism and Fascism. The former's head is tied in a kerchief. The latter wears a big black hat. A more urgent or contemporary note was struck by Low's 'Turkish Bath' cartoon of July 29 in the *Evening Standard*. Under the headline 'Revolution at our Turkish Bath: Blimps Rise', the inimitable Colonel Blimp was depicted broadcasting a proclamation from the Hot Room.

26

Blum returns to Paris – de los Ríos – 'Ah je t'en prie, mon petit, ne vas pas te fourrer là-dedans' – the anguish of Blum – the compromise – Mussolini sends Savoias to Franco – his motives – the diplomacy of Count Ciano – Franco's emissaries in Bayreuth – German aid agreed – its purposes – its organisation – Salazar – Willi Muenzenberg at work – reactions across the Atlantic – Roosevelt and Hull – the Italians crash – stormy meeting at the French Cabinet – a strange request from Madrid

While Eden and Blum were consulting together in London, Fernando de los Ríos, the new Republican representative in Paris, visited Daladier, the War Minister, Pierre Cot, the Air Minister, and Jules Moch, Under-Secretary of Blum's Cabinet. The French undertook to supply pilots to fly the Potez aircraft to Spain. However, 'a member of the French Cabinet' (a Radical without doubt) told Count Welczeck, German Ambassador in Paris[1] that France was preparing to supply to the Spanish Republic 'approximately thirty bombers, several thousand bombs and a considerable number of 75 mm. guns.'[2] Welczeck told this news to Dieckhoff, acting head of the German Foreign Office. Dieckhoff, a solemn career diplomat, told the German Embassy in London to take up this matter with Eden.[3] Despite this, Dieckhoff now informed the German War Ministry that he thought the idea of helping Franco (Beigbeder's request for arms had by then arrived) 'out of the question'.[4] The German Foreign Ministry in fact reacted to the Spanish crisis precisely as did the British. Aid to either combatant would increase the danger of general war. Meantime, Franco's personal messengers to Hitler had got no further than Seville, where they were delayed by engine trouble.[5]

During the evening of July 24, Léon Blum and Delbos returned

---

[1] Welczeck had been Ambassador in Madrid until the preceding April. He had been a friend of King Alfonso, a noted huntsman and a tireless man of the world. He was anti-Nazi.

[2] *GD*, 4.   [3] *Loc. cit*, fn.   [4] *Op. cit.*, 7.   [5] *Cruzada*, X 127.

to Paris. Waiting to meet them at Le Bourget was the silky Radical, Chautemps. He explained that in Blum's absence the news of the Government's decision to aid the Spanish Republic had leaked out to the right-wing publicist, Henry Kerillis, through the Spanish Military *Attaché* in Paris, Antonio Barroso, a convinced supporter of the rebels. Kerillis had already denounced the plan in the columns of *L'Écho de Paris*. 'No one can understand,' said Chautemps, 'why we are going to risk war on the behalf of Spain when we did not do so over the Rhineland.'[1] In fact, a Radical revolt against the idea of aid to Spain had now begun. Both the first rumblings of this and Eden's words were in Blum's ears when at ten that night, he saw de los Ríos, together with Daladier (Minister of War), Pierre Cot, Vincent Auriol (Minister of Finance) and Delbos.[2] De los Ríos pointed out to Blum (just as Franco was pointing out to the Germans) that the Civil War 'could not be looked upon as strictly national' because of Spain's strategic relationship to Italy and Morocco. Now Blum was still passionately in favour of helping the Republic. The contracts for the supply of aircraft were ready. But he did not want to act in the face of Eden's warnings. So he asked de los Ríos whether Spanish pilots could fly the aeroplanes to Spain? This at least would be a compromise. De los Ríos said that the scarcity of Spanish pilots would make this impossible. Anyway, his Government had wanted to retain the French pilots in their service. At this point, Daladier recalled a Franco-Spanish treaty of 1935 – signed for Spain by the then Minister of Commerce, Martínez de Velasco, at that time in the Model Prison in Madrid. A secret clause of this convention had provided that Spain would buy 20 million francs' worth of war material from France. De los Ríos and Blum agreed that the shipments of aircraft and other material should be made under this clause. De los Ríos then went to bed. Blum gave his colleagues an account of the conversations in London, and in particular of the reaction of the British Government to the Spanish War. Alone of the French Ministers, the Radical Delbos was hesitant about helping the Spanish Republic. Later, de los Ríos was roused by Pierre Cot, who telephoned him to come immediately

---

[1] *Les Evénements Survenus*, 217.

[2] The following is based on a letter from de los Ríos to Giral, a copy of which was apparently stolen from the house of Rivas Cherif in Geneva, and published in all Nationalist apologias on the war. Its genuineness is admitted by Republicans and is borne out by other evidence, e.g. Cot and *Les Evénements Survenus*. The letter may be easily seen in Foss and Geraghty, 372–6.

to see him at his house. He did so, and Cot told him that Delbos could not be convinced that French pilots could take the aircraft to Spain. Cot therefore suggested that the French pilots should fly them to Perpignan, thence to be transported by Spaniards.

The next morning, July 25, de los Ríos visited the French Air Ministry. All seemed favourable for the immediate shipment. But, in the meantime, Castillo, the Counsellor at the Spanish Embassy, refused to sign the papers providing for the shipment. Barroso, the Military *Attaché*, refused to sign the cheque paying for it. Both these men now resigned, on the ground that they would not be a party to the purchase of arms for use against their own people. They informed the Press of what they were doing. The uproar was immediate. All the French evening papers, especially *L'Écho de Paris*, published sensational accounts of the 'arms traffic'. Lebrun, the President, became alarmed and warned Blum that he was leading France to war. Herriot, already a veteran ex-Prime Minister and speaker of the Chamber of Deputies, did the same: *'Ah je t'en prie, mon petit, je t'en prie, ne vas pas te fourrer là-dedans'*![1] The Prime Minister was torn between his pacifism and his desire to help the Republic. Never has the dilemma of the intellectual in politics been more cruelly posed. At four in the afternoon, the French Cabinet met. Daladier and Delbos were the spokesmen for a refusal to Spain, Cot for acceptance. Eventually, a compromise was reached. The Government announced in a *communiqué* that it would refuse the Spanish Government's request for arms. But the shipment would be in fact effected through Mexico. Nor would hindrances be placed in the way of private transactions. During the day, £140,000 in gold from the Spanish gold reserve arrived at Le Bourget as guarantee for the payment. Cot, the Air Minister, remained the chief organiser of these transactions. The Byron of the age, André Malraux, then close to the Communists (though he never was a party member) acted as buyer on behalf of the Republican Government.[2] Henceforward, the Spanish Embassy in Paris was a veritable *caravanserai* where at all hours of the day and during many of the night individuals of every nationality came in and out offering all classes of arms, munitions and aircraft, at all prices.[3]

[1] *Les Evénements Survenus*, 217.
[2] Malraux had become world famous in 1934 with the publication of his masterpiece, *La Condition Humaine*.
[3] Azcárate, 20. The effect of French Non-Intervention caused deep fissures and quarrels throughout the Second International, of which the French Socialist party was

Meanwhile, in Rome on the morning of July 25, Ciano saw Goicoechea, accompanied by Sainz Rodríguez. The connection between the plotters of 1934 and the rebels of 1936 was satisfactorily explained.[1] Mussolini and Ciano immediately arranged to send aid, especially transport aircraft. Eleven Savoia 81 were to be flown to Morocco by Italians, in the next few days.[2]

The motives of Mussolini in acting in this way were mixed. He was flattered to be asked. He aspired to dominate the Mediterranean, and he supposed that this ambition would be assisted by the establishment in Spain of a right-wing Government inspired by semi-Fascist ideas. Such a 'new Spain' would perhaps draw off French troops from the Italian border and, in the event of a Franco-Italian war, prevent the passage of French troops in Morocco to France. The triumphant conquest of Abyssinia in April had left Mussolini both anxious to display his personality in some new way, and without any obvious place in which to do it. The Italians, he reflected, have to be 'kept up to the mark by kicks on the shins.' 'When the war in Spain is over,' he was to remark, 'I shall have to find something else: the Italian character has to be formed through fighting.'[3] The public reason for Italian intervention, repeated *ad nauseam* by Italian diplomats during the Civil War, was that Italy was 'not prepared to see the establishment of a Communist State' in Spain. This was the explanation for intervention which Mussolini gave to his wife Rachele.[4] It also probably became a real fear once his aid had started. Although, before July 1936, his propaganda had been more directed against the 'decadent' democracies of France and Britain than Communism, an even moderately left-wing Government in Spain

---

one of the leaders. The split in, for example, the Belgian Socialist party (which at this time had a share in the Government of Belgium) lasted until 1940.

[1] *Cruzada*, X 126. But Attilío Tamaro (Vol III 200) says that Mussolini refused to send aid when twice asked by Franco and only agreed when he heard that Blum was helping the Republic. This was probably a factor but not the decisive one. Cantalupo also mentions three requests of which only the third was successful.

[2] Two of these later crashed (see page 233). And it was alleged by the French officials who investigated the crash that one of the dead Italian pilots had received flying orders on July 15. Apart from Mussolini's pledge and aid in 1934, there is no other evidence of Italian aid before the rising; the papers on the dead pilot either contain a misprint, perhaps for July 25; or the pilot simply returned *from leave* on July 15. Since the planes did not leave Sardinia for Morocco till July 30, and since Franco had needed them from July 19 onwards, it is inconceivable that they were, as alleged, arranged before the rising.

[3] Monelli, 141.   [4] Rachele Mussolini, 91.

would be hostile to his designs. But it was still possible that the Duce might draw closer to the *bourgeois* objects of his particular scorn than to Germany. His relations with Hitler were at this stage still devious, undefined and exploratory. Here, as in his attacks upon Communism, the Spanish crisis forced a change. Spain was to make Hitler and Mussolini allies. Later, Ciano told Cantalupo, his first Ambassador in Nationalist Spain, that the Duce had only 'very reluctantly agreed to lend Franco military support'.[1] And the King, Victor Emmanuel, opposed the idea of large scale aid. Ciano, however, was most enthusiastic for it.[2]

The diplomacy of Ciano, who played an important part in subsequent events, was violently anti-British without the fascination mixed with the hatred felt for Britain by Ribbentrop and even by Mussolini. When three Falangists described to him how all Spanish miseries, since the reign of Philip II, had been caused by England, Ciano encouraged them 'on this wise path', warning of 'the dangerous Anglomania of certain old stagers of diplomacy.'[3] His task during the Spanish War was made easier by the desire of the British Government to achieve an Italian alliance. This increased Ciano's scorn for England, though he always got on well with Lord Perth, the Roman Catholic convert and ex-Secretary-General of the League who was Ambassador to Rome and who so far exceeded his Government's instructions as to show himself to Ciano as 'a man who has come to understand, even to love Fascism.'[4] Throughout this time an Italian spy in the domestic service of Perth gained possession of all British telegrams between Rome and England by the simple device of fitting a removable false back to the Ambassador's private safe. Ciano was thus able to act with unusual freedom in his relations with Britain, so much so that eventually the British realised that there must be a security leak. Perth pooh-poohed the suggestion that it could be in Rome. He was only convinced that it must have been when, on the occasion of the wedding of his daughter, his wife's tiara was placed overnight in the diplomatic safe, among the telegrams. It had vanished by the morning.[5]

Also on July 25 Franco's emissaries from Tetuán, Captain Arranz, Bernhardt and Langenheim at last arrived at Berlin.[6]

---

[1] Cantalupo, 62.   [2] Attilio Tamaro, *loc. cit.*   [3] Ciano, *Diary 1937–8*, 48.
[4] Ciano, *Diary 1937–8*, 206.   [5] Vansittart, 516.
[6] The following account is based on *Cruzada*, X 127, which is substantiated by the German sources available and which are indicated at appropriate points. The account given in the footnote to GD, 2 confirms that in *Cruzada*.

Franco's letter was sent to Hitler through the foreign department of the Nazi party. In the afternoon, at the Foreign Ministry, both Dieckhoff, the acting head of the Foreign Ministry, and Neurath, the Foreign Minister, repeated to their own satisfaction that deliveries of arms to aid the Nationalists in Spain were impossible, since they would become known, and since 'there would be serious consequences to the German colony in Spain.'[1] However, both the Nazi party and Admiral Canaris, head of the Military Intelligence, had other ideas. Canaris immediately recommended[2] Franco to his superiors as a 'tested man' who 'deserved full trust and support', and whom he had met several times on surreptitious visits to Spain.[3]

Goering, chief of the Luftwaffe and of the German five year plan, gave an account of what happened next at his trial at Nuremberg in 1946. 'When the Civil War broke out in Spain,' said the Reichmarshal, 'Franco sent a call for help to Germany and asked for support, particularly in the air. Franco with his troops was stationed in Africa and . . . he could not get his troops across, as the fleet was in the hands of the Communists . . . the decisive factor was, first of all, to get his troops to Spain . . . the Fuehrer thought the matter over. I urged him to give support under all circumstances: firstly, to prevent the further spread of Communism; secondly, to test my young Luftwaffe in this or that technical respect.'[4]

Hitler undertook to see Langenheim and Bernhardt on the evening of July 26, at Bayreuth. The Fuehrer had been made receptive by a performance of *Die Valküre*. Without consulting the Foreign Minister, German support for Franco was agreed.[5]

Hitler later explained to his *entourage* that he helped Franco so as 'to distract the attention of the western powers to Spain, and so enable German rearmament to continue unobserved.'[6] But in 1941 Hitler said: 'If there had not been the danger of the Red Peril's overwhelming Europe, I'd not have intervened in the Revolution in Spain. The Church would have been destroyed,' he added with relish.[7] He gave this as a reason for intervention to Ribbentrop

---

[1] *GD*, 10–11.

[2] No doubt it was for these services in particular that Franco later granted asylum and a pension to Frau Canaris after her husband's disgrace and death in 1944. Mr Ian Colvin says also that in 1940 Canaris advised Franco from his private knowledge as to the best way to resist Hitler's demands that Spain enter the War. (Colvin, 130.)

[3] Abshagen, 112.   [4] *Nuremberg Trials*, IX 280–1.

[5] *Cruzada, loc. cit.*   [6] Liddell Hart, *The Other Side of the Hill*, 34.

[7] *Tabletalk*, 320.

on July 27, 1936.[1] The Fuehrer also said in 1936 that a Nationalist success in Spain would establish a Fascist power 'athwart the sea communications of Britain and France' – so adding a strategic reason for intervention.[2] In 1937, the Fuehrer gave yet another explanation: Germany needed Spanish iron ore, and a Nationalist government would make this available to Germany, whereas a left-wing one would not.[3] This reason was probably urged by Bernhardt at the meeting on July 26. No doubt the true motives of the German Government derive from a mixture of these reasons. Canaris, recalling his experience of the first World War, probably argued that German submarines could not refuel in war if the Spanish bases were in democractic or left-wing hands. Hitler, like Mussolini, was certainly pleased to be asked so deferentially for help by Franco, and treated by another country, for the first time since he came to power three years before, as if he were indispensable. The part played by Bernhardt and Langenheim shows that the policy followed was that of the Nazi party and not that of the Foreign Ministry. Yet there is no sign that even the Nazis desired to set up in Spain a State comparable to that of Nazi Germany in social structure. Like Canaris, they wanted a military, not an ideological, ally.

After the meeting at Bayreuth on July 26, a department in the German War Ministry, COS 'W', was named to superintend the recruitment of 'volunteers' and the despatch of war material. Two holding companies were set up through which all material from Germany to Spain would be sent, along with all payment or Spanish raw materials sent in exchange. These companies were HISMA (*Compañia Hispano-Marroquí de Transportes*) and ROWAK (*Rohstoffe-und-Waren-Einkaufsgesellschaft*). If a German trader wished to sell anything to Spain, he would have to sell it first to ROWAK while HISMA would market it in Spain. A fleet of ships was assembled, and the navy instructed to provide protection. Thirty Junkers 52 transport aircraft were immediately sent to Morocco.[4] At the same time a 'tourist group' (*Reisegesellschafts-union*) was set up under General von Scheele to send volunteers to man these units and to form a training contingent for the Spanish Army. Eighty-five men left Hamburg for Cádiz on July 31 with six

---

[1] Ribbentrop, 59.   [2] Liddel Hart, *loc. cit.*
[3] See below, page 459.
[4] Evidence of General Warlimont, submitted to US Army Intelligence, 1945. (*UN Security Council Report on Spain*, 1946.)

Heinkel fighters. They arrived on August 5.[1] These were followed by engineers, other technicians and some more fighters. In September, more fighters were despatched, with two tank companies, a battery of anti-aircraft guns and some reconnaissance aircraft. Scheele later became the military head of HISMA, Bernhardt, the general manager at Seville, and Colonel von Thoma, commander of the ground troops and tanks. Von Thoma and his officers set out partly to train the Spaniards, partly to gain battle experience themselves. He found, he says, the Spaniards quick to learn – and quick to forget.[2] Henceforward four transport aircraft were despatched to Spain from Germany each week. Cargo boats were sent on an average every five days.[3]

All the above mentioned German officers were appointed, and this elaborate organisation was set up, within a week of the request made to Hitler by Franco through the two Moroccan Nazis. The German Foreign Ministry was taken by surprise. On July 28, Dumont, at the Spanish desk, once again minuted that the Ministry was against aid.[4] This view was shared by the War Minister, Field Marshal von Blomberg, and General von Fritsch, the Chief of Staff. They thought 'Operation Magic Fire', as it was named, militarily wasteful. Ribbentrop, Hitler's special adviser on foreign affairs, shared these doubts.[5] Both the German Foreign and Economics ministries were kept in the dark about HISMA and ROWAK until mid-October – though the Finance Ministry had to know from the start, since it afforded ROWAK a credit of 3 million reichsmarks.[6] Nevertheless, the Foreign Ministry, though taken by surprise,[7] acquiesced without protest in the decisions taken against their advice. When the Spanish Republican Government shortly protested to the German counsellor in Madrid that German aircraft had been reported at Tetuán, the sombre note 'not to be answered' was minuted on the copy of the protest which arrived at the Foreign Ministry.[8] Everything was kept very secret. The air ace Adolf Galland described how 'one or other of our comrades (in the Luftwaffe) vanished suddenly into thin air. . . . After about six months he would return, sunburnt and in high spirits.'[9]

[1] *Cruzada*, X 139.   [2] Liddell Hart, *Other Side of the Hill*, 98.
[3] These last figures derive from the Nationalist historian of the war in the air, Gomá, 66. One hundred and seventy transport ships made the journey to Spain in the entire war, chiefly leaving Hamburg.
[4] *GD*, 14.   [5] Ribbentrop, 60.   [6] *GD*, 114.
[7] Weizsäcker, 112.   [8] *GD*, 16.   [9] Galland, 23.

Nearly all the Germans who went to Spain, especially as pilots, were young Nazis who felt seriously that, in the words of their marching song, 'We shall be marching onwards, if all else crashes about us. Our foes are the Reds, the Bolshevisers of the world.'[1] They were all apparently willing to go to Spain as part of their duties, even if they could not be altogether described as volunteers.

It was through Portugal that the greater part of German aid was at first sent. The part of that country in the Spanish Civil War was simple. Less clerical than the Portuguese corporative *régime*, the Spanish Nationalists stood for almost the same things as 'gracious Salazar', as the South African poet Roy Campbell called him.[2] The military aid which Salazar could give the Nationalists was small.[3] But he gave them many other things as valuable: a place in which to plot; a refuge; a means of communicating between their two zones at the start of the Civil War. Nicolás Franco, the General's eldest brother, with Gil Robles, was permitted to establish his headquarters for the purchase of arms at Lisbon. The Republican Ambassador in that capital, Sánchez Albornoz, swiftly became a prisoner in his own Embassy. Salazar remarked on August 1 that he proposed to help the rebels 'with all available means' – including the intervention of the Portuguese army, if this should be necessary.[4] As a result, Spanish Republicans who escaped into Portuguese territory were usually handed over to the Nationalists. The Portuguese Press served the Nationalists from the start. On August 20, the German Minister at Lisbon reported that war material brought from Germany in the steamships *Wigbert* and *Kamerun* had been despatched onwards to Spain most smoothly. Salazar, he said, had removed 'all difficulties . . . by his personal initiative and handling of details.'[5]

In the meantime, on July 26, the same day that Hitler agreed to

---

[1] *Wir werden weitermarschieren, wenn alles in Scherben fällt, Unsere Feinde sind die Roten, die Bolshevisten der Welt.* (*Deutsche Kämpfen in Spanien.*)

[2] In his poem, 'The Flowering Rifle'. Campbell was caught in his house at Toledo by the outbreak of the Revolution in that city. Narrowly escaping with his life (and that of his family) he later became one of the most ardent apologists for the Nationalists, without, however, actually fighting for them.

[3] Eventually 20,000 Portuguese fought for the Nationalists. Some of them were unwilling conscripts, most volunteers.

[4] *GD*, 25. Portugal offered unconditional support to General Mola on July 26, in reply to a request transmitted to Salazar in person by General Ponte. (Iribarren, 123.)

[5] *GD*, 53. Feeling against Portugal shortly became as strong as against Franco on the international Left. Louis Golding accordingly agitated for a boycott on port.

help Franco, Gaston Monmousseau, chief of the European office of the Profintern, presided over a joint meeting of the Comintern and Profintern at Prague.[1] It was decided that a thousand million francs should be found to aid the Spanish Government, of which the unions of the Soviet Union would contribute nine-tenths. The administration of the fund would be carried out by a committee composed of Thorez, leader of the French Communist party, Togliatti, La Pasionaria, Largo Caballero and José Díaz. The fund and its application would no doubt be kept chiefly in the hands of the first two. An intense and clever propaganda campaign now spread throughout Europe and America for aid to Spain. A large number of organisations for aid were set up, nominally humanitarian and independent, in fact dominated by Communists. Paris, and Willi Muenzenberg, remained the centre of this activity. The most important of these groups was International Red Help, which had been active in assisting the revolutionaries of the Left in Spain since 1934. On July 31, a meeting was held in Paris attended by International Red Help leaders. This formed the *Comité International de l'Aide au Peuple Espagnol*, of which Victor Basch[2] was president. This shortly had branches in every country. For the time being, all these organisations concerned themselves only with the provision of money, food and non-military aid. The committees' nominal leaders were often distinguished and unsuspecting personalities, but were usually served by Communist secretaries. But there was no military aid from Russia. When the Spanish Communists complained at this act of desertion, Togliatti harshly remarked: 'Russia regards her security as the apple of her eye. A false move on her part could upset the balance of power and unleash a war in East Europe.'[3]

The first reactions could now be observed to the Spanish War across the Atlantic.[4] Chile, Mexico, Argentina, Uruguay, Paraguay and Cuba, had received many recent immigrants from Spain. But all the countries of Latin and South America felt to some extent concerned by the events in Spain. There was strong feeling for the Nationalists in Brazil and the Canadian province of Quebec, where, as in Spain, there existed Fascist organisations in a Catholic background. Chile was also strongly pro-Nationalist. The Mexican

---

[1] The source of this footnote is referred to in footnote 4, page 214.
[2] A Hungarian Jewish polymath who had led liberal causes since the time of the Dreyfus case.
[3] Hernández, 36.   [4] Taylor, 39 fl.

Government was from the start an ardent supporter of the Spanish Republic, as might be expected from a country whose Constitution had itself derived from a rising against clerical and aristocratic privilege.

The United States was then preparing to endorse the achievements of Roosevelt's first term of office in the presidential elections of 1936. International affairs seemed far away to most Americans. Neutrality in all 'adventures' in Europe was the policy of both Republican and Democratic parties. During the Abyssinian crisis, in May 1935, a Neutrality Act had been passed in Congress rendering it illegal for American citizens to sell or transport arms to belligerents once the President had proclaimed a state of war. Although this act did not apply to civil wars, the American Government acted from the start of the Spanish conflict as if it did, although President Roosevelt had a natural sympathy for the Spanish Republic – a point of view shared by the American Ambassador in Spain, Claude Bowers, a historian by profession. Mrs Eleanor Roosevelt, Henry Morgenthau, Secretary of the Treasury, Henry Wallace, secretary for Agriculture, Harold Ickes, Secretary of the Interior, and Sumner Welles, the Assistant Secretary of State, were also Republican champions. But the Secretary of State, Cordell Hull, had only sympathy for the cause of impartiality, and always had his way.

Public opinion in the USA became, however, as moved by the Spanish War as it did in Europe. A torrent of propaganda poured from the Spanish Government's information bureau in New York and from the 'Peninsular News Service', the Nationalist headquarters in the same city. American newspapers took sides in the war with even greater vehemence than did those in Britain and France. American Catholics attacked reporters of Republican sympathies and liberals attacked those who wrote in apology for the Nationalists. On the *New York Times*, this controversy extended to two of its leading reporters, W. P. Carney, who wrote from among the Nationalists, and Herbert Matthews, among the Republicans.

On July 30, out of the first consignment of Savoia bombers sent by the Italian Government to help the Spanish Nationalists, two made a forced landing at Berkrane in French Morocco, and one crashed at Zaida in Algeria. Three of the occupants of the latter were killed and two injured. An enquiry made by General Denain, a former French Air Minister, showed that the aircraft

had had their Italian colours painted out, had been fitted with four
machine guns, had left Sardinia at dawn, and had been manned by
Italian Air Force men in civilian clothes. A survivor admitted that
the expedition was being made to assist the Spanish Nationalists.
A short while after the accident, a Spanish aircraft flew over
Berkrane and dropped a sack containing uniforms of the Spanish
Foreign Legion and a message in Italian: 'Put on these and tell
the French you belong to the Legion stationed at Nador.'[1]

Now earlier that day the Quai d'Orsay had denied that the
French Government had sent any war material to the Spanish
Republic: and Blum and Delbos repeated the denial to the
Foreign Affairs Committee of the Senate in the evening. This was
true, at that time – the material had not yet been sent. On August
2, there was a stormy meeting of the French Cabinet. Cot argued
that the proof of Italian aid to the Nationalists showed that the
policy of non-intervention had failed. Delbos, on the prompting
of Léger and 'in consideration of the British position', argued that
all countries who might aid one or other of the combatants in
Spain should be approached for a general agreement on non-
intervention. At eight in the evening, the Cabinet announced that
they had decided to appeal urgently to 'interested Governments'
– Britain and Italy in the first instance – for a 'non-intervention
pact'. But at the same time Cot was told to hasten and, because of
the proof received of Italian aid to the Nationalists, not to worry
about shipment *via* Mexico. His arms deliveries, 30 reconnaissance aircraft and bombers, 15 fighters, and 10 transport and
training planes were sent to the Republic at this time.[2]

Recruitment followed of technicians for the Republic. Special-
ised workmen (to be paid 2,000 pesetas a month, together with a
5,000 peseta gratuity on signature of contract) were secured for
the naval repair workshops at Cartagena and Valencia. The
French Radical deputy, Boussutrot, controlled the recruitment of
pilots (to be paid 25,000 francs a month) for Spain. The lives of
these men were insured at 300,000 francs with the Insurance
Company of which Boussutrot was director.[3] Meanwhile, Mr

---

[1] *L'Écho de Paris*, 1.8.36.

[2] Cot, 343. *Les Evénements Survenus*, 219. Blum testified that this shipment did
not occur till after the Cabinet of August 8. But he seems to have confused the dates.
Cot was later accused at the Riom trial of wasting on Spain aircraft which would have
been useful in France in 1940. Actually, all the aircraft sent were old and would not
have been of use in 1940.

[3] *The International Brigades*, 18.

Philip Noel-Baker had arrived in Paris. Blum told him that a Nationalist Spain would be a military threat to Britain as well as to France. Mr Noel-Baker suggested that the British Cabinet should be approached in this sense, perhaps through Sir Maurice Hankey, Secretary of the Cabinet. And so Blum sent Admiral Darlan, French Chief of Naval Staff to make this unofficial approach to Baldwin's Government.[1] And all the time from Republican Spain, and especially from Catalonia, appeals were being sent out for help: 'Workers and anti-Fascists of all lands! We the workers of Spain are poor but we are pursuing a noble ideal. Our fight is your fight. Our victory is the victory of Liberty. We are the vanguard of the international proletariat in the fight against Fascism. Men and Women of all lands! Come to our aid! Arms for Spain!'

The Government of the Republic were however showing that they would not permit any sentiment to come between them and their search for arms. On August 2, Barcía, Foreign Minister in Giral's Cabinet, asked the German businessman Sturm, of the Independent Airplane Association of Berlin, for pursuit planes and light bombers, with bombs of 50 or 100 kilograms. Payment would be in any currency requested, even in gold.[2] This request explains the peculiar politeness of the Republican Government at this time to Germany (the censorship forbade any derogatory use of swastikas in cartoons) even though they knew of the despatch of war material by Germans to their enemies.[3] The German official, Schwendemann, who received the request, urged its dilatory handling, and not its straightforward rejection. The German merchantman *Usamoro* meantime had left Hamburg with the first sea cargo of aid to the Nationalists. The 'tourist group' now sent its first pilots and technicians. And in Rome Ciano set up a special department in the Italian Foreign Ministry, the Uffizio Spagna, to supervise the Spanish aspect of his master's ambitions.

There was one other aspect of the internationalisation of the Spanish Civil War. Just as the 1850s were the great age of the Ambassador, so were the 1930s the great age of the foreign correspondent. From the end of July onwards, for two and a half years, the greatest names in world journalism were usually to be found south of the Pyrenees. Distinguished writers were hired by news

---

[1] *Les Evénements Survenus*, 219. [2] *GD*, 20.
[3] The Republic also attempted to gain native troops from the foetid Spanish colony of Ifni, before it fell at the start of August.

agencies to represent them at the Spanish War. The Spaniards were very conscious of this and were very proud of their fame. The journalists themselves were to write about Spain much that was inevitably inaccurate and much that could be regarded as brilliant reporting. But many journalists deliberately wrote articles which were intended not so much to be commentary or reporting as pamphlets aimed to help one side or the other. This was particularly true of the Republican side, for the Nationalist press department did not have the gift of exciting much enthusiasm among Anglo-Saxon correspondents. Among the Republicans many journalists went into the lines from time to time, helped train Spaniards in the use of machine-guns, and organised arms supply. And it was even a correspondent of *The Times* who first pointed out to the anti-Fascist Militias Committee that they could not win the war unless they found a way of feeding Barcelona.

27

The war in the Sierras and in Aragón – Durruti – the first foreign volunteers – John Cornford – Lister – Modesto – El Campesino – the Fifth Regiment

By the beginning of August 1936 the two main battlefields of the start of the war in Spain had lost their momentum. In Aragón, the beginnings of a front ran south from the Pyrenees, skirting Jaca, Huesca, Saragossa, Belchite, Daroca and Teruel (all of these were in Nationalist hands), where the front became, so far as the 'anti-Fascists' were concerned, the responsibility of the Valencians. The advanced positions of the Republic were at Tardienta (headquarters of the PSUC column) and Siétamo, taken by the loyal Barbastro garrison, both near Huesca. A large POUM column had its headquarters at Leciñena, to the north-east of Saragossa in the Sierra de Alcubierre. Along the Ebro at Osera and Pina, the Anarchists were established under Durruti. At Montalbán in the south, the ex-carpenter, Ortiz, commanded a heterogeneous group, with Anarchists predominating. Durruti's column was the most formidable of these forces, having advanced within striking distance of Saragossa. Here, Colonel Villalba, Commander of the Barbastro garrison and now in official, if vague, command of the whole front, persuaded Durruti to halt, for fear of being cut off. And there, within sight of Saragossa, the militia would remain, the lights of the town twinkling tantalisingly at night 'like the portholes of a great long liner', as George Orwell later put it, for another eighteen months.[1] The front line would consist of an advanced, partly fortified position on high ground, with about 300 men in the village behind. Such a group, with about six light field guns and two howitzers, would have little or no contact with the column in the next village, or on the next hilltop. In Tardienta, for example, the PSUC column sent back to Barcelona a lorryload of loot. On the way the guards were stopped by the POUM and shot as robbers, the dead men being sent back to Tardiente in coffins. In all the *pueblos* traversed

---

[1] Orwell, 38.

by the militias of Barcelona a helping hand had of course been given to the revolution. Thus, the people of Lérida had decided to spare their cathedral from the flames. Durruti soon put an end to such lukewarm behaviour. The cathedral burned. Durruti's violence, however, had made him actually loathed by

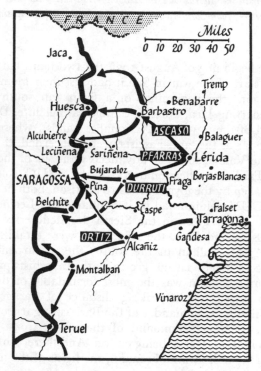

MAP 10. THE ADVANCE OF THE REPUBLICAN
MILITIA IN ARAGÓN

the peasants of Pina (near Saragossa) and his column had been forced to leave by their silent hate.

Opposite, the Nationalists were installed in similar positions, although their regular officers would ensure military discipline. The regular troops lacked the enthusiasm which made up for the absence of discipline on the Catalan side, but *Requetés* and Falangists were possessed of a fury as great as that of their opponents. They were stimulated to a great fury and patriotic zeal when a solitary Republican bomber dropped a bomb which struck the famous effigy of the Virgin of the Pilar at Saragossa, but did not explode. It was not simply a matter of religious outrage. The Virgin had shortly before been solemnly named Captain-General of the city.

In the revolutionary columns there were several groups of foreigners – notably German and Italian *émigrés*, Communists and Socialists, who had come to the 'Workers' Olympiad' at Barcelona after fleeing from Hitler and Mussolini. The Italians formed themselves into the so-called Gastone-Sozzi Battalion, and the Germans under Hans Beimler, a Communist ex-deputy of the Reichstag, into the Thaelmann[1] 'Centuria' (a group of about a hundred men). Certain French and Belgians formed the Paris Battalion. These men (and some women) were of no particular political grouping, though Communists predominated. In late August, another Italian group, the *Giustizia e Libertá* column, under Carlo Rosselli, fought near Huesca. The first English volunteers in Spain were Sam Masters and Nat Cohen, two East London 'garment workers' who were bicycling in France at the time of the rising and immediately went to Barcelona. Both were Communists. In Barcelona, they organised a 'Centuria' named after the English Communist, Tom Mann. However, this did not fight until September. Earlier, Masters fought with the Thaelmann Centuria.[2] The first Englishman who went to the front was John Cornford, a twenty-year-old research student in history at Trinity College, Cambridge, and the great-grandson of Charles Darwin and son of the Laurence Professor of Ancient Philosophy at Cambridge.[3] Conceived in the month of Rupert Brooke's death at Skyros, he was christened Rupert after him – though his matter-of-fact intellect caused him always to be known by his second

---

[1] Thaelmann had been a Hamburg harbour worker, whose hearty but semi-illiterate incoherence commended him to Stalin in the late 'twenties as a Leader of the German Communists. His dumb loyalty to Russia could be contrasted with the traitorous doubts of middle-class intellectuals. Beimler had been imprisoned in a concentration camp and had escaped by strangling his SS guard and walking out in his clothes.

[2] The only full account of the British volunteers in Spain is *Britons in Spain* by Bill Rust (London 1939). It is generally accurate, though, as a good Communist, its author often omits or ignores the part played by non-Communists or by those who left the party before the end of the war in Spain. (E.g. Mr George Aitken or the gallant Major Nathan. See below, page 347.)

[3] Cornford was accompanied (on a different part of the same Aragón front) by Richard Bennett, also from Trinity College, Cambridge. After a short while on the front-line, Bennett joined the Barcelona Radio Services and broadcast as 'Voice of Spain'.

name of John. At twenty, he was already a pillar of the English Communist party.[1] At nineteen, he had married a Welsh miner's daughter. He was a poet, with a double first in history, and a member of the Standing Committee of the Cambridge Union. Despite the rigidity of his Communism, a romantic imagination was constantly breaking through.

The war in Spain greatly developed his poetic talent. Surprisingly, for a Communist, he joined a POUM column on the Aragón front, at Leciñena on August 13. This was because he had brought no papers with him proving his 'anti-Fascist identity', and was thus refused membership of the PSUC column.[2] The first English volunteer to be killed was a woman, Felicia Browne, a Communist painter, shot in Aragón on August 25. Previously living on the Costa Brava, she had fought in the street battles in Barcelona, where she had travelled to attend the 'Workers' Olympiad'.[3]

The battles of the Sierras to the north of Madrid also lapsed into calm at the start of August. Repeated assaults failed to reconquer these heights at the end of July. Here General Riquelme, the military hope of the Republic, had succeeded the unfortunate Colonel Castillo in command of the militia forces. The failure of the attack caused the command to change yet again, this time to Colonel Asensio Torrado,[4] the most brilliant military brain among the officers loyal to the Republic. The Government held all the heights commanding the approaches to Madrid except for the Alto de León and the Somosierra Passes, where General Ponte

---

[1] The Communist party of Great Britain at this time numbered only 7,000. Cornford had been largely responsible for the revival of Communism at Cambridge: from 200 members in 1933, the Socialist Club (always Communist in outlook) rose to 600 in 1936 (Neal Wood, 52). The centre of this interest was Trinity College.

[2] *John Cornford. A Memoir*, edited by Pat Sloan, 199.

[3] These foreign volunteers were supported by a British Medical Aid Unit, of twenty-four persons all under thirty, including doctors and nurses. This unit originated as follows: Isobel Brown the Communist moving spirit behind the British Committee for the Relief of the Victims of Fascism (one of Muenzenberg creations) was receiving many donations labelled 'Spain'. She therefore inspired the creation of a British Medical Aid Committee with non-Communist but left-wing doctors as figureheads which despatched the Medical Aid Unit to Spain under the leadership of a Socialist, a contemporary of Cornford's at Cambridge, Kenneth Sinclair Loutitt. The value of this small unit was considerable since nearly all the army doctors of Spain were with the rebels. As for the civilian practitioners, these seem to have been almost equally divided between the Republicans and the Nationalists. Before the war there were about 10,000 qualified doctors in Spain.

[4] Not to be confused with Colonel (later General) Asensio Cabanillas who was one of the best Nationalist commanders and against whom the Republican Asensio fought.

(taking over from Colonel Serrador) and García Escámez were three and eight miles respectively down the Madrid side of the passes. Due to lack of ammunition Mola had ordered these commanders not to attempt any further advance. Thus both groups, each composed of a mixture of regulars, Carlists, and Falangists, with more Falangists at Alto de León and more Carlists at Somosierra, were fighting defensively against the more numerous Government militia forces opposed to them.

The Republican militia forces in the Sierras, unlike their colleagues in Aragón, were fighters first and revolutionaries afterwards. Even the Anarchists had learned that some orders would have to be obeyed if battles were to be won, and their main column was now commanded by a regular officer, Major Perea. All the militiamen wore the *mono*, with the initials of their trade union (rather than their political party) on their caps. Like the armies which had gone out from Barcelona, the Madrid militiamen were organised in columns of approximately 600 men each. These columns were formed usually of six battalions or *centurias*, of about 100 men each. The battalions would assume distinctive names, many of them evocative of old revolutions and far-off street battles, such as *Commune de Paris*. Others would take the name of contemporary political leaders such as La Pasionaria. There were several battalions known as the Steel Battalion, so-called because it was assumed to be the picked corps of the union or political party which had formed it. However, the most formidable of the Republican forces in the Sierras was that founded by the Communist party, the Fifth Regiment. It was so named because there had customarily been four regular regiments stationed in Madrid, whose military organisation, rather than the revolutionary and enthusiastic indiscipline of the militias, the Communist party from the start tried to emulate.[1]

The force was based upon the Communist-Socialist Youth, but others joined as a result of the recruiting drive led by La Pasionaria. By the end of July, nearly 8,000 members of this group had gone to the front.[2] In addition to its regular organisation, the Fifth Regiment adopted the use of political commissars employed by the Red Army in the Russian Civil War, with the declared aim of making clear to the soldiers precisely what they were fighting for. In Russia, the system had been devised to keep the loyalty of the Tsarist officers fighting for the Red Army. In theory, in the Fifth

---

[1] Cox, 27. [2] *International Press Correspondence* (Inpreccor) Vol XVII No 6, 6.2.37.

Regiment as in the Red Army, there were commissars attached to commanders at all levels down to that of company commander. Also, in theory, the counter-signature of commissars was necessary for every order. But neither of these stipulations was in practice fulfilled. The moving spirit of the regiment was the Italian Communist, Vidali ('Carlos Contreras'). He was as ruthless as he was efficient and imaginative. While, for instance, he early gained a reputation for shooting cowards, he also made the Fifth Regiment march in step by chartering the Madrid municipal band to keep time. Under his guidance, certain Spanish Communist military leaders appeared – notably Enrique Lister,[1] once a quarryman, and Juan Modesto, an ex-woodcutter who had been a Sergeant in the Foreign Legion under Franco. Both of these severe and able men had taken part in the Asturias rising in 1934, and had thereafter escaped to Russia, where they had studied at the Frunze military school. Lister had been taken while a boy to Cuba and he had learnt trade union politics on the building sites of Havana. Later, he had organised bloodshed and revolution in Corunna. A third Communist leader to appear during the battles of the Sierras was Valentín González, always known as *El Campesino* (the peasant), being notorious for his beard, his great size, his volubility and his physical strength. His enemies said that his name, as well as his beard, was given to him by the Communists so as to attract the peasants to the Communist party. He himself said that he had been known by this *sobriquet* ever since the time, when, aged sixteen, he had blown up four members of the Civil Guard in a lonely Estremadura sentry box and then taken to the hills. Later he had fought in Morocco – according to himself on both sides. He was a brilliant guerilla leader, but was hardly up to his subsequent command of a brigade and a division. Though retained for reasons of propaganda as commander, the real work was done by a clever young Major named Medina.

Between Barcelona and Madrid, the two main Republican centres and fronts, the battle-line was uncertain. The militia column which had captured Guadalajara and Alcalá advanced to capture the cathedral city of Sigüenza. But further advances were precluded, as on the Nationalist side, by a lack of ammunition. From Valencia, a militia column drove north-west towards Teruel, the most southerly rebel town of Aragón. The Civil Guard, which formed part of that column, deserted to the Nationalists as

---

[1] A portrait of Lister is given by Malraux in *L'Espoir* as 'Manuel'.

soon as they reached the front. And, though Teruel was surrounded on three sides, and Major Aguado, its first Nationalist commander, was killed, no progress was made towards its capture. Here as elsewhere, revolution occupied the militiamen as much as war. The confusion of the region was increased by the release, in late August, of the common criminals of a penal establishment nearby. These chiefly joined the CNT Iron Battalion before Teruel.

In between these main battlefields all along the line of division everywhere referred to as a 'front', there were many gaps where it was easy, from either side, to cross into the other Spain. Here and there, on hill-tops, look-out posts of militiamen from the nearby town on the Republican side would face groups of Falangists or of the Civil Guard on the Nationalist. Thus gradually the passions in Spain matured into a regular war.

28

The advance of the Army of Africa – Mérida – Badajoz – Medellín
– in the Tagus valley – Talavera

Two main campaigns now altered the complexion of Spain: the advance of the Army of Africa, commanded by General Franco, northwards from Seville; and that of the Army of the North under General Mola, against the Basque province of Guipúzcoa. The former campaign was made possible by the aid of Germany and Italy. The Germans supplied transport aircraft to carry 1,500 men of the Army of Africa to Seville between July 29 and August 5. This was the first 'air lift'.[1] Hitler did not greatly exaggerate when in 1942 he remarked that 'Franco ought to erect a monument to the glory of the Junkers 52. It is this aircraft that the Spanish Revolution has to thank for its victory.'[2] The Italians meantime supplied fighters to cover the merchant ships which ferried 2,500 men with equipment from Morocco to Spain on August 5, 'the day of the Virgin of Africa'. Henceforward Franco was in command of the Straits. The Republican Fleet, incompetently led by its crews, retired to the harbours of Cartagena and Barcelona – where indeed it spent most of the rest of the war. An army could therefore be assembled at Seville, to march due north to cut off the whole Portuguese frontier from the Republicans, to join forces with the Army of the North, and to advance upon Madrid along the Tagus valley. This army was directed by Franco, who flew to Seville on August 6, leaving Orgaz in command in Morocco. It was led in the field by Yagüe, the Falangist chief of the Foreign Legion, and under him Majors

---

[1] In all 10,500 men were flown to Spain from Africa in July and August, and 9,700 in September. Thereafter the need for such airlifts ceased as Franco possessed complete command of the sea (Aznar, 89). The German, Captain Heinichen, apparently acted as technical adviser to Franco on the airlift.

[2] *Tabletalk*, 687. Yet such a final conclusion is hardly possible for the judicious historian. What if Franco had not got transport aircraft from abroad? Who can say that the Nationalists would *certainly* have been beaten? Córdoba might have fallen. But would Seville? Would not the Army of Africa have been transported to the mainland in some other way?

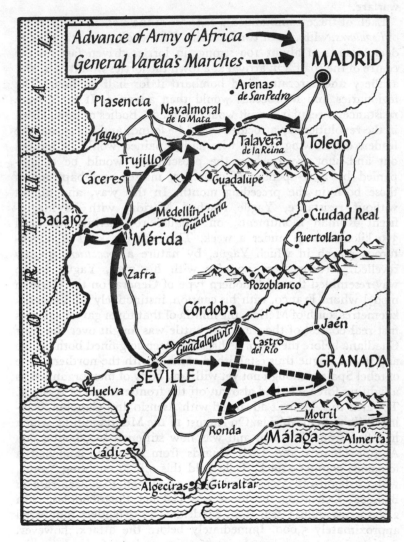

Advance of Army of Africa
General Varela's Marches

MAP II. THE ADVANCE OF THE ARMY OF AFRICA

Asensio, Castejón and Tella, all three veterans of Moroccan warfare.[1]

Each of these commanded a *bandera*[2] of the Legion and a *tabor*[3] of *Regulares*, with one or two batteries. The whole force travelled in detachments of about 100 strong, in lorries driven fast up the centre of the road. On arrival at a town the lorries would halt, and artillery and aircraft would bombard it for half an hour. The legionaries and Moroccans would then advance. If there were resistance, a regular assault would be made. Bodies of those killed in the revolutionary atrocities would be found, and in reprisal the leaders of left-wing parties who had remained would be hunted out and shot. Everywhere the proscription would be accompanied by a re-opening of churches, masses and baptisms of those born in the preceding month. In this way, and almost without resistance, Yagüe reached Mérida, with its magnificent Roman monuments, on August 10, having advanced 300 kilometres in under a week. This was the kind of adventurous march in which Yagüe, by nature a *condottiere*, greatly revelled. Ardent, very popular with his men, Yagüe in no way resembled the cold modern type of General on the German model whom Franco, with his caution, instinctively admired. Six kilometres south of Mérida, the militia of that town gave Yagüe his first real contest of the war. The battle was fought over the river Guadiana before the town. A thrust by Asensio gained both bridge and town. Yagüe thus established contact with the northern zone of rebel Spain – though not yet with any body of men organised as a fighting force. He had also cut off the frontier-town of Badajoz. Towards this, he next advanced with Asensio and Castejón, leaving Tella to hold Mérida. On August 11 the Mérida militia, which had fled from the town and was now stiffened by about 2,000 Assault Guards and Civil Guards from Madrid, launched a ferocious counter-attack. Tella held this off, so enabling Yagüe, with Castejón and Asensio and about 3,000 men, to concentrate on Badajoz. Defending the town was Colonel Puigdendolas, with 2,000 extra militia sent from Madrid. The defenders numbered approximately 5,000. Immediately before the attack, however, they had to expend material, energy and confidence on the defeat of a mutiny of the Civil Guard.

The hot and dusty town of Badajoz is surrounded by walls and,

---

[1] For this campaign, see Aznar, 102 fl; Lojendio, 138 fl; Sanchez del Arco, *passim*.
[2] See above, page 133 fn 3.   [3] A *tabor* consisted of 225 men.

from the east, whence Yagüe was advancing, is further guarded by the broad river Guadiana. After a morning's artillery bombardment, in the middle of the afternoon of August 14, the attack was ordered. A *bandera* of the Legion stormed the Puerta de la Trinidad singing, at the moment of the advance, their regimental hymn proclaiming their bride to be death. At the first assault, they were driven back by the militia's machine guns. At the next, the legionaries forced their way through, stabbing their enemies with knives.

The entry was made, though of the assault force only a captain, a corporal and 14 legionaries survived. At the same time, another column of legionaries assaulted the walls, near the Puerta del Pilar. They won this with less difficulty. The battle then went on in the streets. The two attacking forces met in the Plaza de la República beneath the shadow of the cathedral, and thereafter the town was lost. However, hand-to-hand fighting continued until the night. Badajoz became a city of corpses.

Battle and repression were indistinguishable since, once the town had been penetrated, there was no one to give orders either to continue or to cease fighting. Colonel Puigdendolas had fled into Portugal. The legionaries killed anyone with arms, including two militiamen who were killed on the steps of the high altar of the cathedral. Many militiamen, who though disarmed could hardly be said to have surrendered, were shot in the bull-ring.[1] These executions continued into the next day, August 15, and at a lesser rate for some time afterwards.[2] This conquest sealed off the Portuguese frontier from the Republican Government.

[1] The news of the 'massacre' of Badajoz was first given to the world by two French journalists, Dany and Derthet, and a Portuguese journalist, Mario Neves. Their account was later denied by Major MacNeil Moss in *The Legend of Badajoz*, which was itself effectively countered by Mr Arthur Koestler in *Spanish Testament*, 143–5. En quiries by the author in Badajoz in 1959 have left him convinced of the truth of the story as described above. The exact number of those killed in the bull-ring will probably never be known, though it is more likely to be 200 than 2,000 – the figure named by Mr Jay Allen of the *Chicago Tribune*. The bull-ring is an obvious place for executions in Badajoz, since it is no distance away from the main square. Several of the details added at the time to the story of the fall of Badajoz are false: e.g. the report describing the 'gutters' of the Calle San Juan as running with blood. This could not be true, since that street has no gutters. The rumour that the Nationalist Army was enabled to enter Badajoz by being permitted to go round by Portugal seems without foundation. On the other hand, there was certainly fighting inside the cathedral, as eye-witnesses have separately testified to the author.

[2] Yagüe certainly did not intervene to prevent bloodshed. But on Franco's orders he did restrain the Moors from castrating corpses of their victims – an established Moorish battle-rite. Even so, German officers testified to Robert Brasillach that they saw many bodies so treated – several with crucifixes laid on their breast. (Brasillach, 127.)

On August 20, Yagüe began a new advance, turning east towards Madrid. Tella advanced through Trujillo to Navalmoral de la Mata, which he occupied on August 23. To the east, the valley of the Tagus stretched out with no serious natural obstacles. Asensio and Castejón advanced to the Tagus over the mountains of Guadalupe. Here Madrid's Estremadura army, under General Riquelme, reinforced once again, turned to fight. A section of Asensio's column was nearly destroyed in the town of Medellín, by Malraux's French air squadron.[1] But the militia on the ground were no match for the legionaries and Moroccans who outmanoeuvred them, forcing them to retreat hastily from their position, or risk being cut off. Nine thousand men retreated (including 2,000 Anarchists, who refused Riquelme's orders in battle, and launched useless attacks in the San Vicente hills).

Asensio and Castejón joined Tella therefore at Navalmoral. After some days' rest, the advance began again on August 28 along the north side of the Tagus valley. The campaign resembled that in Estremadura two weeks before. Resistance was rare. The Republican troops, many of whom had been moved from the Guadarrama, were unused to the battle conditions of this thirsty and barren valley. There were desertions. The militia refused to dig trenches, since they considered this undignified and cowardly. The Government could not risk losing all their men in a general engagement and therefore retreated all the time. On September 2, the columns of the Army of Africa reached Talavera de la Reina, where 10,000 militiamen were established, with as much artillery as could be spared (as well as an armoured train) in a fine defensive position on the slopes before the town. At dawn on September 3, Asensio and Castejón advanced to try and surround the town. The aerodrome and railway station, some way out of the centre, were occupied. At midday an assault was launched against the town itself, whose defenders by now had become thoroughly alarmed. In the early afternoon, after very little street-fighting, Yagüe had conquered Talavera. The Under-Secretary of War in Madrid, Hernández Sarabia, telephoned Talavera in the evening to be answered by a Moroccan.[2] The last town of importance between Franco and Madrid had now fallen.

[1] Malraux, 99–105.   [2] Aznar, 174.

29

The campaign in Guipúzcoa – the bombardment of San Sebastián – Irún

The second main campaign of August was that in the north.[1]
Mola's aim was to capture San Sebastián and Irún, thus
cutting off the Basques from the French border at the
western end of the Pyrenees. Four columns of mainly Navarrese
troops operating here were now placed under the command of
their countryman, General Solchaga. On August 11, Colonel
Latorre took the old Basque capital of Tolosa. On the same day,
Colonel Beorlegui seized Pikoketa, a key ridge commanding the
approach of Irún. On August 15, the next-door town of Erlaitz
fell. Telesforo Monzón, an aristocratic Basque Nationalist, went to
Barcelona to seek aid. But the Generalitat could only spare 1,000
rifles. The Basques therefore confiscated the gold in the Bank of
Spain and other banks at Bilbao and sent it by sea to Paris, to
buy arms on its credit abroad.

The rebels now moved the few ships that they possessed towards San Sebastián and Irún. Colonel Ortega, recently a Sergeant-
Major of *Carabineros*, in command at San Sebastián, threatened
to shoot five prisoners for each person killed in sea bombardment,
the prisoners in the town being many, and distinguished, due to
San Sebastián's position as the summer capital of the country. The
rebel ships, *España*, *Almirante Cervera* and *Velasco*, nevertheless began to fire on August 17. The population hid, but four people were
killed, and thirty-eight wounded. Ortega executed eight prisoners
and five rebel officers. The naval bombardment continued on the
following days without causing civilian panic. Irún and San
Sebastián began to be bombed daily, Italian Capronis being fore-
most among the attackers. On August 26 the land assault on Irún
began. The number of men involved were about 3,000 Basques
and Republicans and nearly 2,000 Nationalists (550 legionaries,
450 Carlists, 440 Civil Guards and 400 Falangists). Beorlegui was,
however, supported by nearly all the artillery upon which Mola
could lay his hands. He had also a number of light tanks, manned

[1] This chapter is based on the accounts in Steer, Lojendio, Aznar and *The Times*.

with machine-guns, and armoured cars, all scrawled with '*Viva España*' in white chalk. The Basques on the other hand were strengthened by a number of French and Belgian technicians sent by the French Communist party,[1] and also by some Anarchists from Barcelona. But they had no artillery at all.

The ensuing battle was fought in dazzling sunshine, so close to the French frontier that Beorlegui had to restrain his men from

MAP. 12. THE CAMPAIGN IN GUIPÚZCOA

firing in an easterly direction. Day after day there was prolonged rebel artillery bombardment, followed by an assault, after the Basque positions appeared to be destroyed and evacuated. The defenders would then return and, in hand-to-hand fighting, re-capture the position. After a delay, the artillery bombardment would begin all over again. The Puntza ridge, for example, was destroyed, evacuated and recaptured four times in this way before

[1] On his own admission in the Chambre on March 16, 1939, the French Communist leader André Marty, future leader of the regularly organised International Brigades, was at Irún. For Marty, see below, page 301.

being finally captured on September 2. That day, the Navarrese also took the whitewashed convent of San Marcial, on the windy hill immediately commanding Irún, and the customs post at Behobia. The latter was surrounded, the men within fighting hand to hand to the last man, those who could having leapt into the Bidasoa to swim to France and to safety. All observers testify that both sides fought with complete disregard of personal safety, putting to the lie those accusations of cowardice that both shouted at each other when the firing had ceased, at night, or during the afternoon's siesta-time. Most of the inhabitants of Irún began to flee across the International Bridge on the road to Hendaye. On foot, by wheelchair, by motor-car, by coach, by horse, with domestic and farm animals, with babies, with a few precious articles of cheap furniture or pictures, the refugees fled to the frontier impelled by a blind panic, many in tears and penniless. The militiamen had hitherto been fed and urged on by their wives and families at home. Now they were alone, a rearguard who had, in fact, nothing to defend. On September 3, 1936, Beorlegui, supported now by 1,500 men assaulted the town of Irún. He was watched by crowds of spectators from the French side of the Bidasoa. The attack was not immediately successful. At two in the morning, the frontier village of Behobia was captured. Most of the defenders of Irún, including the committee in charge, fled to France before the sun rose. The Anarchists, led by their colleagues from Barcelona, and the French and Belgians, stayed last. The former set several parts of Irún ablaze. They also shot a number of the right-wing prisoners in Fort Guadalupe at Fuenterrabía, and then escaped, leaving the rest free to cheer Beorlegui the next day, as he occupied the burned and ruined town. Beorlegui suffered a mortal wound in the leg in a final battle at the International Bridge, against a group of French Communist machine-gunners. As for the refugees, those who wished to continue to fight – 560 men, including the French and Belgians – were sent off by train to Barcelona where they attached themselves to the columns in Aragón. The rest were despatched to camps in France.

30

General Varela in Andalusia – Miaja on the Córdoba front – the
Majorca campaign – the Simancas barracks – Aranda holds Oviedo
– Moscardó holds the Alcázar – air-raids on Madrid

Apart from their main strategic venture in the south of
Spain, the Nationalists mounted in August several forays
to establish communications between Seville, Córdoba,
Granada, Cádiz and Algeciras. The dashing and ambitious son of
a Sergeant-Major, General Varela, the ex-instructor of the Carlists,[1] with a *tabor* of Moroccans, marched to Granada.[2] The
province of Málaga, though protected by mountains, was thus
faced to the north as well as to the west by possible rebel advances.
An immediate attack on Málaga was, however, called off. Varela
was ordered north to defend the Nationalist position at Córdoba,
threatened on August 20 by a Republican attack under General
Miaja, so briefly Minister of War on the night of July 18–19, who
was now leading the militia of Andalusia, numbering about
10,000. The attack reached the gates of Córdoba, which would
probably have fallen had it not been for the arrival of Varela with
his Moroccans. Then Miaja and his militia were beaten back,
many men of the militia carrying rifles only for use against those
stopping their flight.[3] Miaja's failure immediately raised the
question of his loyalty to the cause of the Republic. And then, it
began to be asked in Madrid, could any General or ex-regular
officer be loyal?[4] Certainly there was spying on a large scale.
Miaja himself, for instance, heard the news of his relief from command on this front from Burgos Radio – before the announcement
had been made public.

The Republic also launched a campaign in August. On the 9th,
a joint Catalan and Valencian expeditionary force under an Air
Force Captain named Bayo arrived at Ibiza in four transport ships,
escorted by the battleship *Jaime Primero*, two destroyers, a submarine and six aeroplanes. The workers rose against the fifty men

[1] See above, page 75.   [2] Lojendio, 108.
[3] Borkenau, 158.   [4] Zugazagoitia, 110.

of the garrison and the island returned to Republican control. On August 13 Bayo arrived on the west coast of Majorca.

At dawn on August 16 he disembarked with 2,500 men on the east coast near the small town of Porto Cristo, which was itself quickly occupied. However, after the immediate success of the landing, the invaders passed the morning indecisively. In the evening about 10,000 more men had been disembarked. They established themselves at a depth of about 10 to 12 kilometres.

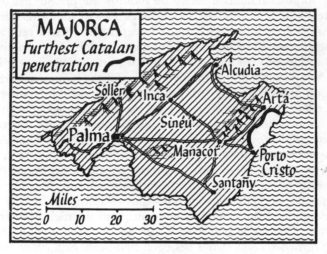

MAP 13

However, perplexity at their own success continued, so allowing the Nationalists to gather themselves for a counter-attack. An Italian fighter air squadron which proudly called itself 'the Dragons of Death', together with three bombers, led by Arconovaldo Bonaccorsi, a fanatical Fascist with a red beard who called himself the Conte Rossi, arrived in their support.[1] Henceforward Republican bombers were unable to get through to bomb Palma. A unit of the Foreign Legion also arrived from Africa. On September 3, the Nationalist counter-offensive, led by Colonel García Ruiz, began. The Catalan Expeditionary Force fled back to their ships. The beaches were covered with corpses, but many of the militiamen managed to get away, leaving the greater part of their

[1] Lojendio, 150. This first Italian shipment to Majorca was financed by Juan March (who had arrived in Rome in late July) and other Spaniards then living in Rome.

arms. Some of the wounded billeted in a convent were shot in the sight of the Mother Superior.[1] Few prisoners were spared execution. So the expedition came to an inglorious end, though Barcelona radio announced: 'The heroic Catalan columns have returned from Majorca after a magnificent action. Not a single man suffered from the effects of the embarkation, for Captain Bayo, with unique tactical skill, succeeded in carrying it out, thanks to the morale and discipline of our invincible militiamen.'[2] Thereafter, Majorca remained for some months the private fief of the 'Conte Rossi' who, dressed in his black Fascist uniform, relieved by a white cross at the neck, roared over the island in a red racing car, accompanied by an armed Falange chaplain. It was now that the murders of working-class Majorcans reached their height.[3]

In Asturias, meantime, the two battles for the Simancas barracks in Gijón and for Oviedo continued into August. Only when the former had been reduced could the Asturian miners concentrate all their numbers on Oviedo, where Colonel Aranda dared not sally out of the town which he had won by such guile. The siege in Gijón was rendered more difficult by bombardment by the cruiser *Almirante Cervera*. The 180 defenders, on the other hand, were constantly lulled by broadcasts from Radio Club Lisbon, Corunna and Seville, into false expectations that relief was on its way. The water supply of the defenders gave out, and the nightly smacking of lips by Queipo de Llano on Radio Seville, after a good glass of wine, turned several of the besieged half-mad. Still, they did not give in. Here, as at Toledo, two sons of the Colonel in command, a fanatical officer named Pinilla, were brought by the militia to demand the surrender of the barracks. Pinilla refused, and both sons were shot. Eventually the barracks were stormed by the miners using dynamite as their only weapon. Pinilla ordered no surrender even until the last moment. Finally on August 16 this remarkable commander sent a Roman message by radio to the Nationalist warships off the town: 'Defence is impossible. The barracks are burning and the enemy are starting to enter. Fire on us!' The demand was obeyed, and the last defenders of the Simancas barracks died in the flames. Thereafter the miners laid close siege to Oviedo. Aranda inside lacked supplies, but the besiegers lacked almost all material except for their infernal dynamite. So neither side made a move. Aranda had to hold a whole city with enemies within as well as without with only 3,000 men. His own relaxed and jovial personality was clearly the main-stay of the defence.[1]

At Toledo the battle was intermittent. The resistance of the Alcázar maddened the militiamen besieging it. Rifle-fire went on all August from both sides. The well-trained and protected defenders were alarmingly good shots, and the militia made no attempt at an assault to end the siege. Insults and boasts were exchanged through megaphones. Occasional bombs dropped made no difference at all to the defence of the ancient fortress, which had been thoroughly reinforced at the beginning of the century – just before, indeed, General Franco had attended the Infantry School there. The strongly Catholic population made the besiegers feel that they were surrounded by treason. The civilian authorities were meantime engaged in squabbling over the protection of the incomparable paintings in Toledo's churches and in the El Greco museum. Although the defenders in the Alcázar possessed all the ammunition they needed, there seemed no hope whatever of their relief. They were entirely cut off from the outside world and had no knowledge of the state of the rest of Spain. There was no electricity and the saltpetre off the walls was used for salt. They behaved nevertheless with amazing serenity. Parades were taken and the one thoroughbred horse inside was looked after as if in a stud. A *fiesta* in honour of the Assumption was even held in the cellars of the Alcázar, with flamenco dancing and castanets. Then on August 17, a Nationalist aeroplane flew over them and dropped messages of encouragement from Franco and Mola and, more important, news. On September 4 came the fall of Talavera de la Reina, only 70 kilometres away down the Tagus.[2]

The proximity of the Nationalists to Madrid was now expressed most vividly. On August 23 the nearby Getafe airport was bombed and on August 25 Cuatro Vientos, an airport somewhat nearer. On August 27 and 28 Madrid itself was raided. Voelckers, in charge at the German Embassy, described the raid on August 27 as being by three Junkers 52. 'Please arrange,' he asked Berlin, 'that as long as Lufthansa traffic continues, no Junkers raid

[1] Pérez Solis *passim*.
[2] Borkenau, 147. *General Cause*, 317–41. The Alcázar also received the following message from the 'young women of Burgos': 'The heroic epic which your valour for God and Spain has written on our glorious Alcázar will be the pride of Spanish chivalry for ever. Gentlemen cadets, we are *señoritas* radiant with joy and hope and, like you, we are the New Spain of the glorious dawn.' It was generally thought everywhere that the Alcázar was entirely held by cadets.

Madrid.' However, on August 29, he had to complain again. Junkers 52 had dropped four heavy bombs on the War Ministry, causing considerable damage and several deaths.[1] There was consequent rising anti-German feeling in Madrid. Voelckers urged that the German Embassy and German colony should leave.[2]

[1] GD, 61.

[2] The air raid caused the formation in Madrid of house committees in each block to organise listeners for the sirens which would be the signal to go down into the cellars. These committees also investigated the obscure texts of the Government's housing decrees, and protection against illegal raids. This led to the development of a kind of special constabulary in which the Socialists and Communists took the lead. Local Communist branches organised groups to paint the street lamps blue and secure a black-out. However, at this time of the year, a black-out was hard to enforce, since closed shutters made the rooms within intolerably hot. People were told to avoid the rooms facing the street and stay in inner rooms with candles. These experiences, of course, were common to those who lived in other parts of Europe at the time of the Second World War. But, except for the modest alarms in the First World War, these raids on Madrid were the first of their kind to occur.

31

The diplomatic battle of August 1936 – in pursuit of a Non-Intervention pact – the USA holds off – trickery of Italy – trickery of Stalin – arrival in Madrid of Rosenberg and his mission – trickery of Germany – Mr Eden's committee

While the Republic thus failed militarily, the diplomatic events of August were as signal a defeat. On August 3, Chambrun, the French Ambassador at Rome, presented his Government's non-intervention plan to Ciano, who promised to study it.[1] Britain, on the other hand, accepted the idea in principle on its presentation. The same day, the German battleship *Deutschland* put into Ceuta, and the Admiral in command lunched with Franco, Langenheim, Bernhardt and Beigbeder. An escort of Falangists cried 'Heil Hitler!'[2] The next day, August 4, François-Poncet, French Ambassador in Berlin, put the non-intervention plan to Neurath, who answered that Germany had no need to make such a declaration. He would, however, be prepared to discuss how the Spanish Civil War could be prevented from spreading to all Europe, provided that Russia was a party to the talks. Neurath added that he knew that the French had delivered aeroplanes to the Republicans. François-Poncet replied by claiming that the Germans had likewise supplied the Nationalists.[3] In Moscow, the French Ambassador made a similar approach to the Soviet Government. On August 6, Ciano, having consulted with Hassell, German Ambassador in Rome, said that Italy agreed in principle to the French plan. But he pointed out the need to 'check all fund raising' for either side; to make the scheme cover all countries; and to establish control.[4] That day's *Pravda* announced that the Russian workers had already contributed 12,145,000 roubles to aid Spain. But the Soviet Government itself, like the Italian, agreed to the French non-intervention plan 'in principle', asking for Portugal to join the group of states subscribing themselves, and demanding that 'certain States' – i.e.

---

[1] Ciano, *Diplomatic Papers*, 25–6. [2] *GD*, 27.
[3] *Ibid.*, 30. [4] *GD*, 30.

Germany and Italy – should immediately cease aid.[1] Nevertheless, on August 7 François-Poncet was back at the Wilhelmstrasse (and Chambrun at the Palazzo Chigi) with a draft declaration of non-intervention, already accepted by Britain, Belgium, Holland, Poland, Czechoslovakia and Russia, which would renounce all direct or indirect traffic in war material or aircraft. Neurath said this would be difficult without a blockade: and what about the Comintern?[2] The same day, the British and French Ministers in Lisbon asked Monteiro, the Portuguese Foreign Minister, to join the Non-Intervention Agreement. Monteiro, like Ciano, held his hand.[3]

All this time the French frontier was open to the transport of aid to the Republic. But on August 8 the French Cabinet changed their policy. A *communiqué* announced that from August 9 all export of war material to Spain would be suspended. This was explained as being due to the 'almost unanimously favourable' reply the Government had received to its ideas for non-intervention. In fact the previous day Sir George Clerk, the British Ambassador, had almost presented Delbos with an ultimatum. If France did not immediately ban the export of war material to Spain, and a war with Germany were to follow, Britain would hold herself absolved from her obligation to aid France under the Treaty of Locarno.[4] Furthermore by this time Admiral Darlan had returned with bad news from London. He had seen an old friend, Admiral Lord Chatfield, who had told him that there was no point in making any unofficial approach to the Government through Sir Maurice Hankey, and that Franco was a good Spanish patriot. The Admiralty, also, were 'unfavourably impressed' by what they had heard of the murder of the Spanish naval officers. Darlan therefore reported that there was no possibility at all of Britain looking favourably on French aid to the Republic.[5] And fear of offending England was the reason why the French Cabinet was brought, on August 8, to reverse its decision of August 2.[6] Blum bitterly regretted this reversal. He was indeed on the brink of resignation, but Auriol and Fernando de los Ríos (acting, with Jiménez de Asúa, as Spanish Ambassador to Paris) persuaded him not to do so.

[1] *The Times*, 7.8.36.   [2] *GD*, 323.   [3] *USD*, 1936 Vol 2 485.
[4] Álvarez del Vayo, *Freedom's Battle*, 70. Confirmed by Azcárate to the present author. Elegant, arrogant, aristocratic, did Sir George recall how in 1898, during the Fashoda crisis, he had been Resident Clerk in the Foreign Office and had received a telegram from the British Consul at Brest that the French fleet had put to sea, bound for England? The news was false, but war was near.   [5] *Les Evénements Survenus*, 219.   [6] Cot, 345–6.

A friendly French Government would, after all, be better for the Republic than one that was hostile.[1] On August 9, Blum, in spite of everything, was cheered at a meeting at Saint Cloud by a great crowd chanting 'Arms for Spain', while aircraft traced the word PAIX in smoke across the blue summer Sunday sky. Both the Socialist and Communist French trade union leaders were now committed to the policy which the crowd demanded. Jouhaux, the Socialist, and Thorez (like English Communists) were as one in declaring that there could be 'no neutrality for the conscientious worker'. Since the despatch of arms was forbidden, funds for clothing, food and medical supplies for the Republic were collected instead. In fact, French aircraft continued to be despatched to Spain *via* countries which were not party to non-intervention. All the time, indeed, that Pierre Cot remained Minister of Air (until June 1937) facilities were made at French airports to help Republican aircraft. Such breaches of non-intervention were officially excused as caused by 'errors of navigation'.[2]

While Blum was speaking at Saint Cloud, the Counsellor of the German Embassy in London was blandly assuring the Foreign Office that 'no war materials had been sent from Germany and none will'.[3] The same day, in Seville, the American Consul noted, however, the arrival of ten new Savoia bombers from Italy, eighteen Junkers, six German fighters and six anti-aircraft guns – together with twenty Italian pilots and thirty Germans.[4] The German Consul in Seville urged to the Wilhelmstrasse that these Germans should not appear in the streets in German uniform, since they were immediately recognised and given 'great ovations'.[5] One Junker made a forced landing in Republican territory, where it was detained, with its crew. The next day, the German Counsellor in Madrid, Schwendemann, on instruction from Berlin, demanded their release. The Spanish Government refused. On August 12, Neurath told François-Poncet that, until the Spanish gave up the aircraft ('merely a transport aeroplane'), Germany could not agree to the Non-Intervention Pact.[6] But, on August 13, Portugal accepted non-intervention in principle, reserving liberty of action if her border should appear threatened by the progress of the war.

The United States Government had by now also been called

---

[1] De los Ríos convinced Blum with a burningly eloquent description of the young militiamen fighting Fascism in the sierras. Blum buried his face in his hands and wept. De los Ríos did the same. The interview ended like that. Azcárate, 257.

[2] Cot, 353–4.   [3] *The Times*, 10.8.36.   [4] *USD*, 1936 Vol 2 481.
[5] *GD*, 38.   [6] *Ibid.*, 37.

upon for the first time to take up an attitude to the Spanish war. On August 5, the Secretary of State, Cordell Hull, allowed it to be generally known (though not announced) that the American Government favoured a rigid policy of non-intervention. On August 10 the Glenn Martin Company, an aircraft firm, asked what the Government's attitude would be to the sale of eight bombers to the Republican Government. The acting Secretary of State replied that such a sale 'would not follow the spirit of this Government's policy'.[1] The State Department next instructed Bowers, the American Ambassador in Spain, to refuse even to join a mediation proposal suggested to the diplomatic corps at St Jean de Luz by the Argentine Ambassador.[2] The US Government also refused on August 20 to take action on a Uruguayan proposal for mediation by the American States.[3] Mexico, meantime, alone of all the Governments of the world, openly began to send arms in limited numbers to the Republicans.[4] President Cárdenas publicly announced at the start of September that he had already despatched 20,000 7-millimetre rifles and 20,000,000 rounds of ammunition to the Spanish Government.

Meantime, the British and French pursuit of non-intervention continued. Britain prohibited exports of war material to Spain on August 15, after news had been received of flights of British aircraft from Croydon to Nationalist Spain. Neurath gave a note to François-Poncet on August 17 agreeing, pending the release of the Junkers and the acceptance of similar obligations by all countries possessing arms industries, to ban arms shipments to Spain and suggesting that this ban should be extended to volunteers.[5] Ciano also took up this last point with the French Ambassador in Rome, Chambrun, but promised, before that question and that of funds were settled, that Italy would prohibit the export of arms.[6] This sudden reversal of policy surprised the French. It was caused by a realisation that it would be as possible as desirable, in the words of the German *Chargé* at Rome 'not to abide by the declaration anyway'.[7] On August 20, Welczeck told Berlin that he thought a postponement of the Non-Intervention Agreement would work to the disadvantage of the rebels, since, if it were

---

[1] *USD*, 1936 Vol 2 474.   [2] *USD*, 1936 Vol 2 488.   [3] *Ibid.*, 498.
[4] The first 'incident' for America arising out of the Civil War was the accidental bombing (Nationalists) of the US destroyer *Kane* while *en route* from Gibraltar to Bilbao to evacuate American citizens there. No damage was done and eventually a somewhat evasive apology from Franco was forthcoming (Taylor, 61–2).
[5] *GD*, 45.   [6] Ciano *Diplomatic Papers*, 31–2.   [7] *GD*, 60.

not concluded soon, Blum would be forced to give unlimited support to the Spanish Government.[1] Admiral Raeder, however, wrote to Hitler the next day urging that, either Germany should support Franco to a much greater extent than at present, so preparing the German Army for a world war and actually risking war, or be more impartial and completely abandon the Nationalists.[2] Neurath, however, pressed agreement to non-intervention on Hitler. It was clearly understood that the flow of men and war materials should continue and increase.[3] On August 24, with the future of the Junkers in Madrid still unsettled, Germany signed the declaration demanded by the French.[4]

The Soviet Union, meantime, did not propose to be left out of these negotiations any more than the German Foreign Ministry wanted her to be. Stalin's motives in joining the Non-Intervention Agreement were chiefly that, in his pursuit of an alliance with France and Britain, he wanted to be a party to all such great power discussions. On August 23, Russia accepted the Non-Intervention Agreement, and on August 28, Stalin issued a decree forbidding export of war material to Spain so as to align the Soviet Union with the other powers. Russian Foreign Ministry officials showed even greater diffidence than usual during these negotiations, and Litvinov had to refer even insignificant details of wording of the Soviet adhesion to Stalin.[5] *Izvestia* turned many logical somersaults in denouncing neutrality as 'not our idea at all' and as 'a general retreat before Fascist Governments', yet explaining that the Soviet acceptance of it was 'due to the fact that the French declaration was aimed at the end of Fascist aid to the rebels'.[6] The dilemma of Soviet policy, desirous of pleasing France, while not appearing to desert the world revolution, was never more difficult. But Stalin's slowness is also explained by his preoccupation at this moment with the trial of the first group of Old Bolsheviks, which began on August 19: Kamenev was condemned to death on August 23 and Zinoviev some days later. Stalin's mind was thus on other things than Spain.

However, at the very moment that the Soviet Government adhered to the Non-Intervention Agreement, diplomatic relations between the Spanish Government and the Soviet Union were

---

[1] *GD*, 49.   [2] *Ibid.*, 51.   [3] See below, page 263.
[4] The crew of the Junkers had already been released. The aeroplane itself was destroyed in a Nationalist air raid.
[5] *USD*, 1936 Vol 2 515.   [6] *Izvestia*, 26.8.36.

being formally, and indeed formidably, established.[1] The old revolutionary, Antonov-Ovseenko, who had commanded the Red Guard which stormed the Winter Palace in St Petersburg in 1917, and had later been a member of the first Bolshevist Government in Russia, arrived at Barcelona as Consul-General on August 25. In recent years he had been in disgrace as a Trotskyist. The experienced Russian diplomat Marcel Rosenberg, ex-Deputy Secretary of the League and Ambassador in London, reached Madrid as Ambassador on August 27. Rosenberg brought with him a large staff, including General Berzin, previously head of Soviet Military Intelligence, who had been a drinking companion of Voroshilov. Berzin was often known in Spain as 'Goriev'. When aged 16 he had led a guerilla force in the Revolution of 1905. Wounded, he was made prisoner, sentenced to death and then, due to his youth, sent to life imprisonment in Siberia. He escaped and continued his revolutionary activities, joining the Red Army in 1917. He was a tall grey-haired man whom some mistook for an Englishman.[2] Antonov-Ovseenko had as his commercial assistant Arthur Stashevsky. This individual was a Pole, short and thick-set, seeming to be an ordinary businessman. He also had served in the Red Army. Later he had taken an active part in the re-organisation of the Russian fur trade, visiting America. These Russians were now added to the group of foreign Communists already in Spain such as 'Carlos Contreras' and Codovilla. The date of the arrival of these missions shows that the double attitude expressed in *Izvestia* was reflected in a double policy, suggesting that, as ever, Stalin intended to keep all courses open. The headquarters of the Soviet mission in Madrid was the quiet Gaylord's Hotel, between the Prado and the Retiro Park.[3]

One further contradictory step was apparently taken by the Soviet Government. The Comintern, it will be recalled, had been occupied with the despatch of non-military aid to the

---

[1] The Republic had set out to establish diplomatic relations with Russia, but the elections of 1933, giving a right-wing majority in the Cortes, prevented this. The exchange of Ambassadors had been planned ever since February 1936, but only now. occurred.

[2] Berzin appears under the nickname 'Starik' in Whittacker Chambers' *Witness*, being then Chief of Intelligence (p. 283–5). American Communists assumed wrongly that 'Starik's' move to Spain signified his liquidation. This did not occur till 1937. See below, page 455, footnote.

[3] For an extraordinary picture of life in this hotel in August 1936–March or April 1937, see Chapter 18 of *For Whom the Bell Tolls* – perhaps the best piece of *rapportage* Hemingway has yet written.

Republic. Many organisations had been set up all over the world with this in view, most of them respectable democratic bodies but with some Communist party members in the background. It seems that now, even while the Soviet Government itself refrained from giving aid to the Republic and while it was watching to see how non-intervention would work, the Comintern was instructed to set up an organisation for the supply of arms. According to General Walter Krivitsky, at this time Chief of Soviet Military Intelligence in Western Europe with his headquarters in The Hague, this decision was taken on August 31, as a result of a delegation from the Republic to Moscow with the offer of 'huge sums of gold'. This date seems a little early, but if correct would explain why so large a staff accompanied Rosenberg to Madrid when the Soviet Government still did not want itself to send *Russian* aid to Spain. Krivitsky was precise in saying that on September 2 he received instructions to mobilise all possible facilities for the transport of arms to Spain from Western Europe.[1]

The Russian double-dealing was closely matched by Germany. On August 25, the day after Germany had signed the Non-Intervention Agreement, the War Minister, Field Marshal Blomberg, summoned Colonel Warlimont, an officer hitherto known in the *Wehrmacht* for his social graces. Hitler, said Blomberg, had decided to aid Franco. Warlimont was henceforth to lead the German contingent. On the 26th, Warlimont and Admiral Canaris visited the head of Italian Military Intelligence, General Roatta, and exchanged ideas about what had to be done in Spain. Warlimont then left for Tetuán, on an Italian cruiser, under the name of 'Waltersdorf'. A German aircraft flew him and Roatta first to Seville where they talked to Queipo, and then to Cáceres, where they met Franco. Warlimont thereupon took up his duties.[2]

While the other Powers were thus busy arranging to break their

[1] Krivitsky's evidence must be regarded as tainted unless corroborated. He later fled to America, denounced his masters and died, probably murdered, in a Washington hotel in 1941. His book, and the articles in the *Saturday Evening Post* of which the book was an expansion, were probably partly written by a well-known American Sovietologist, often thought to be helped in what he writes about Russia by the FBI. There is a no doubt baseless *canard* that the FBI reaches its dates by averaging various estimates. Krivitsky is certainly wrong in suggesting that the Soviet Government now decided to send *Russian* arms to Spain. All other evidence suggests that this did not occur till the beginning of October (see below, page 294). Furthermore, this would not be a matter upon which Krivitsky could have first-hand knowledge – though he would have in respect of Comintern aid. (Krivitsky, 98–9.)

[2] General Warlimont's affidavit to US Military Intelligence in 1946 (*UN Security Council Report on Spain*, 76).

words in respect of non-intervention, Mr Eden took up an Italian suggestion for a commission to supervise its working. After dispute as to its powers, a Non-Intervention Committee was arranged. This committee, deriving from the recollection of the successful Ambassadors' conference under Sir Edward Grey's chairmanship at the time of the Balkan wars, was to be convened at the Foreign Office in London. The first meeting was arranged for September 9. Thus was born the Non-Intervention Committee, which was to graduate from equivocation to hypocrisy and humiliation, and which was to last out the Civil War.[1]

[1] Despite the British policy of non-intervention, from this time the Foreign Office gave instructions to the British Embassy in Madrid to give asylum to Spanish refugees from the 'Red Terror'; and within a matter of weeks the Embassy in Madrid comprised seven buildings. For the rest of the war, the foreign embassies in the Spanish capital remained the home of several thousand upper and middle-class Spaniards, some active members of the Fifth Column, others terrified and broken, all hungry, cold and increasingly pale due to the lack of fresh air. There was a certain amount of 'Scarlet Pimpernel' activity, and later in the war many exchanges of these refugees for Republicans in Nationalist hands.

32

*The Republican defeats and their causes – massacre in the Model
Prison – fall of the Giral Government – Largo Caballero forms his
Ministry*

The beginning of September had brought defeat to the
Spanish Government on all fronts. Yagüe was at Talavera,
Beorlegui at Irún, and threatening San Sebastián; the
Majorcan expedition had failed; Saragossa, Huesca, Oviedo, and
the Alcázar at Toledo remained in rebel hands; in the south, much
of Andalusia had gone, as well as nearly all Estremadura. The
efficiency and experience of the well-armed Army of Africa was
the chief explanation for the Nationalists' success. Bravery and
emotion could win street battles, but were naturally inadequate
against the legionaries and the *Regulares*. The bravest militiamen
showed themselves fearful before the unknown terror of aerial
bombardment. Those who had so proudly marched along the
Castellana every week before the war had never known bombs. A
general flight might be caused by two bombers, half of whose
bombs did not explode at all while the rest did no damage.
Political predilections also affected even tactics. On the Talavera
front, great faith was put in the use of an armoured train, that
favourite development of the Russian Civil War. But in Spain this
'vital shovelful of coal that keeps a dying fire alive', as Trotsky had
called his own train, proved useless. The Russian Civil War was,
however, constantly recalled by the Spanish officers of the Republic in search of some precedent for their own problems of leading a mass army.[1] Their troubles were not only in the fighting line.
The Ministry of War had no organised control and no real central

---

[1] Their followers were equally influenced by a film of the Russian Revolution
portraying the exploits of Chapiaev, the guerilla leader. As before the war, films made
a great impression on the Spanish working class. Shirley Temple in *The Little Colonel*,
which was also shown in Madrid at this time, had an effect on tactics of which Captain
Liddell Hart might have been proud. The greatest possible success was also enjoyed
by Groucho Marx, who was represented as a Colonel in *Duck Soup*. Looking very like
any Spanish regular officer he remarked before a map: 'A child of three could solve
this problem.' A pause. 'Fetch me a child of three.' The militiamen on leave from the
Sierra found this relevant.

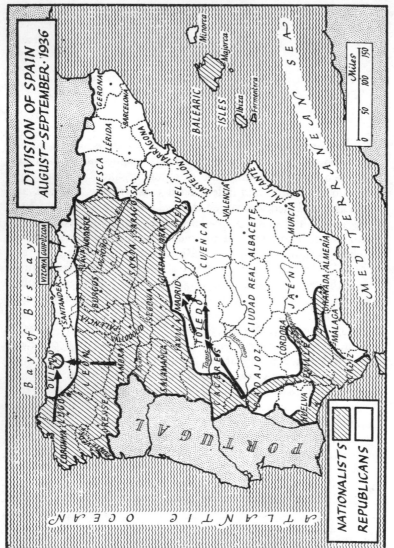

DIVISION OF SPAIN
AUGUST~SEPTEMBER·1936

Bay of Biscay

ATLANTIC OCEAN

MEDITERRANEAN SEA

BALEARIC ISLES

Minorca

Majorca

Ibiza

Formentera

PORTUGAL

NATIONALISTS

REPUBLICANS

Miles
0   50   100   150

CORUNNA
LUGO
OVIEDO
PONTEVEDRA
ORENSE
LEÓN
SANTANDER
VIZCAYA
GUIPUZCOA
NAVARRE
LOGROÑO
BURGOS
PALENCIA
VALLODOLID
ZAMORA
SALAMANCA
SEGOVIA
SORIA
ZARAGOZA
HUESCA
LÉRIDA
GERONA
BARCELONA
TARRAGONA
CASTELLÓN
TERUEL
GUADALAJARA
MADRID
CÁCERES
TOLEDO
CUENCA
VALENCIA
ALICANTE
BADAJOZ
CIUDAD REAL
ALBACETE
MURCIA
CÓRDOBA
JAÉN
HUELVA
SEVILLE
GRANADA
ALMERÍA
MÁLAGA
CÁDIZ
Tagus

MAP 14

staff, and the movement of different militia groups entailed endless bureaucratic delays. There were no opportunities for rifle practice and no rifles for such training – partly because the political parties all kept a proportion of their arms for possible use against their friends. The CNT in Madrid, for example, were believed to possess 5,000 rifles at their headquarters. A food shortage also developed – this being due not only to the loss of Castile, but to the phenomenal waste of food sent to the militias at the front.[1]

The pressure of the defeats, combined with the failure of Giral to obtain arms from the two *bourgeois* democracies, now caused a general demand for a change of the Republican war leadership. In Madrid, this feeling was expressed particularly by the once extreme members of the UGT – the group, that is, around Largo Caballero, now the effective king of Madrid. Every day he and Álvarez del Vayo visited the Sierra to exhort and be welcomed by the militiamen. They wanted, however, to dominate and not simply enter, the Government. They demanded a real proletarian administration. Even Prieto had complained in *Informaciones* that the reading of Socialist newspapers was frowned on at the Ministry of the Interior. Prieto himself worked incessantly for the service Ministries even though not a Minister. The Italian Socialist Pietro Nenni arrived in Madrid in early August and pictured Prieto at this time in shirt sleeves, the centre of ceaseless activity: 'He is nothing; he is not a Minister; he is a Deputy of a parliament in recess. But yet he is everything – the animator and co-ordinator of Government action.'[2] Prieto opposed the idea of his party taking over the administration, still thinking it possible to influence Britain and France to help the Republic by maintaining a purely middle-class Government – and no doubt not wishing to see Largo Caballero assume power. He therefore suggested that Socialist Ministers should simply 'guide' the Giral Government, as he was himself doing. The Communists supported this policy. Largo Caballero criticised Prieto's proposal as being incapable of purging the administration or controlling the economy. It would compromise the Socialists, as their share in Azaña's Governments of 1931 and 1933 had done, and give the Anarchists a new opportunity. Largo wanted, in fact, to lead the Government himself.

By this time, the political prisoners in the hands of the Republic had suffered various fates. In Barcelona, Generals Goded and

---

[1] For Madrid at this time, Barea, *The Clash*, 109–60, is most useful.
[2] Nenni, 146.

Fernández Burriel were tried in early August. A retired expert was engaged to defend the two Generals, who behaved with impassive dignity. General Llano de la Encomienda – who had lost a son fighting for the militias in the Guadarramas – and the Civil Guard General, Aranguren, bore witness against them. The two rebels were accordingly shot for military rebellion in the fortress of Montjuich. The liberal members of the Republican Government agreed to the death sentence only with extreme reluctance. A few days later, General Fanjul and Colonel Quinto were shot after a court-martial in Madrid, the former after being married at the last moment to an unknown woman.

On August 23 a fire broke out at the Model Prison in Madrid.[1] Was this caused by the three thousand political prisoners imprisoned there who attacked their guards with mattresses to which they had set fire? Or was it the work of common criminals in the prison, stimulated by CNT militiamen, who had been searching for arms? The exact origins of the fire will probably never be discovered. But at all events the news that the political prisoners had rebelled spread in the city, at the same time as the news of Badajoz,[2] began also to be rumoured, despite the censorship. A crowd gathered, headed by militiamen on leave. They demanded that the building be stormed so as to massacre the political prisoners. Socialist politicians arrived to urge moderation. But the militiamen refused to listen. Forty prisoners were shot down in the courtyard. Their dead bodies were trundled round to frighten the living. After threatening to kill them all *en masse*, a selection of the most eminent prisoners was made, and another 30 people were shot the next morning. These included Melquiades Álvarez and Martínez de Velasco, two well-known right-wing politicians, Fernando Primo de Rivera, brother of José Antonio, Ruiz de Alda, José Antonio's closest intimate, Dr Albiñana, the leader of the Nationalist party, and General Villegas, one-time leader of the revolt in the Montaña barracks. More surprising than the execution of these men was the fact that among those in the prison at the time and spared were the ex-leader of the CEDA youth, Ramón Serrano Suñer, the Falangist, Fernández Cuesta, and Antonio Lizarza, the Carlist conspirator.

After these terrible events, a first step towards regularisation was

---

[1] For two opposing accounts of this, see *The General Cause* and Borkenau: see also Juan de Córdoba, 105, for Serrano Suñer's account of the events.
[2] See above, page 247.

taken by the Ministry of Justice. This was the establishment of the
Popular Tribunals, which were supposed to fill the gaps caused
by the resignation, flight or murder of the regular judicial authorities. In every province of Republican Spain these courts took a
slightly different character. In general, however, they were composed of 14 delegates from the Popular Front and the CNT, with
three members of the old judiciary. Persons denounced to these
tribunals were able to find some rough form of defence (though
Falangists as such were invariably shot, together, usually, with all
members of the CEDA and those who contributed to their funds).
A doctor, for example, denounced by a patient who owed him
money, was able to disprove the charge and secure the denounce-
ment of the denouncer. An ordinary tradesman, also, only at the
last moment managed to escape being denounced as a spy by a
creditor.[1] 'Unauthorised' executions nevertheless continued,
though with diminishing ferocity. The two brothers, the Dukes of
Veragua and de la Vega, descendants of Columbus, were, for
instance, shot by militiamen who were afraid that the Popular
Tribunal might acquit them. At the end of August the Government told everyone to lock doors at 11 p.m., abolished *serenos*,
instructed *concierges* to allow no one to enter houses, and to telephone the police if 'loud knocks indicate militiamen want to
enter'. This step almost ended illegal killings.

On September 4, Azaña reluctantly accepted Giral's resignation as Premier. Largo Caballero, however, the obvious choice for
his successor, refused to take office unless the Communist party
also did so. (He invited the Anarchists to join: they refused.) No
Communist party had previously ever joined a western Government. The Spanish Communist Central Committee opposed
joining, for fear of being compromised by a non-Communist
policy. Moscow, however, gave instructions to join and Largo
Caballero formed his Government on this basis of collaboration
with the Communist party. The Communists explained this action
by saying that Civil War demanded unity against Fascism and that
the main tasks of the proletarian revolution were already fulfilled.
Accordingly Hernández, editor of *Mundo Obrero*, became Minister
of Education, and Uribe, the Marxist theorist, became Minister of
Agriculture. There were six Socialists in the Cabinet, including
Prieto as Minister of Navy and Air, and Álvarez del Vayo

[1] Between August 1936 and June 1937, the Popular Tribunals judged no less than
46,064 people and imposed 1,318 capital sentences. (Nenni, 73.)

as Foreign Secretary. Juan Negrín, a Socialist without close political associations, became Minister of Finance; he was Professor of Physiology at the University of Madrid and had distinguished himself in university administration. (Araquistain, to his annoyance, was given the post of Ambassador in Paris.[1]) The Cabinet was completed by two members of the Republican Left (including Giral as Minister without Portfolio) and one each of the Republican Union and the Esquerra. Largo Caballero named himself Minister of War, succeeding Hernández Sarabia who was almost exhausted by a month's improvisation of strategy. He was now supported by a regular central staff under Major Estrada; Colonel Rodrigo Gil, an artillery officer of the old school, became Under-Secretary at the War Office. This 'Government of Victory', as it was named, was unusual not only in the combination of Communists in the Government, but in the fact that Hernández, the new Minister of Education, had actually been convicted nineteen years earlier for the attempted murder of the new Minister of the Air and Marine, Indalecio Prieto.[2]

---

[1] The Ambassador in London, López Oliván, who had always been a Monarchist (and made no bones about saying so), now gave up his charge to join the Nationalists. He was replaced by Pablo de Azcárate, Deputy Secretary-General of the League of Nations, who being eminently respectable seemed the best person to represent Republican interests at the all-important London Embassy. On arrival in London, the Marshal of the Diplomatic Corps, Sir Sidney Clive, told Azcárate that the King did not like changes of Ambassador, and if Franco entered Madrid and was recognised as the real Government of Spain, he hoped that Azcárate would be able to remain. Azcárate was received perfectly by all London's diplomatic corps, except for Jan Masaryk, the Czech Minister, who refused to deign to call on the 'Red Ambassador', and for Grandi, the Italian Ambassador. Ribbentrop, who presented his credentials the day after Azcárate, was always very correct. But Azcárate's task was not easy. He had to establish a quite new Embassy, since most of the old staff had left. And Vansittart welcomed him very coldly on his first visit to the Foreign Office, rejecting his request to allow Republican pilots to train in Britain. (Azcárate, MSS 6–9.)

[2] Álvarez del Vayo, *Freedom's Battle*, 203. Hernández, 47. Inprecorr quoted by Cattell, *Communism*, 56. Borkenau, 32. Bowers, 524. Martín Blázquez, 189.

33

The Nationalists had by the start of September begun to imbue their movement with a heroic or spiritual significance which alone could justify the waging of war. Whereas their first manifestos and *communiqués* in July spoke draconically of order and control of anarchy, they now talked of 'a crusade of liberation'. To sustain a war effort, to maintain morale, to justify executions, it was necessary all the time to make frenzied appeals to the past and to the spirit, to excite civilian emotion through patriotic propaganda. Republicans of all complexions were denounced as 'Reds'.

On August 15, the Feast of the Assumption, the Monarchist flag was substituted for that of the Republic. In a solemn ceremony in Seville, Franco came forward on the balcony of the town hall, kissed the flag many times and shouted across the packed square 'Here it is! It is yours! They wanted to rob us of it!' Cardinal Ilundaín of Seville kissed the flag also. Then Franco went on: 'This is our flag, one to which we have all sworn, for which our fathers have died a hundred times covered with glory.' He ended with tears in his eyes. Queipo de Llano spoke next, and went into a rambling discussion of the different flags which Spain had had at different times. Finally, he compared the Monarchist colours with 'the blood of our soldiers, generously shed, and the Andalusian soil, golden with harvests.'[1] He concluded with his customary references to 'Marxist rabble'. During this speech, Franco and Millán Astray, the founder of the Foreign Legion (who had returned from Argentine after the rising), standing nearby, found it difficult to suppress their laughter. Afterwards, Queipo said his in-

---

[1] In *For Whom the Bell Tolls*, Pilar refers to the Republican flag as 'blood, pus and pomegranate', and to the Monarchist flag simply as 'blood and pus'.

tense emotion had prevented him from developing his speech as
he had intended. Next to speak was Millán Astray,[1] a man from
whom there seemed more shot away than there was of flesh remaining. He had but one leg, one eye, one arm, few fingers left on
his one remaining hand. 'We have no fear of them,' he shouted,
'let them come and see what we are capable of under this flag.' A
voice was heard crying '¡Viva Millán Astray!' 'What's that?' cried
the General, 'no vivas for me! But let all shout with me "¡Viva la
muerte!"' (Long live death!). The crowd echoed this mad slogan.
He added, 'Now let the Reds come! Death to them all!' So
saying, he flung his cap into the crowd amid extraordinary
excitement.

José María Pemán, a right-wing poet, and one of the chief
literary apologists for the movement, followed by comparing the
war to 'a new war of independence, a new Reconquista, a new expulsion of the Moors!' The final exclamation must have sounded a
little odd in a city from which an expedition of Moroccan soldiers
had some days previously set out for the north to conquer Madrid,
and whose public building and leading Generals were even at that
moment guarded by Moroccans. 'Twenty centuries of Christian
civilisation,' continued Pemán, 'are at our backs; we fight for love
and honour, for the paintings of Velázquez, for the comedies of
Lope de Vega, for Don Quixote and for El Escorial.' While the
crowd cheered him to the echo, he added: 'We fight also for the
Pantheon, for Rome, for Europe, and for the entire world.' He
concluded this successful oration by naming Queipo de Llano,
'the second Giralda'.[2] And, though perhaps this last comparison of
the drunken General with the enchanting Moorish tower next to
the cathedral of Seville went a little too far even for the crowds
who cheered the speaker, such is the ease with which human
beings can be brought to believe their own propaganda that most
active supporters of the Nationalists in the Spanish Civil War
quickly came to accept such comparisons as true.

With a regular supply of military aid agreed from Germany and
Italy after a week of war (and no question of payment for this was
as yet permitted to sully Nationalist Spain's relations with her first

---

[1] Millán Astray briefly challenged Queipo as chief propagandist of the Nationalists.
He raved excitedly for six nights about death and the purity of Spanish womanhood,
but could hardly be followed by his hearers. Later, he ran the Nationalist propaganda
in Salamanca.

[2] Bahamonde, 36–8. Pemán's speech appears in Enciclopedia Universal Ilustrada,
1936–9 Supplement (Vol 2, 1404).

friends), the chief preoccupation of the Generals was how they could secure credit for essential raw materials such as oil, the small native supply of which from the Canaries was obviously inadequate.

The Republican possession of the Spanish monetary gold caused the Nationalists to start the war with neither the backing for a currency nor the means of obtaining credit from abroad. However, from the start, strict financial measures were imposed forbidding the export of foreign currency, and fixing the peseta at the level which had obtained before the war. The only real backing for this was the expectation of a Nationalist victory. The German agency HISMA helped to stabilise the Nationalist currency. The export trade of the mines of Andalusia and of Morocco, together with the agricultural produce of the Canaries and Andalusia also assisted the Nationalist economy. In addition, the financiers of Europe and America not only expected the Nationalists to win but desired them to. Although the Republic had taken great care to protect all foreign concerns in Spain, the collapse of foreign investments in Russia had occurred too recently to be ignored. So the question of the oil supply was solved by the long-term credit, without guarantee, accorded by the Texas Oil Company.[1]

Relations between the Spaniards and their German allies were already difficult. For example, the HISMA military leader Von Scheele quarrelled with the Nationalist air commander, General Kindelán, at the end of August. Von Scheele supposed that the faster French Breguet aircraft operating in Aragón would overwhelm the Germans, and Kindelán asked that the Heinkels should be flown by Spaniards. Von Scheele replied that Spaniards would be incapable of flying them. The dispute had to be referred to Franco. There was also rivalry between the Nazi Bernhardt and the soldier von Scheele, since the former did his utmost to give the impression that von Scheele was a mere employee of his own and that he, Bernhardt, was Hitler's delegate to Franco. The latent quarrel between the Nazi party and the Germany army was thus

---

[1] Five tankers of the Texas Oil Company were on their way to Spain at the time of the rising. They received orders to deliver to the Nationalists on credit. These shipments continued. After the Embargo Act (see below, page 339) some were made by declaring that they were bound for France. The Texas Oil Company was fined $22,000 for this. It made no difference; 344,000 tons of oil were delivered in 1936, 420,000 in 1937, 478,000 in 1938, 624,000 in 1939. The bill was paid, and credit renewed (Feis, 269).

expressed on Spanish soil. The aircraft manufacturer Willy Messerschmitt, on return to Germany from a visit to Nationalist Spain, meantime urged the Foreign Ministry that the time was ripe to extract pledges from Franco with regard to Germany's 'future economic and perhaps even political influence' over Spain. He suggested a treaty to lay down a quota of raw material deliveries to Germany for a number of years. Bernhardt, anxious to ingratiate himself with Franco, opposed this. But Franco was later induced, against Bernhardt's advice, to start delivery of copper to Germany from the nominally British Rio Tinto mines as part payment for war material.[1] Nor did the Germans see absolutely eye to eye with Franco ideologically. Captain 'Strunk'[2], a top German intelligence officer, later complained that he thought Azaña's policy of 'the middle way' superior to Franco's so-called 'saviour army', since this presaged a return of the old order, with landowners and a strong church.[3]

At this stage, Italian aid was limited to the supply of aircraft flown by Italian pilots. These were assimilated into the Nationalist army as members of the Foreign Legion. With them there were as yet no serious disputes.[4]

Franco's position on the Nationalist side had been greatly enhanced during August. Partly this was the result of the military successes of the Army of Africa, and the preoccupation of Mola with so many small and less spectacular campaigns. Partly, however, it was due to the relations which Franco had established with Germany and Italy. Both nations, especially the former, gained the impression that the 'Young General' was both able and likely to be influenced by them. They decided this without perhaps taking adequate account of the power wielded over Franco by his wife, a fervent Catholic who increasingly saw her husband as the leader chosen by God to save Spain from the enemies of the Church. It was therefore for religious reasons also that Franco was coming to see himself as a great political leader. Nevertheless, for the time being, Nationalist Spain remained without a single command. Mola, Queipo and Franco met several times, but nothing was decided as to whether any of them should be in supreme control. This absence of a central command became

---

[1] *GD*, 84–9.
[2] This was probably Col Funk, later German Military *Attaché* in Nationalist Spain.
[3] *USD*, 1936 Vol 2, 611.
[4] Pini and Susmel, Vol III 357.

more and more serious, and by the end of August, several Generals – especially the commander of the Air Force, Kindelán – were speculating as to how to overcome this difficulty.[1]

[1] Franco established himself on August 26 in a palace at Cáceres as a headquarters. In a cool drawing-room in this hot Estremaduran city he worked with his *aides* and his brother Nicolás, as political adviser. On two occasions, when visiting the Army of Africa at the front, he had to leave his motor-car to take refuge from a marauding Republican aircraft.

34

'The Government of Victory' – Colonel Asensio Torrado – Rojo at the Alcázar – the Army of Africa rests – the Non-Intervention Committee meets – new advances on the Tagus – the final assaults on the Alcázar – Varela arrives in relief – the relief of the Alcázar

The first task of the 'Government of Victory' was to avoid immediate defeat. To the alarmingly near Tagus front, the astute Colonel Asensio Torrado, previously in command in the Sierra, was despatched to meet Yagüe, and his namesake, Asensio of the Legion. The Gastone-Sozzi column of Italian volunteers was transferred from Aragón to the Tagus, together with a group of French volunteers known as the *Commune de Paris* column. Asensio Torrado immediately attacked at Talavera. Though his men fought with courage and, this time, persistence, he could not manoeuvre to meet the fast-moving Nationalist counter-attack. As other Republican commanders had had to do so often, he was forced to choose between retreat and encirclement. His men made up his mind for him. They streamed back past his headquarters, leaving behind much material. However, no immediate Nationalist advance followed this new Republican retreat. The advance of 425 kilometres from Seville had somewhat wearied even the Army of Africa. The Nationalist General Staff knew that, the closer their armies drew to Madrid, the stiffer would be the resistance. In the pause while the main advancing column was reorganised, and Talavera established as a base of operations against Madrid, a newly equipped force under Colonel Delgado Serrano drove swiftly to the north to establish fighting *liaison* for the first time with the southernmost troops of Mola's Army, of the North, Colonel Monasterio's cavalry force coming from Ávila. A junction was made on September 8 at Arenas de San Pedro in the Gredos mountains. This cut off a large portion of Republican territory to the west. The pacification of the area followed in the usual manner.[1]

---

[1] It was at this point that the Army of Africa was joined by two ex-Regular British officers, Lieutenants Nangle and Fitzpatrick. The former, who had been in the Indian

On September 9, the defenders of the Alcázar at Toledo received the news by megaphone from a militia-post in a house across the street that Major Rojo, ex-Professor of Tactics at the Academy of Infantry, wished to call with a proposal from the Government. Since Rojo was known to Moscardó and others of the defending officers, he was received, during a cease-fire, at the Alcázar. He proposed that, in return for the surrender of the Alcázar, life and freedom would be guaranteed to the women and children inside. The defenders themselves would be handed over to court-martial. Moscardó not unnaturally refused these terms. In return, he asked Rojo to ask the Government to send a priest to the Alcázar during another cease-fire. Rojo promised to pass on the request, and departed, after chatting with the officers of the garrison, who unsuccessfully beseeched him to remain with them.[1]

Also on September 9, the Non-Intervention Committee met for the first time in London. W. S. Morrison, Financial Secretary to the British Treasury,[2] led the British delegation and took the chair. The other countries, represented by their Ambassadors in London, were Albania, Austria, Belgium, Bulgaria, Czechoslovakia, Denmark, Estonia, Finland, France, Germany, Greece, Hungary, Ireland, Italy, Latvia, Lithuania, Luxemburg, Norway, Poland, Rumania, Turkey, the Soviet Union and Yugoslavia. The list thus included only European countries and excluded Switzerland, which had banned the export of arms, but whose neutrality, like that of the United States, forbade her intervention even in a Committee of Non-Intervention.[3]

The first meeting of the Committee was concerned with 'the murky tide of procedure', in *Pravda*'s words. The representatives

---

Army, was one of the most professional and efficient officers of all time. His devotion to military life was absolute. Fitzpatrick was a more romantic Irish soldier of fortune, who explained that he was driven to volunteer for Spain, after seeing a famous photograph of militiamen seated on an altar dressed in priests' vestments. Both were given commissions in the Legion – the first foreigners to receive commissions who had not risen from the ranks. Captain (as he now is) Fitzpatrick has kindly permitted me to read his unpublished reminiscences of his experiences in Spain.

[1] Aznar, 202.
[2] Later Speaker of the House of Commons, Viscount Dunrossil and Governor-General of Australia. He had been Chairman of a British Cabinet committee concerned to co-ordinate non-intervention between the different departments. He has kindly given me an account of this meeting.
[3] The Non-Intervention Committee was throughout serviced by the Foreign Office. Papers, documents, etc., were prepared by a British Secretariat.

present agreed to give to Francis Hemming, the British Treasury official who became the Committee's secretary, the texts of the laws their countries had passed banning the export of arms. Apart from the British representative, the dominant figures at the Committee were Corbin, the French Ambassador, Grandi, the Fascist ex-Foreign Secretary whom Mussolini had transferred to the Embassy at London for not being Fascist enough, and Maisky, the Soviet Ambassador. Ribbentrop, the German Ambassador, and his second in command, Prince Bismarck, took a less prominent part from the start than Grandi to whom, indeed, they had been instructed to leave the running. However, Ribbentrop described how difficult he found working with Grandi – 'an intriguer if ever there was one'.[1] Portugal, whose attendance the Soviet Government had insisted upon, was not represented. The Portuguese Minister in Berlin said on September 7 (when the German ship *Usamoro* was refused facilities to discharge her cargo of arms for the Nationalists at Lisbon due, it was thought in Berlin, to British influence) that she would not be represented until after a ban on volunteers.[2] But the Portuguese need not have worried. Grandi had been instructed by Ciano 'to do his best to give the Committee's entire activity a purely platonic character'.[3] Ribbentrop later blandly admitted that a better name for the Non-Intervention Committee would have been 'intervention committee'.[4] The German attitude to the Committee was more ambiguous than the Italian, partly because the German Foreign Office was so ill-informed as to what the War Ministry was doing. The German diplomats had not, indeed, decided whether real non-intervention would aid Franco or not. As for France and Britain, Bismarck accurately reported that the first meeting of the Committee left the impression that, for both countries, 'It is not so much a question of taking actual steps immediately, as of pacifying the aroused feelings of the Leftist parties . . . by the very establishment of such a Committee'.[5] And, although the contemporary reports of British and French Consuls (not to speak of other agents) in Nationalist Spain are not available to historians, it is, perhaps, not absurdly fanciful to assume that they were as well-informed as their American colleagues. The British Consul

---

[1] Ribbentrop, 71.   [2] *GD*, 77.   [3] *GD*, 75.
[4] Ribbentrop, *loc cit*. He added, in his apologia written in Nuremberg between the trial and the sentence, 'I often wished that this wretched Spanish Civil War would go to the devil, for it constantly involved me in disputes with the British Government.'
[5] *GD*, 84.

at Seville must have known, as the American Consul, Mr Bay, reported, that German and Italian soldiers, airmen, aircraft and tanks were in that city and that, so far from making any attempt to leave after the start of non-intervention, their numbers were increased and reinforced. From the start, in fact, the British and French Governments were occupied less with the end of intervention on all sides than with the *appearance* of such an end. In this way the flow of war material to the two sides in Spain might not be prevented, but the extension of the Spanish War might be.

Britain later accused Italy of landing aircraft in Majorca on September 7.[1] On September 12, Ingram, the British *Chargé* in Rome, pointed out that changes in the Mediterranean would 'closely concern the British Government'. Ciano replied that no such alteration had occurred or was contemplated.[2] The incident showed that Britain would protest when she felt her closest interests were threatened by some consequence of the Spanish War, but that she would not do so in respect of a mere breach of the Agreement that she had done so much to secure. However, to give Baldwin's and Blum's Cabinets their due, both believed that their countries, and Spain, and European peace, would be best served by the prevention of military aid to Spain. Both Governments were at this time making every effort to keep the pact, even though in France this policy continued to make trouble for Blum on the Left. But at this time the majority of expressed opinion in both countries supported this policy. The Labour party in England even deplored the delay in bringing non-intervention into being. As for the Communists, Thorez tried to persuade Blum to change his policy on aid to Spain on September 7.[3] Despite his lack of success he nevertheless undertook that the Communists would not vote against the Government in the National Assembly. The Comintern sponsored in London a 'Commission of Inquiry into Alleged Breaches of the Non-Intervention Agreement in Spain'. Such respectable persons as Philip Noel-Baker, Lord Faringdon, Professor Trend of Cambridge and Miss Eleanor

---

[1] Lord Plymouth at meeting of the Committee, 23.10.36.

[2] Eden in the House of Commons, 16.12.36. But Majorca was nevertheless an Italian stronghold throughout the rest of the Civil War. The main street, the Ramblas, in Palma, was renamed the Vía Roma, and statues of two Roman youths in togas with eagles on their shoulders stood at its entry. The Bay of Pollensa became an Italian naval base. War material was poured into the island. The island was mined and refortified by Italians.

[3] Cattell, *Soviet Diplomacy* 24.

Rathbone were members. The two secretaries were Geoffrey Bing and John Langdon-Davies.[1]

In Spain, on September 13, the Basques surrendered San Sebastián to the Nationalists without a fight rather than risk the destruction in battle of its beautiful avenues. They also shot certain Anarchists who wished to set the town ablaze before the entry of the enemy. In the south, General Varela embarked upon a new Andalusian march, to the north of the mountains sheltering the long coastal plain of Málaga. Making for Ronda, Varela occupied *pueblo* after *pueblo* without resistance. In Aragón, fighting continued before Huesca. But no advance occurred. Only in Toledo did matters seem to be improving for the Republic. Conditions had greatly deteriorated inside the Alcázar. There was very little food – the bread ration being reduced to 180 grammes a day for each defender. During a three-hour truce on September 11, a suave priest from Madrid, Vázquez Camarasa, who had escaped death at the hands of the militia due to his known liberalism, arrived at the fortress. Owing to the impossibility of hearing individual confessions, he gave a general absolution to Moscardó and the defenders. In a gloomy sermon, he spoke of the glory which the garrison would gather in the next world. He thus administered a kind of extreme unction to the defenders. Certain of the Civil Guards defending the Alcázar meanwhile talked with the militiamen besieging them. The latter gave the defenders cigarettes and undertook to take messages to their families. Vázquez Camarasa left, and the siege continued. The Republicans now sought to end the resistance by burrowing under the walls from outside and planting a land mine under each of the two towers nearest the city. Civilians were evacuated from the city in preparation for the onslaught planned to follow the explosion. War correspondents were invited to Toledo, to watch the fall of the Alcázar, as if the occasion was a gala matinée.[2]

The next day, September 12, saw an important step towards Franco's assumption of supreme power on the Nationalist side. A

---

[1] Koestler, *Invisible Writing*, 323. The Spanish Republic also said that they would accept 'real non-intervention'. By this they meant no legislation in any country preventing them from buying arms. This was rather different from, for example, the Labour Party's view of non-intervention, which was that neither side should be able to get arms from abroad. Mr. Langdon-Davies has objected to a statement in an earlier printing of this book to the effect that he was at that time a member of the Communist party. I am satisfied that Mr. Langdon-Davies was never a member of the Communist party and I regret this mistake.

[2] *General Cause*, 334; Aznar 204–5. Evidence to the author of press correspondents

meeting of the Nationalist *junta* occurred at San Fernando aero-drome, Salamanca. Generals Orgaz and Kindelán proposed the idea of a single Nationalist command. Mola supported the suggestion with a fervour that raised doubts as to his sincerity, though there is no sign in fact that he opposed Franco in any important way after the beginning of the war. Old General Cabanellas was the only General who opposed the plan. He was outvoted. Kindelán, supported by Mola, proposed that Franco should be the General at the head of the single command. This was agreed, though Cabanellas did not vote. The Generals then separated. For over two weeks, however, nothing more was done.[1]

The second meeting of the Non-Intervention Committee occurred on September 14. It set up a Sub-Committee composed of Belgium, Britain, Czechoslovakia, France, Germany, Italy, the Soviet Union and Sweden, to deal with everyday matters of non-intervention. The smaller States even on the Sub-Committee were only too willing to follow the lead of the great Powers, and the real debates were confined to France, Britain, Germany and Italy. The timidity before Hitler, and before all international responsibility, of the Scandinavian and (as they would now be called) the Benelux countries was indeed in some ways the most distasteful aspect of the diplomatic history of those days. But then, what could they do if Britain continued with 'appeasement'? On September 14, Kagan, the Soviet *Chargé*, alleged that Italian military aircraft had recently landed at Vigo. Grandi denied the story. This coincided with Pope Pius XI's first public reaction to the war in Spain. He spoke of the Republicans' 'truly satanic hatred of God', at Castelgandolfo to 600 Spanish refugees.[2] Soviet aid to Spain, in the form of funds, food and other non-military material, which had lately slackened, now began again. But military aid did not yet come.

Back in Spain, General Varela was able to complete his design of capturing all central Andalusia, by taking Ronda on September 16. Mola, after the capture of San Sebastián, was now turning his

---

[1] Kindelán, 50–3. Iribarren, 216. Prieto was a passionate advocate of a single command on the side of the Republic, but with, for the time being, no success.

[2] The same day, a priest in Madrid who had sided with the Republic, Fr García Morales, adjured the Pope to denounce the rebels. Some days later, José Bergamín, the Catholic apologist who edited *Cruz y Raya*, described the Generals, Bishops, Moors, and Carlists who were fighting the Republic as being implicated in some 'fantastic mumming show of death'.

greatest efforts once more to the south, with the aim of falling upon
Madrid from the extreme north-west, in the Ávila region. In
Asturias, a column of Falangists and regular soldiers at last set out
from Corunna to attempt to relieve Aranda in Oviedo. The battle
also broke out again in the Tagus valley. Once more, the militia
fought with grim courage. This time they had even been persuaded
to dig trenches. From these, however, they now refused to move,
even when Yagüe sent forces on either side to outflank them.
After a seven hours' battle, the militia were once again forced to
choose between retreat and being surrounded. Once again they
chose the former, abandoning their well-prepared defensive position at Santa Olalla, and also the larger town next to it, Maqueda,
which fell to Yagüe on September 21.

Now, however, a critical decision faced the Nationalist Command: should they relieve Toledo now only forty kilometres away;
or continue to march on Madrid? For the position of the Alcázar
was now alarming. The defenders lived entirely in the cellars.
They had run short of water and had to eat their mules and all but
one of their horses – the thoroughbred racehorse who was kept
alive and tended till the end. On September 18 the Republicans
blew up the south-east tower. The whole besieged building began
to resemble a pile of rubble. Militiamen climbed up on the ruins of
the tower and fastened there a red flag on the equestrian statue
of Charles V in the courtyard. But the mine under the north-east
tower did not explode. Four officers repelled the militiamen on the
north turret with only pistols. On September 20, five engines full
of petrol were set up in the Hospital of Santa Cruz, and the walls
of the Alcázar were sprayed with the inflammable fluid. Grenades
were thrown to set it alight. A cadet leapt out of the Alcázar and
pointed the hose at the militia. The cadet was killed, and the
hose turned back to the Alcázar. In the afternoon, the petrol was
set on fire, but no great damage was done. In the evening, Largo
Caballero arrived in Toledo, to insist on the fall of the Alcázar
within twenty-four hours. The next day, Franco resolved to relieve
the city. General Kindelán asked him if he knew that the diversion
might cost him Madrid. Franco agreed that this was possible, but
argued that the spiritual (or propaganda) advantage of relieving
Moscardó was more important.[1] The lure of the Toledo arms
factory was, however, probably the determining cause of the
Nationalist diversion. On September 23, Varela, in command

[1] Kindelán, 54.

because Yagüe had fallen ill, set out for Toledo, with columns under Colonels Asensio and Barrón, both to advance on the city from the north. Meantime, the besiegers laid a new mine beneath the north-east tower. Assault guards were poured into Toledo from Madrid, to make the final onslaught. The mine was exploded on September 25 and the tower tumbled into the Tagus. But the solid rock foundations of the fortress could not be penetrated. And, while the Government issued *communiqués* announcing the fall of the Alcázar, Varela reached a point only fifteen kilometres away.

The annual League of Nations General Assembly was meantime starting in Geneva. By this time, of course, that organisation was crumbling. Its faults were patent. Never, even at the time of its splendour (such as after the admission of Germany in 1925) had it lost the character of an institution dominated by the victors of 1919. Nevertheless, till 1935 it had fulfilled its *rôle* as the expression of a world-wide passion for peace comparatively successfully. It had made peace between Greeks and Bulgars in 1925; it ended the Colombo-Peruvian War of 1934. It had abstained, true, over Manchuria in 1931. But this did not seem irreparable. In 1935, however, the League had failed to take effective action over Mussolini's invasion of Abyssinia. It voted for sanctions, but not any which had any effect. On July 4, 1936, these were abandoned. Mussolini's African adventure was tacitly accepted. The responsibility for all these retreats lay with the British and French Governments whose influence was supreme at the Palais des Nations. At the General Assembly of 1936, the *débâcle* over Abyssinia had to be reviewed. But now there was also Spain. In the wings of the assembly on September 24, Eden persuaded Monteiro to bring Portugal into the Non-Intervention Committee. In his speech in the general debate which opened the Assembly, Eden did not mention Spain at all, though he pledged that British policy would be to co-operate whole-heartedly with the League. Dr Lamas, the Argentinian President of the Assembly, supported by other Latin American delegations, sought to prevent Álvarez del Vayo from speaking on Spain, since it was not on the agenda – though the general debate had been regarded as permitting any discussion. But Álvarez del Vayo made his speech (though he had been persuaded to be moderate by Eden). He deplored that the Non-Intervention Agreement had placed the Government on the same footing as the rebels: whereas, by the established canons of international law, his Government was legally entitled to buy arms abroad and the rebels were not. The Republic would accept real non-intervention, but by this he meant freedom to buy arms.

Before any further speeches were made at Geneva, the Alcázar was relieved. On September 26, Varela cut Toledo's road communication with Madrid. Escape for the Republicans henceforth could only be to the south. In the morning of September 27, the defenders saw the friendly army of Varela massing on the long barren hills to the north. At noon, the attack on Toledo from outside was launched. Once again, the violence and training of the Army of Africa told immediately, although Toledo is easy to defend. The militia broke and fled, leaving behind the entire contents of the arms factory. In the evening, the defenders of the Alcázar heard Arabic words in the street below. The relief had arrived. There remained only the blood-bath that often then attended a Nationalist capture of a town. Lieutenant Fitzpatrick reported that, in reprisal for the discovery of the mutilated bodies of two Nationalist airmen outside the town, no prisoners were taken on entering Toledo, and that the main street was running with blood down the hill to the city gates.[1] Moroccans killed the doctor and a number of wounded militiamen in their beds at the San Juan hospital.[2] Forty Anarchists trapped in a seminary drank large quantities of anisette and then set fire to the building in which they were hiding, burning themselves to death.[3] Varela himself entered the city on September 28. Moscardó, parading before his men, informed him, saluting, that he had nothing to report, using the phrase '*sin novedad*' (as usual) which had served as the password for the rebels on July 17–18. The besieged came out into the open air for the first time for two months. And prayers were offered to 'the Subterranean Virgin, Our Lady of the Alcázar'.[4]

The same day, September 28, Portugal appeared for the first time at the Non-Intervention Committee. Lord Plymouth had now succeeded W. S. Morison as British representative. He quickly angered the Russian delegation by his arrogance – this '*haut*

---

[1] Fitzpatrick MSS.

[2] Cox, 54. This journalist was in Madrid at the time. Others have spoken of killings in this hospital. I think it probable that this terrible incident was partly caused by the fact that certain unwounded militiamen took refuge in the hospital and so drew the fire of the Moors in that direction.

[3] Langdon-Davies, 257.

[4] The seige of the Alcázar has a literature of its own. See especially Muro Zegri, *passim* and Sánchez del Arco, 175–8; Pemán, 190 fl; Aznar, 211; Cruzada, xxix 143-90.

landlord', *Pravda* described him, 'the appraiser of horses and a member of the aristocratic Beefsteak club'. At Geneva, meantime, Litvinov explained, so far as he could, the tortuous official motives of Russian adhesion to the Non-Intervention Pact. The Soviet Government, he said, had joined 'because France had feared otherwise there would be war' – although Russia thought non-intervention as illegal as did Álvarez del Vayo.

35

Nicolás Franco as Lucien Bonaparte -- Franco Head of State – the Anarchists enter the Catalan Government – Durruti and the new world – the Basque statute passed – a dinner in Salamanca – new advance of the Army of Africa – de los Ríos in Washington – institution of political commissars

In preparation for the final advance to Madrid, Franco was named Head of State in Nationalist Spain on October 1. The ground for this step had been prepared by Kindelán, with Nicolás Franco, the latter acting in the *rôle* of Lucien Bonaparte with the analogy of the 18 Brumaire definitely in mind. On September 29, Kindelán, Orgaz, Yagüe and Franco, travelled to Salamanca by air. On their arrival, Franco was greeted as 'Generalissimo' by an escort of Falangists and Carlists detailed to act in this way by Nicolás Franco. At a meeting with the *junta*, Kindelán read a decree confirming this title, to which was added that of Head of Government. But this-time the Generals assembled were cool to the proposal. Why add political, to the military responsibilities of the Generalissimo?[1] Cabanellas said that he wished for time to consider the decree. The conference was suspended for luncheon, at which by a mixture of veiled menace and flattery Kindelán succeeded in establishing Franco as he wished. Cabanellas was permitted two days for his 'consideration', so as not to hurt his pride.[2] The original text of the decree, as accepted by the Generals on the 29th, spoke of Franco as Head of Government. But a special messenger from Nicolás Franco arrived at the printer on a motor bicycle to alter the text at the last moment to 'Head of State', and it was with this wording that the decree was issued.[3]

This was a real *coup d'état* by Franco, though in the tumult of war and emotion that swept Nationalist Spain after the

---

[1] It may be noted that the Generals who complained were anti-Monarchists, afraid that Kindelán and Orgaz, both Monarchists, were really aiming at a Restoration through this manoeuvre.

[2] Kindelán, 54. Ansaldo,73, confirms Kindelán's *rôle*.

[3] Creac'h, 182. Confirmed privately to me.

relief of the Alcázar, no one noticed it as such. On October 1, Franco was installed as Head of State in Burgos. In a speech afterwards, he elucidated his view of the future of Spain: the popular vote would be eliminated in favour of a 'better way of expressing the popular will'; labour would be guaranteed against the domination of capital; the Church would be respected, taxes revised, and the independence of peasants encouraged. Insofar as the speech contained any theoretical basis, it was founded on the more harmless aspects of the Falange's programme. The crowd in the square beneath him cried out 'Fran-co, Fran-co, Fran-co', as they had only a year before been crying 'Je-fe, Je-fe, Je-fe' for Gil Robles – both cries being copies of the Italian cry of 'Du-ce, Du-ce'. But the affair remained more a parody of Italian Fascism, since the short figure of General Franco, surrounded by priests in black cassocks and *bourgeois* persons, could never be very impressive. Henceforward posters all over Nationalist Spain proclaimed the virtue of having 'One State. One Country. One Chief'. Franco was described as 'Caudillo' – a bad translation of 'Fuehrer'. On the streets of Nationalist Spain, the remark 'The Caesars are always victorious Generals' was everywhere scrawled.[1] With their leaders all either dead or in prison, the Falange accepted this change without protest – for the time being. The Carlists also were preoccupied at this moment, by the death of the old Pretender, Alfonso Carlos, in Vienna on September 28. Last of the original line of Don Carlos, his nephew by marriage Prince Xavier of Bourbon Parma acted as Regent till a new member of the Bourbon dynasty could be found who would certainly pledge himself to *Dios, Patria, Rey* and the implacable principles of anti-democratic traditionalism. Fal Conde and other Carlist leaders were actually in Vienna for Don Alfonso Carlos's funeral when Franco was gaining the 'crown' at Salamanca.

On October 2 an administrative *junta* at Burgos was named to carry on the Nationalist administration, headed by an associate of Mola's, General Dávila. Nicolás Franco, a 'great friend of Germany' as the German diplomat Dumoulin reported,[2] stayed by his brother's side as 'Secretary-General'. General Orgaz stayed as High Commissioner in Morocco and Colonel Beigbeder as his Secretary-General. Cabanellas, as a sop, was given the sinecure of Inspector-General of the Army. With Franco named as 'Generalissimo', the two armies already formed, that of the North

---

[1] Ansaldo, 78.　　　　　　　　　　[2] *GD*, 107.

and that of the South, were confirmed in the names of Mola and Queipo de Llano. Queipo de Llano, however, continued to do what he could to discomfort Franco from his private kingdom of Seville. His nightly rabid broadcasts continued, though he had recently ceased to cry 'Viva la República' at the end of them.[1]

The Army of Africa remained under the personal control of Franco, who changed his headquarters from Cáceres to Salamanca. Varela led in the field, beneath him being four columns under Asensio, Barrón, Delgado Serrano and Castejón respectively, each of mixed Moroccans and legionaries and each about 1,200 men strong, supported by technical sections. A battalion of mainly Falangist volunteers from Seville was attached to Delgado Serrano.[2] This still comparatively small force now lay ready for the advance on the capital along a forty-kilometre front from Toledo to Maqueda. The advance did not begin until Franco had assured himself of overwhelming air superiority, achieved thanks to further German and Italian supplies.[3] Also, the Generalissimo assured himself that the Aragón front would remain reasonably stable by sending there certain Moroccan reinforcements.

Political changes also occurred on the Republican side. On September 26, the CNT, having held the reality of power in Barcelona since the rising, accepted it formally by entering the Generalitat. Juan Fábregas became Catalan Councillor for Economics. The Anarchists henceforth referred to the Catalan Government as 'the Regional Defence Council', to avoid giving to their already alarmed extremist followers the impression that they had joined a real Government. The POUM also joined, Andrés Nin becoming Minister for Justice. The PSUC rejoined the Government, Comorera at their head. This new Government declared its aim to be to curb revolutionary indiscipline. The Anarchists, having for the first time in history entered a Government, now daily diminished in importance, as did the anti-Fascist Militias Committee, upon which they had been so powerful. This caused increasing anger among the Anarchist rank and file. Durruti, however, preserved his idealism at the front. 'I do not expect any help from any Government in the world,' he told a Canadian journalist, at the end of September. The Canadian

---

[1] Bahamonde, 57.   [2] López Muñiz, 7-8.

[3] Nationalist historians say that the first sea cargo of Italian aid, including twelve Fiat 32's and 'thousands of cannon projectiles', arrived at Vigo at the end of September. It is probable that this was indeed the first cargo to land at Vigo from Italy. (Aznar, 316.)

replied: 'You will be sitting on a pile of ruins if you are victorious.'
Durruti answered: 'We have always lived in slums and holes in
the wall – we shall know how to accommodate ourselves for a
time. . . . We can also build. It is we who built the palaces and
cities here in Spain and in America and everywhere. We, the
workers, can build cities to take their place. And better ones – we

MAP 15. THE ADVANCE ON MADRID

are not in the least afraid of ruins. We are going to inherit the
earth. The *bourgeoisie* may blast and ruin their world before they
leave the stage of history. But we carry a new world in our hearts.'[1]
The POUM, on the other hand, believed that they had secured a
'workers' majority' in the Catalan Government. But they continued to wonder aloud: 'Are we collaborating with the petty
bourgeoisie? Or are they collaborating with us?'[2]

[1] *Montreal Star*, 30.10.36. But Durruti was shortly converted to the 'discipline of
indiscipline' by Ilya Ehrenburg. The burden of Durruti's comments was, 'You mean
officers should be appointed? Orders should always be obeyed? An interesting idea.
Difficult to introduce, but let us see . . .'
[2] *The Spanish Revolution* (POUM paper), 4.11.36.

A week later, on October 1, a rump meeting of the Cortes assembled at Valencia to approve the Statute of Basque Autonomy. The Basque leader, Aguirre, proclaimed that the Basques, though Catholic, did not fear the proletarian movement, nor its motives – 'for we know how much justice there is in them.' He pledged the new Basque Republic (to be known as Euzkadi), of which he was to become President, to stand by the Government of Madrid 'until the defeat of Fascism'.[1] On October 7, all the municipal Councillors of the three Basque provinces who could attend voted in the sacred village of Guernica for the Presidency of the 'Provisional Government of Euzkadi' to govern during the Civil War. Aguirre was elected nearly unanimously. He then named the Government, which was sworn in under the celebrated oak tree. The Civil Governor of Bilbao handed over authority to Aguirre. In his Cabinet, there were five Basque Nationalists, holding the key posts of the Interior, Justice, Defence and Agriculture; and these naturally dominated the first Basque Government, which also nevertheless included three Socialists, one Communist, and one member each from the two Republican parties. The new Governments first action was humane. They evacuated 130 female political prisoners by His Majesty's Ships *Exeter* and *Esk* to France, through Dr Junod of the International Red Cross.[2] The Basque Civil Guard and *Asaltos* were reorganised, the former being altered into a People's Guard under Major Ortúzar. All of the latter force were Basque Nationalists, and all over six feet in height.[3]

The new offensive of the Army of Africa had by now begun, on October 6. The attack struck directly northward from Maqueda and Torrijos, breaking away, that is, from the latitudinal advance from west to east which had marked this campaign since the fall of

---

[1] *Diario de Sesiones*, October 1. The Basque Nationalist Irujo had joined the Republican Cabinet on September 25 (Lizarra, 99).

[2] This was one of the more harrowing incidents of the Civil War. Bilbao had been bombed on September 29. The fury of the people of the city had caused the consequent murder of a number of the political prisoners kept in appalling conditions in three small cargo boats in Bilbao harbour. Afterwards the Basque Government released the 130 women as part of an exchange previously agreed through Dr Junod. But when Dr Junod first returned to Bilbao, he did so without the children whom he had promised to bring back from where they had been on holiday near Burgos. For the Nationalists had gone back on their word. The church bells of Bilbao were ringing, the mothers and the families of the children thronged the quay, when HMS *Exmouth* sailed in empty-handed. The terrible disappointment nearly caused the lynching of Dr Junod. But later 40 children were sent back. The full exchange, however, was never achieved.

[3] Aguirre and Steer are the basis for this paragraph. I have also been helped by the evidence of Mr Luis Ortúzar.

Badajoz. It coincided, and aimed to join hands, with a campaign from the north, under General Valdés Cabanillas, starting from Ávila. German and Italian aircraft first bombed the Republican supply lines into Madrid. The Republican lines then broke at the attack by Castejón. Asensio, however, was held up by vigorous defence in the hills of San Viente, and Valdés Cabanillas made little progress in the difficult country of the Sierra de Gredos.

That afternoon, the Non-Intervention Committee met in London. Lord Plymouth pointed out to Germany, Italy and Portugal the allegations of aid made by the Spanish Government at Geneva. Maisky accused Portugal of allowing its territory to be used as a Nationalist base of operations, and demanded a commission to patrol the Spanish-Portuguese border. That night in Salamanca, Franco gave a reception for Dumoulin, the German Counsellor in Lisbon, who had arrived with Hitler's congratulations on Franco becoming Head of State. Franco said that he felt complete admiration for Hitler and the new Germany. He said that he hoped soon to be able to hoist his own flag beside the banner of civilisation that the Fuehrer had already raised. He thanked Hitler for 'his valuable material and moral help'. A dinner followed, attended by the highest-ranking German pilot in Salamanca and by Nicolás Franco and Kindelán. Franco, reported Dumoulin, 'permitted not even a moment of doubt as to the sincerity of his attitude towards us, being very optimistic as to the military situation, counting on taking Madrid in the near future'. The Generalissimo permitted himself to speculate on the future political organisation of Spain: a restoration of the Monarchy could not at present be discussed; and it was essential – 'though proceeding with kid gloves' – to create 'a common ideology among the co-fighters for Liberation' – Army, Falange, Carlists, Orthodox Monarchists and CEDA.[1]

The following day, October 7, the offensive against Madrid was resumed. Yagüe, recovered from his illness, returned to the field command acting under Varela. This meant that the Army of Africa was now led by a firm Falangist as well as a romantic Carlist.[2] Aircraft flew over Madrid demanding the evacuation of the city. And Mola announced facetiously that he would be taking a cup of coffee in the Gran Vía in the capital on October 12.

---

[1] *GD*, 107.
[2] The latter, Varela, caught the imagination of foreign journalists. He would receive them at all hours of day or night (unlike other Nationalist Generals), sometimes with his innumerable medals worn on the breast pocket of his silk dressing-gown.

In London, the Soviet *Chargé*, Kagan, now sent a note almost in the form of an ultimatum to Lord Plymouth. Precisely at this time Russian ships were about to leave Odessa and other Black Sea ports with arms for the Republic. So Kagan, alleging that 14 Italian aircraft flew legionaries to the Spanish mainland on September 20, announced that, if such violations of the Non-Intervention Pact did not immediately cease, the Soviet Government would consider herself free from her obligations under the agreement. 'If there is an agreement,' wrote Kagan, 'we want that agreement to be fulfilled. If the Committee ... can secure that ... well and good. If it cannot, let the Committee say so.'[1] The next day, October 8, a Soviet diplomat in Moscow told the American *Chargé* that, unless the Committee did show itself determined to bring about an immediate end of violations, the Soviet Union would withdraw, considering itself free to aid Spain with military equipment. This blunt change of Soviet policy infuriated the British Foreign Office. 'What,' they asked, 'can Russia hope to gain by throwing over neutrality at this time?' But the Soviet action was supported on October 9 by the British Labour Party Conference, which passed a unanimous resolution declaring that Germany and Italy had broken their neutrality and calling for an investigation. That day, the meeting of the Committee lasted seven hours, the exchange of insults between Kagan and Grandi astonishing the other diplomats. The Portuguese Ambassador temporarily withdrew during the discussions of the Russian proposal for the patrol of the Spanish-Portuguese frontier.

Meantime in Spain, the Army of Africa captured San Martín de Valdeiglesias, and merged its offensive with that of Valdés Cabanillas at El Tiemblo. The front once established along a north-south line, Monasterio's cavalry was transferred to the Tagus valley, to join Tella and Barrón. The militia fled towards Madrid, and always along the roads, so making an easy target for the Nationalist aircraft with their machine guns. Bayo, once the commander of the ill-fated Majorcan expedition, harassed the Nationalist Army while it was assembling, by a series of successful guerilla actions.[2]

---

[1] Cattell, *Soviet Diplomacy*, 44. The quotations of this historian from the documents of the Non-Intervention Committee are invaluable since he had had access to copies of the conference papers in the State Department – which are the American copies of the German copies, captured after the war. The British copies themselves of course linger unconsulted in the Foreign Office library. They are still regarded as 'confidential'.

[2] López Muñiz, 5.

Thus, although Mola was late in keeping his rendezvous for a cup of coffee in the Gran Vía (in one of whose cafés a table was thereafter kept with a reservation for him upon it in large letters); at the end of the first ten days of October, the Republic was faced once more with defeats on all sides. Largo Caballero refused to mobilise Madrid's large building industry to dig entrenchments, on the grounds that he had no shovels and no barbed wire. He added that Spaniards might fight from behind trees, never from trenches.[1] Russian arms had not yet arrived, the supply from French and other sources was as small and unreliable as that from the Spanish war-industries themselves. On October 10, de los Ríos, newly appointed Republican Ambassador at Washington, appealed unsuccessfully to Cordell Hull to allow the Republic to purchase arms from the United States, saying that the collapse of the Republic would cause the fall of Blum, and so presage the extinction of democracy. Hull said that America had no law against aid to Spain – only a policy of 'moral aloofness'.[2]

Back in Madrid, in a new attempt to achieve discipline in the army, the Government ended the independence of the militias, making them dependent on the central General Staff. This was done on October 10, but it was a long time before this decree was carried out. They also established, throughout the armies, as a result of demands by Álvarez del Vayo and the Communist party, the system of political commissars which already obtained in the Communist Fifth Regiment. These were intended to maintain the militiamen's political faith in their cause after the disappearance of their own parties, and to diminish their continued suspicions of the loyalty of the regular army officers. It was, however, a victory for the Communist party. From the start, the commissars were mainly Communists, since the party had now established itself as by far the most effective Republican propagandists. An unidentifiable Russian Communist officer described as 'Miguel Martínez'[3] indeed carried out the organisation of these officials.[4] Four days later, a greater change still came over the Spanish War: Russian military aid to the Republic began.

---

[1] Louis Fischer, *Men and Politics*, 353.   [2] *USD*, 1936 Vol 2 536.
[3] He was, perhaps, the future Marshal Rokossovsky, who was certainly in Spain at about this time under one *alias* or another. See below, page 305.
[4] Kol'tsov, 17. Quoted by Colodny, 26.

36

Russian aid – Comintern aid – the vacillation of Stalin – Thorez'
visit to Moscow – formation of the International Brigade – journey
to Albacete – Marty, Longo, and their staff – Kléber – Russian
supply ships – other agitation – Goering calls for more men

The German *Chargé* in Moscow, Tippelskirch, made an estimate on September 28 of Soviet aid to Spain hitherto. He added: 'To what extent "the Soviets" are rendering more than "humanitarian" aid remains open.'[1] No proof of any Russian violation of the arms embargo had been received in Berlin. Already Largo Caballero felt special bitterness towards Russia, who appeared only interested in not jeopardising the Franco-Soviet pact. Jesús Hernández had recently complained to General Berzin, the Russian military attaché, that the failure of Russia to send arms was making things very difficult for the Spanish Communists.[2] Rosenberg, the Russian Ambassador in Madrid, reported that the Republic was lost unless Russian arms were sent soon.[3] And during September, more and more Russian and Comintern leaders went to Spain. Michaél Kol'tsov, *Pravda*'s leading foreign correspondent arrived in the middle of the month, apparently with military as well as propaganda functions. He was followed by Alexander Orlov, previously head of the economic section of the NKVD, now instructed to set up a branch of that distasteful body in Spain to keep a general watch upon the activities of the Comintern and foreign Communists in Spain.[4] Such an

[1] *GD*, 100. Mr D. C. Watt has, however, unearthed two interesting reports in the files of the German Military *Attaché* at Ankara (Annex to report No. 4238 of the German Military *Attaché*, Ankara, February 7, 1938, and Annex 2 to Report No. 7238 of April 4, 1938) which purports to be a statement derived from a German agent with access to Turkish records of the amount of Soviet aid through the Dardanelles (*The Slavonic and East European Review*, June 1960, pp. 536–41). These reports conclude that in September 1936, 3 Soviet ships brought 500 tons given material, with 1,000 tons of ammunition.

[2] Hernández, 42.   [3] *The International Brigades*, 53.

[4] Krivitsky, 101. Krivitsky says that Orlov's appointment was decided at a meeting in Moscow on September 14. This was almost the last conference presided over by Yagoda, the GPU chief who was displaced on the 24th by Yezhov, and later shot. For Krivitksy's allegations that Russian military aid to Spain began from this date see above, page 263.

important and baleful individual would not have been sent to Spain unless something equally important was afoot. But still Stalin vacillated. Everything seemed to point to intervention. But still, with Zinoviev and Kamenev hardly cold in their graves, he delayed, waiting to see how the Non-Intervention Pact would work,[1] and how the Comintern aid already agreed upon would change matters, and perhaps listening to Russian Generals, such as Tukhachevsky who, busy with the task of building a great Soviet army, may be supposed to have opposed the despatch of precious war material so far away from the Motherland.[2]

Stalin's decision was eventually reached apparently as a result of a visit to Moscow on September 21 by Thorez, the French Communist leader. By that time, the aid which General Krivitsky had been ordered to begin from The Hague had only reached a very primitive stage. On September 21 itself, after a delay in keeping with the habits of Comintern as well as Russian bureaucracy, an agent named Zimin visited General Krivitsky in The Hague. Zimin described the supreme importance of keeping the Soviet Government's name from being associated in the Comintern arms traffic. The first move, he said, was to set up an organisation for the purchase of arms throughout Europe. Krivitsky arranged the financial capital and the offices, and guaranteed profits.[3] Agents were easily found. These resembled characters from a novel by Phillips Oppenheim. There was, for example, a mysterious Doctor Mylanos, a Greek subject, established in the Polish port of Gdynia. There was Fuat Baban, another Greek, the representative in Turkey of the Skoda, Schneider and Hotchkiss firms, and who was later arrested in Paris for drug-peddling. And there was 'Ventoura. Of Jewish origin. Born in Constantinople. Found

---

[1] Litvinov's autobiography, 212, gives a description of Stalin at this moment. This document is widely held to be a forgery. But I have found the few entries in it dealing with Spain likely to be accurate. Nevertheless, the following must be read with reservations. On September 10, Litvinov noted Molotov to be still demanding aid to Spain, to 'oblige Blum'. Dimitrov, whom Litvinov disliked and whom Stalin allegedly called 'a poor Marxist version of an Anarchist', argued as usual that Russia would lose influence with the Popular Front in Paris if she did not aid Spain. Litvinov described this argument as 'drivel'. He said that the Soviet Union's first task was to achieve international security, in the form of a convention in which France and Britain would participate. Stalin vacillated, said Litvinov, adding 'he rarely does this'.

[2] It was customary then, as now, to regard all such delays and contradictory moves by the Soviet Government as being evidence of sinister Machiavellianism. In fact, Soviet policy is very often simply explicable as being carried out by inefficient and dilatory Russians.

[3] Krivitsky, 103–5.

guilty of a swindle in Austria. False passport. Lives with a woman in Greece. Domicile in Paris in a hotel in Avenue Friedland'.[1] It is such persons as these who must be pictured, during the rest of the Spanish War, carrying out their profitable missions behind the backs of the dignified gentlemen of the Non-Intervention Committee and supplying somewhat obsolete weapons to the militiamen of the Spanish plains and sierras. A chain of import-export firms was set up in Paris, London, Prague, Zurich, Warsaw, Copenhagen, Amsterdam and Brussels, with always a NKVD member as a silent partner controlling funds. Arms were procured from Czechoslovakia, France, Poland, Holland and even Germany; and here, in some instances, Admiral Canaris purposely secured the despatch, through Communist hands, of faulty war material to Spain.[2] With the French frontier closed, the best way of transporting the arms was by sea, securing Consular papers from other Governments, Latin American or Chinese, certifying that the goods were for those countries.[3] However, this organisation was not properly working before October. Before the effects of Comintern aid could be seen, on September 22, Thorez visited Moscow.[4] He supported arguments put by Rosenberg, Russian Ambassador in Madrid, for military aid from Russia direct. He also suggested that aid should be given to the Republic in the form of volunteers raised internationally by foreign Communist parties (though they would welcome non-Communists). They could be organised by the Comintern, and led by foreign Communists exiled from their own country, now in Russia. These 'International Brigades' would have a great propaganda value for the Communists and might form a nucleus of an international Red Army, besides giving stiffening, alongside the Spanish Communist Fifth Regiment, to the Republican Army. Such an international force had been suggested at the meeting of Comintern and Profintern on July 26, which had started to arrange 'humanitarian' aid to Spain. The English Communist military expert, Tom Wintringham, in Spain with the British medical aid unit, had also suggested the idea. Since then, hundreds of foreigners had joined the Re-

---

[1] This evidence derives from a German Foreign Ministry note of October 8, 1938, to the Spanish Nationalist Foreign Ministry quoted in *The International Brigades*, 43.
[2] Though some genuine German material got through to the Republic, and the Nationalist Ambassador in Berlin had to complain, this was not till 1938.
[3] *International Brigades*, 34.
[4] Willi Muenzenberg, the Comintern propaganda chief, also went to Moscow at this time to argue the Spanish Republicans' case. He was only able to return

publican Army – many in the POUM. Thorez's suggestion[1] was to capitalise on the goodwill caused by the arrival of these international volunteers, and ensure that as many as possible should join the forces led by the Communist party. Such an organisation could be the chief recipient of any Soviet aid in Spain. If, for example, the Spanish Government did not pay for the aid, it could be withdrawn. Soviet arms, even in Spain, could in this way be secured in the hands of reliable party members.

The Bulgarian head of the Comintern, Dimitrov, apparently now became enthusiastic for the idea. Stalin himself realised that in this way he could dispose of the large numbers of Communist *émigrés* in Soviet Russia who were best out of the way at a time when the great purge was beginning. Furthermore, it is possible that certain leading Russian Generals made the despatch of arms to Spain conditional on the sending of a shock force, even if composed of foreign Communists. For in this way at least some military lessons and experience might be gathered, even at the expense of some Russian war material. Henceforward Russian military papers, such as *Krassnaya Zvezda* and *Krassnaya Armii*, gave as much attention to the fighting in Spain as the German *Wissen und Wehr* and *Kriegskunst*. Earlier in the month, Randolfo Pacciardi, an Italian Republican *émigré* (never a Communist), had approached the Spanish Government with the aim of forming an Italian Legion in Spain, independent of political parties, out of all Italian political exiles, to be recruited at first in Paris. But Largo Caballero had opposed the idea.[2] Now, after new disasters on the battlefront, he altered his view.[3] Togliatti said bluntly to Jesús Hernández that Soviet aid would be not only effective for the Republican Army but for the Communist party: 'We will tell the Socialists and Anarchists that the arms are inadequate so that they will blame

---

to Paris by good fortune. Shortly afterwards, he finally quarrelled with his chiefs, and left the party, to be murdered mysteriously in Southern France in 1940.

[1] It is in principle unlikely that such an idea could have come to Thorez himself, who is not a man of vast imagination, and it is at least possible that Wintringham should be given more credit for it than he. Togliatti, Vidali and Rosenberg must have been consulted and perhaps used their influence in favour of the scheme.

[2] Pacciardi, 17–19.

[3] It would seem that this was arranged by a definite treaty, in which Luigi Longo, an Italian, Stephan Wisniewski, a Pole, and Pierre Rebière, a Frenchman, concluded negotiations in Madrid on behalf of the Comintern (*L'Epopée d'Espagne*, 50) with Martínez Barrio. Rosenberg of course could not have been left out of the discussions.

Blum and the Non-Intervention Committee . . .'[1] Stalin, entering upon the whole project with misgivings, took no risks in Spain. Before Soviet weapons were actually used on Spanish soil, the entire remaining Spanish gold reserve had been despatched to Russia as security for payment. To the few Russian technicians and military experts whom he sent to Spain Stalin gave the order 'stay out of range of artillery fire.'[2] This meant that they should neither be killed nor, more compromising, captured.

The formation of the International Brigades now became the main work of the Comintern. Each Communist party was instructed to raise a given number of volunteers. In many cases, the prescribed figure was higher than local parties could possibly attain. Most of the ablest leaders of the Comintern, not already involved, like Togliatti, in Spain, were employed in this way. The future Marshal Tito, Joseph Broz, at first was at Paris organising, from a small left bank hotel, the flow of recruits through his so-called 'secret railway', which provided passports and funds for East European volunteers.[3] Where the volunteer was not a Communist he was usually investigated by a NKVD representative and by a Communist doctor – the latter perhaps only at the French-Spanish border.[4] Many escaped this security checking, however, especially those who joined the volunteers in Spain or *en route*. Some sheer adventurers in search of excitement joined – such as Nick Gillain, the Belgian who gave his reason as 'spirit of adventure, lassitude and this rainy autumn of 1936'.[5] About 60% were Communists before volunteering, and a further 20%, approximately, became Communists during their experiences in Spain. From all countries (including Britain) 80% (or even a higher percentage) of the Brigades were members of the working class.[6] Most were young men, though many of the Germans and Italians,

---

[1] Hernández, 49.   [2] Krivitsky, 126.

[3] When, after the secret assassination of Gorkič and other Yugoslav leaders at the end of 1936, he became chief of the Yugoslav Communist party, he supervised the despatch of Yugoslavs. According to one of his biographies, Tito wanted to fight in Spain himself, but the Comintern refused to permit this (Bilantan, 24). Tito denies having ever been in Spain but it seems probable that he at least visited the Brigades' headquarters for one reason or another. His reluctance to admit this is no doubt explained by some aspect of the Gorkič murder.

[4] The fact that the Spanish Republican Government were under no illusions about the connexion between the Communist parties and the volunteers is attested by the advice of Spanish Consuls to would-be volunteers to make contact with Communist parties.

[5] Gillain, 7.

[6] Approximate figure worked out after questioning of survivors.

militant refugees from Fascist *régimes*, were veterans of World War I. Many, especially among the French, were at this time unemployed[1] and nearly all had had experience of street fighting against 'the Fascists' in Berlin, Paris and even London. Many of the British volunteers appear to have been persons who desired some outlet through which to purge some private grief or maladjustment. An English Communist volunteer summed up the motives of his countrymen in Spain by saying 'undoubtedly the great majority are here for the sake of an ideal, no matter what motive prompted them to seek one.'[2] The qualification is significant. But let not posterity impugn the sincerity of these men. Some may have been adventurers. Many of the leaders were time-serving Stalinists. But the majority were neither. Perhaps as many as a third of them died in action in Spain. Many more later suffered political or professional ostracism because of their Spanish experiences. Many were executed simply because they had been to Spain in the purges in Eastern Europe of 1949.

The central recruiting office of the Brigade was in the Rue de Lafayette in Paris. Karol Świerczewski, a Pole known as 'Walter' was military adviser, at the head of a *bureau technique* in the nearby Rue de Chabrol. Świerczewski had fought in the first World War for Russia. He then took part in the Russian Revolution and Civil War, later becoming a Professor in the Moscow Military School.[3] Recruitment was directed by the Italian Communists Nino Nanetti and Giuseppe di Vittorio (known as 'Mario Nicoletti'). The theme of recruitment propaganda was based on the slogan that Spain should be 'the grave of European Fascism'. The main recruiting centre was at the *Maison des Syndicats* at No 8 Rue Mathurin-Moreau. There were branches in the *Maisons des Syndicats* throughout Paris, France and Belgium. From France the International Brigade volunteers were sent to Spain either by train or boat. The first group was to arrive on October 14 at their base at Albacete, halfway between Madrid and Valencia, surrounded by the endless wastes of La Mancha, and known for several centuries for the manufacture of knives.[4]

The first contingent of volunteers, five hundred strong, left

---

[1] Many unemployed Frenchmen from Lyons were despatched into the Brigades.
[2] Tomalin MSS, 7.
[3] He appears in *For Whom the Bell Tolls* as General Goltz.
[4] See *The International Brigades, passim*; Wullschleger, 21 fl; Colodny, 178.

the Gare d'Austerlitz, in Paris, by train 77 (later nicknamed 'the train of volunteers') and travelled *via* Perpignan and Barcelona, to find on arrival at Albacete that no preparations had been made. The barracks of the Civil Guard had been made over to them. The rooms on the ground floor were still stained with the blood of those killed there on July 25. The International Brigaders squeamishly preferred, therefore, to crowd into the rooms upstairs to sleep.[1] The first group were nearly all Frenchmen, with some Polish and German exiles from Paris. There were also some White Russians who hoped to use this roundabout method of returning to their own land. These were shortly afterwards joined by many of the foreign volunteers who had fought in Aragón and in the Tagus valley, including the German Thaelmann *Centuria*, the Italian Gastone-Sozzi *Centuria*, and the French Paris Battalion. John Cornford was among these, though he had returned home to England on leave after his fighting in August. Communist party members predominated among these new recruits. Socialists and liberals, however, existed among them and were greeted with special welcome by the Communists as representing the spirit of the Popular Front. The day after arrival at Albacete, all volunteers would be identified and registered. A clerk would ask if there were officers, non-commissioned officers, cooks, typists, artillerymen, riders or machine-gunners present. Many replied according to their ambitions rather than to their abilities.[2] The volunteers were then organised in language groups, with appropriate names. The English volunteers were as yet too few to form a separate battalion and some were therefore joined to the Germans and some to the French.

The supreme '*troika*' in command of the base was André Marty as Commander, Luigi Longo ('Gallo') as Inspector-General, and Giuseppe di Vittorio ('Nicoletti') as Chief Political Commissar. The two latter, Italians, were men of marked ability and even humanity.[3] Marty lacked both. He was the son of a worker condemned to death in his absence for his part in the Paris Commune. He had first come to prominence in 1919 when as a seaman-machinist he had led the mutiny of the French Black Sea Fleet in

---

[1] Gillain, 18.   [2] *Ibid.*, 19.

[3] Luigi Longo is at the time of writing Vice President of the Italian Communist party, and Giuseppe di Vittorio was till his death in 1958 Secretary-General of the General Confederation of Italian Labour, the Communist trade union which is the largest in Italy. Longo's *nom de guerre* was taken from the name of a famous and elegant matador, El Gallo, who had recently retired from the bull-ring.

protest against orders received to support the White Russian armies. At that time he was not a Communist, though he became one in 1923. His rise to the top of the French Communist party in the succeeding years was largely due to his conspicuously anti-militarist record. He owed his appointment at Albacete to his supposed military knowledge and to his constant favour with Stalin as a man who had refused to take up arms against the struggling Soviet Union seventeen years before. By 1936 he had become obsessed with an imaginary fear of Fascist or other spies.[1] He was also arrogant, incompetent and cruel. He was followed to Spain by his wife, Pauline – whom even he seemed sometimes to try and avoid. He was an appropriate agent of Soviet policy in the age of purges. Even Stalin had a less suspicious nature than André Marty. The military commander of the base was a crony of Marty's, a Parisian municipal councillor, Gayman,[2] who went by the common Spanish name of 'Vidal'. A French artillery Major, Hagar, established specialist schools of artillery, observers, commissars and cartographers. Captain Alocca, an Italian tailor from Lyon, was in command of the cavalry base at the nearby town of La Roda, while another French Captain Etienne, nephew of the General of that name, set up an artillery base at Almansa. André Malraux organised the International Brigade's air squadron at Alcantarilla and Soviet technicians undertook the development of a training airfield at Los Alcázares. Here Russian instructors trained both Spaniards and international volunteers for air fighting. Albacete became too full for all the trainees, and the neighbouring *pueblo* of Madrigueras was taken over by the Italians, Tarazona de La Mancha by the Slavs, La Roda by the French and Mahora by the Germans. Dr Oscar Telge, a Norwegian, controlled the medical services, with a staff of many Nationalities beneath him, and Pauline Marty acted as inspector of the hospitals. Louis Fischer, the American journalist, acted at first as Quarter-Master General until he quarrelled with Marty, when his post was taken by a Bulgarian, Kapov.[3] Gottwald, the Czech Communist, served in Albacete for a time as general political adviser. The German Ulbricht organised a German division of the NKVD, where he investigated German, Swiss and

---

[1] Though undoubtedly the International Brigades did include some spies.
[2] For the following, see the *International Brigades*, pamphlet issued by the Spanish Foreign Ministry 1953.
[3] Louis Fischer, *Men and Politics*, 366.

Austrian 'Trotskyists'.[1] The Brigade were provided with uniforms by the French Communist party, including an Alpine round woollen hat. Discipline was enforced with an iron hand. 'The Spanish people and the Spanish People's Army have not yet conquered Fascism,' Marty told the Brigade. 'Why? Is it because they have lacked enthusiasm? A thousand times no. Is it because they have lacked courage? I say ten thousand times no. There are three things they have lacked, three things which *we* must have – political unity, military leaders and discipline.'[2] When he spoke of military leaders, he indicated a short figure with grey hair, his overcoat buttoned up to his neck – 'General Emilio Kléber'. Kléber was now forty-one, a native of Bucovina, now part of Rumania, at his birth Austria-Hungary. His real name was Lazar Stern, and his *nom de guerre* was that of one of the ablest of the French Revolutionary Generals.[3] In the first World War he served as a Captain in the Austrian Army. Captured by the Russians, he was imprisoned in Siberia. At the Revolution he escaped and joined the Bolshevik party, and he was alleged to have been present at the murder of the Czar at Ekaterinburg. After taking part in the Russian Civil War, he studied at the Frunze Military Academy and joined the Comintern Military Section. He was sent on various confidential missions in the Chinese wars and perhaps also to Germany. Now he arrived in Spain, as the leader of the International Brigades. He was built up by Communist propaganda to be a soldier of fortune of naturalised Canadian nationality. On being introduced to his future command by Marty, he stepped forward and gave the salute of the clenched fist, amid a roar of applause. Marty went on: 'There are some who are impatient, who wish to rush off to the front at once. These are criminals. When the first International Brigade goes into action, they will be properly trained men, with good rifles.' So the training at Albacete went on. The difficulties of language were surmounted. The different ways in which the nations carried out their left and right turns in drill were co-ordinated. Only the Germans, however, took drill seriously or were any good at it. Irishmen enlivened the dark barracks with their customary songs. And in a dozen languages slogans were scrawled on walls: '¡Proletarios de Todos Países! ¡Uníos!' 'Proletariar, Alle Länder, Vereinigt Euch!'

[1] Ruth Fischer, 500 footnote.   [2] Romilly, 72–3.
[3] The French Marshal Kléber had also acted for a time as a mercenary, in the armies of Austria in the 1780s.

'Prolétaires de Tous Pays, Unissez-vous!' 'Proletari di tutti i Paesi Unitevi!' 'Workers of the World, Unite!'

During the next few months, volunteers continued to stream into Albacete. W. H. Auden[1] described the urgency of the appeal of Spain in words still irresistible.

> *Many have heard it on remote peninsulas,*
> *On sleepy plains, in the aberrant fishermen's islands*
> *Or the corrupt heart of a city,*
> *Have heard and migrated like gulls or the seeds of a flower.*
>
> *They clung like burrs to the long expresses that lurch*
> *Through the unjust lands, through the night, through the alpine tunnel;*
> *They floated over the oceans;*
> *They walked the passes. All presented their lives.*
>
> *On that arid square, that fragment nipped off from hot*
> *Africa, soldered so crudely to inventive Europe;*
> *On that tableland scored by rivers,*
> *Our thoughts have bodies; the menacing shapes of our fever*
>
> *Are precise and alive. For the fears which made us respond*
> *To the medicine ad. and the brochure of winter cruises*
> *Have become invading battalions;*
> *And our faces, the institute-face, the chain-store, the ruin*
>
> *Are projecting their greed as the firing squad and the bomb.*
> *Madrid is the heart. Our moments of tenderness blossom*
> *As the ambulance and the sandbag;*
> *Our hours of friendship into a people's army.*

Some volunteers came by sea from Marseilles, some across the Pyrenees by secret paths unknown to, or unwatched by, the French Police carrying out the orders of their non-interventionary Government. Those who crossed the Pyrenees would stay one night in the old castle of Figueras. By both routes nearly all went through Barcelona, or through Alicante, where they were greeted with enthusiasm by crowds shouting *'salud'*, *'no pasarán'* and 'UHP'. The streets would fill with Spaniards singing the *International*, as the

---

[1] He himself worked with an ambulance unit for a short while in 1937. See below, page 392.

volunteers marched to their train. A reception would be held at
the Town Hall, where a band would give the *International*,
The Young Guard, *The Red Flag*, or the *Hymn of Riego*, or
all of them. The train onwards would stop at small stations, where
peasants would press forwards offering wine and grapes, giving the
clenched fist salute, and shouting '*Viva Rusia*' – even though
they might know that the men in question were not Russian, but
Frenchmen or Englishmen. Bands, even in these stopping places,
would play the *International*, while local Communist and other
Popular Front parties would crowd the platforms with the names
of their villages inscribed on banners. Frequently, not surprisingly,
the recruits would arrive drunk. One Irish recruit from Liverpool,
who afterwards wrote a *Candide*-like description of his experiences,
began on his first night at Albacete a period of recurrent illnesses,
drinking bouts and visits to the Brigade penitentiary that lasted for
six months.[1]

At precisely the same time as the nucleus of the International
Brigades arrived in Albacete, the first Russian ships bringing arms
began to arrive at Cartagena and at Alicante. The date of the first
arrivals was apparently October 15, when *Pravda* was still demanding, like Maisky, that either the 'Fascist' countries should be forced
to respect non-intervention, or the Spanish Government should
be given every facility to purchase arms. The same day, Stalin
sent an open letter to José Díaz, the Spanish Communist leader,
published in *Mundo Obrero* on October 17, saying that the 'liberation of Spain from the yoke of the Fascist reactionaries is not the
private concern of Spaniards alone, but the common cause of all
progressive humanity'. And twelve cargo vessels carrying arms to
Spain passed the Bosphorus between October 1 and October 24,
being officially declared bound for Mexico, London and Hamburg.[2] Among them, on October 11, the *Georgi Dimitrov*[3] loaded
60 trucks at Odessa for Spain; on October 12, the *Neva* left Odessa
with 151 trucks; on October 13, 150 Russians disembarked at
Alicante in the *Ciudad de Barcelona*, and the *Bolshevik* landed at

[1] The Anarchists distrusted the International Brigades at the beginning and gave
orders to their militants who controlled the French frontier passes to oppose their
entry. But 'after requests by international personalities we desisted, though continuing
to believe that these persons were not wanted. Arms were needed, not men' (Abad
de Santillán, *La Revolución y la Guerra de España*.)

[2] *GD*, 126. *New York Times*, 24.10.36.

[3] Other Nationalist sources say that the *Georgi Dimitrov* unloaded 6 planes, 48 trucks
and 1,106 tons of ammunition on October 23 at Alicante.

Cartagena 18 aircraft, 15 tanks and 300 cases of munitions; the same day the Spanish *Campèche* landed munitions of Russian origin at Alicante, and the *Transbalt* loaded 100 trucks and munitions boxes (with food) at Odessa; on October 16 the *Komsomol* landed 50 tanks at Cartagena, with men to operate them, and other material, while the Spanish *Lavamendi* loaded a number of unmounted aeroplanes on the high seas from an unidentified Russian ship; 150 Russians landed that day at an aerodrome 150 miles south of Alicante, and 'early in October' an unknown Russian steamer was said to have landed 6 aircraft at Alicante. The Russian personnel were almost all pilots, or flying instructors. The head of the Russian air force was an officer named Jacob Schmutchkievich who went under the name of General 'Douglas'.[1] Other Russian officers appeared in Madrid at this time, with various missions. They are not easy to distinguish since they went under false names. One of them was certainly the tank General Pavlov. The future Marshals Rokossovsky, Konev and Malinovsky apparently all appeared in Spain at one time or another.[2]

By this time, organisations for aid to the Republic had sprung up in nearly every country in the world. Friends of Spain, Spanish Medical Aid Committees, Committees for Spanish relief were set up everywhere. Behind them all lurked the shadow of the Comintern or of the local Communist parties. Mr Philip Toynbee, then a Communist at Oxford, described later how his orders that Michaelmas term were 'to proliferate Spanish Defence Committees throughout the university, as a moth lays its eggs in a clothes cupboard'.[3]

Not all these organisations were concerned to aid the Republic

---

[1] Tinker, 53. This *nom de guerre* was inspired by the fighter of that name then much in demand. The identity of 'Douglas' was revealed in the Soviet periodical *Questions of History*, No 7, 1956 by 'José García' of the Soviet Academy of Sciences.

[2] The same issue of *Questions of History* admits the existence of Malinovsky in Spain. Other Russians admitted in that periodical to have been in the Spanish War include – General Stern, who went under the name of Grigorevitch, and who (apparently) was quite different from Kléber, whose real name, as we have seen, was Lazar Stern. The article also mentions Generals Meretzkov and Rodimtsev and a pilot, A. Serov, as having been in Spain either at this time or later. The only evidence for the appearance of Rokossovsky and Konev, apart from rumour, is El Campesino, *Comunista en España*, 73–85. According to El Campesino, Rokossovsky was charged with espionage in Nationalist Spain – chiefly allegedly to discover for Stalin the character of certain German arms. Konev, under the name of 'Paulito', is said by El Campesino to have trained terrorists in Spain. There is nothing inherently improbable in this story. El Campesino says he got on very well with Malinovsky, who was known as 'Mañolito', adopted the rank of Colonel, and revelled in eating chick-peas.

[3] Toynbee, *Friends Apart*, 87.

win the war. Many were aimed simply at humanitarian work, regardless of who gained the victory. The greater part of the money available, however, went to Republican Spain, since their need was greater than that of the Nationalists, who had adequate food and medical supplies throughout most of the war. This caused the Nationalists to conclude that all the foreign agencies at work in Republican Spain were politically subversive. And indeed the Communist party lay behind most of even these selfless committees of English humanitarians. But such aid was in fact more needed by the Republic than by the Nationalists because the Spanish Military Medical Corps had been mainly with the rebels since the start of the rising.[1]

At the same time, in Berlin, Goering was complaining that he did not have adequate personnel to handle deliveries to and from Spain. Hess then put the whole of the Nazi party's foreign organisation at his disposal for this, Eberhard von Jagwitz at its head. Jagwitz thenceforth worked directly under Goering, twelve rooms being provided for him in the Nazi party offices. And now at last the German Foreign and Economic Ministries also heard of the existence of ROWAK and HISMA, on October 16.[2]

[1] There were, however, general relief funds which gave aid to both sides. The English General Relief Fund for Spain was supported by the Archbishops of Canterbury and of Westminster, the Chief Rabbi, the Moderator of the Church of Scotland and the Free Churches. It was formed in December 1936.

[2] *GD*, 113–14.

37

In Spain itself, on October 16, the Nationalist garrison in Oviedo was relieved after suffering terrible privations – and, indeed, only just in time to prevent its fall to the Asturian miners, who had already penetrated into the town.[1] The monastery of Santa María de la Cabeza near Córdoba, held by Captain Cortés and a Civil Guard detachment, was henceforth the only Nationalist outpost inside Republican territory. Varela now launched the next stage of his assault on Madrid. On October 15, the whole thirty-kilometre front was driven forward fifteen kilometres. The advance continued on October 16 and 17, when a new attack was made from the south by Barrón and Tella. Major Domingo, the Republican field commander, shot himself in despair after two hours of fighting. The road junction of Illescas, halfway between Toledo and Madrid, fell on October 17. Largo Caballero telephoned the town to speak to his commanding officer, to be answered, to his horror, by Varela. The next day, the weary Republican Army, only partly heartened by the assurance of their new commissars that Russian help was really coming, launched a counter-attack upon Castejón at Chapinería. Six thousand militiamen broke Castejón's lines and surrounded the town by the morning of October 19. Castejón then personally led a sally out of the town through its cemetery, and changed the Republican victory into a defeat. On October 20, another Republican attack, directed by General Asensio Torrado[2] in person, with Majors Rojo, Mena and Modesto leading 15,000 men, was launched at Illescas, where Barrón was established with his Moroccans and legionaries. The Republican forces were brought up to the front by double-decker Madrid buses plainly visible across the flat land from Barrón's command post. Illescas was plastered with artillery

---

[1] Aznar, Villegas and Lojendio are the basis for the following military descriptions.
[2] He had been promoted General after Talavera.

bombardment, and the town surrounded. Monasterio's cavalry and Tella's column from Toledo were thrown into the battle, and the Nationalists once again outflanked the militiamen, who were finally driven back beyond their point of departure by October 23. Behind the Nationalist lines, aid from Italy and Germany continued. The American Consul at Gibraltar noted the arrival of the first Italian infantrymen sent to the mainland of Spain – 23 Abyssinian veterans – on October 23.

The sound of battle could now be plainly heard in Madrid. An atmosphere of gloom pervaded. Azaña, like many other citizens, gave up the capital for lost, and, unlike them, fled to Barcelona – without even telling the Cabinet. The first the Ministers heard of this escape was an urgent request from Barcelona as to what entertainment would be proper for the President. The Cabinet hastily announced that the President had left for an extended tour of the fronts; this remark was celebrated as the only joke in Madrid during the Civil War. Henceforward Azaña lived at the spectacular mountainous monastery of Montserrat outside Barcelona, conveniently far from likely aerial attack and conveniently near the French frontier in case of a general collapse. Incapable of abandoning his sensitivity, Azaña increasingly infuriated his Ministers. He totally refused to listen to intelligence reports, which he named 'bad detective stories'. His sincerity always impelled him to speak the truth, even on telephone calls to other countries which could easily be tapped. And when his Cabinet expostulated he would simply reply: 'I am not to blame that I am of an analytic spirit and you are not.'[1]

The approach of the battle brought closer fraternity than ever between Anarchists and Socialists. The UGT and CNT in Barcelona sealed their differences for a while at least in a declaration of common purpose on October 22. While large capitalists should be expropriated without compensation and their concerns collectivised, small proprietors should not be disturbed, unless their firms were needed for war production: in which case (like all foreign concerns) they would be compensated. The Anarchists were also prevailed upon to support a single Republican command, obligatory military service, discipline, and a 'unified war industry'. Although the statement omitted any consideration of agriculture, it represented one more victory of the UGT over the CNT, and therefore, for the PSUC or for the Communists, over

[1] Álvarez del Vayo, *The Last Optimist*, 173.

the Anarchists – and also, implicitly, of the Madrid Government over that of Barcelona.

In Madrid, a committee of the Popular Front and CNT was set up to intensify the search for members of the Fifth Column. Illegal murders, which had almost ceased, broke out again. One so killed was Ramiro de Maeztu, once counted among the Generation of '98, later a theorist of Spanish Fascism. Loyalty was everywhere suspect. Asensio Torrado was blamed for the defeat of Illescas, and he was fortunate to be given the post of Under-Secretary on October 24, while General Pozas took command of the Army of the Centre. The same day, General Miaja, the old scapegoat for the collapse of the Córdoba offensive, was brought from retirement in Valencia and named commander in Madrid in succession to General Castelló, the ex-Minister of War, who now became finally insane. A rapid easterly advance by Monasterio's cavalry from the Illescas-Toledo road meantime caused the fall of Borox, Esquivias, Seseña and Cuesta de la Reina, so threatening Madrid's communications with Valencia.

During these new battles around Madrid, Russian aid continued to stream through the Bosphorus. At least nine large cargo ships reached Spain from Russia between October 20 and 28. They carried altogether at least a hundred trucks, twenty-five tanks, thirty pieces of artillery, fifteen hundred tons of ammunition, six thousand of grain, three thousand of other food, and a thousand tons of diesel oil. But it is impossible to make an accurate, or even an approximate estimate of the extent of Russian assistance. According to the Nationalists the inventory of Soviet war material of all sorts from October 20 until November 20, 1936, was 100,000 rifles, 3,000 million cartridges, 1,500 machine-guns, 6,000 shell guns, 300 bombers, 200 cannon, 75 anti-aircraft guns, 20,000 incendiary bombs and 25,000 air bombs.[1]

All Republicans would regard this estimate as being so exaggerated as to be laughable. The Russians and Communists deliberately sought to exaggerate their material. As in the miracle of the loaves and fishes, every six Russian aircraft was made out to be six hundred. The Nationalist figures quoted seem certainly exaggerated somewhat. But, nevertheless, the aid was undoubtedly a great injection of life into the Republican defences.[2]

Partly in order to give guarantee for payment for these shipments and others to come, partly to make certain that it would not

[1] *The International Brigades*, 30.   [2] See Appendix III.

fall into the hands of the rebels if Madrid should fall, the bulk of the Spanish monetary gold – 1,581,642,400 pesetas worth (£63,265,684) out of the total 2,258,569,908 pesetas worth (70% being in gold pounds sterling) – was despatched on October 25 from Cartagena[1] to Odessa. Much of the rest of the monetary gold was already in Paris, but some remained in Madrid till the end of the war. Russia was chosen because she seemed to be the Republic's only friend, for delivery to London or Paris might risk confiscation under the Non-Intervention Agreement. The allegations made later that the Soviet Union cheated the Republic out of this money have a slightly unreal character, since the goods supplied had no market price. However there is no doubt that Russia drove a hard bargain for her goods. In addition to the gold, Spanish raw materials were despatched to Russia in bulk. Largo Caballero and the Finance Minister, Dr Negrín, were party to these transactions, and Azaña also gave his consent. Prieto later claimed that he did not know where the gold was going. The question remains undecided, but it seems in fact likely that Prieto helped with the shipment at Cartagena.[2] The night before the shipment took place, Italian bombers bombed Cartagena. Prieto, frightened, insisted on taking refuge in an old naval headquarters. In the morning he discovered that he had been standing all night in a *patio* under a glass-roof. This faery gold, as it later appeared to be, left for Russia on October 25, travelling by way of Tunis and arriving at Odessa on November 6.

The Non-Intervention Committee met again on October 23. The Soviet Government, declared Maisky, could not consider themselves bound by the Non-Intervention Agreement 'to any greater extent than any of the remaining participants' in the Committee. The chief upshot of this meeting was Portugal's breach of diplomatic relations with the Spanish Government because of Soviet charges against it. The Soviet Union did not, as the Soviet Press had suggested was probable, now leave the Committee. This may have been due to Litvinov's return from Geneva. He no doubt pointed out that an abandonment of the Committee would mean a breach with France and Britain and, therefore, a blow to the policy of collective security. Lord Plymouth meantime circulated a note in the Committee's Sub-Committee on October

---

[1] Where it had already been taken some weeks before.
[2] Álvarez del Vayo, *The Last Optimist*, 284. I prefer this account to that of Prieto, who at this time (and until well into 1937) was by no means an anti-Communist.

24 accusing Russia of three breaches of the agreement and Italy of one. He also proposed the control of the supply of war material to Spain by, for example, establishing observers at Spanish ports who could report what they saw to the Committee.

During these exchanges in London, the Italian Foreign Minister, Count Ciano was visiting Berlin. There he discussed Spain with Neurath and Hitler. They all agreed that Germany and Italy should recognise the Nationalists as the official Government of Spain after the fall of Madrid – which Neurath imagined could be counted upon within a week. Both Germans and Italians discounted any idea of influencing Spanish internal affairs or of taking over any part of Spanish territory. They also exchanged rumours: Ciano said he had heard nothing of the German report that 400,000 Russians were on their way to Spain. However, he said, he was instituting an observation service between Sicily and Africa. He added that Italy was finishing two submarines for the Nationalists – the association of ideas indicating that the completed vessels would be useful in this Mediterranean vigil. This meeting brought the Germans and Italians far closer together on all matters. Within a week, Mussolini would launch for the first time the phrase 'Berlin-Rome Axis' to describe their association.[1]

1 Ciano, *Diplomatic Papers*, 60–1. *GD* 122, 117.

BOOK IV
THE SIEGE OF MADRID

38

Arrival of Russian arms – the Condor Legion formed by the German Government – the 'Fifth Column' – the Nationalists prepare their triumph – the Anarchists enter the Government – Mola's plan of attack – flight of the Government from Madrid – General Miaja and the Communists in control – Kol'tsov – massacre of the political prisoners at Paracuellos – the Government escape assassination at Tarancón[1]

O n October 28, the diplomats met again in the Locarno Room in the Foreign Office. Maisky repeated, with a plethora of double negatives, that those countries who considered it just to supply the Spanish Government (that is, the Soviet Union) were 'entitled not to consider themselves more bound by the Non-Intervention Agreement' than did Germany, Italy and Portugal.[2] The British Trades Union Congress and Labour party followed the Russians by dropping non-intervention. Henceforth 'Arms for Spain' was a cry which united the Left[3] in Britain as elsewhere. At the same moment, Largo Caballero was broadcasting over Madrid Radio. 'The time has come to deliver a death-blow,' he began. 'Our power of taking the offensive is growing. We have at our disposal a formidable mechanised armament. We have tanks and powerful aeroplanes. Listen, comrades! At dawn, our artillery and armoured trains will open

---

[1] I must repeat my acknowledgments for help in this Book to the research of Mr R. G. Colodny. He is especially valuable for his quotations from the diaries of Michael Kol'tsov which, republished in Moscow in 1957, have not been translated into English. The works of López Fernández and Somoza-Silva, Miaja's *aide*, which are of great value, are well summarised in Colodny. His account is inclined to be over-favourable to the Communists but, since the Communists played a major part in the battle of Madrid, this does not matter so much. Valuable evidence by eye-witnesses on the Republican side is given in Buckley, Cox, Regler (*The Great Crusade*), Pacciardi and Malraux. On the Nationalist side, I have here found, as always, the trio of Lojendio, Aznar and Villegas (supplemented by López Muñiz) most helpful. *La Cruzada* henceforward becomes a little weary – but then it has already reached its twenty-ninth volume.

[2] *USD*, 1936 Vol 2 546.

[3] At the Labour Party Conference, held that year in Edinburgh, 519,000 votes had been cast against the party line of support of non-intervention. These included Sir Charles Trevelyan, Christopher Addison, Philip Noel-Baker and Aneurin Bevan.

fire. Immediately, our aircraft will attack. Tanks will advance on the enemy at his most vulnerable point.'[1] Madrid had heard such optimistic predictions before. This time, however, Largo Caballero was speaking the truth: Russian tanks and aircraft had arrived.

The attack took place at dawn on October 29. A group of Russian tanks, driven by Russians, led by the tank specialist, General Pavlov, smashed into the Nationalist cavalry. These tanks were used in the new *blitzkrieg* style evolved in Germany by Colonel Guderian and admired in Russia by Tukhachevsky. They were, that is, massed together for a shock attack rather than, as favoured by the French, spread out in support of infantry.[2] A strange quixotic battle ensued between tanks and horsemen in the narrow streets of Esquivas. Since the Fifth Regiment could not advance fast enough, the tanks were shortly forced to retire. The effect of the attack was to suggest to the Nationalists that the south of Madrid was better guarded than it actually was.

The following day – though apparently without specific news of the Russian tank attack – the German Foreign Minister, Neurath, despatched an urgent instruction to Admiral Canaris who had recently arrived in Spain, where, under the name of 'Guillermo', he was enjoying himself driving fast about the bumpy and deserted roads. 'In view of possibly increased help for the Reds,' Neurath said, 'the German Government does not consider the combat tactics of White Spain, ground and air, promising of success.' He therefore instructed Canaris formally to propose to Franco that Germany should send powerful reinforcements. If Franco wanted these, he would have to agree that they should be placed under a German commander responsible solely to him and guarantee that the war would be more systematically and actively conducted.[3] Franco accepted these terms. By November 6, the so-called 'Condor Legion', with General von Sperrle as commander, and Colonel Richtofen as Chief of Staff, had been assembled at Seville. This force comprised at first a battle group of 4 bomber squadrons of 12 bombers each, a fighter group of the same strength, and a seaplane, reconnaissance and experimental squadron. It was supported by anti-aircraft and anti-tank units, and two

---

[1] *Solidaridad Obrera*, 30.11.60.
[2] The Russian admiration for this 'revolution in warfare' partly derived from the fact that it seemed akin to their own political and economic revolution.
[3] *GD*, 123–5.

armoured units of four tank companies of four tanks each.[1] The personnel of this force amounted to some 6,500 men.[2] Although this was undoubtedly a most revolutionary unit its equipment and armament were primitive. The Condor Legion flew mainly without radio. Their machine-guns had to be reloaded by hand. The bombers were Junkers 52. The fighters were Heinkels 51 and Messerschmidts 109.[3] There was also later attached to the Condor Legion a 'North Sea Group' composed of gunnery, mine and signal specialists. These operated from the battleships *Deutschland* and *Admiral Scheer*.[4] Thus precisely when Russia was committing herself to the help of the Republic, Germany was increasing and reorganising hers. By a grim paradox, the Russian and German officers who in the years before Hitler had come to power had secretly trained together on the plains of White Russia were now able to carry out experiments in actual contest in the larger war-game of the Spanish War, with Spaniards their victims.

Despite, or perhaps because of this new commitment to their German allies, the Nationalist Generals were now supremely confident. Mola took over the whole command on the Madrid front for what was expected to be the final assault. He established his headquarters at Ávila. When asked by a group of foreign journalists which of his four columns he expected would take Madrid, he replied, in words repeated incessantly during the twenty-five years of treachery and espionage since that time, that it would be that 'Fifth Column' of secret Nationalist supporters within the city.[5] A heavy bombing campaign against Madrid was mounted from October 29 onwards, partly to satisfy the German advisers who were curious to see the civilian reaction. The attack upon Getafe on the 30th was particularly severe, 60 children being counted among the deaths. From that time onwards, every day until fighting began in the outskirts of the city on November 6 a small *pueblo* described by journalists as a 'key' to Madrid was captured by the Army of Africa. On November 4 the airport of Getafe fell. The next day the Nationalists entered the nearby suburbs of Alcorcón and Leganés, the bus and tram terminals of Madrid.

---

[1] The tanks were commanded by von Thoma, who had already been in Spain for three months training Spaniards and giving general military guidance.

[2] *Loc. cit.*   [3] Galland, 26.

[4] *Völkischer Beobachter*, May 1939, quoted by Toynbee, *Survey 1938*, Vol I 358.

[5] Mr Noel Monks, then of the *Daily Express*, has described this press conference to the author. But Lord St Oswald (at the time a reporter on the Republican side) has a claim to have coined the phrase some weeks before.

Franco announced that the liberation of the capital was near, and told Madrileños to keep to their houses, which 'our noble and disciplined troops will respect'. A threat that 'we shall know the guilty and only upon them will fall the weight of the law' accompanied these words.[1] Lists of persons to be arrested were made ready, and a municipal administration for the conquered city was formed in Ávila. Lorries of food for the population were assembled only a little behind the artillery. Radio Lisbon even broadcast a description of Franco entering Madrid on his white horse.

On the Republican side, after the high hope of the day of the Russian tank attack, there was gloom everywhere. The streets of the capital were filled with refugees and their cattle, goods and domestic animals. The Government was re-formed to include, in this hour of final crisis, the Anarchists, as the Catalan Generalitat had been re-formed a month earlier. García Oliver became Minister of Justice, Juan Peiró, a glazier, Minister of Industry, Juan López Sánchez, Minister of Commerce and Federica Montseny, the bespectacled female intellectual from Barcelona, Minister of Health. These working-class leaders entered the Government with scarcely a ripple of surprise caused. The rest of the Ministry, which was enlarged from 13 to 18, remained much as previously. Azaña opposed the inclusion of the Anarchists, but he was brought to agree by telephone.[2] García Oliver, probably the only genuine anarchist ever to have held the portfolio of Justice in any country, immediately impressed even Republicans by his efficiency.[3] But his obsession at the start of his tenure of office was to destroy the archives of convicts at the Ministry of Justice. This he did. It was later said that the compromising files had been burned in an air-raid.[4] The Anarchist paper *Solidaridad Obrera* spoke of November 4 as 'the most transcendental day in the political history of the country', and announced that the Government had 'ceased to be an oppressor of the working class'. All demands for a Nationalist Council, not a Government at all, were immediately dropped. The Socialist Araquistain explained from Paris that the UGT had become converted to revolutionary Socialism, and that the CNT now recognised the State as 'an instrument of struggle'.[5] But Federica Montseny was told by her

[1] Valdesoto, 183. [2] Álvarez del Vayo, *Freedom's Battle*, 206.
[3] Martín Blázquez, 298. [4] *General Cause*, 371.
[5] *Socialist Review* VI No 6 (May–June 1938) 17, quoted Cattell, *Communism*, 66.

father that this meant 'the liquidation of Anarchism. Once in power, you will not rid yourselves of power'.[1]

The Anarchists gave no new fire to the Cabinet. On the contrary they surrendered to the prevailing gloom. Only the Communists stayed resourceful. It was they who monotonously but hearteningly proclaimed '*no pasarán*' on the radio, and in the streets. It was they who warned Madrid that its fall would presage the massacre of half the population. Their prestige, and that of the Fifth Regiment, was bound up with the survival of the city.

With a mixture of over-confidence and caution, Mola, Varela and Yagüe delayed their great attack until dawn on November 7. The plan was that an arrow-like attack should be launched between the University City and the Plaza de España into, that is, a middle-class area on the heights immediately above the valley of the Manzanares. Such an attack would entail a difficult climb up the hill covered by West Park, from across the River Manzanares and the Casa de Campo. Of Yagüe's columns, the first, Asensio's, was to cross the Manzanares directly below the Paseo de Rosales, the long terrace-like street running along the top of West Park, and climb up to capture the Model Prison and the Don Juan barracks. Castejón was to cross to the left and establish himself at a student hall of residence known as the Fundación del Amo, on the Madrid side of the University City. Delgado Serrano, on the right, was to capture the Montaña barracks and bring the Royal Palace and the Gran Vía under fire. Meantime, Barrón and Tella were to advance in the suburb of Carabanchel to suggest that the main attack was coming from the south.[2]

Largo Caballero's Government now decided to leave Madrid for Valencia. It was announced that administration could not be carried on in a war zone. However, the timing of the decision suggested that the Government thought the city about to fall. At three o'clock on November 6 Largo Caballero told the commander of the Madrid Division, General Miaja, of the plan, and that he was henceforth in control. The leading Ministers, civil servants and politicians of all parties, except the Communist, thereupon left Madrid taking with them all the Government files, including those of the Ministry of War. Miaja and General Pozas, commander of the Army of the Centre, were sent for by the Under-

---

[1] Señorita Montseny in a speech in Toulouse (International Bulletin of the MLE-CNT in France September-October 1945). Quoted Richards, *Lessons of the Spanish Revolution*, 59.   [2] López Muñiz, 25 ff.

Secretary of War, General Asensio who gave them each an envelope marked 'very confidential, not to be opened till 6 a.m.' Asensio then left for Valencia also. Miaja insisted that the orders be opened immediately. He and Pozas then discovered that both sets of instructions had been put in the wrong envelope. Pozas was ordered to establish a new headquarters of the central Army at Tarancón. Miaja was charged to set up a *junta* of defence with representatives of the Popular Front parties, to be responsible for Madrid.

This was the opportunity of the Communists, and the Russian advisers. These rapidly assumed the executive functions abandoned by the regular civil servants. While Russian aircraft dropped leaflets calling on Madrileños to emulate Petrograd, *Mundo Obrero* exhorted wives to be ready to take their men's lunches 'not to the factory but to the trenches'. And, while Republican officials and commanders were reluctant in their gloom to co-operate with Miaja, the Communist Antonio Mije said that the Fifth Regiment was unreservedly at the General's disposal. He added that the Communists would defend Madrid house by house. The *junta* of defence which General Asensio had proposed was formed, almost all young men. Though proportionate, as stipulated, to the governmental parties, as in the *pueblos* of the first days of the war, power remained with the strongest group .– now the Socialist-Communist Youth and the Communist party. Michael Kol'tsov, the *Pravda* correspondent, seemed for a while the chief inspiration of the *junta*.[1]

A new General Staff was also set up, composed chiefly of officers considered too unimportant to be taken to Valencia. Rojo, who had taken the Republic's surrender terms to the Alcázar, became Chief of Staff. He began the difficult task of discovering what army, and what arms, still existed. For the confusion in the War Ministry attendant on Largo Caballero's departure had caused a breakdown in communications with the fighting units, who were more or less carrying on on their own. All the commanders, and then the trade union leaders, were summoned to the War Ministry. Miaja spoke to them in heroic terms, not concealing the extreme gravity of the situation, and demanding that 50,000 trade unionists be mobilised for the Front the next day. The commanders returned to their men heartened, knowing at least that Madrid would not fall without a fight. The Communist-Socialist

[1] Barea, 174.

Youth, meantime, organised searches for Fifth Columnists. 'Miguel Martínez', the Russian Chief Commissar, sent away the political prisoners in the Model Prison. In the moment of alarm, nearly all of these were butchered by their guards, officially while being 'transferred to a new prison', at the small nearby village of Paracuellos de Jarama. During the next few days mass executions occurred of nearly all the political prisoners in Madrid, at that same village, at San Fernando de Henares nearby and at Torrejón de Ardoz. Among the thousand or so killed at this time was Ledesma Ramos, the first of the Spanish Fascists.[1]

The Government itself narrowly escaped a similar fate. On the way to Valencia, several Ministers were held up at Tarancón by the 'Iron Column', the *cagoulards* of the Spanish Revolution, who did not accept the entry of their leaders into the Government. The Ministers were unceremoniously forced out of their seats at rifle-point and told to return to their posts in Madrid or be shot. Álvarez del Vayo enabled the Government to proceed by feigning to return to Madrid and then driving very fast past the Anarchist picket. UGT officials met with similar difficulties on the other road to Valencia, at Cuenca.[2] Such was the decay of the prestige of the Government at the moment when the Army of Africa was at the gates of Madrid.

[1] Galíndez, 66; *General Cause*, 236.
[2] Álvarez del Vayo, *Freedom's Battle*, 208; Borkenau, 196.

39

The battle of Madrid – mobilisation of the populace – arrival of the first International Brigade – their rôle in the defence – the Nationalists held – Durruti arrives in Madrid – Asensio crosses the Manzanares – battle of the University City – the fire raids on Madrid

The battle which began on the west of Madrid on November 7 was one of the most extraordinary in modern war. An army, well-equipped but only about 20,000 strong, mainly Moroccans and legionaries, engaged in a fierce struggle against an ill-armed but enormous urban mass. The former were supported by German and Italian, and the latter by Russian, tanks and aircraft.

At dawn, Varela began a heavy artillery bombardment. At the same time, Madrid Radio transmitted orders to build barricades. Masses of workers left for the front lines, many without arms, ready to take up the rifles of those killed. La Pasionaria's voice was heard incessantly on the loudspeakers in the streets, exhorting women to prepare to pour boiling oil on those who came to attack their homes. Women played as great a part as they had done in the early days of the war, appealing in demonstrations that all men should be sent to the front. A women's battalion even fought before the Segovia bridge.[1] Children also helped with building barricades. Russian fighters appeared for the first time to combat German and Italian bombers. Undoubtedly, however, it was not weapons but tenacity that held up the Nationalist advance. The militiamen, given extra fire by pamphlets, speeches and poems proclaiming that those who did not believe in victory were cowards, carried out almost to the letter their orders not to retreat an inch. In the Casa de Campo, the Nationalist advance planned to reach the Montaña barracks only reached the high ground known as Mount Garabitas. From thence a magnificent view, and also an artillery firing point, can be gained across the valley to Madrid. All the time the Republic commanders sent back appeals for more ammunition, or news that half their men

---

[1] This group infuriated the Irish Lieutenant Fitzpatrick then serving with Castejón. Women at the battle seemed to him the final degradation of the Republican side.

had fallen. All the time, Miaja replied that reinforcements had been sent. But it was impossible to know how much of the spirit of resistance, emanated from the cellar headquarters of the Ministry of War, derived from Miaja and how much from the Russian

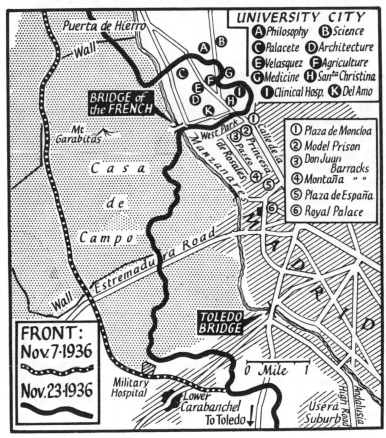

MAP 16. THE BATTLE OF MADRID

General Berzin whose office was a few doors away. Certainly the resistance owed much to the propaganda and administration of the Communists, Spanish as well as Russian.

The battle had been engaged once again on the morning of November 8, Varela's artillery was pounding away at King Alfonso's prized buildings in the University City and the wirelesses of Madrid were issuing orders for total mobilisation at two-minute intervals when, at last, the first units of the International Brigade marched in perfect order along the Gran Vía towards the front.

The first of these was a battalion of Germans, with a section of British machine gunners.[1] It was first named after its leader, an ex-Prussian Colonel, Hans Kahle, now a Communist, and its name was then changed to the Edgar André Battalion, in honour of the German Communist leader of that name executed at the start of this month by Hitler.

Secondly, there was the Commune de Paris Battalion, composed of French and Belgians under Colonel Dumont,[2] a French ex-regular officer but a long-standing Communist all the same. To these French-speaking combatants was attached a British machine gun group. The third battalion was the Dabrowsky Battalion, under a Pole, Colonel Tedeusz Oppman, chiefly composed of Polish miners recently living in France and Belgium. All three groups included most of the survivors of those Germans, Frenchmen and Poles who had fought in Aragón and in the Tagus valley. The entire Brigade was commanded by the engaging and able Hungarian, 'Kléber'. It had arrived after being cheered across La Mancha by peasants shouting '*no pasarán*' and '*salud*', to which its members had replied with a cry of '*Rot front*' and '*Les soviets partout*'. And now these apparently disciplined men, in their corduroy uniforms and steel helmets, followed by two squadrons of French cavalry, greatly impressed the Madrileños, who had supposed the capital lost. Many thought that the Soviet Union was at last intervening. So the cry of 'Long live the Russians' rang from the balconies of the Gran Vía.

By the evening the brigade was in position. The Edgar André and the Commune de Paris Battalions were sent to the Casa de Campo. The Dabrowsky Battalion went to join Lister and the Fifth Regiment at Villaverde. Kléber took command of all the Republican forces in the University City and the Casa de Campo. He immediately startled the Spanish commanders with his efficiency. In the Casa de Campo the International Brigade was spread out, one brigader to four Spaniards, to raise morale and to

[1] These included John Cornford.
[2] Described as Colonel 'Kodak' because of his pleasure at being photographed. Twenty years previously, Dumont and 'Hans' had been facing each other in the German and French armies on the Western Front.

give lessons in firing to the dogged militiamen. The Army of Africa now met machine-gunning as good as its own.

It has often been argued that the International Brigade saved Madrid. This view was so widespread that the British Ambassador Sir Henry Chilton, assured his colleague Bowers at St Jean de Luz that there were 'no Spaniards in the defending army of Madrid.'[1] This XIth International Brigade, however, probably comprised only about 1,900 men.[2] The XIIth International Brigade, which eventually arrived at the Madrid front on about November 12, comprised about 1,600. This force was too small to have turned the day by numbers alone. Furthermore, the militia and workers had checked Varela on November 7, before the arrival of the Brigade. The victory was that of the populace of Madrid. The bravery and experience of the Brigades was, however, crucial in several later battles. The example of the International Brigades fired the militiamen to continue to resist, while giving to the Madrileños the feeling that they were not alone, that there was some substance for the stirring utterances of, say Fernando Valera, a Republican deputy who, in the night of November 8, proclaimed on Madrid Radio: 'Here in Madrid is the universal frontier that separates Liberty and slavery. It is here in Madrid that two incompatible civilisations undertake their great struggle: love against hate, peace against war, the fraternity of Christ against the tyranny of the Church. . . . This is Madrid. It is fighting for Spain, for Humanity, for Justice, and, with the mantle of its blood, it shelters all human beings! Madrid! Madrid!'[3] Most of the world, nevertheless, accepted the despatches of the many eminent journalists, such as Sefton Delmer, Herbert Matthews, Henry Buckley and Vincent Sheean quartered in the Gran Vía or the Florida Hotels, who now reported Madrid likely to fall.

The next day, November 9, Varela, checked in the Casa de Campo, mounted a new attack, no longer a feint, in the Carabanchel sector. But the street-fighting baffled the Moroccans, who made no progress. In the Casa de Campo, Kléber assembled the whole of the International Brigade. In the misty evening they launched an attack. 'For the Revolution and Liberty – forward!'[4]

---

[1] *USD*, 1936 Vol 2, 603.
[2] Cox, 144; Fischer, 393. Colodny agrees with Zugazagoitia, 195, who puts the number of this first Brigade at 3,500. (Colodny, 64; 180.)
[3] Somoza Silva, 183.   [4] Malraux, 332.

Among the ilex and gum trees, the battle lasted all night and into the morning of November 10. By then, only Mount Garabitas in the Casa de Campo was left to the Nationalists. But one-third of the first International Brigade was dead. Varela now abandoned the direct attack on Madrid through the Casa de Campo. A sanguinary battle, however, continued in Carabanchel. Hand-to-hand fighting occurred in the Military Hospital. At the same time, the bombing of the capital, which had been continuing intermittently since the start of the assault, was increased. Incendiaries particularly were used, since fire was considered to be the best means of spreading panic.

On November 12, the continuing battle in Carabanchel convinced Berzin, Kléber, Rojo and Miaja (the directors of the defence) that the next attack by Franco would be against the Madrid-Valencia highway. They accordingly sent to that sector of the front the new XIIth International Brigade, comprising the Thaelmann, André Marty and Garibaldi Battalions of Germans, French and Italians. This was commanded by General 'Lukacz'. He was, in fact, the Hungarian writer Mata Zalka. Like Kléber, he was a Hungarian who had served in the Austrian Army in the First World War, had been captured by the Russians and had joined the Red Army. Earlier he had appeared as 'Kémeny', the hero of Smyrna. He was a man full of what the casual traveller supposes to be typical Hungarian gaiety. The German Communist writer Gustav Regler, handsome as Siegfried, was Commissar of the Brigade. He had previously directed the Republic's cultural loudspeaker van, a task coveted by the French Communist poet, Louis Aragon. In this Brigade, the Thaelmann Battalion of Germans was led by Ludwig Renn (Arnold Vieth von Golssenau), celebrated for his pacifist novel *Krieg* based on his experiences in the First World War. The Bavarian Communist and ex-deputy, Hans Beimler, was his Commissar as well as acting as general Commissar to all the Germans in Spain. Attached to the Battalion were 18 Englishmen, including Esmond Romilly, the wild and anarchic nephew of Winston Churchill. The Garibaldi Battalion of Italians was led by the non-Communist Republican Randolfo Pacciardi, who proved himself from the start an outstanding leader. The Socialist ex-comrade of Mussolini, Pietro Nenni, was one of his company commanders.

This force was less well-prepared for war than the XIth Brigade. When the Brigade entered battle, commands were confused, since the language problem presented difficulties in giving orders. (Lukacz was a less good linguist, as well as a less able commander, than Kléber.) The Brigade had to fight when weary from marching 14 kilometres. The artillery support was inadequate. Certain companies got lost. Fighting went on all day; but the object of the attack, the hill in the geographical centre of Spain known as Cerro de los Angeles, remained impregnable. The Brigade then withdrew and was transferred to the Madrid front.[1]

At the same time as the XIIth International Brigade arrived, Durruti also came to Madrid, with a column of 3,000 Anarchists, having been persuaded to leave Aragón by Federica Montseny on behalf of the Government. He demanded an independent sector of the front, so that his men could show their prowess. Miaja unwisely agreed to allot to the Anarchists the Casa de Campo. Berzin attached to him his expert incendiarist, the Macedonian Communist Santi, as adviser. Durruti received orders to attack on November 15, with all the Republican artillery and aircraft in support. However, when the hour came, the machine guns of the Moroccans so terrified the Anarchists that they refused to fight. Durruti, furious, promised a new attack the next day. However, Varela chose this moment to advance once again. Three times the van of Asensio's column reached the Manzanares, and three times it was driven back. Eventually, Asensio gained a foothold on the edge of the river beneath the Palacete de la Moncloa. After a heavy artillery and aerial bombardment, two Moroccan *tabors* and one *bandera* of legionaries charged across. They found that the Anarchists had fled, and that their way up to the University City was clear. The heights were swiftly scaled. The School of Architecture and other neighbouring buildings were captured. The XIth International Brigade was sent from the Casa de Campo to defend the Hall of Philosophy and Letters. But more and more of the Army of Africa, including men from the columns of Delgado Serrano and Barrón, at the same time crossed the river.

A bloody battle began in the University City. Its destruction seemed in strict accordance with the slogan of the founder of the Foreign Legion, Millán Astray – 'Down with Intelligence'. The babel of tongues, the frequent multilingual singing of the *International*, the insults exchanged between the Nationalists and Republicans, added to the macabre confusion. The marching songs

[1] Romilly, 85 fl.

of the German Communists brought to the crumbling masonry of the laboratories and lecture halls a wild Teutonic sadness. Muffled commands sounded in the darkness addressed to men who had never seen the city which they had come to defend: '*Bataillon Thaelmann, fertig machen!*' '*Bataillon André Marty, descendez vite!*' '*Garibaldi, avanti!*'[1] Hours of artillery and aerial bombardment, in which neither side gave way, were succeeded by hand-to-hand battles for single rooms or floors of buildings. In the Clinical Hospital, the Thaelmann Battalion placed bombs in lifts to be sent up to explode in the faces of the Moroccans on the next floor. And, in that building, the Moroccans suffered losses by eating inoculated animals kept for experimental purposes. Great courage was shown on both sides. A company of Poles from the Dabrowsky Battalion resisted in the Casa de Velázquez (so-called because it was from that site that the master had painted the Guadarrama) to the last man. An advance-guard of Moroccans drove back Durruti's Anarchists once again at the Plaza de la Moncloa, the first square inside Madrid proper, and began to fight their way along the long Calle de la Princesa. Some drove desperately down the Paseo de Rosales to reach the Plaza de España. All were killed. But the rumour that 'the Moors are in the Plaza de España' was not easy to staunch. Miaja appeared on the battle line to re-establish the courage of the militia. 'Cowards!' he cried, 'die in your trenches! Die with your General Miaja!'[2]

The battle of the University City continued until November 23. By this time, three-quarters of the area was in Mola's hands. The Clinical and Santa Cristina Hospitals, with the Institutes of Hygiene and Cancer, were his furthermost points of penetration. His advance towards the Plaza de la Moncloa was prevented by the continued defence in the Hall of Philosophy and Letters. The two almost exhausted armies now dug trenches and built fortifications. The Nationalists realised that any further advance into Madrid would cost too much. The Republicans understood that a dislodgement of their enemies would be equally costly.

On November 21, while the battle was still raging, Durruti was killed in front of the Model Prison. His death was said to have been caused by a stray bullet from the University City. It seems more probable, however, that he was killed by one of his own men, an 'uncontrollable', who resented the new Anarchist policy (termed 'the discipline of indiscipline' since August advocated

---

[1] Regler, *The Great Crusade*, 4.   [2] López Fernández, 175.

vigorously by Durruti) of participation in government. Durruti's funeral in Barcelona was an extraordinary occasion. All day long, a procession of 80 to 100 people broad marched down the Diagonal, the widest street in the city. In the evening a crowd of 200,000 pledged themselves to carry out the dead man's principles. But the death of Durruti marked the end of the classic age of Spanish Anarchism. An Anarchist poet proclaimed that Durruti's nobility while living would cause 'a legion of Durrutis' to spring up behind him. He was wrong.

In the meantime, Franco, having remarked before Portuguese journalists that he would destroy Madrid rather than leave it to the 'Marxists', greatly intensified the aerial bombardment. The German officers of the new Condor Legion were interested to see the reaction of a civilian population to a carefully planned attempt to set fire to the city, quarter by quarter. The bombing concentrated as far as possible on hospitals and other buildings such as the Telefónica, whose destruction would cause special panic. The air raids were accompanied by artillery bombardment from Mount Garabitas. From November 16 until November 19, the bombing, especially at night, continued and 1,000 people were killed. No great city in history had then been so tested – though the attack was a foretaste of what was to happen in a few years in London, Hamburg, Tokyo and Leningrad – as commentators in Madrid at the time eloquently prophesied. The terrible flames caused the capital to appear like some elemental place of torture. Over the crackle of fire, there could be heard the monotonous refrain, repeated syllabically, like a beat on a distant drum, '*No pas-ar-án! No pa-sa-rán! No pas-ar-án!*' Many fled to the middle-class Salamanca district. But there was no room for all. Twenty thousand persons lived on pavements, preferring to stay in Madrid rather than leave for the coast. As it was, 15,000 persons a week were being sent away to the Levante. Both the military and psychological effects of the air attacks can be considered nugatory, since they inspired greater hatred than they did fear. The Palacio de Liria, the town house of the Duke of Alba, was bombed, but militiamen succeeded in carrying off most of the innumerable art treasures within.[1] The correspondent of *Paris Soir*, Louis Delaprée,

---

[1] The Duke was among those who voiced complaints of 'Red Vandalism'. In 1937, Sir F. Kenyon, former Director of the British Museum, and James (now Sir James) Mann, Keeper of the Wallace Collection, visited Republican Spain to report that the art treasures of the Prado and elsewhere in the Republic were in excellent keeping.

wrote apocalyptically in his diary: 'Oh, old Europe, always so occupied with your little games and your grave intrigues, God grant that all this blood does not choke you.'[1] He was mortally wounded in an aerial battle a few days later when flying home to complain that his editor had not published his most sensational despatches.[2]

During these weeks, Madrid had been cut off from the rest of the world.[3] Almost the only communications, indeed, with Valencia had been when Miaja had demanded more munitions from Largo Caballero, to receive a counter-request for the ministerial table silver left behind in the Capital.

[1] Delaprée, 14.

[2] Delaprée's plane was almost certainly attacked accidentally by Republican aircraft. Delaprée died a few days later in Guadalajara hospital.

[3] On November 23 the US Embassy was transferred to Valencia from Madrid though the *Chargé*, Wendelin, was evidently reluctant to leave. Most of the other Embassies had also left by this time, though leaving behind skeleton staffs in Madrid—many of them looking after Spanish right-wing refugees.

40

Intervention and non-intervention – Nationalist blockade – German and Italian recognition of the Nationalists – Spanish-Italian Agreement of November 28 – Italian and German aims discussed – Faupel – Spain before the League – Britain's mediation plan – her volunteer plan – American volunteers – the Embargo Law in the USA – the Mar Cantábrico – the Control plan – Mussolini and Goering

The Non-Intervention Committee continued its deliberations in London. On November 12 Maisky happily remarked 'after weeks of aimless wandering, our Committee . . . has elaborated a scheme for the more or less effective control of the Non-Intervention Agreement'.[1] For, on that day, a plan of Lord Plymouth's to discover breaches of the pact by posting observers at Spanish frontiers and ports was approved. But Portugal, Germany and Italy argued that, before the plan could be put to the two Spanish contestants, control by air should be included. The near-impossibility of this made it obvious that these countries were really concerned to prolong negotiations rather than reach agreement quickly. All this time, the German Consul at Odessa, and newspaper correspondents at Istanbul, reported the shipment of arms and other material from Russia. Nor did the Consul miss the arrival of a grey ship of 4,000 tons, its name made illegible, which lay in Odessa roadstead without a flag, and which was unloaded at night.[2] This vessel had brought the monetary gold of Spain. 'If all the boxes of gold that we piled up in Odessa,' said Krivitsky, who later spoke with one of the NKVD officials who unloaded them, 'were laid side by side in Red Square they would cover it from end to end.'[3] When the gold eventually reached Moscow, the counting was made as if to last for ever – so that the Spanish officials accompanying it should remain in Russia as long as possible. When they were eventually allowed to go free, one

---

[1] Cattell, *Soviet Diplomacy*, 54. November 12, 1936, it may be recalled, was the day of Baldwin's famous admission to the House of Commons that he had 'been less than candid' to the electorate over rearmament for fear of losing the election.
[2] *GD*, 128.   [3] Krivitsky, 132.

was transported to Washington, one to Buenos Aires, one to Mexico. Of the Soviet officials who knew of the transaction, Grinko, the Commissioner of Finance, was later shot, and Marquiltz and Cargan, Director and sub-Director of the Gros Bank were sent to Siberia with Ivanovski, the Treasury representative at the Gros Bank. Not long after, the Soviet Government spoke of new mines in the Urals and became an exporter of gold.[1]

The shipment of Russian military aid was, of course, noticed by Consuls other than the German. On November 15 Eden, in the House of Commons, bluntly announced that there were countries 'more to blame for the breach of non-intervention than Germany and Italy'.

On November 17 Eden was, however, faced with a new Spanish problem. The Nationalists declared that they intended to prevent war material reaching the Republic, and to do so would even attack foreign ships in Republican harbours. Now under international law British ships could carry arms to Spain from foreign ports and demand aid from the Navy if interfered with.[2] But interference would be made legal if Franco were recognised as possessing belligerent rights in the Civil War. Though the British Government would have liked to have made such an act of recognition (they believed that this would more easily keep Britain out of the conflict) the French Government opposed it.

Before announcement of this blockade had been digested, Germany and Italy announced their recognition of the Nationalists as the true government of Spain. Franco received the news by describing Germany and Italy, with Portugal and Nationalist Spain, as bulwarks of culture, civilisation and Christianity in Europe. 'This moment,' he added, 'marks the peak of life in the world.'[3]

Largo Caballero's Government replied to the German and Italian 'act of perfidy' by using the same emotive language as Franco: 'Spain's historic rôle as the bulwark of democracy assumes an even greater importance.' However, Eden said in the House of Commons on November 20 that it was 'quite possible to follow a policy of non-intervention while recognising a Government of one

---

[1] Madariaga, 392. Hernández, 48.

[2] Unless the interference were to occur within Spanish territorial waters, where the Navy was not entitled to follow.

[3] This was on November 18. The previous day Germany and Japan had affirmed their friendship in the Anti-Comintern Pact, ostensibly directed against Communism but in reality an offensive military alliance. Italy joined a year later (see page 503).

side or another'. French diplomats became more and more gloomy. American journalists thought European war was near.

Eden announced the British attitude towards the Nationalist blockade on November 23.[1] Legislation would be introduced prohibiting the export of arms to Spain in British ships from all ports. This was done on November 27 and the bill became law on December 3. The French Government ordered their fleet not to help merchant ships if molested under the blockade, but took no legislative measures. An air of crisis continued.

On November 27 the Italian Ambassador in Paris told his American colleague Bullitt that Italy would not cease to support Franco even if Russia were to abandon the Republic – 'Franco's effectives being insufficient to enable him to conquer the whole of Spain'.[2] Mussolini was thus gambling all on a Franco victory. Accordingly, Ciano sent his henchman Anfuso to Franco proposing that Italy should send a division of Black Shirts (and further aid until victory was assured). In return, Franco would agree to support Italy in her Mediterranean policy. Neither party would support collective measures under the League against the other, and trade connections would be made as favourable as possible.[3] Franco agreed in principle with this arrangement which committed him to so little, and the division of Black Shirts began to be fitted out in Italy. Meantime the first German *Chargé* to the Nationalist Government arrived at Burgos. This was General von Faupel, a corps commander in the first World War, and sometime Inspector General to the Peruvian army. Hitler had told him not to concern himself with military matters, but he took one man with him for propaganda, and one for the 'organisation of the Falange'. Presenting his credentials, Faupel dressed himself up in the cap and gown of a professor rather than a uniform. From the start, he and his wife – 'gross, intelligent and maternal' – were disliked by the Spanish leaders.[4] Faupel, in his turn, found Franco

---

[1] On November 24, Robert Graves, previously (like Bernanos) resident in Majorca, called on Winston Churchill begging him to denounce German and Italian policy in the western Mediterranean. The following conversation ensued:

> Churchill: Both sides have imbrued their hands in blood. You wish for intervention? The country wouldn't stand it.
>
> Graves: Not intervention in the sense of taking sides . . . but of safeguarding British interest in the Mediterranean.
>
> Churchill: Seven French deputies have just been to see me – making frantic appeals for intervention. The best brains in France . . . (Graves, 411).

[2] *USD*, Vol 2 1936 576.   [3] *GD*, 139. Ciano, *Diplomatic Papers*, 75–7.
[4] Serrano Suñer, 44–7.

'likeable' but 'incapable of measuring up to the needs of the situation'.[1] General Faupel was anti-religious and disliked the upper class – thinking that only a man of low birth could make a Fascist revolution. Accordingly his propaganda agents associated with, and encouraged, the more radical members of the Falange, particularly its new leader, the anti-intellectual Hedilla.[2]

Almost Faupel's first report to Berlin was to urge (with General Sperrle, the commander of the Condor Legion, agreeing) that Germany should either now leave Franco to himself or send additional forces. In the latter case, Faupel said that one strong German, and one Italian Division was needed.[3] A concentrated combat force of 15–30,000 could, he said, break through the Republican lines at one point in overwhelming strength and win the war. Dieckhoff at the Foreign Ministry warned against this, arguing that more than one German Division would be needed, and that if such forces were sent Germany and Italy would incur the same odium as the French had gathered in Spain in 1808. The question remained in suspense for some weeks.

The situation was now complicated by several new international moves. Delbos, fearing that Italy was about to attack Barcelona, proposed to Eden that they should ask Germany, Italy and Russia for a 'gentleman's agreement' to cease arms-traffic and then mediate in Spain. Delbos also asked for support from Roosevelt. Bullitt, on receiving the request, took the opportunity to warn Delbos 'not to base his foreign policy . . . on an expectation that the United States would ever again send troops or warships or floods of munitions and money to Europe'.[4] The Republic at the same time appealed to the Council of the League of Nations on the grounds that Germany and Italy had committed aggression against Spain. The Non-Intervention Committee meanwhile agreed on December 2 (Portugal abstaining) to put Plymouth's control plan to the two Spanish parties. On December 4 France, now joined by Britain, officially approached Germany, Italy, Portugal and Russia for mediation. Eden explained that his idea was that the six powers most closely concerned would call an armistice, send a commission to Spain and, after a plebiscite, set up a Government under a group of men who had kept out of the Civil War, such as Salvador de Madariaga.[5] The Foreign Office, whatever her Consuls had told her previously, had now definitely

[1] GD, 159.   [2] See below, page 353.   [3] GD, 159–60.
[4] USD, 1936 Vol 2 578–81.   [5] GD, 158–9.

heard from her Seville Consul that 5,000 Germans (the nucleus of
the Condor Legion) had passed through that city and that on
about November 20 a German anti-aircraft detachment of 700
men had landed at Cádiz.[1] On the same day as the French mediation proposal was put forward, Lord Plymouth, therefore, brought
up for the first time the question of non-Spaniards fighting in the
Spanish War, which he urged should be considered before all other
non-intervention matters. Grandi, pointing out with truth that
Germany and Italy had suggested a ban on volunteers in August,[2]
opposed the isolated consideration of the matter.[3]

There were thus now three Franco-British plans for at least
ameliorating the conditions of the Civil War; the control plan, the
mediation proposal and the suggestion for giving priority to stopping volunteers going to Spain. On Sunday, December 6, while
they were supposed at least to be considering these ideas, Mussolini, Ciano and the Italian Chiefs of Staff met to consider the
intensification of aid to Spain.[4] The ubiquitous Canaris was
present, to tell the Italians that the German Government had
decided to cut down participation in Spain as compared with
Italy. The German War Ministry had in particular decided against
Faupel's suggestion of sending complete units to Spain. No such
qualms, however, beset the Italians. Mussolini desired to share ever
more closely in the 'crusade'. Three thousand Black Shirts with
good modern war material left for Spain at the start of December.
But a few days later Blomberg, the German War Minister, told
the American Ambassador in Berlin, Dodd, that the Spanish crisis
was now over. Germany, having tested some of her war material in
Spain, did not want further commitments there. He spoke, unfortunately, two years too soon.[5]

On December 10, to the annoyance of Litvinov (who advised
Álvarez del Vayo against taking Spain to the League) and of the
French, who had not been consulted at all, Álvarez del Vayo put
the Republic's case before the League Council at Geneva. He

---

[1] *USD*, 1936 Vol 2 586.   [2] See above, page 260.
[3] The British public were occupied with other matters than the possibility of non-
intervention in Spain. On November 26 Baldwin told the Cabinet that the King
wished them to take legislative action to permit him to marry Mrs Simpson. On
December 1 the Crystal Palace burned down. On December 3 the Abdication crisis
broke in the Press. Mr Pollitt assured his readers that 'there is no crisis in all this for
the working class. Let the King marry whom he likes.' Sir Oswald Mosley called on
the British Union of Fascists to stand behind the King. On December 12 Baldwin
told the House of Commons of the King's decision to abdicate.
[4] *GD*, 165.   [5] *USD*, 1936 Vol 2 612.

could scarcely have expected that, after so many failures to take collective action, the League would now act over Spain; but at least the question was placed on the agenda. On December 11, Álvarez del Vayo demanded that the League condemn Germany and Italy for recognising the rebels. He pointed out that foreign warships had attacked merchantmen in the Mediterranean, that Moorish troops had been used, that the war in Spain was a general danger to peace, and that the Non-Intervention Agreement was ineffective. Lord Cranborne, for Britain, and Vienot, for France, denied the total ineffectiveness of non-intervention and appealed to the Council to welcome the Franco-British mediation plan. In the end the Council passed a resolution condemning intervention, urging those members of the League who were on the Committee to do their utmost to secure non-intervention, and commending mediation. Spanish Nationalist and Republican newspapers however rejected mediation in editorials. Though Russia and Portugal declared their willingness to support any mediation plan which could be agreed, Germany and Italy, while offering support, said that they thought the idea unlikely to be accepted by either side. The mediation plan was in fact dropped, Eden and Delbos pressing forward with their less ambitious schemes. The Republic accepted the control plan in principle on December 16, at the same time setting out in detail their familiar views on non-intervention and reserving their right to reject the plan in whole or in part after further examination. The Nationalists replied on December 19 by asking questions on the working of the plan. These answers were considered by the Non-Intervention Chairman's Sub-Committee on December 23, in an atmosphere of apprehension at the renewed possibility of general war. This had been caused by the news of Italians arriving daily in Spain, by the Spanish Republic's seizure of the German vessel *Palos*, bound for Nationalist Spain, and by the Italian sinking of a Russian supply ship, the *Komsomol*. In Paris, Delbos had a solemn talk with Welczeck. The whole French people wanted an understanding with Germany, he said.[1] The way to achieve this was collaboration in Spain. On Christmas Eve, 1936, the British and French Ambassadors in Berlin, Rome, Moscow and Lisbon insisted, over the heads of the Non-Intervention Committee, on the urgent need to ban volunteers from early in January. François-Poncet said that the question had earlier not seemed to France important enough to justify such an interference

[1] *GD*, 180.

in personal freedom as a legislative ban on volunteers.[1] The prospects of this were hardly helped, however, when Blum was assured by the Italian Minister that if only he allowed Franco to be installed in Spain a period of Italian-French friendship could begin. Mussolini, added the diplomat, perhaps with truth, really hated Hitler and only wanted an opportunity to break away from him.[2]

Foreigners were undoubtedly now flocking into Spain – 'armed tourists', as Winston Churchill named them. The second expedition of 3,000 Italian Black Shirts and 1,500 technicians arrived at Cádiz. These were all to go into action in battalion units under Italian officers in the uniform of the Spanish Foreign Legion. Italian troops and pilots in Spain now totalled 14,000.[3] Troops received two sets of wages: two pesetas a day from Franco, twenty lire a day from Mussolini. The Germans in Spain remained the same – about 7,000. All were paid only by Berlin. On the last day of 1936, the American Consul-General in Barcelona estimated that 20,000 foreign volunteers had arrived by rail from France since October, 4,000 having passed through Barcelona and Albacete between Christmas and New Year's Eve.[4] Meantime, in Moscow, on January 1, 17 Russian pilots were named 'heroes of the Soviet Union' for 'difficult Government tasks' – that is, for Spanish service. Throughout, Russia made no formal acknowledgement of its aid to Spain but, since the power of Soviet tanks and aircraft was noted by all the journalists in Spain, the Soviet Government was content to remain in the position of being regarded as the 'one country which had come to the aid of Spanish democracy'.

[1] *Ibid.*, 186. The Germans believed that the British wanted only to safeguard their commercial interests in Spain. To this end, Faupel reported, not only did the commercial counsellor at the British Embassy frequently visit Burgos to discuss such matters but Chilton kept the Nationalist authorities so well informed as to what was going on that the text of a statement to be made by Eden at 3 o'clock in the House of Commons was communicated to Franco by 10 o'clock in the morning of that day. This was not surprising, since Chilton was still very pro-Nationalist. 'I hope,' he told the American Bowers, 'that they send in enough Germans to finish the war.' (*USD*, 1937 Vol 1 225.)

[2] An extension of this positive appeasement was seen in the Anglo-Italian 'gentleman's agreement' of January 2, 1937. This affirmed the independence of Spain and freedom of passage through the Mediterranean. It was expected that the agreement would lead to detailed negotiations, but these did not begin till 1938 (when they caused the fall of Eden – see below, page 514).

[3] The Italian Ministry of Air noted on January 23 that 'by January, Italy had 211 pilots, 238 specialists, 777 ground officers, 995 NCOs and 14,752 troops'. (Quoted by Cattell, *Soviet Diplomacy*, 4.)

[4] *USD*, 1936 Vol 2 625.

The first organised group of 96 Americans to volunteer for Spain left New York on December 26.[1] It was already an offence under American law for an American to enter the army of another State. This did not, however, apply to Americans who volunteered abroad – only to those who were recruited on American soil. All sorts of evasions of this law were obviously possible, though from January 11 all US passports were marked 'Not valid for Spain'.[2] This made little difference, since from Paris onwards the volunteers could be looked after by the Brigades' organisation. In fact, no prosecutions were made of US citizens volunteering for the Republic (none volunteered for the Nationalists throughout the war).

The American 'moral embargo' on aid of war material to Spain had been effective until December 28. On that day Robert Cuse, a nationalised Latvian of the Vimalert Company of Jersey City, acting for the Comintern, applied for a licence to ship $2,775,000 worth of aircraft engines to the Spanish Government. The State Department granted the licence but publicly regretted that an American firm had wantonly insisted on its legal rights against the Government's policy. The State Department sent notes to the Governments on the Non-Intervention Committee describing the facts, and saying that the shipment could not begin before two months. But, rightly fearing that the US Government might quickly act to prevent shipment at all, Cuse began to load his cargo on to the Spanish ship *Mar Cantábrico* immediately. The President swiftly arranged that Senator Pittman and Representative McReynolds should introduce resolutions to ban arms shipments to Spain into the two Houses of Congress as soon as they re-assembled on January 6. On that day, in the Senate, only Senator Nye opposed the resolution. He urged that the embargo was not neutral in that it harmed the Republic more than the Nationalists. Several members of the Lower House also criticised it. However, the Senate passed the new law by 81 to 0 and the House of Representatives by 406 to 1. The dissentient, Representa-

---

[1] Rolfe, 18. This group arrived on January 6 at their base at Villanueva de la Jara, near Albacete, in the flat plain of La Mancha, whose bleakness recalled home to two Wisconsinites among them. Since they were accompanied by a number of Cubans, easy relations were soon opened with the villagers.

[2] The passports of these men may have played a greater part in history than the men themselves. For the NKVD secured the passports of all dead (and some alive) members of the International Brigade, and they were despatched to Moscow: here a pile of nearly a hundred of them 'mainly American' were observed by Krivitsky. Then new bearers were issued with these, and entered America as, apparently, reformed citizens.

tive Bernard, declared the act sham neutrality since its effect was
'to choke off democratic Spain from its legitimate international
rights at a time when it was being assailed by the Fascist hordes'.[1]
A technical error in the Senate, however, prevented the resolution
becoming law until the 8th and, on the 7th, the *Mar Cantábrico*,
though with only part of Cuse's cargo, left New York in great
haste.

This was not the end of the adventure. Two American pilots,
Bert Acosta and Gordon Barry, who had flown aircraft for the
Republic in the autumn, claimed that they were owed pay of
1,200 dollars. They persuaded the Coastguard to serve a writ on
the Captain of the *Mar Cantábrico* in Long Island Sound.[2] But the
writ applied only to the personal property of Prieto, the Spanish
Air Minister. So, accompanied by a Coastguard cutter and
aeroplane as far as the three-mile limit (in case the arms embargo
should become law quicker than was expected), the *Mar Cantábrico* set off for Vera Cruz in Mexico, where she picked up further
cargo and sailed for Spain. Although then disguised as a British
ship, the vessel was captured by the Nationalists in the Bay of
Biscay and the material on board (which Queipo de Llano announced to be useless) was eventually used against the Basques in
the Battle of Bilbao. The Spaniards among the crew were executed.[3]

Franco announced that over the Embargo Act President
Roosevelt had behaved like a 'true gentleman'. Germany also
praised the act. American Socialists and Communists protested
violently, as did many liberal intellectuals in the United States.
With varying intensity during the rest of the Spanish War, the
President was begged by liberals to declare that, because of the
presence of so many foreign troops in Spain, a state of war
existed. Therefore, the liberals urged, the Neutrality Act of 1935
should be made to apply – so preventing any export of war
material to Germany and Italy. The Secretary of State, Cordell
Hull, continued, however, to doubt the existence of German and
Italian intervention, although he was constantly informed of its
extent by his Ambassadors. And Roosevelt was persuaded that

[1] Representative Bernard later introduced a resolution demanding support of the
Republic, suggesting at least equal restrictions against the Governments of Germany
and Italy.
[2] The Spanish Consul General in New York later denied that any moneys were due
to these men.
[3] Senator Nye later accused the owners of a steamship company in New York of
spying for Franco and causing the arrest of the *Mar Cantábrico*.

such a declaration might increase the likelihood of general war. He therefore refrained from this step.[1]

On January 5 Portugal, and on January 7 Germany and Italy, answered the Anglo-French proposal on volunteers. (Russia had replied in the affirmative on December 27.) The German note was drafted personally by Hitler. What was the point of by-passing the Non-Intervention Committee? And was it not unfair to make such a proposal now when the Republican side was well supplied with foreign volunteers? However, Germany would co-operate, provided that the plan was effectively controlled and that it was not isolated from related problems.[2]

Germany, having seemed to be leaving the affairs of Spain all to Italy, suddenly took provocatory action. The German vessel *Palos* had been released after its seizure by the Republic on December 27, but one Spaniard on board was retained, along with a cargo of celluloid and telephones, on the grounds that it was war material. Germany's demand for the release of the man and the material was not accepted. The German Navy therefore proposed the bombardment of a Republican port or convoy in reprisal. Neurath agreed to threaten 'sterner measures' if the demand was not immediately complied with. When it was not, three Republican merchant ships were captured and two of them handed over to the Nationalists. The bombardment of a port was kept for future use.

Another crisis followed. The French Government heard on January 7 that 300 Germans had landed in Spanish Morocco. Blum instructed an immediate protest. Léger reminded Welczeck, the German Ambassador in Paris, of the Franco-Spanish Moroccan Agreement of 1912, forbidding the fortification of either Spanish or French Morocco against each other. Welczeck denied that there could be German troops in Morocco. The French Press meantime became excited. Vansittart pledged British support to France if the reports should prove correct. The next day, French troops began to concentrate along the border of French Morocco. Faupel reported to Neurath that there was a German unit in Melilla – a Spanish *presidio*[3] to which the Moroccan agreement did not apply. Hitler meantime summoned François-Poncet and told him that Germany had no territorial ambitions in Spanish territory. The statement was given to the Press, and the crisis died down. The incident thus passed into history as one war-scare more,

---

[1] Taylor, 75–95.   [2] *GD*, 210–12.   [3] See above, page 59 fn.

easily created and easily damped, in the chain of anxiety which destroyed the nerves of France between 1918 and 1939.[1]

Despite its volume, German and Italian aid to the Spanish Nationalists did not even yet have its purpose and its limitations clearly defined. On January 13 the Italian Ambassador in Berlin, Attolico, a scholarly man of intelligence and low birth who did not know German, called on Neurath urging Germany to send more men to Spain. Neurath replied that that would seriously endanger the general European situation. 'Unless,' he added, 'we want to risk war, we will have to realise that the time is drawing near when we must abandon further support for Franco.'[2] A new Franco-British note had been delivered on January 10, urging that to volunteer for the Spanish War should generally be made a crime, as it already was in Britain and France. Neurath appeared genuinely to accept that, if an agreement on volunteers were reached, then Germany would loyally carry out whatever obligations it might involve: 'We would not only have to demand actual control measures but also have to adhere to them.' On the other hand, when Attolico said that Franco intended to reject control as 'an intolerable limitation of national sovereignty', Neurath urged that, to preserve the Non-Intervention Committee, Franco should agree in principle but stipulate conditions. On January 14, Weizsäcker told a member of Ribbentrop's private information service that 'the Spanish adventure is to be abandoned. It is only a question of drawing Germany out of the affair gracefully,' he added.[3] Yet Goering said the same day that Germany would never tolerate 'a Red Spain'.[4] Amid these conflicting points of view, Goering, Mussolini and Ciano met on January 20 at Rome. They agreed that, now that Franco was 'amply supplied', Germany and Italy should support the British-French plan to prevent volunteers entering Spain. The last military aid should be despatched by January 31. They also agreed that the Civil War should under no circumstances lead to world war. Schmidt, interpreter for Goering at this meeting, observed that both Germans and Italians spoke of their forces in Spain as if they were genuine volunteers – even to each other.[5]

Finally, what of Stalin? During this period merchant ships, some sailing under Spanish flags, some under Russian, some under

[1] USD, 1937 Vol 3 217 fl; GD, 215 fl.   [2] GD, 222.
[3] GD, 225.   [4] Ibid., 226.
[5] Schmidt, 62. Ciano, Diplomatic Papers, 85 6.

Mexican, continued to bring Soviet war material to Spain,[1] across the Mediterranean. Yet the ensuing months cannot be understood unless it is realised that Russia was about to embark upon the most terrible year of her history. During 1937 ninety of the leading Soviet Communist party leaders at the very least, were killed in the *Yezhovshchina* – the bloodbath carried out by Yezhov on Stalin's orders. Thousands – without exaggeration – followed them to their secret graves. Japanese intelligence reports estimated that 35,000 Army officers – half the whole Soviet officer corps – were also executed in 1937, allegedly for conspiracy with Germany. Most of those Soviet officers and other Russian officials who had been in Spain from August 1936 onwards were to be caught up in this obscure, silent and remorseless holocaust. In January 1937, apparently, some members of the Central Committee of the Soviet Communist party tried to halt the tide of massacre – only to pay for it with their lives. At the same time also it is now clear that Stalin, beginning to despair of any attempt to establish an alliance with France and Britain, once again turned his attention to the possibility of an alliance with Hitler: Kandelaki, Soviet Trade Commissioner in Berlin, was instructed to make feelers towards Germany, only to be rebuffed. For the time being, therefore, Soviet foreign policy continued in support, *faute de mieux*, of the idea of democracy and of the Popular Front.[2] But these curious facts throw an ironic light on André Marty's obsession with 'Fascist spies' at Albacete.

Thus, at the start of the new year, as in the first weeks of the war, Germany and Italy could be expected to prevent the Nationalists from losing. Weizsäcker, head of the political department in the German Foreign Ministry, noted: 'Germany's goal, as well as Italy's, is in the first instance a negative one. We do not want a Communist Spain.'[3] Russian aid was correspondingly still aimed to prevent Republican defeat. It was clear that the intervention of forces large enough to ensure victory for either side would have risked a general European war. And the only unchanging motive in

[1] According to the German Military *Attaché* in Ankara (this is the source referred to on page 294 fn. 1 above), eight ships (five Spanish, three Russian) reached Spain in January, bringing six aircraft, thirty-five cannon, twelve tanks, 3,150 tons of war material and 3,250 tons of ammunition. (See Appendix III.)

[2] These negotiations were described in Krivitsky, 37–9. A despatch from Neurath to Schacht of February 1937 found in the German Foreign Ministry archives confirms that Krivitsky was telling the truth. See Schapiro, 485; 420.

[3] Weizsäcker, 113.

the minds of the German, Italian and Russian leaders (as of those of Britain and France) was that none desired such a war as a result of the conflict in Spain. But the obvious falsity of the development of the non-intervention policy continued to revolt most liberals and Socialists in western countries – provided, however, that they were not in the Government, when the agonising dilemma of Blum might have troubled them also.

41

Stalemate around Madrid – battles of Villarreal, Boadilla, Lopera, and the Corunna Road

Events in Spain had not been affected in any way by these grave intrigues in the capitals of Europe. Madrid itself settled down to what was accepted as a siege, though only a small part of the city was invested. Measures continued against the Fifth Column, especially those suspected of firing at nights from the so-called 'phantom cars'. The police knocked one night at the Finnish Embassy in the Calle Fernando el Santo to be refused admittance. From inside someone opened fire (one policeman being hit). Finally breaking in, the police disclosed 525 quivering Spanish *bourgeois* within. The Embassy officials, save one Spanish-born employee, had all left for Valencia.[1] Another characteristic event at the start of the winter was the murder of the Baron de Borchgrave, the Belgian *Chargé*. He was believed to have persuaded several of his compatriots in the International Brigade to desert. One night, his body was discovered outside Madrid.

While the two armies of the Madrid Front tried to reassemble for a new trial of strength, the Basques, commanded by Generals Llano de la Encomienda and Martínez Cabrera, set out to capture Vitoria, capital of their southern province of Álava. The Republic of Euzkadi had now raised 46 infantry battalions each of 660 men. Of these 27 were raised by the Basque Nationalists (these being known as *Gudaris*), 8 by the UGT, the remainder by mixed Communists, Socialist-Communist Youth, left-wing Republicans and Anarchists. This army was attended by a Corps of Almoners, composed of 100 priests, whose duties were unique in the Republican army: they were to celebrate mass, to watch the *Gudaris'* morality, to be present at the last moments of the dying and to 'form the minds of the conscripts in the Christian tradition'.[2] Be-

---

[1] After this a false Embassy was opened under the national flag of Siam. The aim was to attract secret Nationalists. Various persons (apparently only six) came to seek refuge. Their conversations were listened to by secret microphones, and they were later murdered.

[2] *Le Clergé Basque*, 27.

hind these forces, the Basque arms industries were not yet at full strength. They needed certain minerals from abroad, and their purchase was hampered by the Nationalist blockade and by the Non-Intervention Agreement – for even cotton-wool was, under that agreement, banned for export to Spain, since it might be used for filling shells. A Hamburg (Comintern) shipment of arms had reached Bilbao in September and, at the end of October, there were large shipments from Russia – 12 single seat fighters accompanied by Russian pilots, 25 armoured cars, 12 other cars, 12 anti-aircraft guns, some small arms, and light bombs. Except for replacements and some artillery, however, no more arms came to the Basques from Russia.

The Basque attack began on November 30 on Villarreal de Álava. This Nationalist position was held by Colonel Iglesias and 600 men. By December 2 the town was surrounded but on December 5 Colonel Alonso Vega arrived from Vitoria in relief. The Basques were driven back by superior artillery and aviation. Having omitted to provide for defeat, they had forgotten also to establish advance guard hospitals or adequate medical supplies. In a single night, 400 men died from gangrene in improvised hospitals in the sanctuary of Saint Antony of Urquiola. So ended the one and only Basque offensive of the Civil War.[1]

This attack nevertheless represented the greatest period of self-confidence of the Basque Republic. Despite treachery among certain of his officers, Aguirre reorganised the defences. His lieutenant Aldasoro had almost solved the problem of securing food both for the Basques and for the 100,000 refugees who had fled to Bilbao from Guipúzcoa. Most food had to be imported. The food ships were escorted by a fleet of fishing boats, converted into a navy, by mounting two 101 mm. guns on each boat. In this way essential food supplies were secured, including much from other parts of Spain.

On December 13 the Madrid front burst once again into battle. The Nationalists sought to continue an offensive tentatively begun ten days earlier, aiming to cut off the Republicans in the Guadarramas and secondly to surround Madrid from the north.[2] The battle took the form of a struggle by the Nationalists to reach

---

[1] Lojendio, 264 fl.

[2] In the beginning of this first engagement Hans Beimler, the Communist Commissar of all the Germans in Spain, had been killed – though not, as is sometimes alleged, liquidated by his Communist comrades. The true story is in Regler, *Owl of Minerva*, 286. He was replaced by the more sinister figure of Franz Dahlem.

the Madrid-Corunna road some miles short of El Escorial; Orgaz, newly appointed supreme commander of the Madrid front, directed operations. Varela commanded in the field. Beneath him were assembled 17,000 infantry and cavalry, organised into four mobile brigades under García Escámez, Barrón, Sáenz de Buruaga and Monasterio.[1] The Nationalists began as usual with a heavy artillery bombardment. On December 14, the advance began on Boadilla del Monte, a lonely *pueblo* apparently far out in the plain

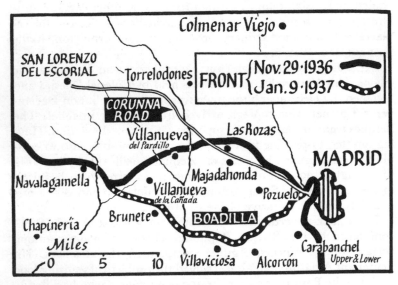

MAP 17. THE BATTLE OF THE CORUNNA ROAD

of Castille (though in fact only twenty kilometres from Madrid) and dominated by a small monastery. By night the town had fallen. The Republican force here consisted of a series of hetero-geneous battalions under Major Barceló, a Republican army officer who, like many other regular soldiers, had joined the Com-munist party since he was attracted by its discipline. The Russian tanks under General Pavlov and both International Brigades were flung into the battle as reserves. The two British groups attached to the Thaelmann and the Commune de Paris Battalions, Cornford's group and Romilly's, met for the first time beneath the ilex trees on the road to Boadilla. The Nationalists retired from

[1] López Muñiz, 56.

Boadilla, and the Dabrowsky and Thaelmann battalions entered it. Then the Nationalists surrounded them. A terrible fight ensued. Casualties on both sides were high. The Dabrowksy and Thaelmann Battalions left seventy-eight corpses behind in the town itself. All but two of the ten still remaining[1] English members of the Thaelmann Battalion's first company were killed, Esmond Romilly being one of the survivors, Bert Ovenden,[2] a Communist from Stockport, being the other. Another violent hand-to-hand battle occurred for the nearby castle of the Duke of Sueca, held by Republican members of the Civil Guard, who eventually retired leaving behind a hundred bodies. After this the Nationalists, having won only Boadilla and Villanueva de la Cañada, 8 kilometres to the north, called off their attack.

No sooner had these battles been concluded than the Republic launched an abortive attack on the Córdoba front. It was during this battle that the famous *communiqué* was issued: 'During the day the advance continued without the loss of any territory.' By this time, the British volunteers for the International Brigade had been numerous enough to permit the formation of a full British company, the 'No. 1 Company', 145 strong which was now attached to the French Marseillaise Battalion of the newly organised XIVth International Brigade, commanded by the Polish General 'Walter'.[3] The British Company was commanded by Captain George Nathan who, having risen to the rank of CSM during the First World War, became in 1918 the only Jewish officer in the Brigade of Guards. Resigning his commission after a dispute in the officers' mess over the pay of privates, he passed much of the 1920s and 1930s unemployed, though he was for a time doorman at Peter Jones. By hard work he had by this time developed a British upper-class accent of which he was very proud. In Spain, where he invariably appeared immaculately dressed, his boots being polished to the point of dazzlement by one or other of his invariably good-looking batmen, he genuinely found himself a mercenary leader – resourceful, brave as a lion and respected by all. The very sight of Nathan with his gold-tipped

---

[1] Eight (out of the original eighteen) had been killed in their two previous actions, south-east of Madrid and in the University City.

[2] Ovenden was killed at Brunete in July 1937. Romilly (who shortly returned to England) lived on to be killed fighting as a bomber pilot in the Battle of Britain. Romilly's *Boadilla* is an excellent description of this battle.

[3] A XIIIth International Brigade had been formed and was at this time established before Teruel. It was chiefly composed of East Europeans.

swagger stick was an encouragement to his men. One section of
the British was composed of Irishmen who had all, it was said,
'experience of warfare in Ireland'. Their absurdly chivalrous
leader, Frank Ryan, had been a member of the IRA since 1918.[1]
The company left by train for the Andújar front on Christmas Eve
and fought with the rest of the brigade between December 28 and
29, without success, to capture the small village of Lopera. In this
battle Ralph Fox, the Commissar of the Company, was killed. He
was the leading English Communist man of letters, once of
Magdalen College, Oxford.[2] The poet John Cornford was also
killed on the day following his 21st birthday. At all times he had
been oppressed by the gloom of the Norse sagas, in which all the
heroes fight with extraordinary gallantry, but knowing that they
will be defeated. It was a strange myth to find expression among
the endless olive trees of the valley of Guadalquivir.

After the failure of the action, André Marty appeared at
General Walter's headquarters, and Major Lasalle, commander of
the Marseillaise Battalion, was accused of spying for the Nationalists, tried and shot. The Major died protesting his innocence,
shouting imprecations at Marty and begging the intervention of
the Alsatian Colonel Putz, the president of the council of war which
had condemned him. In fact, Lasalle appears to have been a
coward, though not a spy.[3]

After Christmas, a new attempt was made by Orgaz to cut the
Madrid-Corunna road. The four columns engaged in the battle of
Boadilla had been reinforced by new conscripted troops and
Falangists trained by German officers at Cáceres. These were
faced, at the start, by Republican brigades led by El Campesino,
Barceló, Cipriano Mera and Durán. Cipriano Mera was the lead-
ing Anarchist General produced by the war and Durán was a
composer by profession, who had found himself as a commander.

[1] Acier, 113. There is thus the macabre paradox that Nathan, the ex-Black and Tan
officer, fought as a commander of ex-members of the IRA, in Spain.
[2] Fox was aged 36 when he died. In an introduction to a memoir published in his
memory, Harry Pollitt claimed Byron as Fox's precursor in dying for a foreign cause.
(See Fox, 6.) He even went so far as to quote in elegy the famous lines:

> Yet freedom, yet thy banner, torn but flying, streams like
> The thunderstorm 'against the wind'.

Byron seems to have been an obsession with Pollitt at this time. Having urged Mr
Stephen Spender to join the Communist party purely to be able to help over Spain,
he advised him that the best way he could help the party was 'to go and get killed,
comrade, we need a Byron in the movement'.
[3] Wintringham, 83–6.

On January 3, the attack began. Barrón advanced along the road from Villanueva de la Cañada and, on January 4, reached the first houses of Las Rozas, on the Madrid-El Escorial railway. On the right, García Escámez and Sáenz de Buruaga fought against tenacious resistance at Pozuelo. The advance was slow since the number of summer villas in the area afforded good cover to the defenders. General Kléber sent as reinforcements the Commune de Paris Battalion to Pozuelo and the Edgar André and Thaelmann Battalions to Las Rozas. On January 5, after a day of inaction, due to heavy fog, a new Nationalist attack began. Bombing was followed by the advance of tanks and mobile artillery, then by the first two infantry waves, and then by more tanks. The Republican front broke everywhere. This *blitzkreig* attack was of interest to those German officers on the Nationalist side who, with ruthless objectivity, could still regard Spain as the 'European Aldershot'. The brigades of Barceló, El Campesino and Cipriano Mera lost touch with each other, and munitions ran out. Miaja, in general command of the defence, was forced to send blank rounds to the front on the assumption that men who heard their rifles firing would go on defending themselves. He even staged a mock execution of deserters to prevent weakness in the trenches. The impending disaster caused the transfer of Lister's brigade from south Madrid, and persuaded Largo Caballero to send the XIVth International Brigade up from Córdoba.

The advance continued. The Nationalists reached the high road at Las Rozas and beyond Pozuelo (though the town itself held on). But Orgaz's columns suffered very heavy casualties from the machine guns of the International Brigade. On the 6th, the Thaelmann Battalion was sent to hold out at Las Rozas, and not to retreat an inch farther. These orders were later revised, but by then messages could not get through since the battalion was surrounded. All day the Thaelmann Battalion held their ground, against tanks, aerial attack and infantry. The Moors stormed several of their trenches and as usual bayoneted the wounded they found there. But the Germans did not give way. The next day Kléber sent a new order to the battalion, to advance. The survivors had reluctantly to send back the following message: 'Impossible. The Thaelmann Battalion has been destroyed.'[1] Walter, leader of No. 1 Company of the Thaelmann Battalion,[2]

---

[1] Lindbaeck, *Internationella Brigaden* 87–90. Quoted Colodny, 214.
[2] Not to be confused with the Polish General 'Walter'.

had during this battle the eerie experience of coming upon the body of a Condor Legion pilot with whom he had once served in the same air squadron.[1]

By January 9 the Nationalists had conquered, at great cost, ten kilometres of the coveted highway, from just beyond the last houses of Madrid at the Puerta de Hierro to Las Rozas. On January 10, there arrived in Madrid the XIVth and XIIth International Brigades, including the British No. 1 Company, commanded by Jock Cunningham, a Communist since 1922 when he had been freed after two years of prison for leading a mutiny of the Argyll and Sutherland Highlanders in Jamaica two years earlier.[2] Nathan commanded the whole Marseillaise Battalion in succession to the ill-fated Lasalle. A German group of the XIVth Brigade asked for 12 hours' sleep after their 48-hour journey following on their battles at Córdoba. 'Walter', their Polish commander, appealed to them: 'The Government has called for the best troops. That is you. Or could there have been a mistake with regard to the XIVth Brigade?' The recalcitrant troops went on to the front, this being perhaps the only time in history that a Polish commander has rebuked a German force. The next day, the Republic counterattacked in heavy mist and fierce cold. The XIIth International Brigade reached Majadahonda and the XIVth reached Las Rozas – a battalion of the latter being lost in the mist and being never seen again. Russian tanks, led in person by General 'Pavlov', drove wildly about, destroying men but unable to gain ground. The battle continued till January 15, when each side dug fortifications. Both had lost 15,000 men in ten days. Orgaz retained his ten kilometres of high road, Miaja had prevented the isolation of the Sierras. The military stalemate thus appeared complete.[3]

The remainder of the 2,000-kilometre front was quiet, since neither side had enough forces for more than one battle at the same time. The fronts themselves consisted in most places simply of 'a system of narrow trenches hewn out of the rock with extremely primitive loopholes made out of piles of limestone. Twelve sentries

---

[1] Acier, 82.

[2] Cunningham had the reputation of being the only soldier in a military gaol in England who made such a fuss that the authorities freed him to rid themselves of the trouble of looking after him. He was a man of great physical strength and, at a low level of command, possessed marked qualities of leadership. He was nicknamed the 'English Chapiaev' – after the guerilla leader of the Russian Civil War – and there could not at that time have been a greater compliment.

[3] Regler, *Great Crusade*, 219–41. Colodny, *passim*.

were at various points in the trench, in front of which was the barbed wire, and then the hillside slid down to a seemingly bottomless ravine; opposite lay naked hills'.[1] On every hill-top, in Aragón, for example, there seemed to be a knot of ragged, dirty men, Nationalist or Republican, 'shivering round their flag', with occasionally bullets wandering between them – and sometimes voices, encouraging desertion, painting a rosy picture of the comforts to be had on the other side, and shouting insults. Nationalists would, indeed, desert, sometimes five a night before a single company's sector. The Republic offered every deserter from their enemies 50 pesetas and 100 if they brought their arms with them. There were occasional instances of desertion by Republicans. In most cases, the deserters were men who had been caught in the wrong place at the start of the war, had pretended to belong to the side for which they were fighting to save their lives, and who had been waiting ever since for an opportunity to cross the lines.

The character of the winter of 1936 in Spain was, however, best expressed by the long convoy of lorries, laden with food brought by the Nationalists to feed Madrid once it had fallen. Their contents slowly rotted in the snow and rain. A mile away, behind the Republican lines, the Madrileños stoically put up with rice bread and increasing hunger.[2]

ADDITIONAL NOTE TO CHAPTER 41

A League of Nations mission visited the Republic that winter to enquire into health conditions. They found no epidemic but there were over a million refugees fleeing from one province to another. (Minutes of 96th Session of Council, p. 94.)

---

[1] Orwell, 20–3. Orwell reached Barcelona at the end of December and joined a POUM column on the Aragón front, with whom he stayed till April. He returned to the front a month later but finally returned to England in June.

[2] Dr Junod of the Red Cross meantime had established himself at St Jean de Luz in order to try and effect exchanges of prisoners. Red Cross branch offices were set up in Salamanca and Valencia which communicated *via* Geneva. Lists of prisoners were compiled and occasionally individuals were exchanged by Red Cross agencies between prisoners in one camp or the other and their relations. Friends and enemies rubbed shoulders in the Red Cross offices, irreconcilable even in their sorrow. Dr Junod tells the story of Isabela, a fierce Monarchist, on behalf of whose brother he had pestered the Republican authorities for months. At last the news came: 'Executed with ten others. Buried in the cemetery.' Tearless but deadly pale she passed on her way out Carlota, whose fiancé had been missing. Each knew the story of the other. They saw each other and they understood at once. With the same movement of contempt and hatred they avoided each other as they passed. But Carlota said afterwards: 'At least she can visit his grave. But I shall never know, never.'

42

The repercussions of one event in particular extended over both sides of these battle lines. This was the trial of José Antonio in Alicante. The decision to bring the leader of the Falange to trial seems to have been inspired by the fear that, if the Republic collapsed, one of their chief enemies would go unscathed. As always, fear showed itself the father of ruthlessness. During the trial, a militiaman appeared as a witness for the prosecution. 'Do you hate the defendant?' asked José Antonio, who was defending himself. 'With all my heart,' replied the witness. Dignified and eloquent throughout, the founder of the Falange was condemned to death. His brother Miguel and his brother's wife received a similar sentence. But José Antonio, with the chivalry which even his enemies have never denied ·him, appealed on their behalf. 'Life is not a firework one lets off at the end of a garden party,' he concluded. As a result, they were reprieved. No such clemency was possible for José Antonio himself. Princess Bibesco, Asquith's daughter, who when wife of the ex-Rumanian Minister in Madrid had been celebrated as the one woman friend of Azaña, telephoned the President to beg him to prevent the execution. Azaña gloomily answered that he could do nothing since he also was a prisoner.[1] So José Antonio was shot on November 19. His final request was that the patio in which he was to be shot should be wiped clean after his death 'so that my brother Miguel will not have to walk in my blood'.

For a long time this execution was not confirmed. He was referred to by Nationalists as the 'absent one'. (Always when names of Falangist martyrs were read out at ceremonies, the Falange would cry 'Present', in imitation of a similar Nazi rite.) His execution removed from the scene yet one more person who might have been a rival to Franco. Fernández Cuesta and Serrano Suñer, his

[1] Ximénez de Sandoval, 588–617.

possible successors, were still in Republican prisons. The leadership of the Falange was in the next four months taken by Manuel Hedilla, an almost illiterate mechanic from Santander. His working-class background caused him to be looked upon as the leader of those who desired to develop the Falange into a party with a mass following among the working class and with radical aims.

In reprisal for José Antonio's death, the Nationalists shot Largo Caballero's son, who had been a prisoner since the officers of his regiment at El Pardo drove north to join Mola on July 19. The loss increased the gloom of the Republican Prime Minister, who was daily growing more jealous of La Pasionaria, Miaja and others who had stayed behind in Madrid and were now reaping the glory in the world's headlines.

One other notable occurrence straddling the battle lines was the change of attitude of the most prominent intellectuals of pre-war Spain. Most of these had found themselves in Republican Spain at the time of the rising. They signed a manifesto pledging support of the Republic. The signatures had included those of the physician and historian, Dr Marañón; the ex-Ambassador and novelist, Pérez de Ayala; the historian, Menéndez Pidal; and the prolific writer and philosopher, José Ortega y Gasset. However, the effect of the Republican atrocities and of the increasing influence of the Communists caused all these men, who had had so much to do with the foundation of the Republic in 1931, to take what opportunity they could find of fleeing abroad. There, they repudiated their support of the Republic.[1] An exactly contrary course was taken by the great and garrulous Basque philosopher, Miguel de Unamuno, author of *The Tragic Sense of Life*, and arch-priest of the Generation of '98. As Rector of the University of Salamanca, he had found himself at the start of the Civil War in Nationalist territory. As late as September 15, he was still supporting the Nationalist movement in its 'struggle for civilisation against tyranny'.[2] But by October 12 he had changed. On that date, the day of the Festival of the Race, a great ceremony was held in the ceremonial hall of the University of Salamanca. There was the Bishop of Salamanca. There was the Civil Governor. There was Señora Franco. There was General Millán Astray. And, in the chair, was Unamuno,

---

[1] The novelist Pío Baroja fled from the Republic to Nationalist Spain, which he also abandoned.

[2] He was reported as saying this in an interview in *Le Petit Parisien* of that date.

the Rector of the University. After the opening formalities, Millán Astray made a violent attack on Catalonia and the Basque provinces describing them as 'cancers in the body of the nation. Fascism, which is Spain's health-giver, will know how to exterminate both, cutting into the live healthy flesh like a resolute surgeon free from false sentimentality'. A man at the back of the hall cried Millán Astray's motto: '¡Viva la Muerte!' Long live death! Millán Astray then gave the now customary rabble-rousing slogans: 'Spain!' he cried. Automatically, a number of people shouted 'One!' 'Spain!' shouted Millán Astray again. 'Great!' replied the still somewhat reluctant audience. To Millán Astray's final cry of 'Spain!' his followers gave the answer 'Free!' Several Falangists, in their blue shirts, gave a Fascist salute to the inevitable sepia portrait of Franco which hung on the wall over the däis. All eyes were now turned to Unamuno, who slowly rose and said: 'All of you are hanging on my words. You all know me and are aware that I am unable to remain silent. At times to be silent is to lie. For silence can be interpreted as acquiescence. I want to comment on the speech – to give it that name – of General Millán Astray, who is here among us. Let us waive the personal affront implied in the sudden outburst of vituperation against the Basques and Catalans. I was myself, of course, born in Bilbao. The Bishop,' here Unamuno indicated the quivering prelate sitting next to him, 'whether he likes it or not is a Catalan from Barcelona.' He paused. There was a fearful silence. No speech like this had been made in Nationalist Spain. What would the Rector say next? 'Just now,' Unamuno went on, 'I heard a necrophilous and senseless cry: "Long live death." And I, who have spent my life shaping paradoxes which have aroused the uncomprehending anger of others, I must tell you, as an expert authority, that this outlandish paradox is repellent to me. General Millán Astray is a cripple. Let it be said without any slighting undertone. He is a war invalid. So was Cervantes. Unfortunately there are all too many cripples in Spain just now. And soon there will be even more of them if God does not come to our aid. It pains me to think that General Millán Astray should dictate the pattern of mass psychology. A cripple who lacks the spiritual greatness of a Cervantes is wont to seek ominous relief in causing mutilation around him.' At this, Millán Astray was unable to restrain himself any longer. 'Abajo la Inteligencia!' he shouted. 'Long live death.' There was a clamour of support for this remark from the Falangists. But Unamuno went on:

'This is the temple of the intellect. And I am its high priest. It is you who profane its sacred precincts. You will win, because you have more than enough brute force. But you will not convince. For to convince you need to persuade. And in order to persuade you would need what you lack: Reason and Right in the struggle. I consider it futile to exhort you to think of Spain. I have done.' There was a long pause. Then, with a brave gesture, the Professor of Canon Law went out with Unamuno on one arm, and Señora Franco on the other. But this was Unamuno's last lecture. Thereafter, the Rector remained under house arrest. He might have been imprisoned had not the Nationalist authorities feared the international consequences of such an action. Unamuno died brokenhearted on the last day of 1936.[1] The tragedy of his last months was a natural expression of a society in which, by a law of September, all books of 'Socialist or Communist tendencies had been ordered to be destroyed as a matter of public health'. In December all such books (or any 'generally disruptive' matter) were ordered to be handed in within forty-eight hours.

The situations in the two Spains continued to differ absolutely – save in one thing: thousands of Spaniards first supported one side or the other entirely because of the accident of where they were in July 1936. Later these were inflamed by propaganda and generous emotion to abandon this opportunism for a real devotion to the cause which they had come to support. Among the Nationalists the war, the army and its organisations were everything. Political or social change was hardly considered except among those Falangists who had been the closest followers of José Antonio. The vast numbers of new Falangists known as 'new shirts', who had joined the movement since the rising, were much less eager to try and base their movement on a sound social programme. The 'new shirts' were, of course, still trying to find their political bearings. No political party, after all, has ever grown so fast as the Falange – not even the Communist party in the Republic. From 75,000 as a maximum in July, there were nearly a million members at the end of the year. Many of these were ex-CEDA men. Nationalist Spain was nevertheless found 'optimistic' and 'frivolous' by the German Voelckers who arrived at Seville after the closing of the German Embassy at Alicante. He complained that no programme had been begun for the solutions of 'the social questions which were at the root of the Civil War' and that there had been no general conscription, which he thought (erroneously) pertained in Republican Spain.[1]

Even so, the war inevitably brought radical changes in Nationalist Spain. The most remarkable Falangist institution was a body named *Auxilio Invierno* ('Winter Help') founded in Valladolid by the widow of Onésimo Redondo, the Falangist leader killed at Alto de León. It began in October in a single room in Valladolid as a centre for children. Within a few months, it had branches throughout Nationalist Spain.[2] Since its title seemed too close to that of the similar Nazi body in Germany, it shortly changed its name to *Auxilio Social* ('Social Help'). Other bodies grew out of *Auxilio Social*. These included the *Cocinas de Hermandad* ('Brotherhood Kitchens'), organisations for making clothes for the destitute and maternity homes. At the same time, there was an absolute necessity to expand production in every sphere in order to win the war. This brought change willy-nilly. Queipo de Llano, for example, for all his *braggadocio*, supplied 9,000 farmers with wheat to sow a quarter of a million acres in Andalusia which would not otherwise have been cultivated.

The numerically small but well-armed forces along the battle line expressed the character of the Nationalist society.[3] The Nationalist leaders still feared disturbances at the rear, and consequently still shot all the possible enemies of the *régime*, including, haphazardly, prisoners. Cantalupo, the new Italian Ambassador, began his mission by asking for an end of the slaughter of prisoners. Franco told him firmly that the shooting of prisoners had stopped.[4]

It was indeed possible to trace four stages in the manner of Nationalist executions. At the beginning, shooting occurred without any judicial proceedings whatever. After a while, various subterfuges such as executions 'while trying to escape' were substituted. From October 1936 until February 1937 the detained were given a chance of self-defence before an emergency tribunal, though mostly witnesses were not heard. From February 1937

[1] *GD*, 137.

[2] By October 1937 it had 711 branches; in October 1938, 1,265, in October 1939, 2,847. It was a voluntary organisation, though of course backed by the authorities.

[3] Conscription was never introduced on the Nationalist side of the Civil War. It was on the side of the Republic, though, since there were never enough arms to go round, it was not always effectively enforced.

[4] Cantalupo, 130.

until the end of the war all cases were tried by a court-martial. This created an appearance of justice, but sentences continued to be given for political reasons. Many remained under sentence of death for long and arbitrary periods.[1]

By this time most of the irregularities of conduct which had earlier marked Nationalist Spain had become formal. For example, just as courts-martial now habitually heard trials, so special sequestration commissions were set up to confiscate property, whereas previously this had occurred arbitrarily.

At the end of 1936, the failure of the direct attack on Madrid and the hardening of the fronts everywhere caused military gloom among Nationalists and their foreign supporters. But economically Nationalist Spain was in fine fettle. Their peseta was quoted internationally at double the rate of that of the Republic. They possessed all the food they needed, and were still backed by all the old Spanish financiers and bankers. Their credit continued good for essential supplies, including, above all, oil from the Texas Oil Company.

Nationalist Spain was at this time administratively divided. Burgos was the official seat of government. The Treasury and Ministers of Justice and Labour were established there. It represented the Catholic, traditional and generally right-wing aspect of the Nationalist cause. Salamanca was the home of the Head of State, the Falangist organisations, the Foreign Office, the Ministry of War, the Embassies and the political staffs of Germany and Italy. Disputes between the Ministries in the two cities expressed the underlying disputes of the *régime*.

The atmosphere of Nationalist Spain was dominated by propaganda, quite as much as Republican Spain. This was aimed at exacerbating hatred. Lists would be mysteriously discovered on Republican prisoners or corpses, naming all those to be eliminated in the Nationalist zone. The impression of the Republic that was fostered in Nationalist Spain was of an anarchic terrorism controlled entirely by 'the paid assassins of Moscow'.[2] There were rumours everywhere. A group of Carlists assured some French journalists in Saragossa that Thorez, helped by Blum and Daladier, had staged a *coup d'état* in France, that Pétain was fighting them in the south, and that, once the French civil war was over, Laval would place an army at the Spanish rebels' disposal.

[1] Cf. Bahamonde, 85–90; Ruiz Vilaplana, 149 fl.   [2] Ruiz Vilaplana, 234.

The Spanish Church remained the close ally of the Nationalist
régime. Divorces and civil marriages concluded under the Republic
were annulled. One Sunday in the Church of Our Lady of Mercy,
during High Mass, the priest broke off apparently spontaneously
in the middle of administering the sacrament. 'O, you that hear
me!' he said. 'You who call yourselves Christians! You are to
blame for much that has happened. For you have tolerated in
your midst, yea, and even employed in your service workmen
banded together in organisations hostile to Our God and our
country. You have heeded not our warnings and have consorted
with Jews and Freemasons, atheists and renegades, so helping to
strengthen the power of the very lodges whose aim it was to hurl us
all into chaos. Be warned of the tragedies of today! You should be
to all these people – as we must all be – as fire and water . . . no
dealings with them of any kind . . . no pardon for criminal destroyers of churches and murderers of holy priests and ministers.
Let their seed be stamped out – the evil seed – the seed of the
Devil. For verily the sons of Beelzebub are also the enemies of
God!'[1] It will be observed that the Church still believed itself to
be fighting Masonry above all else. Yet there was a difference between the commitment of the Spanish hierarchy to the Nationalist
cause, and the attitude of the Vatican. True, when in September
Pope Pius XI had received 600 Spanish refugees from the Republic he had spoken of the 'satanic' behaviour of the godless in
Spain.[2] But now, at the end of December, General Franco complained to the Italian Ambassador Cantalupo of the Pope's attitude to the Nationalist cause. His representative at the Vatican
suggested to the Pope that he should publicly condemn the
Basques. But Pius refused, due to the influence of the Basque
Bishop of Vitoria. The furthest he would go would be to issue a
general condemnation of Catholic co-operation with Communists.
He also complained of the execution of certain Basque priests by
Nationalist troops and showed himself very gloomy about Franco's
prospects.[3] Presumably this attitude on the part of the Pope was
caused by the alarmingly close relations of Franco with the
heathen Mussolini and Hitler.

[1] Ruiz Vilaplana, 191. There were undoubtedly dissentient voices. The Bishop of
Vitoria had already been dispossessed for too great sympathy with his Basque flock.
The Bishop of Pamplona was for a short time under house arrest. It was said that the
Archbishop of Santiago responded to a Falangist speech demanding sterner measures
against the Asturians with the remark: 'There have been enough crimes:'
[2] To the Spanish Refugees. Speech of September 14, 1936.   [3] *GD*, 189.

General Franco's most serious difficulties in the winter of 1936–7 were, however, with the Carlists. On December 8, a decree by the Carlist authorities had established a 'Royal Military Academy' for the training of young officers to fill the place of those killed in action. On the surface, this might seem a perfectly sensible plan. But its initiators had not consulted General Franco. It was not surprising, therefore, that Franco should tell the Carlist leader, the Count of Rodezno, that he was 'annoyed' by this apparent act of insubordination. He next instructed General Dávila, head of the administrative *junta* at Burgos, to inform Rodezno that the creation of the Military Academy could only be considered an attempted *coup d'état*. As a result, Fal Conde, the Carlist supreme leader in Spain, whom Franco believed to be the chief inspiration of the plan for the Academy, was ordered to leave the country within forty-eight hours. The Carlist war *junta* considered this peremptory instruction on December 20. They decided to agree, under protest, chiefly to prove their innocence of any attempt at a *coup*: and Fal Conde left for Lisbon, the favourite resort of all right-wing exiles from Spain.[1] Franco was later to explain to the German Ambassador, Faupel, that he would have had Fal Conde shot had he not been afraid of the effects upon Carlist morale at the front.[2]

---

[1] All the above derives from the Carlist Archives, Seville.

[2] The fighting spirit of the Carlists cannot be gainsaid. One *Requeté* was asked who should be advised if he were to die. 'My father, José María de Miguerarena of the Montejurra militia, aged 65.' 'And if he should be killed too?' 'My son, José María de Miguerarena, of the Montejurra militia, aged 15.' I myself have seen casualty returns in the Carlist Archives speaking of grave wounds being incurred by boys of fifteen. Between July and October 1936, 40,000 volunteers from Navarre had joined the Nationalist Army – a tenth of the population.

43

*Republican Spain – its political and regional fragmentation – the
Communists and the Republicans – jealousy and decline of Largo
Caballero – the new army – achievements of the Republican reforms –
a riot in Bilbao*

By January the Republic could look with pride at its winter's work hitherto. But the very diminution of the crisis caused fragmentation, partly geographical, partly political. Barcelona, for instance, presented the appearance of a city at peace. Valencians would be heard grumbling that the 'Catalans are not at war'. Barcelona's worker-dictatorship of August had also vanished. Was Marx right after all in saying that Anarchism inevitably degenerated into petty *bourgeois* habits? The Anarchists were certainly in decline. The Communists' air of possessing the future, their dynamism, their political attitude of no-nonsense, and, of course, the prestige of Russian arms made them the obvious party for ambitious people to join.[1] Their numbers had increased to about 250,000 by the end of 1936. But had it not been for 'the propaganda by sight' (Russian aircraft), as González Peña put it, they would have been far less successful. The Communists of Barcelona, thanks additionally to their championship of individual ownership and opposition to revolution, were everywhere gaining ground. The PSUC agitated for the dissolution of the revolutionary committees, so as to place all executive organs, both nominal and actual, under the Generalitat, which with the Esquerra, they dominated. Rivalry between the Anarchists and PSUC became acute at the start of January, when the latter managed to place a veteran anti-Anarchist, their Secretary-General Comorera, as Food Minister. Comorera immediately abolished the bread committees, led by the CNT, which had hitherto supervised the food supply of Barcelona. Henceforward,

---

[1] Even General Miaja told Pietro Nenni that he preferred the Second to the Third International. 'I like the Communists,' he said, 'because they are more resolute. The Socialists talk first, then act. If the Communists talk, they do so *after* acting. Militarily speaking, it is an advantage.' (Nenni, 171.)

there was no State intervention in the food supply in Catalonia. Even rationing was abandoned. This brought immediate hardship, since the price of bread had gone up far more than wages. There followed a bread shortage caused by the inadequate harvesting of the previous year, but attributed by the Anarchists to Comorera's inefficiency. A poster war ensued, CNT posters demanding Comorera's resignation, PSUC posters calling for 'Less talk! Less Committees! More bread!' and 'All power to the Generalitat'. Meantime, bread queues, of 300 or 400 persons, outside closed bakeries, became a pathetic daily sight. Sometimes, when no bread could be distributed, *Asaltos* had to disperse the queues with rifle butts. Life seemed a far cry from the Utopian dreams of July 19, 1936.

Down the coast at Valencia, conditions appeared more revolutionary than at Barcelona. Nearly all factories and shops were managed by their workers. But the effect of the Government's move to Valencia had been to give them control over the Levante which, before November, had been almost independent. As for the dissident Anarchists of the Levante, a force was despatched against the 'uncontrollables' of Tarancón and Cuenca, who had so nearly brought the Government to a tragic end. After fighting, both towns became model Socialist centres, whereas in neither had the UGT previously been strong. Here too, however, the Communists and Anarchists were in conflict – especially over the question of the marketing of oranges from the Valencian *huerta*. Since July 1936, the marketing had been done by a committee of the UGT and CNT, representing all the trades who handled the crops though not the orange growers themselves. The Ministry of Agriculture paid this body 50% of the international price of the crop on delivery, and 50% after sale and deduction of expenses. The orange growers, with the support of the Communist Uribe, Minister of Agriculture, argued that this committee took the profits, and that they got nothing. The committee contended that, if the orange-crop were handed over to private commerce, not only would the trade unions be destroyed, but the private merchants would keep abroad the foreign currency. The violent hatred of the orange growers for the committee was shown by the revolt in January of the *pueblo* of Cullera, which suddenly declared itself independent, burned flashlights towards the Mediterranean to attract Nationalist ships, and turned guns against Valencia. The Government then had to take the same repressive measures against these peasant enemies of the Anarchists as they had earlier done over different matters against the Anarchists themselves.[1]

In Madrid, hostility between the Communists and Anarchists had different implications. On the one hand it was an aspect of the quarrel between Madrid and Valencia, and on the other the start of a dispute between the Communists and Largo Caballero. After the battle of the Corunna high road, Kléber argued that the Republic should launch an attack, the International Brigades leading the offensive. But here Kléber came up against the jealousy which he had inspired in Miaja and other Spanish commanders. Largo Caballero, already jealous of the international prestige of La Pasionaria and other Communists who had remained in Madrid during the siege, concluded that Kléber wished to use the International Brigades to stage a Communist *coup d'état*. The Anarchists of Madrid supported Miaja, and therefore indirectly, for the first time, Largo Caballero. Even so Kléber's ideas might have triumphed had he not incurred the suspicion of André Marty. As a result, Kléber left his command and went to live in a small hotel in Valencia. At the same time, Rosenberg for no obvious reason (he was, however, a Jew at a time when Stalin's perhaps always latent anti-semitism came to a head) left his post as Ambassador at Valencia and went back to Moscow, where he was shortly to 'disappear' in the purges now developing at cumulative speed. Other Russians in Spain were called home with similar consequences. Parties would be given in Madrid, attended by General Berzin, to bid farewell to officers summoned back in this way.[2] Eventually Berzin himself, guest of honour at these macabre gatherings, would also be recalled, with the usual results. Meantime in Spain, the Communists suddenly ceased their most outspoken attacks on their enemies. Instead they struck through the NKVD, which was staffed mainly by foreign Communists, since Spanish Communists were considered less sound. The number of Russians in Spain never exceeded 2,000, but those who were there were placed in key positions. Barcelona radio services were under one Kolzov-Ginsberg. A certain Vladimir Birchitski was a central figure in arms production. And the general rumour of 'the Russians are in control' was henceforward heard everywhere in the Republic. Undoubtedly their lack of knowledge of Spain, as well as their secretiveness, led these Russians (and other foreign Communists) into grave mistakes.

---

[1] Borkenau, 198–204.   [2] Regler, *Owl of Minerva*, 294.

The use which the Communist party made of its power was to establish itself as deeply as possible in the Republican administration, to arrange that, through the agency of Orlov, the NKVD's tentacles should crowd out all private *checas*, both of the Socialist-Communist Youth and others, and to prepare the way for the same purge of Communists and other Marxists in Spain as had now reached its second stage in Russia.[1] The first move in the Spanish purge was the PSUC's campaign to manoeuvre the POUM out of the Catalan Generalitat. Nin eventually left on December 16. The Anarchists gave this their blessing since, like all the other parties, they also did not love the POUM's aggressive and self-assertive arrogance. The Anarchists must, however, have been a little anxious not only at the spread of the Communist party's power, but also at its threats. 'So far as Catalonia is concerned', thundered *Pravda* on December 17, 'the cleaning up of Trotskyists and Anarchists has begun and it will be carried out with the same energy as in the USSR'. However, no action was yet taken: and Antonov-Ovseenko, the Russian Consul-General (who, as an ex-Trotskyist, must have had his own fears of the future at this time), expressed publicly his admiration of the Catalan Anarchists on December 22. By this time also the violence of the Popular Tribunals and *checas* had been greatly diminished, perhaps chiefly because their work was almost completed. There were indeed few prominent members of the old right-wing parties of before the Civil War left in Republican Spain. But wild crimes by militiamen continued sporadically, especially in backward provinces.

The Communists maintained their campaign against collectivisation of land, and the Anarchists continued in favour of its general application. Neither were strong enough to force their own solution. So the question of expropriated property was left suspended, most large estates being run by municipalities (or committees where these still existed separately) with the old labourers working under much the same conditions as of old. Where the Anarchists had established themselves first, in Catalonia, Aragón and in certain wheat farms in La Mancha and sugar-cane farms near Málaga, collectivised methods persisted. In Aragón, this included 75% of the small properties. There, all crops were placed under the control of a local committee. Wages were paid in pro-

---

[1] Radek, Piatakov and others were tried in Moscow between January 23 and 30, and thirteen were executed.

portion to needs. The Anarchists claimed, in respect of wheat in Aragón, a 30% increase in production.

The argument as to the relative advantage of the militia system or the army system continued as the chief bone of contention between Communism and Anarchism. Republican staff officers had suggested that the mixed brigade – a self-contained unit, with its own artillery, mortars, supply and medical services, developed during the wars in Morocco, was the best type of organisation for the war. It was in fact adopted because the Communist party, and the Soviet advisers, favoured it. A decree ending the militias, and reorganising the army in mixed brigades was published at the end of December. The inspiration of these steps towards the formation of a regular army was the efficient Under-Secretary, General Asensio, and his advisers of the old regular Army such as Martín Blázquez. The Anarchists disliked passionately these developments. The Libertarian Youth spoke of the dangers of just such an army as had rebelled in July: 'a shock force knowing nothing of the cries for liberty, bread, justice of the cannon fodder.' The General Council of the FAI demanded the suppression of the salute, equal pay for all in the army, newspapers at the front, and soldier councils, at all levels. *Solidaridad Obrera* grumbled about 'obsession of discipline', 'neo-militarism', and 'psychosis of unity'. The Iron Column before Teruel rebelled against the financial implications of the decree against militias. Hitherto, the column had been paid *en bloc*. Now the men were to be paid individually. Fighting occurred before the Anarchists submitted to the new regulations. The Anarchists (and UGT) were naturally dubious about abandoning their militias, particularly when the dissolution of the Communist Fifth Regiment was followed by the nomination of that body's commander, Lister, to lead the first mixed brigade. In fact, for some months longer, the militiamen still existed, though beginning to be classed under numbers not names. The separate political flags were still seen as often as that of the Republic. On the Aragón front, separate political columns lasted until the middle of the year. Uniforms were still non-existent, though everyone wore corduroy knee breeches and a zipper jacket. Training continued rudimentary since all the rifles were at the front; and even these continued, except for parts of the Madrid front, to be old and unreliable, while artillery was everywhere scarce. Grenades were still as liable to explode in the hands of the thrower as upon the enemy. In many places there were no maps, range-finders, periscopes, field-glasses, or cleaning materials. Orwell discovered, with the horror of a trained member of the Eton OTC, that no one in his POUM column had heard of a pull-through.[1] Bad marksmanship continued to be the rule. Discipline in most places continued to be based upon class loyalty, rather than orders by officers – though General Asensio Torrado, the Under-Secretary at the War Ministry and the moving spirit in the creation of the new Republican 'People's' Army, insisted on correct military uniform for officers.[2]

Largo Caballero meanwhile continued to be jealous of everyone in Madrid, especially of La Pasionaria who had had such great popular success there. His relations with Miaja and Madrid's commanders remained bad. He also began to dislike the presence of the Russian Ambassador, Rosenberg. On December 21, Stalin sent a letter to him full of brotherly and moderate advice: the parliamentary method might in Spain be more revolutionarily effective than in Russia; even so, the Russian experience might be useful in Spain – hence the despatch of certain 'military comrades' who had received orders to follow Spanish instructions and act only as advisers. Stalin begged Largo Caballero 'as a friend' to report how successful the advisers had been, and to say whether he found Rosenberg satisfactory. The letter ended with the advice that peasants' and foreigners' property should be respected, that partisan forces should be formed behind the Nationalist lines, that the small *bourgeoisie* should not be attacked and that Azaña and the Republicans should not be cold-shouldered.[3] And in fact the political moderation of the Communist party in Spain now brought them a working alliance with the liberal Republicans. The Republicans' policy, insofar as one existed apart from the general aim of winning the war, was nearly that of the Communist party in both military strategy and economics. It was thus in language almost identical with that of La Pasionaria that Azaña, in one of his rare public appearances, at Valencia on January 21, demanded 'a war policy . . . with only one expression

---

[1] Orwell, *loc. cit.*

[2] For all the above, see Martín Blázquez, 279–90.

[3] This letter was published for the first time in the *New York Times* on June 4, 1939, by the then ferociously anti-Communist Araquistain, Ambassador in Paris 1936–37. When this letter arrived in Largo Caballero's office, no one could read the illegible signatures. Codovilla, the Comintern agent, was summoned. He could not read the signatures either. It took a member of Rosenberg's staff of the Russian Embassy to decypher the names of Stalin, Molotov and Voroshilov (Gorkin, 85).

– discipline and obedience to the responsible Government of the Republic'.[1]

Social and other reforms, Azaña and the Communists could now agree, should await victory. And it was the adoption of this policy which gave the Communist party much of its power. If the war was to be won, this was the way to win it. Their moderation gave them the friendship not only of the Republicans but also of many of the regular officers in the Army who thought the Communists sane and well organised. The Anarchists seemed genuinely puzzled by the Communists' close alignment with *bourgeois* democracy. At a National Youth Congress in Valencia in January, the Secretary-General of the Socialist-Communist Youth, Santiago Carrillo, remarked 'we are not Marxist Youth. We fight for a democratic, parliamentary republic'. *Solidaridad Obrera* named this 'Reformist Quackery'. 'If the United Socialist Youth are neither Socialist, Communist, nor Marxist, what are they?'

As for the Socialists, the UGT (whose membership had risen to two million) was now well stocked with Communists, though it is impossible to know precisely how many. All winter, the Communists were urging the unification of the Socialist and Communist parties, on the model of the existing union in Catalonia and the two youth movements. Both wings of the Socialist party, Largo Caballero's as well as Prieto's, were, however, now wary of these approaches.

Even so, by the spring of 1937, Largo Caballero's Government was everywhere seeking to slow down the process of revolution. The political committees which had sprung up in all *pueblos* in July were being replaced by municipal councils. The nationalisation of foreign firms ceased and of others was delayed. The Government also did all it could to end the collective management of factories. It sought to bring such concerns under State control, whether nationalised or privately managed. To ensure this, credit was made difficult for Anarchist factories. Some mills therefore stopped when cotton was exhausted.

Yet when all these quarrels are understood, and this increasing stranglehold over the Republic exercised by the ruthless Communists, Spanish and foreign, is taken into account, it needs also to be realised that this Government of Largo Caballero was fumbling towards a better Spain. The war might be taking up most of the Republican resources, but attention was being

[1] Quoted by Cattell, *Communism*, 135.

paid to education as never before. One hundred and forty-three million pesetas would be spent on education in the Republic in 1937 compared to only three million in 1936. That figure represents less of an increase than would appear immediately, because of the inflation of the Republican peseta. Nevertheless, the real increase must have been over fivefold.[1] The number of new schools opened in 1937 approached 1,000. There were 60,000 teachers in Republican Spain in 1937 compared with 37,000 in all Spain in 1931. In 1937, there were to be 2,000 military schools, at which over 200,000 previously illiterate militiamen learned to read. Despite the disputes over collectivisation or private management, the decree of October 1936 legalising the expropriation of land owned by Nationalists revolutionised the life of Spain. By May 1937, nearly four million hectares (15% of the whole area of Spain) had been taken over by the Institute of Agrarian Reform. Credits of 80 million pesetas, and implements and fertilisers, had been afforded. The amount of land under cultivation increased by 6% between July 1936 and October 1937. In almost every case, the peasants of Republican Spain were by early 1937 either owners of their own land or labouring for a collectivised farm. The tenant farmers and the landless labourers dependent upon a negligent landlord had vanished. In industry, despite the uneasy compromise achieved in those concerns still nominally under private ownership,[2] production had generally increased by 30% and 50% in those industries (such as textiles) directly concerned with the war. In health, despite the demand for doctors and medical services at the front, there were over a thousand more beds for tubercular patients in the Republic than in 1936. Later in 1937, compulsory inoculation for smallpox, diphtheria and typhoid was instituted. By the end of 1937, there were as many child welfare centres in Republican Spain as there had been before the war in all Spain.[3] The remarkable and devoted work of the foreign medical aid organisations indeed radiated throughout the Republic, setting new standards of hygiene and efficiency. These achievements gained in the teeth of war should not lightly be ignored. In the field of ordinary (as opposed

---

[1] Figures in *Education in Republican Spain* (pamphlet), published by United Editorial, 1938.

[2] In Catalonia, a decree of January 9 made it obligatory for private owners to submit questions of wages, hours, new employees, production and distribution quotas, and monthly accounts to a committee of workers.

[3] Margaret Stewart, *Reform under Fire* (Fabian Society, 1939).

to political) justice, there was also a marked increase in the speed of the hearing of ordinary cases. The unusual figure of García Oliver, the Anarchist Minister of Justice, stood behind such changes. He made, on January 3, 1937, perhaps the most remarkable speech of any law Minister at any time: 'Justice,' he announced, 'must be burning hot, justice must be alive, justice cannot be restricted within the bounds of a profession. It is not that we definitely despise books and lawyers. But the fact is that there were [sic] too many lawyers.[1] When relations between men become what they should be there will be no need to steal and kill. For the first time, let us admit here in Spain that the common criminal is not an enemy of society. He is more likely to be a victim of society. Who is there who says he dare not go out and steal if driven to it to feed his children and himself? Do not think that I am making a defence of robbery. But man, after all, does not proceed from God, but from the case, from the beast. Justice, I firmly believe, is so subtle a thing that to interpret one has only need of a heart.'[2]

The northern Republican territories remained generally apart from the quarrels of the south. Yet they had their own difficulties. On January 4, Bilbao was raided by 9 Junkers 52, escorted by Heinkels. Two of these were shot down by Russian Boeing fighters. Two Germans parachuted to the ground. One was killed by the crowd infuriated by this wanton attack. The other was saved from a similar death by a Russian pilot. In the meantime, Bilbao turned mad with anger. The rage of the people was exacerbated by hunger, since few food ships had recently managed to penetrate the Nationalist blockade. A furious mob, composed chiefly of non-Basque refugees from Asturias, Castile and Galicia, marched to the buildings where the political prisoners of Bilbao were being kept. The prison governors telephoned the Basque Government. They said they could not much longer prevent the warders from opening the gates to the crowd. A UGT battalion was sent to hold the prison gates. But the battalion joined with the people, who were now shouting imprecations against those who had 'brought the Germans to kill our children'. First, the gates of the Larrinaga prison were thrown open, and the men of the UGT battalion began a massacre in which 94 prisoners were killed. In the second

---

[1] The use of the past tense is ominous. According to *The General Cause*, 127 judicial functionaries had been killed in Republican Spain.

[2] Quoted by Berryer, *Red Justice* (London 1937).

prison, at the Convent of the Angeles Custodios, 96 prisoners were killed. At the Convent of the Carmelites, which had also been converted into a prison, the prisoners, allied with six Basque guards, barricaded the staircase. Then, at a given signal, all the electric bulbs in the convent were knocked out. The crowd concluded that the convent was being bombed, and fled, having killed only four prisoners. The motorised Basque police now arrived. By tragic irony, they were commanded by Telesforo Monzón. He had recently conducted negotiations for the exchange of these same political prisoners with the Nationalists and, due to Franco's insistence on dealing with the Valencia Government, had failed in his mission. The UGT militiamen implicated were arrested, and the crowd vanished. The Basque Government now sought to atone for this act of mob insanity. The families of the dead (most of whom were from Bilbao) were permitted to arrange funeral services and processions in the streets. Six members of the UGT battalion responsible were condemned to death and, as a public act of abasement, censorship of journalists' reports on the massacre was dropped.

On January 13, the Anarchists of Bilbao sought to profit from the inevitable atmosphere of tension. Their posters demanded for them a share in the Government. They were easily controlled. A few weeks later, their newspaper, the *CNT del Norte*, was banned and their meetings were henceforward only permitted by licence. The Government had purposely not sent the all-Basque police to control the mainly non-Basque crowd at the prisons, for fear of worsening relations between the Basques and the others. The ultimate consequence of the riots was that the Basque Nationalists became supreme in Vizcaya.[1]

[1] Steer, 110–22.

44

The battle of Málaga

Málaga, with 100,000 inhabitants, is the chief city of a narrow coastal plain running between the sea and the Sierra Navada. Its superb climate and natural harbour has given it three thousand years of commercial eminence. At the start of 1937, the front, from a point on the coast thirty kilometres from Gibraltar, ran inland up to Ronda and continued along the mountains to Granada. The Republic held thus a long coastal strip thirty kilometres wide, with Málaga as its centre. The only road to the north was blocked by a flood at Motril. Málaga itself had been incessantly bombed and workers had earlier destroyed the fashionable district of La Calata. The town, therefore, presented an appearance of desolation. A Nationalist campaign against it began on January 17, commanded by Queipo de Llano, leading the so-called Army of the South. Colonel the Duke of Seville, a Bourbon prince, was in field command. He began by cutting off the most westerly part of Republican territory as far as, and including, Marbella in the first three days. Next, troops from the garrison at Granada under Colonel Muñoz advanced to capture Alhama and the surrounding territory, to the immediate north of Málaga. Both these two preliminary attacks were accomplished almost without resistance.

Though refugees from the newly lost territory crowded into the city and slept on the stone floor of the cathedral, the Republican command at Málaga had no suspicion that these events foreshadowed a general campaign. Nothing was done to reinforce Málaga from Valencia. Since the road was still cut at Motril, artillery could therefore not have come anyway. Largo Caballero himself meanwhile was toying with the idea of an attack from the Madrid-Valencia road on the Nationalists south of Madrid. A week passed.

To the immediate north of Málaga, the mechanised forces of the Italian Black Shirts, 9 battalions in all, had now been assembled under General Roatta, one of Mussolini's most trusted sup-

porters in the army who had previously been head of Italian
military intelligence. He was now in command of units mounted
chiefly in tanks and armoured cars. Unlike the pilots of July-
August 1936 (who had worn Foreign Legion uniforms), these
Italians had a special uniform of their own. The Italians operated
under separate leadership so that they could if possible by themselves realise the grand victory so desired by the *Uffizio Spagna* set
up by Ciano to deal with Spanish affairs. Originally, the Italians

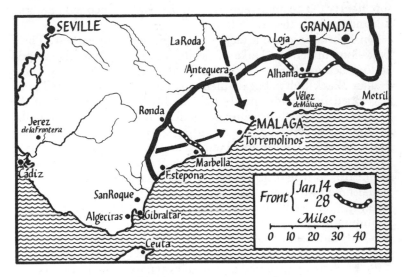

MAP 18. THE BATTLE OF MÁLAGA

had proposed that this attack should be the prelude to a drive on
Valencia, accompanied by a landing there. Mussolini next told
Franco that he could send no further aid after the forthcoming
Non-Intervention Agreement on the end of volunteers. Franco
replied on January 25 that since non-intervention control could
not cover States such as Mexico, who were not party to the agreement, it should be rejected. He also gave a new list of war needs.
Generals Faupel and Roatta, with Anfuso, temporarily in Spain,
called on Franco to ask which of these were the most urgent. 'All,'
said Franco. To secure this, the Generalissimo said he would
agree to set up a joint Italian-German General Staff, consisting of
five German and five Italian officers. The two allies went away to

confer on the implications of this suggestion. Meanwhile, the Málaga campaign became fully under way.[1]

The Republican commander at Málaga was Colonel Villalba, the turncoat of Barbastro and recently transferred from Catalonia. His troops numbered 40,000, almost all Andalusians and all militiamen, untouched by Asensio's reforms. They were confident, and warmly supported by the local peasants. For example, outside Málaga in a *pueblo* too poor ever to have had large estates, Dr Borkenau was assured by a peasant that he was fighting for 'liberty'. The man agreed that he had gained no material advantage from the revolution.

On February 3, the attack on Málaga began in earnest. Three battalions under the Duke of Seville advanced from the Ronda sector, meeting fierce resistance. On the night of February 4, the Italian Black Shirts began their advance. A panic immediately developed in Málaga, partly because of the unfamiliarity of the Italian tanks, partly because of the fear of being cut off. Villalba was unable to communicate a fighting spirit to the men of Málaga, and anyway his conventional temperament was not such as to make him believe that a civilian population could, or should, fight to the death, as it had in Madrid. In these circumstances, after the initial break-through of the front by the Duke of Seville on February 4, and the Italians on February 5, the Nationalist advance continued with rhythmic regularity. On February 6, the Italians reached the heights of Ventas de Zafarraya, dominating the escape road to Almería. The bombing of Málaga continued all day. Villalba therefore ordered a general evacuation, believing the last moment to have been reached. In fact, the Nationalists did not cut the road of retreat. They did not relish the fight of desperation upon which an encircled city would inevitably embark. All that day and during February 7, the Republican high command, the political and trade union leaders, and others who feared the consequences of Nationalist occupation, struggled to escape up the coast. The fortunate fled in the few available motor-cars, the remainder on foot. The *Canarias*, *Baleares* and *Velasco* bombarded the town, while the German *Graf Spee* stood nearby. In the evening of February 7, the Italians reached the outskirts of Málaga. The next day, with the Spaniards under the Duke of Seville, they entered the desolate and ruined town. There ensued the most ferocious proscription that had occurred in Spain since the fall of

[1] *GD*, 231, 236.

Badajoz. Thousands of Republican sympathisers were left behind, some being immediately shot, the rest imprisoned. One eye-witness alleged that 4,000 people were killed in the first week after the entry into the city. As usual, this figure must be regarded as an exaggeration. But certainly the first group were shot without trial on the beach, the second after brief examination by the newly established council of war.[1] The only Republican journalist left behind, Arthur Koestler, then of the *News Chronicle*, was imprisoned in Seville for several months, being much of the time under sentence of death.[2]

On the road to Almería, Nationalist tanks and aircraft caught up with the refugees. Letting the women go free, so as to increase the Republic's food difficulties, they shot the men, often in the sight of their families. Many of those who escaped lay down exhausted and starving.

So ended the inglorious battle of Málaga. The Republican fleet might have assisted the resistance had not Italian ships made to look like the *Canarias* and *Baleares* drawn the Republican vessels away from the battle. The XIIIth International Brigade, then at Murcia, might have been sent to the aid of the beleaguered town, had not the Communists feared that the Anarchists would take the opportunity of rising in Valencia. At all events, the fall of Málaga led to the fall of Asensio Torrado, the Under-Secretary of War and Largo Caballero's favourite General, whom the Communists accused of being in a Valencian night club while the city was about to collapse. Largo Caballero had saved Asensio from disgrace in October when he had been pilloried as the 'General of defeat'; he was unable to do the same again, though Asensio was largely responsible for the organisation of the People's Army and was no more blameworthy than anyone else in Valencia for the defeat at Málaga. He was succeeded as Under-Secretary for War by Baráibar, editor of *Claridad* and of no military experience whatever. The dismissal of Asensio, insisted upon by the Communists, was one more bone of contention between them and the 'Spanish Lenin'.[3]

---

[1] Bahamonde, 117.

[2] He was later exchanged through the good offices of Dr Junod for the beautiful wife of a Nationalist pilot held in Valencia.

[3] For the battle of Málaga, see Borkenau, 211 fl; Aznar 339 fl; Koestler, *Invisible Writing*, 338 fl; Worsley, *passim*.

45

The battle of the Jarama

The defeat at Málaga coincided with a new Nationalist offensive to the south-east of Madrid, in precisely the area where Largo Caballero had himself been contemplating an attack – the valley of the Jarama. The Nationalists attacked with five mobile brigades, each with a majority from the Army of Africa, under García Escámez, Sáenz de Buruaga, Barrón, Asensio and Rada (the Carlists' old instructor), supported by six 155 mm. batteries and a Condor Legion artillery group of 88 mm. guns.[1] The aim of the offensive was to cut the Madrid-Valencia high road. It was undertaken along an eighteen kilometre front running north to south from a line some hundred yards to the east of the Madrid-Andalusia high road.

The attack, a surprise to General Pozas, the Republican commander of the Army of the Centre, began on February 6. García Escámez drove furiously into Ciempozuelos, defended by the newly formed Republican 18th Brigade, whose advance elements were totally overwhelmed. Rada advanced in the north to capture a 697-metre peak, La Marañosa, where two Republican battalions fought to the last man. On February 7, Barrón reached the junction of the Rivers Jarama and Manzanares, bringing the Madrid-Valencia high road under fire. The Republican defence was hampered by a number of confused new brigades who had been intended to take part in Largo Caballero's projected offensive and now found themselves in retreat. On February 8, Miaja sent the crack brigades of Lister and El Campesino to aid Pozas. The XIth International Brigade (now, as a result of reorganisation, formed of the German Thaelmann and Edgar André Battalions, and known by the former name) was ordered to the Jarama. On February 9, the Republican defence was reorganised all along the heights on the east bank of the Jarama. A division (including the XIIth chiefly Italian International Brigade, now reorganised to be composed of Italians and known as the Garibaldi Brigade) was established

[1] López Muñiz, 73.

as a reserve to prevent any general break-through. At dawn on February 11, however, the Nationalists succeeded in forcing the Jarama. A group of Moroccans silently worked their way in the dark to the Pindoque bridge, where they knifed the sentries of

MAP 19. THE BATTLE OF THE JARAMA

the French André Marty Battalion (now of the XIVth Brigade) one by one while standing at their posts. Immediately, two regiments of Nationalist cavalry rode across the river. The Pindoque bridge was blown up by mines operated from the local Republican command post but, having risen a few feet in the air, descended on the same spot and so still afforded a crossing. At the same time, a force under Barrón personally crossed the Jarama some miles higher at the Arganda bridge. By three in the afternoon, a brigade was across, despite heavy Republican air attacks. Here they met the bulk of the André Marty Battalion, whom they surrounded but who resisted until their ammunition was exhausted. Then the Moroccan cavalry charged and killed most of the survivors. The Slav Dabrowsky Battalion, however, now held the line before Arganda. In the area of the Pindoque bridge, the Garibaldi Battalion, from high ground, concentrated their fire on the bridgehead and held up any further advance. Farther south still, Asensio had at dawn stormed the small whitewashed *pueblo* of San Martín de la Vega. Machine guns held him up all day at the bridge here, but at nightfall he got across by a stratagem similar to that practised at dawn at the Pindoque bridge. A Moroccan *tabor* killed the Spaniards on guard. Asensio spent the night consolidating his position and, the next day, the 12th, stormed and captured the heights of Pingarrón, on the other side of the river. Sáenz de Buruaga's Brigade crossed also at San Martín and joined Asensio in a new offensive at the south of the front towards Morata de Tajuña.

The ensuing battle was marked by Republican control of the air for the first time. Nationalist Junkers were driven out of the sky by Russian fighters. It also marked the first fight of the XVth International Brigade, commanded by Colonel 'Gal', a naturalised Russian, of Hungarian birth like Kléber and Lukacz. Gal was incompetent, bad-tempered and hated. The central figure in the formation of the brigade was the Chief of Staff, the gallant English Captain Nathan – shortly promoted to the rank of Major. The Political Commissar was a French Communist, Jean Chaintron, who passed under the name of 'Bethel'. The brigade comprised volunteers from 26 nations. The first battalion of the brigade consisted of 600, chiefly Englishmen of the Saklatvala Battalion – so called after the Indian Communist of that name who had been briefly a Member of Parliament in the 'twenties, but usually known as the British Battalion. In command was the 'English Captain', Tom Wintringham, once of Balliol College, Oxford, more recently editor of *Left Review*, a Communist and military correspondent of the *Daily Worker*.[1] The Political Commissar was a rugged Scottish Communist, George Aitken.

---

[1] Wintringham, 16. The leader of the English Battalion in training had been Wilfred Macartney, a flamboyant journalist of the Left, who was not a Communist – though

The British Battalion included a large number of Scots and some Welshmen. There were some Americans in the battalion at this stage, sixty Cypriots (from London), an Abyssinian, an Australian, a Jamaican, a South African and a Cuban. The company commanders and the Political Commissars were all Communists. The other three battalions of the XVth Brigade were 800 mixed Balkans of the Dimitrov Battalion; 800 French and Belgians of the 6th of February[1] (or Franco-Belgian) Battalion; and 550 Americans of the Abraham Lincoln Battalion, including many Negroes. The Abraham Lincoln Battalion was still training at the village of Villanueva de la Jara, near Albacete. The Irish were divided between the Abraham Lincoln and the British Battalions. Those who joined the former did so because they had objected to the British *Daily Worker*'s omission to mention that many of the fallen on the Córdoba front at Christmas had been Irish. They had then been serving with the British No. 1 Company, and had rioted when their first request for transfer had been refused. Frank Ryan, their leader, also had a public quarrel at this time with Marty.[2] There were also about 160 Greeks in the Dimitrov Battalion. Of those who fought with this Brigade few (especially among the Americans and British) had seen action before. They contrasted, therefore, with the experienced men of the other Brigades.

An Irish group of volunteers had by this time been also gathered on the Nationalist side. Their Commander, General Eoin O'Duffy, was leader of a semi-Fascist Irish movement known as the Blue Shirts. He expected that the exploits of his 600 men in Spain would bring him to political eminence in his own country. At this moment, they had completed their training at Cáceres and had received orders to advance to the Jarama front.[3]

---

he had been to prison for giving military secrets to Russia. Already a rich man, he had grown richer on the profits of the book he then wrote on his experiences, *Walls Have Mouths*, published in 1935, after leaving prison, with an introduction by Compton Mackenzie. He had to abandon command of the Brigade because he was shot in the leg by Peter Kerrigan, Commissar of all the British in Spain, who was apparently merely cleaning his gun.

[1] So named after the riots in Paris on February 6, 1934, but actually formed by coincidence on February 6, 1936.

[2] Copeman, 83.

[3] O'Duffy, 135. O'Duffy had been Commissioner of the Irish Civic Guards till relieved of that post by De Valera. The blue shirts had been founded by ex-President Cosgrave after his defeat by De Valera in 1932. About half the rank and file, and nearly all the officers of O'Duffy's group in Spain were blue shirts. Those who were not were chiefly out-of-work adventurers. (See the pamphlet by Seumas McKee, *I was a Franco soldier*, London 1938.)

The British Battalion bore the brunt of Asensio's and Sáenz de Buruaga's assault on February 12. They defended the so-called Suicide Hill for 7 hours against artillery and machine gun fire from Pingarrón high above them. Nearly all the Nationalists' reserves were flung into the battle, while Lister arrived on the left of the British Battalion. A British volunteer, John Lepper, described the scene in a poem:

> *Death stalked the olive trees*
> *Picking his men*
> *His leaden finger beckoned*
> *Again and again.*[1]

The battle continued all February 12. The International Brigades suffered very heavy losses, including most of their officers. Only 225 out of the original 600 members of the British Battalion were left at the end of the day.[2] Wintringham, the battalion commander, was wounded in the thigh and was eventually replaced by Jock Cunningham.[3] A Protestant clergyman from Kilkenny, the Rev R. M. Hilliard,[4] and Christopher Caudwell, an indefatigable Communist writer aged 29, were the most notable deaths.[5] One company of the British Battalion (including the commander, Fry) was tricked into capture by admitting to their trenches a group of Moroccans who advanced singing the *International*.

The next day the survivors of the British Battalion retreated. They were, however, sent back to recapture their positions, being rallied by the Commissar, Aitken, and Ryan and Cunningham, their only two remaining officers. It seems also that at this moment the commander of the Brigade, the mysterious Colonel Gal, at last played his part in infusing a certain fire to his men. Possibly, however, his Chief of Staff, Nathan, was more responsible.

Further north, meanwhile, Sáenz de Buruaga, after launching an assault towards the Arganda-Colmena road, was driven back to the Jarama by the Germans of the XIth International Brigade,

---

[1] Spender and Lehmann, *Poems for Spain*, 33-4.   [2] Wintringham, 151 fl.

[3] Though for a few unhappy moments the command was in the hands of ex-Sergeant-Major Overton, who had seemed to his comrades previously the model of military knowledge, but who panicked when his boasting led to his promotion.

[4] Known as 'the Boxing Parson'.

[5] His real name was Christopher St John Sprigg. He had written seven detective stories, five books on aviation, and three more works on philosophy and economics, including *Illusion and Reality*, which put forward succinctly the Marxist view of aesthetics.

the Dimitrov Battalion and a unit of Russian tanks. Nationalist artillery on Marañosa could not give adequate support, because this would risk firing on their own men. On February 15, Miaja assumed command of the battle of Jarama, thus linking its outcome to the Madrid command. All the forces in the Jarama were grouped together as the 3rd Army Corps, under the command of Colonel Burillo, who had been in command at Pontejos barracks on the night of Calvo Sotelo's murder. He hated the International Brigades and treated their messengers with extreme rudeness.[1]

The arrangement of the battle line nevertheless meant that four International Brigades now held the front line from Arganda to Morata (the XIIIth Brigade at this time had been sent to the Granada Front).[2] To the south was Lister with his ex-Fifth Regiment Communists. Sáenz de Buruaga succeeded in winning his way back from the Jarama to the first heights on the other side, but henceforward there was no other advance.

The front was not, however, entirely without incident. On February 16, General O'Duffy's Irish Nationalists had reached the Jarama front at Ciempozuelos. No sooner were they in position than they observed a force advancing towards them. The Irish officers concluded they were friends and went to meet them. Eight paces away from the Captain of the advancing troops, the Spanish liaison officer with the Irish saluted and announced: '*Bandera Irlandesa del Tercio!*' The Captain advancing drew his revolver, fired, and in a few moments the exchange became general. The Irishmen lost four killed, including the Spanish liaison officer. It later transpired that their opponents had been a *bandera* of Spanish Nationalists from the Canary Isles. An enquiry was held, by which the Irish were held blameless and the Spaniards allotted all responsibility. Thereafter the Irish were quartered at Ciempozuelos. On one occasion, the German von Thoma requested Irish infantry protection for a German tank advance – an event generally assumed to be unique in the history of war.[3]

---

[1] At the same time, the hated Colonel Gal was promoted to the rank of General, to command a division. He was replaced with the XVth Brigade by a Croat, Čopíc, a saturnine chess addict and musician, who had briefly been a Communist Deputy in Yugoslavia.

[2] These were now commanded as follows: Hans Kahle led the XIth Brigade, Lukacz the XIIth, Gómez (the German Zeisser) the XIIIth, the Alsatian Colonel Colonel Putz the XIVth, and Čopíc the XVth. The XIth henceforth consisted chiefly of German speakers, the XIIth of Italians, the XIIIth of Poles and other eastern Europeans, the XIVth French, and the XVth English and American. But see below, Appendix III.

[3] O'Duffy, 157.

On February 17, meanwhile, the reorganised Republican Army mounted a counter-attack. One division struck to push Barrón back across the Valencia road. Another, from the north, crossed the Manzanares west of Marañosa. But attacks by Gal, on the 23rd and 27th, at the Nationalists' strongest front between Pingarrón and San Martín were, not unnaturally, unsuccessful. Here the Americans of the Abraham Lincoln Battalion, 450 strong, saw their first action. Their commander was Robert Merriman, twenty-eight years old, a Communist, the son of a lumberjack, who had worked his way through the University of Nevada to a lectureship at the University of California. He had originally come to Europe on a travelling scholarship to investigate agricultural problems. Alone of the brigades, a majority of the Americans was composed of students. Seamen were the next largest group. The Americans were in other ways curiously innocent beside the rest of the Brigades. They did not come from war-torn cities now ruled by dictators as did many of their comrades. None of them had done national service in the American Army. They were younger than most of those in other brigades. Yet they fought with great gallantry, without artillery cover. 120 were killed, 175 wounded. Among those killed was Charles Donnelly, a young Irish poet of great promise.[1] Well might they later sing, to the tune of 'Red River Valley':

> *There's a valley in Spain called Jarama*
> *It's a place that we all know too well,*
> *For 'tis there that we wasted our manhood*
> *And most of our old age as well.*[2]

Henceforward, as had occurred in the battle for the Corunna road, each side was too strong to be attacked. Fortifications were therefore prepared. The battle of Jarama was over – resulting in yet another stalemate, in which the Republicans had lost land to the depth of 15 kilometres along a front of some 20 kilometres, but had retained the Valencia road. Both sides, therefore, claimed the victory. The Republicans suffered about 25,000 casualties and the Nationalists 20,000.[3]

---

[1] Rolfe, 57–71. Wintringham, 259.   [2] Rolfe, 71.
[3] The chief source for this battle is Colodny, *op. cit.*; Aznar, 357–64; Wintringham, 151 fl; Lojendio, 198–206; Ruiz Albeniz *passim*; Rolfe.

46

The battle of Guadalajara

The start of March 1937 found Republican Spain with its morale considerably raised by the battle of the Jarama. Although its own counter-attacks there had not been successful, efforts by Orgaz to renew the offensive had also failed – two attacks on February 23 and March 1 costing 6,000 casualties and gaining no ground. The newly organised Republican Army, with the International Brigades as models, had for the first time held the Nationalists in open country. Soviet fighters had established at least temporary air mastery. A campaign for volunteers for the new army had begun, launched by Azaña, Largo Caballero and Companys. Each of the three politicians, all sinking in power, made emotional speeches at the campaign's inauguration. Companys demanded an 'act of devotion' from the people, in the Plaza de Cataluña. 'Catalans!' he exclaimed, 'do you promise, for the honour of your regiments, to endure every sacrifice, and put forth every effort, in order to conquer Fascism?' The great crowd roared, '*Si*'. 'Catalans,' said Companys, 'your promise has ascended into the infinite, has been heard throughout the world and by generations to come. Remember this! *Visca la Llibertat*.'[1] Politically, the Communists had strengthened their hold over the administration and the Army so much that they were now – as they had earlier been in Madrid alone – almost the real executive power of the State. A grumbling tension with the Anarchists remained, but for a time the Communists were careful to confine their attacks to the 'incontrollables' among the Anarchists, though of course they could easily so call all their Anarchist enemies. In these attacks, they were fully supported by the Republican and Socialist Press. At their annual conference on February 21, the FAI threatened that their Ministers would be withdrawn from the Government unless the Aragón front, still manned mainly by Anarchists, was supplied with arms.[2] Though some supplies were sent, they were

[1] Quoted in Peers, *Spain in Eclipse*, 14–15.
[2] FAI minutes published Barcelona 1937. Quoted Cattell, *Communism*, 110.

not adequate to start an offensive against the ever elusive Saragossa. The Anarchists nevertheless climbed down and remained in
the Government. Militarily indeed, the Aragón front was obviously
not so crucial as that at Madrid, which had only been held with
extreme difficulty, and by the use of all the material available.

The Communist party held a conference from March 5 to 8
at Valencia. The speeches were all moderate, except about the
POUM. Díaz gave a bouquet to the 'pure' Republicans for participating in the 'anti-Fascist movement hand-in-hand with the
proletariat'. He spoke of freedom of religion – denying that the Republic stood for a battle against religion. As for agriculture, he left
open, as if the matter needed further discussion, the question of
whether the confiscated estates should be collectively or individually run. But he, and all speakers, urged speed in unifying the
Army and organising industry for war. Otherwise, he added threateningly, 'the Government will cease to be the Government'.[1] As for
the POUM, their leaders, as ex-Communists, could hardly expect
to be anything but vilified. They had proposed that Trotsky should
come to Catalonia. They had attacked the show trials of Radek,
Piatakov and others. They spoke of 'Stalinite Thermidorians' who
had established in Russia 'the bureaucratic *régime* of a poisoned
dictator'. They insisted that they were fighting for Socialism
against capitalism, and that '*bourgeois* democracy in this country'
had had its day – dangerous attacks on the party line of defence
of 'the democratic republic'.[2] Díaz denounced them as 'agents of
Fascism who hide themselves behind the pretended slogans of
revolutionaries to carry out their major mission as agents of our
enemies in our own country'. POUM newspapers and radio stations
outside Catalonia were seized as being harmful to the war effort.
But in Barcelona, the PSUC did not yet feel strong enough to take
these steps. Nor were they strong enough to force the unification
of all the parties of the Popular Front, as their leaders demanded.[3]

The ease with which Málaga had been captured, meanwhile encouraged the Italian commanders in Nationalist Spain to

[1] Díaz, *Por la Unidad, Hacia la Victoria*, 13–15. Quoted Cattell, *Communism*, 92.
[2] *The Spanish Revolution* (POUM newspaper) 3.2.37.
[3] A committee of liaison between Communists and Socialists was created. It is
instructive to note that Prieto was at this time in favour of a Socialist-Communist
unification. Russia, he believed, was the Republic's only help. The majority of the
Socialist executive, however, were against this move. (Álvarez del Vayo, 288.) This is
confirmed by Nenni, who also notes that the future violent anti-Communist Araquistain, Ambassador in Paris, shared this view. (Nenni, 67 footnote.)

aspire to further military exploits. The idea of landing near Valencia – rumours of which had caused alarm in the Republican Government – was abandoned. The new plan was that an attack should be launched on Madrid from a new direction – the north-east.[1] This would aim to capture Guadalajara, the capital of the province of that name, fifty miles from Madrid. Orgaz would at the same time continue the Jarama offensive and if possible meet the advance from the north-east at Alcalá de Henares, so finally encircling Madrid. The idea of the campaign had indeed been first suggested on February 13, when the battle of the Jarama was at its height. The Guadalajàra attack was undertaken on the right by the Soria Division under Moscardó, the hero of the Alcázar, with 20,000 legionaries, Moroccans, and some Carlists. On the left, 30,000 Italians were under the orders of Roatta. These were divided into four divisions: the Black Shirts under General Rossi, the Black Flames under General Coppi, the Black Arrows under General Nuvolari and the Littorio Division under General Bergonzoli. These were supported by 250 tanks and 180 varied pieces of mobile artillery, together with a chemical warfare company, a flame-thrower company, and 70 lorries per battalion. This force was accompanied by about 50 fighters and 12 reconnaissance aircraft. The important aspect of the plan from Mussolini's point of view was that they would act together, so that the great victory to be gained would redound only to the Italian credit. The military plan was accompanied by a bizarre proposal from Mussolini to Franco, made by the Fascist Farinacci, that Spain's troubles might be solved by the Duke of Aosta's assumption of the Spanish throne.[2]

Guadalajara in peacetime is a stagnant provincial capital commanding the gorge through which the river Henares runs swiftly down from the Guadarrama. The airport of Barajas is nearby. In 1937, it was the headquarters of the Russian air squadron. The advance against Guadalajara opened early on March 8. The front was then held by two new Spanish divisions. It was broken at the first assault by Coppi's Black Flames Division, composed entirely of trucks and armoured cars, operating those tactics later celebrated as the *Blitzkrieg*. At the same time Moscardó broke

---

[1] Thanks to the kindess of Mr F. W. Deakin, Warden of St Antony's College, Oxford I have been able to see the report on Guadalajara sent to Rome by the Italian Commander, General Roatta, at present in the library of the Foreign Office. Lojendio, 212 fl, Anzar 380 fl. Regler, *Owl of Minerva* and Colodny are the other chief sources.

[2] Cantalupo, 85–6, 147 fl. Farinacci made no attempt to bring Cantalupo into these discussions, and the two only met accidentally at a special *corrida*.

through the Republican lines on the Soria road. However, in mid-morning, the temperature lowered, and rain fell heavily. Sleet, ice and fog followed. The Nationalist aircraft were unable to leave their improvised landing-grounds. But the Republican Air Force, operating from nearby Barajas, hampered the advance from the start. In the meantime the Republican High Command were busy sending reinforcements. The vile weather, as well as the

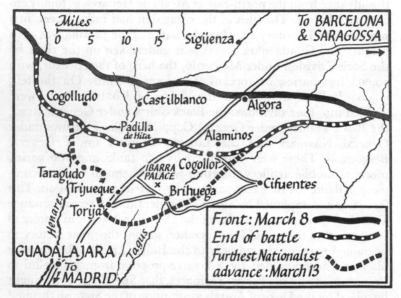

MAP 20. THE BATTLE OF GUADALAJARA

fatigue of the men, prevented Orgaz from embarking on his attack in the Jarama valley. The next day, the 9th, the Italian advance began again, despite continued bad weather. Coppi's Black Flames entered Almadrones at half-past ten in the morning, and then moved to the left flank to widen the gap in the Republican lines, capturing Masegasa. Nuvolari and the Black Arrows took over in the centre. Moscardó also continued to advance and captured Cogolludo. The situation thus appeared critical for the Republic. But, by the evening, a 4th Army Corps had been hastily assembled from the best Republican regiments, under the overall command of Colonel Jurado. The 11th Division, led by Lister, and composed of the German XIth International

Brigade, El Campesino's brigade, a Basque brigade, and an ex-Communist 1st Brigade, was established in the woods along the road from Trijueque to Torija. Along the Brihuega-Torija road, the Anarchist Cipriano Mera, had established himself with a division which included Lukacz's XIIth International Brigade, headed by the Garibaldi Battalion. The old, partly walled town of Brihuega thus lay halfway between the two armies. Here, in 1710, the French General Vendôme had defeated Lord Stanhope in the last battle of the War of the Spanish Succession. Here again an international battle now occurred. At dawn on March 10, half-asleep, as it had been since the last conflict around it, Brihuega fell to the advancing Italian Black Flames and Black Arrows. Bergonzoli's Littorio Division followed as a reserve. At the same time, Moscardó, advancing down the banks of the Henares, had reached Jadraque.

About noon, the Garibaldi Battalion – accompanied by the formidable trio of Vidali (Carlos Contreras) as Inspector-General of the whole front, Luigo Longo (Gallo), holding the same position for the International Brigades, and Nenni, who commanded a company in the battalion – advanced along the road from Torija towards Brihuega. They had no idea that Coppi and Nuvolari had already taken that town. Reaching the so-called palace of Don Luis, they advanced on foot, accompanied by a motor cyclist patrol. Five kilometres short of Brihuega, this patrol encountered a motor cyclist from Coppi's Black Flames who, hearing the Italian voices of the Garibaldi Battalion, asked if he was right in supposing he was on the the Torija road. The Garibaldi motor cyclists said that he was. Both groups now went back to their headquarters. Coppi assumed that the Garibaldi scouts were part of Nuvolari's division. He therefore continued to advance. Ilse Barontini, the Commissar and acting commander of the Garibaldi Battalion,[1] continued also. He established his men in woods on the left of the road, where they made contact with the similarly far advanced XIth International Brigade. Coppi's tanks now appeared. They were attacked by the machine guns of the Garibaldi Battalion. The Black Flame infantry was sent in to attack. Two patrols of the opposing Italian forces met. The Black Flame commander asked why the other Italians had fired on him. '*Noi siamo Italiani di Garibaldi*' came the answer. The Black Flame patrol then surrendered. But, for the rest of the day, the Italians fought a civil war of their own around a

[1] Pacciardi had been wounded at the Jarama.

country house known as the Ibarra Palace. Vidali, Longo and Nenni meantime arranged a propaganda machine. Loudspeakers called out through the woods: 'Brothers, why have you come to a foreign land to murder workers?' Republican aircraft dropped pamphlets promising safe-conduct to all Italian deserters from the Nationalists, with a reward of 50 pesetas. One hundred pesetas were pledged if they came with arms. Meantime in Rome, Count Ciano was assuring the German Ambassador, Hassell, that Guadalajara was going well. 'Our opponents,' he added, 'are principally Russian.'[1] The next day, the 11th, the battle began again. The Italian Fascist commanders were favoured by an Order of the Day from General Roatta instructing them to keep their men in a state of the greatest exaltation. 'This is an easy matter,' went on Roatta, 'if they are frequently spoken to with political allusions, and are always reminded of the Duce, who has willed this conflict.'[2] The Black Arrows on this day broke the front of Lister's 11th Division, capturing Trijueque, and began to drive fast in their armoured cars along the road to Torija. The Thaelmann Brigade suffered heavy casualties and complete defeat was only prevented by the personal will-power of Ludwig Renn, the new Chief-of-Staff of the brigade. Rallying, it held the road to Torija from Trijueque. The road to Trijueque from Brihuega was also held all day by the Garibaldi Battalion. On the 12th, a storm permitted the Republican bombers, rising from their permanent runways, to pound away unmolested at the Italian mechanised columns. Among the casualties was General Luizzi, Roatta's Chief-of-Staff, killed by an incendiary bomb. Lister then ordered his division to counter-attack. General Pavlov's Russian tanks attacked first, to be followed by infantry. Trijueque was recaptured at bayonet point by the Thaelmann and El Campesino Brigades. Many Italians surrendered. The Republican attack continued along the road to Brihuega. The Garibaldi Battalion stormed their compatriots in the Ibarra Castle and captured it at nightfall. The following day, March 13, the Republican Government telegraphed the League of Nations that documents and statements by Italian prisoners clearly proved 'the presence of regular military units of the Italian army in Spain' in defiance of Article 10 of the Covenant.[3] General Roatta

---

[1] *GD*, 251.   [2] *Spanish White Book*, 275.

[3] The documents captured at Guadalajara included many poignant letters from Italian wives and mothers to their serving sons: one wife wrote to her husband: 'What a beautiful honeymoon mine has been! Two days of marriage and twenty-five months of interminable waiting. First comes the country, I know, and afterwards love, but I

now despatched his other two divisions, Rossi's Black Shirts and the Littorio Division under Bergonzoli. Both attacks were beaten off. On the 14th, Pavlov's tanks drove up the road beyond Trijucque towards the cathedral city of Sigüenza, captured a great deal of material, and might even have taken Sigüenza itself had they been supported by mobile infantry. There was a pause in the battle for three days on March 15, 16 and 17. Roatta issued orders of the day, but made few preparations, preferring to complain of the continued inactivity of Orgaz on the Jarama.[1]

On March 18, the whole Republican Army on the Guadalajara front was put on to the offensive. It was an unfortunate moment for the Italians, since Roatta had that morning gone to Salamanca to ask Franco for aid, and to urge him to order Orgaz to attack at all costs. At half-past one, 80 Republican aircraft bombed the surroundings of Brihuega. Heavy Republican artillery fire followed. At 2 o'clock, Lister's and Cipriano Mera's two divisions, with 70 of Pavlov's tanks, attacked, the one in the west, the second in the east, aiming to encircle the town. They had almost achieved this when the Italians received orders to retreat. They did so, so fast that the action must be named a rout, down the only road still open to them. The pursuit continued for several miles. Moscardó also was ordered to retreat to Jadraque.[2]

In this ill-named battle of Guadalajara, the Italians lost about 2,000 killed, 300 prisoners of war and about 4,000 wounded. Moscardó's losses were insignificant. The Republic lost about the same number of men killed and wounded as the Italians, but very few prisoners. After the battle, the apologists for the Republic claimed it as a great victory over Mussolini. Ernest Hemingway, who arrived in Spain at this time accompanied by Sidney Franklin, the American matador, wrote: 'I have been studying the battle for

---

am an egoist, and with reason, for you were one of the first volunteers to go to Africa, and are among the last to return. I pray God that one day He will make it possible for you both to serve the country and also provide bread for your family.' (Document No 267 in the folio presented to the League of Nations.) A mother writes: 'Dear Armando, I can only pray that God and the saints keep you and if you return in good health we can go back to Rome and open the shop.' Other documents give lists of those shot as cowards for giving themselves self-inflicted wounds, and for bandaging themselves when they had nothing wrong with them. These enforced and ill-paid mercenaries who were sacrificed to Mussolini's pride were surely the most pitiable of all the participants in the Spanish War.

[1] Actually, several attempts at offensives were made in Orgaz's sector, without success. O'Duffy's Irishmen went into action for the first time on March 13: the killed included Sergeant-Major Gaselee of Dublin and two 'légionnaires' from Kerry.

[2] Hemingway, Spanish War, 7–13; Regler, Great Crusade, 315 fl.

four days, going over the ground with the commanders who directed it, and I can state flatly that Brihuega will take its place in military history with the other decisive battles of the world.'[1] Herbert Matthews, of the *New York Times*, reported that Guadalajara was to Fascism what the defeat of Bailén had been to Napoleon.[2] Militarily, it would be more accurate to see the battle as similar to that of Jarama and the Corunna road. A Nationalist attempt to complete the encirclement of Madrid was thwarted at the cost of 20 kilometres – for the Nationalists did gain about that depth of territory along the road from where they started. Politically, however, the retreat of the Italians and the clear proof that organised Italian units were being used by the Nationalists was of great propaganda value to the Republic. The battle had been intended to be an exhibition of how the Italians could carry out the most modern techniques of war. But it was an object lesson, in fact, of how a mechanised attack should not be launched. The Italians had not maintained fighting contact with their enemies and had not taken the weather into account at all.

Guadalajara also had the effect of angering Mussolini so much that he announced that no Italians could return alive from Spain unless they won a victory. To Hassell, he blamed the Spaniards, who had 'hardly fired a shot during the decisive days'.[3] The Falangist, Fernández Cuesta (later a Nationalist Minister), remarked to Angel Baza, an agent of Prieto sent to visit him in prison to negotiate the idea of a compromise peace, that the Italian defeat at Guadalajara was the 'sole satisfaction he had experienced in the war'.[4] The gloom of Cantalupo the Italian Ambassador at Salamanca became so great that he had to be recalled. The battle also led the General Staffs of Europe (notably the French) to conclude that motorised troops were not as effective as had first been suggested. The Germans were perhaps restrained from drawing this conclusion by their contempt for the Italians as soldiers.[5]

---

[1] Hemingway, *The Spanish War*, in *Fact* June 1937. The author of *Death in the Afternoon* thereafter took an active part in the war on the Republican side, exceeding the duties of a mere reporter by, for instance, instructing young Spaniards in the use of rifles. The first visit of Hemingway to the XIIth International Brigade was a great occasion, the Hungarian General Lukacz sending a message to the nearby village for all its girls to attend the banquet he was giving. (Regler, *Owl of Minerva*, 298.)
[2] Matthews, *Two Wars*, 264.   [3] *GD*, 258–60.
[4] Zugazagoitia, 241.   [5] Miksche, *Blitzkrieg*, 37.

47

Stalemate around Madrid – dissatisfaction in the International
Brigades – Hemingway, Spender and Auden in Spain

Guadalajara brought to an end the series of conflicts around Madrid. Apart from intermittent bombardment, the capital remained quiet. Professor J. B. S. Haldane arrived to give advice on gas attacks.[1] The chief anxiety of the defenders was the question of food supplies. In Valencia the population ate well throughout the war and visitors were often served with ten different hors d'oeuvres and ten courses, but in Madrid meat was almost unknown. Foreign visitors ate horse meat, though Hemingway once procured three tins of caviare and half a camembert at the Hotel Florida. In the University City, 'illiteracy and rats' were the enemies most vigorously pursued, for each unit had its schools for reading and writing.

The International Brigades now had their first rest from action. The volunteers had discovered in battle that 'a war of ideas' is much the same as any other conflict. In Spain as elsewhere there was confusion of orders, jamming of rifles at the critical moment, uncertainty about the whereabouts of the enemy and of headquarters, desire for cigarettes (or sweet-tasting things), fatigue, occasional hysteria.[2] One unknown member of the British Battalion wrote:

> *Eyes of men running, falling, screaming,*
> *Eyes of men shouting, sweating, bleeding,*
> *The eyes of the fearful, those of the sad,*
> *The eyes of exhaustion, and those of the mad.*

[1] His concern, and that of his wife Charlotte, in Spain had been begun by the enlistment of her sixteen-year-old son in the British Battalion of the International Brigade. Haldane became among the most assiduous of all the supporters of the Republic. He travelled about Spain incessantly between now and the end of the war. Charlotte Haldane also visited Spain, but her main work was to act as a kind of matron for the reception of British volunteers for the International Brigades at the staging point in Paris. Both became secret members of the Communist party.

[2] Certain middle-class intellectuals among the volunteers prided themselves on the greater grumbling among the working-class volunteers than among themselves.

Eyes of men thinking, hoping, waiting,
Eyes of men loving, cursing, hating,
The eyes of the wounded, sodden in red,
The eyes of the dying and those of the dead.

From the start, the wilder volunteers had got into trouble with the authorities, if only for drunkenness. But now trouble was incessant.[1] Those who wished to return home were not permitted to do so when they wished. Some complained that they had volunteered on the assumption that they could go home in three months' time. Here the principles of a volunteer army fighting allegedly for ideals conflicted with military needs. The punishment for attempted desertion or escape was at least confinement in a 're-education camp', for whose cruel rigours many idealistic but easily disgusted young men from Anglo-Saxon or Scandinavian countries were not prepared. The Foreign Office in London eventually negotiated a settlement which exempted British volunteers from the death penalty, but this was undoubtedly several times imposed on others.[2] The Communist leadership of the Brigades showed itself harsh to humanitarian needs, and favoured party members – in matters of leave and conditions – to the exclusion of all the others.[3] Uniforms were so scarce that the British Battalion seemed almost in rags. The dissatisfaction with the Communists in Spain reflected the general disillusionment with Stalin's *régime* following the first news of the purges beginning in Moscow.[4]

While Anglo-Saxons became disillusioned, however, Eastern European volunteers continued to flow into Spain, many through Tito's 'secret railway'. Many were arrested on the way, since (after the end of February) to volunteer for Spain was now illegal

---

[1] Venereal disease was very high among the French volunteers, chiefly because no one had taken any precautions against its spread. The British Battalion leaders early gave lectures to their troops on contraception.

[2] Thompson, 118.

[3] Though, in an effort to put the Popular Front policy fully into effect, all cell meetings of the Communist party inside the International Brigades ceased about this time for about 9 months.

[4] Nor were international relations inside the brigades always happy. For instance, Gal, now a General, gave a banquet one night for the XVth Brigade. On his right at dinner he placed the new brigade Commissar, George Aitken. On his left sat the new commander Čopić. The Chief of Staff, Colonel Klaus, a Prussian who had fought as an officer in the World War, was placed next to Čopić down the table. Klaus was so angry at this *placement* that in true German fashion he walked out and had to be brought back under armed guard. (Evidence of Mr George Aitken.)

in all the non-intervention countries.[1] The chiefly right-wing
Governments of the Balkans and East Europe made every effort
to enforce this. Nevertheless the recruitment continued. And the
future Yugoslav Communist heretic Djilas acted as executive head
of the flow of volunteers from Yugoslavia.[2]

While the battles were temporarily over, and a rest-period
had come, discipline became increasingly hard to keep in the

MAP 21. THE BATTLES AROUND MADRID
NOVEMBER 1936–MARCH 1937

Brigades. Leave in Madrid could not overcome the feeling
among many that they would never return home. Food became
bad. Men began to desert in small groups. A lorry would disappear
from the cookhouse. It would be found that the driver and three or
four men had gone with it. Some months later, it would reappear

---

[1] These laws were passed as part of the Non-Intervention Control Agreement. See
below, page 395.
[2] Dedijer, 106–8.

in Barcelona where the men had gone to catch a boat home to England.[1]

The American battalions[2] of the International Brigade were by now known for the excellence of their canteen. They were also visited by numerous American journalists. At one bedside in a hospital financed by American sympathisers,[3] Ernest Hemingway comforted a casualty by literary talk.

'They tell me Dos Passos and Sinclair Lewis are coming over too,' said a wounded American, a would-be writer. 'Yes,' said Hemingway, 'and when they come I'll bring them up to see you.' 'Good boy, Ernest,' said the man in the bed. 'You don't mind if I call you Ernest?' 'Hell no,' replied Hemingway.[4]

The ambulance units of the Republican army were now filled with many foreign writers. W. H. Auden served as a stretcher bearer. But he went home 'after a very short visit of which he never spoke'.[5]

Later, in June, a Dependants Aid Committee was formed in Britain for the welfare of the families of British volunteers in Spain. This was formed by the then Communist Mrs Charlotte Haldane. Her clerical staff were all paid Communists, but the body was sponsored by non-Communists such as: the 'Red Duchess' of Atholl (then a Conservative MP, who ruined herself

---

[1] Stephen Spender, one of the most active apologists of the Republic, appeared in Spain at this time, in search of a former secretary who had volunteered for the Brigades and who, being disillusioned, had tried to escape. For a time, there seemed a possibility that this young man might be shot. Rather in the style of a novel by Kafka, Spender dined with the Commissars of the British Battalion who were his judges and who were eventually persuaded to relent. The story of young Coope also shortly engaged the attention of England. He was an English youth of eighteen, who volunteered for the Brigades after hearing a speech by Miss Ellen Wilkinson, and who later escaped *via* a ship which left him in Greece. The boy's father went out to Spain to search for him, and joined the Brigade to do so.

[2] There were now two American battalions, the Abraham Lincoln Battalion, now commanded by Martin Hourihan from Pennsylvania, and the George Washington Battalion, led by a Yugoslav American, Marko Markowicz.

[3] The American Medical Aid Fund to the Spanish Republic, headed by Dr Cannon of Harvard Law School, had already raised 100,000 dollars. It had six hospitals in Spain with 18 ambulances. For a time the State Department refused, under the Embargo Act, to permit even doctors and nurses to go to Spain. Later they relented. (Taylor, 133.)

[4] Hemingway, *Spanish War*. Hemingway shortly became busy directing a propaganda film, *The Spanish Earth*, with Dos Passos and Archibald Macleish.

[5] Spender, *World within World*, 247. The experience of Auden in Spain is curiously similar to that of Simone Weil. Both (unlike everyone else who visited Spain) were uninformative when they arrived home. Simone Weil, who spent some time in Catalonia in August–October 1936, seems to have undergone conversion as a result of her experiences.

politically by her championship of the Republic),[1] H. N. Brailsford, Will Lawther, Lord Listowel, J. B. Priestley, Clement Attlee,
R. H. S. Crossman, Emanuel Shinwell, Miss Eleanor Rathbone,
G. R. Strauss, Miss Ellen Wilkinson, Sir Norman Angell, Vernon
Bartlett, Victor Gollancz, Professor Laski, Sean O'Casey, H. G.
Wells and Sybil Thorndike.[2] The Committee raised £41,847
between then and October 1938. Meanwhile in the United States
the Government, ever in search of the refinement of purest
neutrality, promulgated regulations which prevented the gathering of funds for one or other of the two Spanish parties unless these
were for *bona fide* relief purposes. In fact, none of the 26 bodies
which registered under these arrangements was refused a licence.

ADDITIONAL NOTE TO CHAPTER 47

It is of interest that the Chapaiev battalion was composed of 231
industrial workers, 68 agricultural workers, 36 sailors, 7 civil
servants, 13 peasants, 18 miscellaneous employees, 8 intellectuals
and 7 artisans (Kantorowioz, *Chapaiev*, p. 7).

---

[1] Her book *Searchlight on Spain* was among the most successful of all the books on the
Spanish War. She also wrote a preface for Arthur Koestler's *Spanish Testament*. In
1938 she resigned her Conservative seat, and stood again as an Independent Conservative in protest against the Government's non-intervention policy. She lost the
ensuing by-election.

[2] Charlotte Haldane, *Truth Will Out*, 106.

48

The Non-Intervention Control Plan – apparent sincerity of Germany
– effects of Guadalajara – an outburst by Count Grandi

The Non-Intervention Committee was now apparently about to achieve its first victory. On January 28 Faupel in Salamanca had been told by the German Foreign Ministry that Germany desired 'as effective a control as possible and to cut off Spain from supplies after it is established'.[1] Such a control was agreed in the Committee's sub-committee. There would be observers on the non-Spanish side of Spanish frontiers, and on ships of the non-intervention countries going to Spain. There would also be non-intervention warships patrolling Spanish waters.

Ribbentrop was instructed not to make air control a condition of acceptance of the control plan – for fear of ruining the prospects of agreement.[2] Grandi too was told by Ciano to be 'positive',[3] since all essential Italian shipments to Spain had been finished. The only stumbling-block was Portugal who refused for reasons of 'sovereignty' to accept international observers on her side of the Spanish frontier. Russia now said she wished to participate in the naval patrol. She was offered an area off north Spain. Maisky suggested the east coast. This was rejected by Germany and Italy (who had been allocated that area) since they did not desire the Russian Navy in the Mediterranean, as this would make possible Russian breaches of control. Portugal finally agreed to accept a number of British observers officially attached to the British Embassy in Lisbon, who would not be recognised as 'international controllers'. And Russia agreed not to insist on participating in the naval control. The cost of a year's operation of the scheme was estimated at £898,000. Britain, France, Germany, Italy and Russia would each pay 16% (£143,680), while the other 22 countries divided the remaining 20%.[4] The naval patrol was

---

[1] *GD*, 237.   [2] *GD*, 241-2.   [3] *Ibid.*, 243.
[4] Britain's 16% was docked by £64,000, the estimated cost of the Portuguese frontier control.

undertaken by the four participants at their own expense. The final scheme was agreed on March 8. An International Board, with Britain, France, Italy, Germany and Russia (and later Poland, Greece and Norway) represented, and with the Dutch Vice-Admiral van Dulm as chairman, would administer the scheme. Britain would be responsible for the Portuguese-Spanish frontier. 130 observers under a Chief Administrator (the Danish Colonel Lunn) would be on the French frontier. There would be five observers on the Gibraltar frontier and 550 observers at ports, headed by the Dutch Rear-Admiral Olwer, to supervise all unloading of cargoes. The naval patrol would be controlled by Britain from the French frontier to Cape Busto at the north-west tip of Galicia in the south, and from the Portuguese frontier to Cape de Gata. France would patrol from Cape Busto to the Portuguese frontier, the Spanish Moroccan coast, Ibiza and Majorca. Germany was responsible for the east coast of Spain from Cape de Gata to Cape Oropesa, and Italy from Cape Oropesa to the French frontier. Minorca was also the responsibility of Italy. The setting up of the scheme and the legislation needed in the various countries to ensure that their citizens complied, took until the end of April. The observers and the non-intervention patrol ships were by then in place. The non-intervention flag, two black balls on a white ground, waved hopefully henceforward off the harbours of Spain. Yet this plan seemed inevitably to the Republic to add insult to injury. Not only were Germany and Italy bringing arms to the Nationalists without abatement, but they were now allotted a task policing the prevention of this. The mockery was complete.

The presence of organised Italian divisions at the battle of Guadalajara came before the Non-Intervention Committee before the start of the scheme. It came up not, however, as a breach of the agreement, since all events previous to the adoption of the control plan were now tacitly forgotten, and it was not suggested that the Italians had all arrived since then. The matter arose in discussions of the possibility of withdrawing 'volunteers' from Spain. On March 23, the atmosphere of the Committee, already heated by reports of Italian disaster at Guadalajara, was excited by new reports that Italian troops had left in the *Sardegna* for Cádiz after the agreement on control. Grandi said that he was unable to discuss volunteers and, carried away by his bad temper, added that he personally hoped that no Italian volunteer would leave Spain till the end of the war.[1] This caused general consternation. The next day, Maisky accused Italy of 'ever-increasing military intervention', saying that there were at least 60,000 Italians in Spain in mid-February, that this figure had since been increased, and that a commission should examine the matter on the spot.[2] Grandi's speech was discussed, in the meantime, in the chancelleries. German diplomats displayed marked tact. They acted separately from their military colleagues, since they apparently desired to realise the control agreement. Cerruti, the Italian Ambassador in Paris, assured Delbos that Italy would not break up non-intervention. By the start of April, the Committee had obviously been preserved, though it was not yet being used.

[1] Cattell, *Soviet Diplomacy*, 73.   [2] *Ibid.*, 74.

BOOK V
THE WAR IN THE NORTH

49

The start of the Basque campaign – the Nationalist Army – the Basque Army – the bombing of Durango – Togliatti proposes the political assassination of Largo Caballero – the crisis in Barcelona – the Basque attempts at mediation

On March 22, 1937, Franco put his plans to his air chief, General Kindelán. First, the Guadalajara front would be fortified. The Italians would be reorganised at Palencia. The University City salient would be withdrawn. Two new divisions would be formed. Forty new aircraft and twenty batteries would be bought from abroad. And Mola would embark on a campaign against the Basques. Kindelán advised against a withdrawal from the University City. He suggested the doubling of the number of aircraft and batteries to be bought. Franco took his advice. The plan as amended was then acted upon.[1]

Mola's Army of the North was reorganised and re-equipped. All the Nationalist mobile artillery and aircraft were despatched to Vitoria in support. This change of front represented a stern and terrible realisation by the Nationalist Generals that Madrid could not be taken and that the war could not be won quickly, even though, as a result of a vast recruiting campaign, their total number under arms would soon approach 400,000 men. The change caused particular dissatisfaction among those leaders of the Falange, such as Hedilla, who were impatient for victory so as to prove the sincerity of their social aspirations. The Falangists were anyway nettled by the prevalence of priests around the Generalissimo. There was a similar restlessness among the Carlists, for whom the length of the war was beginning to suggest that the

[1] Kindelán, 76. General Orgaz, Nationalist Supreme Commander at Jarama, and long ago one of the first military plotters against the Republic, was now given the task of forming a series of military academies for officers and NCOs to fill the emptying ranks caused by casualties. Young soldiers who had served six months at the front spent two months studying and returned as officers. Thanks to Orgaz's efficiency, nearly all the young men of the middle classes of Nationalist Spain served as officers. The assistance of German officers in these academies was very great. The first Commander of the Condor Legion, General Sperrle, noted in *Die Wehrmacht*, May 1939, that 56,000 Spanish officers had passed through the hands of German military instructors.

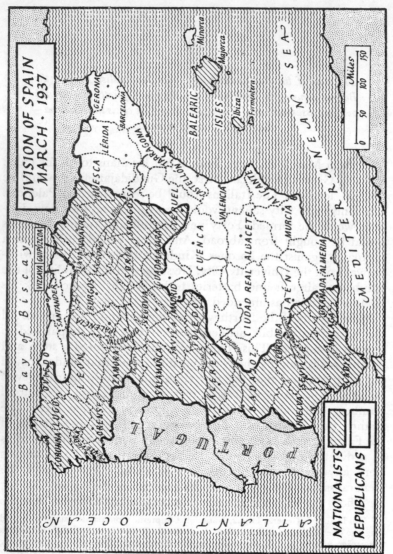

DIVISION OF SPAIN
MARCH · 1937

Bay of Biscay

MEDITERRANEAN SEA

BALEARIC ISLES

Minorca
Majorca
Ibiza
Formentera

ATLANTIC OCEAN

PORTUGAL

Miles
0   50   100   150

NATIONALISTS
REPUBLICANS

VIZCAYA GUIPÚZCOA
SANTANDER
OVIEDO
LUGO
CORUÑA
PONTEVEDRA
ORENSE
LEÓN
PALENCIA
BURGOS
NAVARRE
LOGROÑO
SORIA
GUADALAJARA
ZAMORA
VALLADOLID
SEGOVIA
MADRID
SALAMANCA
ÁVILA
TOLEDO
CÁCERES
CUENCA
HUESCA
LÉRIDA
GERONA
BARCELONA
TARRAGONA
SARAGOSSA
TERUEL
CASTELLÓN
VALENCIA
ALICANTE
ALBACETE
MURCIA
CIUDAD REAL
BADAJOZ
CÓRDOBA
JAÉN
GRANADA
ALMERÍA
HUELVA
SEVILLE
MÁLAGA
CÁDIZ

MAP 22

Generals would remain in power for ever, if they won, rather than restore the Monarchy.

The decision to attack in the north was, however, mainly suggested by the suspicion that it could be conquered quickly, and so provide a victory badly needed to bolster Nationalist prestige. The lure of Basque iron ore, as well as the other industries of Bilbao, was an additional motive, particularly to the Germans of HISMA. Many thought that Bilbao could be taken within three weeks of the start of operations. For Mola knew the quantity, as well as the deployment, of the Basque defence forces, through the treachery of Captain Goicoechea, a Basque officer, who had taken part in the building of Bilbao's defences, the so-called 'ring of iron', and who had driven over to the Nationalists in his own motor-car early in March.

Some days before the Basque war began, a sea-fight occurred outside Bilbao which was an enactment of what was to follow. A merchant ship laden with war material for Bilbao was intercepted by the new Nationalist cruiser *Canarias* five miles from the shore. Three small Basque trawlers fought the cruiser until they had lost two-thirds of their crew and had been almost shot to pieces. Of this struggle, C. Day Lewis wrote his celebrated narrative poem, the *Nabara*, beginning:

> *Freedom is more than a word, more than the base coinage*
> *Of statesmen, the tyrant's dishonoured cheque, or the dreamer's mad*
> *Inflated currency. She is mortal, we know, and made*
> *In the image of simple men who have no taste for carnage*
> *But sooner kill and are killed than see that image betrayed.*

The last three lines accurately describe the Basque tragedy.[1]

Mola's offensive began on March 31. The attack was undertaken by 50,000 infantry of the 61st Navarre Division, under General Solchaga. The Monarchist General Vigón was Mola's Chief of Staff.

Four Navarrese brigades were established between Vergara and Villarreal, on the borders of the two Basque provinces of Vizcaya and Álava. They were all heavily armed. On either side of them was an Italian division – the 23rd March Division and the Black Arrows. The former was entirely composed of Italian Fascists, the latter of mixed Italians and Spaniards with Italian officers. In support, there was the Spanish Air Force, the Italian

[1] Steer, 141; Aguirre, 48–53.

Expeditionary Air Force and the Condor Legion. Sixty aircraft altogether were assembled at Vitoria, and another sixty at other northern Nationalist aerodromes. Forty-five pieces of artillery were in support.[1]

The Basque Army was commanded by Llano de la Encomienda, the loyal General at Barcelona at the start of the war. He was pessi-

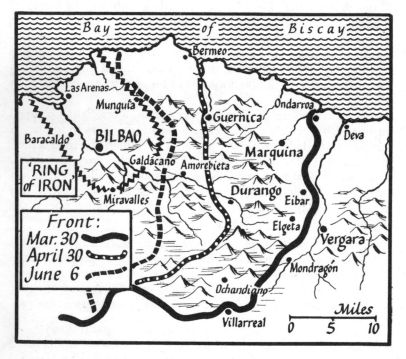

MAP 23. THE CAMPAIGN IN VIZCAYA

mistic of victory. His troops were estimated by the friendly *Times* correspondent, George Steer, at 45,000. This force was far less well-armed than that of their opponents. There were 20 battalions without machine guns. The Basques possessed 25 comparatively obsolete aircraft, 20 pieces of artillery and 12 tanks.

Mola issued a preliminary ultimatum reminiscent of the Athenians' threat to Melos: 'I have decided to terminate rapidly the war in the north: those not guilty of assassinations and who

[1] Aznar, 397.

surrender their arms will have their lives and property spared. But, if submission is not immediate, I will raze all Vizcaya to the ground, beginning with the industries of war.'[1]

On March 31 this threat began to be put into practice. The Condor Legion dive-bombed not only the villages of the front line, but also the country town of Durango, a road and railway junction between Bilbao and the front. There, one bomb killed fourteen nuns in the chapel at St Susana. The Jesuit Church was bombed at the moment the priest was communicating the Body of Christ. In the church of Santa María, the priest was killed while elevating the Host. The rest of the town was also bombed and machine gunned. 127 civilians, including 2 priests and 13 nuns, were killed that day, and 121 died later in hospitals.[2]

Durango had previously been known as the town where Don Carlos had decreed, in 1834, that all foreigners taken in arms against him should be executed without trial. From 1937 it has enjoyed the equally cruel renown of being the first defenceless town to be mercilessly bombed.

The same day, after heavy air and artillery bombardment, the Nationalist General Alonso Vega advanced on the right of the front to capture the three mountains of Maroto, Albertía and Jacinto. North of Villarreal, in the centre of the front, violent fighting occurred in the suburbs of Ochandiano. This battle continued until April 4. Forty to fifty aircraft bombed the town each and all day. The Navarrese nearly encircled it. Terrified of being cut off and so falling alive into the hands of the enemy, the Basques withdrew, leaving 600 dead. Four hundred prisoners were taken. After April 4, there was a pause in the offensive, due to heavy rain. Mola therefore reorganised his troops for the next phase of the campaign, which had already seemed likely to be longer than he had at first prophesied. General Roatta, the failure at Guadalajara, was recalled from command of the Italians and General Ettore Bastico, who had made a name in Abyssinia, replaced him.[3]

The Basques also hastily fortified their new positions, and made further adjustments to the ring of iron. The tactical use of aerial bombardment, however inaccurate, had caused great alarm, and

[1] Steer, 159.
[2] *Ibid.*, 162. The Dean of Canterbury arrived on the scene shortly after the destruction.
[3] Aznar, 400 fl; *GD*, 269.

great hatred against Germany. The commanders in the field were assured that Republican aircraft were on their way. But the Government at Valencia found it difficult to send such support. The Nationalist blockade prevented transport by sea. The distance between the Basques and the main Republican front made a direct flight across Nationalist territory risky. There were also few airfields in the mountainous district of Vizcaya.

The Republican Government was also reluctant to aid this front, which they naturally considered less important than that of the centre. Even if the Basques and all the north were conquered, the war would still be won and lost in the south. The Communist party hated Aguirre, and the whole Basque experiment was disliked by most Socialists also. Even Republicans at Valencia thought that, now the Basques were independent, they should fend for themselves.[1]

The Governments of Valencia and Barcelona were both at this time weakened by political troubles. At the start of April no less than the chief Russian economic adviser in Spain, Stashevsky, visited Moscow and criticised Orlov's NKVD tactics in Spain. His colleague, Berzin, had made a similar complaint the month before to the terrible Yezhov, head of the NKVD itself. Yezhov, busy with a whole programme of political executions, did nothing.[2]

An astonishing meeting of the Spanish Communist party executive was shortly held, attended by Marty, Togliatti, Codovilla, Stepanov, Gerö, Gaikins, the Russian *Chargé*, and Orlov himself. Togliatti bluntly announced that he wanted Largo Caballero removed from the Premiership. Díaz and Hernández protested. Díaz added that Spanish Communists ought not always to have to follow the lead of Moscow. Fear or ambition kept the other Spaniards from speaking. Stepanov said that it was not Moscow, but 'history' which condemned the Prime Minister, both for his defeatism and for his defeats. Marty agreed with him. Díaz called Marty a bureaucrat, and Marty growled that he was a revolutionary. 'So are we all,' said Díaz. 'That remains to be seen,' answered Marty. Díaz told Marty that he was a guest at meetings of the Spanish Communist party. 'If our proceedings do not please you,' said Díaz deliberately, 'there is the door.' Uproar followed. Everyone stood up. La Pasionaria shrieked 'Comrades! Comrades!'

[1] Steer, 173.
[2] The only evidence for this is Krivitsky, 125–7. But in view of what happened to both the complainers within three months it seems eminently likely.

The Hungarian Gerö sat open-mouthed in astonishment. Orlov
appeared imperturbable. Togliatti looked serene. Codovilla tried
to calm Marty. Such scenes were unheard of at meetings of Communist parties, especially when the potentates of the Comintern
were present. Eventually, Díaz was brought to accept Togliatti's
proposal if the majority voted for it. Needless to say Díaz and
Hernández were alone in voting against. Togliatti next said that
the campaign to destroy Largo Caballero should begin at a meeting in Valencia. He blandly suggested that Hernández should
make the keynote speech. As for the next Premier, Juan Negrín,
the Finance Minister, would be the best choice. He was less
obviously pro-Communist than Álvarez del Vayo, and less actually
anti-Communist than Prieto.[1]

Before Hernández's speech was made, the tension in Barcelona
between the Anarchists and the POUM on the one hand and the
Esquerra and PSUC on the other once again became acute.
Companys' lieutenant, Tarradellas, wanted to fuse all the Catalan
police into one body by dissolving the so-called Patrols Committee upon which all the political groups were represented. This survival from the early days of the war was still dominated by the
CNT. In this matter, as in so many others, the aims of the Communists and of those Republicans or Catalans who placed the
efficient conduct of the war above all else once more coincided.
When on March 27 Tarradellas solemnly forbade any police to
have political affiliations, the Anarchists resigned from the
Generalitat. The succeeding Government crisis lasted so long that
the Plaza de la República (now renamed Plaza San Jaime)
became nicknamed the Plaza 'of the permanent crisis'.

Eventually, on April 16, Companys, by one of his rare decisive
acts, arbitrarily formed a new Government under Tarradellas of
only five members, one each from the Esquerra, CNT, UGT and
Rabaissaires. But the tension in Barcelona continued. Throughout
the crisis, the Anarchist Ministers in the Government at Valencia
had done their best to restrain their Barcelona comrades; but the
result was that the Anarchist leaders themselves lost further influence with the extremists among their followers.

Perhaps in the knowledge of the difficulties between the
Basques and the Republican Government in Valencia, various

[1] This meeting was described by Jesús Hernández, 66–71. No one else has confirmed
it. Since the decisions which Hernández described as being taken shortly followed, there
is no reason to doubt his account – save perhaps that of his own part in the affair.

proposals were now made to the Basque Government for a mediated and separate peace. The most important resulted from an initiative of the Argentinian Ambassador to Spain, then established with the rest of the diplomatic corps at San Jean de Luz. He suggested to the Vatican that the Pope should try and arrange a separate peace. As a result, Cardinal Pacelli, Secretary of State, wrote a conciliatory letter to President Aguirre, suggesting terms for peace in the northern provinces. Unfortunately, the letter was despatched by ordinary mail. The Paris Post Office, seeing a letter for Spain, sent it to Valencia, where it fell into the hands of the Republican Government. A meeting of the Republican Cabinet met secretly without the Basque Minister Irujo being present. They sent a bitter telegram denouncing the Basques for trying to arrange a separate peace. The Basque Government, not knowing of the misdirection of the letter from Rome, concluded that the affair was a manoeuvre of the Communists to discredit them. The Basque Minister of Justice, Leizaola, therefore, sent a telegram couched in such strong terms that Prieto, reading it, thought that it demanded that he should be shot. And in this state of misunderstanding the relations between the Basque and Republican Governments remained throughout the rest of the war. The Basque Government rested in ignorance of the truth of the affair until February 1940, when a Jesuit priest exposed part of the story in the *Revue de Deux Mondes*.[1]

---

[1] *Revue de Deux Mondes*, 10.2.40. The above account was told to me by Señor Jesús María de Leizaola, and confirms the account in Aguirre, 34–6. The telegrams from Faupel to Berlin giving a version of the tale current in Salamanca should be discounted. In May 1937, another *démarche* was made from Italy to secure a mediated peace – this time by Mussolini himself. Count Cavalletti arrived in the south of France suggesting that Aguirre should ask the Duce to arrange a mediated peace. The Duce would then try and achieve this 'perhaps by establishing an Italian protectorate over the Basque provinces!' But Aguirre rejected the proposal firmly (Aguirre, 31–3).

50

*The blockade of Bilbao – 'Potato' Jones – the Seven Seas Spray –
Hedilla's coup d'état – formation of the Falange – the Carlists –
Serrano Suñer*

Now, in mid April, the Basque front remained comparatively quiet. But behind the Basque lines a new crisis arose over the food supply. On April 6 the Nationalists announced that they would in future prevent food supplies from entering Republican ports in the north of Spain. The British steamer *Thorpehall*, with a cargo of provisions for Bilbao from Santander,[1] was immediately stopped some five miles off shore by the Nationalist cruiser *Almirante Cervera* and the armed trawler *Galerna*. Eventually, however, the *Thorpehall* was allowed to pass, since the Nationalist vessels showed a marked disinclination to quarrel with two British destroyers, HMS *Blanche* and HMS *Brazen*, which hastened to the scene.

The announcement of this blockade placed the British Government in a difficult position. By international law, a blockade (including the right of search on the high seas) could be carried out by belligerents in war. But specifically because they did not wish to subject British merchantmen to the search of Spanish naval vessels, Baldwin and his Ministers were opposed to the recognition of the two Spanish warring parties as belligerents. Nearly all British trade with Spain was now carried on with Republican ports. But the Nationalists had command of the seas. There-

---

[1] The ensuing narrative will not be understood unless it is realised that British ships now carried most of the trade to and from Spain. British exports to Spain fell heavily during 1937. Coal exports went down by 37%, machinery by 90%, motor-cars by 95%, cutlery by 90% (figures for all Spain, since the Board of Trade did not separate statistics for the two Spains). UK imports, however, increased except in respect of nuts and potatoes. The decrease in the export figures was due to Spain's concentration on imports of raw materials and war material. For those British persons who worried about their investments in Spain, that genius *manqué* of the epoch, Brian Howard (often regarded as the original of Anthony Blanche in Evelyn Waugh's *Brideshead Revisited*) wrote a poem, urging them to

> *Spare a thought, a thought for all these Spanish tombs,*
> *And for a people in danger, grieving in breaking rooms,*
> *For a people in danger, shooting from falling homes.*

407

fore, if belligerent rights were granted, it would be mainly Nationalist naval vessels that would be doing the intercepting and mainly British merchantmen which would suffer. But here was a blockade declared of northern Spanish ports. Unless belligerent rights were admitted, British merchant ships would be entitled to ask for the aid of the Royal Navy if they were interfered with outside the Basque territorial waters of three miles from the shore. How much less trouble, therefore, it would be if there were no British merchant ships going to Basque ports at all!

This last reflection, perhaps made only subconsciously, no doubt disposed the British Admiralty to believe certain new reports. The captain of HMS *Blanche* bluntly signalled that the Nationalist blockade was effective. Sir Henry Chilton reported the same from Hendaye. There were other similar naval reports: not only was a Spanish Nationalist naval group outside Bilbao in a position to prevent the entry of all merchantment; but the Basque territorial waters were mined. Thus (reported Chilton and the Navy) it would be actually dangerous for British merchant ships to try and enter Bilbao. Inside the three-mile limit, of course, the Royal Navy had no right to protect merchantmen. And since the Basques had obviously lost command of the sea, attacks might well be carried out against British ships within the territorial waters. So on April 8 the Admiralty instructed all British merchant vessels within a hundred miles of Bilbao to repair to the French fishing port and resort of St Jean de Luz, and to await further orders. The following day, Sir Henry Chilton was told by Troncoso, the Nationalist Military Governor of Irún, on instructions from Burgos, that Franco was determined to make the blockade effective. The voyage of four British merchantmen known to be bearing food cargoes and now at St Jean de Luz would in particular be prevented by force. Meantime, more mines would be laid across Bilbao harbour.[1] This determined statement reached London on the morning of Saturday April 10. It caused Mr Baldwin to summon the Cabinet for Sunday. Back from their week-ends came among others Mr Duff Cooper, Secretary of State for War, Sir Samuel Hoare, the First Lord of the Admiralty, Sir John Simon, the Home Secretary and Mr Eden, the Foreign Secretary. As a result of the Cabinet, the Board of Trade 'warned' British ships not to go to Bilbao, and intimated that the Navy could not help

---

[1] Nationalist note of April 9, referred to by Eden in the House of Commons April 19 (*Hansard*, Vol 322 col 1404).

them if they tried to do so. Mr Baldwin explained this decision to an angry House of Commons on the Monday. There were risks, he said, against which it was impossible to protect British shipping.

Throughout the following week there was mounting uproar in Parliament. All that spring Spain had been an incessant topic for question-time and for debates on foreign affairs. Eden and Cran-borne, the Foreign Secretary and his lieutenant, had been hard pressed both by Labour and Liberal sympathisers of the Republic and by the handful of Conservatives who supported the National-ists. Had the Government heard of the arrival of new Italian divisions at Cádiz? How many Russians were there at Madrid? How many British volunteers had been killed while fighting with the International Brigades? To most of these questions, the Govern-ment, concerned above all to maintain and develop non-inter-vention, had always professed ignorance of exact information. Now the interest of the House of Commons in the cause of Spain reached a climax. On April 14, Mr Attlee for the Labour party moved a vote of censure. The British Government, the greatest maritime power in the world, had given up trying to protect British shipping; yet the Basque President had said that the mines in Bilbao har-bour had been cleared, that at night armed trawlers (aided by searchlights) protected the port. Where did the Government gain its information of the dangers? Did it do so from 'those curious people, our consular agents, who seem so silent on the question of Italian troops landing?' Sir John Simon, the Home Secretary, next argued that if British ships were to be allowed to go to Bilbao, there would have to be mine-sweeping. That would constitute intervention in favour of the Republic. Sir Archibald Sinclair, the Liberal leader, argued that the Government's acceptance of the Nationalist blockade spelled intervention. The Germans, after all, he said, recalling incidents of the winter, had always looked after *their* ships. Mr Churchill spoke next. He reiterated his Olympian detachment from either side in the war and indulged in a day-dream of mediation through 'some meeting in what Lord Rose-bery once called a "wayside inn" which would give the chance in Spain of peace, of law, of bread and of oblivion'. Then indeed these 'clenched fists might relax into the open hands of generous co-operation'. Mr Harold Nicolson described the refusal to risk British ships in Basque waters as a 'bitter pill. It is not pleasant. It is a potion which is almost nauseating', but it had to be accepted. Mr Duncan Sandys urged the grant of belligerent rights, as only then could one expect the two sides to obey the rules of war. Mr Noel-Baker recalled that it was the first time since 1588 that the British had been afraid of the Spanish fleet. Mr Eden ended the debate (which was of course won by the Government) by saying that if British merchant ships did leave St Jean de Luz, and so disobeyed the Board of Trade warning, they would be given naval protection as far as the three-mile limit. 'Our hope is that they will not go because in view of reports of conditions we do not think it safe for them to go.'[1]

All this time, the masters of the merchantmen at St Jean de Luz were growing impatient. Their cargoes (for which they had been paid handsomely)[2] were rotting. Three vessels, all commanded by Welsh captains named Jones (therefore differentiated from their cargoes as 'Potato Jones', 'Corn Cob Jones' and 'Ham and Eggs Jones') gained notoriety by pretended attempts to set out from port. 'Potato Jones' in particular gained a sudden reputation, from a series of breezy answers to a reporter of the *Evening News*, as a rough salt in the Conradian tradition. However, it was not he (he eventually delivered his cargo in Valencia) who made the great attempt to break the Bilbao blockade. This was done by the *Seven Seas Spray* which, with a cargo of provisions from Valencia, sailed out of St Jean de Luz at ten o'clock at night on April 19, ignoring frantic messages from the shore. Her master, Captain Roberts, also turned a blind eye to the warnings of a British destroyer ten miles off the Basque coast. The destroyer told Captain Roberts that he must proceed at his own risk, and then wished him good luck. At half-past eight in the morning the *Seven Seas Spray* reached Bilbao without having seen either mines or Nationalist warships. As this valiant vessel moved slowly up the river to dock, the captain and his daughter standing on the bridge, the hungry people of Bilbao massed excitedly on the quayside and cried 'Long live the British sailors! Long live Liberty.'

The British Admiralty now publicly admitted its former error in advising that the blockade was effective. For the truth about Bilbao was as Mr Attlee had described it in the debate: the Nationalist blockade at Bilbao was ineffective.

Other ships at St Jean de Luz therefore set out for Bilbao. One

---

[1] All this debate, which was punctuated by points of order, cries of 'withdraw', and other interruptions, is to be seen in *Hansard*, Vol 322 cols 1029–1142.

[2] Certainly, special profits (up to 100% more than usual) were earned by British shipowners who ran the risk of helping to provision the Republic.

of these, the *MacGregor*, while ten miles out, was ordered to stop by
the Nationalist *Almirante Cervera*. The *MacGregor* sent an SOS to
HMS *Hood*, which had been despatched from Gibraltar in case of
trouble. Her Commander, Vice-Admiral Blake, requested the
Almirante Cervera not to interfere with British ships outside territorial waters. The *Almirante Cervera* replied that Spanish territorial
waters extended six miles. Admiral Blake said that Britain did not
recognise this claim (which had long been a British bone of contention with Spain), and told the *MacGregor* to proceed if she
wished. The *MacGregor* did so. A few yards short of the three-mile
limit, the Nationalist trawler *Galerna* fired a shot across the
MacGregor's bows. HMS *Firedrake* ordered the *Galerna* not to attack
a British ship. From the coast, the Basque shore-battery loosed a
salvo, and the *Galerna* withdrew. No further attempt was made to
prevent British shipping from arriving at Bilbao.

What was the explanation of this curious incident in the history
of British shipping? Not certainly the imputation of Mr A. V.
Alexander when he alleged that he saw Dr Leslie Burgin, Parliamentary Under-Secretary of the Board of Trade, smiling when he
spoke of the starvation in Bilbao. Mr Eden was no doubt telling the
truth when he told the House of Commons in passing on April 20
that 'if I had to choose in Spain, I believe that the Basque Government would more closely conform to our own system than that of
Franco or the Republic.' But it would certainly seem that the
Navy gave incorrect information to the Government. It is clear too
that some at least of the Navy's information derived not from a
careful examination of the facts but from none other than the
Nationalist warships. The *Daily Telegraph* of April 20 published an
interview with a Nationalist Captain Caveda who remarked how
pleasant it had been to work with the British fleet 'on questions
arising from the blockade of Bilbao'.[1] Sir Henry Chilton, anyway a
strong sympathiser with the Nationalist cause, could hardly gain
any information save from the Nationalists at Hendaye. And Mr
Baldwin's Government, led by Sir Samuel Hoare at the Admiralty,
seems to have been pleased to accept the false information and to
act precipitately upon it.

[1] Yet it would be quite wrong to conclude that the British Navy were as a service on
the side of Franco. The fleet at Gibraltar were admittedly on excellent terms with the
loyal Nationalists; but Admiral Burrough, the commander of the *Exmouth*, responsible
for evacuation of many prisoners and refugees from Bilbao, was a firm friend of the
Basque Government. The truth seems to have been that the Navy was friendly with
everyone with whom they came into contact.

Behind the Nationalist lines, meantime, before the renewal of the offensive in the north, certain events, long brewing, had come to a head. These stretched back to the preceding winter when the Carlist leader Manuel Fal Conde had been exiled by Franco to Portugal.[1] The Carlists had naturally been very critical at the harsh measure. The Carlist War Council had unsuccessfully demanded a public revision of the sentence. This discontent on the part of the Carlists struck a responsive note in the breasts of certain of the Falangists most out of sympathy with General Franco's leadership.[2] Accordingly, it was not altogether surprising when Fal Conde in Portugal received an invitation from the Falange to open discussions on the idea of a unification between the two parties. The idea was accepted.[3]

These negotiations lasted three weeks. They produced some interesting documents, but no results.[4] The Carlists concluded that the Falangists were merely aiming at consuming the whole traditionalist movement. The two parties therefore parted, though amicably, at the end of February. The way to a resumption of discussions was to be kept open by the Count of Rodezno. In fact, however, the idea of the unification of the two parties was taken up by General Franco himself, who had been following these developments from afar. Since he had assumed power as Head of State he had successfully manipulated the disparate supporters of the national movement as if they had been the warring chieftains of the Riff during his early manhood. Would not a simple act of unification, from above, lead in the end to that amalgamation of ideologies of which he had hopefully spoken to the German diplomat Dumoulin five months before?[5]

[1] See above, page 359.

[2] Despite the apparent extremes of difference between the Carlist and the Falangist movements, their leaders had always been comparatively close together, united in their hostility towards liberalism, democracy and 'the nineteenth century'. José Antonio and Fal Conde had been on good terms before the war. See above, page 87 fn 2 for the suggestive role of Colonel Rada.

[3] All the above and the following derives from the Carlist archives, Seville. The Falangists taking part in the discussions were Sancho Dávila, Rafael Garcerán and Escario. The Carlists were Fal Conde, the Count òf Rodezno and José María Arauz de Robles. Hedilla, the provisional head of the Falange, knew of the negotiations but disapproved of them (GD, 268).

[4] The most remarkable document was a series of 'bases for a union' of the two groups, included in a Falangist note of February 1. By this the Falange would 'agree to install, at an opportune moment, a new Monarchy as a guarantee of the continuity of the National-Sindicalist State and as the basis for its Imperium. The new Monarchy would break all links with the liberal Monarchy'.

[5] See above, page 291.

One other influential voice was also strongly in favour of this idea: Ramón Serrano Suñer, the Generalissimo's brother-in-law, who as leader of the CEDA Youth had brought that movement to merge in early 1936 with the Falange. This able and ambitious lawyer had escaped in February from Republican Spain. Through the help of the humane Dr Marañón, he had succeeded in being sent from a firing squad to a tubercular sanatorium. From thence flight was eventually made possible. He arrived at Salamanca full of terrible stories of the Model Prison, where he had observed the shooting of his friends, Fernando Primo de Rivera, and Ruiz de Alda. His hatred of the Republicans was sharpened by the execution of his two brothers at their hands. Since he always maintained that they had died because they were refused asylum in the French Embassy, he also now nursed a particular passion against France, bolstering his already strong dislike of democracy. There was, therefore, now little left of the politician of the CEDA which he first had been. Henceforward, this dandy with prematurely white hair and blue eyes – rare in Spain?– was the dominant influence on his brother-in-law. Nicolás Franco became less and less important till he was quietly posted away as Ambassador to Portugal. Serrano Suñer owed much of his political success to his remarkable charm; but while he magnetised a small circle he alienated the masses. He was a sensitive man of varying moods – a contrast to the reserved Franco. The relations between Franco and Serrano were cemented by their two wives, Zita and Carmen, who met incessantly. Thus began in Spain the rule of *cuñadisimo* (literally, super brother-in-law) which was to give rise to countless jokes in the next few years and would eventually lead Serrano almost to supreme power in the State.

At this time, however, Serrano had no official position whatever. But from the moment of his arrival in Salamanca Franco used him as a political guide. And also from that date Serrano occupied himself in trying to find some theoretical and, if possible, ideological, basis for the new Nationalist State. He had interviews with Monarchists, Falangists, churchmen and Generals. He saw Cardinal Gomá, and the Count of Rodezno, and General Mola. And, afterwards, he took a walk one day with Franco in the garden of the bishop's palace at Salamanca. He told the Generalissimo that his discussions suggested that none of the existing parties in Nationalist Spain answered to the needs of the moment. But, even so, something would have to be done. The Army was the basis of the existing power. Yet 'a state of pure force', he said, could not be indefinitely prolonged. The National movement had been formed as a purely negative reaction against the criminal weakness of the Republican Government and before the menace of a Communist revolution. But a return to parliamentary government was impossible. 'In other places, thanks to an intelligent series of conventions, democracy may give effective results. But in Spain it has been amply indicated that it is only possible in a brute or explosive state and in a form leading to suicide.'[1] Here surely was an opportunity of creating a State free of all engagements, precedents and burdens, a State truly new, the sole State of this kind which had ever been able to appear. Was not the position in Spain in 1937 much the same as it had been in the fourteenth century at the start of the reign of the Catholic kings?[2]

With such ideas did Serrano beguile the Generalissimo in the garden of the bishop's palace one fine spring afternoon in 1937. And this was the first of many such talks between the two men. Franco meantime busied himself with studying the statutes of the Falange – of which, of course, he was not a member. He analysed the speeches of José Antonio and of Víctor Pradera, the Carlist theoretician, who like José Antonio, had been shot in Republican territory. However, the statute unifying the Carlists and the Falange, and indeed affiliating all the parties which supported the Nationalists into one movement (even *Acción Española*), would have been delayed had it not been for certain curious events in Salamanca in early April.

The truth of this *affaire ténébreuse* seems to have been that the group of right-wing Falangists who had taken the lead in the abortive negotiations with the Carlists now plotted the overthrow of Hedilla, the provisional leader of the Falange. On April 16 the National Council of the Falange elected a new triumvirate to manage its affairs. This was composed of Sancho Dávila (the leader of the right-wing group) and two friends of Hedilla, José Moreno and Agustín Aznar. The new Secretary-General of the movement was Rafael Garcerán. Hedilla, left in a somewhat undefined position as provisional leader of the movement, vacillated. That evening, Franco received the triumvirate and the new Secretary-General, and asked them all, somewhat obscurely,

---

[1] This is the reflection profoundly held by many Spaniards of the present.

[2] Serrano describes the above conversation in pages 29–31 of his autobiography. He disowns fathering the analogy of the Catholic kings which had already been much used.

to refrain from violence. Later, in the middle of the night, a riot broke out around the lodgings in Salamanca of Sancho Dávila and Garcerán. Armed youths began firing. Whether these had been sent by Hedilla or Nicolás Franco or by anyone else remains uncertain. But the affair gave an excuse for the arrest of Sancho Dávila and Garcerán, who were charged not only with attempting to overthrow Franco but with negotiating with Prieto. The next day, the National Council of the Falange re-affirmed their support of Hedilla. But now Franco struck too. He sent instructions to all local heads of the Falange to take orders in future only from him. Hedilla was at last provoked into action. His closest friends persuaded him that Franco's act spelled the end of the Falange.[1] He therefore despatched telegrams, ordering that the provincial leaders of the Falange should, on the contrary, only follow him. Some of his followers, the 'Old Shirts', prepared public manifestations in his favour. They also proposed to establish a *junta*, of which Pilar Primo de Rivera, José Antonio's sister, and General Yagüe were to be members, though these two apparently had not agreed to serve. But Franco was informed of what was afoot by the Falangist chief at Zamora, to whom one of Hedilla's telegrams had been addressed. When Hedilla swaggered down to Franco's headquarters to exact conditions for his continued support of the Nationalist movement, he was arrested. Twenty other 'Old Shirts' were also apprehended. All Falangists elsewhere in Nationalist Spain were forbidden for the time being from going to Salamanca. Franco took the opportunity to decree the establishment of his new party, uniting the Falange and Carlists, with the vast portmanteau name of *Falange Española Tradicionalista y de las JONS*. The Generalissimo, of course, would be the head of the new party though he had never been either a Falangist or a Carlist. Rodezno and his more moderate Carlists agreed, with almost absurd lack of forethought, though without much enthusiasm.[2] Their three radio stations were closed. Neither

---

[1] The German Ambassador Faupel had agreed with Danzi, the Fascist representative at Salamanca, and the local Nazi *landsgruppenleiter* that if there were to be a clash between the Falange and Franco they would support the latter (*GD*, 269). But it would seem that Faupel's propaganda chiefs, Kohn and Kroeger, encouraged Hedilla to act precipitately. The Finnish Military *Attaché*, the soldier of fortune Karl von Hartmann, was understood by Franco's authorities to have promised military help!

[2] The official party uniform henceforth consisted of the blue shirt of the Falange and the red beret of the Carlists. Neither party liked the compromise, and the Falangists put the Carlist beret into their pockets whenever they could. On one celebrated occasion, a group of Falangists with bare heads were greeted by the Carlist Rodezno in

Fal Conde nor the Carlist Regent Xavier of Bourbon Parma were consulted by Franco. The aged widow of old Don Alfonso Carlos (herself a veteran of the Second Carlist War) wrote to Fal Conde on April 23: 'It is an infamy that has been done to us. With what right . . .?' (The Carlist War Council was not officially told what had happened by Franco till April 30.)[1]

But what, it will be asked, of General Mola, the commander of the Army of the North, the old conspirator of Pamplona? He was present at the reading of the decree uniting Falangists and Carlists from the balcony of Franco's headquarters at Salamanca. But he only expressed his alarm at the great power which Franco had gathered to himself by a petty objection to the use, in the decree, of a verb not registered by the Spanish Academy.[2] Quaipo de Llano was also summoned from Seville and his adhesion – reluctantly, one can presume – obtained. Hedilla meantime was condemned to death 'for rebellion', though the sentence was later commuted to life imprisonment.[3] Serrano stepped into the position which he had held, and became, on Franco's insistence, Secretary-General of the new movement. He thereafter spent his time coordinating and palliating the different sections of the movement, and in particular the few discontented Falangists who remained free and who gathered to squabble in the drawing-room in Salamanca of Pilar Primo de Rivera. The orthodox Monarchists were also shortly affiliated, by a supplementary text, to the new party.[4]

Franco no doubt considered that since Serrano was a man without followers and owed everything to himself, he would be easily

---

ordinary clothes'. Asked why he was so dressed the old cynic answered: 'It is because I cannot put my blue shirt into my pocket . . .' (Ansaldo, 78).

[1] This account of this obscure crisis is based on Faupel's despatches (GD, 277, 284); Serrano Suñer op. cit; the Carlist archives; Alcázar de Velasco; and Pagés Guix. See also Emmett Hughes, Creac'h and Claude Martin's Franco.

[2] Serrano Suñer, 41–2.

[3] There were later rumours that some of Hedilla's friends had tried to rescue him from Pamplona jail (where St Ignatius had conceived the idea of the Society of Jesus) and that he was unwilling to escape. Some of his associates apparently did escape, being brought back and shot. This incident is described by the French Fascist historian Brasillach, 385, but I have not been able to confirm it.

[4] It may be added that Franco apparently had interpreted the first (Sancho Dávila, etc.) plot as Monarchist. In an interview in ABC de Sevilla, he stated clearly that he personally would decide when the Monarchy should be restored. Gil Robles, the ex-leader of the CEDA, shortly announced his support of Franco, but he rather spoiled the effect of this by aligning himself firmly at the same time with the (orthodox) Monarchists. He remained in exile throughout the war, taking no part in politics (though he occasionally helped with the arms traffic), and did not return to Spain till 1957.

manageable. And indeed no dispute between the two seems to have occurred till after the end of the Civil War. He remained isolated, distrusted and somewhat feared. At this stage, and until late into the Second World War, he was fanatically and ideologically pro-German, even though he was hated by the German Ambassador. Yet what precisely did he stand for, the *cuñadisimo*?

He himself described his views ten years later, when in disgrace and retirement. This new State which had never previously existed, and which he described with such enthusiasm to his brother-in-law was, of course, 'what it is convenient to name the authoritarian State, the unique type of modern State which appears expedient, the only form of society which could carry out the re-education and reorganisation necessary for the political life of Spain. Perhaps, in its outward form, this State offers some resemblance with *régimes* already adopted by certain other peoples, but what, truly, varies from people to people is the dogma which covers this form, and the spirit with which it is obeyed. There can, as in totalitarian Russia, be a complete divergence between Government and governed. The form can, as in the case of Germany, have an immoral side. We, on the other hand, have nothing to do with such doctrinal points. Our position derives from our national tradition and our confessional faith. We reject political relativism and political agnosticism. Outside the vast field left to discussion and doubt, there exist permanent truths, certainties, of which political life is composed, and which give limits to governmental action. These are the great and unchanging principles which affect the "to be or not to be" of the country and of the whole of civilised society'.[1] These were the ideas of the man who among a disparate group of Generals of the King, admirers of Germany and of Italy, bishops and old-time politicians, was the conscience of Nationalist Spain during the remainder of the Civil War.

Faupel and the Italian General, Roatta, met to discuss these developments. Roatta thought that, unless Germany and Italy intervened to exercise a decisive influence on operations and upon Spanish society, the war could not be won. Faupel therefore gave Franco a Spanish translation of the Nazi labour law. He urged him to start social legislation, and offered to place 'social experts' at his disposal. The Italian Fascist representative in Spain, Danzi, gave Franco a draft Constitution for Spain on the Italian model. But the Generalissimo paid no attention to either Danzi or

---

[1] Serrano Suñer, 38.

Faupel.[1] Serrano Suñer added that these schemes and their inspirers (especially the Nazi group attached to the German Embassy) would have been more welcome if they had taken the trouble to translate what they had to say into Spanish.[2]

Meanwhile, on April 20 a new Nationalist advance began in Vizcaya. When the artillery and aerial bombardment had ceased, and the Basques in the first line came up from the shallow trenches in which they had sheltered, they heard machine guns from the rear. Once more, as at Ochandiano, the cry was 'we are cut off'. Many of the defenders retreated while they still could. Before the village of Elgeta, however, among the lion-shaped hills of Inchorta, good deep trenches had been dug. Led by Major Beldarrán, the Basques here successfully held off the attack. But two CNT battalions now withdrew from the front, apparently to try and blackmail the Basque for a place in the Government. This defection completed the collapse. All the Basque commanders now longed to retreat to the prepared trenches of the 'ring of iron'. Constant bombing blocked roads and prevented movement. The General Staff in Bilbao showed a laxness that brought accusations of treachery. On April 24 all the heights on that part of the front chosen for the offensive fell to the Nationalist General García Valiño. Beldarrán had to fall back from his well-defended position at Elgeta. An atmosphere of chaos persisted. Artillery did not know where to fire. Trenches were silently evacuated. General defeat for the Basques thus seemed imminent six days after the renewal of Mola's offensive.

[1] GD, 274.   [2] Serrano Suñer, 49.

51

Guernica – Santa María de la Cabeza

Guernica is a small town of the Basque province of Vizcaya, lying in a valley ten kilometres from the sea and thirty from Bilbao. With a population of some 7,000, Guernica appears simply one more village in a hilly countryside of friendly villages and isolated farmhouses. It has nevertheless been celebrated since before records began as the home of Basque liberties. For it was before her famous oak that the Spanish Monarchs or their representatives customarily swore to observe Basque local rights.

On April 26, 1937, a Monday (and, therefore, like all Mondays at Guernica, a market day) the small farmers from nearby were bringing into the main square the fruits of the week's toil. At this time Guernica lay some thirty kilometres from the front.

At half-past four in the afternoon, a single peal of church bells announced an air raid. There had been some raids in the area before, but Guernica had not been bombed. At twenty minutes to five, Heinkels 111 began to appear, first bombing the town and then machine gunning its streets. The Heinkels were followed by the old spectres of the Spanish War, Junkers 52. People began to run from the town. These also were machine gunned. Incendiary bombs, weighing up to 1,000 lbs, and also high explosives, were dropped by waves of aircraft arriving every twenty minutes until a quarter-to-eight. The centre of the town was then destroyed and burning. 1,654 people were killed and 889 wounded. The Basque parliament house and the famous oak, lying away from the centre, nevertheless remained untouched.[1]

This story as here described was attested by all witnesses, including the Mayor of the town, who were present at the time. It was confirmed by the Basque Government and by all the political parties, from Anarchists to Republicans. It was vouched for by *The Times*, *Daily Telegraph*, *Reuter*, *Star*, *Ce Soir* and *Daily Express* correspondents, who visited the scene that night and who picked up bomb fragments made in Germany. Twenty Basque priests, of

[1] *Le Clergé Basque*, 151–3.

whom nine were eye-witnesses of the bombing, and including the Vicar-General of the diocese, wrote to the Pope giving this version of what happened.[1]

The chief of Nationalist propaganda at Salamanca, however, said on April 27 that the Basques had destroyed the town. The next day the Nationalists solemnly announced that none of their aircraft had left the ground on April 27. But Guernica had been destroyed on April 26. On April 28 Durango and Guernica both fell without resistance (though Guernica offered fine natural defensive positions). Foreign journalists with the Nationalists were next told that, while 'a few bomb fragments' had been found in Guernica, most of the damage had been caused by Basque incendiarists, presumably to inspire indignation and a new spirit of resistance. On May 4 a new Nationalist report said that Guernica naturally showed signs of fire after 'a week's bombardment by artillery and aircraft'. It admitted that Guernica had been intermittently bombed over a period of three hours. Ten days later, the word 'Garnika' was found in the diary for April 26 of a German pilot shot down by the Basques. The pilot explained that this referred to a girl he knew in Hamburg. Some months later another Nationalist report admitted that the town had been bombed, but alleged that the aeroplanes were Republican. The bombs were said to have been manufactured in Basque territory and the explosions to have been caused by dynamite in the sewers.

But the truth of this story has long since been known.[2] In

---

[1] Two Basque priests, Fathers Mancheca and Augustín Souci, went to the Vatican with a copy of this letter. On arrival, Mgr Mugica (the exiled Bishop of Vitoria) went to Mgr Pizzardo, the Under-Secretary of State at the Vatican, and requested an interview with the Pope. Pizzardo said that this was unnecessary since he had the letter. Mugica wrote to Pacelli saying that the two priests had arrived, but for a long time received no answer. One day, however, a messenger arrived post-haste from the Vatican, at a moment when the priests were eating their lunch in a small restaurant. Without being able to finish their meal, the priests were whisked off to the presence of Cardinal Pacelli, whose secretary told them that they would be received provided that they said nothing about it, and that they did not mention the subject which had brought them to Rome. Pacelli received the two Basques standing up. They mentioned the letter to the Pope, and Pacelli, coldly remarking 'The Church is persecuted in Barcelona,' showed them the door immediately. (Evidence of Fr Alberto Onaindía.) One has the impression that Pacelli as Secretary of State was much more hostile to the Basques than the Pope, Pius XI.

[2] The Basque account is confirmed by conversations the present author carried out in Guernica in the summer of 1959. Many who experienced the tragedy still live in the new rebuilt town. In 1945, the Basque Government in exile attempted to bring a case against Germany at the Nuremberg War Crimes Tribunal. The attempt was unsuccessful, since no events which occurred before 1939 were taken into account at Nuremberg.

October 1937, a Nationalist staff officer told a *Sunday Times* correspondent: 'We bombed it, and bombed it and bombed it, and *bueno* why not?' The German air ace, Adolf Galland, who shortly afterwards joined the Condor Legion, admitted that the Germans were responsible.[1] (He added that the attack was a mistake, caused by bad bomb sights and lack of experience.) Goering himself admitted in 1946 that Germany had regarded Guernica as a testing ground.[2] In fact, Guernica might have been regarded as a military target, since it was a communications centre not far from the battle line, but it is difficult not to conclude that the Germans deliberately bombed the town in an attempt to destroy it, observe in a clinical way the effects of such a devastating attack, and thus carry out the instruction of Mola of March 31. (Whether or not Mola knew what was afoot remains a matter of doubt.)

An international controversy began immediately to rage over Guernica. Picasso[3] had earlier in the year been commissioned to paint a mural for the Spanish Government building at the World's Fair in Paris. He now immediately began work on a representation of the horrors of war expressed by the destruction of Guernica, in the painting that is generally regarded as his masterpiece.

On April 30, the day when Non-Intervention Control had begun (and the British Foreign Secretary no doubt imagined that he would have been free for a while from considering what he named the 'War of the Spanish Obsession'), Eden told the House of Commons that the Cabinet were considering what could be done to prevent another Guernica. Ribbentrop from London urged Berlin to get Franco to deny that German pilots were responsible.[4] In the Condor Legion itself, 'great depression' was caused by the consequences of the attack.[5] On May 4 Plymouth suggested to the Non-Intervention Committee that it should call on both Spanish parties not to bomb open towns. Ribbentrop and Grandi disingenuously argued that Guernica could not be discussed apart from a consideration of the general humanitarian aspect of the war. Maisky naturally protested against this extension of the area of debate. A conference was held the same day of Church of

[1] Galland, 26.   [2] Ansaldo, 81.
[3] Before the Civil War, Picasso had shown no great interest in politics. But, from July 1936 onwards, he had championed the Republican cause, financially and otherwise. He accepted the (honorary) post of Director of the Prado and reported on the condition of the paintings which had been removed from Madrid to Valencia. In January, he had etched a series of comic strips, *The Dream and the Lie of General Franco*.
[4] *GD*, 279.   [5] Galland, *loc. cit.*

England leaders including William Temple, Archbishop of York. It made a formal protest to Eden against the bombing of non-military targets.

The Basque collapse behind the destroyed city, meantime, was staunched, although the fishing port of Bermeo was captured on April 30 by the Black Arrows numbering 4,000. On this day, the Basque morale was given a fillip by the destruction of the Nationalist battleship *España* by a mine off Bilbao. On May 1 Mola attacked all along the front. But the Italians were held, and then driven back, by a UGT battalion. The Italians in Bermeo were surrounded, and forced to beg relief. Bombing had now lost some of its terror for the Basque militia, since they observed that the noise it caused was invariably worse than its effects. So no more ground was lost for the time being.

While Guernica occupied the headlines of the world, events as dramatic were occurring in the Sierra Morena, the magnificent range of mountains which divides the tableland of Castile from Andalusia. Here, on two mountain tops around the shrine of Santa María de la Cabeza, 250 Civil Guards, most of their families, 100 Falangists and about 1,000 members of the *bourgeoisie* of Andújar had held out for the rising for nine months. Throughout most of the early part of the war there had been no attack launched against this Nationalist enclave in the heart of Republican Spain. Indeed, for some time the Popular Front Committee of Andújar had been uncertain whether the Civil Guard in the sanctuary were friends or enemies. After living in this equivocal security for some time, and after they had gathered a good supply of food, the rebels decided that it was morally impossible not to let the 'Reds' know where they stood. So they despatched a letter by hand giving a declaration of war. Major Nofuentes, who wanted to surrender, was deposed from command in the sanctuary, though his life and that of certain other pro-Republican officers was respected. The siege then began. A Civil Guard Captain, Santiago Cortés, whose wife and family were political prisoners in Jaén, led the defenders. Carrier pigeons communicated news and exultant messages with the Nationalists at Córdoba and at Seville. Nationalist pilots trained specially so as to be able to drop supplies into the small area which was being defended – a technique which they found to be curiously similar to dive-bombing. Altogether 80,000 kilos of food were sent from Seville and 70,000 from Córdoba. More delicate supplies (such as medical appliances) were dropped by turkey, whose flight had been remarked to be heavy, majestic and comparatively vertical. Inside the sanctuary, there were improvised schools and hospitals. Meantime, while 10,000 militiamen surrounded the rocky natural fortress no major attack was launched.

In early April, however, the Republic decided to overwhelm this island of resistance, and despatched the XIIIth International Brigade led by General 'Gómez' (the German Communist, Zeisser) to lead the attack. After fierce fighting, the small encampment of defenders was divided into two. Lugar Nuevo, the smaller encampment, sent its last pigeon to Captain Cortés to say that it could no longer hold out. But torrential rain followed and during the night Lugar Nuevo was evacuated without loss, all the defenders (including 200 women and children) being taken into the sanctuary. Next, Franco gave permission to Cortés to surrender if resistance became impossible. He also gave orders for the evacuation of women and children under the guarantee of the Red Cross officers who had recently arrived. But Cortés and the defenders, inflamed by the passions which had been necessary in order to carry on resistance, could not but speculate about the power of the Red Cross to carry out any such guarantee. The defenders were surrounded by 20,000 Republicans, who seemed likely to be as savage as Red Indians. Doubts and difficulties arose. The attacks began again. Aircraft and artillery led the way. The heroic Cortés was wounded on April 30, and on May 1 the International Brigade and the militia of Jaén broke into the sanctuary. For a while slaughter was general. The sanctuary was burned. Flames engulfed the Sierra. Eventually, the majority of the women and children were taken away in lorries and the remaining armed defenders taken prisoner. Cortés died of wounds in hospital some days later. The defence of Santa María de la Cabeza, more than the successful defence of the Alcázar and of Oviedo, had gained the admiration of Spaniards of all sides.[1]

[1] The literature on the defence of Santa María de la Cabeza is considerable. I have chiefly used Reparaz and Luis Martín, *Defensa y Mártirio de Santa Maria de la Cabeza* (Seville 1939).

52

The Barcelona civil war – the visit to the Telefónica – responsibility for the crisis – negotiations – end of the riots

The main battlefield of the Civil War now became, tragically, Barcelona. On April 25 the Anarchist paper *Solidaridad Obrera* published a violent attack on the Communists. It particularly attacked Cazorla, the Communist Commissar for Public Order in Madrid, who had closed the Anarchist newspaper there. During the day, Roldán Cortada, a prominent member of the Socialist-Communist Youth in Barcelona, was murdered, presumably by Anarchists. Rodríguez Sala, the PSUC Chief of Police, ordered a police demonstration in the suburb where the crime had been committed. That night, an Anarchist was killed in Barcelona, and the Anarchist Mayor of Puigcerda was shot on the French frontier, because he and his followers had attempted to take over the guard of the frontier by force. Admittedly the Mayor of Puigcerda had been a notorious brigand who had insisted on the total collectivisation of all products and goods, while maintaining his own cattle. Yet open fighting in Barcelona between Anarchists and POUM on the one hand against the Catalan Government and the PSUC on the other was all the time expected.[1] Arms were gathered and buildings fortified. The Voroshilov (previously Atarazanas) and Pedrera Barracks were Communist citadels. The Marx Barracks was the stronghold of the POUM. The CNT proudly held out at the Chamber of Commerce.

A week passed, full of rumours. May 1, traditionally a day of great proletarian rejoicing, was quiet since the UGT and CNT agreed that in the circumstances the customary demonstrations would lead to riots. On May 2 Prieto telephoned the Catalan Government from Valencia. The Anarchist operator answered

---

[1] This was the impression of George Orwell who returned to Barcelona on April 26 from the front, where he had served with the POUM (*Homage to Catalonia*, 169 fl). His account of the following riots, marvellously written though it is, should be read with reservations. It is more accurate about war itself than about the Spanish War.

that there was no such thing as a Government in Barcelona, only a defence committee. The Telefónica at Barcelona was run by a committee of UGT, CNT, and one Government delegate, but dominated by the CNT. The Government and the Communists had believed for some time that the CNT tapped their telephone calls, which they were certainly in a position to do. So at half-past three in the afternoon on the next day, May 3, Rodríguez Sala, accompanied by the Generalitat representative on the Telefónica committee, went to the Telefónica, and visited the Censor's department on the first floor. The CNT workers, roused from their late lunch, thought that this was an attempt by the Government to gain control of the Telefónica, and from the second floor they opened fire down the stairs to the Censor's department. Rodríguez Sala telephoned for aid. The Civil Guard appeared, and also a moderate FAI leader, Dionisio Eroles. Dionisio Eroles persuaded the CNT workers not to shoot again. They accordingly gave up their arms, but first fired their spare ammunition through the windows. A great crowd had by now gathered below in the Plaza de Cataluña. It was first assumed that the Anarchists had captured the Telefónica. Then the word 'provocation' spread among the CNT. Within a few hours, all the political organisations had brought out their hidden arms and had begun to build barricades. Shop owners hastily shuttered their windows.

The spark which fired this crisis was undoubtedly the visit of Rodríguez Sala to the Telefónica. Yet it would be wrong to assume hastily that this was a step in a carefully worked out policy to provoke the CNT into violent action, carefully plotted by the Russian Consul-General Antonov Ovsëenko and the Hungarian Communist, Gerö, the chief Comintern representative in Catalonia. Until this moment, the Communists in Barcelona had gained all their ends chiefly by a mixture of secret terror and common-sense. Their political tactics and their military and economic policy had the support of both the Catalan Government and the Republican Government at Valencia. An open clash with the CNT in Barcelona was the one contest which the Communists could not have been sure of winning. Togliatti had embarked upon the delicate manoeuvre of the destruction of Largo Caballero, with all his prestige among the working class in Spain. This task required the undivided attention of the Communists. Certainly they would have taken more trouble, and even taken men from the front, if they had actually planned a *coup*. But of course, once the shooting had begun, the Communists would be expected to reap the fullest advantage from what was happening – to take the opportunity, for example, to discredit and destroy finally their old enemies in the POUM. Certainly, the Communists were waiting for an opportunity to do this, and in April 1937 the feeling was high enough in Barcelona to suggest that the time was ripe.

The Communist party later alleged that the crisis had been caused by the agents of Franco in the CNT and the POUM. Documents were said to have been found in hotels in Barcelona proving this, and Faupel, the German Ambassador at Salamanca, reported to Berlin that Franco told him on May 7 that the Nationalists had thirteen agents in Barcelona. One agent had reported that 'the tension between the Communists and Anarchists was so great that he could guarantee to cause fighting to break out there'. Franco said that 'he had intended not to use this plan until he began an offensive in Catalonia but, since the Republicans had attacked at Teruel[1] to relieve the Basques, he had judged the present moment to be right for the outbreak of disorders in Barcelona. Actually the agent had succeeded, within a few days of receiving such instructions, in having street fighting started by three or four persons'.[2] This evidence cannot be ignored. Falangists did join the FAI, POUM and CNT at the start of the Civil War to save their skins; and, undoubtedly, the tension in Barcelona was such that it required little to set it off. It might have been the spy who first cried 'provocation' in the Plaza de Cataluña. But spies are boastful men, and this one may have attributed the really spontaneous outbreak of the fighting to his own intrigues.

In the meantime, the CNT did nothing to prevent the worsening of the situation. In the evening of May 3 CNT representatives visited the Catalan Premier, Tarradellas, and his Home Secretary, Ayguadé. The two Ministers promised that the police would leave the Telefónica. The CNT went on to demand the resignations of Rodríguez Sala and Ayguadé. This was refused. The fact that negotiations continued, however, further suggests the lack of planning for any *coup* by either side. But, by nightfall, Barcelona was a city at war. The PSUC and the Government controlled Barcelona to the left of the Ramblas, proceeding from the Plaza de Cataluña. The Anarchists controlled the area to the right of

---

[1] A minor attack which had no consequences.   [2] *GD*, 286.

the Ramblas. The suburbs were all with the CNT. In the centre of the city, where Union and political headquarters were near to one another in large buildings or hotels which had been requisitioned, machine guns were placed on roofs, and firing began along the housetops. All cars were shot at by both sides. Yet at the Telefónica, a truce had been agreed, and the telephone itself was working. The police on the first floor even sent sandwiches up to the CNT workers above. Several police cars however were blown up by grenades dropped from roofs. Henceforward, any journey by car was dangerous.[1]

On May 4, Barcelona was silent save for sporadic machine-gun and rifle fire. Shops and houses were barricaded. Bands of armed Anarchists attacked *Asalto*, Civil Guard or Government buildings. These were followed by Communist or Government counterattacks, carried out by the Barcelona Civil Guard, *Asaltos* or other Catalan soldiers. The atmosphere was that of July 19, 1936. The angles of fire were the same as on that epic day. And once again the police fired against their late comrades in arms, in July the soldiers, now the Anarchists, without quite knowing why, obeying only the 'implacable and ironic laws of revolutionary confusion'.[2] In the meantime, the political leaders of the Anarchists, García Oliver and Federica Montseny, broadcast from Valencia an appeal to their followers to lay down arms and return to work. *Solidaridad Obrera* made the same appeal. The two Ministers then travelled to Barcelona with Mariano Vásquez, Secretary of the National Committee of the CNT. They all wished to avoid an engagement against the Communists. Furthermore Largo Caballero had no wish at all to use force against Anarchists. The Durruti column, with 500 militiamen, had meantime assembled at Lérida to march on Barcelona. On hearing García Oliver's speech they stayed where they were. But the CNT workers, excited by an extreme Anarchist group who had named themselves the 'friends of Durruti', did not obey their leaders. The POUM ranged itself with the Anarchist extremists. Their paper, *La Batalla*, issued slogans for the re-awakening of the 'spirit of July 19'.

Inside the Generalitat, negotiations went on all the time. Tarradellas, backed by Companys, refused to dismiss Rodríguez

---

[1] Mr Richard Bennett (with Barcelona Radio) has described to me how at this time his door in Barcelona was opened by two men carrying bombs who bluntly asked him: 'Whose side are you on?' 'Yours,' he wisely answered.

[2] Brasillach, 329.

Sala and Ayguadé. On May 5 a solution was apparently reached. The Catalan Government would resign, to be replaced by a Provisional Council in which Ayguadé would not figure. The Anarchists, the Esquerra and the *Rabaissaires* would each be represented as before. But confused firing nevertheless continued, raking along the empty broad streets and bringing death to those who unwisely ventured out of their houses or refuges. A leading Italian Anarchist intellectual, Professor Camillo Berneri, was murdered.[1] The 'Friends of Durruti' issued a pamphlet announcing that a revolutionary *junta* had been formed. All responsible for the attack on the Telefónica would be shot. The Civil Guards must be disarmed and the POUM, having 'established itself beside the workers', must be given back a place in the Government. *La Batalla* republished this manifesto without comment. The atmosphere of alarm was heightened by the arrival of British destroyers in the bay, which the POUM feared, for no reason, might immediately begin a bombardment.[2]

On May 6 a truce proclaimed by the CNT was observed all the morning. But all appeals to return to work were disregarded, from fear rather than from obtuseness. In the afternoon, fighting began again. Police and Esquerra bands attacked Anarchist buildings. A number of Civil Guards were blown up in a cinema by 75 mm artillery brought by members of the Libertarian Youth from the coast. Antonio Sesé, General Secretary of the Catalan UGT, and newly appointed a member of the Generalitat, was killed on his way to take up his appointment (probably accidentally, since all moving cars were still automatically shot at). However, in the evening, two cruisers, followed by the battleship *Jaime Primero*, arrived with armed men from Valencia. The reluctance of Largo Caballero to act at all in the crisis had been overcome by Prieto. 4,000 *Asaltos* also arrived from Valencia by road, having overcome risings at Tarragona and Reus on the way. At a quarter-to-five in the morning of May 7 the CNT broadcast a desperate appeal for a return to normality. The presence of *Asaltos* from Valencia in the streets ensured that this now occurred. The natives of the city appeared again, to stroll along the Ramblas, and discuss the fighting. On May 8 the CNT broadcast: 'Away with the

---

[1] Who by? Despite allegations that the murder was the work of the OVRA, Mussolini's secret police, everything points to Communist guilt. Since Berneri was apparently hailed in Italian, while walking home, the assassins may have been Italian Communists.

[2] Orwell, who was with a POUM firing post, shared this apprehension.

barricades! Every citizen his paving stone! Back to normality!'
The Barcelona riots were over. The official estimate of the
casualties was 400 killed and 1,000 wounded.[1]

[1] H. N. Brailsford gave figures for 900 dead and 2,500 wounded (*New Statesman*,
21.5.60). The Anarchist leaders regretted afterwards that they had secured this cease-
fire, since it merely led to their final surrender before the Communists. (Abad de
Santillán, 140–4.)

53

The Estremadura offensive – the campaign against the POUM –
political crisis at Valencia – the fall of Largo Caballero – Dr Negrín –
Negrín's Government

The Barcelona riots led directly to the last stage of the Communist attack upon Largo Caballero. Feelings between the Prime Minister and the Communists had been made worse than ever by a dispute on strategy. Several Republican officers of the high command proposed to test the new Republican army as now formed by launching an attack in Estremadura, towards Peñarroya and Mérida. They argued that 75,000 men should be concentrated, with heavy air support. Largo Caballero supported the idea. The Communists opposed the plan. The new Russian chief adviser, General Kulik, proposed striking down from the Republican positions along the Corunna road towards the little town of Brunete, cutting off the Nationalists in the Casa de Campo and the University City.[1] Miaja, who, as a result of his experiences in Madrid, was much under Communist influence, declared his disapproval of the Estremadura plan. Finally, when the Republican officers proved recalcitrant, the Soviet advisers simply announced that there would be no aircraft for the proposed offensive.[2] Here, once more, the Communists were arguing for a policy which, as well as being likely to serve their own ends, was also militarily more sensible than that of their opponents in the discussion. For, whatever the shortcomings of the Brunete plan, it was certainly more practicable than the fanciful Estremadura scheme.

This military quarrel merged into the larger Communist feud with Largo Caballero. Galarza, Minister of the Interior and an

---

[1] Hernández, 80–1. General Berzin was in Bilbao. Kulik's identity is uncertain. Hernández describes him as 'rough, strong, sympathetic, tall, a polar bear of a man'.

[2] An unpublished State Department Memorandum (sent from Valencia) estimated that at this moment the Republic possessed 460 aircraft. Of these, 200 were said to be Russian pursuit planes, 150 Russian bombers (bi-motor Martin type), 70 Russian observation planes, 8 French Bloch 210 bombers and 32 miscellaneous aircraft. (Cattell, *Communism*, 228.)

old enemy of the Communists, was denounced for permitting the Barcelona crisis to arise – for failing 'to see the open preparations for a counter-revolutionary *putsch*'. On May 11 the POUM's Valencian paper *Adelante* was, in reply, openly provocative in comparing the Government, because of its repressive measures, to one led by Gil Robles. On May 14 the Government ordered the surrender of all arms, except those held by the regular Army, within 72 hours. The Barcelona Civil Guards, PSUC and *Asaltos* began to round up arms. Finally, on May 15, at a Cabinet meeting in Valencia, Jesús Hernández and Uribe proposed the dissolution of the POUM.[1] Largo Caballero replied that he was, above all, a worker, and would not dissolve a brotherhood of fellow workers. The Anarchist members of the Cabinet supported the Prime Minister and argued that the Barcelona riots had been provoked by the 'non-revolutionary parties'. The two Communists, followed later by Giral, Irujo, Prieto, Álvarez del Vayo and Negrín, walked out of the meeting, pointing out that a crisis therefore existed. The Cabinet crisis thus broke. Some time that day, Hernández, on behalf of the Communists, proposed to Negrín that he should become Prime Minister. Negrín answered that he would do so if his party accepted the idea, adding that he was unknown and not popular. Hernández replied that popularity could be created. If there was one thing the Communist party could do well, he said, it was propaganda. Negrín protested that he was not a Communist and Hernández answered that was 'all the better'.[2] The next day, May 16, Largo Caballero gave his resignation to Azaña. The President asked the Prime Minister to remain in office until after the planned military operation – either at Brunete or in Estremadura. Largo Caballero agreed and Azaña began to plan a Cabinet without the Communist party. So great a break with the past administration would have needed, in effect, a new executive. In consequence, Largo Caballero, supported by the executive committee of the UGT, approached the Anarchists with the idea of forming a purely trade union Cabinet of CNT and UGT. The way to the pure syndicalist State was thus opened. At this point, however, Negrín, Álvarez del Vayo and Prieto told Largo Caballero that the Government could not do

[1] For this crisis see Periats, II 231 fl; Cattell, *Communism*, 153 fl; Álvarez del Vayo, *Freedom's Battle*, 212; Gorkin, Araquistain and Hernández. I have also consulted Señor Irujo and Señorita Montseny present at this Cabinet.
[2] Hernández, 86–8.

without the Communists, because of the need for Soviet aid. The Communist party now sent a note to Largo Caballero naming their conditions for support of a Government headed by him. All problems of war would be dealt with by a supreme war council. The Prime Minister would cease to be War Minister. All the Ministers would have to please all parties supporting the Government (Galarza would therefore be dismissed). A Chief of Staff would be named to plan the war. The Political Commissars would be responsible only to the War Commissariat, though that body would be responsible to the War Minister and War Council. These conditions were rejected by Largo Caballero, who insisted (somewhat like Asquith in 1916) on retaining control of the war in his own hands. He was fully supported by his old Anarchist enemies. Azaña himself now sought a compromise candidate. Prieto seemed too controversial, since his enmity with Largo Caballero was so long standing and so well known. Negrín, whom the Communists had let it be known that they would support, stood out as the obvious choice.

Juan Negrín came from a prosperous middle-class family of the Canary Isles. Trained as a doctor in Germany, he had later been closely associated with the Nobel prizewinner for Medicine, Ramón y Cajal. He himself became, when still very young, Professor of Physiology at the University of Madrid. In Madrid he had had much to do with the organisation of the University City. He did not join a political party, and indeed had no interest whatever in politics, till the last years of Primo de Rivera's dictatorship, when it seemed to him clear that it was his duty, if he wanted a better Spain, to join the Socialist party. However, though he became a deputy under the Republic, he did not take an active part in politics till the Civil War, being still too concerned with his own work. Indeed almost the only political act which was remembered of him during the Republic, was his vote in 1932, in his party group, against a reprieve for General Sanjurjo.

Despite this lack of political experience, he was named Minister of Finance by Largo Caballero in September 1936. His proved efficiency in university administration and his interest in financial matters inside the Socialist party recommended him for this arduous post. At this time, he was thought to be, if anything, a follower of Prieto. But he had hardly ever made a speech in the Cortes and was still very much of a political unknown. In the

Ministry of Finance he was a most successful administrator. He had handled the complicated questions of paying for Russian aid with skill, and established excellent personal relations with the Russian economic adviser, Stashevsky. But he had remained a man without a personal following, and without any apparent political prejudices or loyalties of any sort. This, combined with his admitted efficiency and his excellent academic background – which might seem likely to recommend him to the favour of Britain and France – caused him to be accepted without question by so many disparate groups as the new leader of the Republic in succession to Largo Caballero. Not unlike Franco, many of the politicians of the Republic (by no means only the Communists) thought that it would be comparatively easy to influence Negrín as they wished.

However, at the start of his premiership, he told Azaña that if he were to be Prime Minister (which he had not wished), he would be so 'one hundred per cent'.[1] And he insisted on being so for the rest of the war. His intellectual arrogance, the inevitable consequence of the entry of such a first-class brain into politics, made him, needless to say, ten enemies a day. Other politicians, especially members of his own Socialist party, were furious that a newcomer to politics should behave so dictatorially towards them – and should have such genuinely *political* success. Members of his Cabinet were angered by his irregular habits of eating and drinking, and of calling conferences at all hours – somewhat as Churchill was to enrage his military advisers. His enemies privately accused Negrín of a lack of those Roman virtues which they said were necessary to win the war. And there is no doubt that the new Prime Minister was almost incapable of working with a team of Ministers, especially a coalition of such disparate individuals as was necessary in the Republic. But he was a man for whom personal freedom was a veritable passion. This, he believed, was at stake in the Spanish Civil War. There is certainly no sign that his lavish spending and living, his delight in pretty women and his gargantuan eating and drinking at all hours (the outward signs of his enormous energy and vitality) prevented him from working far harder than any other Minister.

The policy of Negrín as Prime Minister was throughout a realistic opportunism. A moderate Socialist with a predilection for 'planning', he was ready to make any political sacrifice in order to

[1] Statement made to me by Julio Álvarez del Vayo.

win the war. This of course led him, as it had led Largo Caballero and Prieto, into close relations with Russia, since, as before, Russia remained the only source of arms. Furthermore their political moderation and ruthless realism in face of the war made the Spanish Communist party, throughout Negrín's Ministry, the most useful political party in Spain. Thus Negrín had to accept many things from the Russian Ambassador and from the Spanish Communist party which he disliked. As Minister of Finance Negrín had been specially concerned with the dispatch of the Spanish gold to Moscow. His consequent relations with Russia resembled those of Faust with Mephistopheles.

But it would be quite wrong to conclude that Negrín was a mere instrument of Soviet policy. It is true that few politicians have successfully used a Communist party, and not been later swallowed by it. But in the 1930s and in Spain the possibility did not seem so far-fetched. Negrín's personal self-confidence and his reserved secret nature perhaps led him to think that he could slough off the Communist connection when necessary. And when, from the early summer of 1938, he was seeking some kind of compromise peace with the Nationalists, he does not seem to have confided in the Communists or anyone else. It would in fact be ludicrous to suppose that so tough and independent-minded an intellectual, with so bad a temper, could ever be subservient to anyone. Though he was on excellent terms with the Russian economic adviser, Stashevsky, on one occasion (when Minister of Finance) he had told him forcibly not to try and dictate the internal affairs of Spain. Otherwise, added Negrín, 'there is the door'.[1] At least once, Negrín had to be restrained from breaking diplomatic relations with the Soviet Union, probably on the occasion of the murder of Andrés Nin.[2] Whereas Largo Caballero received the Russian Ambassador Rosenberg at all times without appointment, Negrín insisted that Rosenberg's successors, Gaikins and Marchenko, should telephone to arrange a meeting beforehand.[3] While Largo was referred to by the Russians as 'comrade', Negrín insisted on being named 'Señor Prime Minister'.[4] Negrín had no close relations with the leaders of the Spanish Communist party and he had a strong dislike for La Pasionaria. And, indeed, despite the continued eclipse of the Anarchists, the Communist party increased its power far less under Negrín than it had under Largo.

---

[1] Evidence of Pablo de Azcárate.
[3] *Ibid.*
[2] *Ibid.* See below, page 454.
[4] Evidence of Álvarez del Vayo.

Hernández admits that a time would have come when it would have been necessary to 'liquidate' Negrín.[1]

This was a mortal struggle. No quarter would be offered to the vanquished. If the wilder and more engaging revolutionaries on the Republican side were repressed by the Communist-controlled police, this might have to be accepted, provided that the Republic's reputation abroad was not greatly injured. Negrín was surrounded by the wrecks of the reputations of men like Azaña, the 'strong man of the Republic', and 'the Spanish Lenin' Largo Caballero. They were shortly to be joined, among the broken reeds of Spain, by Indalecio Prieto. The Anarchists were also crushed in spirit. Negrín assumed appalling responsibilities when becoming Prime Minister. He made mistakes. But for the rest of the Civil War, this arrogant physiologist, with the disorderly private life, represented the spirit of the Spanish Republic.

The Cabinet which Negrín formed included two Socialists besides himself – Prieto as War Minister and Prieto's *protégé*, Zugazagoitia, as Minister of the Interior. The Communists Hernández and Uribe retained their old Ministries of Education and Agriculture. Giral and Giner de los Ríos, Republicans, became Foreign Minister and Minister of Communications and Public Works. The Basque Irujo became Minister of Justice and a Catalan, Jaime Ayguadé, brother of the ex-Catalan counsellor, became Minister of Labour. Thus, no members of Largo Caballero's wing of the Socialist party were included in the Government. Araquistain, Largo Caballero's chief remaining supporter, even resigned from the Embassy in Paris. He was replaced by Ossorio y Gallardo, a Catholic ex-Minister of the Monarchy who, it was hoped, would please the French Right.[2] Álvarez del Vayo, no longer a political follower but still a friend of the outgoing Premier, remained Chief Political Commissar and Spanish representative at Geneva. Negrín asked the Anarchists to join the Cabinet but they refused, saying that they had not provoked the crisis, which they considered 'unwise, inopportune and harmful to

[1] Hernández, 135. This may have been said because Negrín from an early stage placed hope in a world war which he thought inevitable, but which Stalin was always trying to stave off. On one occasion Negrín angered Stalin by insisting that the Republican Ambassador in Moscow, Marcelino Pascua, should either be received immediately (to demand aid) or should return home. (Private information.)

[2] The most influential Republican representative in Paris during Negrín's Government was the American journalist, Louis Fischer, who from his headquarters at the Lutetia Hotel, near the Sèvres-Babylone metro station, directed an elaborate organisation for the purchase of arms and the diffusion of pro-Republican propaganda.

the conduct of the war'. To join Negrín, they said, would prove a lack of nobility. The Communist party stretched out a hand of friendship to the CNT, urging 'discussion of problems' between them, but the advance was rejected. Despite this, on May 30 García Oliver, followed by the other three Anarchist ex-Ministers, made speeches in which they showed how proud they were of their achievements during their time in the Government.

With the Communist party still the strongest opponents of social revolution, Negrín's Government was thus further to the Right than its predecessor. The dominant member was undoubtedly Prieto, who now controlled the whole of the machinery of war. Since he was a known anti-Communist, the Communist party, despite its machinations, could not be regarded as having gained greatly from the change. As is so often the case with Communist policy, a brilliantly successful political manoeuvre was thus concluded without any immediate advantage at the end of it.

54

New war in Vizcaya – Besteiro in London – the mediation proposal –
the Barletta *incident – the* Deutschland *incident – the German*
fleet at Almería – Prieto proposes war with Germany

Dr Negrín's Government accidentally but appropriately included five men (Prieto,[1] Zugazagoitia, Irujo, Uribe and Hernández) from the Basque provinces. There the front continued slowly to crumble. The Basques were now almost back to the Ring of Iron. The bombing continued, the Germans experimenting now with the idea of dropping large numbers of small incendiary bombs on woods to force the Basques to leave their positions. Two Asturian and Santander battalions abandoned easily defensible positions. A new Navarrese brigade relieved the Italians surrounded at Bermeo.

At this moment, Neurath, visiting Rome, was being told by Mussolini that Germany and Italy had 'made enough sacrifices' for Franco. The Duce said that he would tell Franco that he would withdraw the Italians the next month if the Spaniards did not prosecute the war more energetically.[2] Aircraft sent to the help of the Basques from Valencia *via* France were held up at Toulouse by the Dutch Colonel Lunn of the Non-Intervention Committee. They were then returned to Valencia with their machine guns confiscated. But eventually, on May 22, the risk was taken of sending ten fighters across Nationalist Spain to Bilbao. Seven arrived safely. A rumour was now heard that Mola had threatened to raze Bilbao to the ground. He was thought to have added: 'and its bare and desolate site shall make the British forever regret their help to the Basque bolshevists'. This tale, together with the widespread horror at the destruction of Guernica, probably inspired the British Government to join the French in agreeing to escort Basque refugee ships (including British merchant ships) once they were outside the Spanish three-mile limit. The first refugees were to be evacuated children, to be parcelled out

---

[1] Prieto was born in Oviedo, but went to Bilbao as a boy.   [2] *GD*, 287.

among those who agreed to look after them. The CGT in France agreed to take 2,300 and the Soviet Government undertook the care of Communist children. A Basque children's relief committee in England, supported by the British branch of the Roman Church, agreed to look after 4,000 children. These, after being carefully examined by four doctors from the Ministry of Health, were boarded at a camp in Stoneham in Lincoln-shire. The Nationalists protested, believing that these steps im-plied that the Basques were preparing to destroy Bilbao. But the evacuation of 'our brave expeditionary infants', as the Bilbao Press described those who went away, continued without difficulty.[1]

Mr Anthony Eden had meantime been visited by the Socialist reformist, Professor Besteiro, who represented the Republic at the Coronation on May 12 of King George VI. Besteiro came to Eden on behalf of the unhappy Azaña, begging the British Foreign Secretary to mediate in the Civil War. Azaña suggested that, after the successful withdrawal of foreign volunteers, the great powers should then impose a settlement on Spain.[2] The idea was one with which Eden had himself toyed. But the British *Chargé* at Valencia, Mr Leche, reported that the hatred in Spain was such that media-tion would not now prosper.[3] Eden nevertheless persevered. The British Ambassadors at Rome, Berlin, Paris and Moscow, and the Minister at Lisbon, approached the Foreign Ministers in those capitals in precisely the sense that Azaña had suggested.[4] On May 19, however, Bastiniani, Ciano's second-in-command at the Palazzo Chigi, angrily complained to Hassell that Eden's plan was typical of 'the British desire to prevent a Fascist victory at all costs'.[5] On the 22nd, Franco told Faupel that an armistice and free elections would mean a 'Leftist Government' and mark the end of white Spain. He 'and all Nationalist Spaniards would rather die than place Spain in the hands of a Red or a democratic Government'. Serrano Suñer believed that a compromise of any sort would simply 'leave open the door to a return to that state of affairs which had made war inevitable'.[6] The Generalissimo told Faupel that the Republic might accept mediation, because of what

[1] Cloud, *passim.* Steer, 263. Britain also made a proposal to the Basques that they should name a series of neutral zones which would be guaranteed against attack. The Republican Government protested against Britain's act in thus dealing with the Basques as if they were a regular Government.

[2] de Madariaga, 416.   [3] *USD*, 1937 Vol 1 295.   [4] *GD*, 291.
[5] *GD*, 291.   [6] Serrano Suñer, 70.

he believed (wrongly) to be Prieto's part in its origins. The British, said Franco, wanted an armistice because they had advanced large sums to the Basques.[1] The conversation between Franco and Faupel ended with both agreeing on the trouble caused by the Vatican. Franco said he had told Cardinal Gomá, the Archbishop of Toledo, that no mention should be made in Spain of the recent encyclical, *Mit Brennender Sorge*, delivered against Nazi Germany, and read in German churches in March.[2] On May 24, Ciano told the American Ambassador that the armistice plan was unfair at this time since Franco was about to enter Bilbao.[3] In Geneva, the League Council now met. Álvarez del Vayo requested the discussion of Italian intervention in Spain. Eden arrived in Geneva and the British delegation which he led there openly confessed that the armistice plan had failed.[4] And indeed nothing more was heard of it. On the 28th, the League Council considered the Spanish complaint. Álvarez del Vayo spoke eloquently of German and Italian intervention. He doubted whether Non-Intervention Control would really prevent the influx of material and agreed to the withdrawal of volunteers. Litvinov supported him in all particulars. Delbos and Eden proclaimed their 'fervent belief' that they had made progress since the previous December, when the Council had last been seized of the Spanish question. Their policy both at the conference table and in the corridors was, as ever, to keep the matter in a low key so as not to drive the Germans or Italy from impatience out of the Non-Intervention Committee.

In that body in London the same day, Grandi raised a new incident, that of the Italian cruiser *Barletta*. This vessel, part of the Non-Intervention Naval Control, had been sheltering in the harbour of Palma de Mallorca. It could not have been carrying out its patrol duties there, since Majorca was part of the French responsibility. Its presence in Palma could not have been entirely innocent. During a Republican air raid on May 24 on the island, the *Barletta* was hit. Six Italians were killed. The Non-Intervention Committee passed a resolution deploring the incident and suggesting that there should be a safety zone for all naval patrol vessels in Palma. The next day, the League Council passed an

---

[1] This was not true, though admittedly Britain had extensive financial and commercial interests in Bilbao.

[2] *GD*, 295. This encyclical was never read in Spain.

[3] *USD*, 1937 Vol 1 302.　　　　　　　　[4] *Ibid*., 303.

innocuous resolution regretting that its previous resolution of December had not been better carried out, welcoming the start of Non-Intervention Control, urging the withdrawal of volunteers, condemning the bombing of open towns, and approving such humanitarian acts as Britain and France had undertaken in respect of the Basque children. These pious sentiments were, needless to say, doomed to remain as aspirations. The same day a new naval incident occurred in the Balearics.

The Ministry of Defence at Valencia had pointed out that non-intervention naval patrol could not legally be exercised inside Spanish territorial waters. Palma harbour was a known centre of Nationalist arms trading. The Republicans would therefore continue to attack it. Patrol ships would, however, be safe enough outside Spanish territorial waters. On May 26 the air raid on Palma had been repeated, and bombs fell on the German patrol ship *Albatross*, also lying off duty in Palma. In the morning of May 29, the commander of the German naval patrol protested that Republican aircraft had approached several German patrol ships in the posture of attack. He announced that repetition of such behaviour would produce 'counter-measures'.

That evening, the German battleship *Deutschland* lay at anchor off Ibiza. Suddenly, two Republican aircraft, at first unidentifiable against the dying sun, appeared overhead and dropped two bombs. One fell in the seamen's mess, killing 22 and wounding 83 of the ship's company. The other hit the side deck and caused little damage.

The Republican Ministry of Defence claimed that the *Deutschland* fired first at the aeroplanes, who thereupon retaliated. This seems not to have been the case. 'Reconnaissance aircraft' which the Ministry claimed them to be, do not carry bombs.[1] It is possible that the raid was due to Republican Air Force indiscipline.[2] But anyway to bomb the *Deutschland* was not an illegal act. Ibiza harbour was a perfectly natural object for attack by Republican aircraft.

All the next day, the Germans deliberated what to do. Hitler was in a great rage at the death of so many Germans, and the Foreign Minister Neurath passed six hours with him seeking to moderate his anger.[3] The *Deutschland* itself sailed to Gibraltar

---

[1] Blum said to the American Ambassador that his information was that the Germans were telling the truth (*USD*, 1937 Vol 1 309).

[2] Salvador de Madariaga, 388.   [3] *USD*, 1937 Vol 1 317; *GD*, 297 fl.

where it disembarked the wounded. Nine more died, bringing the total death roll to 31.[1]

At dawn on May 31, the Germans took their revenge. A cruiser and four destroyers appeared off Almería and fired 200 shots into the town, destroying 35 buildings and causing 19 deaths. The same day, before the Non-Intervention Committee, Ribbentrop announced that Germany would withdraw from the non-intervention discussions, and from the naval patrol, until she had received guarantees against the repetition of any such incidents. Grandi said that Italy would act likewise. On June 1 Eden showed 'obvious ill humour' when Azcárate called on him, clearly indicating he believed the German version of the incident. In Berlin, Neurath argued to François-Poncet that Germany had shown 'exceptional restraint', and the Ambassador agreed.[2] Sir Nevile Henderson, who had recently arrived as British Ambassador, begged Neurath 'not to do the Reds the compliment of expanding the Spanish situation into a world war'. By his language he clearly expressed his own views formed, no doubt, in his last post at Buenos Aires. Neurath replied that the incident should cause Britain to change her previous 'benevolent attitude' towards the Spanish Republic.[3] In Paris, Delbos pointed out to Welczeck that France too had been provoked in several incidents, by the Nationalists, but had taken no reprisals.[4] Even Cordell Hull summoned the new German Ambassador in Washington, Dieckhoff. With his usual caution, the Secretary of State told him that the United States 'desired that Germany might see its way to make peaceful adjustments' of its Spanish difficulties.[5] In Geneva, Álvarez del Vayo played momentarily with the idea of putting the Spanish case before the League Council. But Eden and Litvinov both opposed the plan.

In Valencia the Republican Cabinet met.[6] Prieto wished the Republic to bomb the German fleet in the Mediterranean. This, he said, might start a world war but that was worth risking since it would inevitably draw off German aid from Franco. Negrín said that Azaña would have to be consulted. This gave all the Ministers time to consult their consciences – and their

---

[1] The *Deutschland*'s victims were looked after by the Governor of Gibraltar, General Sir Charles Harrington, whose chief care hitherto in the Spanish War had been how to restore the Royal Calpe Hunt to its ancient glory. Meets had been resumed after the fall of Málaga.

[2] *GD*, 298. [3] *Ibid.*, 299. [4] *loc. cit.*
[5] *GD*, 302. [6] Hernández, 114.

friends. Hernández and Uribe went to the Central Committee of the Communist party. The proposal flung the Comintern advisers into a fine flurry. Codovilla went to the Soviet Embassy. Togliatti went to the Russian advisers at their headquarters, in a beautiful orange grove at El Vedat. Moscow[1] was consulted by wireless. And Stalin answered that the Soviet Government had no desire for world war. Prieto's plan should therefore at all costs be defeated. If necessary, Prieto would have to be murdered. But the Republican Cabinet, with Azaña, also opposed Prieto's plan in the end. A real war against Germany might after all have brought the annihilation of the Republic before Britain and France could be induced to give them aid. The 'incident' of Almería, therefore, was allowed to be forgotten.[2]

[1] *La Casa* (home) was the Spanish Communists' word for Moscow.
[2] There was one other occasion when a world war was nearly provoked by the Republic. The dismembered body of a Republican pilot was dropped on to the airfield at Barajas near Madrid with scornful comments added in Italian. The incensed Republican Air Force wished to take off to bomb Rome. Hidalgo de Cisneros, the commander, announced that he would accompany his men. But once again the Republican Cabinet restrained the impetuous. The advantages to the Republic of a general conflict was always equivocal if it were to arise out of the Spanish War. The impression I get is that the Republic simply did not know what would be the consequences for them if they became involved in an actual war with Germany or Italy. It is certainly unlikely that Britain and France would have wanted to assist them if they could help it. This was evidently also a pre-occupation of Russia, who presumably knew that if she sent to Spain enough arms to win the war for the Republic, the odds would be that a world war would follow, with Britain and France at least neutral and perhaps actually aligned against her.

55

The Basque defences – renewed Huesca offensive and the death of Lukacz – Segovia offensive – the death of Mola – last stage of the Bilbao campaign – decision to resist – the militiamen fall back into the city – the fall of Bilbao

Bad weather had held up Mola's operations against Bilbao. Inside that city a new General Staff arrived from Valencia (to act beside the Russian Berzin) under General Gamir Ulíbarri. He had once been director of the school of infantry at Toledo and since the start of the war Republican commander at Teruel. This able officer introduced greater efficiency into the Basque General Staff. The Russian General Berzin remained as general adviser. A new shipment of Czech arms, including 55 anti-aircraft guns, also arrived *via* the Comintern at the start of June. But no more aeroplanes came and those recently sent were destroyed on the ground.

In the meantime, the Republican Government undertook two offensives in other parts of Spain to attempt to draw the Nationalist fire from Bilbao. The first was yet another attack against Huesca, on the Aragón front. This was carried out by the reorganised Catalan army, which since the May riots had been under Valencian control. Led by General Pozas, the attack was unsuccessful. There were 10,000 Republican casualties, mainly Anarchists, in the week which the attack lasted. They included, however, the gay General Lukacz and many Italians serving under him in the Garibaldi Brigade.[1] These Italians, mostly singing *Bandiera Rossa*, were observed in their train on the way to the front by the recently wounded George Orwell. From his hospital train he saw 'window after window of dark smiling faces, the long tilted barrels of the guns, the scarlet scarves fluttering – all this glided slowly past us against a turquoise-coloured sea. . . . The men who were well

---

[1] Hungarian anti-Communists have alleged that Lukacz committed suicide on Moscow's orders. This tale is scotched by the account of his death given by Gustav Regler, who was wounded at the same time. (Regler, *The Owl of Minerva*, 312.)

enough to stand moved across the carriage to cheer the Italians as they went past. A crutch waved out of the window; bandaged arms gave the red salute. It was like an allegorical picture of war – the trainloads of fresh men gliding proudly up the line, the maimed sliding slowly down.'[1]

The other attack at this time was by General Walter on the Segovia front. On May 31, with the XIVth International Brigade under Colonel Dumont as a shock force, he broke through the Nationalist lines at San Ildefonso. The attack reached La Granja before being halted by Varela, with units transferred from Barrón's division to the south of Madrid. The attack occasioned a quarrel between Walter and Dumont as to who was to blame for the defeat.[2] Since Dumont was so well supported by the French Communists, Walter could do no more than protest against Dumont's well-known vanity and inefficiency. But henceforth Dumont and Walter shared in no further operations, the XIVth Brigade being moved to another front.[3]

There was one further preliminary to the final act of the Bilbao campaign. The death occurred on June 3 of General Mola. The aeroplane in which he was flying to Burgos crashed on the terrible hill of Buitrago, where the political prisoners of the capital of Castile had, in July and August 1936, been so indiscriminately and ruthlessly killed. Inevitably a question mark surrounds the manner of Mola's death. Was there, perhaps, a time bomb in the aeroplane? Certainly there were many who might have desired the death of Mola – Franco among them. For many years afterwards a Colonel sat in Valladolid with two loaded pistols before him on his table, waiting till he found out who killed his son – the pilot of Mola's aircraft. Faupel described Franco as 'undoubtedly relieved by the death of Mola'. The Generalissimo's last words on his brother-in-arms were: 'Mola was a stubborn fellow! When I

[1] Orwell, 260.

[2] Our Lady of Fuencisla, patron saint of Segovia, was later named a full Field-Marshal for her part in the defence of the town. This was when General Varela had become Minister of War in the Nationalist Cabinet in 1942. The news caused Hitler to say that he would never under any circumstance visit Spain. (*Tabletalk*, 515.)

[3] This was the Republican offensive described by Hemingway in *For Whom the Bell Tolls*. He suggests that it was betrayed but, due to Marty's obstinacy, it was nevertheless allowed to continue. The action of this book covers 'the 68 hours between Saturday afternoon and Tuesday noon of the last week of May 1937' (Baker, 225). Hemingway himself, oddly enough, was by then back in New York, campaigning to raise funds for the Republic. His old friends in America thought that they were seeing the transformation of a previously uncommitted writer. Hemingway returned to Spain later in the year.

gave him orders differing from his own proposals, he often asked, "Don't you trust my leadership any more?" [1]

General Dávila, head of the administrative *junta* at Burgos, known to resemble Mola in his Monarchist and Catholic views, succeeded as commander of the Army of the North. He was a bureaucratic General and, in stature, even shorter than Franco. General Jordana succeeded Dávila at Burgos. He was a man who hitherto had had little to do with Franco's movement. A member of Primo de Rivera's Governments, High Commissioner of Morocco under the King, he was already old, and therefore recommended himself as being beyond personal ambition. Although a Monarchist at heart, he regarded himself as a liberal. In truth he was a man of an age far away from that of Fascism, Communism and the industrial revolution. Courteous, loyal, very hard-working, he was later as Foreign Secretary to do much to commend the *régime* to foreign Ambassadors.

On June 11 the new commander Dávila ordered the Army of the North to return to the attack. The preliminary artillery bombardment was very heavy and the general shock broke the Basque defenders of the last high point before the Ring of Iron. By nightfall, Generals García Valiño, Bautista Sánchez and Bartomeu, with three Navarrese brigades, had reached this famous line of defences. All night the bombardment continued. One series of incendiary bombs dropped in a cemetery and caused a fiery resurrection of the dead.

On June 12, after forty-five batteries had pounded away at the Ring of Iron for several hours, Bautista Sánchez's brigade attacked at the spot where the defence system had hardly been constructed at all. The treachery of Goicoechea had no doubt suggested this point for the assault. The attack followed immediately upon the artillery bombardment. The defenders could thus hardly tell when firing from tanks succeeded the shelling. Confusion, smoke, movement seemed suddenly everywhere in the Ring of Iron. Once again, various Basque units found that they were in danger of being surrounded and hastened to retreat. By dusk, Bautista Sánchez had broken the Basque lines on a front one kilometre long. He was ten kilometres only from the centre of Bilbao. The Nationalists could therefore shell Bilbao as well as bomb it. On

---

[1] *GD*, 410. One allegation at the time was that Mola had been killed by the Germans because he had protested against the bombing of civilian targets. The protest and alleged outcome are equally unlikely.

June 13 all the Basques beyond the Ring of Iron were withdrawn inside. In Bilbao, many prepared to flee to France. A conference was held at the Carlton Hotel, at which Aguirre and his Ministers asked the military commanders if Bilbao could be defended. The chief of artillery, Gerricaechebarria, thought not. The Russian General Berzin, recalling his defence of Madrid and his own part in it, advised resistance. During the night of June 13–14, the Basque Government decided to defend Bilbao. But as many as possible of the civilian population were evacuated to the west, towards Santander. This foreshadowed the abandonment of the city. For the defence of a city is made immeasurably more difficult if civilians do not share with soldiers in the defence, and if all do not feel that they are fighting for their homes and their families.[1]

On June 14 certain changes of the Basque commanders gave new life to the defence. The Alsatian Colonel Putz, previously commander of the XIVth International Brigade, took over command of the 1st Basque Division. The flight of refugees from Bilbao went on all day and with a controlled emotion that might have been employed for the defence of their city. The road to Santander was machine-gunned from the air by the Condor Legion. Two vessels full of refugees were captured by the Nationalist fleet. The Basque Government withdrew to the village of Trucios, in western Vizcaya. They left behind a *junta de defensa* for Bilbao composed of Leizaola (the Minister of the Interior), Aznar (a Socialist), Astigarrabia (a Communist) and General Gamir Ulíbarri. On June 15, thanks to Putz's reorganisations, a line at least was presented to the advancing Nationalist army. Beldarrán was in the north, Putz in the centre and, in the south, Colonel Vidal, a regular officer who had joined the Basques in San Sebastián at the start of the war. It was at the point where the treacherous Major Goicoechea had revealed the fortifications to be incomplete that the next attack was made. Vidal's men immediately broke and fled across the river Nervión without even blowing up the bridges behind them. They thus laid open the road into Bilbao. The next day, June 16, Prieto telegraphed to Gamir Ulíbarri to hold Bilbao at all costs, especially the industrial region of the town. On this morning, certain members of the Fifth Column began to fire indiscriminately into the streets of the suburb of Las Arenas. An Anarchist group effectively silenced this outburst. But, throughout the day, the Nationalist advance continued. Vidal's division re-

---

[1] Steer, 307; Aznar, 422 fl.

treated still further. Putz's incurred heavy casualties. On June 17 the headquarters of these two commanders were in the centre of Bilbao. During that day 20,000 shells dropped on the city. The militia lines were continuously bombed. High points and isolated houses changed hands several times. Throughout June 18 the Basque militia were falling back. Within Bilbao, men and material were being transported along the railway line and the last two roads to Santander. These were now beginning to come within artillery range of the advancing Black Arrows. In the evening, Leizaola, chivalrous to the end, arranged for the delivery to the enemy of the political prisoners in Basque hands to avoid their being left without Basque guards in the last stages of the resistance. He also guaranteed the preservation of Bilbao by preventing the Communist and Anarchist battalions from blowing up the University and the church of St Nicolás, which they had thought would make good enemy machine-gun nests. The Nationalists now gained all the right bank of the river Nervión from the city to the sea and most of the left bank as far as the railway bridge. It was time to leave. At dusk on June 18 all the Basque fighting units were ordered to evacuate their capital. In the morning of June 19 the last militiamen did so. At noon, Nationalist tanks made a preliminary reconnaissance across the Nervión to find Bilbao empty. The Fifth Column, the opportunists and the secret agents emerged cautiously, to hang out red and yellow Monarchist flags from their balconies. A crowd of two hundred Nationalist sympathisers gathered to sing and shout. A Basque tank suddenly appeared from nowhere, dispersed the crowd, tore down, with bursts from its guns, three flags from the balconies, and drove along the last road of escape. Between five and six o'clock in the evening the Vth Navarrese Brigade under Bautista Sánchez entered the city and placed the Monarchist flag on the town hall. In the moment of victory the conquerors might have recalled that it was the Carlists' failure to take Bilbao that lost them both the nineteenth-century civil wars of Spain.[1]

According to Faupel, Franco had learnt his lesson from the 'senseless shootings' after the fall of Málaga. He accordingly forbade large troop detachments from entering Bilbao, so avoiding excesses.[2] The Basque leaders, of course, had left. Immediate reprisals did not occur and few civilian prisoners were made. But the fall of Bilbao marked the end of Basque independence. The

---

[1] Aznar, 425–6. Steer, 336–71.   [2] GD, 409.

conquerors made every effort to extinguish Basque separatist feeling. All schoolmasters were dismissed unless they could prove their political negativism. The Basque tongue was officially forbidden. And, within a fortnight, Herr Bethke of ROWAK had visited all the iron mines, blast furnaces and rolling mills of Bilbao. He found them undamaged. Work could start immediately to provide both for Franco's present and Hitler's future offensives.[1]

The news of the fall of Bilbao was given by a priest to the Basque children in England at their camp at Stoneham. The assembled children were so appalled that they fell upon the bringer of such bad tidings with stones and sticks. Three hundred children out of the three thousand five hundred broke out of the camp in wild and grief-stricken purposelessness.[2]

[1] *Ibid.*, 412.   [2] Cloud, 8.

56

The fall of Bilbao intensified an already heated world-wide controversy over the religious implications of the Spanish Civil War. The Republican affiliation of the Basques, admitted by even fervent supporters of the Nationalists as 'the most Christian people in Spain',[1] caused all Catholics to look to their loyalties. In the early spring, two very eminent French Catholics, François Mauriac and Jacques Maritain, had issued a pro-Basque manifesto.[2] The destruction of Guernica further strengthened the hands of those whom the right-wing French Catholic Press dubbed the *'Chrétiens Rouges'*. On May 15 two Spanish Dominicans in Rome, Fr Carro and Fr Bertrán de Heredia, published a violent pamphlet denouncing the idea 'prevalent in too many Catholic homes' that one could be neutral in the Spanish Civil War. For this meant giving equal rights to 'the murderers, the traitors to God and to the Fatherland'. Sin, like crime, had no rights. The Archbishop of Westminster described the war as 'a furious battle between Christian civilisation and the most cruel Paganism that has ever darkened the world'.[3] The figure of 16,500 nuns, bishops, monks and other religious persons for murdered priests was given by *Osservatore Romano*, and the Pope officially declared all those priests who had been murdered to be martyrs. Claudel thereupon wrote his famous ode *Aux Martyrs Espagnols*, as a verse preface to a pro-Nationalist tract by one of the Nationalist agents in Paris. On July 1, Maritain replied with an article in *La Nouvelle Revue Française*, in which he named those who killed the poor, 'the people of Christ',

---

[1] *La Guerre d'Espagne et le Catholicisme*, a pamphlet by Vice-Admiral H. Joubert in answer to the article of July 1 by Maritain (Paris 1937), page 26.

[2] This document was also signed by Georges Bidault, Claude Bourdet and Maurice Merleau Ponty.

[3] Quoted by Fr Bayle, SJ, *¿Que pasa en España?*

in the name of religion as being as culpable as those who killed priests by hatred of religion.

On July 1 also the Spanish hierarchy, led by Cardinal Gomá, Archbishop of Toledo, took the extraordinary step of despatching a joint letter to the 'Bishops of the Whole World'.[1] In this, they explained that they had not wished an 'armed plebiscite' in Spain, though thousands of Christians 'had taken up arms on their personal responsibility to save the principles of religion'. They argued that the legislative power since 1931 had sought to change 'Spanish history in a way contrary to the needs of the national spirit'. The Comintern had armed 'a revolutionary militia to seize power'. The Civil War was therefore theologically just.[2] The bishops recalled the martyred priests and comforted themselves with the reflection that when their enemies who had been fascinated by 'doctrines of demons died under the sanction of law, they had been reconciled' in their vast majority to the God of their fathers. In Majorca only 2% had died impenitent; in the southern regions no more than 20%. The bishops concluded by naming the National Movement 'a vast family, in which the citizen attains his total development'. Despite this remark (which would have sounded well on the lips of José Antonio) they added that they 'would be the first to regret that the irresponsible autocracy of Parliament should be replaced by the more terrible one of a dictatorship without roots in the nation'. And they finally reproved (though in words moderate enough to suggest that they sought a compromise) the Basque priests for not having listened 'to the voice of the Church'. This letter was not signed by the Archbishop of Tarragona (who undoubtedly opposed its ideas) nor by the Bishop of Vitoria.[3] This last prelate, now in exile, championed the Basque priests. It was not true, he said, that there was religious freedom in Nationalist Spain (even the Germans had complained

---

[1] Published in London by the Catholic Truth Society. It seems probable that the letter was written on the suggestion of General Franco. It was certainly drafted by Cardinal Gomá and circulated for signature by the bishops.

[2] Fr Ignacio Menéndez Reigada added, in *La Guerra Nacional Española ante la Moral y el Derecho* (Salamanca 1937), that the rising had been 'not only just but a duty'.

[3] The Bishop of Orihuela was ill, so his representative signed on his behalf. As one might have expected there is no truth in the tale that the Bishop of Oviedo was purposely run down in a motor-car to prevent him from signing the letter. The Archbishop of Tarragona, though refraining from ever commenting on the attitude of the Spanish Church in the Civil War, never made any public statement of his position. He never returned to Spain, however, and dying in exile in the Chartreuse Convent near Zurich had inscribed on his tomb the laconic epitaph reminiscent of that of Hildebrand: 'I die in exile for having too much loved my country.'

about persecution of Protestants),[1] nor was it true that death sentences were only administered after trial.[2] Despite this championship by their bishop, the Basque priests were accused before the Pope by the Spanish hierarchy of having acted as politicians and of carrying arms. The Basque clergy replied that no Basque priest had ever been affiliated *qua* priest to the Basque Nationalist party and that none, not even the corps of almoners, had carried arms.[3] But on August 28 the Vatican formally recognised the 'Burgos authorities' – as the British Foreign Office referred to them – as the official Government of Spain. A nuncio was despatched to the Castillian capital. Henceforward any Catholic who sided with the Republic or who even, like Maritain, preached that the Church should be neutral, became technically rebels against the Pope.

The pamphlet war nevertheless continued during the rest of the Spanish conflict, above all, in France. Mauriac continued his articles in favour of the Republic. Maurras replied in *L'Action Française* by proclaiming that the Church was the only real International. Bernanos published his *Les Grands Cimetières sous la Lune*, which gave so terrible an account of the Nationalist repression in Majorca. A right-wing writer replied with *Les Grands Chantiers au Soleil*. In Liège a prayer of the exiled Spanish priests to the Virgin of the Pilar appeared: 'To You, O Mary, Queen of Peace, we always return, we the faithful sons of Your best-loved Spain, now vilified, outraged, befouled by criminal Bolshevism, deprived by Jewish Marxism, and scorned by savage Communism. We pray You, tears in our eyes, to come to our help, to accord final triumph to the glorious armies of the Liberator and Reconqueror of Spain, the new Pelayo, the Caudillo! *Viva* Christ the King!'[4]

In America, the Basque priests relied chiefly upon Protestants for active championship. But polls of American Catholics suggested that only four out of ten Catholics were with the bishops. Opinion was nevertheless so cautious in America that even a project to bring certain Basque children there was dropped as a possible breach of neutrality.[5] In the meantime, in the Basque provinces themselves a campaign of persecution had started. 278 priests and 125 monks (including 22 Jesuits) suffered deprivation, imprisonment, deportation to other parts of Spain or, later (in the case of 16[6]) death.[7]

[1] GD, 236.   [2] *Le Clergé Basque*, 10.   [3] *Le Clergé Basque*, 33–8.
[4] Don Antonio Berjón, *La Prière des Exilés Espagnoles à la Vierge du Pilier* (Liège 1938).
[5] Taylor, 157.   [6] See below, page 484.   [7] *Le Clergé Basque*, 110–43.

57

The fall of the POUM – arrest and murder of Nin

During the last days before the fall of the Basque capital, the Republican Government had been equally preoccupied with the fall of the POUM. After the formation of Negrín's Government, all the skill and energy of the Communists had been concentrated upon the persecution of this sect. They were accused of Fascism and of conspiring with Franco.

The truth about this affair seems to have been that in April the Communist-controlled police in Madrid unearthed a genuine conspiracy by the Falange. One of the conspirators, named Castilla, was induced by threats to become an *agent provocateur*. Castilla prevailed upon another Falangist in the capital, Golfín, to prepare a fraudulent plan for a military rising by the Fifth Column. Golfín did this, and he, and his plan, were then apprehended. Next someone, probably Castilla, wrote a letter purporting to be from Nin to Franco on the back of Golfín's plan. At about the same time, another genuine Falangist agent, named José Roca, who kept a small bookshop in Gerona, was discovered by the Catalan Communists controlled by Ernö Gerö. Roca's task was to pass on messages to a Falangist named Dalmau, a *hotelier* in the same town, the Venice of Catalonia. One day, some time after the dissolution of the POUM, a well-dressed individual called at the bookshop, left some money for Roca and a message for Dalmau and asked if he could leave a suitcase in the shop for three days. Roca agreed to this request. Not long after, the police arrived to carry out a search. Naturally they came upon the suitcase which, when opened, was found to contain a pile of secret documents all sealed, oddly enough, with the stamp of the POUM military committee.

It was upon these documents, the letter from Nin to Franco and the suitcase found in Gerona, that the Communist case against the POUM rested. Of course, all were forgeries.[1]

[1] The above account derives from what Golfín and Roca told the POUM leaders when they met in prison. See Gorkin, 252–3 and 258–60. The *provocateur* Castilla was allowed to escape with his life and a certain amount of money to France. The chief Catalan police agent acting for Gerö, Victorio Sala, once a member of the POUM,

By mid-June the Communists judged their position strong enough to take final action. It is instructive to note that on June 12 Marshal Tukhachevsky and seven other senior Russian Generals were shot for 'intrigues with Germany'. A wave of arrests spread through the Russian administration and army throughout the rest of 1937 and all of 1938. It could hardly have been a surprise to Jesús Hernández when, on June 14, he was told by Colonel Ortega, the Communist Director-General of Security, that the NKVD chief in Spain, Orlov, had given orders for the arrest of all the leaders of the POUM.[1] Hernández went to Orlov, who insisted that the Cabinet could know nothing of the matter, since the Minister of the Interior, Zugazagoitia, and others, were friends of those detained. There was certain proof, Orlov added, of the POUM's involvement in a Fascist spy-ring. Hernández went to Díaz, who was furious. Together, they went to the Communist party headquarters, where a violent quarrel occurred. Díaz and Hernández denounced the foreign 'advisers'. Codovilla suggested smoothly that excess of work was making Díaz ill. Why did he not take a holiday for a while? In Barcelona meanwhile, on the orders of Antonov-Ovsëenko, the Russian Consul General, the POUM headquarters at the Hotel Falcón was closed. It was immediately, and conveniently, turned into a prison. The POUM itself was declared illegal, and 40 members of its central committee arrested. Andrés Nin was taken off separately, but his friends all found themselves in an underground dungeon in Madrid. All members or associates of the POUM went in fear of arrest, since the Stalinist habit of visiting the alleged crimes of the leaders upon all possible followers was well known. The Communist newspapers daily screamed accusations against those whom their party had arrested but did not bring to trial. They announced that all sorts of evidence had been discovered giving irrefutable proof of the POUM's guilt. And a rumour spread that Andrés Nin had been murdered in prison.

Negrín sent for Hernández. He asked Nin's whereabouts. Hernández said that he knew nothing. Negrín complained that the

---

later broke with the Communists, whom he has since accused of atrocious crimes. All these documents were published in an anti-POUM tract, *Espionaje en España*, written by 'Marc Reisser' (a pseudonym for the Comintern propaganda department). The Communist point of view can also be seen in George Soria, *Trotskyism in the Service of Franco*.

[1] For all the following, see Hernández, 124–6. An account of events from the POUM side is given in Gorkin.

Russians were behaving as if Barcelona were their own country. What would happen in the Cabinet that afternoon when Nin's disappearance would inevitably be raised? Hernández promised to investigate the affair. But Codovilla told him that Nin was being interrogated. Togliatti said that nothing was known of Nin at the Soviet Embassy. The Cabinet meeting followed. At the door, journalists asked news of Nin. Inside, Zugazagoitia demanded if his jurisdiction as Minister of the Interior was to be limited by Soviet technicians. Prieto, Irujo and Giner de los Ríos supported this protest. Hernández and Uribe replied that they knew nothing of Nin. No one believed them, not realising that there could be secrets even among Communists. Negrín then suspended the discussion until all the facts were known.

Had they been able to purchase and transport arms from American, British and French manufacturers, the Socialist and Republican members of the Spanish Government might have cut themselves loose at this point from Stalin. But the strict non-intervention of the British, French and American Governments meant that the alliance of the Republic and the USSR could not be broken.

A widespread campaign in Spain and abroad now began asking 'Where is Nin?' Negrín begged the Communist party to end the discreditable affair. The Spanish Communists, who were in no better position to answer these questions than their interrogators, replied that Nin was no doubt in Berlin or Salamanca. In fact, he was in Orlov's prison in the dilapidated ex-cathedral city of Alcalá de Henares, Cervantes' birthplace and Azaña's, for centuries the centre of Spanish learning. He was there undergoing the customary Soviet interrogation of suspected deviationists. His resistance to these methods was apparently amazing. He refused to sign any documents admitting his guilt and that of his friends. Orlov was at his wits' end. What should he do? His own position as a prosecutor loyal to Stalin was at stake. He himself went in deadly fear of Yezhov, the chief of the NKVD who had once been his protector.[1] Eventually, Vittorio Vidali (Carlos Contreras) suggested that a 'Nazi' attack to liberate Nin should be simulated. So, one dark night, ten German members of the International Brigade assaulted the house in Alcalá where Nin was held. Ostentatiously, they

---

[1] So he himself says in his own memoirs which, however, make no reference whatever to Nin or the POUM. It is possible that the memoirs are a forgery. See below, page 503 fn.

spoke German during the pretended attack, and left behind some German train tickets. Nin was taken away in a closed van and murdered. His refusal to admit his guilt saved the lives of his friends. Stalin and Yezhov may have planned a staged trial in Spain on the model of the Moscow trials, with a full paraphernalia of confessions; if so they were thwarted.[1]

But now there disappeared all those Russian leaders who had arrived in the dangerous and exciting days of September and October 1936. Antonov-Ovsëenko, Stashevsky, Berzin, Kol'tsov – even Gaikins, the *Chargé*, all vanish not only from Spain but also from history. Many other Russians who had been in Spain under false names also left. What terrible apprehensions must have been theirs as they travelled back across the Mediterranean, and by train across the Ukraine! How much more terrible must have been the reality of what awaited them! Why were they killed? At least partly because they objected to the policy followed by Stalin towards the Spaniards with whom they had worked so much.[2]

[1] The elimination of the POUM was accompanied by the arrest of the Generals who had been associated with Largo Caballero: Asensio, Martínez Monje, Martínez Cabrera.

[2] Kol'tsov was not shot till the very end of the purges, in late 1938. Stashevsky was shot because of his impolitic criticisms of the NEVD in Spain – apparently returning to Moscow in June 1937 (evidence of a former Soviet officer in the possession of Mr John Erickson of St Andrew's University).

58

Germany and Italy return to non-intervention – Anglo-German
rapprochement *– the* Leipzig *incident – Negrín goes to Paris –*
Eden and Delbos patch up non-intervention – Hitler at Wurzburg

By now, Eden and Delbos had procured the return of Italy
and Germany to non-intervention and to naval patrol.
The two Spanish contestants would be formally asked to refrain from attacking foreign warships and to name safety-zones for
refuelling patrol ships. Breaches of this agreement would be examined by all four parties to the naval patrol. Self-defence (not
retaliation) would be permitted to ships attacked. Delay would
enable each country to resume their freedom of action. The
Spanish Republic, however, condemned the whole control system
for treating them on the same level as the Nationalists, and demanded the freedom to carry out 'legitimate acts of war', such as
air attacks in Palma, without 'Almería incidents'. Russia, fearing
a general line-up against her, announced that patrol should be a
matter for all powers on the Non-Intervention Committee. Ciano,
suddenly suspecting a German *rapprochement* with England, complained to Berlin (as did Ribbentrop himself in London) at being
told, at the last minute, of a projected visit by Neurath to Britain.[1]
Mussolini boasted to Hassell on the 12th that England still under-
estimated him. In any war between him and England, the leopard
(Italy) might be defeated in the end but the lion (England) would
be severely wounded in the process.

Italy now increasingly dropped her reticence with regard to her
intervention in Spain. Open casualty lists and embarkation notices
began to be published in Rome. *Popolo d'Italia* announced on
June 4 that 'one day the veil will be lifted on events in Spain. The
world will then see in the most clear way that the legionaries of
Fascism have written a new page of history and glory'. But in Germany it was a crime to mention the existence of German troops
in Spain. If those who had served in Spain had spoken of their

---

[1] *GD*, 339.

experience, it would have been regarded as a very serious matter indeed.

No sooner had the Germans, with the Italians, agreed to return to non-intervention, than the captain of the German patrol cruiser *Leipzig* reported that, on June 15, three torpedoes had been fired at his ship off Oran. They did not register hits. Then, on June 18, a new submarine attack occurred. The captain of the *Leipzig* alleged that this torpedo had either glanced the ship's side or that the cruiser had come into contact with part of the submarine. This news reached Hitler at a bad moment. He had just returned from a memorial service to the sailors, now numbered at 32, who had been killed in the *Deutschland*. He demanded first that Neurath cancel his proposed visit to London; secondly, he wanted a demonstration of protest by the fleets of all the naval patrol powers.[1] The Republic denied responsibility for the attack on the *Leipzig*. Prieto formally offered to give Eden all facilities for an enquiry into the incident. Eden, who had tended to believe Germany's story over the *Deutschland*, seemed to accept Prieto's denial and his offer. But Germany and Italy refused an enquiry. Eden, reported Azcárate to Valencia, 'could not hide his shame and disgust at Germany's behaviour'.[2] Nevertheless, nothing could make the Non-Intervention Committee agree what to do. Germany and Italy formally withdrew from the naval patrol, though remaining in the committee.

Negrín and Giral, his Foreign Minister, now visited Paris. Blum had recently been defeated, and had been succeeded as Premier by Chautemps, the Radical Socialist. Blum was Vice-Premier and Delbos still at the Foreign Ministry. The two Spaniards set out to try and persuade this Government to end non-intervention. For Soviet aid to the Republicans had recently been considerably reduced: firstly because of the increasingly effective Nationalist blockade in the Mediterranean, secondly because of the continued closing of the French frontier (which prevented shipment *via* France) and thirdly, from the start of July, be-

---

[1] *GD*, 366.

[2] Azcárate, 80. In a foreign affairs debate in the House of Commons on June 25, Chamberlain, making his first speech as Prime Minister, described Germany's behaviour over the *Leipzig* as 'showing a degree of restraint that we ought to recognise'. On non-intervention he said: 'Each side is being deprived of supplies of material of which it feels itself in urgent need.' This was not true. The Nationalists hardly felt deprived of material. One of his supporters, Sir A. Southby, followed with the remark: 'I think Germany is sincere in her desire for peace' (*Parliamentary Debates*, Vol 325 col 1586), a statement which inspired Mr Lloyd George almost to apoplexy.

cause of the war between China and Japan, in which Stalin decided to aid the ill-equipped armies of the former. The idea that, by buying arms from the democracies, he could detach himself somewhat from Russia and from the Communists probably played its part in Negrín's mind.

The Republican position had been rendered worse still by the Portuguese abandonment of all control, until the naval patrol should be restored. Britain and France, after Germany and Italy had left the naval patrol, offered to carry out all of it themselves, with neutral observers on board their ships. Grandi and Ribbentrop alleged that this would be a very partial patrol. They proposed instead that while land control should be maintained, belligerent rights, including the rights of search on the high seas, should be granted to both Spanish parties as a substitute for naval patrol. This proposal would certainly have favoured the Nationalists. So far from its being acceptable to the French, Chautemps and Delbos were considering following Portugal's example and abolishing all frontier control. Negrín and Giral urged this as second-best to a total end to non-intervention. But the French reliance on the British in all matters of foreign policy prevented even this. All the French Ministers realised that any breach with Britain on the subject of opening the frontier would merely help Italy. The tragic actor in the drama remained Léon Blum. '*Je n'en vis plus,*' he would murmur to his friends in the Second International such as Nenni or de Brouckère.[1] He felt remorse for the policy which he had undertaken to support for the rest of his life. The Nationalists meantime sent a note to all foreign powers, threatening that those countries (England and France, for example) who did not agree to grant belligerent rights 'should not be surprised' if Spain were henceforward economically closed to them.

The British and French Governments were, in fact, once more laboriously patching up the elaborate fabric of non-intervention. The control system, despite the German and Italian abandonment of naval patrol, was judged to be working adequately. But the Non-Intervention Board estimated that 42 ships escaped inspection between its inception in April and the end of July. Nor was the air route covered. The control board could not prevent the despatch of military supplies in ships flying a Spanish or a non-European flag. In fact, German, Italian and Russian material continued to flow into Spain. The Spanish Nationalist debt to Ger-

[1] Nenni, 83.

many, for instance, had now attained 150 million reichsmarks. For what purpose? Brutally, and certainly simplifying the question, Hitler announced in a speech at Wurzburg on June 27 that he supported Franco to gain possession of Spanish iron ore.[1]

[1] In 1937 Germany was to import 1,620,000 tons of iron from Spain, 956,000 tons of pyrites, 2,000 tons of other minerals. In the single month of December, she took 265,000 tons of iron and 550,000 of pyrites. The monthly average of German imports from Spain in late 1937 was to be 10,000,000 reichsmarks. Meanwhile, on June 21, the second (Socialist) and third (Communist) International had one of their periodic meetings, this time at Annemasse near Geneva. Louis de Brouckère and Fritz Adler represented the former, and Marcel Cachin, Luigi Longo, Franz Dahlem, Pedro Checa, and Florimond Bonte the latter. They demanded the end of non-intervention but issued no reproof to the French Socialists (and indeed Communists) who continued to support a Government which was one of the mainstays of that policy.

59

*The battle of Brunete – the Republican Army – the XVth Inter-
national Brigade – the offensive – the offensive halted – death of
Nathan – deadlock in London – Plymouth's compromise control plan
– the German-Spanish economic agreements – the Nationalist counter-
offensive at Brunete – end of the battle – Republican losses – insubordination in the International Brigade*

After the final capture of the Basque provinces, General
Franco paused before falling upon Santander, the next
Republican centre in the north. The Republican Army
now launched its long-discussed offensive. This, of course, turned
out to be the Communist choice of Brunete. Two army corps had
been gathered, under the supreme command of Miaja. These
were the Vth Army Corps under the Communist Modesto, and
the XVIIIth Army Corps, under the Republican regular, Colonel
Jurado. The former comprised Lister's 11th Division, El Campesino's 46th Division and Walter's 35th Division. The last-named
included the XIth International Brigade. Jurado's corps included
Gal with the 15th Division (the XIIIth and XVth International
Brigades). In reserve, Kléber returned from Valencia to command
the 45th Division and the ex-musician Durán was in command of
the 69th Division. This army numbered 50,000 in all. It was supported by 150 aircraft, 128 tanks, and 136 pieces of artillery. The
aim of the offensive was to advance towards the stagnant village of
Brunete from the north of the El Escorial-Madrid road so as to cut
off all the besiegers of the capital from the west.[1]

The XVth International Brigade, still led by the Croat Communist Čopíc, was used in this battle as a shock force. It was composed of six battalions, grouped in two regiments, one commanded
by George Nathan, the other by Major 'Chapaiev', a Hungarian
who had taken this then sought-after pseudonym. Nathan had
underneath him the British, the Abraham Lincoln and the George

[1] Rojo *¡Alert a Los Pueblos!*, 104; Aznar, 435; López Muñiz. In writing of this battle I
have drawn on the memories of Mr Malcolm Dunbar, Mr Giles Romilly, Mr George
Aitken and Mr Miles Tomalin, who fought here with the British Battalion.

Washington Battalions, and Chapaiev the Franco-Belge and Dimitrov Battalions, together with one Spanish battalion. Fred Copeman now commanded the British Battalion. He was a powerful ex-sailor who had led the so-called naval mutiny at Invergordon on HMS *Resolution*.[1] Merriman led the Lincoln Battalion and Oliver Law, a negro, the Washington Battalion.[2]

The Nationalists were surprised by the offensive of Brunete, though it had been discussed in the cafés of the Republic for

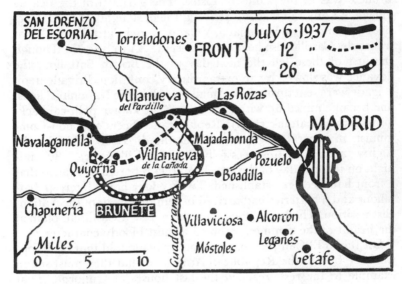

MAP 24. THE BATTLE OF BRUNETE

three months. On the line which was to bear the brunt of the attack there were certain depleted elements of the 71st Division, mainly Falangists, and about 1,000 Moroccans. After being exhorted on the eve of the attack by Prieto and La Pasionaria, the 11th Republican Division under Lister struck at dawn on July 6, after an artillery and aerial attack. Lister's method resembled that of

---

[1] According to his own account, Copeman did not become a Communist till he had left Spain. He was, nevertheless, so closely associated with the party that this really made no difference. The fact that the leader of the British Battalion was formally not a Communist suited the Communist leaders, who could thus deny that the International Brigades was a branch of the Comintern.

[2] The 'English Chapaiev' (Cunningham) who earlier had been wounded, was now on the brigade staff.

the Nationalists at Bilbao. Within a few hours he had advanced ten kilometres and surrounded Brunete. Immediately, the Nationalists sent reinforcements[1] to the broken front. Varela was named the commander, with his headquarters at that old battlefield of the preceding winter, Boadilla. Asensio's 12th Division, Barrón's 13th, and Sáenz de Buruaga's 150th were transferred from Guadalajara. The Condor Legion and heavy artillery were despatched from the north.[2] These fresh reinforcements arrived at midday. By then, Brunete was in the hands of Lister. The garrison of the nearby village of Quijorna was still resisting the onslaughts of El Campesino. Villanueva de la Cañada, Villanueva del Pardillo and Villafranca del Castillo also held out against the XVth Brigade. Though the first of these fell the next day to the British Battalion, the advance was slowed by an extraordinary confusion. Brigade upon brigade were sent through the small breach in the Nationalist lines, and became mixed up with each other. The known political background to the attack caused Republican officers and non-Communists in general to grumble about the direction of the battle. Eighty tanks were unsuccessfully flung at Villafranca.[3] By midnight on the first day of the attack, Varela reported to Franco that a front had been re-established. Twenty-four hours later, 31 battalions and 9 batteries had arrived in reinforcement of the Nationalist position. The battle, fought on the parched Castillian plain at the height of the summer, assumed a most bloody character.[4]

On July 8 El Campesino, egged on by being told that his troops were the best in the Republican Army and that they must set an example to the rest, reached the last houses of Quijorna. That village fell the next day. Villanueva del Pardillo and Villafranca del Castillo fell in the early morning of July 11. But Boadilla, constantly attacked, was held by Asensio. By July 13 the offensive of Brunete was over. Henceforward the Republicans would be attempting to defend the positions which they had won. On July 15, after further fierce fighting around Boadilla, orders were given for trenches to be dug. The Republic had gained a pocket of land about twelve kilometres deep by fifteen wide. Lister was three kilometres south of Brunete on the road to Navalcarnero. In the British Battalion Copeman had been wounded and his place was

---

[1] Among those sent there could not be 'General' O'Duffy's Irishmen since, in accordance with their original six months' engagement, these were withdrawn in May. Nine remained to fight with the Legion in other battles.

[2] Galland, 27.   [3] Miksche, 38.

[4] Aznar, 443; López Muñiz, 171.

briefly taken by Joe Hinks. His name seemed oddly homely to be commanding a battalion among those yellow hills. At the end of this battle the gallant English Major George Nathan was killed. Earlier that day he had personally rallied a battalion of fleeing Spaniards with his gold-tipped swagger-stick in hand. He was mortally wounded by a bomb. In his last moments he ordered those around him to sing him out of life. At nightfall he was buried in a rough coffin beneath the olive trees near the River Guadarrama. A funeral oration was pronounced by the Brigade Commissar, George Aitken. Gal and Jock Cunningham, two tough men who had been jealous of Nathan, stood listening with tears running down their cheeks.

There was now three days' pause in the battle of Brunete. Back in London, the deadlock in the Non-Intervention Committee continued complete. On July 9 the Dutch Ambassador proposed that Britain should attempt to reconcile the opposing points of view. After consulting the Cabinet, Plymouth accepted the task. On July 14 he presented to the Committee a British 'compromise plan for control of non-intervention'. Naval patrol would be replaced by observers at Spanish ports. There would also be observers on ships. On land, the control system would be restored. Belligerent rights at sea should be granted when 'substantial progress' had been made in withdrawal of volunteers. Germany accepted the plan 'as a basis for discussion'. Delbos, not having been consulted, was angry. Britain, he complained, was now mid-way between France and Italy, instead of co-operating with France.[1] Azaña emerged from his lonely eminence at Montserrat to denounce the plan as helping Franco. Belligerent rights could only favour the Nationalists and a partial withdrawal of volunteers would enable Franco to dispense with certain inefficient Italians, while the Republic would have to give up invaluable members of the International Brigade. Discussion of the plan had not begun, however, before the Nationalists launched a counter-attack at Brunete.

On July 18[2] Sáenz de Buruaga attacked on the left, Asensio on

---

[1] *USD*, Vol 1 1937 360. This remark was made at a lunch at which the new British Ambassador in Paris, Phipps, and Bullitt were present.

[2] On the 18th Julian Bell, son of Clive Bell and nephew of Virginia Woolf, was killed, aged 29, by a bomb when driving an ambulance for the British Medical Unit. He had only been in Spain a month. His motives for going to Spain seem to have been simply a general sympathy for the Republic, but also 'the usefulness of war experience in the future and the prestige one would gain in literature and – even more – Left politics.' (Bell, 176.)

the right, and Barrón towards Brunete itself, in the centre. Fighting was very violent. The battle continued in much the same way between July 19 and 22. During these days, two hills on either side of the front were occupied by Sáenz de Buruaga and Asensio.

In London, meantime, Count Grandi succeeded in beginning the interment of the new British control plan. He demanded that the points in it be discussed in numerical order. Thus belligerent rights which, by hasty drafting, had been placed prior to volunteers, should be discussed first. Maisky insisted on discussing volunteers first. Deadlock thus returned to the Locarno Room in the Foreign Office. On the 26th, Britain asked for other Governments' views in writing on its plan. Léger in Paris complained that the British 'were prepared to accept anything rather than have a showdown'.[1] A final humiliation occurred when Grandi produced a questionnaire which, he said, made the British questions clearer than the British document itself had done. This, incredibly, was accepted by Plymouth.[2]

Back in Castile on July 24, Asensio and Sáenz de Buruaga succeeded at last in breaking the lines of the Republic on its two flanks. Barrón broke through in the centre to recapture all of Brunete, save its cemetery, where Lister maintained himself until the morning of the 25th. Then he retreated. Varela wished to pursue the Republicans onwards to Madrid. But Franco restrained him, pointing to the prior need of taking Santander.[3] The Republic retained Quijorna, Villanueva de la Cañada and Villanueva del Pardillo, but at a cost of an estimated 25,000 deaths and about 100 aircraft. The Nationalists lost 23 aircraft, and about 10,000 men.[4]

The battle may be regarded as similar to that of Jarama, Guadalajara or the Corunna Road, in reverse. Both sides claimed a victory. The attackers – in this case, the Republicans – gained an area of five kilometres deep along a front of fifteen kilometres. But they failed to attain their objectives. In fact, the Republican Army lost so much valuable equipment and so many veteran soldiers that the battle of Brunete should properly be regarded as a defeat for them. It was thus also a setback to the Communists who had sponsored it.

The losses of the International Brigades were very heavy at Brunete. The Lincoln and Washington Battalions lost so many

[1] *USD*, 1937 Vol 1 366.   [2] *Loc. cit.*
[3] Kindelán, 99.   [4] Aznar, 461. Kindelán, 100.

men that they had to be merged into one.[1] Among the Americans who fell were Oliver Law, the negro commander of the Lincoln Battalion, and a particularly high number of Jewish members of the American battalions. During the campaign there was insubordination among the brigades. Captain Alocca, in command of the brigades' cavalry, deserted in the face of the enemy and drove to the French frontier. Returning later to Madrid, he was shot for cowardice. The British Battalion, which had been reduced to about 80 men, also grumbled about returning to the battle. Commissar Aitken and Klaus (the Chief of Staff, who had taken over the command of the brigade when Čopic was wounded) went to expostulate both to Gal and to Jurado, the corps commander. They were finally successful.[2] But the XIIIth Brigade, composed mainly of Poles and Slavs, absolutely refused to return to the battle. Its commander, Colonel Kriegger, former Italian Communist Deputy for Trieste, sought to re-establish himself by brandishing his revolver. Pointing this weapon at one of the mutineers, he ordered obedience. 'No,' answered the other. 'Think well of what you are doing,' returned the Colonel. 'I have.' 'For the last time!' 'No,' answered the man. The Colonel shot him dead. The men became furious and Kriegger narrowly himself escaped death. The mutineers were only subdued after the arrival of some *Asaltos* with tanks. The Brigade thereafter had to be thoroughly reorganised and 're-educated'.[3]

Military theorists were later at pains to point out the tactical significance of the battle of Brunete for the use of the tank. The Czech Miksche, for example, who commanded a group of batteries on the Republican side, later reflected, in his *Blitzkrieg*, that the Republican tanks were unsuccessful since they were used spread out in support of infantry, in accord with French theories; but Varela, on the insistence of the German von Thoma, concentrated his tanks to find a tactical thrust-point (*schwerpunkt*) and so gained the day.[4]

During these days, the Germans, partly because of the crisis at the front, succeeded in eliciting from the Nationalists certain economic concessions. In a document signed by Jordana and Faupel on July 12 the Spaniards promised that they would conclude with Germany their first general trade agreement, would

---

[1] Wintringham, 260.   [2] Mr Aitken's evidence.   [3] Lizón Gadea, 35–6.
[4] This controversy over the use of tanks can be traced back to their very first operational use, in the battle of Cambrai on the Western Front in 1917.

tell Germany of any economic negotiation with any other country, and give most-favoured nation treatment to Germany.[1] This was supplemented by a declaration, on July 15, that both countries would help each other as much as possible in the exchange of raw materials, food and manufactured goods.[2] On the 16th, Spain agreed to pay its debts for war material in reichsmarks, with 4% annual interest. As guarantee of the debt, raw materials would be sent to Germany. And Germany would participate in Spanish reconstruction and redevelopment.[3]

These good relations were a contrast with those between the Nationalists and the Italians. The Italian commanders as ever wanted to use their troops in a decisive action where they could win 'a great triumph'. Danzi, the Italian Fascist director in Spain, had allegedly 240,000 pesetas a month to spend on propaganda for the legionaries. But, said Faupel, everyone really knew that, for example, the battle of Bilbao was decided by German fliers and anti-aircraft batteries, not by the Italian forces on the ground. And Franco himself had recently described the whole history of Italian troops in Spain as a 'tragedy'.[4]

[1] GD, 413.   [2] Ibid., 417.   [3] Ibid., 421.   [4] Ibid., 410.

60

Non-Intervention in decline – start of Italian submarine campaign –
the Santander campaign – the Basques of Santoña – infamy of
the Italians

T he battle of Brunete ended at a moment when the great
European powers had almost abandoned non-intervention. In public, the Germans and Italians might both declare that they wanted simultaneously to grant belligerent rights
and start the withdrawal of volunteers: in private, Ciano was complaining to Hassell that the Italians had been ready for action for
some time in Spain but were not being used. The Soviet Union
meantime opposed even the discussion of belligerent rights until
after volunteers had been withdrawn. Delbos was, at this time,
thinking of proposing mediation in Spain by Roosevelt and the
Pope. But nevertheless he had arranged that the French Army
was ready to attack Sardinia and Spanish Morocco if there were
any more Italian aid. France, he said, could not allow Italy to
control Spain. Brave words! But the main aim of British diplomacy,
under the new Prime Minister, Neville Chamberlain, was to
secure friendship with Italy.

Under Chamberlain the British Government were to seek the
appeasement of Hitler and Mussolini more vigorously than they
had done under Baldwin. The change of emphasis (though not of
policy) was seen in the olive branch sent in the form of a private
letter suggesting 'talks' from Chamberlain to Mussolini on July 29.[1]
Spain, for Chamberlain, was a troublesome complication which
should, if possible, be forgotten. This now briefly seemed possible.
Even Eden told Delbos that he hoped Franco would win, since
he thought he could reach agreement on an eventual German
and Italian withdrawal.[2] On August 6 Maisky asked pointblank in
the Non-Intervention Committee if Germany and Italy would

---

[1] Ciano, *Diplomatic Papers*, 132. This letter was written without consultation with
Eden at the Foreign Office. (Churchill, *Gathering Storm*, 189.)

[2] *USD*, 1937 Vol 1 369. This was no doubt a hasty aside by Eden, for the evidence is
that the Foreign Secretary was throughout perplexed as to who to champion in the
Civil War.

agree to the withdrawal of all volunteers on the two sides in Spain. He received a generally vague answer. During the rest of August there was only one non-intervention meeting. This was on the 27th, when it was concluded that the naval patrol did not justify its expense and that, therefore, the British idea for observers at ports should be substituted for it.

However, there were new alarms from Spain. Exaggerated rumours of the extent of Soviet aid to the Republic caused Franco to send his brother Nicolás to Rome and to ask the Italian fleet to strike against Russian and other vessels in the Mediterranean.[1] Mussolini agreed. He would not use surface vessels, but submarines, 'which would raise a Spanish flag if they had to surface'.[2] As a result, due partly to bad management, partly to the knowledge that Russian material was transported under other flags, many British, French and other neutral ships, as well as Spanish vessels, were attacked in the Mediterranean by Italian submarines and by Italian aircraft operating from Majorca. A British, a French and an Italian merchant ship were bombed on August 6 near Algiers. On August 7 a Greek ship was bombed. On the 11th, the 13th, and the 15th, ships of the Republic were torpedoed. On the 12th a Danish cargo boat was sunk. The Foreign Office in London became perturbed once again over Spain.

These developments coincided with the start of the Nationalist offensive against Santander. The Army of the North was still led by Dávila. The Italians under General Bastico were grouped as the Littorio Division, the Black Flames and the March 23 Division. There were 6 Navarrese brigades under Solchaga. To these were added 30 battalions of Castillian volunteers, anxious to win back Castille's only port. The Army of the North amounted to 106 battalions in all. It was supported by 63 batteries and the Condor Legion. Before this campaign, Franco transferred his headquarters from Salamanca to Burgos.[3]

The XVth Republican Army Corps of 3 divisions, under General Gamir Ulíbarri, was the nucleus of the defence of Santander. To this were added a division each of Basques and Asturians. This force was supported by some 50 batteries, 33 fighters and bombers and 11 reconnaisance aircraft. The Republican army numbered about 50,000.[4] However, the bare figures give an inaccurate idea of the disproportion of the forces. Except for 18

[1] GD, 432.   [2] This visit occurred on August 4. Ibid., 433.
[3] Aznar, 475.   [4] Ibid., 466.

Russian fighters, Santander's aircraft were all slow and old. The Nationalists' air support included the latest German models which were being used to test their efficiency; the same was true of the artillery.

The campaign began on August 14. The battle lines lay across the Cantabrian range, whose highest points were in the hands of the Republic. The field of war was thus, throughout the campaign, of splendid and rugged beauty. The Republicans were over-

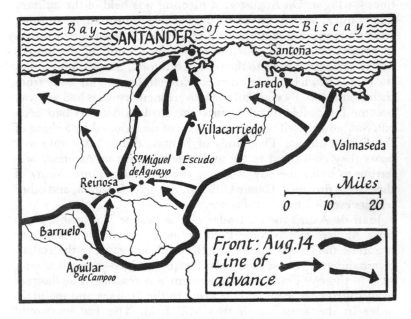

MAP 25. THE SANTANDER CAMPAIGN

whelmed by the aerial bombardment. On the very first day of the attack, the front in the south was broken. The Navarrese brigades rolled up the foothills of the Cantabrians. Reinosa, with its armament factory, was captured on August 16. Next, backed by their own great weight of artillery, tanks and aircraft, the Italian Black Arrows broke the front by the sea on August 18. The March 23 Division, in the centre, captured the critical pass of Escudo. Henceforward there was no real front. The army of Santander retreated steadily before the overwhelming power of their adversary. The Basques fought better for Santander than the Santanderinos had for Bilbao, but even they could not maintain their hold.[1] In Santander itself, all industry and commerce was closed down so that workers could be free to build fortifications. Once again a Spanish city became filled with the cattle, the domestic animals and the few personal belongings of peasants flying from the battle raging round their homes. The Basque *Emigré* Government, as it had now become, once again occupied itself with evacuation. Many of the Basques refused to fight any more and made preparations for flight. On August 22 a meeting was held of the military and political leaders, including the Basques. The soldiers, as usual, were more gloomy than the civilians. From Valencia came orders to retreat to Asturias. But the next day the bulk of the Basque armed forces withdrew to the port of Santoña, thirty kilometres to the east. They had no desire to continue to fight so far away from their homeland. By nightfall the Government's orders had anyway become impossible to fulfil, since the road to Asturias had been cut. Santander itself became the scene of riots caused by a rising of the Fifth Column. Thousands of Santanderinos leapt into any boats they could find to try and reach France or Asturias, preferring to brave the Bay of Biscay than to risk capture. Many of these were drowned. Gamir Ulíbarri, Aguirre, Leizaola, and other leaders escaped by air to France.

Juan de Axuriaguerra, leader of the Basque Nationalist party since Aguirre had become Premier, now went from Santoña to negotiate the Basque surrender. He went, however, to the Italian commander, in whose hands the Basques judged themselves safer than in those of Franco. An agreement was reached. The Basques would surrender, deliver their arms to the Italians and maintain order in the areas which they still held. The Italians would guarantee the lives of all Basque fighters. The Basques would not be forced to take further part in the war on the Nationalist side. All Basque politicians and civil servants would be free to go abroad. The Italians also gave an assurance that the Basque people would not be persecuted. In the meantime, Dávila and his army entered Santander. The Italians entered Santoña and the Italian Colonel Fagosi took over the civil administration. The Basques now awaited the fulfilment of the Italian part of the Armistice. The British vessels *Bobie* and *Seven Seas Spray* were in Santoña harbour ready to carry refugees to France. But no instructions came to begin the

---

[1] Aguirre had wanted to move all the Basque forces to the Catalan front, but the idea had been rejected in Valencia. (Aguirre, 59 fl.)

transportation. On August 27 the commander of the *Bobie*, a French captain named Georges Dupuy and Costa e Silva, a Latin American non-intervention observer on the *Seven Seas Spray*, received permission to embark all those in possession of a Basque passport. The embarkation therefore began. But at ten in the morning, Italian soldiers surrounded the ships and the waiting Basques with machine guns. Colonel Fagosi informed Dupuy and Silva of Franco's orders that no one was to leave Santoña, foreign or Basque. All the Basques already on board the two ships were ordered to disembark. The ships were then searched by five Falangists. At dawn the next day, August 28, Dupuy saw those who had so briefly been his passengers being marched as prisoners along the road towards Santander. An Italian Colonel, Farina, openly expressed his disgust at his superior's apparent renegation on his word of honour. The ships of hope then raised anchor, certain Basques hiding in the machinery. Those left behind were treated simply as prisoners of the Nationalists. Summary trials and executions followed.[1]

Mussolini telegraphed his congratulations to the Italian commanders. The text of this document and the names of its addressees were published in the Italian papers on August 27. Ciano instructed Bastico to secure 'guns and flags captured from the Basques'. He recorded in his diary 'I envy the French their Invalides and the Germans their Military Museum. A flag taken from the enemy,' added this fellow-countryman of Leonardo, 'is worth more than any picture.' The next day he wrote: 'This is the moment to terrorise the enemy. I have given orders for the aircraft to bomb Valencia.'[2]

The Germans in Spain, meantime, were quarrelling among themselves. General Sperrle, commander of the Condor Legion, and Faupel, the Ambassador, hated each other. Sperrle even refused to see Faupel when he called to see him at San Sebastián. Sperrle also publicly criticised the monopoly held by HISMA, so encouraging the Spaniards to criticise it too. And Franco now applied, through Sperrle, to have Faupel replaced, partly because of his relations with the Falange, but chiefly because of his heavy-handed arrogance.[3]

---

[1] Steer, 388-90. This account is confirmed by Señor Jesús María de Leizaola.
[2] Ciano, *Diaries 1937-8*, 5.
[3] *GD*, 434. This recurred in mid-August. Sperrle was himself also shortly recalled, being succeeded in command of the Condor Legion by General Volkmann.

61

General Franco received the news of the capture of Santander while attending to the start of another Republican diversionary offensive, this time on the Aragón front. This was undertaken by the Catalan Army – now renamed the Army of the East – commanded by General Pozas; Colonel Cordón, a Communist regular officer, was his Chief of Staff. Under him were General Kléber with the 45th Division, Colonel Trueba with the 27th, and the Communist Major Modesto's formidable Vth Army Corps, comprising the 11th, 46th and 35th Divisions of Lister, El Campesino and Walter. These had been transferred from the Brunete front. Walter's Division included four International Brigades (not the XIVth, because of his quarrel with its commander, Colonel Dumont). While the Croat Ćopić remained leader of the XVth Brigade, the Chief of Staff was Robert Merriman. Steve Nelson, a tough but engaging shipyard worker from Philadelphia, was Brigade Commissar, in succession to Aitken who had returned home. These appointments signified a period of American predominance in the XVth Brigade. There was even some American resentment when the post of Chief of Operations in the Brigade went to Malcolm Dunbar, an elegant and efficient young Englishman who three years before had been leader of an advanced aesthetic set at Trinity College, Cambridge. The American Lincoln-Washington Battalion was led by an engineer from Wisconsin, Hans Amlie, once of the IRA. The British Battalion was now led by Peter Daley, an Irish Communist. The leading British survivors of Brunete, such as the commander Copeman, the Commissar, Tapsell, and the Chief of Staff, Cunningham, returned to England.[1] The XVth Brigade had recently been enlarged by the addition of the Mackenzie-Papineau Battalion, formed from Canadians who had previously been with the Americans. This was named after the two Canadian leaders of the revolt of 1837 against Britain. Less than a third of the battalion were in fact Canadians, the remainder being American. The first commander was the efficient Captain Thompson, the Commissar Joe Dallet.[2] Both were Americans.

Opposing this array was General Ponte, in charge at Saragossa, with General Urrutia at Huesca and General Muñoz Castellanos at Teruel. A mobile column commanded by Colonel Galerna also assisted with the Nationalist defence. The front was not continuous, since only strategic heights were fortified.

On August 24 the Republican attack began at eight points, without aerial or artillery preparation. Three attacks were made north of Saragossa, two between Belchite and Saragossa, and three to the south. The two villages of Quinto and Codo, north of Belchite, were the first to fall. The Ebro was crossed near Fuentes del Ebro, and Mediana fell on August 26. The XVth International Brigade played a major part in these battles. The British Battalion's commander, Daley, died of wounds received here, being succeeded by another Irishman, Paddy O'Daire. Both the commander and Commissar of the Mackenzie-Papineau Battalion were also killed. The brigade Commissar, Nelson, was wounded, along with Amlie, commander of the Lincoln Battalion. The former was succeeded by Leonard Lamb, a student, the latter by a tough American trade unionist, Doran. Belchite, meantime, held out.[3]

This small, well-fortified town had an extraordinary fascination for the Republic, whose troops had been watching it for months. The siege of Belchite, now surrounded, continued, and took up the vitality of the attackers, as well as their time. Inside Belchite, the defenders' water supply was cut off. They could

---

[1] These three returned to England with a specific purpose in mind – to discuss the nature of Communist control over the British Battalion. A quarrel ensued at a meeting of the Central Committee of the Communist party, at which Cunningham had to defend himself against insinuations of Fascism. Copeman and Tapsell returned to Spain in the autumn, but Cunningham shortly afterwards left the party.

[2] First husband of Mrs Robert Oppenheimer. Both he and Steve Nelson played a subterranean *rôle* in the Oppenheimer hearing in 1954. Dallet was the son of rich parents and had become a longshoreman to 'throttle the evidence of his earlier sheltered life'.

[3] Aznar, 504. For this battle I have once again been assisted by survivors, notably Mr Malcolm Dunbar.

hardly have felt better for the knowledge that they were demon-
strating the use of 'the island of resistance, organised for all-round
defence.' The heat was appalling. The Nationalist mayor, Alfonso

MAP 26. THE ARAGÓN OFFENSIVE OF THE AUTUMN
OF 1937

Trallero, was killed with a rifle in his hands on the walls of the
city. The 13th and 150th Nationalist Divisions of Barrón and
Sáenz de Buruaga were now despatched from Madrid, to meet in
Aragón the remains of those same picked forces led by Lister,

Walter and El Campesino against whom they had fought in Castile. The former held up the Republican advance north of Saragossa. The latter sought to relieve Belchite, now 15 kilometres behind the Republican front lines. After a gallant resistance, however, Belchite eventually surrendered on September 6. But the Republic now returned to the defensive. After one daring and unsuccessful dash by Lister using Russian cruiser tanks gathered in a group into Fuentes del Ebro, the campaign slowed to a standstill.

The Italian attacks upon neutral shipping had now become too frequent to be ignored by Britain and France. The two Governments were further angered by Mussolini's boasts about his part in the Santander campaign. The two events caused the *Entente Cordiale* to act, for once, with some decision.

On August 26 a British ship was bombed off Barcelona. On August 29 a Spanish steamer was shelled by a submarine off the French coast. A French passenger steamer reported that she was chased by a submarine into the Dardanelles. On the 30th the Russian merchantman *Tuniyaev* was sunk at Algiers, on its way to Port Said. On August 31 a submarine attacked the British destroyer *Havock*. It replied with depth charges. On September 1 the Russian steamer *Blagaev* was sunk by a submarine off Skyros. On September 2 the British merchantship *Woodford* was sunk near Valencia. 'Three torpedoings and one prize,' Ciano remarked in his diary on that day, 'but international opinion is getting very worked up, particularly in England, as the result of the attack on the *Havock*. It was the *Iride*,' the Italian Foreign Secretary admitted – though only to himself.[1] Britain sent four more destroyers to the Mediterranean. Chamberlain and the Cabinet also agreed to Delbos's suggestion for a conference of 'interested powers'. On September 6, all States with Mediterranean frontiers, except Spain, together with Germany and Russia, were invited by Britain and France to a Conference on the 10th. This was to be held at Nyon, not far from Geneva (where it was not proposed to hold it for fear of angering Italy, who associated Geneva with the League's condemnation of her Abyssinian expedition). 'The full orchestra,' Ciano now noted, 'the theme: Piracy in the Mediterranean. Guilty – the Fascists. The Duce is very calm.' García Conde, the Spanish Nationalist Ambassador, brought a message from Franco saying that, if the blockade lasted throughout September, it would

[1] Ciano, *Diaries 1937–8*, 7–8.

be decisive. 'True,' Ciano admitted, but he nevertheless ordered Admiral Cavagnari to suspend it, until further orders.[1]

The Soviet *Chargé* in Rome, Helfand, now formally accused Italian submarines of sinking the *Tuniyaev* and *Blageav*. He claimed irrefutable evidence of Italian guilt – 'from intercepted telegrams, I expect', wrote Ciano airily, doubtless recalling the use which he himself made of that source of information.[2] This Russian move was probably chiefly due to a desire to edge Germany and Italy out of the Nyon Conference. Ciano anyway immediately disclaimed responsibility and disputed the right of Russia to make such a judgment. Both Italy and Germany proposed that the Non-Intervention Committee, not a special Conference, should handle the matter. But Eden and Delbos pressed on with their arrangements for Nyon. Churchill and Lloyd George, from the south of France, wrote to Eden that now was 'the moment to rally Italy to her international duty.'[3]

The conference followed, with Italy and Germany absent. It was immediately successful. First, Delbos and Eden proposed that the Mediterranean should be patrolled by warships of all the riparian States, with Russia (and Italy) allotted the Eastern Mediterranean. But the smaller countries had no warships to spare for this task and did not wish to risk war. So it was decided that the British and French fleets should patrol the Mediterranean west of Malta and attack any suspicious submarine. All this was decided on the first day of the Conference. The agreement was signed on the 14th. Mussolini was furious, and Litvinov spoke of his pleasure at an international agreement 'with very considerable backing'. Churchill wrote to Eden that the agreement had shown the possibility of British and French co-operation. Further agreements, between naval experts, were planned to consider the other problem of attacks by aircraft on surface vessels. Ciano now sent a note requesting 'parity of duties' with all the other States of Nyon. On September 15, nevertheless, he sent two submarines to Franco and promised two more. The wits in the Café Bavaria at Geneva suggested that the 'unknown statesman' – Mussolini – should erect a monument to the 'unknown submarine' in Rome. On September 17 the Nyon Conference's naval experts gave the

---

[1] Ciano, *Diaries 1937–8*, 9. The blockade was very nearly successful as it was. Whatever credence one can give to the incomplete figures reported by the German Military *Attaché* at Ankara, he clearly *reflects* the truth when he reports no Russian material reaching Spain at all during September, by the sea route. (See Appendix III.)

[2] *Ibid.*, 11.   [3] Churchill, *The Gathering Storm*, 191.

naval patrol the same power against aircraft as they had against submarines. Warships which attacked neutral ships would be counter-attacked by the patrol, regardless of whether they were in Spanish territorial waters or not. On the 18th, the French and British *Chargés* in Rome gave Ciano the texts of the Nyon Agreements and asked for an interpretation of his request for 'parity'. They thus made possible the return to more friendly relations with Italy which Chamberlain still so much desired.

The same day, Negrín was before the League of Nations Assembly requesting that its Political Committee should examine Spain. Once again he demanded the end of non-intervention. But, once again, only Litvinov and Mexico supported the Republic. Eden claimed that non-intervention had stopped European war. With his usual fondness for earthy metaphors, he compared non-intervention to a leaky dam, 'better than no dam at all.'[1] Italy was now invited to send experts to Paris so as to 'adjust' the Nyon Agreement in accordance with Italian wishes. Ciano therefore felt that he had achieved a diplomatic triumph. On September 22 Delbos talked with Bova-Scoppa, the Italian Representative at Geneva, who said that no more Italian troops would go to Spain and that Italy had no designs on Spanish territory or resources. Eden received from Grandi a similar assurance. On September 27 the British, French and Italians began naval talks in Paris. Italy was allotted a patrol zone between the Balearic Islands and Sardinia and in the Tyrrhenian Sea. This enabled the Italians to continue sending supplies to the Nationalists at Majorca without any fear of being watched. Also on the 27th, the League's Political Committee took up the question of Spain. Álvarez del Vayo spoke with his customary eloquent bitterness at the news of Italian reinforcements to General Franco. Walter Elliott, now the British Representative, successfully persuaded the committee to omit any denunciation of Germany and Italy from the resolution which would be put forward. But this document did refer to the 'failure of non-intervention', to the consideration of ending it if no agreement could be reached on the withdrawal of volunteers in 'the near future' and to the 'existence of veritable foreign army corps on Spanish soil'. However much the British might dislike such comparative forcefulness, they could hardly object. For Mussolini, even while the resolution was being discussed, was, in

---

[1] Compare his likening of the Suez Operation in 1956 to the extinction of a 'forest fire'.

Germany, publicly mourning the deaths of thousands of Italians on Spanish soil. Privately, the Duce told Hitler that, Nyon or not, he would continue his torpedoing operations. He even boasted to Rudolf Hess that he had already sunk nearly 200,000 tons of ships.[1] These remarks gave an ironic quality to the apparently successful end, on September 30, of the naval talks in Paris, with Italy now included in the Nyon patrol.

It was hard now to represent the Nyon Conference of three weeks before as a triumph of 'strength'. But then, the British would have been worried if it had been. A note was at this moment being prepared in the Foreign Office and in the Quai d'Orsay to invite the 'pirate now turned policeman' (as Ciano boasted himself to be)[2] to general talks on Spain. This was put to Ciano on October 2. The same day, the carefully drafted resolution of the League was passed. Álvarez del Vayo only agreed to the vagueness of the phrase 'in the near future' on the understanding that Britain and France needed ten days to see if Italy would reply amicably to their equally carefully drafted invitation of the same day. Also on October 2, however, Franco told Ciano that he wanted more and not less 'volunteers'. He also asked that Bastico should be recalled, presumably for his arrogance in the Santander campaign in going so far as to negotiate individually with the Basques. Meantime, America was preoccupied with the case of Harold Dahl, a former US Air Force pilot, who had enlisted (with a false Mexican passport) in the Republican Air Force. He had been forced to bale out over Nationalist territory. A court-martial there sentenced Dahl to death for 'rebellion'. The United States Government had to exert itself, and an American Colonel who had fought in Morocco by Franco's side telegraphed to his ex-comrade in arms to appeal for clemency. The death sentence was later commuted to life imprisonment.[3]

The Aragón front, calm since Pozas had ordered entrenchment at Belchite, had now burst once again into life. On September 22, in a climate less torrid than Saragossa, the Republic attacked across the swift-flowing river Gallego, in the foothills of the Pyrenees. This was a magnificent and picturesque countryside to which the nobles of Aragón had, in the past, repaired for the sum-

---

[1] *Documents Secrets du Ministère des Affaires Etrangères d'Allemagne*, 1936–43 Vol III 22 (Moscow 1946).
[2] Ciano, *Diaries 1937–8*, 15.
[3] Dahl eventually returned to America in 1940.

mer. The fall of the valleys in a north-south direction made an
advance in an east-west direction almost impossible. Yet this was
the only practicable route for either army. On September 25, 26
and 27 the battle continued nevertheless with extreme ferocity.
Aircraft were used on both sides with singular ineffectiveness.
Thereafter, the volume of the attack decreased. Though pressure continued until mid-October, the whole Aragón offensive was really over by the end of September.

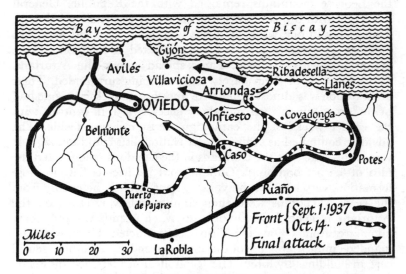

MAP 27. THE ASTURIAS CAMPAIGN

At the same time Dumont's XIVth International French and
Belgian Brigade launched an attack on the enemy lines near
Madrid. The men were given champagne before the offensive
began. The battle eventually became a massacre of the intoxicated. Later, an investigating committee alleged that Dumont
had spent his time in 'meetings, celebrations and the persecution
of the Trotskyists'.[1]

Another more important mountain campaign was begun
on September 1 by Nationalist forces under Aranda against
Gijón and the rest of the Asturias. This was accompanied by an
effective blockade of the coast. But progress was slow. The
Leonese mountains, a natural protection to Gijón, provided con-

[1] Gillain, 208–12.

tinuous magnificent defence positions. Vertigo was a weapon of war in the hands of the Republic. The absence of the Condor Legion, then stationed on the Aragón front, prevented the swift victory of machine over nature that had characterised the battle for Santander. Franco may also have kept back armaments from Aranda for some time to prevent that clever General from gaining too swift and magnificent a victory. At all events by October 14, after six weeks' battle, several of the highest points of the Leonese mountains remained with the Republic. General Solchaga, with the Navarrese on the coast, was similarly slow.

Suddenly in one week, Asturias was finally lost and won. On October 15 Aranda and Solchaga effected a junction at the mountain town of Infiesto. Panic spread among the Asturians. Large numbers of them barely escaped being surrounded. Their ammunition was almost exhausted, and the six weeks' struggle had made inroads upon their morale. Henceforward, in contrast with the earlier weeks of the campaign, resistance was feeble. The advance continued as swiftly as the Nationalists could manage. It was at this time that the Germans in the Condor Legion tested the idea of 'carpet bombing'. Galland and his friends flew in close formation, very low, up the valleys, approaching the enemy from the rear. All bombs were then simultaneously released on the Asturians' trenches.[1] On October 20, when Aranda was only forty kilometres from Gijón, the Fifth Column acted. One group demanded immediate unconditional surrender. Another seized certain buildings by force. The Republican leaders, led by Belarmino Tomás, immediately fled to France by sea. Twenty-two Republican battalions surrendered. On the evening of October 21, Aranda and Solchaga's forces entered Gijón. Though the whole northern front had now disappeared, 18,000 men maintained themselves as guerilla forces in the Leonese mountains until March, so delaying new offensives by the Nationalist armies. 209 persons were officially reported shot in January 1938 and until the end of the war Asturias was closely patrolled.

The war in the north had been remarkable for the use of an overwhelming superiority of aerial and artillery armaments. Yet neither in the Basque, the Santander nor the Asturias campaigns did the bombardments really cause the Nationalist victory. The existence of three practically independent states on the Republican side, the centres of quite different theories of government and

[1] Galland, 30.

themselves internally divided, was a fatal source of weakness. The conquest of all this territory brought the Nationalists the Asturian coal fields and the industries of Bilbao. It gave them 18,600 square kilometres of land and about $1\frac{1}{2}$ million people, including many war prisoners who were put to work in conditions little better than those of concentration camps. They also gained all the north coast of Spain, enabling the entire Nationalist Navy to be concentrated in the Mediterranean. Finally, it freed 65,000 men of the Army of the North, and its armaments, to fight in the south.[1]

[1] Villegas, 220.

62

The pacification of the north – execution of 16 Basque priests – ill-behaviour of the Italians – Germany's quarrels with Franco over mines – the Nationalist Army

During the lull which followed the Asturias and Aragón campaigns, and which lasted from mid-October until mid-December, the apparent stability of both Spains seemed such as would preserve a stalemate. Compared with the 'lyrical illusion' and the chaos, the atmosphere of euphoria and massacre of July 1936, the comparatively coherent organisation of the two Spains, with armies of about half a million men each, was astonishing. War had in both zones forged an order of which Peace might have been proud.

Nationalist Spain (two-thirds of the whole country) remained a military State. General Jordana was still head of the *junta* at Burgos which wielded all the administrative power, but its departments were spread about in several cities. Serrano Suñer, with vague and undefined powers, was the political leader of the country. Fernández Cuesta, an 'old shirt' of the Madrid Falange who had recently been exchanged (for a cousin of Azcárate) from a prison in Republican Spain, became Secretary-General of a new National Council, whose forty-eight members were finally named on December 2. This body remained more advisory in character even than most advisory organisations. It resembled the Italian Fascist Grand Council, since all its members, though their duties were legislative, were nominated by General Franco himself. Though there were Falangists on the council, there were also Carlists, Monarchists and old members of the CEDA. There were two women – Pilar Primo de Rivera and Mercedes Sanz Bachiller, widow of Onésimo Redondo and founder of *Auxilio Social*. But the need for a purely military *régime* was accepted by even the remaining old shirts of the Falange because, as Stohrer, the new German Ambassador, put it, 'Forty per cent of the population in the liberated regions are thought unreliable'.[1]

---

[1] *GD*, 462. Faupel had finally left in late August. Stohrer was a career diplomat who had been a junior member of the German Embassy in Madrid during the first World

All the Carlist representatives on the National Council were of the moderate wing who, following the Count of Rodezno, had wanted a treaty with Alfonso XIII in 1931 and who in April 1937 had accepted the Unification decree. Fal Conde, though still in exile, was several times asked by Franco to join the Council, but he refused. On December 5, Prince Xavier, the Carlist Regent, condemned all who took the oath demanded by the Council without asking his permission. He followed this announcement with a journey to Spain – his usual headquarters being in France. In San Sebastián he told Serrano Suñer that it was wrong to try and give to Spain a Gestapo on the German model. In Burgos he told Franco: 'If it were not for the *Requetés*, I very much doubt whether you would be where you are.' The Prince then went on a tour of the battlefronts. Having received a wildly enthusiastic welcome in Seville, he had reached Granada before he was give a peremptory order to quit Spain. He succeeded nevertheless in having another interview with Franco who told him: 'You are waging a campaign in favour of Monarchy.' The Prince replied: 'I have not spoken a word of politics. But my name is Bourbon. And, after all, I thought you also were a Monarchist.' 'Much of the Army is for a Republic,' answered Franco, 'and I cannot ignore that state of mind.' 'I believe that the main reason why you want me to leave Spain is that the Germans and Italians insist,' said Prince Xavier. Franco finally agreed, by saying: 'If you remain in Spain, your Highness, neither the Germans nor the Italians will give us any more war material.' Prince Xavier therefore left Burgos for France, remarking, 'Do not forget that I am the last link between you and the *Requetés*; nor that I shall always work for Spain but not for you personally.'[1]

The Nationalists only began upon the systematic 'pacification' of the north of Spain after the final conquest of Gijón. It is impossible to find accurate figures for the number of those executed. In November, it was said at Burgos that 200 Basque executions had occurred. Aguirre, a man not given to wanton exaggeration, said that 1,000 had been executed by then, that 11,000 were under sentence of death and that 10,000 were in prison. It was reported that 80 Basques were shot between December 14 and 16. These

War. He had been expelled because of being implicated in a plot to assassinate the pro-Allied Prime Minister, Count de Romanones.

[1] From an unpublished series of notes for a life of Prince Xavier de Bourbon, in the Carlist Archives at Seville.

included some of those who had so unwisely surrendered to Italy at Santoña. The executions included those of several women and of sixteen churchmen.[1] None of the latter appeared before a tribunal. The announcement of the death sentence was made to all of them minutes only before it was carried out, so that they had no time to prepare for death. All were buried without coffins, funeral services or official registration. One of those shot was a Carmelite monk, the remainder priests. The most eminent were Joaquin Arin, Archpriest of the parish of Mondragón, aged sixty, and Father Aristimuño, a distinguished writer on Basque culture. On the justification for their death, the exiled Bishop of Vitoria later remarked to the Primate of all Spain, Cardinal Gomá: 'What, shoot the Archpriest of Mondragón and these other priests whom I know so well? Everyone in Franco's army, from the Generalissimo downwards, would have done better to kiss their feet'.[2]

Yet among the *bourgeoisie* of most of Nationalist Spain there was little slackening of enthusiasm for the great 'crusade'. The leaders might not be on such good terms as they made out. The defeated might be maltreated. But this was war, was it not, and these ugly matters were the obverse side of one's own sacrifices. Economically, Nationalist Spain was in far better shape than the Republic. The currency was stable, food prices had not risen much and stocks would have been adequate to provision the whole of Republican Spain. The terrible spectre of hunger in the cities did not exist. Coal and fuel were in ample supply. Thus, away from the fronts, middle-class life was carried on without too great an interruption. In the evening, for instance, one would as of old walk up and down the main street of the town at the hour of the *paseo*, and notice perhaps a number of uniforms, though not so very many. There would be placards encouraging patriotic service. One would hear news of so-and-so's daughter who was working with the *Auxilio Social*. One would have to give, before the evening was out, at a café or in the cinema, a small contribution to war victims or to subsidise state meals or to aid refugees. Indeed, the sum might be

---

[1] The number may have been twenty. Four more unidentified but probably ecclesiastical bodies were found at Vera, Navarre.

[2] See Aberrigoyen *passim*; *Le Clergé Basque*, 94–107. These executions were undoubtedly carried out by the whim of the local Military Governor rather than by the orders of the Nationalist authorities. When Cardinal Gomá heard of the shootings he went to Franco to complain, and only one more Basque priest was shot thereafter; but many were imprisoned and others exiled to other parts of Spain. (Evidence of Fr Onaindía. The whole question of the Basques' theological position *vis-à-vis* Franco and the Vatican is exhaustively examined in Iturralde, Vol II.)

large, since much money was certainly gathered for these and other services. And, as the evening progressed, war might seem nearer. At ten o'clock there would be Queipo de Llano on all the radio services, in cafés and in private houses, accusing perhaps a British journalist like Noel Monks of being drunk at the time he wrote for the *Daily Express* that Guernica had been destroyed by the Germans; or giving the latest news of the 'Jew Blum' or Doña Manolita, as he always referred to Azaña, in a high-pitched voice; or there might even be a song, for Queipo sometimes suddenly interrupted his talks to give a rendering of some favourite Spanish jingle. And then, at midnight, there would be the daily *communiqué*, and the list of casualties and of prisoners; and then, with the *Royal March* and the Fascist salute, to bed.

As for the lives of the combatants on the Nationalist side, one gains a curiously frivolous and amateur impression from the pilot Ansaldo's account of a day on the Northern front:

8.30 a.m.	Breakfast with the family.
9.30 a.m.	Departure for the front. Bombardment of enemy batteries. Machine-gunning of trenches and convoys.
11 a.m.	A little golf at Lasarte . . .
12.30 p.m.	Sun-bath on Ondarreta beach and short swim in the calm sea.
1.30 p.m.	Beer, shrimps and conversation in a café.
2 p.m.	Luncheon at home.
3 p.m.	Short siesta.
4 p.m.	Second war mission, similar to that of the morning.
6.30 p.m.	Cinema. Old but fine film of Katherine Hepburn.
9 p.m.	*Apéritif* at the Bar Basque. A good 'Scotch'. Animated scene.
10.15 p.m.	Dinner at Nicolasa's, war songs, company, enthusiasm . . .[1]

But then, the air force was always rather favoured in Nationalist Spain.

1937 had seen the general rehabilitation of religious teaching in Spanish Nationalist schools. In September 1936, it had been declared obligatory. In April 1937 all schools were ordered to have images of the Virgin. All pupils were, as in the past before the

[1] Ansaldo, 74.

coming of the Republic, to repeat, on reaching and leaving school, an *Ave María*. The crucifix was later also made obligatory. Staff and pupils were henceforth obliged to go to mass on festivals. Readings from the gospel were to be given at least once a week. The Catholic Church indeed permeated every aspect of Spanish Nationalist culture.

The more socially-minded of the Falange nevertheless continued their work. Throughout 1937, the demands of war continued to bring radical changes into the Nationalist economy. On August 23 a National Wheat Council was established to control the price, production and distribution of Spain's chief agricultural activity. A decree of October 7 obliged all fit women between the ages of seventeen and thirty-five who were not occupied by their families, other war-work or hospital duties, to undertake some kind of social service (*servicio social*). A certificate of social service became essential to secure almost any employment for Spanish women. Queipo de Llano meantime continued to busy himself with the economic development of Andalusia. His most successful measure was the establishment of a Committee of Agricultural Loans in Seville for assistance to farmers. He also made grandiose plans for the industrial revival of the region. And in the spring of 1938 a number of textile factories were set up in Seville. There is no doubt that for all his faults, Queipo de Llano had a powerful dynamising influence on Andalusia as a whole.

The troubles of the Nationalists at this time were in fact less among themselves than with their Italian and German allies. Ciano's creature, Anfuso, returned from Spain in mid-October to tell his master that the Italian troops in Spain were tired and that Franco could hardly wait for them to go away, though he still needed their artillery and aircraft. Ciano supposed that the Generalissimo 'must be jealous of our success'.[1] The boastful arrogance of the Italian officers and troops, however, especially in San Sebastián, angered all Spaniards with whom they came into contact. A violent scene occurred between Franco, Viola (the new Italian Ambassador) and General Bastico (shortly before being recalled on Franco's insistence) because the Generalissimo desired to flank the Italians by Navarrese in the next battle.[2] There was also a squabble in respect of the bill for the two submarines sold by Italy to Spain, which had not been paid.[3] These difficulties, however, were smoothed over by the despatch of 100,000 tons of Spanish

[1] Ciano, *Diaries 1937–8*, 22.   [2] *GD*, 521.   [3] Ciano, *Diaries 1937–8*, 32.

steel to Italy.[1] But Mussolini was still owed three billion lire for war material at the end of November, with little prospect of an early settlement of the debt.[2]

The dispute between the Nationalists and the Germans was also an economic one. Germany was now affording to the Nationalists credit of 10 million reichmarks a month, of which 4 million was for war materials, $5\frac{1}{2}$ million for other exports and 350,000 cash credit. There had been no sign that the Spaniards intended to pay any of these debts. Worse, German financiers were becoming fearful lest Britain should step in to take the coveted iron ore. The busy officials of HISMA and ROWAK had been occupied with the so-called Montaña project, designed to guarantee to Germany a steady supply of Spanish minerals. The project provided for German control of no less than 73 Spanish mines. The Ambassador Stohrer advised that German interest in Spain must be 'the deep penetration' into agriculture and mining. The former question solved itself since, whatever happened, Spain would have to find a market. The mines, on the other hand, were more difficult. Upon them must be based all German diplomatic, military and cultural efforts. 'The solution,' he added threateningly, in his recommendation, 'would have to be forced, if it could not be obtained by reasonable means.' On October 9, however, a decree issued by the Burgos *junta* nullified all titles to mines obtained since the start of the Civil War. The Germans anxiously asked the meaning of this. Nicolás Franco replied evasively that only a fully-fledged Spanish Nationalist Government could conclude so important a matter as the Montaña project. Nothing now was done. Goering and Bernhardt (recently named as Goering's agent in Spain for the four-year plan) became impatient.[3] Impatience changed to suspicion when Britain, the suspected rival and the probable enemy in war, exchanged diplomatic agents with Franco – mainly for commercial and economic reasons: for Sir Henry Chilton had at last retired, leaving the *Chargé* in Valencia, John Leche, to be named Minister with the Republic. Sir Robert Hodgson (whose experience as Consul in Russia in 1917 no doubt recommended him as a fervent opponent of Bolshevism) went to Burgos on November 16 as agent.[4] The Duke

---

[1] *Ibid.*, 37.   [2] *GD*, 512–16.

[3] For all the above see *GD*, 496–503 and 541–2.

[4] The British mission was very unpopular. 'It was assumed,' Sir Robert Hodgson said, 'that we were against the movement and *España, una, grande, libre*. This was proved

of Alba went to London in a complementary capacity. For reasons still obscure, Mr Eden was hostile to the idea of receiving Alba in England as Franco's official representative, and only consented when the Nationalist Spaniards demanded his reasons – which he did not give.[1] On December 2 Stohrer told Franco that Germany had heard that England had received considerable concessions from Spain, and asked for an explanation. Germany insisted on a major part of the ore production of Bilbao and Asturias, and an unlimited concession to buy scrap. Otherwise, she would have 'to re-examine her attitude to the Spanish Nationalist Government'. Franco described the German allegations as 'fabrications', saying that he personally was surprised that Britain paid so little attention to Spain. The delay over the Montaña project, said Franco, was due to the Nationalists' lack of copies of previous laws, archives and trained officials.[2] But still the question of a formal contract was left to *mañana*.

The Nationalist Army now numbered about 600,000 men. This was composed of 650 battalions of infantry and one division of cavalry, supported by 290 artillery batteries and 600 aircraft. These forces were still organised in three: the Army of the North under Dávila; of the Centre under Saliquet; and of the South under Queipo de Llano. 200 battalions and 70 batteries (commanded by General Orgaz) formed the reserve.[3] All the aircraft were either German or Italian, the bombers being Junkers 52 or Savoias 73, the fighters being Fiats 32, Heinkels or Messerschmitts.

---

by our obstinate denial of belligerent rights and by the continued description in the British press of the Nationalists as insurgents.' Hodgson did not have an interview with Franco till February, 1937. Hodgson, 84–5.

[1] The French Government did not establish even these limited relations with Nationalist Spain. All they did, as *L'Action Française* ironically commented, was to restore the *Sud Express*, the main daily train from Paris to Hendaye. However, Charles Maurras (who – and this was a clear sign of the times – had been elected in 1938 to the Académie Française) was a little later received in Saragossa 'not even as a diplomat but as a Head of State'; and visiting right-wing or Fascist French journalists and politicians, from Doriot to Pierre Gaxotte, and even the Archbishop of Chartres, showed to Franco 'the Christian friendship of the true France'.

[2] *GD*, 522.

[3] Aznar, 536. Generally speaking all young men between 18 and 29 were called up in Nationalist Spain.

63

The Republic in the autumn of 1937 – Negrín and the Communists – final discomfiture of Largo Caballero – Prieto dismisses the Commissars – La Pasionaria's hatred for Prieto stimulated by her relations with Antón – the SIM – the 'tunnel of death' – a scandal at Albacete – 'qui a volé les soldats de la liberté?' – economic condition of the Republic – Hemingway writes The Fifth Column *– the writers' congress – Malraux, Hernández and Spender – a mistake by Bertolt Brecht – peace rumours*

Under Dr Negrín's Government, a degree of unity had been achieved in Republican Spain which was itself a revolution in Spanish history. On October 31, Negrín announced the transfer of the central government to Barcelona. Catalonia thus passed more and more under central control. Henceforward, the Catalans played a diminishing part in events. Protesting, their leaders toyed with the idea of peace and mediation. The most serious criticism of the Republican Government came from those Anarchists who still aspired to forge a syndicalist State out of the Civil War. Their criticism was more national than regional. It was linked with that of Largo Caballero and his band of sour Socialists. Madrid, the fief of the Communist party, presented no regional problem, since the Communists remained the proponents of central control, even if wielded from Valencia or Barcelona.

While Dr Negrín had successfully overcome the regional differences in Spain, his position in relation to political opposition was also strong. On October 1, the UGT elected Rodríguez Vega as their new Secretary-General in place of Largo Caballero. The old man was thus dislodged at last from the position which he had held since 1925. The Communists henceforward blamed Largo Caballero for all the defeats in the Civil War, both while he was in office and since. The ex-Premier was now irretrievably lost. On October 17, he made a speech at Madrid in general criticism of Dr Negrín's conduct of the war. The Government had permitted this speech to be made so that, if possible, Largo Caballero could

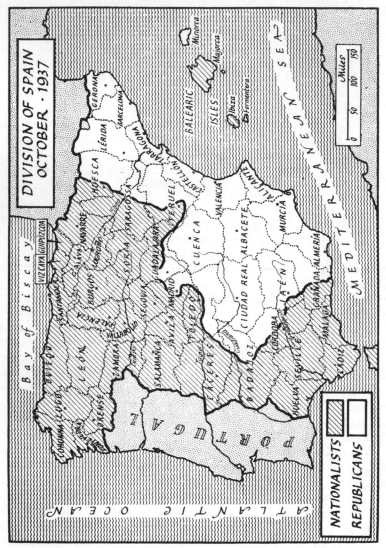

DIVISION OF SPAIN
OCTOBER · 1937

NATIONALISTS
REPUBLICANS

MAP 28

·make himself appear foolish. When he did not do so conclusively, his further activities were prohibited. He denounced Negrín as a dictator, but the Government had no more to fear from him. The extinction of Largo -was above all a victory for Negrín and those Socialists who supported him in a policy of extreme social moderation while subordinating everything to the war effort.

But, while Dr Negrín used Communist support against Largo Caballero, he was not absolutely the prisoner of that party. The Defence Ministries were dominated by Prieto. After a long equivocal period, he was now developing into a passionate anti-Communist. Although the first memorable event during the administration had been the dissolution of the POUM, the Communists were no longer hourly increasing in power and prestige, as they had been throughout the time of Largo Caballero. Indeed, they were even alarmed at the extent to which they had antagonised the CNT, whom Jesús Hernández now tried to placate with soothing words. But again he castigated the FAI, this time as a 'dishonourable political party', thus alleging a false division (for purposes of attempting to hasten a real one) between FAI and CNT.

The Communist party had begun in the summer elaborate negotiations for their unification with the Socialists and a working pact between the two parties was published on August 17. This repeated the declared war aims of Dr Negrín's Government, and added an agreement that the extreme revolutionary Left should be purged. It approved close co-operation between the parties both at home and internationally. But this, and another later declaration by all five Popular Front parties on October 10, made no concession to the Communists.

At the end of October, Negrín ended the discussions between Socialists and Communists about prospective unity, saying that such a rigid framework was more suitable to Nationalist than to Republican Spain. This rebuff was not offset by the Communist success in November in establishing, by a moderate programme, an alliance (though not an amalgamation) of all the youth parties, including the Anarchists. The Socialists did not object, since their youth had long ago been swallowed up.

Prieto was meantime busy attempting to restrict the power of the Communists in the Army. In October officers were forbidden to engage in political proselytisation and even to attend party meetings. In November the post of Chief Political Commissar was abolished. Many of the commissariats at the fronts were also abolished. This step meant the transfer of Antón, a Communist Commissar on the Madrid front, to take command of a regular battalion. This young man was La Pasionaria's lover, and occupied a house with her and Togliatti in Madrid. (Her miner husband was all the time at the front with her son.) La Pasionaria accordingly became more ardently an enemy of Prieto, but as yet his prestige was such that she could not touch him.[1]

On October 1 the Cortes met. It had decided to meet twice a year for the duration of the war, so as to preserve the outward form of democracy at least, and had done so in October 1936 and February 1937. Two hundred of those elected in February 1936 were present. Among these were several radicals and one member of the CEDA. Even Portela Valladares, the Prime Minister at the time of the elections of 1936, attended. He had in 1936 rallied to Franco and narrowly escaped death at the hands of the Anarchists in Barcelona. Now he described how Franco had tried to persuade him to hand over power to him after the elections. The Communists, who now claimed 300,000 members, apart from the PSUC and the united Socialist-Communist Youth, demanded new elections. Certainly their parliamentary representation of sixteen members did not reflect their following, but this demand was refused by Negrín. The Communists even began to wonder whether they should continue to support Negrín. This was the main question at their congress held on November 12 and 13. Díaz urged elections but no delegate wanted the party to leave the Government. Furthermore, though the political power of the Communists might be decreased, the party still retained its attraction for army officers. And, rather as the potentially subversive character of much of Nationalist Spain prevented the Falange from quarrelling with Franco, so the lack of supplies, of food as well as arms, kept together the Republic.

The Communists, of course, were still very powerful. In addition to their continuing control over military aid to the Republic, they contrived to fill the prisons with their own enemies. The POUM leaders, arrested in June, had not yet been brought to trial. Orlov's men were still at work and in addition there was a new body, the SIM (*Servicio de Investigación Militar*). This new secret police was from the start led by Communists. Its nominal duty was to investigate spies. It was not modest, however, in exceeding

[1] Hernández, 160.

these functions. From the start of its activities, the SIM employed all the odious tortures of the NKVD. Cells were made so small that prisoners could hardly stand, being paved with bricks set on edge. Powerful electric lights were available to dazzle, noises to deafen, baths to freeze, irons to burn, clubs to beat. The SIM was undoubtedly responsible for the murder of many conscripted into the Republican Army who were not merely cowardly or inefficient but also unwilling to follow the orders of Communist commanders. Among various actions supposed to have been taken by this body was a peculiarly distasteful scheme in Madrid. It was allowed to be rumoured that a tunnel had been dug to run from a house in the suburb of Usera to the Nationalist lines. A number of Nationalist sympathisers, including several sheltering in foreign embassies, paid heavily to avail themselves of this scheme. When they arrived at the mouth of the tunnel, clutching a few valuables and keepsakes, they were shot down. Sixty-seven bodies were identified as having been duped by this tunnel of death at the end of the war.[1]

The Republican Army now numbered about 450,000. Vicente Rojo, the ex-Professor of Tactics at Toledo and Miaja's *aide* in the defence of Madrid, was now its Chief-of-Staff. This army was at this time supported by 350 aircraft and 200 batteries – with 90 battalions and 35 batteries in reserve. The Army of the Centre was commanded by Miaja; of the East (once of Catalonia) by Hernández Sarabia, the regular officer who had been War Minister at the start of the war; and the Army of the Levante was under Menéndez, Hernández Sarabia's old adjutant. Both these last two officers were close friends of Prieto.[2]

At this time the International Brigades were formally incorporated into the Republican Army. Officially the Brigades were to take the place of the Foreign Legion in the regular Spanish Army. Great attention had now to be paid to discipline and dress. A five-point justification of the salute appeared in *Our Fight*, a weekly paper published in English by the XVth International Brigade:

(1) A salute (of course, this meant the clenched fist) is the military way of saying 'hello'.

(2) A salute is the quickest way for a soldier to say to an officer, 'What are your orders?'

(3) A salute is not undemocratic: two officers of equal rank, when meeting on military business, salute each other.

[1] *General Cause*, 304.   Aznar, 542-9.

(4) A salute is a sign that a comrade who has been an egocentric individualist in private life has adjusted himself to the collective way of getting things done.

(5) A salute is a proof that our Brigade is on its way from being a collection of well-meaning amateurs to a steel precision instrument for eliminating Fascists.[1]

Early in 1937, these admonitions were followed up by an appeal to all to learn Spanish. *Volunteer for Liberty* named this 'our anti-Fascist duty'.

The Brigades now found it hard to gain new recruits from abroad. The tales of the volunteers who returned home disgruntled and the reports of the liquidation of the POUM played a great part in this. The gaps in the ranks of the Brigades were filled by Spanish volunteers. Most of these were Communists. A crisis was also brewing in the Brigade organisation. The Frenchman Gaymann (Vidal), who was the Commander of the base at Albacete, under Marty, was accused of embezzlement. He left for Paris allegedly for reasons of health. His successor was 'Gómez', the German Communist whose real name was Zeisser and who had earlier led the XIIIth International Brigade. This appointment intensified the already existing quarrel between the German and the French Communists at Albacete. Kapov, the Quartermaster-General (in succession to Louis Fischer), and a French Communist, Grillet, with his wife, were also accused of embezzlement. The Grillets were intimates of Madame Marty. At last, the cry came that Marty had himself '*volé les soldats de la Liberté*'. The scandal grew so that the great man had himself to go to Moscow to justify himself. He did not return to Spain for a long time.[2]

Economically, the Republic was much less well off than Nationalist Spain. There was a continued shortage of food and, after the fall of the north, also of fuel. As to arms, Prieto told the American *Chargé* at Valencia that, thanks to Russia and Mexico, the essentials were now acquired fairly satisfactorily. But, he went on, Russia was growing diffident. Stalin apparently feared that what all the world already knew would be discovered – namely, that he was selling arms to the Republic. The War Minister added that the Republic received no favours from Russia, since she paid the full market price for goods. Apart from these sources the Re-

---

[1] Quoted in Rust, 98. Pamphlets on 'Leadership' were published in considerable numbers from about this time in Barcelona: e.g. *El Mando* by 'General W.W.W'.

[2] *The International Brigades*, 125.

public had to buy from intermediaries and adventurers. All of them, Prieto complained, exacted vast profits.[1] In the centre of this world of gun-runners, Comintern agents, and crooked traders, Louis Fischer continued to direct the chain of arms purchasing bodies from the Hotel Lutetia, at the crossroads of the Rue de Vaugirard and the Boulevard Raspail, in the 7th Arrondissement in Paris.[2]

The Basque leaders moved to Barcelona after the fall of Santander, and there set up their *Emigré* Government. One consequence was that Catholic services were again held in the Catalan capital, at the Basque headquarters. The Basques continually urged religious toleration upon the Government. The Government, however, while agreeing in principle, argued that public opinion was 'not yet ready' for this step. But permission was given for services to be held in private homes licensed by the Government. By the winter about 2,000 priests had returned from exile to Barcelona. These had to go about in lay dress, though henceforth they were not, as heretofore, called up for military service. The Vatican, additionally, were not at all enthusiastic for the formal re-establishment of religion in the Republic – since this would have weakened the catholic writing of Franco's cause. The Archbishop of Tarragona, for instance, apparently was willing to return to his cathedral but was refused permission to do so.[3]

Meantime, Madrid continued in siege and in near famine. Bombardments were frequent. Mr Ernest Hemingway busied himself by writing a play entitled *The Fifth Column* while his hotel, the Florida, was hit over thirty times. In the summer of this year, a writers' congress was held at Madrid whose declared purpose was to discuss the attitude of intellectuals to the war. One concealed aim, however, of the Communist organisers of the Congress was to condemn André Gide. In his recent book, *Retour de l'URSS*, Gide had attacked the Soviet Union, where he had been received as a friend of the Government. This congress was attended by

[1] *USD*, 1938 Vol I 149–50. The arms profiteers at the expense of the Republic came from all classes. Who in those days had not heard of the English peer who, having received payment from the Republic for a cargo of ammunition, sold it again to the Nationalists?

[2] The enormous variety of makes of arms in the Republican Army was a source of great inefficiency. There were rifles of six different calibres, machine guns of five, mortars of six, while there were twenty-eight models of artillery.

[3] Álvarez del Vayo, *Last Optimist*, 317–18. The Vicar-General of Barcelona forbade the opening of any church and allowed it to be known that he would refuse licences to priests who heard Mass. (Evidence of Señor Irujo.)

Hemingway, Spender and most of the leading literary apologists for the Republic. It was dominated by Malraux 'with his nervous sniff and tic'.[1] The delegates drove about in Rolls Royces and talked with the Spanish poets of the war – Rafael Alberti, Bergamín, Machado and Miguel Hernández. Of these, Rafael Alberti was undoubtedly the most prolific. There were few editions of *Volunteer for Liberty*, the paper of the XVth International Brigade, which did not contain one of his verses. The most remarkable poet was, perhaps, Miguel Hernández, a Communist member of the Fifth Regiment at the start of the war. He was a shepherd who had been taught to read by a priest in the hills through examples of sixteenth and seventeenth-century writing. The outbreak of the Civil War had caused in him a sudden outburst of poetic activity.[2] A speech by Bertolt Brecht was read at the Congress.[3] As on many occasions of this kind, the national anthems of the different nations were played, so that Stephen Spender found himself at Barcelona giving the salute of the clenched fist while the band trumpeted 'God save the King'.

As 1937 drew to its end there were rumours of attempts to arrange a compromise peace. Ossorio y Gallardo, the Republican Ambassador in Paris, was said to be negotiating with Nationalist agents in Brussels.[4] Stories were told that Companys, who had little to do now that the Republican Government had moved to Barcelona, was planning a federation of two Spains, to be brought about by persons uncommitted to either side in the war, such as

---

[1] Spender, *World Within World*, 496.

[2]   *The winds of the people sustain me,*
    Spreading within my heart.
    The winds of the people impel me,
    And roar in my very throat . . .
    I come not from a people of oxen,
    My people praise
    The lion's leap,
    The eagle's rigid swoop,
    And the strong charge of the bull
    Whose pride is in his horns.

(Translation, slightly altered, by A. L. Lloyd, in Spender and Lehmann, *Poems for Spain* 37.)

[3] He shortly wrote his play *Señora Carrara's Rifles*, satirising the idea of neutrality on the model of J. M. Synge's *Riders to the Sea*. The theatrical effectiveness of the play is not diminished by the playwright's mistake in giving his characters Italian instead of Spanish names.

[4] There were similar rumours that Pablo de Azcárate, Ambassador in London, was negotiating with these agents. The ex-Ambassador has specifically denied these to the present author (*GD*, 519–20).

Salvador de Madariaga and Miguel Maura. All such ideas were violently opposed by Republican army officers who feared that their former colleagues would have no mercy if they were allowed any power over them. The only actual contact between the two sides seems to have been Angel Baza, a secretary of Prieto, who maintained relations at Hendaye with Troncoso, the Nationalist Military Governor of Irún.[1]

[1] One other contact was through the Red Cross. Dr Junod, helped by the British Embassy at Hendaye, succeeded in arranging the exchange of small groups of prisoners. But this hardly made any inroad upon the thousands of prisoners who were now in Spain. Even most of those who had taken refuge in foreign Embassies in Madrid at the start of the war were still held there. In January 1938 most were transferred to Valencia with the Embassies concerned and a little later 500 persons who had taken refuge in the French Embassy were sent away. There remained, however, over 2,000 left in Embassies in Valencia. (Toynbee, A., *Survey 1938* Vol I 391–2,393.)

BOOK VI

THE WAR OF ATTRITION
December 1937 – November 1938

64

Ciano's musings – Eden at the Non-Intervention Committee – the French Government opens the frontier – Hitler and Stalin agree on the Spanish War – Italy joins the Anti-Comintern Pact

The continuing political moderation of Negrín's Government was partly due to the Republican illusion that this could even now help to bring France at least, if not Britain, to assist them with arms.

On October 10 Ciano had replied to Eden and Delbos's proposal for consultations about Spain[1] by saying that he could not act without Germany. So far from wishing to settle Spain, Ciano was at this time wondering whether he could despatch Alpine troops there – 'to break through to Valencia'.[2] He had also just named General Berti as the new commander of the 60,000 Italian troops in Spain in succession to Bastico, the 'hero of Santander'. Further commitments were in fact prevented by troubles in Libya and Abyssinia, where Italian troops had to be sent to put down local risings. When, at the end of October, a ceremony was held for the presentation of medals to men who had fought in Spain and to the widows of those who had fallen, Ciano 'examined his conscience' to ask if this blood had been shed in a good cause. 'Yes, the answer is yes,' he comforted himself, 'at Málaga, at Santander, at Guadalajara we were fighting in defence of our civilisation and our revolution!'[3]

The French reaction to Ciano's refusal to talk was to consider opening the Pyrenean frontier to the passage of arms for the Republic. But Eden persuaded Delbos to go back to the Non-Intervention Committee. At the Foreign Office Vansittart made an excuse not to see the Republican Ambassador in London, Azcárate, on October 11: for, after all, Ciano's refusal made nonsense of the Republic's concession at Geneva ten days before. Meantime Delbos insisted that if an agreement was not reached on volunteers within one week, France would open her frontier.[4] On October 15

[1] See above, page 478.   [2] Ciano, *Diaries 1937-8*, 18.   [3] *Ibid.*, 26.
[4] *USD*, 1937 Vol 1, 420. Here as usual, the best source for French policy is in these reports by the American Ambassador in Paris.

Eden told Grandi that this new appeal to the Committee was 'a last attempt'. The Foreign Secretary later told an audience at Llandudno that his patience with Italian intervention in Spain was 'well-nigh exhausted'.

On October 16 the Non-Intervention Sub-Committee at last met once more. Between then and November 2 the British plan of July 14, which proposed the grant of belligerent rights subject to the withdrawal of a 'substantial proportion' of volunteers in Spain, became the basis for discussion. After prolonged, wearisome and confusing negotiations in which the patient Eden played the most important rôle, this plan was finally accepted on November 4. The two Spanish parties were to be asked for their co-operation with the plan, and to agree to accept two commissions to number the foreigners in their zones and put into effect the withdrawal. In the meantime, since far more than one week had passed since Delbos made his stipulation, the French frontier was left open for the passage of arms by night. Eden had rather cryptically told Delbos, 'Don't open the frontier but allow to pass what you want'.[1] Henceforward, in Blum's less ambiguous words, 'we voluntarily and systematically shut our eyes to arms smuggling and even organised it'.[2]

On November 5, the day after the Committee approved the withdrawal plan, Hitler, while unfolding his desire for a war of extermination against Britain and France to an alarmed Neurath, Blomberg and Beck, said that in the Spanish War, 'from the German point of view, a 100% Franco victory is not desirable. We are most interested in the continuance of the war'.[3] Only thus, he

[1] Azcárate, 122.

[2] Les Evénements Survenus en France, 219. On October 28 Azcárate had a curiously interesting interview with Eden in the House of Commons. Azcárate urged firmness.
Eden: What you want is a preventive war against Italy.
Azcárate: No, simply a clear political line which, if maintained with energy and determination, would be enough to calm the intemperance of Mussolini.
Eden: It is not easy to decide that line.
Azcárate: With respect to Spain it is easy: it is to make certain that the UK preserves Spain free from foreign entanglement and free from a Fascism which would interfere with British strategic interests.
'Eden,' reported Azcárate, 'heard me with his head low, saying that it was easier for me to say this than for him to convince his colleagues. I asked him what the Republic ought to do to give a guarantee that there was no Communist danger in Spain. Eden merely said that it would be unreasonable to insist that the two Communists leave the Government.' (Azcárate, 129–30.)

[3] This was the celebrated 'Hossbach Memorandum' (Nuremburg Trials, Vol XXV 403–14). It was also the time when the Germans in Spain were becoming excited over the Spanish mining project – see below, page 487.

went on, could the Italian position in the Balearic Islands – which was important from the overall strategic point of view – be preserved. Some months before, a Russian General returned to Spain to tell Orlov that the Politburo had adopted a policy almost the same as that proposed by Hitler: that is, that it would be best if the war in Spain dragged on and tied Hitler down there.[1] Thus, for mutually hostile reasons, the two leading *aficionados* of the Spanish War had reached the same conclusion. On·November 6 Italy joined Germany and Japan in signing their so-called Anti-Comintern Pact. Although Ciano desired it to remain a 'pact of giants', he nevertheless planned to bring Spain in, so as to link the 'Axis to the Atlantic'.

On November 20, Franco accepted the British 'volunteer' plan in principle. He made reservations, however, about the rights of the commission to guarantee the withdrawal. He suggested that the withdrawal of 3,000 volunteers would constitute the 'substantial withdrawal' upon which belligerent rights would be conditional. The figure no doubt occurred to Franco since precisely that number of Italian troops were now withdrawn, regardless of agreements, because they were sick and unreliable.[2] On December 1 the Republic also accepted the plan in principle – though for different reasons: Azaña and Giral thought that acceptance would mean the suspension of hostilities, which would thereafter not be renewed. Negrín and Prieto agreed that the start of a volunteer plan would mean suspension of fighting but liked the idea because it would give them time to re-group their forces.[3]

---

[1] Orlov, 241–2. Orlov names this soldier General 'N'. I have been unable to establish whether this work is a forgery or the work of a ghost.
[2] *GD*, 550.   [3] Azcárate, 120.

The battle of Teruel – Attlee with the British Battalion – Colonel Rey d'Harcourt holds out – his fall – Paul Robeson sings – Ciano worries – the 'Farce of non-intervention' – the Germans reproved – Franco forms a Government – the Italians sink the Endymion *– battle on the Alfambra – fall of Eden – fall of Teruel – El Campesino surrounded – Togliatti demands the removal of Prieto*

65

The military lull in Spain came to an end in December. The aim of Franco was to launch a new attack at Guadalajara, and then at Madrid.[1] This never occurred, since the Generalissimo's plans were betrayed. Instead the Republic launched an attack at Teruel on December 15, a week before the Guadalajara attack had been planned. Teruel was chosen because it was thought not to be strongly held, and because its capture would give a shorter line of communications between New Castile and Aragón and threaten the road to Saragossa. It was also, however, like Belchite, Huesca and Saragossa itself, a town which had held the Republican troops fascinated since the start of the war. Prieto wanted a spectacular capture to reflect well upon his tenure of the War Ministry and to show how successful the Army could be without a Commissar-General. It was rumoured also that Prieto wanted to capture Teruel, and then, from a position of strength, try and arrange an armistice. Such a victory might further give Dr Negrín's Government the additional prestige it needed to take over without difficulty control of Catalan industry.

For political reasons, the offensive was to be carried out only by Spaniards, with no International Brigades. The Army of the East, under Hernández Sarabia, would effect the main part of the assault on Teruel, and would be assisted by the Army of the Levante. The whole Army totalled 100,000 men. Hernández Sarabia's force was composed of two Army Corps, the XVIIIth under Herédia

---

[1] The idea of attacking in Catalonia was never entertained at this time in Franco's headquarters, because it was supposed that Catalonia was the centre of Republican resistance and would never give in. The supposition indicates the poor intelligence system operated by the Nationalists.

and the XXIInd under the Basque Ibarrola. The latter included Lister's XIth Division which, as usual, was selected for the first attack.[1]

The International Brigades rested during the early part of these operations. The British settled down at Mondéjar. Fred Copeman and Walter Tapsell returned from Britain to be the Commander and Commissar again of the British Battalion. They brought with them 350 new volunteers. Early in December the battalion received a visit from the British Labour leaders, Clement Attlee, Ellen Wilkinson and Philip Noel-Baker. A great dinner was given to these persons, at which Major Attlee promised to do his utmost to end the 'farce of non-intervention'. Mr Noel-Baker recalled how Britain had sent 10,000 men to assist the Spanish liberals in the Carlist wars. Then the visitors took a parade by torchlight. Henceforth the No. 1 Company of the British Battalion was known as the 'Major Attlee Company'. Major Attlee wrote back: 'I would assure (the Brigade) of our admiration for their courage and devotion to the cause of freedom and social justice. I shall try to tell the Comrades at home of what I have seen. Workers of the World unite!'[2]

Teruel is the bleak, walled capital of a poor province, with a population of 20,000. Each winter it records the lowest Spanish temperature of the year. The town is celebrated for the glum legend of the *Lovers of Teruel*, which often attracts those who desire a melancholy theme for a short ballet. This gloomy history was a suitable background for the atrocious battle of Teruel, which lasted for over two months.

On December 15, 1937, with snow falling, and without artillery or aerial preparation (so as to avoid giving notice of his intentions) Lister began his attack. He and Herédia set out to surround the town.[3] This they did by advancing immediately to the ridge on its west side known as the Muela de Teruel – Teruel's tooth. By seven o'clock in the evening the encirclement was accomplished. The Commander of the garrison at Teruel, Colonel Rey D'Harcourt began to withdraw his defences into the town. On the 17th he gave up attempting to maintain a foothold on La Muela. Franco, however, did not decide until December 23 to suspend the Guadalajara offensive with which his German and Italian advisers

---

[1] Aznar, 549. Rojo, *España Heroica* 150.   [2] Rust, 100–1.
[3] The best accounts of this battle from the Republican side were by Buckley and Matthews. Lojendio, Aznar and Villegas are sources for the Nationalist counteroffensive.

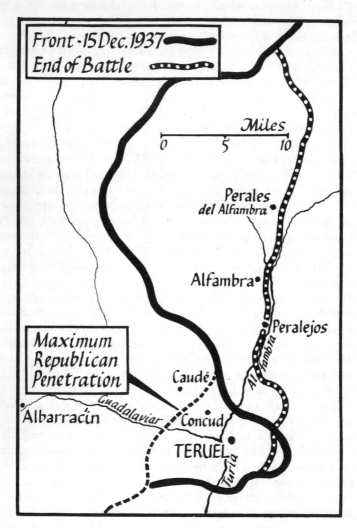

Front · 15 Dec. 1937
End of Battle

Miles
0   5   10

Perales
del Alfambra

Alfambra

Peralejos

Maximum
Republican
Penetration

Caudé

Guadalaviar

Albarracín

Concud

TERUEL

Alfambra

Turia

MAP 29. THE BATTLE OF TERUEL

urged him to continue. But the political failure to save Teruel would have cost Franco too much – especially in credits abroad.

By Christmas, after continuous fighting, Barcelona Radio had announced the fall of Teruel. In fact, the town had indeed by then been penetrated, while the 4,000 defenders (half were civilians) had established themselves in the Civil Governor's office, the Bank of Spain, the Seminary and the Convent of Santa Clara. These buildings were clustered together in the south part of the town. Ciano noted on December 20: 'The news from Spain is not good. Franco has no idea of synthesis in war. His operations are those of a magnificent battalion commander. His object is always ground, not the enemy.'[1]

Franco's counter-offensive to relieve Teruel began on December 29. Rey D'Harcourt was telegraphed to 'trust in Spain as Spain trusts in you', and to defend at all costs. After a day of artillery and aerial bombardment, Generals Varela and Aranda, with the Army Corps of Castille and Galicia, began to advance. They were protected as ever by the Condor Legion, whose personnel by this time had begun to weary of the constant changes of front. Their headquarters had now been established in a twelve-carriage train.[2] The Republican lines were pushed back, but did not break, continuing to offer furious resistance. Still no International Brigades were used. The Republican Armies were all ex-militia men, now acting as a formidable and disciplined Army. Inside the town, Rey D'Harcourt maintained his resistance. On New Year's Eve, with the weather worsening, the Nationalists made a supreme effort, reaching La Muela de Teruel in the afternoon. The city and its environs could now be easily shelled but the Republicans maintained their defence until visibility was non-existent. The roads and the engines of all machines of war froze. Teruel, maintaining its reputation for bad weather, registered a temperature of 18 degrees below zero. Fighting itself froze to a standstill. Men who, at Brunete, had cursed the remorseless sun of Castile, now went down with frostbite, and many limbs had to be amputated. The Nationalists probably suffered the most from cold, since their lack of a textile industry prevented the despatch of warm clothes. The Moors especially lacked winter clothing and longed for the sun of Africa. A blizzard lasted four days, leaving behind four feet of snow and cutting both armies off from their supply-depots. Six hundred vehicles were snowbound between Teruel and Valencia.

[1] Ciano, *Diary 1937–8*, 46.   [2] Galland, 32.

In the meantime, fighting continued inside the city itself. Prieto had insisted that civilians among the Nationalists should not be harmed. This excluded the use of large land mines. Nevertheless, the Republicans flung grenades into the already ruined cellars of the buildings in which the shivering defenders were clustered. By New Year's Day, 1938, all the defenders in the Convent and Hospital were dead. On January 3 the Civil Governor's residence fell. The remaining defenders now had no water, few medical supplies, and little food. Their defences were piles of ruins. Yet they maintained themselves till January 8 when the weather still prevented a heavy Nationalist attack. The bombing and artillery had, however, begun again. The heavy snow on the ground lent to the explosions a primaeval wildness. Colonel Rey D'Harcourt, with the Bishop of Teruel at his side, now gave in. A simple soldier, he was immediately accused by the Nationalists of both military errors and of treason. In the circumstances, however, he had resisted for far longer than might have been supposed humanly possible. After his surrender the civilian population of Teruel was evacuated. The Republicans became the besieged and the Nationalists the besiegers.

The Republican army was now joined by several International battalions, including the British. This had just been visited by Mr Harry Pollitt and Professor and Mrs Haldane. Paul Robeson had been with the brigade on Christmas Eve. He sang Negro spirituals in the snow. The British Battalion had been taken over by William Alexander, since Copeman had retired ill. The XVth Brigade Commissar was now Hugh Slater.[1] The removal of Copeman meant the removal also of the strongest influence against the death penalty for punishments in the British Battalion. Hitherto, none had occurred. Now, despite the agreement reached between the Foreign Office and the Republic, two battle-shocked Englishmen were shot for cowardice.[2]

At the New Year, Franco received a personal message from Mussolini. The Duce said that he would continue to send Italian aid, but could it not be used in accordance with its quality – in engagements in which decisive results could be expected? During this time, Berti and the other Italian commanders were deliberately misleading their Government about developments in Spain.

---

[1] Also known as Humphrey Slater. He used the Christian name of Hugh in his days as a Communist, because he thought it sounded more proletarian.
[2] Copeman, 147.

The field commander, General Frusci, telegraphed the news of the capture of Teruel on January 1. On the 7th, the day before Rey D'Harcourt gave in, Anfuso reported that the reason why the city was not completely occupied was because, 'when the Generals reached the Archbishop's [sic] palace, they wasted two hours dining with him'.[1] In fact, the Bishop was captured by the Republic the next day, when the Nationalist Generals were still two miles outside the town. The Italian over-confidence was perhaps excited by Franco's own haste in declaring the fall of the town. On January 1 he announced that the 'brooch of Teruel' was the 'clasp to the year's victories'.[2]

While such difficulties were clogging the Nationalist advance, differences among Republicans were further diminished. The two warring elements of the UGT were brought together on January 3 after skilful diplomacy by Léon Jouhaux, sent from France. Largo Caballero continued to sulk, and the Communist party continued to reserve for him their most vituperative attacks. He and Araquistain were accused of 'criminal, disrupting attacks on the unity of the People's front'.[3]

Stohrer, the German Ambassador in Salamanca, however, noted how the political and economic strength of the Republic had increased and told Berlin that, if Franco were to win by military success, Germany would have to send not only more material, but a much greater number of technical personnel and officers with a general staff training.[4] Ciano too was worried for the first time. He feared 'a Republican offensive to push back the whole Nationalist front'. And what would happen to the Italian Expeditionary Force then? 'Either we strike the first blow,' he mused on January 14, 'or skilfully disengage ourselves, and rest content with having inscribed on our banners the victories of Málaga and Santander.'[5] By the end of the month an air of frenzy had come over Ciano – preoccupied as he was with Hitler's designs on Austria, and his own more distant ones on Albania. 'We *must*,' he wrote, 'get to the end of the Spanish adventure.'

As for the non-intervention negotiations, Plymouth, in reply to Franco's idea of belligerent rights after 3,000 'volunteers' were withdrawn, proposed it after the withdrawal of 75% of them. But Plymouth was not inclined to be hasty. The German representa-

[1] Ciano, *Diary 1937–8*, 62.   [2] Quoted Peers, *Spain in Eclipse*, 36.
[3] Quoted Cattell, *Communism*, 178.   [4] *GD*, 553.
[5] Ciano, *Diaries 1937–8*, 64–5.

tive Woermann (who acted most of the time as Ribbentrop's understudy) accurately described the work of the Committee in late January as 'unreal, since all participants see through the game of the other side, but only seldom express this openly. The non-intervention policy is so unstable, and is such an artificial creation, that everyone fears to cause its collapse by a clear "no", and bear the responsibility. Therefore, unpleasant proposals are talked to death, instead of rejected. It proved tactically clever to bring up belligerent rights at the same time as volunteers,' he added, 'since this made it possible to drag out the discussion again and again.' He thought Britain was interested in volunteers only because they believed this to be a way of removing Italy from the Balearics. Volunteers, he comforted his superiors, could not be expected to be withdrawn before May – and then further delays would always be possible.[1] It was, therefore, with justified bitterness that the English Communist Edgell Rickword satirised the Committee in his poem 'To the Wife of any Non-Intervention Statesman':

> *Permit me, Madam, to invade,*
> *Briefly, your boudoir's pleasant shade:*
> *Invasion, though, is rather strong,*
> *I volunteered, and came along.*
> *So please don't yell or make a scene*
> *Or ring for James – to intervene.*

The German Foreign Ministry (the chief expert on Spain now being Weizsäcker) replied to Woermann with equal realism. German policy was to prevent a Republican victory (though not necessarily to secure a Nationalist one). Its aim in the Committee was to gain time, deferring 'for as long as possible the time when we might have to commit ourselves to a fundamental decision'.[2] However, at the end of January the British Government, partly alarmed by news of a new shipment of arms from Italy, proposed strengthening the naval patrol by placing additional observers at Spanish ports. The German Admiralty at first objected, 'since the sea was the one route by which Franco could receive reinforcements'. Eventually, the Foreign Ministry persuaded the Admiralty to drop their objections.[3]

In Burgos, the German diplomats continued arguing about their mines. Jordana told Stohrer on January 25 that he had to stand by old Spanish laws in dealing with the matter because 'the mentality

---

[1] *GD*, 564.   [2] *GD*, 573.   [3] *Ibid.*, 574–5.

of the Spanish people is such that it tends to call members of previous Governments to account for its actions. . . . One never knows what might happen', he added, with the wisdom of an old Monarchist. The *Chef du Protocol*, Sangróniz, the next day, told the Ambassador: 'I want to tell you that it was not correct to arrange the matter as Germany wanted to do. It was a psychological error to alarm and, in a sense, mobilise the interested parties, and the entire Spanish administration, by the purchase of numerous mining rights. This aroused opposition, which would not have appeared if Germany had purchased only a few to begin with.'[1] It was not the first time that the German nation had been discomfited by its own greed.

On January 17 a new stage began at Teruel. Aranda and Varela sought first to capture the high ground around the city. Heavy Italian artillery was first used to prepare the way for the advance. After an hour's fighting, accompanied overhead by aerial combats between Fiats and Russian fighters, the Republican line broke. On the 19th, for the first time, the International Brigades under General Walter were flung into the battle. The newly named Major Attlee Company now received its blood-christening, thirteen of these men dying on the first day. Slowly the Republicans continued to retreat, and the heights of La Muela were lost. However, on January 25, 26 and 27, Hernández Sarabia launched holding counter-attacks all along the front to the north of Teruel.

By the end of this battle, the Nationalists had at last organised a regular Cabinet. Franco became President of the Council, with Jordana Vice-President and Foreign Minister. Dávila, though keeping command of the Army of the North, was Minister of Defence. General Martínez Anido, the tyrannical Civil Governor of Barcelona after 1917 and later a member of Primo de Rivera's Cabinets, became Minister of Public Order. The other members of the Government were non-military. Andrés Amado, a close friend of Calvo Sotelo, became Finance Minister. A naval architect, Juan Antonio Suanzes, an old friend of Franco, became Minister of Industry and Commerce. The Carlist Count de Rodezno became Minister of Justice, Sáinz Rodríguez, the Monarchist intellectual, became Minister of Education. These represented the old political parties, but the most powerful member of the Cabinet was Serrano Suñer, with his hold over the new Falange. He became Minister of the Interior and Secretary-

[1] *GD*, 570.

General of the Falange, thus establishing real power over that
organisation. Fernández Cuesta, the only 'old shirt' in the
Government, became Minister of Agriculture in addition to his
honorific post of Secretary-General of the National Council.
Pedro González Bueno, a typical member of the new Falange,
became Minister of Labour. The last member of the Cabinet,
Alfonso Peña y Boef, was an engineer who had played no previous
role in politics. Once again the ex-Colonel of the Foreign Legion
had brought the tribes under his leadership to uneasy agreement.
The Cabinet took an oath of allegiance to Franco and to Spain in
the romanesque monastery of Las Huelgas: 'In the name of God
and His holy evangelists, I swear to fulfil my duty as Minister of
Spain with the most exact fidelity to the Head of State, Generalissimo of our glorious armies, and to the principles which constitute the Nationalist *régime* in service of the destiny of the country.'

One obvious omission among the Ministers, of course, was
Queipo de Llano. Gradually, though not yet entirely, his private
fief in Seville was to be taken away from him.[1] He was not unnaturally angry at his exclusion, and out of pique brought to an
end his inimitable nightly broadcasts. Nationalist Spain was much
duller thereafter. Thousands of Spaniards had listened to him
every night at 10 p.m.,[2] and loved and believed everything that he
said. Barcelona Radio constantly accused him of being drunk.
'Well why not,' he once bellowed in answer. 'Why shouldn't a real
hombre enjoy the superb quality of the wine and women of Seville?'
He was also taxed by Barcelona with his Republican past. He
admitted that he had thought at one time that the Republic could
solve the problems of Spain. But now the future lay with Franco.
But, he assured his listeners, if he should see that Franco was not
acting in Spain's best interests (an eventuality he considered
impossible) then his patriotism was such that he would fight even
the Caudillo. Not unnaturally this reflection was not popular at
Salamanca. What finally entranced his hearers as a rule, however,
was his custom, at the end of a specially violent attack on the
'rabble' for one vice or another, of introducing an irrelevant
personal message, such as, 'And now if my wife and daughter who

---

[1] Serrano Suñer, 66.
[2] For two nights Queipo had changed to 10.30 p.m. This was, he told his hearers,
because a delegation of Sevillian girls had complained that his broadcasts at 10 o'clock
gave them only half an hour at their window with their *novios*. So Queipo changed his
time, thereby disrupting the whole of Nationalist Spanish radio programmes: for all
stations were automatically linked with Radio Seville for Queipo.

are in Paris happen to be listening, I should like to say I hope they are well and to assure them that we here in Seville are thinking of them. *¡Buenas noches señores!*[1]

The new Spanish Nationalist Government (which transferred its headquarters, though by no means all its Ministries, to Burgos) received on February 6 a note from none other than Prieto. He proposed an agreement banning the aerial bombardment of rearguard towns on both sides. The Nationalists replied that Barcelona would continue to be bombed unless its industries were evacuated. Prieto's approach had been made because of the recent, unceasingly violent raids on Barcelona. Seville and Valladolid were bombed by the Republicans on January 26. These raids were against Prieto's instructions, being carried out by Communist pilots.[2] These, in their turn, caused a heavy Nationalist raid on Barcelona on January 28, killing 150. These air attacks were, in fact, not launched by Spaniards at all, but by Italians from Majorca without consultation with any Spanish commander. With satisfaction, Ciano recorded a somewhat melodramatic eye-witness account of the raids: 'I have never read a document so realistically horrifying. Large buildings demolished, traffic interrupted, panic on the verge of madness, five hundred wounded. And yet there were only nine S79's and the whole raid lasted one and a half minutes.'[3]

There was now a new burst of Italian submarine activity in the Mediterranean. On January 11 the Dutch merchantman *Hannah* was sunk. Two unsuccessful attempts were made on British ships on January 15 and 19. On February 1 the British ship *Endymion*, with a cargo of coal for Cartagena, was torpedoed and sunk, ten lives being lost including that of the Swedish observation officer on board. Eden told Grandi that the British Navy reserved the right henceforth to destroy all submerged submarines in its patrol zone. This had some effect, and no further submarine sinkings were reported, but sporadic aerial attacks continued on British merchant ships bringing supplies to the Republic.

On February 7, a Nationalist attack began north of Teruel

[1] There is a good study of Queipo as propagandist in Dundas, *Behind the Spanish Mask*, 59 fl.
[2] Prieto, *Yo y Moscú* 197–200.
[3] Ciano, *Diaries 1937–8*, 72. Eden promised Azcárate to try and intervene with Franco against these raids (Azcárate, 209). While it presumed that this *démarche* was being considered, the Republic refrained from all reprisals. But later, after Eden had resigned, Britain denied that she had ever taken any initiative in the matter.

towards the line of the River Alfambra where the Republican defences were weak, since the main part of their army was concentrated in the south, at Teruel itself. This battle lasted two days. The front was immediately pierced by three attacks. Monasterio's cavalry on this occasion swept all before it in the most spectacular cavalry action of the war. But Aranda and Yagüe, the latter with the Army of Africa, advanced with almost equal swiftness. By February 7 the victory was complete, and achieved before Hernández Sarabia had managed to send any reinforcements. In these two days, the Republic lost one thousand square kilometres, seven thousand prisoners, fifteen thousand other casualties and a vast amount of material – munitions, arms and ambulances. Those who were not cut off by this highly successful manoeuvre fled in disorder, and were machine-gunned from the air as they did so.

Before the next onslaught, Lord Plymouth had presented in London his revised ideas for the withdrawal of volunteers. The Powers should choose between a proportionate or numerical withdrawal. Twenty thousand or fifteen thousand 'might represent a figure to be regarded as 'substantial'. Grandi and Woermann commented politely. More important talks were now going on in London than these, between Grandi, Eden and Chamberlain. It shortly became clear that these were in fact three-sided. Eden made the start of negotiations for an Anglo-Italian agreement conditional on the withdrawal of at least some volunteers from Spain. Chamberlain thought that this insistence would waste too much time. On February 18 Grandi refused to discuss separately the volunteers in Spain (or Austria). He suggested 'general conversations' in Rome. Chamberlain agreed. Eden did not. And so the latter resigned with his Under-Secretary of State, Lord Cranborne, on the 20th, to the delight of Ciano and Mussolini – and apparently also, of Lord Perth.[1] Eden had throughout seemed uneasy and unhappy – as well he might – at having to be the advocate of the policy of non-intervention, which turned out, in effect, to be a policy of discrimination against the Republic.[2] The crowds who gathered outside No. 10 Downing Street to cheer the 'strong young figure' of the outgoing Foreign Secretary – the words are those of Churchill – shouted, 'Arms for Spain!' with new, but unjustified optimism.

---

[1] Feiling, 337. Ciano, *Diaries 1937–8*, 78.
[2] Azcárate always gained the impression in interviews with Eden that he found non-intervention repugnant.

The last battle for Teruel began on February 17. Yagüe on this day crossed the Alfambra and, advancing southwards along its east bank, cut off the city from the north. On the 18th, he and Aranda began a movement of encirclement, like that carried out in December by the Republicans, at several kilometres distance from the city. Yet another Commander of the British Battalion had to be named in succession, since Alexander was now wounded. This was Sam Wild. Like Fred Copeman, he had served on HMS *Resolution*. A Communist of long standing, Wild had fought with the Brigade from December 1936 till May 1937 and then since December 1937.

By February 20, the Republican road and rail communications to Valencia were threatened on both sides. Teruel itself was being penetrated by other Nationalist units. Hernández Sarabia gave orders for withdrawal. Most of the Republican army was out of danger before the line of retreat was cut off, but they left behind much material. Fourteen thousand five hundred prisoners were taken. Ten thousand Republican corpses were discovered by the Nationalists in Teruel, apart from those who had fallen in the Alfambra battle.

Among those surrounded in Teruel were El Campesino and his staff. They managed, however, to force their way out through the enemy lines. This bearded man of action later claimed that he was purposely left in Teruel to die by Lister and Modesto, his chief rivals among the Communist soldiers. He also reported that Teruel itself was deliberately starved of ammunition by the Russian General 'Grigorivich', and allowed to fall, so as to discredit Prieto.[1]

Prieto's prestige, along with his own self-confidence undoubtedly diminished after the fall of Teruel. But the full attack upon Prieto by the Communists did not begin until after the fall of Teruel, when '*le seul grand homme de la république*', as French journalists were fond of describing him, surrendered to pessimism. Until then, the Communists had been compelled to conceal their dislike of Prieto. It was only, indeed, on February 24 that Hernández's first article appeared in *Frente Rojo*, denouncing 'the defeatists'. The decision by the Communists to launch one of their deadly campaigns against the War Minister must have been taken only shortly before that.

It seems that the Bulgarian Stepanov (representative of the Comintern in Spain) returned about this time from a visit to Moscow. Russia, he said, was contemplating sending a great deal

---

[1] El Campesino, *Listen Comrades*, 11; *Comunista en España*, 65-70.

of new aid to Spain. For this, Prieto would have to be ousted. Thereafter a policy of grim resistance would be followed. Hernández argued that Prieto was surely the man for this, since he could gain the support of the Communists, the CNT and the UGT. But Togliatti, as so often, closed the argument by announcing that Negrín would have to take over full power.[1]

[1] Hernández, 159.

66

The situation in March 1938 – attacks on Prieto – sinking of the
Baleares – *the Aragón offensive and the Republican rout – the*
Nationalist labour charter

Nineteen months had now passed since the Generals had
risen in July 1936. Neville Chamberlain, freed from the
embarrassing virility of Eden at the Foreign Office, was
ready for arrangements with Mussolini. Hitler had told Schuschnigg, the Austrian Chancellor, that if he did not yield to German
demands Austria would become 'another Spain'.[1] The question of
the withdrawal of volunteers in Spain had brought Eden's quarrel
with Chamberlain to a head, but seemed otherwise certain to remain an academic matter – as Franco earnestly hoped it would be.
Half-way through this 'Second Triumphant Year',[2] the Generalissimo would not mind losing the Italian infantry, said the Marqués
de Magaz, his Ambassador in Berlin; but he required the Condor
Legion and the Italian 'specialists' (presumably the bombing
pilots in Majorca) till the end of the war. Mussolini nevertheless
wanted his precious infantry to be used, so he pettishly ordered the
air force in Majorca to cease operations till it was.[3] For this reason
Barcelona enjoyed, at the start of March 1938, some peace from
aerial attack. Bruno Mussolini, the Duce's son, was meantime
withdrawn from the air force engaged in Spain, after twenty-seven
actions. He had volunteered to take part, but withdrew on
Franco's suggestion when special efforts were undertaken by the
Republic to shoot him down.[4]

Inside Barcelona, the Communist campaign against Prieto was
beginning. On February 27 La Pasionaria publicly criticised his

[1] Schuschnigg, *Ein Requiem in Rot Weiss-Rot* 37 fl. Quoted Churchill, 205.
[2] It had become customary in Nationalist Spain to date public decrees and even
private letters by the terminology Year I, Year II after the Rising of July 18, 1936.
[3] Ciano, *Diaries 1937–8*, 80. Ciano too was almost frantic: 'Franco must exploit his
success. Fortune is not a train which passes every day at the same time. She is a
prostitute who offers herself fleetingly and then passes on to others.'
[4] Rachele Mussolini, 71.

518 THE SPANISH CIVIL WAR

conduct of the war. Hernández began a series of attacks upon him in *Mundo Obrero* under the pen-name of Juan Ventura. The Communist party of Cartagena named Prieto 'enemy of the people', while blaming him for the explosion the previous June which had destroyed the battleship *Jaime Primero*. Prieto complained to Negrín. At a meeting of the Socialist party executive in his own house, Negrín sought to belittle the differences between Prieto and the Communists. The Minister of the Interior, Prieto's old *protégé* Zugazagoitia, intervened dramatically. 'Don Juan,' he said, 'masks off! At the front, our comrades are murdered because they refuse to accept the Communist party's commands. As for Don Indalecio, look at the articles in the *Frente Rojo* and *La Vanguardia* by "Juan Ventura", a *nom-de-plume* of the Minister of Education!'¹ *La Vanguardia*, a Republican paper which invariably supported Negrín, had that day indeed named Prieto an 'impenitent pessimist'. Negrín answered that he could do without neither the Communists nor Prieto. Some days later, *Frente Rojo* published another article by Hernández this time suggesting Prieto's dismissal. Zugazagoitia protested at a Cabinet meeting that this was published after the censor had struck it out. Hernández replied that a Minister could not be censored by officials. Negrín successfully calmed both the opponents. The quarrel simmered. During this time, Prieto made new efforts to achieve, through Angel Baza at St Jean de Luz, that compromise peace at which he had been for so long aiming.

On March 6 the Republic received the encouragement of a victory at sea. The Nationalist fleet, led by the cruisers *Baleares*, *Canarias* and *Almirante Cervera*, were sailing past Cartagena, at midnight on March 5. For once, no German or Italian destroyers shadowed their movements. The Republican cruisers *Libertad* and *Mendez Nuñez*, and the destroyers *Lepanto*, *Sánchez Barcáiztegui* and *Admiral Antequera* came broadside against this force. The Republican destroyers loosed their torpedoes and immediately left the scene. The *Baleares* was hit amidships and blew up. The other Nationalist ships did not go to the rescue of those wrecked. So HMS *Kempenfelt* and *Boreas*, on non-intervention patrol nearby, picked up 400 out of the 1,000 who were aboard and took them to the *Canarias*. Republican aircraft appeared overhead and dropped

---

¹ i.e. Jesús Hernández. For confirmation of Communist murders at the front, *see* Peirats, III 102–30. The CNT and FAI sent a complaint on this question to Prieto on March 25.

bombs. A British able-seaman was killed. The Nationalist Admiral went down with his ship.

Franco, meanwhile, had prepared his next offensive into Aragón. The attacking army would be commanded by Dávila, with Vigón as his second-in-command. Solchaga, Moscardó, Yagüe and Aranda would command army corps, alongside the Italian General Berti. Divisions under García Escámez and García Valiño would form the reserve. Varela, with the so-called Army of Castile, would hold himself ready in the wings of the general attack, at Teruel. The Condor Legion also held itself in readiness, although at this time there was considerable restlessness among these hard-worked fliers. The slogan, 'We are fighting on the wrong side' even began to circulate among them, half-humorously but with a real feeling of respect for the military skill of their adversaries.[1] As for the German tanks, Franco wanted to parcel them out among the infantry – 'in the usual way of Generals who belong to the old school', von Thoma scornfully commented. 'I had to fight . . .' he said, 'to use the tanks in a concentrated way.'[2]

The attack, as usual preceded by devastating artillery and aerial barrage, began on March 9. The best troops of the Republic were weary after Teruel. Their war material was exhausted – units were observed going into battle with half the men lacking even rifles. The Aragón front was broken in several points on the first day. Yagüe advanced down the right bank of the Ebro, sweeping all before him. On March 10, Solchaga's Navarrese conquered Belchite. The XVth International Brigade were the last out of that dead town.[3] The Italians under Berti encountered momentary stiff

---

[1] The Condor Legion now consisted of two Messerschmitt 109 groups of four squadrons; two Heinkel 51 groups of two squadrons; a reconnaissance group of Heinkels and Dornier 17s, of three squadrons; four bomber groups of three squadrons of Heinkels III and Junkers 52. Fighters and reconnaissance groups were of nine aircraft, bomber groups of twelve (Miksche, 81).

[2] The tank corps under von Thoma now comprised four battalions, each of three companies with 15 light tanks a company. This was accompanied by 30 anti-tank companies, with six 37 millimetre guns apiece. (Liddell-Hart, *Other Side of the Hill*.)

[3] The bespectacled and now veteran American Major Merriman and the Brigade Commissar Doran were killed in the retreat. Merriman was succeeded by the English Malcolm Dunbar. Doran's successor was Johnny Gates, a steel workers' leader, then aged twenty-four. A huge Brooklyn art student, Milton Wolf, took over command of the Lincoln Battalion. The Commissar of the British Battalion, Wally Tapsell, was also killed near Belchite. It was said that he was shot in the back. He had been an outspoken critic of the changes of front in the Communist policy towards Spain. He had, also, many enemies, since it had been he who, in 1929, had upset the then Communist party of Great Britain leadership, and installed Pollitt. But at this distance of time, it is not easy to distinguish the truth of his death.

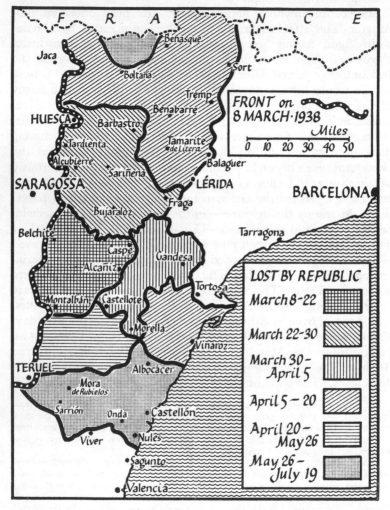

MAP 30. THE CAMPAIGNS IN ARAGÓN AND THE LEVANTE
March–July 1937

resistance at Rudilla and then, with the Black Arrows leading, broke through the line. 'It is full speed ahead,' crowed Ciano in Rome.[1] Aranda had to endure harder fighting, before breaking through, on March 13, to capture Montalbán. The defence had hardly yet begun. Rojo named Caspe as its centre and there assembled all the International Brigades. But, even as he did so, news arrived of the Italian approach towards the next town of Alcañiz. Even where Republican units fought effectively they were obliged to fall back due to the collapse of the units next to them. The rout appeared absolute.

The day of the start of this offensive saw the promulgation in Nationalist Spain of the Falangist Labour Charter. This was a culmination of the political reflections of Serrano Suñer. Many of the proposals were admirable in themselves. Hours and conditions of work were to be regulated. A minimum wage was to be guaranteed, accompanied by increased social insurance, family allowances and holidays with pay. Labourers' wages were to be raised and every peasant family was to be allowed a plot of land adequate to supply their primary needs. Tenant farmers were to be safeguarded against eviction. These aims remained, however, chiefly in the realm of aspiration. The only fully applied sections of the Charter were those providing for respect for private property and the threat that acts which disturbed production would be regarded as treason. The economic life of the country was to be controlled by the organisation of 'vertical' syndicates, whose officials would all be Falangists. These prescribed a hierarchy of assemblies rising from local corporations in each district to five national chambers of agriculture, shipping, industry and commerce, public and national service, and culture, and ultimately to a national corporative assembly.

This law was followed by a Press Law in April, by which the State assumed control of the whole structure of the Spanish Nationalist press. Only registered journalists would be allowed to practise this craft, just as only registered newspapers and periodicals would be allowed to appear. No doubt the already subservient newspapermen of Nationalist Spain were persuaded to accept this law without protest by the introduction of a regular minimum salary scale for journalists of different grades.

[1] Ciano, *Diary 1937–8*, 87.

67

Negrín in Paris – Blum forms his new Government – opening of the
frontier – heavy raids on Barcelona – Mussolini's satisfaction –
collapse in Aragón continues – Yagüe enters Catalonia – the SIM's
murders – Negrín and Prieto – a riot in Barcelona – the fall of Prieto –
Negrín forms a new Government – the Nationalists reach the
Mediterranean – the Anglo-Italian Pact

The collapse of the Aragón front had caused **Negrín** to fly
urgently to Paris to beg for the re-opening of the French
frontier. This had been closed once more since January,
when the Radical Chautemps had been abandoned by the
Socialists. The leader of the Republic arrived in the French capital
at an opportune moment – as indeed he had been led to expect by
a letter he had received from Blum.[1] For the sudden change in the
Spanish War occurred when the rest of Europe were occupied by
the outrage of Hitler's rape of Austria. On March 13, Chautemps's
Ministry was brought down by the Socialists. Blum formed his
second Popular Front Government with the moderate Paul-
Boncour as his Foreign Secretary. Many in Paris now believed war
with Germany to be inevitable. Even the customarily cautious
Massigli, Political Director at the Quai d'Orsay, went so far as
to call non-intervention a farce.[2] Monsieur Comert, Director of
Information at the Quai d'Orsay, was overheard to say, 'We will
avenge Austria in Spain'.[3] At a meeting of the French National
Defence Committee on March 15 Blum suggested an ultimatum to
Franco. This would state: 'If within 24 hours you have not re-
nounced the support of foreign forces, France will . . . reserve the
right to take all measures of intervention which she judges useful'.
General Gamelin pointed out, however, that the General Staff
did not have a separate mobilisation plan for the south-west of
France. Daladier said that world war would clearly follow from
direct intervention in Spain. Léger, Secretary-General of the
Quai d'Orsay, remarked that intervention would certainly be a

[1] Álvarez del Vayo, *Last Optimist*, 300.   [2] *USD*, 1938 Vol 1 163.
[3] Brasillach, 397.

casus belli for Germany and Italy, while Britain would separate from French policy.[1]

On March 17 the French Cabinet agreed to Negrín's request to open the frontier.[2] Blum wept in open sympathy with Negrín as arms, purchased from Russia, private adventurers, the Comintern, and some even from the French Government itself, began to flow across the Pyrenean frontier into Spain. But all further steps were rejected. The idea that a French motorised corps might go to the aid of Catalonia was disallowed by the Chiefs of Staff when they realised that such a step would probably have to be accompanied by general mobilisation. Blum was assured by Colonel Morell, the French Military *Attaché* in Barcelona, a Monarchist and a member of *Action Française*, '*Monsieur le Président du Conseil! Je n'ai qu'un mot à vous dire: un roi de France ferait la guerre.*'[3] But Ribbentrop was right when on March 21 he told the Italian *Chargé* in Rome, Magistrati, that France would not intervene in Spain without Britain's support. He was as perspicacious when he added that he doubted that Chamberlain 'was bent on a policy of adventure'.[4]

On March 16 Barcelona was once again bombed by the Italians. The German Ambassador in Salamanca, Stohrer, reported the effects as 'terrible. All parts of the city were affected. There was no evidence of any attempt to hit military objectives.'[5] The first raid came at about ten o'clock in the evening. Six Hydro-Heinkels flew across the city at 80 miles an hour and 400 metres up. Thereafter raids followed at three-hourly intervals until 3 o'clock in the afternoon of March 18. There were seventeen raids in all. About 1,300 were killed and 2,000 injured.[6] Ciano reported that orders for the raids were given directly by Mussolini and that 'Franco knew nothing about them'. Stohrer reported Franco furious.[7] On March 19, indeed, the Generalissimo asked for their suspension, for fear of 'complications abroad'. This did not prevent Ciano from

---

[1] This meeting is described in Gamelin, *Servir*, Vol II 322–8.

[2] They were perhaps partly stimulated to do so by the appearance of a news story that a military rising had taken place against Franco at Tetuán. This was the fabrication of the Comintern propaganda department, the work being inspired by Otto Katz and carried out by Claud Cockburn. The fraud aimed to give the impression that Franco might still be defeated and that therefore it was worth the French effort to open the border.

[3] *Les Evénements Survenus en France*, 253.

[4] *GD*, 622. Ribbentrop had succeeded Neurath as German Foreign Minister in February.

[5] *GD*, 625.

[6] Report of US Military *Attaché*, Colonel Fuqua (Bowers, 376.)

[7] *GD*, 626.

telling both the American Ambassadors in Rome that Italy had no control over Italian aircraft operating in Spain. Mussolini, thinking, like his own ex-General Douhet, that aircraft could win a war by terror, declared his delight that the Italians 'should be horrifying the world by their aggressiveness for a change, instead of charming it by the guitar'.[1] Though the people of Barcelona were at first terrified, and many went up into the hills at night to sleep, as in Madrid no military advantage was gained by the attackers. Many of the wounded from their stretchers exhorted the public with clenched fists to resist.

The consternation caused abroad was considerable. Meetings of protest were held in London.[2] The most eloquent protest was perhaps George Barker's poem 'Elegy for Spain'. Cordell Hull abandoned his customary caution to express horror 'on behalf of the whole US people'. But such indiscriminate raids on Republican towns continued from time to time during the rest of the war. The contribution they made to the Nationalist cause was not, however, worth the trouble and damage which they brought. For instance, the petrol storage station in Barcelona was bombed 37 times before being hit. Nor did the Nationalists seriously interfere with the loading and unloading of Republican supply ships in the Mediterranean harbours.

The Aragón advance meantime continued. On March 16 three Nationalist divisions, commanded by Barrón, Muñoz Grandes and Bautista Sánchez, surrounded Caspe. In the South, Aranda finally broke the Republican lines and captured Montalbán. On March 17 Caspe fell, after two days of heavy fighting in which the International Brigades, including the XVth, performed prodigies of valour. The British Battalion's commander, Sam Wild, and others, narrowly escaped capture. By now, the Nationalist army was 100 kilometres east of their starting point eight days before. Before the natural defences of the broad rivers Ebro and Guadalupe, the advancing armies were allowed a pause for reorganisation.

On March 22, 1938, the Nationalists' offensive began again, this

[1] Ciano, *Diary 1937–8*, 91–2.
[2] A public letter of protest was signed by a mixed group of eminent Englishmen, including both Archbishops, Cardinal Hinsley, the Lord Chief Justice, the Chairman of I.C.I. and Lloyds, Lords Horder and Camrose, the Headmasters of Rugby and Haileybury, Maynard Keynes and many others. These were the days when the slaughter of innocent civilians could still shock public opinion. On one occasion H. G. Wells gave his name to one of these protests. The Nationalist agent, the Duke of Alba, wrote to him in genuine astonishment that so great a writer should have such truck with the 'rabble'.

time against those battle lines before Saragossa and Huesca which had been held for so long by the Catalan army. All these familiar fortifications were lost in a day. Generals Sòlchaga and Moscardó launched five attacks on the 150 kilometres from Huesca to Saragossa in one morning (one being to the north of the former city). Huesca was relieved at last. Tardienta and Alcubierre fell. The next day, Yagüe crossed the Ebro and captured Pina, that *pueblo* whence so long ago Durruti had been frozen away by the silent hostility of the inhabitants. All those revolutionary Aragonese villages which in August 1936 had given birth to such a varied political anthropology were now captured. Pursued by machine-gun fire from the air, the inhabitants, where they could, fled eastwards in an all too familiar stream, with their cattle, their chickens, and their carts carrying loved objects. On March 25, Yagüe captured Fraga, and thus entered the golden land of Catalonia. At Lérida, the next town, El Campesino's division made a brave and militarily most valuable stand for a week. To the north, Moscardó entered Barbastro. Farther north still, Solchaga was for a while pinned down in the Pyrenees. As they wound their way through the valleys, his columns presented an easy target to Republican artillery and aircraft. To the south, meanwhile, Aranda, García Escámez, Berti and García Valiño drove through the high plain known as the Maestrazgo, in southern Aragón, before preparing to advance to the Mediterranean. The fronts indeed hardly existed. There were desperate but isolated acts of resistance by one or other of the Republican units. In general, however, the campaign seemed lost, and it was not at all clear where the rout would end. While superior artillery and leadership played its part in these rapid Nationalist advances, air superiority was the most notable cause of victory. The plains of Aragón provided easy landing fields. Aeroplanes thus could carry out the one-time functions of cavalry in driving Republican units from their positions as in a charge. From these battles the Germans learnt a great deal about the use of fighters for the support of infantry – and the Russians did the same.[1] So too did the increasingly skilful pilots of the Spanish Nationalist Air Force.[2]

---

[1] The German air ace Galland, with the Condor Legion, recalled that it was from this time that a clear division could be made between combat and offensive aircraft. (Galland, 29.)

[2] The Spanish pilots were accustomed to think of an air battle in the same terms as a bull-fight. Always they would refer to the stage of actual battle by the bull-fight cheer, 'al toro!'

At this period of military crisis the SIM came into its own in Barcelona. Officially designed to find spies, it now sought 'defeatists' as well. These were named to include those guilty of profiteering, food-hoarding and robbery. Summary tribunals were set up to deal with these 'offences'. The SIM undertook a brief private murder campaign of vengeance. Forty people had been 'taken for a ride' before the Government intervened to end this development. The special prisons of the SIM in Barcelona, especially that in the convent of San Juan, nevertheless remained full of strange tortures which might have been devised by the ghost of Edgar Allan Poe. A spherical room painted in black, with a single light at the top, gave a mad feeling of vertigo. Some cells were so small that one could not sit down.

Negrín now returned from his partially successful mission in Paris. He found Barcelona overwhelmed with gloom. The fountainhead of this defeatism was, inevitably, Don Indalecio Prieto. Stretched in his armchair in the Ministry of National Defence, he would blandly announce to journalists and sycophants in the tones of a victor: 'We are lost!' Prieto infected everyone with this mood, including the easily influenced Giral, the Foreign Minister. Giral even expressed his gloom to the French Ambassador, Labonne, recently arrived in Barcelona. Almost before Negrín had returned, therefore, the French Government was being informed by their representative in Barcelona that any war material they might send to Catalonia might quickly fall into the hands of Franco – or Hitler or Mussolini. It required all Negrín's skill to convince Labonne that he personally was still resolved to fight on. Meantime, what was to be done with Prieto?[1] A Cabinet meeting had been arranged at the Pedralbes Palace in Barcelona under Azaña's chairmanship. Before it began, Negrín called Prieto and Zugazagoitia, Prieto's chief follower, and begged them to support him if, at the Cabinet, anyone should mention negotiations. Both agreed to do so, apparently thinking that the Prime Minister himself was going to propose mediation – which Prieto had been pursuing assiduously in recent weeks. Prieto suggested that Republican funds abroad should now be blocked so as to help those who might be forced into exile after a mediated peace. Negrín replied 'all that is taken care of'. At a preliminary meeting of Ministers before the Cabinet, Negrín said that he had heard it said that some of the Ministers

[1] Álvarez del Vayo, *Last Optimist*, 301.

were for peace. No one replied. Giral, the Foreign Minister, said that Labonne, the new French Ambassador, had offered the members of the Government a refuge at the French Embassy in the event of complete collapse. The Republican fleet, Labonne had added, could sail to Bizerta or to Toulon. This latter point made everyone angry, for the Cabinet thought that, once more, the French were thinking only of themselves and desiring to remove from the Mediterranean a potentially hostile Spanish fleet in Nationalist hands. The Ministers then moved into Azaña's room. Here, however, the angry noise of a great multitude of people could be heard moving towards the palace. A demonstration was being held to protest against peace, and Prieto. Organised by the Communists it was nevertheless joined by the Anarchists. The crowd carried banners on which were written 'Down with the treacherous Ministers!' and 'Down with the Minister of National Defence'. The gates of the Pedralbes Palace gave way and this Barcelona mob, inspired by the Communists, arrived beneath the French windows of Azaña's room. Prieto, the particular object of the crowd's anger, could thus hear La Pasionaria, his particular enemy, haranguing her incensed followers. Negrín eventually persuaded the crowd to go away, having reassured them that the war would go on. Prieto later accused the Prime Minister, probably truthfully, of organising this demonstration. Yet it would have been difficult to see that Prieto could have made headway with any negotiations. For the Nationalists would only, then as later, have accepted unconditional surrender. This would have included the freedom to exterminate the 'absolute enemy' – the phrase used by Serrano Suñer to describe every shade of left-wing opinion, from liberal to Anarchist.[1]

On March 28 a fateful meeting occurred of the War Council. Prieto's gloom dispirited everyone present. Negrín had to intervene to assure the Generals that they retained his confidence. On March 29, while El Campesino was still battling with great courage for Lérida and the XVth International Brigade equally gallantly for Gandesa, the Republican Cabinet met in Barcelona. Prieto (in Negrín's words) 'with his suggestive eloquence, his habitual pathos, completely demoralised the Cabinet by falsely representing the conclusions of the previous day's meeting of the Council for

[1] The above derives from Negrín and Prieto, *Epistolario*; Álvarez del Vayo, *Last Optimist*; Zugazagoitia; Prieto's apologia, *Cómo y por qué salí del Ministerio de Defensa Nacional*; see also the commentary on these in Madariaga.

War'. On the night of March 29–30, 'a painful and violent struggle surged up' within the mind of Negrín. As a result he decided to transfer Prieto from the Ministry of Defence, though retaining him in the Government.[1]

On April 3 Lérida and Gandesa fell to the Nationalist armies. In Gandesa 140 British and American members of the XVth International Brigade were taken prisoner. The Brigade had, however, successfully held back Yagüe for several days, so permitting regroupment and the safe withdrawal of material. Two days later came the fall of Indalecio Prieto.

It has often been alleged that Negrín was at this time black-mailed by the Communists. They are accused of having told the Prime Minister that, unless Prieto were dismissed, there would be no more Soviet aid. But since March 17 aircraft and medium-calibre guns had been coming from Russia, being landed at Bordeaux and transported overland across the Pyrenees to Barcelona. In truth, Negrín himself, without Communist encouragement, was determined to move Prieto from the Ministry of National Defence because of his defeatism. He desired that he should be Minister Without Portfolio or of Public Works. But Prieto refused these posts and so left the Government. The question at issue had been whether or no Don Indalecio should fill the most important position in the Cabinet while despairing of victory and all the time seeking mediation. Yet, as he must by this time have discovered, the only means to secure peace with the Nationalists was by capitulation.

Prieto later explained that he abandoned the Ministry of Defence because he was weary of Communist control. He described his contests with Communists over matters of strategy and tactics. He revealed how two shipping companies, France Navigation and the Mid-Atlantic Company, had been founded to purchase arms abroad but were later used for making commercial profits for the Communists.[2] Yet he did not suggest that from the point of view of carrying on the war, a social or military policy different from that of the Communists would have been more advantageous. He did not explain what policy, other than one of friendship with Russia, could have been followed when Russia remained the only sure

[1] *Epistolario*, 24.
[2] Other shipping companies created in England by the Republican Government were those of Howard Tenens Limited, the Prosper Steamship Company, the Burlington Steamship Company, 'Southern Shipping', and the Karfish Company. The Entreprise Maritime, also created by the Republic, was registered at Marseilles.

source of war material – apart from the flagging industries of Catalonia. Nor did he suggest what else could be done other than carry on the war when the Nationalists offered only unconditional surrender. After all, his own plans for a negotiated peace with Franco had failed. The truth seems to be that Prieto was mentally exhausted by the war and its troubles, as well as by his own disputes with the Communists.

The Communists had, in fact, their own private crisis at this moment. The Soviet Government wished the Spanish Communists also to withdraw from Negrín's Government. The caucus immediately assembled in its customary atmosphere of jealousy and cigarette smoke. Did Moscow want the Republic to lose, demanded Hernández? The Bulgarian Stepanov replied that this move was aimed to convince English and French public opinion that the Communists were not interested in the conquest of power in Spain. If European war came, a Russian alliance with Britain and France would thus be easier to achieve.[1] Moscow's orders were, however, partially disobeyed. Uribe remained at the Ministry of Agriculture but Hernández left the Ministry of Education to become Commissar-General of the Armies of the Centre and South, a post of far greater power. This purely superficial change in the Cabinet was anyway more than recompensed for by the return of the Russian apologist Álvarez del Vayo to the Foreign Ministry.[2] The other Socialists in the Cabinet, apart from Negrín, were González Peña, who became Minister of Justice and Paulino Gómez Sainz, who became Minister of the Interior. The Basque Irujo became Minister Without Portfolio and the Catalan Ayguadé remained as Minister of Labour. The Government was strengthened by the entry into it of Segundo Blanco of the CNT, who became Minister of Education and Health. The Anarchists agreed to this support of Negrín (as they had supported Largo Caballero in the far-off and heroic days of November 1936) because of the extremity of the crisis. The other four posts went to Republicans – Giral (Minister without Portfolio), Giner de los Ríos (Minister of Transport), Velao Oñate (Minister of Public Works) and Méndez Aspe, an

[1] Hernández, 166–8. On March 18 the Soviet Government had proposed a 'grand alliance' within the League against Hitler. This idea was firmly rejected by Chamberlain.
[2] Furthermore the following other Communists now held key positions: Nuñez Maza (Under-Secretary for Air); Cordón (Under-Secretary for War); Hidalgo de Cisneros (Chief of Air Force); Prados (Chief of Staff of the Navy); Cuevas (Director General of Security); Marcial Fernández (Director General of *Carabineros*).

intimate of Negrín's (Minister of Finance). The ex-Minister of the Interior, Zugazagoitia, somewhat surprisingly became Secretary-General of Defence.

The same day that Prieto fell, General Aranda's troops gained their first sight of the Mediterranean. A few days later the Italians almost reached the sea at the mouth of the Ebro. They were held up at Tortosa by stiff resistance by Lister. Colonel Gambara, in field command, reported differences with the Spanish. Ciano for once agreed that his countrymen were not blameless. 'So often Italian officers show a stubborn and provincial intolerance, explicable only by their ignorance of the world,' he remarked.[1] To the north the advance of the Nationalists continued into Catalonia. By April 8 Balaguer, Tremp and Camarasa had fallen. This cut off from Barcelona her electric current generated from the Pyrenean waterfalls. The old steam-generating plants of the city had to be put to work again.

By April 15 it did seem that the end of the war must be near. On this day, Good Friday, General Alonso Vega, leading the 4th Navarrese Division, took Vinaroz, a fishing town known for its lampreys. He was thus able to make the sign of the Cross on the shores of the Mediterranean. His men waded out into the sea in a mood of exultation. The Republic, despite furious and now well-equipped resistance to this last attack, were now cut in two. While the Government remained in Barcelona, Miaja, accompanied by Hernández as Chief Commissar, became Supreme Commander of all the centre and south-west of Spain still in Republican hands. He was increasingly built up by propaganda as the real strong man of the Republic, 'the Joffre of Spain'.[2]

The next day, April 16, Chamberlain achieved his Anglo-Italian Mediterranean Pact. Italy undertook to withdraw her troops from Spain when the war was over. Only then would the pact come into force. The two countries also agreed to guarantee the *status quo* in the Mediterranean. Perth, noted Ciano, was moved. He said: 'You know how much I have wanted this to come.' 'It is true,' added Ciano, 'Perth has been a friend – witness dozens of reports which are in our hands.'[3] Azcárate sent a protest to the Foreign Office expressing his horror that the public exchange of letters between Italy and Britain should calmly accept Italian troops in Spain till the end of the Civil War – while at the same

[1] Ciano, *Diary 1937–8*, 99.   [2] Miravitlles, 41.
[3] Ciano, *Diary 1937–8*, 102.

time Britain was nominally maintaining the Non-Intervention Pact and a plan for the withdrawal of volunteers.[1] *Pravda* denounced the Anglo-Italian pact as giving its blessing to Mussolini in 'his war against the Spanish people'. Churchill echoed the same in a letter to Eden – 'a complete triumph for Mussolini, who gains our cordial acceptance for his fortification of the Mediterranean against us, for his conquest of Abyssinia, and for his violence in Spain'.[2] The English Conservative opponents of Chamberlain, headed by Winston Churchill, came during the summer of 1938, to be Republican sympathisers.[3]

But there was no sign that Italy had any more intention of keeping the Non-Intervention Agreement than in the past. It was to no effect whatever that Álvarez del Vayo began his new term as Foreign Minister with an eloquent appeal to Britain and France to end non-intervention. Three hundred more Italian officers went to Spain on April 11. For her part, Germany had concluded that the approaching Nationalist victory would prevent any action on the volunteer plan. The Foreign Ministry, therefore, instructed their London Embassy to agree to any formula for withdrawal of volunteers. Hitler now wanted to withdraw the German troops in Spain. The Austrian Air Force needed development, and 'our soldiers cannot learn any more'.[4] Franco suggested that the Condor Legion might be withdrawn, provided that the aircraft, anti-aircraft guns and other equipment were left behind for the Spanish pilots, whom the Germans had trained to fly. The Generalissimo, meantime, had begun to prepare for victory – as well he might. On April 5 he abolished the Catalan Statute. The use of Catalan was officially prohibited. These measures, like the air raids on Barcelona, created anger without causing fear.

[1] Azcárate, 153. The Republican Ambassador added that thereafter 'shame and indignation' at British policy caused the Republic to keep relations with the UK to a minimum.
[2] Churchill, 221.
[3] Churchill, for instance, was even brought to have an amicable conversation with the Republican Ambassador, Azcárate, showing sympathy for the Republic, after dinner at the Soviet Embassy. The apparent conversion of Churchill to the Republic was the work of his son-in-law, Mr Duncan Sandys, who visited Barcelona in the Spring of 1938. However, his Republicanism was never ideological. See for instance his interview with Luis Calvo, published in *La Nación* of Buenos Aires, August 14, 1938: 'Franco has all the right on his side because he loves his country. Also Franco is defending Europe against the Communist danger – if you wish to put it in those terms. But I, I am English, and I prefer the triumph of the wrong cause. I prefer that the other side wins, because Franco could be an upset or a threat to British interests, and the others no.'
[4] *GD*, 635.

68

Yet the Republic, despite appearances, was not beaten. This was chiefly due to the reopening of the French frontier on March 17. It was partly due to the reorganisation of the General Staff carried on under the shadow of imminent defeat. Negrín's new Government brought forward a new commander-in-chief in place of Rojo, in the person of the efficient and hard-working Communist ex-Sergeant of the Legion, Modesto. Whether it was simply that Rojo was tired and had permitted himself to be influenced by the pessimistic Prieto, a new spirit marked the Republican General Staff from this time. These changes were reflected immediately in the course of the battles. Perhaps also the Nationalist commanders and their troops were somewhat weary after their brilliant campaign.

Working-class unity had meanwhile been greatly encouraged by the serious military situation. On March 18 the UGT and CNT signed an agreement marking a further retreat from Anarchism. Industry would henceforth be entirely subject to central economic planning. Collectivisation of agriculture would be voluntary. On the other hand, the UGT agreed to urge the Government to cease the dissolution of collective farms and to support workers' control in those industries which desired it. Both unions also agreed that their tasks were, above all, to promote greater production. In fact, collectivisation was everywhere giving way to State control. The Government increasingly appointed 'mediators' as supervisors of those concerns still run by committees of workers. The Economics Ministry would then provide such concerns with raw materials which they might otherwise lack. The Republic also attempted, without great success, to persuade businessmen in exile to return to Spain.

In the Pyrenees, Generals Solchaga, Moscardó and Yagüe had advanced as far as the river Segre and its tributary, the Noguera Pallaresa, which runs up to the French border.[1] They had, however, to leave an enclave of one Republican division under Colonel Beltrán, nicknamed *El Esquinazado* (The Dodger), in the Valle del Alto Cinca, up against the frontier. The course of the Ebro from the junction with the Segre to the sea completed the northern front. It presented a natural line of defence for Catalonia upon which the Republicans swiftly improved by fortifications.

At the mouth of the Ebro, the Italians were held up at Tortosa till April 18. Though the town then at last fell, the Italian troops were good for no more fighting for a while. Their commander, General Berti, desired them to rest away from the battleground but Franco insisted that they man 'a quiet sector of a quiet front', farther up the Ebro.

On the south side of the Nationalist salient to the sea, the Nationalist advance was also greatly slowed. Here Varela, leading divisions under Generals Bautista Sánchez, Delgado Serrano and García Escámez, sought to press down from Teruel across the dull plain of the Maestrazgo. A breach of the Republican lines was made at the first assault. But, immediately, the weather changed to continual rain. This greatly helped the defenders, who were also reinforced by new weapons, especially fighters and anti-aircraft guns. The advance was halted altogether on April 27. On May 1, in one more attempt to clinch the victory which had seemed so short a while ago to promise so brightly, General Aranda mounted a new assault 35 kilometres to the east of Varela and 20 kilometres from the Mediterranean. In between Varela and Aranda, General García Valiño led a small mobile force to press forward whenever the two flanks should be held. But along all three lines of advance, the fighting was very hard. The advance, contested at every hill, nevertheless continued, but its slow pace caused new political murmurings inside Nationalist Spain. There is nothing like a thwarted hope of triumph for the swift manufacture of general resentment. Franco was criticised for not attacking eastwards to

---

[1] Thousands of the inhabitants of northern Aragón fled into France. Twenty thousand were estimated to have crossed in April, 8,000 of them at a height of 7,000 feet and through heavy snowdrifts. The French Government refused to keep those who had fought in the war. A poll was therefore held among these men at Luchon as to where they wished to go. Over 5,000 agreed to return to Catalonia and 254 decided to go to Nationalist territory. The civilian refugees were given temporary asylum in France, but eventually they also were returned to Spain.

Catalonia instead of south to Valencia. Yagüe, speaking on April 19 at a Falangist banquet at Burgos commemorating the anniversary of the foundation of the united Carlist-Falangist party, praised the fighting qualities of the Republicans and termed the Germans and Italians 'beasts of prey'. For this, he was punished by being sent on a long leave from his command. A fortnight later, the Falange was antagonised anew by a decree which not only officially permitted the Jesuits to return but gave them a position such as they had not enjoyed even under the Monarchy. Two polemical priests – Fr Menéndez Reigada and Fr Lauciríaca, apostolic administrator of the Basque diocese in the place of the disgraced Bishop of Vitoria – were now close advisers of Franco. Normal relations with the Vatican were shortly restored.

In the Republic, administrative arrangements for the long expected and feared bisection of the territory had by now been put into effect. The International Brigades' base at Albacete was transferred to Barcelona. Several towns in the province of Tarragona acted as local supply depots. A submarine mail service was established between Barcelona and Valencia, along with a passenger and freight service. Republican leaders regularly flew over the rebel lines between their bases. General Miaja received both civil and military charge of the central provinces. The consequences of the bisection were indeed far less serious than might have been supposed. Daladier's new French Government[1] opened the canals of south France to enable the Republic's vessels to pass from the Mediterranean to the Atlantic. At the start of May, Daladier told the American Ambassador in Paris, Bullitt, that he had opened the French frontier as wide as possible. Russia, he said, had agreed to send 300 aircraft to Catalonia provided the French transported them across France. Daladier did this, in large trucks, and even though he had to cut down miles of trees along the roads of Aquitaine to let the wings pass.[2] Flandin, a member of the Cabinet, later publicly revealed that 25,000 tons of war material (chiefly sent from Russia but much of it bought in France) crossed the Pyrenean frontier in April and May. And no progress was made in the discussions which Daladier's Foreign Secretary, Georges Bonnet, had begun with Italy, on the model of Chamberlain's. The talks were indeed broken off when, on May 15, Mussolini publicly an-

[1] Though this mainly Radical Socialist Cabinet stood much to the Right of those of Blum and Chautemps, it was nevertheless supported by the Socialists.
[2] *USD*, 1938 Vol 1 192–3.

nounced that he did not know what could come of them, because the two countries were 'on different sides of the barricades' in Spain.

It was in this atmosphere, somewhat more hopeful for the Republic, that on May 1 Negrín issued a declaration listing the war aims of his Government, on the model of President Wilson's fourteen points. Negrín's points stipulated the need for absolute independence for Spain; the expulsion of all foreign military forces; universal suffrage; no reprisals; respect for regional liberties; encouragement of capitalist properties, without large trusts; agricultural reform; the rights of workers guaranteed; the 'cultural, physical and moral development of the race'; the army outside politics; renunciation of war; co-operation with the League of Nations; and an amnesty for enemies. Ten of these points were framed by Álvarez del Vayo and three by Negrín.[1]

Partly also Negrín's thirteen points were a list of conditions of peace. From this time onwards Negrín, this subtle and elusive personality, was attempting to achieve peace by negotiation. He had several meetings with the German Ambassador in Paris, Count Welczeck, but did not succeed in making contact with Franco. He also sought mediation through a cousin of Serrano Suñer but again he was unsuccessful. It is hard to blame him for continuing the war when there was in fact no alternative save surrender. From the time of these unsuccessful essays, he increasingly placed his hopes for Spain in the outbreak of a general war in which, he supposed, Spain's troubles would be ultimately purged. The Communist party was not apparently apprised of these approaches.[2] Also at this time Rivas Cherif, the Republican Consul-General in Geneva, brother-in-law and intimate of Azaña, was known to be attempting a negotiation – once more unsuccessfully.[3]

[1] The moderation of the Republican *régime* itself remained in the realm of aspiration. There was, for instance, no general opening of churches. The only concession was that from March onwards conscripted priests were drafted into the medical corps. It was understood that they would be permitted to tend souls as well as bodies. On June 26, however, commanders were ordered to allow their men access to a minister of religion. Despite occasional lapses, this appears to have been generally upheld.

[2] Nevertheless, even La Pasionaria, in a speech at the plenary session of the Central Committee of the Spanish Communist party on May 23, appealed to all 'proud of being Spaniards' who were on the other side of the battle line to try and drive out 'the invader' and struggle for the thirteen points 'as a basis for a new Spain'.

[3] Zugazagoitia, 387. The Republican Cabinet had earlier been greatly disconcerted by the publication on the Nationalist side of certain memoirs of Azaña stolen from Rivas Cherif's house in Geneva. They gave clever and malignant descriptions of Azaña's old colleagues in the Governments of the Republic.

On May 13 Álvarez del Vayo once again appeared before the Council of the League. He demanded that those States who, in October, had resolved that non-intervention should be reconsidered if it were not shortly made effective, should now carry out that reconsideration. But Chamberlain's new Foreign Secretary, Lord Halifax, pressed a quick vote on the matter. He was anxious, no doubt, to concentrate his energies on the developing crisis in Czechoslovakia. Some delegations, such as those of China and New Zealand who might this time have supported Spain, did not have time to consult their Governments. They therefore abstained. When the vote came, on the evening of the day when the matter had first been raised, Spain and Russia voted for the resolution calling for action, Britain, France, Poland and Rumania voted against, while the other nine States of the Council abstained. The increase in the number of abstentions reflected the increasing sympathy felt for the Republic, even in traditionally right-wing groups. There was also pressure upon the American Government from all kinds of groups to end the embargo on arms to Spain. The columnist, Drew Pearson, remarked that 'Washington has seen all kinds of lobbying ... but seldom before has (it) seen people spend money to come from all over the country in a cause from which they would receive no material benefit'.[1] The former Secretary of State, H. L. Stimson, and the recently retired Ambassador to Germany, William Dodd, signed a petition against the embargo. Einstein and other interested scientists also joined the campaign. Resolutions were introduced in Congress urging the end of the embargo by Representative Byron Scott and Senator Nye. And, on May 3, the Secretary of State, Cordell Hull, met his advisers in the State Department to consider Senator Nye's resolution. Hull and the officials agreed that the embargo should be lifted. A no doubt carefully planned leak about this decision appeared in the *New York Times*. Immediately, the new American Ambassador in London, Kennedy, a Catholic and a firm supporter of Chamberlain's Government, telegraphed his alarm lest this measure should cause an extension of the Civil War. The Catholics in the United States made passionate protests against such assistance to 'Bolshevists and atheists'. Roosevelt, on a fishing holiday in the Caribbean, told Hull to delay and, when he returned to Washington, the decision to end the embargo was reversed.[2]

---

[1] *New Orleans States*, 9.5.38. Quoted Taylor, 169.
[2] Taylor, 174; Bendiner, 59–62; *USD*, 1938, Vol 1 183–95.

Litvinov meanwhile was complaining to Louis Fischer, the American journalist acting as arms purchaser for the Republic, of his friends' incessant reverses. 'Always defeats,' he complained, 'always retreats.' 'If you gave them 500 more aircraft, they could win the war,' said Louis Fischer. Litvinov protested that these would help Russia more in China than in Spain. He personally, anyway, had no aircraft. 'I merely hand on diplomatic documents,' he added. However, he promised to ask his superiors.[1] But, even if he had been successful in procuring the despatch of 500 aircraft, it would have been almost impossible to get them to Spain. For on June 13 Daladier, under pressure from Britain, once again closed the frontier. This was partly done to induce Franco to accept the plan for withdrawal of volunteers. The Mediterranean route from Russia had by now been rendered impossible because of the Nationalist blockade. The months during which arms supplies could freely be brought to the Republic were thus at an end. A month later, the First Chamber of the French Court of Appeal decided that certain gold belonging to the Bank of Spain, which had been deposited in France at Mont de Marsan, belonged to 'a private society' and could not therefore be remitted to the Republic. Though this judgment was not a political act (indeed, Paul Reynaud at the Ministry of Finance and Gaston Palewski, his Under-Secretary of State, were among the strongest supporters of the Republic), its timing certainly suggested the tide of feeling in France towards the Spanish War.

On the Nationalist side, new Italian forces were being despatched to Spain from June 1 onwards. Ciano assured Millán Astray and a party of Spanish pilots visiting Rome that 'notwithstanding all committees, Italy will not abandon Spain until the Nationalist flag is flying from the loftiest towers of Barcelona, Valencia and Madrid'.[2] The Italian divisions were at this time resting in the inferior cabarets and brothels of Saragossa.

The British Government now had, however reluctantly, to return to the 'Spanish question'. For there occurred a further outbreak of Nationalist bombing over Republican Spain. Towards the end of May, the Italian bombing of Barcelona was resumed. It was accompanied by raids on other Mediterranean coast towns, including Alicante and Valencia. On June 1 the houses of the British Vice-Consul and US Consul in Alicante escaped being hit by a half mile. On June 2 Granollers, a town of no obvious military

[1] Fischer, 470.   [2] Ciano, *Diaries 1937-8*, 123.

significance 30 kilometres from Barcelona, was bombed. Between 350 and 500 people (mainly women and children) were killed. Halifax sent several telegrams of protest to Burgos. Sir Nevile Henderson begged Weiszäcker to use German influence to secure an end of these indiscriminate attacks.[1] Ciano was similarly approached by Perth. So too was Pacelli by the British Minister to the Holy See. Ciano, bland as ever, promised to do what he could. Pacelli explained that the Vatican was constantly using its influence in this way with Franco.[2] Eventually Britain decided to sponsor a scheme for a commission to investigate such attacks to see if they were really directed at military targets. Not one of the countries whom Britain approached (the USA, Sweden, Norway, Holland) to share in the scheme was willing to stir from its timid and indolent isolation to take part. Britain therefore sent two officers of her own to carry out the enquiry. Though they found that in almost every case the bombing was aimed at non-military targets, nothing came of their conclusions.

The situation was further complicated by renewed attacks upon British ships in Spanish waters. (By this time nearly all the sea-borne trade with the Republic was carried in British ships, for Scandinavian merchants had apparently decided that the risk of being bombed or seized was too great.) Between mid-April and mid-June 22 British ships (out of 140 then trading with the Republic) were attacked, of which 11 were either sunk or very seriously damaged. Twenty-one British seamen died, and so did several Non-Intervention Committee observers. Chamberlain's Cabinet, according to Sir Alexander Cadogan, the new Permanent Under-Secretary at the Foreign Office in succession to Vansittart, was 'almost distracted'.[3] British shippers were crying out for protection. Daily the Government was attacked in the House of Commons by the Opposition for permitting this state of affairs to continue. The Opposition had been especially incensed by the appointment of Mr Alan Lennox-Boyd, an admitted supporter of General Franco, to the post of Parliamentary Secretary to the Ministry of Labour, an act which (considering the continued inflammatory tragedy of unemployment) they regarded as a deliberate provocation. Even the subtle vocabulary of Mr R. A. Butler, Parliamentary Under-Secretary at the Foreign Office (with Lord Halifax in the Lords, he was the chief Government spokesman on foreign affairs in the House of Commons – other

[1] GD, 674.   [2] USD, 1938 Vol 1 208.   [3] USD, 1938 Vol 1 215.

than the Prime Minister), was taxed to explain why the Government would not permit the export of anti-aircraft guns to Republican Spain, nor the merchant ships to carry their own arms. Yet it became evident that the attacks on British ships, mostly by Italian aircraft based in Majorca, were deliberate. Several Conservatives such as Mr Duncan Sandys were at one with Mr Noel-Baker in the House of Commons in protesting against the ignominy of the position. Mr Bevan evoked memories of what Clive of India would have done, and Mr Lloyd George demanded reprisals by bombing Italian air bases in Majorca.[1] Mr Churchill said: 'I think it could be perfectly safely said to General Franco, "If there is any more of this, we shall arrest one of your ships on the open sea" . . . I can quite understand undergoing humiliation for the cause of peace. I would have supported the Government if I felt that we were making towards greater security for peace. But I fear that this abjection is woefully misunderstood abroad. I fear that it will . . . actually bring us nearer to all those dangers which we desire above all things to withhold from our people.'[2] Lord Cecil of Chelwood resigned the Conservative party whip in the House of Lords because of the Government's ineffectiveness. The Archbishop of York, Dr Temple, with other prelates, pleaded for 'effective action'. But Chamberlain noted in his diary: 'I have been through every possible form of retaliation, and it is absolutely clear that none of them can be effective unless we are prepared to go to war with Franco . . . of course it may come to that if Franco were foolish enough.'[3] Chamberlain meant, of course, that war with Franco – which would hardly have presented overpowering difficulties to the British nation even at that time – would have signified war with Germany and Italy also. Once again the Government was not prepared to risk any part of its policy of 'general appeasement'. The Nationalists eventually suggested that Almería might be made a safety zone. This proposal was rejected by the Republic and by the Committee of British Shipowners, since only one-seventh of the shipping at that time frequenting Republican ports could be accommodated in Almería. The situation was permitted to continue. All the various solutions proposed by Sir Robert Hodgson in Burgos proved ineffective.[4] And the British ship *Dellwyn* was sunk in the sight of a British warship. 'The first

[1] *Parliamentary Debates*, Vol 337 Col 1011 (June 21, 1938).
[2] *Ibid.*, Col 1387 (June 23, 1938).   [3] Feiling, 352.
[4] Toynbee, *Survey*, 1938 I 364–86.

time in history,' mourned Bowers, the American Ambassador and a devoted friend of democracy.[1] And Prieto, in a speech at Barcelona, reflected 'Who would have thought it possible, we who in our study of international relations have come across mention of the arrogance and pride of England, who would not tolerate the least harm to its material interests nor an attack on the lives of one of its subjects? Yet here in our cemeteries are the bodies of English sailors who have paid with their lives for the confidence they had in the protection of the Empire.'

The continuance of attacks eventually caused Lord Perth to tell Ciano that he feared that Chamberlain 'might fall if the raids continued'.[2] The raids were called off for some six or seven weeks from the start of July, simply to prevent such a disaster to Franco and Mussolini. The crisis made bad relations between the Spanish Nationalists and their allies. For if Germany and Italy denied responsibility, they were in fact placing it upon Franco. Stohrer was instructed to tell Franco that Germany had expected that he would protect the Condor Legion from odium.

The Germans, at this time, were involved in their most serious quarrel with Franco. Despite protestations that he would not do so, Franco signed the Spanish mining law before showing it to Stohrer. Concessions included to please the Germans permitted 40% foreign capital investment, and the possibility of exceptions higher than this percentage. The law satisfied Germany, but not the manner of its publication. Stohrer furiously demanded whether he was no longer *persona grata*. He was told that Franco was very busy. Stohrer demanded whether he could not spare half an hour to see the German Ambassador. Later, he was received by Jordana, who explained how he and Franco had championed Germany in the Cabinet and had even gained amendments in Germany's favour. Enemy propaganda, he added, would have claimed that Germany had forced concessions if Franco had received Stohrer just before the decree was published. 'But Spanish Nationalist newspapers never report when I call,' Stohrer pointed out. With bad temper, Germany accepted the apology as well as the concessions.[3]

Meantime, the Nationalist offensive in the Maestrazgo and along the Mediterranean continued with painful slowness. The

---

[1] *USD*, 1938 Vol 1 231. Typical of the reaction was Low's cartoon of June 16 in which he causes Colonel Blimp to remark: 'Gad sir, it is time we told Franco that if he sinks another 100 British ships, we shall retire from the Mediterranean altogether.'
[2] Ciano, *Diary 1937–8*, 132.   [3] *GD*, 675–81.

Republic, its forces commanded by General Menéndez, resisted with skill and valour. The Condor Legion's commander, General Volkmann,[1] reported that its material was exhausted.[2] Only on June 14 did Castellón, sixty miles south of Vinaroz, fall to Aranda after several days of ferocious fighting in its suburbs. Forty political prisoners were murdered and the town sacked before the last Republican units left. The Nationalists henceforward boasted of a large Mediterranean port in El Grao de Castellón. They were also only 50 miles north of Valencia. However, a military stalemate was now reached, eight miles north of Sagunto. The only Nationalist success now obtained was General Iruretagoyena's conquest of El Esquinazado's enclave in the Valle del Alto Cinca. The Pyrenean town of Bielsa fell on June 16. Four thousand men escaped into France. These were each asked by the French authorities to which side in Spain they wished to be sent. One hundred and sixty-eight volunteered to go to the Nationalist side.[3]

The situation in mid-June did not suggest to anyone in Spain or outside that the war would soon be over. Within the Nationalist camp the optimism of the spring had entirely vanished. War weariness was everywhere. According to Stohrer, 'the terror practised at present in the Nationalist zone by Martínez Anido' was 'unbearable even to the Falange'.[4] Once again, as at the start of the war, the methods of the old *régime* in Spain shocked the new terrorists of the Falange. Negrín, speaking in Madrid on June 18, said that not one more second of war could be tolerated if Spain's existence as a free country was to be preserved. But surrender, not moderation, was still the only way that peace could be obtained from General Franco. Abroad, Litvinov announced that Russia would be only too glad to withdraw from Spain on the basis of 'Spain for the Spaniards' and Ilya Ehrenburg in *Pravda*, on June 17, stretched out the 'hand of conciliation' towards the Falange, whom he named 'the Spanish patriots'.

On June 27 Maisky finally agreed to the plan for the withdrawal of volunteers which had been worked out in the Non-Intervention Committee. Two commissions were to be sent to Spain, first to enumerate the numbers of foreigners, then to supervise their withdrawal. The cost, estimated at between £1,750,000 and £2,250,000, would be borne by the non-intervention countries. The plan was sent for comment to the two sides in Spain.

---

[1] Sperrle's successor in command of the Condor Legion. [2] *GD*, 689.
[3] Aznar, 704; Buckley, 375. [4] *GD*, 711.

The Nationalist attitude was expressed by Jordana. He explained to Stohrer that 'a way must be sought of strengthening Neville Chamberlain's position by accepting the plan in principle, but, by skilful reservations and counter-proposals, to win as much time as possible to prosecute the war in the meantime'.[1] The minds of all were best expressed by Maisky (inculpating his own country) when he said that 'the whole demeanour of the interventionist powers compels me to doubt whether the actual evacuation of the "volunteers" will take place'.[2]

On July 5 the Nationalist army in the Levante, began a great effort to force a way to Valencia.[3] García Valiño pressed down from the north outside Castellón, but here the Sierra de Espadán reached almost to the sea and the Government forces under Durán could not be dislodged. On July 31 Varela, with Berti and three Italian divisions alongside Solchaga's Navarrese, attacked southwards from Teruel. The heavy armour of the Italians decided the first days of the battle, but the Republican resistance was as cool as ever. A force of *carabineros* held out for a long time at Mora de Rubielos. Then Sarrión fell, and with it the easily defensible Republican positions along the Sierra de Toro. The front now began to crumble in a fashion alarmingly reminiscent of Aragón. Protected by heavy aerial and artillery bombardment, the Navarrese and Italian infantry in five days advanced 100 kilometres, along a front 30 kilometres wide. All that barred the way to the soft country of the Valencian *huerta*, so prosperous in peace, so easily conquered in war, were certain fortifications constructed before the small *pueblo* of Viver and running into the Sierra de Espadán. These fortifications, however, were brilliantly and imaginatively conceived. Trenches had been constructed capable of withstanding 1,000 lb bombs. The advance was held. Artillery bombardment and bombs made no impression upon the defenders, all Spaniards, led by Menéndez. Every Nationalist infantry assault was repelled by a devastating hail of machine-gun fire. Between July 18 and 23, the Nationalists suffered heavy casualties, estimated by the Republic at 20,000. By the last date, the attack showed clear signs of abating. Valencia was saved.[4]

[1] GD, 725.   [2] Cattell, *Soviet Diplomacy*, 119.
[3] Ansaldo, 63, says that this attack was the result of a personal initiative of Franco. Certain alarmists in Nationalist Spain were convinced that the Germans were at the back of this campaign, in order to prolong the war. The Monarchist General Vigón, by now Franco's Chief of Staff, retorted that Franco was quite capable of such foolishness, because of his pre-occupation with the techniques and strategy of World War I.
[4] Buckley, 379–81.

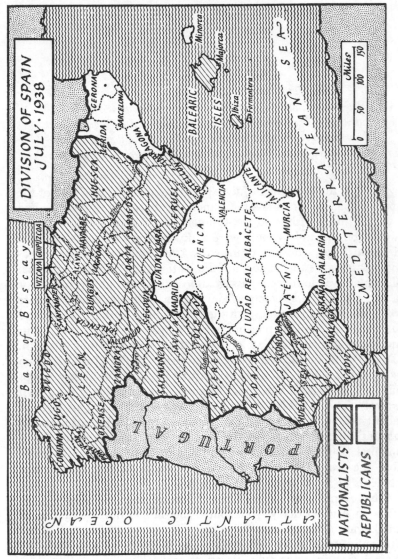

DIVISION OF SPAIN
JULY · 1938

Bay of Biscay

VIZCAYA GUIPUZCOA

CORUNNA LUGO OVIEDO SANTANDER

ORENSE LEON PALENCIA BURGOS ALAVA NAVARRE HUESCA GERONA

ZAMORA VALLADOLID SORIA LERIDA

SEGOVIA GUADALAJARA ZARAGOZA BARCELONA

SALAMANCA AVILA MADRID TERUEL CASTELLON

CACERES TOLEDO CUENCA VALENCIA

BADAJOZ CIUDAD REAL ALBACETE ALICANTE

CORDOBA JAEN MURCIA

HUELVA SEVILLE GRANADA ALMERIA

CADIZ MALAGA

PORTUGAL

GERONA
BARCELONA

BALEARIC ISLES
Minorca
Majorca
Ibiza Formentera

MEDITERRANEAN SEA

Miles
0 50 100 150

ATLANTIC OCEAN

NATIONALISTS
REPUBLICANS

MAP 31

69

*The battle of the Ebro – its unwisdom – its beginning – the
Nationalists caught by surprise – advance to Gandesa – the war of
attrition – the Republican internal crisis – Dr Negrín's new
Government – separatist attempts at peace – the withdrawal plan –
Mussolini agrees to withdraw some forces – the Czech crisis and Spain*

On the morning of July 24, 1938, a meeting was held of the
Republican War Council in Barcelona. Negrín had
previously told the Council that Sagunto and Valencia
would be lost unless there were a diversionary attack elsewhere.
General Rojo, who had returned as Chief of Staff, therefore proposed an attack to the north of the Nationalists' salient to the sea.
The plan was to force a passage across the Ebro at several points
about a hundred kilometres from the sea. The aim was to confuse
the communications between the Nationalists in the Levante and
in Catalonia and, if possible, strike across to restore land communications between Catalonia and the rest of Republican Spain.
To carry out this bold scheme, a new army 'of the Ebro' had been
constituted under Modesto, consisting of the Vth Army Corps
under Lister and XVth under Tagüeña (once leader of the Dawn
Patrol). The XVIIIth Army Corps was in reserve. This force of
about 100,000 men was supported by 70 to 80 field batteries and
27 anti-aircraft guns. All the leading commanders were Communists. Tagüena, like Lister, had had no military experience before the war. He had been merely leader of the Communist
students at the University of Madrid.

The Republican War Council considered the Ebro plan.
Though Álvarez del Vayo disputed the danger of the situation in
the Levante, the plan was accepted.[1] It was, however, rash of the
Republic, with their slender supplies of material and with the
French frontier once more closed, to embark upon an offensive –
as the examples of Brunete, Belchite and Teruel should have
proved to them. And the pattern of those battles – the immediate

[1] Bowers, 388. Álvarez del Vayo, *Freedom's Battle,* 131.

success of the attack, its containment by Nationalist reinforcements hurried from other fronts, and a Nationalist counter-attack – was exactly followed in the battle of the Ebro, though with more terrible consequences than in those other engagements.[1]

Nevertheless, at a quarter past midnight on the night of July 24–25, with no moon, the crossing began at a point proposed in a manoeuvre by the elegant Chief of Staff of the XVth Brigade, Malcolm Dunbar. Units under Tagüeña started to cross the river between Mequinenza and Fagón. Lister and the Vth Army began to cross at several points in the great arc between Fagón and Cherta, notably at Flix, Mora la Nueva, Miravet and, fifty kilometres to the south, at Amposta, near the sea. One hundred boats (each of which carried 8 men), 5 pontoon bridges, and 5 others of various construction, had been assembled. Officers crossed at the head of their men. Material would follow across the bridges, once these could safely be swung across the river.[2] The first unit across was the Hans Beimler Battalion of the XIth International Brigade, composed of Scandinavians and Catalans, whose commanders led the way with a cry of 'Forward sons of Negrín!' in unfamiliar accents.[3]

The other side of the river from Mequinenza to the sea was guarded at this time by the Army of Morocco, to whose command Yagüe had recently returned. The officers had heard rumours that good troops had been assembled across the river but their surprise in the early hours of July 25 was complete. At half-past two in the morning, a message from Colonel Peñarredonda (in command of the sector of Mora) reached Yagüe. The Republicans had crossed the Ebro, some of Peñarredonda's units had heard firing from behind, and he and his divisional headquarters had lost contact with their flanks. This Colonel was one of the most unpleasant and inefficient in the Nationalist army. He had a particular hatred of the International Brigades and, on his own responsibility, gave orders that any of them captured should be shot. He even forced Peter Kemp, serving in his battalion, to shoot a fellow Irishman as

---

[1] The following narrative of the battle of the Ebro is based on the account in Lojendio (409 fl.), Aznar (727 fl.), Rojo, *España Heroica* (172 fl.), Buckley, Kindelán (156 fl.) and the valuable advice of Mr Malcolm Dunbar. Julián Henríquez, Chief of Staff of the Republican 35th Division has also written an interesting book from his point of view, *La Batalla del Ebro*. For the history of air tactics, see Gomá, 337 fl.

[2] A tank became jammed on one of these bridges and delayed the shipment of material. It is the view of Mr Malcolm Dunbar, an usually excellent witness, that had it not been for this, the Republican attack would have reached Alcañiz – at least.

[3] *Reconquista*. (Newspaper of the Army of the Ebro.)

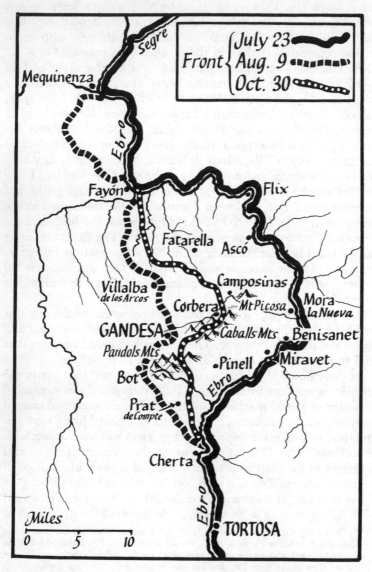

Front { July 23 ⸺
Aug. 9 ▬▬▬▬
Oct. 30 ○○○○○○

Mequinenza

Segre

Ebro

Fayón

Flix

Fatarella

Ascó

Camposinas

Villalba
de los Arcos

Corbera

Mt Picosa

Mora
la Nueva

GANDESA

Caballs Mts

Benisanet

Pandols Mts

Pinell

Ebro

Miravet

Bot

Prat
de Compte

Cherta

Miles
0   5   10

Ebro

TORTOSA

MAP 32. THE BATTLE OF THE EBRO

a special blood protest against intervention on either side.[1] Meantime, the XIVth (Franco-Belgian) International Brigade had crossed the Ebro near Amposta and were engaging forces led by General López Bravo. This crossing failed, though it had anyway been regarded as an advance of secondary importance. The battle nevertheless continued there for 18 hours, after which those who remained retreated in disorder across the river as best they might, leaving 600 dead and much material behind them. Higher up, the first stages of the attack were successful. All the riparian villages in the central part of the front had been occupied by daybreak. A huge bridgehead had thus been established. Those who had crossed, including the XVth International Brigade, continued inland to out-flank, surround and capture the demoralised troops of Colonel Peñarredonda. By evening, that officer had received permission to retreat, with those of his staff and men whom he could take with him. The Colonel himself retired to Saragossa and was seen no more in the war. To the north, at Mequinenza, Tagüena had by then advanced five kilometres from the Ebro. In the centre, Lister had advanced 25 miles, and had almost reached the communications centre of Gandesa. Between Gandesa and the river, all the main observation points on high ground were captured. Four thousand Nationalist prisoners were taken. General Franco had meanwhile ordered the reinforcement of the region by the divisions of General Barrón, Galera, Delgado Serrano, Rada, Alonso Vega, Castejón (from Andalusia) and Arias. Such reinforcements were easy since, between the Pyrenees and Teruel, Franco possessed over half a million men under arms.

The main battle occurred at Gandesa. This town was assaulted by Lister day and night during the suffocatingly hot days of the Aragón summer. On August 1 the XVth International Brigade launched their most fierce attack upon Hill 481, named by them 'The Pimple', immediately before Gandesa. Once again the death-roll was very heavy as it had been inside Gandesa during fighting for that town in March. Among those killed was Lewis Clive, Lieutenant in the brigade, Socialist councillor in South Kensington, educated at Eton and Christ Church, Oxford. A direct descendant of Clive of India, he had rowed No. 4 in the Oxford

---

[1] Kemp was wounded by a stray shell just before the battle of the Ebro began. For months previously he had been facing a one-time contemporary of his at Trinity College, Cambridge, Malcolm Dunbar who was acting as Chief of Staff to the XVth International Brigade.

boat in 1931 and 1932 and sculled for England in the Olympics of the latter year. In Clive's company, there was also killed David Haden Guest, aged twenty-seven, son of the Labour peer Lord Haden Guest, once of Oundle and Trinity College, Cambridge, one of the first pupils of Wittgenstein at Cambridge, who had become a Communist after studying at the University of Göttingen. A lecturer at what was then University College, Southampton, he was scholarly, untidy and very unmilitary.[1]

By August 2 the Republican advance had been contained. The front lay straight from Fagón to Cherta, along the base of the Ebro's arc, but scooping eastwards to leave the Nationalists with Villalba de los Arcos and Gandesa. In the north, the pocket between Mequinenza and Fagón was ten kilometres at its widest. The Republic began feverishly to dig trenches. Methodical and devastating Nationalist attacks began from the air. High-altitude bombing, dive-bombing and low-flying attacks were used in turn. The Nationalist task was, however, the unenviable one of storming heights held by Republicans. German observers noted that, not surprisingly, the troops showed little fighting spirit. On August 14, the HISMA chief, Bernhardt, telegraphed to Goering for more 88 millimetre ammunition, to meet 'the acute military danger'.[2] The orders issued by Lister and Tagüena remained – 'vigilance, fortification and resistance'. These words were repeated incessantly throughout the following weeks. Officers and men were shot for retreating. Sergeants were ordered to kill their officers if they gave the command to retire without written orders from above. 'If anyone loses an inch of ground,' Lister ordered, 'he must retake it at the head of his men or be executed.'[3]

Because of the ground, Franco's tactics were to make an intense artillery and aerial attack upon a given point, small in area, so that resistance would be almost impossible. Then the attack would

---

[1] When a child, Sir James Barrie once asked him: 'Do you want to grow up?' 'No,' said David Haden Guest. 'Why not,' asked the author of Peter Pan. 'Because I might look like you,' answered the future hero of Hill 481. (Guest, 20.)

[2] Immediately before the start of the Ebro battle, the Spanish Nationalist Ambassador in Berlin, Count Magaz, had complained that the German Government were consciously selling arms to the Republic. Rifles at £1 a piece and also aircraft had been sold by Germany nominally to China and Greece, in fact to Republican Spain. Magaz alleged that Goering knew of the transaction, wishing to prolong the Civil War by this trickery. After two months, Germany officially denied that the Nazi Government was officially implicated. (Documents quoted in The International Brigades, 44.)

[3] Aznar, 744–5 prints several Republican orders later captured which show that this threat was often carried out.

be carried out by small bodies of men – perhaps only two battalions. For this reason the Battle of the Ebro became an artillery contest – the unique occasion when in Spain the classic formula 'Artillery conquers the ground, infantry occupies it' was applied. The first Nationalist counter-attack in this manner came on August 6 and 7, when Delgado Serrano reconquered the northern pocket between Mequiñenza and Fagón. The Republic left behind 900 dead, 1,600 rifles and over 200 machine guns. On August 11 Alonso Vega and Galera mounted a counter-attack against the Sierra de Pandols, the blue slate mountains in the south of the front. By the 14th Lister had been forced to surrender the high point of Santa Magdalena. On the 19th, another counter-attack was launched, by Yagüe, on the Republican position on the north slopes of Mount Gaeta, with softer, undulating slopes overgrown with ilex trees. This was also ultimately successful. On September 3 an attack was made by the two army corps of Yagüe and García Valiño (who had been transferred from the Levante and who now commanded the newly formed army of the Maestrazgo, composed of the divisions of Galera, Delgado Serrano, Arias and Mohammed el Mizzian – the one Moroccan who rose to be a divisional commander in the Nationalist Army). Gandesa was partially relieved and the Nationalists recaptured the village of Corbera in the cultivated valley between the Pandols and Mount Gaeta. In this way the Republic lost, after six weeks, about 200 square kilometres of the land which it had won. But these statements of bare fact give an inaccurate picture of the slow and relentless battle fought in the fierce August heat. All day and every day the Nationalist aeroplanes, sometimes 200 at the same time, circled over the Republican lines with hardly any interference from the diminished antiaircraft defences and fighters of their opponents. The Republic had quite lost command of the air by the start of August. This more than cancelled out the advantage gained from their possession of the high ground. During the first five weeks of the counter-offensive the Nationalist aircraft dropped an average of 10,000 bombs every day. But the Republican engineers, who consistently repaired the bridges under aerial bombardment, showed themselves as tenacious as the fighting men ahead of them. This aspect of the battle was most remarkable, however, for the difficulty found in hitting small targets. It was estimated in Barcelona that as many as 500 bombs were needed to destroy one pontoon bridge.

The Republic was jubilant at the immediate success of the Ebro attack. Even Azaña was persuaded that the tide had turned in favour of the Republic. This summer was indeed a moment of hope for all Republicans. The crisis of Czechoslovakia threatened a general European conflict and the Republic set out to show Britain and France that, in war, it might be a worthy ally. This indirectly caused a Governmental crisis in early August. Negrín, in a final effort to mobilise all Republican Spain, proposed to take over the war industries of Catalonia (until then run by the Generalitat). He also proposed that the sinister SIM should be controlled by the Army and that there should be set up a special chamber at Barcelona under the Ministry of Justice to prevent smuggling and the export of capital. Both Ayguadé and Irujo, the Catalan and Basque Ministers, protested against these measures which they suspected of pointing towards the demise of home rule. Negrín knew that Azaña supported these two Ministers, though from dislike of his policy of 'resistance' not from love of separatism. In consequence, the Prime Minister provoked a crisis. Fifty-eight death sentences for espionage and sabotage were pending, and were matters for dispute within the Cabinet. Negrín demanded that these be approved. This brought down the Cabinet and Negrín suggested that Companys, as chief leader of the opposition to him, should form the new Government. Azaña toyed with an appeal to his old peace emissary, the Socialist Besteiro, who would perhaps have formed a Government of mediation or, possibly, of capitulation. At this point, *La Vanguardia*, which invariably presented Negrín's policy, published a list of Besteiro's proposed Cabinet, Negrín being placed in an unimportant Ministry. The Prime Minister himself now announced that he was leaving Spain for some time. At this the Communist party, with whom Negrín had been constantly in touch, arranged for a shower of telegrams of protest to be sent from commanders in the field – including the leaders of the Army of the Ebro and of the units in Catalonia[1]. A parade of Russian tanks along the Paseo de Colón

---

[1] A secret FAI circular of September 1938 pointed out that of 7,000 promotions in the Army since May 5,500 had been Communists. In the Army of the Ebro out of 27 brigades, 25 were commanded by Communists, while all 9 divisional commanders, 3 army corps commanders, and the supreme commander (Modesto) were Communists. This was the most extreme case of Communist control, but the proportions for the Anarchists were nearly as depressing elsewhere. In all six armies of Republican Spain the Anarchists believed the proportions to be 163 Communist brigade commanders to 33 Anarchists, 61 divisional commanders to 9 Anarchists, 15 army corps commanders to 2 Anarchists (with 4 Anarchist sympathisers), and 3 Communist army commanders, 2 sympathisers and one neutral. (Peirats, III 230–3.)

was arranged for the same time. Negrín was then asked by Azaña to form a new Government. In this, a Catalan PSUC politician and a Basque Socialist took the positions left vacant by Ayguadé and Irujo. The crisis was represented as a quarrel between Azaña with Prieto in the background, against the Communists and Negrín over the question of an end of the war.[1] It was also the last flicker of the old flame of Catalan separatism, against a central Government, now led from the Catalan capital itself.

This continued compromise with the Communists has damned Negrín in the eyes of history. Yet, in August 1938 as before, he had no alternative than to sup with the devil. His attempts to secure a mediated peace – which he had concealed from the Communists – had been fruitless. The only victory that Franco would envisage was a total one, giving him absolute powers over the defeated. What knowledge Negrín had of Nationalist justice did not suggest that he, as leader of the Republic, would be justified in giving Franco a free hand over all those thousands who had fought under him. The only hope for the Republic was to continue to resist until the general situation in Europe exploded – as it surely eventually would. Then, perhaps, German and Italian aid to the Nationalists would be diminished or abandoned. Then, surely, France, and perhaps Britain, would be drawn into the Spanish War, as the Republic would be drawn into theirs. In the meantime, the most efficient and tenacious advocates of the policy of resistance remained the Communists. They had to be used. The fact that Negrín did not take the Communists into his confidence in his search for a negotiated peace proves that he was not absolutely their tool. His political aim was indeed to have been that of Stalin himself – to be willing at all times to play a double game. To do this against the Communists may be dangerous but it is not impossible that it could have been successfully achieved in so unorthodox a country as Spain. Perhaps he recalled General Chiang Kai-Shek's successful deception of the Chinese Communists in Shanghai in 1926.

The worsting of the Separatists in the August crisis caused them also to seek, independently of Negrín, a negotiated peace. At the start of September, Aguirre conferred in Paris on the subject with Georges Bonnet, the French Foreign Minister. In London, Catalan

---

[1] For this rather obscure crisis I have relied on the account in Salvador de Madariaga (405–6) and Zugazagoitia, neither of whom are at all friendly to Negrín. I have also discussed the event with Señor de Irujo.

and Basque representatives discussed the question with Lord Halifax. Halifax and Bonnet agreed that neither Spain could now beat the other, and that peace could only be gained by mediation. Once the Czech crisis was over, Bonnet assured Aguirre, Britain and France would attempt to settle the war by an armistice, to be followed by a plebiscite.[1]

The Republic had by now accepted in principle the British volunteer plan. But they made many reservations to its acceptance. They proposed, for example, that Moroccans in the Nationalist Army should be classified as foreign volunteers, that technicians should be withdrawn first, and that, after the withdrawal, non-intervention should be made watertight by aerial control. The Republic also deplored the grant of belligerent rights to the Nationalists under the plan. The Nationalists demanded the immediate grant of belligerent rights, and the withdrawal of 10,000 volunteers from each side afterwards. But this could not be supervised internationally, since 'foreign observers would usurp, in a humiliating way, the sovereign rights of Spain'. The Non-Intervention Committee's Secretary, Francis Hemming, was then sent off to Nationalist Spain to get General Franco to change these uncompromising views. This Nationalist note, as it stood, amounted to a rejection of a withdrawal of volunteers. Azcárate wrote a personal and passionate letter to Vansittart, pointing out the injustice of maintaining non-intervention when Germany and Italy were obviously party to Franco's rejection of the volunteer plan. The French-Spanish frontier had been closed in June in order to help persuade Franco to accept the plan. Could the frontier at least not be re-opened? Vansittart never answered.[2]

The Italian General Berti now approached Franco on Mussolini's orders. The Italians supporting Franco numbered at this time 48,000. Berti made every kind of proposal. Italy was willing either to send two or three more divisions to Spain, or 10,000 more men to make up for losses, or withdraw partially or totally. Franco chose a partial withdrawal.[3] So Mussolini decided to concentrate the Littorio and March 23 Divisions into one large division and withdraw the rest of the Italians. This withdrawal

---

[1] *USD*, 1938 Vol 1 239. The Carlist Fal Conde was also in London that year busily propagating his views on Spain's prospects. (Evidence of Fal Conde.)

[2] Azcárate, 174. Azcárate told his Government that he thought Halifax saw the injustice of the non-intervention discrimination, but that he could do nothing to counter Chamberlain's desire not to offend Italy.

[3] *GD*, 765–6.

could be pointed out to Britain, and Ciano could argue that the Anglo-Italian agreement should be put into effect.[1] But Mussolini was now very angry with the Generalissimo over the Ebro battle. 'Put on record in your diary,' Mussolini thundered to Ciano, 'that today, August 29, I prophesy the defeat of Franco. . . . The Reds are fighters, Franco is not.'[2]

The Republican offensive across the Ebro caused gloom everywhere in Nationalist Spain. Defeatism was talked, even at Burgos. The Falangists were murmuring against Franco and Martínez Anido. Stohrer reported scenes between Franco and his Generals 'who do not carry out attack orders correctly'. The Generalissimo was as alarmed by the Czech crisis as Negrín was elated. The possibility of a general war, and one which he might have to fight against France, caused him to send 20,000 prisoners to work on border fortifications, both in the Pyrenees and in Spanish Morocco. Germany caused Franco great annoyance, and even fear, because no one told him the Fuehrer's intentions. German aid temporarily stopped in mid-September, due to possible needs in central Europe. Magaz, the Nationalist Ambassador in Berlin, was told on September 19 that there would be no changes in German aid to Spain, even if war did come.[3] But, a week later, Franco was still angry. Could not Nationalist Spain, he asked, do something to help? Were Spanish ports needed by Germany for supply?[4]

[1] This plan was not agreed with Franco till the end of September.
[2] Ciano, *Diaries 1937–8*, 148.
[3] GD, 742.   [4] *Ibid.*, 747.

70

The Munich crisis – Franco declares his neutrality – effects of Munich in Spain – the Nationalists unyielding – the Soviet Union changes its policy – withdrawal of the International Brigades – Mussolini withdraws 10,000 men – parade of the 'Internationals' at Barcelona – La Pasionaria speaks – the League of Nations Commission – Sir Philip Chetwode in Spain – the last Ebro offensive – casualties on the Ebro – the Anglo-Italian Mediterranean Agreement in force

The Czech crisis wore on to its melancholy conclusion. The General Assembly of the League meantime assembled, for the last time, as it turned out, at Geneva. Here Negrín and Álvarez del Vayo once more prepared to put the Spanish case. They left behind them the war at its grimmest and least conclusive. For, after the capture of Corbera, the battle of the Ebro had become a terrible exercise in trench, artillery and aerial warfare. The front remained stationary, though appallingly active, until the end of October. Negrín himself (unknown to the Communists, as to the Basques or Catalans) had embarked upon a new project of compromise. On September 9, he secretly met the Duke of Alba, Nationalist agent in London, in the Sihl forest outside Zurich.[1] But, as he suspected, there was no possibility whatever of securing a compromise while Franco was in power. Ten days later, Mussolini nevertheless concluded that a compromise peace in Spain was inevitable and that he would thus lose his '4 billion lire of credit'.[2]

The Duke of Alba was also approached at this point by Britain and France. He was told at the Foreign Office that the French General Staff would take no action if Franco declared himself neutral. Otherwise, if war came, there would be an immediate attack on Morocco and across the Pyrenees. Franco therefore declared promptly that he would be neutral in a European war. He explained to Germany and Italy how, unfortunately, this was essential in the present condition of Spain.[3] 'Disgusting!' remarked

[1] *USD*, 1938 Vol 1 239. (Partially confirmed to me by a private source.)
[2] Ciano, *Diary 1937-8*, 159.   [3] *GD*, 479.

554

Ciano, 'enough to make our dead in Spain turn in their graves!'[1] In pursuance of this policy the Generalissimo announced, as a sop to France, that no German and Italian units would be permitted within 130 kilometres of the French frontier.

The conference of Munich followed. The fate of Czecho-slovakia is well known. As for Spain, Mussolini (roaming around the room with 'his hands in his pockets', as Ciano described him 'his great spirit always ahead of events and men. . . . He has al-ready passed on to other things') told Chamberlain that the swift withdrawal of 10,000 men would 'create the atmosphere' for the start of the Anglo-Italian Agreement. He added that he was 'fed up' with Spain where, he said (untruthfully), he had lost 50,000 men, and that he was weary of Franco, who had thrown away opportunities of victory. Chamberlain, delighted with his diplo-matic success in 'solving' the Czech problem, suggested a similar conference to 'solve Spain'. This would be done by calling on the two sides to observe a truce, while the four Munich Powers would help to work out a settlement.[2] News of this proposal leaked out and caused the Republic to fear that it was about to suffer the same fate as Dr Beneš's Czechoslovakia. Within a few days, the lull in the Italian attacks on British shipping in Republican ports, which had been tolerated by Franco to prevent Chamberlain's fall, came to an end. Eight ships were damaged in the first fortnight of October. British ships carrying food to Republican ports were also seized and held up.

Hodgson, the British agent in Salamanca, now told Stohrer that Britain was intending to mediate in Spain.[3] Stohrer himself questioned whether compromise might not now be in Franco's favour, when his troops were being 'bled white on the Ebro'. But the Generalissimo himself, sitting next to Stohrer at dinner on October 1, talked enthusiastically only of the Fuehrer's triumph at Munich. He was silent when the Ambassador suggested that the 'Czech method' might be the model for the solution of other inter-national questions.[4] On October 2 Negrín broadcast a speech from Madrid declaring that Spaniards must come to an under-standing with each other. He publicly demanded whether the Nationalists desired to carry on war until the country was des-troyed. This made clear to the world for the first time his aspira-tion to seek a negotiated peace. But Hodgson's attempts – aimed at

[1] Ciano, Diary 1937–8, 163.
[2] Ciano, Diary 1937–8, 167–8. Feiling, 376.
[3] GD, 754.
[4] Ibid., 756.

'compromise with the appearance of complete victory' – were as unfruitful as all similar proposals had been in the past. On October 4, Schwendemann, at the Spanish desk in the Wilhelmstrasse, admitted that Germany's 'negative aim' of preventing a Bolshevist Spain could in fact be achieved by compromise. So could their economic interests. But, he added, 'a strong Spain leaning towards Germany' could only be secured by Franco's total victory.[1] And on October 6 Jordana once more told Stohrer that a compromise would mean that the whole Civil War would have been fought in vain. The Republic must be forced absolutely to capitulate.[2] A Nationalist pamphlet published in Paris at this time actually declared that 'the Civil War itself was caused by the attempt at mediation between the rival forces of the Spain embodied in the Republic.'[3] Far from considering compromise, Franco was demanding from Germany shipments of 50,000 rifles, 1,500 light and 500 heavy machine guns (one month's total German production of machine guns) and a hundred 75 millimetre guns. These, he assured the Germans would really result in a Nationalist victory. The Germans were willing – on the condition of the formal recognition of all their mining rights. The matter was not, however, agreed until November.[4]

After Munich, the Soviet Union had finally despaired, not unnaturally, of being able to arrange an alliance with France and Britain against Hitler. From October, the Soviet Government toyed increasingly with the only other solution open to it to avoid being involved in war. This was friendship with Hitler, at the democracies' expense. It was a policy which Stalin had indeed contemplated as a possibility even at the most enthusiastic period of the Popular Front. But now this policy became the only way, as it seemed. This change naturally had its effect on the Spanish Civil War. Stalin's Government desired to have its hands free to take any action which it judged necessary for its self-defence. This would demand an end to Russia's continued commitment in the Spanish war, and particularly of the Army of the Comintern, the International Brigades. Russian spokesmen had already publicly suggested that they would be pleased to withdraw from Spain.[5] Hence Stalin's agreement that, before the final understanding in the Non-Intervention Committee on the with-

[1] *Ibid.*, 758.
[3] *Médiation en Espagne*, AIE, Paris, 1938.
[4] *GD* 776, 784–6. See below, page 566.

[2] *Ibid.*, 760.

[5] See above, page 541.

drawal of volunteers, the International Brigades should be independently withdrawn.

The rôle of the brigades was indeed now over. Their organisation had been successfully copied in the rest of the Republican Army. Furthermore, a majority of the members of the Brigades were now Spanish, some volunteers, but many of them men from prison, work camps and disciplinary battalions. Several of the officers in command of foreign volunteers were also Spanish. The XVth Brigade, for example, was led by the Spanish Major Valledor.[1] Even the Lincoln Battalion comprised a three-to-one majority of Spaniards.[2] Thus Negrín was able, without military risk, to propose at Geneva, during the Munich crisis, the withdrawal of all foreign volunteers in Republican Spain. He asked the League to supervise this step. In so doing he demonstrated his contempt for the Non-Intervention Committee, and gave a much needed fillip to the spirits of the League. The Secretary-General of the League, the usually cold Anglophil Avenol, was unable to repress his delight. 'A master-stroke!' he exclaimed, when meeting Azcárate in the corridors of the Palais des Nations. It hardly seems conceivable, but Hungary and Poland actually voted against giving League assistance to this project. Those two little States were petrified at giving any cause of annoyance to Hitler or Mussolini. But on October 1 it was agreed that the League should supervise the withdrawal, through a commission of 15 officers headed by a General and two Colonels.

The Soviet Union and Comintern now gradually diminished the propaganda appeals on behalf of the Republic, but they continued to send aid, in diminished quantities. This can partially be explained by the fact that, with the French frontier closed once again, it was very difficult to make sure that any aid would arrive. The sea route (even that between Marseilles and Barcelona or Valencia) was increasingly impracticable, due to the effective Nationalist blockade.

The grim battle of the Ebro continued. Behind the lines, Franco prepared his main counter-attack. On the Republican side, 'resist – resist' continued to be cried by the Commissars. The battle was still continuing when the International Brigades were withdrawn. Their last action was on September 22, when the XVth

---

[1] One of the leaders of the revolt in the Asturias in 1934, Valledor, had also fought in Asturias in 1936-7. He had escaped from prison in Nationalist Spain in 1938.
[2] Rolfe, 234.

Brigade went into battle for the last time. The British Battalion once again suffered heavy casualties. The son of the American writer, Ring Lardner, who had been among the last Americans to enlist, was killed in this battle.[1] At a parade of farewell to the Brigades at Barcelona on November 15, Negrín and La Pasionaria spoke words of thanks. La Pasionaria's speech revived for a moment all the ideals of those who had cared so much for the Spanish cause in the heroic days. First, she addressed the women of Barcelona: 'Mothers! Women! When the years pass by and the wounds of war are staunched; when the cloudy memory of the sorrowful, bloody days returns in a present of freedom, love and well-being; when the feelings of rancour are dying away and when pride in a free country is felt equally by all Spaniards – then speak to your children. Tell them of the International Brigades. Tell them how, coming over seas and mountains, crossing frontiers bristling with bayonets, and watched for by ravening dogs thirsty to tear at their flesh, these men reached our country as Crusaders for freedom. They gave up everything, their homes, their country, home and fortune – fathers, mothers, wives, brothers, sisters and children, and they came and told us: "We are here, your cause, Spain's cause, is ours. It is the cause of all advanced and progressive mankind." Today they are going away. Many of them, thousands of them, are staying here with the Spanish earth for their shroud, and all Spaniards remember them with the deepest feeling.'

Then she addressed the assembled members of the Brigades.

'Comrades of the International Brigades! Political reasons, reasons of State, the welfare of that same cause for which you offered your blood with boundless generosity, are sending you back, some of you to your own countries and others to forced exile. You can go proudly. You are history. You are legend. You are the heroic example of democracy's solidarity and universality. We shall not forget you, and when the olive tree of peace puts forth its leaves again, mingled with the laurels of the Spanish Republic's victory – come back!'[2] The parade heaved with controlled emotion. It was true, surely, as Pietro Nenni reflected, that all unknowing they had 'lived an Iliad'.[3] The crowds cheered beneath large photographs of Negrín, Azaña – and Stalin. Flowers were thrown. The volunteers of the International Brigade began to leave by boat and rail for France, for home – wherever it might be.

[1] Sheean, 237.   [2] From a pamphlet printed in Barcelona 1938.   [3] Nenni, 172.

The League of Nations Commission, led by the Finnish General Jalander, the British Brigadier Molesworth, and the French Colonel Homo, counted 12,673 foreigners in the Republican forces. Of these, some 7,000 had been at the front at the battle of the Ebro. There were many more who had assumed Spanish nationality. By mid-January, 4,640 men of 29 nationalities had left Spain. Of these, 2,141 were French, 407 British, 347 Belgian, 285 Poles, 182 Swedes, 194 Italians, 80 Swiss and 548 American. The other 6,000 remained to be engulfed in the catastrophe in Catalonia, and to encounter hardships and trials greater than they had known in the Civil War.[1]

One other Commission was also in Spain at this time. In October 1937 the Republic had proposed to the British that they should negotiate an agreement for the exchange of those Spanish civilians who wanted to leave Nationalist territory, for Nationalist prisoners in Republican hands. It was eventually agreed that a commission led by Field-Marshal Sir Philip Chetwode should visit Spain to arrange a general exchange of prisoners – though Chetwode did not arrive till September 1938. The commission was not very successful. It did secure several small-scale exchanges, such as that of 100 British prisoners in Nationalist hands for 100 Italians held by the Republic. When Sir Philip returned to London at the end of the war, he claimed that he had persuaded the Republic to stop executing their prisoners and that he had gained the remission of 400 death sentences by General Franco. The latter achievement appears genuine, the former less so, since the Republican Government had already promulgated it.[2] Sir Philip, a soldier of the old school, found Republican Spain extraordinary because Negrín wore a dinner jacket.[3]

On October 30, meantime, the long-awaited Nationalist counter-offensive began on the Ebro. The point of attack was the one-kilometre wide northern stretch of the Sierra de Caballs. For three hours after dawn, the Republican positions were subjected to incessant bombardment by 175 Nationalist and Italian batteries and over 100 aircraft. 50 Republican fighters made no impression upon this aerial armada. Then the whole army corps of the

---

[1] Three hundred and five members of the British Battalion were greeted, amid scenes of great excitement, at Victoria Station on December 7 by Major Attlee, Sir Stafford Cripps, Mr Gallacher, Tom Mann and Will Lawther. Sam Wild then gave the battalion its last dismissal. The Dependants Aid Committee looked after the families of those killed as best it could.

[2] Toynbee A, *Survey*, 1938 Vol I 392–3.   [3] De la Mora, 374.

Maestrazgo under García Valiño went into the attack. Mohammed el Mizzian, with the Navarrese of the 1st Division, captured the Republican positions abandoned during the very heavy bombardment. The battle on the heights of the Caballs continued all day, but, by night, these mountains were in Nationalist hands, including 19 carefully fortified positions and the whole Republican defence network. The Nationalists claimed 1,000 prisoners and 500 dead, as well as 14 aircraft. The loss of the Caballs was a terrible blow to the Republic, since it commanded the whole region.

Worse was to follow. On the night of November 1–2, Galera stormed the heights of the Pandols remaining to the Republic. On November 3, advancing through the village of Pinell, he reached the Ebro. All the right flank of the Nationalist Army had now achieved its objectives. On November 7 Mora la Nueva fell. Next, the Nationalists launched a massive attack in the centre of the front, towards the hill known as Mount Picosa. In this sector, the Republic had entrenched itself with the greatest skill. After the fall of Mount Picosa, the overwhelming pressure of the Nationalist armour convinced the Republic that the battle of the Ebro was as good as lost. It had become a question as to how far the Republic could withdraw without disaster. That it was enabled to do so in any order at all was due to the calm of Lister. By November 10 only 6 Republican batteries remained west of the Ebro. They supported six divisions to whom the monotonous orders – 'resist, resist, resist' – had been repeated with extraordinary success. With deliberation the last Republican defence points were abandoned. The hill village of Fatarella fell on November 14 to Yagüe. The last stages of the conflict were delayed by the first snows of winter falling upon a battlefield which had earlier been rendered intolerable by the heat of summer. On November 18 the last Republican left the right bank of the Ebro. Shortly afterwards, Yagüe entered Ribarroya, the last Republican village and bridgehead. The intrepid Anglo-Saxon reporters, Hemingway,[1] Buckley, Matthews and Sheean, were among the last to cross the river.

Republicans have named their casualty figure in this battle at

[1] Hemingway had gone back to America earlier in the year. One night in the summer, however, the friends of the Republic were rejoiced to hear on the wireless the announcement: 'The writer, Ernest Hemingway, has suddenly left his home in Key West. He was last seen in New York, boarding a ship, without hat or baggage, to rejoin the Spanish Republican troops at the front.' (Regler, *Owl of Minerva*, 298.)

70,000 and this may be regarded as being a likely figure. 20,000 of these were prisoners. Deaths may have reached 30,000. Some of the Republican divisions suffered 50% casualties. Of the International Brigades which crossed the Ebro, 75% fell. The German Embassy in Salamanca estimated Nationalist casualties at 33,000 and this figure seems probable. The Republicans lost about 200 aircraft. They also abandoned a great store of material of all kinds, including 1,800 machine guns and 24,000 rifles. In truth, the Republic had lost all its army in the North of Spain.

The same day that the last Republicans left the right bank of the Ebro, November 16, the Anglo-Italian Agreement came into being. This was one further consequence of Munich. The British Foreign Office agreed to the implementation of the Anglo-Italian Agreement, once the 10,000 Italians, of whom Mussolini had spoken to Chamberlain at Munich, had been withdrawn from Spain. On Chamberlain's insistence, the implementation itself was delayed until November. The Italians remaining in Spain would be about 12,000 men of the Littorio Division, consisting of picked men, to be commanded by Gambara. Berti was dismissed. There also remained pilots, the tank corps and artillerymen, as well as officers and NCOs to command 4 mixed divisions of Spaniards. The other Italians prepared to leave Spain. Ten thousand men arrived at Naples on October 20. King Victor Emmanuel and the populace received them without warmth. But Ciano soon forgot his consequent annoyance when he received from Franco, as a souvenir, a painting by Zuloaga of *The Oldest Requeté* with a pleasant background of war and flames.[1] So Chamberlain's Cabinet judged that the long sought agreement could now come into force.

A fortnight later, in the House of Commons, Eden recalled how Lord Perth had said, when the agreement was signed in April, that a settlement of the Spanish question was a 'prerequisite' for its entry into force. Now, Eden said, there had been no Spanish settlement and, instead, an Anglo-Italian deal at the expense of Spain. Such a remark was shown to be justified when, in the House of Lords on November 3, Halifax announced that Mussolini had always 'made plain that, whether Britain approved or not of his reasons, he would not be prepared to see Franco defeated'. The previous day, the Spanish Civil War had even flared up in the

[1] Ciano, *Diary 1937–8*, 180–1.

North Sea. Seven miles off Cromer, a Nationalist armed merchant-man, the *Nadir*, sank the *Cantabria*, a steamer used by the Republic for food supplies.[1] Eleven British ships, furthermore, had been attacked in Republican ports during the month of November. But the British public were generally too preoccupied by the appearance on these shores of the Giant Panda, by their new game 'Monopoly', and by the homely sight of the Royal Family singing 'Under the Spreading Chestnut Tree' to care greatly about their shipping losses. And now, on November 16, here in Rome was Lord Perth 'moved', as the master-toady Ciano put it, at this last act in toadying to Italy.[2]

---

[1] *The Times*, 5.11.38.

[2] Of course the aim of the Anglo-Italian Agreement was to attempt to wean Italy a little away from Germany. Halifax wrote to Sir Eric Phipps in Paris: 'Although we do not expect to detach Italy from the Axis, we believe the Agreement will increase Mussolini's power of manoeuvre and so make him less dependent on Hitler and therefore freer to resume the classic Italian role of balancing between Germany and the Western Powers'. (*British Foreign Policy, 3rd Series*, Vol. III, No. 285.) Mussolini's response was to launch a renewed campaign for cession of the French territories of Nice, Savoy and Corsica.

BOOK VII

THE END OF THE WAR

71

Nationalist and Republican Spain after the end of the Ebro campaign – Republican misery and moderation – the end of the POUM – plans for a compromise peace – the campaign in Catalonia – the two armies – the initial resistance – the collapse – the fall of Barcelona

At the end of the battle of the Ebro, Nationalist morale had risen, though 'Red' agitation in the rear continued. The British Vice-Consul in San Sebastián, Mr. Goodman, was arrested, accused of being a Republican spy.[1] General Martínez Anido, Minister of Public Order, died of pneumonia, and it was said untruthfully that he had been murdered – probably by Serrano Suñer, who disliked him cordially. There was said to be a plot to murder Franco. There were certainly innumerable arrests. 'The prisons', wrote the German Ambassador Stohrer, 'are overflowing as never before. In the prison here (i.e. at Salamanca), which is intended for 40 persons, there are supposed to be about 1,800 at the present'.[2] In September the Nationalists had announced that they had taken 210,000 prisoners since the war began, of which 134,000 were at 'liberty' – usually in some kind of 'national service'. The rest were in prison. There were two bouts of executions of so-called spies, one running into several hundreds. The Falange and the clergy grumbled at each other, though they did not openly quarrel. Despite his Jesuit training, Serrano Suñer had not successfully bridged the gap between these two departments of Spanish society. The text, for instance, of the new secondary education law of September 20, 1938, was an uneasy compromise between Falange and Church: one hour a week was for 'the patriotic formation of youth', while there would be two hours' religious teaching a week. Whereas Catholicism was declared 'the essence of Spanish history', of the two foreign languages which could be studied, one had to be either German or Italian. The economic situation in Nationalist Spain was also

---

[1] The gullibility of Mr Goodman had indeed resulted in the Consular bag being used as a means of communication by 'Red Agents'. He was reproved but released.
[2] *GD*, 796.

less favourable than previously. There was food enough for those who could buy it, but wages generally had not kept up with prices, despite the official policy of strict price control. Due to the difficulties of civilian transport, prices varied from district to district. Manufactured goods were almost non-existent. Production in essential industries had increased during 1935. The iron ore output from Vizcaya, for example, mounted to 154,000 tons in 1938, in place of 115,000 in the last year of peace. Movement in the port of Bilbao increased by 50% over peace time. But then one might have expected the increases to have been even larger.

The Nationalist Government, needing new war supplies desperately for any new offensive upon which they might embark, had meanwhile agreed at last to the German conditions for fulfilment of their request. German capital would be permitted to participate in Spanish mines to the extent of a basic 40%. But 60% would be permitted in one mine and 75% in four others. In Morocco, where the Spanish mining law did not apply, German participation was permitted up to 100%. The Spanish undertook to pay all the expenses in Spain of the Condor Legion and to import 5 million reichsmarks worth of mining machinery. This would be repaid in ore.[1] This refurbishment of the Condor Legion and other supplies sent by Germany to Nationalist Spain was the most important act of foreign intervention in the course of the Spanish Civil War. It enabled Franco to mount a new offensive almost immediately, and so strike the Republic when they had exhausted their supplies. Had it not been for this aid (itself the consequence of the German realisation that after Munich nothing they did in the Spanish War would cause Britain and France to go to war over any of its implications), a compromise peace, despite all Franco's protestations, might have been inevitable.

On the Republican side, the comparative success of the withdrawal from the right bank of the Ebro masked the destruction caused. After all, the Nationalists had taken three months to win back what they had lost in two days. Moderation continued to grow. There was an increased use of slogans of national honour, fatherland, and the past. There was a revival of propaganda for Catalan autonomy. As for religious freedom, permission was at last given for the reopening of churches, though only for funerals and marriages. On October 17 a private funeral procession passed

---

[1] *GD*, 795–6. The date of the agreement was November 19.

through Barcelona in memory of a dead Basque Officer, Álvarez del Vayo being present. On December 9, a commissariat of religion was even set up, to provide ministers for the various armies, but the outbreak of the Catalan campaign prevented this from being put finally into effect.

Food was now appallingly short in the Republic. In Madrid, over half a million persons existed during the winter of 1938-9 on a daily issue of two ounces of lentils, beans or rice, and an occasional ration of sugar or salt cod. Lentils, the commonest food, were named Dr Negrín's 'little victory pills'. The Republic had to buy its food from abroad and supplies were naturally irregular, due to the continued bombing of supply ships. Sir Denys Bray and Mr Laurence Webster reported to the League of Nations that the whole population of the Republic were living on minimum rations and that even those were not being distributed. In Barcelona, where there were a million refugees, the problems were truly appalling. The International Commission for the assistance of child refugees, set up by the Quakers in December 1937, could only help 40,000 out of 600,000 child refugees, even though they were being financed by 17 Governments.[1] The British Government had already contributed £20,000 to this fund. In 1939 they gave another £100,000. But funds were still inadequate, for the cost of giving even a third of these children one meal a day throughout the winter was estimated as nearly £150,000. The Nationalists sought to point out the contrast between the hungry Republic and their own territory by an air-raid of loaves of bread on Madrid and Barcelona. The Republicans replied with an air-raid of shirts and socks, to demonstrate their superiority in manufactured goods.

But even in manufactured goods the Republic could not boast of its position. The chief cause of this was no doubt the blockade. Yet the collapse of production in the Republic in late 1938 cannot entirely be explained by that, nor by the general financial hostility of Europe towards the Spanish Republic. The political decay of the Anarchists and the loss of self-confidence of the CNT before the Communists was at least partly responsible for the economic failure of the Republic. Only in one sphere, indeed, was the Republic still able to preserve its optimism. This was education. 'I have visited,' reported Antoine St Exupéry, 'on the Madrid front, a school installed five hundred metres

[1] Toynbee, A., *Survey*, Vol I 1938, 271, 389.

from the trenches, behind a small wall, on a little hillock. A Corporal was teaching botany. He was carefully peeling away the petals of a poppy. Around him were gathered bearded soldiers, their chins sunk in their hands, their brows knitted in the effort of concentration. They did not understand the lesson very well, but they had been told: you are brutes, you have only just left your holes, we must save you for humanity. And with heavy feet they were hurrying towards enlightenment.'[1] It was the survival of this ardent spirit to the very end that led, for instance, a delegation of French journalists and politicians to confirm, in the words of Raymond Laurent: 'You are fighting for the noble cause of humanity as for the security of France itself.'

In October 1938 the leaders of the POUM (except, of course, for Nin) were at last brought to trial. Not long before, the various real Falangists who had been implicated in their affairs had also been tried. Thirteen of these, including Golfín, Dalmau and Roca, were condemned to death and shot for what, given the circumstances of a civil war, was genuinely espionage. When the POUM leaders came to the tribunal, the case against them almost collapsed. All, including Nin, had succeeded in resisting all Communist pressure upon them to confess. Stalin and Yezhov may have planned a show trial with sensational confessions on the model of those in Moscow. If so, they were thwarted. Republican Ministers and ex-Ministers, headed by Largo Caballero and Zugazagoitia, gave evidence in the POUM's favour. The judgment found the POUM to be true Socialists and absolved them of treason and espionage. But they were condemned to various terms of imprisonment for their part in the May rising of 1937 and for revolutionary activities prejudicial to the war effort.[2]

The German Ambassador, Stohrer, concluded an analysis of the situation at this time with the remark that mutual fear was the chief reason for the continuance of the war. Franco had, for instance, told an American correspondent that he had a list (with witnesses) of a million persons on the Republican side who were guilty of crimes. The Ambassador nevertheless concluded that the oppor-

---

[1] St Exupéry, *La Terre des Hommes*, 210.

[2] Gorkin, 269–80; Peirats, III 297–300. One of the POUM leaders, Rey, was freed. He was later shot by Franco after the end of the war. After the end of this trial, three leading Anarchists – Federica Montseny, Abad de Santillán, and García Birlán – visited Azaña to denounce Negrín as a dictator and demand a change of Government. But Azaña, as usual, would do nothing definite though agreeing with his visitors. (Peirats, III 318.)

tunity for a compromise peace would suddenly come.[1] At the same time, Adolf Berle, Assistant Secretary of State, reported to President Roosevelt, on instructions, how compromise might be achieved in Spain. He proposed associating an American approach with the forthcoming conference of South American countries at Lima. The plan was never carried forward, due to quarrels among the South Americans and to the cautious spirit of Cordell Hull. Cuba, Mexico and Haiti, however, declared themselves in favour of an approach such as Roosevelt had contemplated.[2]

In fact, the possibility of peace was far removed. The Nationalists had even refused to co-operate with a proposal by Negrín in August that each side should suspend the execution of military prisoners for a month.[3] Even on the question of the removal of volunteers (which could be regarded as a touchstone for his pacific intentions) Franco was unyielding. He would accept no such agreement as Britain had proposed, unless he were first granted belligerent rights. In the meantime, with his new supply of German arms, he was preparing a new offensive. This would strike the Republicans hard and fast, after the conclusion of their own assault of the Ebro, just as the run-away Aragón campaign had followed the battle of Teruel. The pick of the Spanish Nationalist divisions were assembled all along the line from the Pyrenees to the Ebro and the sea. These were, from north to south, a new Army Corps of Urgel under Muñoz Grandes; the Army of the Maestrazgo under García Valiño, and the Army of Aragón under Moscardó. Then came the Italian General Gambara's four divisions. These were the picked Littorio Division of Italians, the Black Arrows and Blue Arrows (these being Spanish soldiers under Italian officers in the higher grades and mixed in the lower) and Green Arrows (mixed Italian and Spanish soldiers under Italian officers). Artillery, aircraft and tanks were attached to Gambara, all controlled by Italians. Farther to the south, there was the Army of Navarre under Solchaga and Yagüe with the Army of Morocco. This army consisted of 300,000 men and was supported by 565 pieces of artillery. The offensive, planned for December 10 and postponed till the 15th, was finally named for the 23rd.[4]

---

[1] GD, 796.   [2] USD, 1938 Vol 1 255.
[3] Though the Chetwode Commission (see above, page 559) persuaded the Nationalists to delay 400 executions.
[4] Aznar, 814-5.

The Republican battle lines of Catalonia were commanded by
Hernández Sarabia. Beneath him were the Armies of the East and
of the Ebro, now under Colonels Perea and Modesto respectively.
These forces numbered 220,000 in all. Nationalist historians claim
that their enemies were supported by 250 pieces of artillery, 40
tanks, 80 armoured cars, 46 anti-aircraft guns, 80 aircraft and
26 bombers.[1] The defending Republican army in Catalonia suffered, however, from a general shortage of arms and ammunition.
If the Nationalist figures are correct, they undoubtedly include
material which was worn out. Dr Negrín himself was, as he confessed, tired, 'spiritually and physically'.[2] Rojo, once again Chief of
Staff, believed that General Franco needed several months to prepare a general attack and the Republican leaders hence were toying, when attacked, with a plan to disembark a brigade at Motril,
which would march to Málaga and raise all Andalusia.

On December 23 the attack began, after the Papal *Nuncio* had
vainly requested a truce for Christmas in the name of the Pope.[3]
The main assault was launched by the Navarrese and the Italians,
across the river Segre, twenty kilometres north of its junction with
the Ebro at Mequinenza. The crossing made, the surprised defenders – a well equipped company of *Carabineros* – were deserted
by their officers. The front was thus broken at the first moment of
contact. Higher up the Segre, in the foothills of the Pyrenees,
Muñoz Grandes and García Valiño also broke the Republican
lines. These breaches caused the abandonment of the whole of the
rest of the line of the Segre. At Barcelona the attack was at first
thought insignificant but soon Lister's 5th Army Corps – as usual
in the case of a Nationalist offensive – was thrown into the battle,
to try and hold the attack. With headquarters at Castelldans, in
the first line of hills east of the Segre, Lister maintained himself for
nearly a fortnight. Thus 1938, the year of Munich, gave way to
1939 which was eventually to be the year of general war.

On January 3 the overwhelming Nationalist armour finally told
against Lister and he was forced to abandon his whole line of defence to the Italians. In the north, García Valiño and Muñoz
Grandes, now supported by Moscardó, captured the communications centre of Artesa de Segre. On January 4 Borjas Blancas, a
town now totally wrecked, fell to the Navarrese and Italian armies.

---

[1] Villegas, 351. Aznar, 815.   [2] Zugazagoitia, 447.
[3] See Buckley; Álvarez del Vayo, *Freedom's Battle*, 262 fl.; Aznar, 816 fl.; Villegas,
loc. cit.; Rojo, *España Heroica*; Lojendio, 547 fl.

The front was generally open. Ciano, noting that the only danger seemed the possibility of French intervention, instructed his Ambassadors in Berlin and London to say that this contingency would bring 'regular' Italian divisions to Spain – even if this should

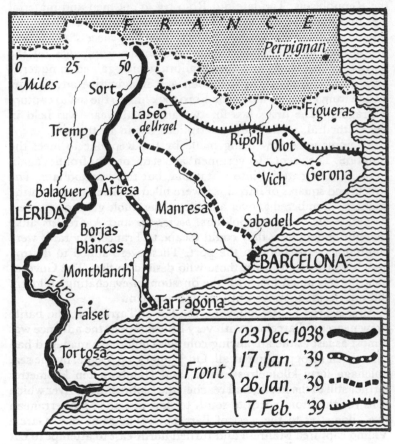

MAP 33. THE CAMPAIGN IN CATALONIA

unleash world war.[1] But, with the British Cabinet still bent on making friends with the dictators (Halifax suggested to Ciano in Rome on the 12th that he hoped Franco 'would settle the Spanish question')[2] there was no likelihood whatever that the French

[1] Ciano, *Diary 1939–43*, 5.   [2] *Ibid.*, 10.

Cabinet would act boldly to save the Spanish Republic. The Republican Commander-in-Chief Hernández Sarabia, informed Negrín that he had only 37,000 rifles left for all Catalonia.[1] At all events, after the fall of Borjas Blancas, the battle of Catalonia became a rout. The swiftness of the Italian mobile divisions astonished the Republicans. Too late did Rojo try to get men and material sent up by boat from Valencia. Uselessly did the Government call up all men from the ages of 17 to 55. The only successful countermeasure of the Republic was a diversionary campaign on the borders of Andalusia and Estremadura, which gained some territory. But on January 14 a sudden and imaginative advance by Yagüe from Gandesa along the Ebro took him to the sea to capture Tarragona. The first Mass for two-and-a-half years was held in the Cathedral, while the proscriptions began in the city.

Attempts were now being made by the Republic to meet the situation. The French Government at last opened the frontier again to allow war material into Catalonia, but this was too late. The streets and squares of Barcelona were filled with refugees from the country – numbered at over a million. The whole great city wore a desperate air of defeat. Soldiers, *bourgeoisie* and Anarchists alike thought only of how they could escape to France. Air raids were continuous, especially on the port. These were aimed to destroy vessels which might assist those who desired to flee. The Government, preoccupied first with the question of evacuating children, did not decide to move until the last moment.

After a brief pause, following the fall of Tarragona, the battle drew nearer to Barcelona with very little fighting; the advance was almost as fast as the advancing columns could have managed had there been no opposition at all. On January 24, Yagüe, by the sea, Solchaga forty kilometres inland, and Gambara ten kilometres farther still to the north, had reached the Llobregat, the river which runs roughly from north to south to flow into the Mediterranean five kilometres to the west of Barcelona. The same day, García Valiño captured Manresa and turned north-east to attempt to cut off Barcelona from the border. Negrín, the Government, the Communist leaders, the chiefs of the Army and of the Civil Service now hastily moved from Barcelona to Gerona, along with the Catalan and *Emigré* Basque Governments. In the Catalan capital, there was no spirit of resistance. The Communist party might cry out that the Llobregat should become the Manzanares of Catalonia, but the

---

[1] Álvarez del Vayo, *Freedom's Battle*, 262.

Catalans, Separatists and Anarchists included, had no intention of fighting. Those foreigners who remained either joined the flood of refugees which fled northwards or tried to find shipping in the heavily bombed harbour. The streets of the great city were filthy after the flight of the municipal cleaners. Mobs had begun to pillage food shops. Many official Republican documents were burned.

In Rome, Barcelona was held to be so certainly lost that Lord Perth was already asking Ciano to prevent reprisals by the Nationalists.[1] In France, a debate raged for a week in the National Assembly, in the course of which Daladier and Bonnet said that it was too late to try and save Spain, while Blum and the united Left, including the Communists, denied that all was lost. Yet Blum's criticism of the Daladier Government for continuing even now to maintain non-intervention could have applied to his own Government, at least since February 1937. On January 25 Yagüe, followed by Solchaga and Gambara, crossed the Llobregat. Resistance was isolated and without any general plan. By the following morning, the north and west of Barcelona had been enveloped. The Navarrese and Italians established themselves on Mount Tibidabo and Yagüe on Montjuich (where he liberated 1,200 political prisoners). At midday, the occupation of the city began. On the first tank which entered Barcelona, a laughing German Jewess was perched, giving the Fascist salute. She had recently been in the women's prison at Las Cortes as a Trotskyist. The incongruity of the spectacle gave a curiously mocking commentary to the *vivas* of triumph at the 'liberation' of Catalonia. Meantime the streets were silent and empty. Almost half a million persons had left the city for the north by all means possible. By four o'clock the main administrative buildings were occupied, untouched by incendiaries. In the evening, those citizens of Barcelona who had all the time secretly supported the Nationalists came into the streets to rejoice.

[1] Ciano, *Diary 1939-43*, 15.

72

The Flight from Catalonia

The conclusion of the campaign of Catalonia was not an offensive but a victory parade preceded by a flight. The world was astonished at the swiftness of the collapse, in reality caused by the depletion of men and material on the Ebro. Mr Duncan Sandys expressed the views of many sympathisers with the Republic (or at least enemies of Franco's allies) when he urged upon the Ambassador in London, Azcárate, that resistance was necessary in Catalonia for the world to suppose that the war was not in fact over.[1] Mr Henry Stimson, ex-Secretary of State, wrote a long letter to the *New York Times*[2] citing legal and political reasons for lifting the embargo on arms to Spain. A correspondence on the subject ensued, which was nonetheless passionate for being too late to be of any assistance. Nor did it help the Republic to know that in England 72% of persons questioned in a public opinion poll supported them, against only 9% for General Franco.[3] All Catalonia was now in total disorder. The flights from Irún, Málaga, Bilbao – all those terrible movements of a terrified population paled into insignificance when compared with the flight from Catalonia along what even Stohrer named 'this road of suffering'.[4] This was a movement of hysterical panic, for only a small percentage of those who fled would have been in mortal danger if they had remained in Catalonia. But the whole of Catalonia now seemed to be on the move. All the towns on the way to the French border were crammed to overflowing. At night, the pavements were choked with hunger-stricken and shivering human beings of

[1] Azcárate MSS.   [2] On January 23.
[3] From an unpublished PhD thesis, *The Spanish Civil War* by H. J. Parry of the University of California, quoted by Taylor, 195. There were three other polls of British opinion, collected by the British Public Opinion Institute, during the Civil War. In January 1937, 14% considered that the Burgos *junta* should be considered the true Government of Spain, against 86% who did not. In March 1938, 57% considered themselves in sympathy with the Government, 7% with Franco and 36% neither. In October 1938, the answers were much as in the previous March.
[4] *GD*, 844.

all ages. Typical of the chaos of the time was the fate of the prisoners of the POUM. Their SIM captors had wanted to leave them behind in Barcelona for Franco to find. Then, however, they were moved northwards. At a certain point near the French border their gaolers placed themselves at their disposal. They therefore at last made good their escape from the prisons of Republican Spain.

At first, the French Government had refused for financial reasons[1] to permit the entry of the refugees. They proposed instead a neutral zone on the Spanish side of the frontier where refugees could be maintained by foreign relief. The Nationalists, however, refused to consider this plan. So the French Government reluctantly permitted the opening of the frontier, though at first only to civilians and wounded men. Under these conditions the first crossings began at midnight on January 27–28. Fifteen thousand crossed on January 28. On the succeeding days, this figure was far exceeded. In the first week of February, it became evident that the retreating Republican army had no intention, and no means, of resisting the Nationalist advance. The French, therefore, were faced with a choice between permitting the entry of the soldiers or resisting them by force. On February 5 the French Government decided to admit the Army, subject to the surrender of their arms. Thus, to the 10,000 wounded, the 170,000 women and children and the 60,000 male civilians who had crossed since January 28, there were added about 250,000 men of the Republican Army between February 5 and 10.

The frontier was a scene of consummate tragedy. The fugitives were worn out by hunger and fatigue. Their clothes were damp from rain and snow. Yet there were few complaints. Crushed by disaster, the Spanish Republicans walked on upright, erect and dignified. Children carried broken toys, the head of a doll or a deflated ball – symbols of a happy childhood which they had lost. At the border, what laughter, what happiness! But what disillusion![2]

On the French side of the frontier, a large camp was opened as a clearing centre at Le Boulou. Here, there was no shelter, though most of the women and children were quickly removed, along with some wounded soldiers, to other parts of France. Families were separated who had never been apart before, even in the disaster of

---

[1] The French Government had already spent 88 million francs on aid to refugees since the start of the war.

[2] Kersher, 24.

the flight. Large camps were established at Argelès, at St Cyprien and at four smaller places in the area for the reception of the Republican Army. These were simply open spaces of sand dunes near the sea, enclosed by barbed wire. Men dug holes for themselves like animals, to find some shelter. There were eventually 15 of these camps, guarded by Senegalese and members of the *Garde Mobile*. Some refugees crossed the border with a handful of earth which they had taken as they left their villages. One *Garde Mobile* forcibly opened one of these gnarled clenched hands, and scattered the earth of Spain in disdain into a French ditch.[1]

In the camps, for ten days there was no proper water and food supply, and the wounded who stayed with their comrades were left uncared for. Among these was the poet Machado, who shortly died of neglect, not of wounds. Food supplies were later secured, but there continued to be a total lack of sanitation and shelter, and meagre medical services. The French Government was vehemently criticised for permitting these conditions but the difficulties of providing for about 400,000 refugees at short notice were, after all, herculean. On the other hand, it is certain that the French Government hoped, by neglect, to force as many as possible of the refugees to throw themselves on General Franco's mercy. (Callousness was also shown by persons comfortable in America or England. Mr Herbert Matthews, for example, was told by the editor of the *New York Times* not to send emotional reports of the conditions of the camp.[2]) It was said that the cost of providing for one refugee was 15 francs a day, and for the wounded 60 francs. The French Government gave 30 million francs for this purpose early in February. At the same time, they not unnaturally asked other Governments to help with the burden. The Belgians agreed to accept two to three thousand Spanish children, but the British and Russian Governments at first would not accept any refugees at all. Later, Britain agreed to the entry of a selected number of leaders. Russia later gave £28,000 for aid to the refugees, and Britain £50,000 to the Red Cross for work in the camps.[3]

---

[1] Regler, *Owl of Minerva*, 321.   [2] *Ibid., loc. cit.*

[3] Toynbee, A., *Survey*, 1938 Vol I 397-9. There were inevitably several settlements of private scores in these camps. In the camp at Argelès, for example, Astorga Vayo, once a leading executive of the hated SIM, was one day greeted by several acquaintances from earlier in the war. He walked with them for a while discussing old times. Suddenly he realised that they had led him to an unfrequented part of the camp. Before him he observed a deep trench dug beneath some pine trees. He turned in dismay. His companions smiled grimly. They buried him alive. (Gorkin, 237.)

Meantime, on February 1, a rump of 62 members of the Cortes, elected three years before with such high enthusiasm, met in a dungeon of the old castle of Figueras, the last town in Catalonia short of the border. Diego Martínez Barrio sat at a table draped in the flag of the Republic. Negrín made a speech naming three conditions for peace: a guarantee of Spanish independence, a guarantee of the right of the Spanish people to choose their own Government, and freedom from prosecution. Nobody opposed these conditions, although it was certain that they would not be accepted by General Franco, and that therefore the Government was in effect recommending the continuance of the war.[1] The Cortes broke up. Its members, including most of the Government, left for France. Azaña, Aguirre and Companys, with Largo Caballero and other Republican leaders, had preceded them there. Álvarez del Vayo and Negrín remained in Catalonia for some days more. On February 2 they approached Stevenson and Jules Henry, the French and British Ministers, to try and arrange with the Nationalists a mediation on the conditions of the Prime Minister's speech at Figueras. The two diplomats agreed to try and do so. Negrín added that, if the terms were rejected, the Republic would continue the war from Valencia.[2] Álvarez del Vayo busied himself with the safe conduct from Figueras of the Prado paintings. They were taken in lorries to Geneva, where they were held temporarily on behalf of the Spanish people by the Secretary-General of the League. The broken refugees stood aside while the incomparable canvases of Velázquez, Goya, Titian, Rubens passed by.[3]

At the same time, the Navarrese and Italian advance continued irresistibly. Gerona, the Venice of Catalonia, fell on February 5, after heavy incendiary bombing which infuriated the retreating Republicans into a show of resistance. A certain number of Nationalist prisoners were massacred – including Colonel Rey D'Harcourt, the hero of Teruel, and the Bishop of Teruel with him.[4] André Marty was also only narrowly forestalled in an attempt to shoot a number of his old staff at Albacete, who might, so he feared in his narrow insanity, tell the world of some of his maniacal acts.[5] To the west, García Valiño entered the old cathedral city of Vich. In fact, as the Nationalists suspected, the

[1] *Diario de Sesiones*, 1.2.39.
[2] *USD*, 1939 Vol 2 739–40.
[3] Álvarez del Vayo, *Last Optimist*, 294.
[4] *General Cause*, 178.
[5] Regler, *Owl of Minerva*, 325.

last resistance was over in Catalonia. While Sir Robert Hodgson, on behalf of Britain, was putting Negrín's three peace points to the Spanish Nationalists, four army corps were advancing towards the French frontier. On February 8 the Navarrese entered Figueras. The same day, their advanced units came into contact with the rearguard of the retreating Republicans. On February 9 Solchaga and Moscardó reached the French frontier, the former at Le Perthus, the latter in the mountains of Nuria. By the 10th the whole frontier was lined by units of Nationalist armies. Earlier in the day, Modesto had led the last units of the Army of the Ebro into France. It was at this moment that Giménez Caballero, then serving under Moscardó, recalled Louis XIV's famous boast, and made the ludicrous proclamation to his comrades: 'At last, there are Pyrenees!'

Thus ended the campaign of Catalonia. The casualties are difficult to estimate. According to the Nationalists,[1] the Republic lost 143 aircraft. The total number of Republican prisoners taken in this campaign was estimated at 200,000. In their flight, the Republic are alleged to have left behind 242 pieces of artillery, 3,500 machine guns and 3,000 vehicles. Such figures seem certain to be exaggerated. Behind, in Barcelona, apart from the inevitable reprisals, Catalan autonomy was, as expected, immediately rescinded, and the Catalan tongue was solemnly banned as an official language.[2]

[1] Aznar, 834.
[2] Propaganda was ruthlessly harnessed to the service of proscription. 'A woman of Barcelona,' newspaper readers were shortly informed, 'recently killed thirty of her lovers because they were Marxists'.

73

Negotiations for peace – their failure – General Franco's conditions –
Senator Bérard's mission to Burgos – French and British recognition
of the Nationalist Government

After the fall of Catalonia, the world concluded that the Spanish war was over. The Nationalist peseta rose on the Paris Bourse to seventy times the value of the Republican – though its real value was thought to be nearer the unofficial rate of 100 to the pound than the fixed one of 42.[1] Inside Nationalist Spain, no more was heard of plots of assassination. At Chicote's bar in San Sebastián (the most famous bar in Nationalist Spain), pessimists had sometimes been the most fashionable clients. Now optimists sternly discouraged even those who laughed at notices announcing 'keep quiet, be careful, enemy ears are listening'. Quarrels were fewer. Serrano Suñer was now the unquestioned leading adviser of Franco. The death of old General Martínez Anido on December 24 had removed his chief enemy in the administration, and on January 24 the Ministries of Public Order and the Interior were merged into one under his own leadership. The question of the relationship between the *régime* and the Church was discussed by Serrano Suñer in a press conference on February 6. While praising Catholic tradition, he proposed a division of powers, especially in education. He also demanded the right of episcopal investiture which the State had enjoyed since the *Concordat* of 1851. But in everything Serrano Suñer did not have his own way. Cardinal Segura, now returned to Spain as Archbishop of Seville after the death of Cardinal Ilundáin, had denounced the Falange as irreligious, and deplored the influence of the Nazis. A little later the Primate, Cardinal Gomá of Toledo, returned to the matter rather more discreetly (as was his custom) in his Lenten Pastoral letter in which he criticised 'exaggerated nationalism'.

---

[1] 52 for imports. The *vales*, issued by municipalities, by Popular Front Committees, and by the Generalitat in early days of the war (nicknamed 'pyjamas' because they could only be used at home), were no longer accepted in most places.

A Monarchist restoration in Nationalist Spain now once again seemed a possibility. A decree of December 15 had given back to the royal family their property and rights of citizenship taken from them by the Republic. King Alfonso and his son Don Juan, however, announced that they wished to be regarded as soldiers of General Franco until further orders. The Nationalist *régime* was now also courted by those who previously had scorned it. The French Government, for example, despatched Senator Bérard to Burgos to negotiate diplomatic relations. Bérard was treated coldly. Jordana demanded first recognition *de jure*, the return of Republican war and merchant ships in French waters, of Spanish art treasures taken by the Republic to France, and of Spanish money in France. The Nationalists, not unnaturally, refused to pay anything for the upkeep of the Republican refugees in Southern France or to allow the French Government to reimburse their expenses in this matter from Spanish assets in France.[1]

The Government of the Republic, meantime, assembled in Toulouse. Negrín and Álvarez del Vayo arrived there on February 9 from Figueras to discover the rest of the Cabinet waiting for permission from the French authorities to fly to Valencia. After a brief Cabinet meeting in the Spanish Consulate, the difficulties over transport were smoothed over. Negrín and Álvarez del Vayo flew to Alicante in an aeroplane belonging to Air France. As could be expected, they found the military leaders of the remains of Republican Spain low in spirit.[2] The same day that Catalonia passed finally into Nationalist hands, Minorca had surrendered. General Franco had let it be known in London that he would occupy Minorca without Germans or Italians. As a result, HMS *Devonshire* had brought negotiators from Majorca to Port Mahon. Its captain had helped to negotiate the surrender of the island and had transported 450 Republicans to Marseilles. Some felt in central Spain that this might be the model for their own capitulation.[3]

On February 12 Negrín explained to the Generals of the Centre the conditions of surrender which he had put to Franco. His audience listened in silence.[4] They still held a third of Spain, in-

[1] Salvador de Madariaga, 431.   [2] Álvarez del Vayo, *Freedom's Battle*, 275.
[3] *GD*, 835. Captain Hillgarth, British Consul in Majorca, had been asked to arrange the surrender by the Nationalists. The Foreign Office agreed with the request but stipulated that neither Germany nor Italy should be told and that no German or Italian troops should be allowed on the island for two years. These conditions were kept.
[4] Álvarez del Vayo, *Freedom's Battle*, 278.

cluding Madrid and Valencia. Their armies numbered 500,000 men but they possessed little war material. The Army of the Centre, for example, had only 95,000 rifles, 1,600 machine gun rifles, 1,400 machine guns, 150 pieces of artillery, 50 mortars and 10 tanks. The civilian population was nearly starving and the Generals themselves had been for a long time out of contact with their Government. All were weary of war. The policy of continued resistance was only urged with any seriousness by the Communist party – whose chief leaders La Pasionaria, Lister and Modesto, with the inevitable Togliatti, also returned to Spain at this time.[1]

Álvarez del Vayo now flew from Madrid to Paris to try and persuade Azaña to return to Spain also. But Azaña told him: 'My duty is to make peace. I refuse to help, by my presence, to prolong a senseless battle. We must secure the best possible guarantees, and then conclude as soon as we can.' The President had already tried to get from Generals Rojo, Jurado and Hidalgo de Cisneros a written recommendation against continuing the war. They had refused. Álvarez del Vayo gave up his task as useless.[2]

On February 13 Franco promulgated a decree applying to all guilty of 'subversive activities' from October 1934 until July 1936 as well as to those who since had 'opposed the Nationalist Government in fact or by vexatious passivity'. It was evident that this gave to the Nationalist authorities wide powers of vengeance. The proscription had, indeed, begun. General Gambara reported to Ciano that Franco had unleashed in Barcelona 'a very thorough and drastic purge'. Many Italians – émigrés of all kinds – were taken. Mussolini, asked for his views, ordered: 'Let them all be shot. Dead men tell no tales.'[3] Those shot included several imprisoned by the Communists.

The issue of reprisals was, of course, the most important one for the Republic. If guarantees against them had been given, the Republic would have made peace a year before. On February 17, Azcárate and Álvarez del Vayo, who was still in Paris, telegraphed to Negrín to suggest that this should be the only condition of peace, and to allow them to put this to Lord Halifax for transmission to Franco. Lord Halifax had even proposed this simple condition to Azcárate before he had left for Paris. Due to telegraph delays (attributed by Azcárate and Álvarez del Vayo to the wilful inter-

---

[1] Díaz had been in Moscow since November, working for the Comintern.
[2] Álvarez del Vayo, *Freedom's Battle*, 278 fl.   [3] Ciano, *Diary 1939–43*, 34.

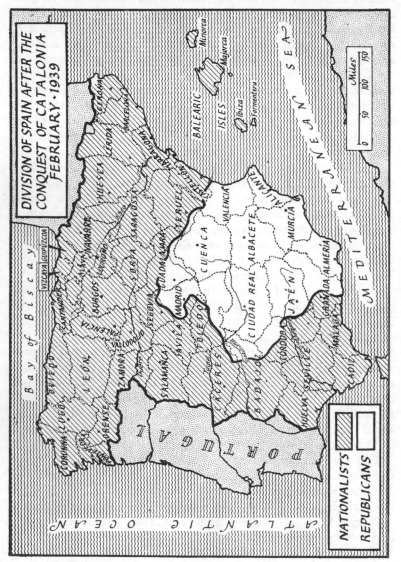

DIVISION OF SPAIN AFTER THE CONQUEST OF CATALONIA · FEBRUARY · 1939

NATIONALISTS

REPUBLICANS

MAP 34

ference of Colonel Casado, the Republican commander of the
Army of the Centre) Negrín's affirmative reply did not reach Paris
until February 25. Halifax meantime, on February 22, gave up
waiting for the agreement to his proposal. He began to arrange an
unconditional recognition of the Nationalist Government.[1] However, on February 18 General Franco had already ended all ideas
of a conditional peace, whether put by Britain or France or by any
Republican. 'The Nationalists have won,' he declared, 'the Republicans must therefore surrender without conditions.' On the
22nd, Franco despatched a telegram to Neville Chamberlain
assuring him that his patriotism, his honour as a gentleman, and
his generosity were the finest guarantees for a just peace. He later
announced that the tribunals to be set up after the Republican
surrender would deal only with criminals – 'reprisals being alien
to the Nationalist movement'.[2] This bland remark, along with the
telegram to Chamberlain, was considered by Britain to be the
only condition obtainable for her recognition of the Nationalist
Government. On February 26, meantime, Senator Bérard completed his mission in Burgos. All the Nationalist demands were
accepted. France and Nationalist Spain would live together as
good neighbours, co-operate in Morocco, and prevent all activities
directed against the security of each other. The French Government undertook to return to Spain all Spanish property taken to
France against the wishes of its true owners. This would include
£8 million in gold kept in Mont de Marsan as security for a loan
made in 1931. The Bank of France had refused to return this to the
Republic, although the loan had been repaid. All Republican war
material in France, all battle, merchant and fishing vessels, works
of art, vehicles and documents, were also to be sent to Spain. In
return, the Nationalists merely agreed to receive a French
Ambassador at Burgos.

The official recognition by France and Britain occurred on
February 27. Mr Chamberlain read out Franco's telegram
on February 22 to the House of Commons. Both the Liberal

---

[1] These facts have been related to the author by Señor Azcárate. They are described
on pages 221 ff. of his unpublished memoirs. *Cf.* also Álvarez del Vayo, *Freedom's
Battle*, 285.

[2] Franco had stated in November 1938 that there would be no question of an
amnesty. 'Those who are amnestied are demoralised.' He (no doubt through the
persuasion of Serrano Suñer) appears to have genuinely believed in 'redemption
through the penalty of labour'. That is, those who were not to be executed would have
to 're-educate' themselves by work in labour camps.

and Labour parties strongly opposed recognition and forced a debate denouncing the action. Mr Attlee condemned Mr Chamberlain's devious way of agreeing the act of recognition with Daladier before telling the House of Commons. 'We see in this action,' he concluded, 'a gross betrayal of democracy, the consummation of two and a half years of the hypocritical pretence of non-intervention and a connivance all the time at aggression. And this is only one step further in the downward march of His Majesty's Government in which at every stage they do not sell, but give away, the permanent interests of this country. They do not do anything to build up peace or stop war, but merely announce to the whole world that anyone who is out to use force can always be sure that he will have a friend in the British Prime Minister.' Mr Chamberlain answered this violent attack by saying that General Franco had given pledges of mercy and that, short of war, Britain could not ever enforce any conditions on him. There followed, as very often in the course of the Spanish War, a heated violent exchange between Sir Henry Page Croft, a Conservative supporter of General Franco, and Miss Ellen Wilkinson. Eden supported the Government from the back benches, urging that to delay recognition might prolong the war. Yet other Conservative back benchers such as Mr Vyvyan Adams deplored unconditional recognition. And Mr Churchill was absent. The Communist Mr Gallacher suggested that the Prime Minister should be impeached. Mr Herbert Morrison and Sir Thomas Inskip closed the debate for the Opposition and for the Government respectively, and closed also the long series of passionate discussions of Spain in the Mother of Parliaments. No foreign issue since the French Revolution had so occupied the House of Commons. And rightly so, since, from a negative point of view, the Government, through the policy of non-intervention which they had maintained (and forced successive French Governments to maintain) had contributed to the defeat of the Republic. They had done this in order to promote that policy of a 'general appeasement in Europe' which meant to try and flatter Hitler and Mussolini into good behaviour.[1]

---

[1] The Opposition, ever since they had decided in October 1936 that non-intervention was 'a farce', had actively supported the Spanish Republic, and had close relations with Azcárate at the Spanish Embassy. But they had always stopped short of non-constitutional action such as organising a trade union boycott on Spanish Nationalist trade and doing what they could to prevent credit facilities being made available from the City to Franco.

Meantime Azcárate paid a final unsuccessful visit to Lord Halifax to urge that Britain secure some guarantee of moderation by Franco as a condition of recognition.[1] Russia denounced the falsity of 'the capitalist policy of capitulation before the aggressor' but took no other action. No act of recognition of Franco was yet prepared in Washington but most other countries now followed the lead of Britain and France.

[1] Later he handed over the Spanish Embassy in London to the Foreign Office who rendered it to the Nationalist agent, the Duke of Alba. Similar scenes were taking place in other capitals. According to Azcárate, the new incumbents followed Alba's example of dismissing, with a few hours' notice, all the employees of the Embassy, including servants who had been there since the Monarchy. This, however, is denied by the Marqués de Santa Cruz, who was then Alba's second-in-command. Some servants were undoubtedly kept.

74

Genereal Franco's statements on February 18 and 22 brought two reactions in Republican Spain. Negrín and the Communists braced themselves towards the idea of further resistance. The leading army officers who were still simply Republican rather than Communist or Socialist, concluded that the harshness of Franco's terms derived from the Communist backing of Negrín's Government and from the Communist complexion of the Republican army. They reckoned that they, as members of the old Spanish army, could conclude an agreement with Franco more advantageous than that possible for Negrín. Partly this conclusion derived, consciously or unconsciously, from a jealousy of the prowess, as well as the predominance, of the Communist officers. Around these Republican officers gathered other Republican opponents of Negrín – supporters of Azaña, Prieto, Largo Caballero among them. All those leaders, however, were now abroad. The only political figure of any consequence among the plotters was Professor Besteiro, the long-dissident reformist Socialist. The plot, in preparation and development, would have been unsuccessful had it not been for the support of the Anarchists in Madrid, who, acting separately from the disintegrating general Anarchist movement, seized the opportunity to settle their long-standing accounts with the Communists. In this way, the last tragedy of the tragic Civil War began. Two and a half years after the military rising led by Sanjurjo, Mola and Franco, the war ended, as it had begun, with a rebellion by a group of officers against their Government.

On the evening of February 23,[1] Colonel Casado, commander

---

[1] The following account of the end of the war in Spain and the *coup* of Colonel Casado is pieced together from, chiefly, the narratives of Colonel Casado himself,

of the Army of the Centre in Madrid and the leading spirit among the officers opposed to Negrín, banned the publication of the Communist paper *Mundo Obrero*, because a manifesto due to appear in it attacked Largo Caballero for leaving Spain and urged continued resistance.[1] This was an obviously bold step for Casado to take, especially when three out of four of the commanders of army corps in his own army – Barceló, Bueno and Ortega – were Communists. (The fourth, Cipriano Mera, was an Anarchist, and the best commander the CNT produced in the war.) Uribe, the Communist Minister of Agriculture in Madrid, protested. Casado still refused to permit publication. The following day, the manifesto was circulated by hand. Casado recalled it so far as was possible. Resolving now to take action on his own, he conferred with deputies of Azaña's party. They agreed to go to Paris to try and persuade Azaña to return to Spain and to take command of the Republic. As Álvarez del Vayo could have told them was inevitable, Azaña refused. Meantime, Negrín himself reached Madrid in the evening of February 24. The next morning, he had an interview with Casado lasting four hours. Casado, speaking of the hunger and lack of fuel in Madrid, said that the war must be brought to an end. Negrín promised to send fifteen days' worth of provisions. Casado replied with further complaints. He had no transport. Britain and France had finally abandoned the Republic. The fall of Catalonia had cut the raw materials of the Republic by 70%. Many of the troops had no shoes and no overcoat. There were only 40 aircraft in the whole Army of the Centre, little artillery and very few automatic weapons. Opposed to this, the Nationalists had thirty-two divisions south of Madrid, with masses of artillery, tanks and at least six hundred aircraft. Above all, and this perhaps told most with Casado, the Communist party had shown itself 'disrespectful'. Negrín ignored the last charge. He told Casado that Russia had sent 10,000 machine guns, 600 aircraft and 500 pieces of artillery. They were now in Marseilles, and despite the great difficulties would be sent on to Spain. The peace negotiations with Franco, he added, had failed. Casado

---

Álvarez del Vayo, García Pradas, Carrillo and Jesús Hernández. Also Negrín's speech in the Cortes Committee in Paris on March 31; Bouthelier and Edmundo Domínguez.

[1] Casado had been a regular Army officer before the Civil War. There persists a rumour that he was an English agent, i.e. presumably that he was paid a certain sum by the British Government to try and bring the war to an end. This anyway unlikely story is disproved to my satisfaction by the manner in which he was received when he arrived in Britain at the start of April.

said that these Russian supplies would never arrive, since the only route was across the sea from Marseilles to Valencia. He urged Negrín to begin negotiations again, and offered his own services in assistance. Negrín accepted the offer. He added that he would remove the Communist party from the Government if necessary. Promoting Casado to the rank of General, Negrín later met the leaders in Madrid of the popular front parties. He was vague as to his general aims. Casado also saw the same politicians, and before them vented his irritation against the Communists.[1]

The situation in Madrid was indeed now terrible. The Quaker International Commission for the Assistance of Child Refugees reported that the average food supply was such that even if the existing level were maintained it could not support life for more than two or three months more.[2] There was no heating, hot water, medicines or surgical dressings. These conditions defeated such international help as was being mobilised. 'Food for Spain' funds were being gathered in England. Gifts were made by several Governments. The Governments of Canada, Norway and Denmark bought surplus food supplies and gave them to Spain. Belgium gave about £10,000 worth of food, and Sweden £75,000 (in addition to an earlier £50,000). The French Government agreed to send 45,000 tons of flour to the Republic, though not as a gift. The United States had sent 60,000 barrels of flour in September. Now they sent 600,000 barrels through the Red Cross.[3] Indeed, the nearer the Republic drew to its end, the greater public interest there was in its fate – especially in the United States.

On February 26 Negrín called a meeting of Republican military leaders at Los Llanos aerodrome near Valencia. There were present all the veteran commanders of the Republican Army – men who, as Captains or Majors, had rallied to the Republic in July 1936 and who now held, if precariously, the *bâtons* of General

[1] Casado, 104 fl.
[2] *The Times* of February 14 had reported that between four and five hundred people were dying from starvation each week in Madrid alone.
[3] But this last cargo of aid was shunted about the Mediterranean from one port to another before being finally delivered. The shipowners attempted to make the bill for transport of the flour as large as possible, justifying themselves by saying that each time a port was named for delivery, it fell to the Nationalists. Thus the hungry children of the Republic waited three months after delivery of the US aid at Le Havre. The Quaker commission meantime continued to give aid to territory conquered by the Nationalists even though they insisted on extracting strict conditions for this. (Kersher, 47.)

officers. To them Negrín spoke for two hours. He described the
failure of his peace negotiations of the last month. He described
also how, since May of the previous year, he had been seeking
peace on honourable terms through intermediaries. He said that
now there was no other course but resistance. Next to speak was
General Matallana, in command of military transport, who
argued that it was madness to continue to fight. He appealed to
the patriotism and the humanity of the Prime Minister to bring an
end to the war. Generals Menéndez, Escobar and Moriones,
commanders of the Armies of the Levante, Estramadura and
Andalusia respectively each agreed with Matallana. Admiral
Buiza, commander of the Navy, said that a commission representing the crews of the Republican fleet had decided that the war
was lost and that the intolerable Nationalist air attacks would force
the fleet to leave Spanish waters, unless peace negotiations began.
Negrín told Buiza that the leaders of the commission should have
been shot for mutiny. Buiza said that, while in principle he agreed
with Negrín, he had not so acted because he personally agreed
with the commission's views. Next Colonel Camacho spoke on behalf of the Air Force. He said that he had only three squadrons of
Natacho aircraft, two of Katuskas and twenty-five fighters. He also
proposed peace. General Bernal, Military Governor of Cartagena,
spoke likewise. Miaja, the 'hero of Madrid', intervened to complain
that he had not been permitted to speak. Negrín now gave him the
floor, saying that he had wanted him, as Commander-in-Chief, to
speak last. And Miaja bluntly demanded resistance at all costs.
Thereupon, Negrín summed up the discussion without making
firm suggestions as to the action to be followed; but he plainly
believed that, since negotiations had failed, the war would have
to continue. In his house nearby at Yeste, he planned to replace
Casado by Modesto. Lister would take Escobar's place, and Galán
that of Moriones. Jesús Hernández, Commissar of all of the Republican forces, would be named Inspector-General of the Armed
Forces. Hence, except for Menéndez, in the Levante, the Republican Army would have commanders who might be Communists but who still firmly believed in the war's continuance.
However, in Valencia, passports were being issued to all political
leaders, for fear of an immediate and general collapse. Miaja himself ensured that he was so provided, despite his brave words
earlier. In the evening, Negrín named General Matallana as
Chief of Staff to the whole Army (so as to remove him from the

more politically dangerous post of commander of communications),
and Modesto a General – a long overdue promotion, delayed because of the Government's desire to keep a semblance of old
seniority in the new army.

The next day, February 28, after the news of the recognition
of Franco by Britain and France, Azaña, in Paris, resigned from
the Presidency of the Republic. The Permanent Committee of the
Cortes assembled at La Perouse, the great restaurant on the Quai
des Grands Augustins, and Martínez Barrio assumed his duties.
The Civil Governor of Madrid meantime told Casado that he had
received orders for his relief, though these had been held up.
Negrín, however, assured Casado by telephone that he had *not*
ordered his relief, and summoned him to Yeste for a meeting the
next day, March 1, with Matallana. Here Negrín proposed the reorganisation of the General Staff. Matallana and Casado would be
heads of the 'General' and the 'Central General' Staff respectively.
Both officers repeated their arguments against further resistance.
After the meeting, Casado and Matallana went on to Valencia.
There they met General Menéndez and Colonel Ruiz-Fornell,
Chief-of-Staff of the Estremadura Army. Casado described to these
officers his resolve to rebel against the Government and to make
peace. Both promised full support but warned against the Communist party. Despite this, on March 2, Casado made a similar approach to Hidalgo de Cisneros, whom he knew to be a Communist,
at luncheon outside Madrid. Presumably he supposed that the air
leader's loyalty to his old colleagues was greater than that to his
new comrades. 'Only we Generals can get Spain out of the war,'
said Casado, who had already given orders for his new insignia as a
General to be placed on his uniform. 'I give you my word,' he
added, 'that I can get more out of Franco than Negrín's Government ever can.' Hidalgo de Cisneros told Casado to go and see
Negrín.[1]

Meantime, also on March 2, Admiral Buiza at Cartagena summoned the commanders of the ships and the political commissars.

[1] Álvarez del Vayo, *Freedom's Battle*, 291. Hidalgo presumably told the Communist
party leaders of this interview. Hernández therefore argued that the official direction
of the party, now completely in the hands of La Pasionaria and Togliatti, desired an
open breach among the Republicans, so as to bring about the swift end of the war and
free Stalin from a tiresome entanglement. This argument presupposes a policy directly
opposite to the one publicly followed – resistance to the end. A more likely explanation
is that the Communists did not act because they thought that to do so first would play
into Casado's hands. After he had acted, the Communists would be able to claim to
represent the legal authority.

He told them that a *coup d'état* against Negrín was being prepared and that a National Council of Defence would be formed, representing the armed forces, all trade unions and political parties. No one at the meeting objected and Buiza concluded that agreement had been achieved. On March 3, however, Paulino Gómez, the Minister of Marine, arrived to tell the commanders that the Government knew what Buiza had said the previous day, but that it was determined to prevail. In Madrid, Casado continued his plotting and received the support of most of the non-Communist Colonels and of the non-Communist political parties. General Martínez Cabrera (Military Governor of Madrid), the Director General of Security, and Pedrero, chief of the SIM, also pledged their support. Casado told Cipriano Mera to make ready to take over the Central Army. A telegram arrived from Negrín summoning Casado to yet another conference at Yeste. Casado told Matallana by telephone that he would not go because he feared arrest. Miaja, somewhat surprisingly, agreed with Casado. He too feared arrest. Casado therefore telephoned Negrín saying that his health prevented him from making so long a road journey again. Negrín promised to send his private aeroplane to fetch him.

The next day, March 4, saw the culmination of the plots in Madrid. At ten o'clock in the morning the head of Barajas Airport informed Casado that Negrín's Douglas aircraft had landed. Casado gave orders that the pilot should be sent home. At noon Negrín once more telephoned to Casado. The Colonel said in explanation that his health made it impossible to leave Madrid. Negrín, brushing this aside, said that he needed Casado immediately, regardless of health. Another aeroplane would arrive at six in the evening, to carry several Cabinet Ministers, who were at Madrid, to Valencia. Casado, said Negrín, should travel with them. Casado answered that he would 'arrange matters' with the Ministers.

Negrín's nomination of the Communist Colonel Galán to be Military Governor at Cartagena now fired strange events in that port. First, General Bernal passively agreed to hand over to Galán. The officers of the artillery under Colonel Armentía came out to protest. There was similar indignation in the fleet. They decided to put to sea, at the disposal of Casado and his friends, news of whom Buiza had told them two days before. Finally, in Cartagena, the Fifth Column of Falangists emerged. Supported by mobs wishing to show enthusiasm for the obvious victors of the Civil War, they surrounded the artillery barracks. A regiment of Marines joined the Falangists and together they proceeded to take over the Naval Broadcasting Station. From thence they sent demands for reinforcements to Cádiz. Italian aircraft bombed the fleet at the same time. Admiral Buiza thereupon ordered the whole fleet to sea just after noon. Meantime, the mercurial Communist, Jesús Hernández, acting on his own responsibility as Inspector-General of the Army, despatched the 4th Division under a securely loyal officer, Major Rodríguez, to bring help to Cartagena. The Major joined forces with Galán. By mid-afternoon, both the Falangist and the anti-Communist rising had been suppressed. But the fleet remained at sea.

In Madrid, six Ministers of Negrín's Government – Giner de los Ríos, Velao, Paulino Gómez, Segundo Blanco, Moix and González Peña were lunching in the central Government building. They were joined for coffee by Casado. The Colonel (he had now dropped his General's rank for fear that it might prejudice his relations with Franco) later reported that each Minister privately expressed to him his despair at Negrín's policy. Casado explained that he had no intention of accompanying them to Yeste. Giner de los Ríos telephoned to Negrín to suggest a postponement of the Cabinet. Negrín answered so fiercely that the Ministers set off immediately. At seven o'clock Negrín telephoned Casado yet again, ordering his presence the next day. Casado replied that he would be there if the situation were no worse. Half an hour later, Casado moved his headquarters to the Treasury, an easily defended building in the Calle Alcalá, near the Puerta del Sol. There he met with Besteiro, the Socialist reformist, who old, ill and depressed as he was, nevertheless still counted greatly as a name. Casado allowed himself, after a show of modesty, to be named President of the future National Council. Besteiro agreed to act as Foreign Secretary. Casado later voluntarily gave way to Miaja, who, through a mixture of fatigue, timidity and opportunism, had been persuaded to join the plotters. Casado then took upon himself the portfolio of defence. The other members of the Council were Wenceslao Carrillo, a Socialist; González Marín and Val, of the CNT; Pérez, of the UGT; and San Andrés and del Río, both Republicans. These took respectively the portfolios of the Interior, Finance, Communications, Labour, Justice and Education. This *junta* broadcast a manifesto at midnight:

'Spanish workers, people of anti-Fascist Spain! The time has come when we must proclaim to the four winds the truth of our present situation. As revolutionaries, as proletarians, as Spaniards, as anti-Fascists, we cannot endure any longer the imprudence and the absence of forethought of Dr Negrín's Government. We cannot permit that, while the people struggle, a few privileged persons should continue their life abroad. We address all workers, anti-Fascists and Spaniards! Constitutionally, the Government of Dr Negrín is without lawful basis. In practice also, it lacks both confidence and good sense. We have come to show the way which may avoid disaster: we who oppose the policy of resistance give our assurance that not one of those who ought to remain in Spain shall leave till all who wish to leave have done so.' After this statement, calculated to gain the sympathy of all the disaffected without suggesting any positive course, both Besteiro and Casado spoke. Besteiro demanded the support of the legitimate power of the Republic which, he added (as if he were General Mola), was now nothing more than 'the power of the army'. Casado concentrated on an appeal to all in the trenches, on both sides. 'We all want a country free of foreign domination. We shall not cease fighting till you assure us of the independence of Spain,' he added for Franco's benefit, 'but, if you offer us peace, you will find our Spanish hearts generous.'[1] Immediately after this broadcast Negrín telephoned: 'What is going on in Madrid, my General?'[2] 'I have revolted,' answered Casado. 'Against whom? Against me?' 'Yes, against you.' Negrín told him that he had acted insanely. Casado answered that he was no General, but a plain Colonel, who had done his duty as 'an officer and as a Spaniard'.[3]

Next day, Casado arranged – as ever, by telephone – that Miaja should come to Madrid to take over as President of the National Council. He also told Menéndez to inform Negrín that, unless Matallana (who had been placed under house arrest) were released within three hours, he would shoot the entire Cabinet. Matallana was consequently released – though not before he had declared himself at Negrín's disposal in respect of the revolt at Cartagena.

Negrín indeed could do little else than accept Casado's action as a *fait accompli*. Jesús Hernández arrived at Yeste to ask what was to

[1] Casado, 150.
[2] An echo of Casares Quiroga's question, so long before, to General Gómez Morato: 'What is going on in Melilla?' (see above, page 133).
[3] Álvarez del Vayo, *Freedom's Battle*, 224.

be done. 'For the moment,' said the Prime Minister, 'nothing. We are thinking of what to do.' And this deliberation continued all day. The Russian advisers, however, knew very well what to do. Hernández discovered General Borov's palace in total disorder and the General, who had succeeded General Kulik as head of the Soviet military advisers, in a high state of excitement. 'We are leaving, we are leaving,' he told Hernández without ceremony.[1] Hernández also found La Pasionaria and Togliatti at Yeste. He accused them of provoking a quarrel with Casado.

The Communist party itself now had to deliberate what was to be done. Casado had been far more successful than they could have expected. Even if Stalin desired to abandon Spain to its own resources, the Spanish Communists could not contemplate, after such expense of energy and resources, that Colonel Casado should simply take over the situation, ignoring the Communist party completely. Yet the only possible course seemed the risky one of using the divisions around Madrid under Communist commanders against Casado; and these divisions were by no means so loyal to the Communist party as the old Fifth Regiment would have been. The whole project seemed uncertain since many Republicans, who would not otherwise have taken sides at all, would rally to Casado if there were to be a civil war within the Civil War. It must be admitted that the Communist party in Spain, the Comintern, and Stalin himself were dumbfounded by the success of Colonel Casado. Prolonged discord within the Republic would, of course, be an opportunity for Franco to break through the last lines of resistance. During this time the Nationalists were in fact, somewhat slowly, reorganising their armies for the *coup de grâce*.

On the morning of March 5, Major Ascanio, the Communist commander of the 8th Division, began to move on Madrid. Communist risings occurred at Alcalá de Henares and at Torrejón de Ardoz, but the three Communists' army corps commanders in the Army of the Centre, Bueno, Barceló and Ortega, pledged their support to Casado just as did the supreme commanders of the Armies of Estremadura, the Levante, and Andalusia. Casado nevertheless took precautions against Communist troop movements. All the roads from the east and north were watched. All the main buildings of Madrid, including the Civil Government building, the War Ministry, the Telefónica, and the Ministry of the Interior, were occupied by his men. In Cartagena, meantime, the

[1] Hernández, 197.

revolts on the shore had been curbed. The fleet, however, remained in mutiny and set sail for French North African waters. On March 6 it arrived at Bizerta where it was interned by the French.

Negrín was making last-minute attempts to prevent strife within the Republican camp. Casado, on the other hand, was attempting to secure the arrest of the Government and of the Communist leaders. Chaos prevailed throughout Republican Spain. The commanders of the different armies were the effective rulers. No one knew even the whereabouts of his colleagues. At Dakar air base Negrín and his supporters were assembled. These were Álvarez del Vayo, Uribe and Moix, of his Government; Hidalgo de Cisneros, the air chief; and Lister, La Pasionaria, Modesto and Cordón. All were Communists save Negrín, Moix and Álvarez del Vayo. Hidalgo de Cisneros telephoned a message calling on the *junta* at Madrid to settle its differences with Negrín. Until half-past two in the afternoon, the small band waited at the airport for Casado's answer. Álvarez del Vayo played chess with Modesto. Then they heard that Alicante had passed to Casado. They waited no longer, giving up the fate of Spain for lost. At three o'clock they flew to France.[1]

[1] Álvarez del Vayo, *Last Optimist*, 316.

75

The civil war within the Civil War – Barceló in control at Madrid –
Cipriano Mera wins back the centre of the city – cease-fire – negotia-
tions with the Nationalists – the Burgos talks – their failure – the
Nationalists' advance – evacuation of the capital – the flight to the
coast – the end of the war

Back in Madrid, the cause of continued resistance was not yet lost.[1] On March 7 Barceló, despite his earlier statement of adhesion to Casado, moved in with his army corps to close all the entrances to the capital. He occupied all the Ministries at the end of la Castellana, the Retiro Park and the headquarters of the Army of the Centre. Three of Casado's Colonels were killed during the assault. Colonels Bueno and Ortega sent troops from the 2nd and 3rd Army Corps to support Barceló. Thus most of the centre of Madrid passed into Communist control. In the afternoon, Cipriano Mera's 4th Army Corps marched to relieve Casado, now holding out in the south-easterly suburbs. His 12th Division captured Alcalá and Torrejón from the Communists established there. Hence Mera rapidly assumed the *rôle* of strong man in Casado's party.

Throughout March 8 there was continuous and at times heavy fighting in Madrid. The Communists remained in control. In the rest of Spain, Jesús Hernández succeeded in dispossessing Ibarrola from the command of the 22nd Army. He used it to prevent the despatch of food to Madrid until his comrade Pedro Checa had been released from the prison into which the *junta* had cast him. Hernández (though Togliatti was still in Spain) now assumed the virtual leadership of the Communist party outside Madrid. The extent of the Communist victory was such that if they had wished they could now have dictated terms. But abandoned by their leaders, they did not know precisely what to do. Their declared aim, after all, was to continue to fight for as long as possible against Franco. How could they do this if they

---

[1] The same sources have been used in this chapter as in chapter 74.

were fighting in the capital? As a result the Communist commanders merely waited to be defeated.

On March 9 Cipriano Mera assaulted the Communist positions in the capital. He captured the headquarters of the Army of the Centre. On March 10 Casado advanced one column as far as the Puerta del Sol and another to Ciudad Lineal. The Plazas Manuel Becerra and Independencia fell back into his hands, together with the headquarters of the 2nd Army Corps and the Ministries in the Castellana.

The following day, Colonel Ortega came forward to offer to mediate between the two sides in this new civil war. Miaja and Casado, already preparing to negotiate with the Nationalists, agreed to this mediation. In the meantime there was a cease-fire, with the two groups still facing each other in postures of hostility. Outside Madrid, even Jesús Hernández and his group had given up hope of a prolonged continuance of the war. They busied themselves with preparations for an escape and for the organisation of the Communist underground which would remain behind in Spain. The Nationalists meantime had advanced some way, during the fighting in Madrid, across the Casa de Campo towards the Manzanares.

It still remained to be seen whether Casado would be any more successful than Negrín in securing terms from Franco. On March 9 his National Council had approved peace terms. Except that they did not demand freedom for Spaniards to choose their own Government, they were more extensive than those proposed by Negrín, which had already been rejected by Franco. There were to be no reprisals, Spanish 'independence' should be guaranteed, and respect should be shown for fighting forces (including officers). Twenty-five days should be permitted during which all who wished to leave Spain would be enabled to do so. The same day, Lord Halifax was defending in the House of Lords his recognition of the Nationalists. No country outside Spain, he said, could judge whether any Spaniard was guilty or not of any crime. He also said that British help in the evacuation of the Republicans would prejudice her reconciliation with the victors.

On March 11 Casado's peace terms were leaked secretly, by unknown persons, to the Fifth Column in Madrid. That afternoon, Casado received a request for an interview from Colonel Centaños, chief of the artillery workshop number 4. The next morning, after a routine discussion about the manufacture of telemeters for the Levante coastal batteries, this officer revealed himself as the representative in Madrid of General Franco. He placed himself at Casado's disposition to open negotiations. Casado, restraining an impulse to arrest him, requested him to return the following day. That night Miaja and Besteiro, with other members of the Defence Council, agreed to accept Centaños's offer. It was not, however, till the 13th that Centaños called again. The 12th was taken up with the end of the Communist revolt. Casado stipulated that all units should return to their positions of March 2. All prisoners taken were to be given up and all commanders would be dismissed. This would leave Casado free to make his own nominations for the three Communist army corps. In return, Casado pledged himself to free all 'non-criminal' Communist prisoners and to listen to the points of view of the Communist leaders.

The Communists agreed to use all their influence to secure a cease-fire. If there were no reprisals, they would act as previously against the Nationalist 'invaders'. In the same morning of March 12 the Communist forces did return to their positions of March 2. Colonel Barceló and his Commissar, Conesa, were the last to leave their advanced positions in Madrid. Both were arrested and shot within a few hours, by order of Casado's council. These executions can only be regarded as acts of retribution for the deaths of those officers on Casado's staff previously shot by the Communists. No other death sentences were given. Outside Madrid, General Escobar crushed Communist reistance in Cuidad Real and Almadén. Menéndez restrained the 22nd Army Corps, still controlled by Hernández, from moving upon Valencia.

On March 13 Centaños and Casado conferred again on the question of the end of the main Civil War. Casado said that he and his friends would negotiate on the conditions previously named. Centaños replied that, since Franco had demanded unconditional surrender, it only remained for the Republicans to agree with the Nationalists the method of surrender. Casado refused unconditional surrender. He added, as Negrín might have done, that if General Franco were wholly intransigent, the Republican Army was ready to fight to the end. Centaños then gave Casado a memorandum from Franco intended to appear full of concessions. There would be free pardon to 'all non-criminals and those deceived into fighting'. Officers who were not criminals would be 'benevolently treated'. Those 'guiltless of murder' could apply for a safe conduct beyond the Spanish frontier. No one would be kept in prison for a period longer than would be necessary 'to correct or re-educate'.

While the National Council considered this discouraging document, Casado himself planned the retreat of the Army of the Centre to the Mediterranean and the expatriation of those who wished to leave. It must thus have been clear to the Colonel that there was little hope of serious negotiation. His task, therefore, was to gain time so as to allow those who wanted to escape to do so. During the ensuing fortnight, many managed to do this, though the means of escape were few, even for those who managed to reach the east coast ports. On March 19 Franco agreed to the start of negotiations with Casado. He and the remainder of the Nationalist command had been busy with the re-deployment of their armies, so as to be ready for a new offensive if it should be necessary. (The three main armies were now those of the Levante under Orgaz, the Centre under Saliquet, and the South under Queipo. Dávila kept to his position of Minister of Defence.) During the last month, indeed, the Nationalist leaders had only had to watch the disintegration of their enemies. Franco expressed his pleasure that he was being saved 'the trouble of crushing the Communists'.

The two emissaries named for negotiation by the Republic were Colonels Garijo and Leopoldo Ortega. These two officers left for Burgos by air in the morning of March 23. Their conditions were not even discussed by Colonels Gonzalo and Ungría, their colourless Nationalist co-negotiators, who merely handed them a document for transmittal to Casado. This provided for the flight of the Republican Air Force to Nationalist aerodromes on March 25. As for the Army, there would be a cease-fire on all fronts on March 27. Commanding officers, with white flags, were to come to the Nationalist lines with documents describing the position of their forces. This formal surrender no doubt seemed to the disciplinarians at Burgos to be the most humiliating conclusion of Republican resistance. In addition, Franco named two ports on the Levante for the expatriation of those who wished to flee. He did not mind if British ships transported these refugees, and would put no difficulties in the way of the departure of these ships. But there was to be no pact, no signature of any document naming these concessions. The Republic would have to trust to the Generalissimo's good intentions. On March 25, Garijo and Ortega returned to Burgos, to demand both that these terms should be put in writing and that a delay of twenty-five days should be granted for the expatriation of those who wished to leave. The latter was refused but the former was accepted. Garijo began to draw up such a document. At six o'clock, however, the Nationalist Colonel Gonzalo bluntly announced that negotiations were considered broken off because the Republican Air Force had not surrendered. Garijo and Ortega returned to Madrid. Casado's council decided that any attempt at further negotiations would be in vain.

Thus ended Casado's ill-fated attempt to secure a more honourable end to the war than Negrín had been able to achieve. By his action he had also ruined the possibility of any further Republican resistance although, for all those who had taken part in the war on the Republican side, continued fighting, however despairing, might have been more advantageous than unconditional surrender into the hands of Nationalist justice. All that can be said for Casado is that his negotiations gained time for many Republican leaders, though not the rank and file, to escape. This would have been possible anyway, since the Nationalist Army would not have been ready for a final offensive until late March.

At one o'clock in the morning of March 26, Casado telegraphed to Burgos to announce that the Air Force would be surrendered the next day. In reply, Franco announced that the Nationalists armies were about to advance. He demanded that units in the Republican front line should show a white flag before the start of artillery and aerial bombardment. Casado and his friends did not answer this message. At five o'clock in the morning the Nationalists launched an attack in the south, preceded by light artillery bombardment.[1] Yagüe, once again in Estremadura where he had won his first laurels, advanced in the Sierra Morena. All day the the advance continued. Pozoblanco fell at noon, Santa Eufemia at dusk. Thirty thousand prisoners and 2,000 square kilometres were captured during the course of the day. At four in the afternoon Franco broadcast those 'concessions' which his two Colonels had put forward at Burgos on March 21. They sounded well enough. So there followed the self-demobilisation of the Republican Army. The men abandoned the front for their homes, and their officers did not stop them. This spontaneous act, all along the front, was not halted by a description on Madrid Radio of the true story of the negotiations at Burgos.

On March 27 a new Nationalist advance began from Toledo.

[1] Aznar, 845.

The Navarrese under Solchaga, the Italians under Gambara and the Army of the Maestrazgo under García Valiño made a free passage of the Tagus. Here, as in the south, the Republic abandoned the front. During the day the Army of the Centre swiftly disintegrated. General Matallana, in command of all these forces, told Casado in the evening that several units had gone over to the Nationalists and that soldiers of both sides were embracing each other in the Casa de Campo. By nine in the evening, the staff only of the first three army corps remained. Casado told the members of his Council to leave quickly for Valencia, whither Miaja had already gone. At ten o'clock, representatives of the UGT, the Socialist party, the Republican Union and the CNT broadcast appeals for calm. Then, when not a single Republican soldier remained in the front line except in the Guadalajara sector, Casado ordered Colonel Prada to negotiate surrender with the Nationalist commander in the University City. That officer accepted a rendezvous with the Nationalist commander at the battle-scarred Clinical Hospital at eleven o'clock in the morning. Casado telegraphed to President Lebrun to beg that all Republicans who wanted should be able to land in France (if they got there). He made the same request to President Cárdenas in Mexico. Next, he told General Matallana to authorise retreats by all the Republican armies in the manner of that of the Central Army. Then he flew to Valencia, accompanied by his wife and by Matallana and Val of his Council. They passed over streams of lorries and groups of Republican soldiers going home. Behind in Madrid, Besteiro remained, agreeing to the certain sacrifice of his freedom in order to stay where he was. The creeping optimism of his tubercular condition no doubt caused him to anticipate fair treatment. Colonel Prada surrendered the Army of the Centre at eleven o'clock. Another Nationalist army meantime broke through the Guadalajara front, to link up with those advancing from Toledo. Thus at long last the strategic aims of the battles of Guadalajara and the Jarama were fulfilled. In the capital itself, the Fifth Column emerged from its hiding places in foreign embassies and elsewhere. But an Anarchist municipal councillor, Melchor Rodríguez, was accepted even by the Falangists as temporary mayor till the final surrender.[1] At midday the Nationalist 1st

---

[1] He was responsible for saving many lives in Madrid when Director of Prisons. (Fonteriz, 61.)

Army under General Espinosa de los Monteros, who had himself for a time been a refugee in the French Embassy before being exchanged, entered Madrid and occupied the Government buildings. Behind, there followed both the representatives of *Auxilio Social* and 200 officers of the Nationalist Army's Juridical Corps, with lorry loads of documents relating to crimes allegedly committed by the Republic. '*¡Han pasado!*' (they have passed), cried the rapidly assembling pro-Nationalist crowds. Those right-wing Spaniards who had passed the war behind the blinds of foreign embassies emerged into the light of day for the first time for two and a half years, blinking, with faces pale as ghosts. On the other fronts, in Estramadura, Andalusia and the Levante, mass retreats were also taking place all day.

Meanwhile, Casado had arrived at Valencia. Here, at Alicante, at Gandía, at Cartagena and at Almería, there were gathered Republicans clamouring for expatriation. During the day, Togliatti, Hernández, Uribe and Checa, the Communist leaders, left by air for Oran from Cartagena. At noon the next day, March 29, Casado, established in the old Captaincy-General, was visited by the Valencian Fifth Column, who demanded their own immediate establishment in the administrative buildings. The town was now running with persons making the Fascist salute. Casado appealed for calm over Radio Valencia and left for Gandía, where he embarked in a British ship bound for Marseilles. During the day, Jaén, Ciudad Real, Cuenca, Sagunto and Albacete were occupied by the Nationalists. On March 30 Gambara's Italians entered Alicante and General Aranda entered Valencia, which by then was entirely under the control of the Falange. Women and children ran forward to kiss the hands of the conquerors, and roses, mimosa and laurels were flung from middle-class balconies. On March 31 Almería, Murcia and Cartagena were occupied. In all these coastal towns, many thousands of those who had wished to leave their country were captured by the advancing armies. The scenes of anguish and fear before the Nationalists' entry were pitiful to see. There were several suicides. General Franco, suffering from a cold in the head, was at last informed by an *aide* that the Nationalist troops had occupied their final objectives in the early evening of March 31. 'Very good,' he replied without looking up from his desk, 'many thanks.'[1] Later he received a telegram from the new Pope Pius XII: 'Lifting up our heart to God, we give sincere thanks

[1] Villegas, 384.

with your Excellency for Spain's Catholic victory.' But despite this approval, the Vatican had not condemned the Basque priests as heretics – nor were they ever to do so, though a special mission to Rome was despatched by General Franco headed by José María de Areilza to secure such a condemnation.[1] Yet the Axis powers could feel themselves well satisfied with the conclusion of the Spanish War; on March 26th Spain had adhered to the anti-Comintern pact and on the 31st a treaty of friendship was formally signed at Burgos by Jordana and Stohrer to cement a five-year friendship between the Nationalist Government and Nazi Germany.[2] On March 31st a non-aggression pact was signed between the new Spain and Portugal.

[1] Evidence of Fr Alberto Onaindía. Areilza became notorious because of his authorship, with Fernando María de Castiella (present Spanish Foreign Minister), of *Revindicaciones de España*, stressing Spain's African ambitions and demanding the return of Gibraltar. Another reaction in Rome was Mussolini's comment to Ciano, pointing to an atlas open at the map of Spain: 'It has been open in this way for nearly three years, and that is enough. But I know already that I must open it at another page.' Ciano, *Diary, 1939–43*, 57. In fact Italy attacked Albania the following week (April 6).

[2] *GD*, 880, 884. This pact was ratified on November 29, 1939.

76

Conclusion

The remaining questions of the Spanish War were quickly settled. Already Marshal Pétain, who had fought alongside Franco in Morocco in 1925, had arrived at Burgos as French Ambassador. His reception by his ex-comrade-in-arms was cool, because of the French Government's delay in handing over the Republican warships gathered at Bizerta. This eventually occurred on April 2. Spanish *objets d'art* and money which had been taken to France by the Republic, together with arms and rolling stock, were returned to Spain during the next few months. The paintings from the Prado were sent back to Madrid from Geneva, after a brief exhibition. It was later found that the collection had lost nothing in the war.

On April 1, meanwhile, the United States had recognised the Nationalist *régime*. Russia was thus the only Great Power which had not done so. The American Ambassador, Claude Bowers, received on returning home to Washington the bitter consolation of being told by Roosevelt that he thought that after all the embargo policy had been wrong. On April 20 the Non-Intervention Committee, which had not met since July 1938, solemnly dissolved itself. On May 19 a Nationalist Victory Parade was held in Madrid. General Gambara's Italians occupied a place of honour. On May 22 a farewell parade occurred at León for the Condor Legion. Four days later 6,000 of its personnel embarked at Vigo for Hamburg. On May 31 about 20,000 Italians set off from Cádiz. Both Germans and Italians were fêted in their own countries: the former were greeted at Hamburg by Goering. On June 6 Hitler reviewed 14,000 members of the Condor Legion in Berlin. The Italians were welcomed at Naples by Ciano and King Victor Emmanuel. By the end of June the evacuation of German and Italian military forces from Spain was complete.

As for the Republican refugees, many of those who succeeded in escaping from the Spanish Mediterranean ports found asylum hard to come by. Eventually, after waiting on British or French ships in Marseilles or North African ports in appalling conditions, most found themselves on French soil. Of those who had earlier fled from Catalonia, 50,000 male civilian refugees and Republican soldiers eventually agreed to go to Nationalist Spain. The rest remained in the concentration camps of southern France. By the end of March, conditions in these places had somewhat improved. Food supplies were now almost adequate. Sanitation and medical services were no longer non-existent. There had been no large-scale epidemics. But the inmates still had nothing to do. Their general situation remained purgatorial.

The leaders of the exiles were by this time quarrelling fiercely among themselves. On March 31 Negrín gave a fiercely contested account of his activities since the fall of Catalonia to a pathetic meeting of the Permanent Committee of the Cortes in Paris. Martínez Barrio, Araquistaín, La Pasionaria, fiercely disputed. At the same time, the ship *Vita* left Boulogne for Mexico piled with precious stones and other treasures, mainly confiscations from Nationalist sympathisers at the start of the Civil War.[1] Negrín was despatching this hoard for the safe-keeping of President Cárdenas in order to finance the Republic in exile. When, however, the *Vita* arrived in Mexico, Prieto, who had gone to South America for the inauguration of the new Chilean President, was there to receive it. He persuaded Cárdenas that he had a title to the treasure. He also succeeded later in establishing a committee of the Permanent Committee of the Cortes, known as the *Junta de Auxilio a los Republicanos Españoles* (JARE) to administer the funds in question. Negrín, maintained as Prime Minister by a narrow majority of the same permanent committee, placed the funds which he had saved in the SERE (*Servicio de Emigración para Republicanos Españoles*). This group was increasingly compromised in the eyes of the world because of its support by the Communist party. Its trading company, the Midatlantic Company, financed by the Republican treasury, was banned by the French Government as a Communist organisation at the start of the World War. However, the two groups, which inevitably quarrelled fiercely, did transport about 150,000 Republican refugees either to Mexico or South America, especially Argentina. About the same number remained in southern France, to be eventually partly absorbed in the community of that area.

[1] The Spanish Republicans were alleged to have carried away funds and money abroad. Much of this, however, had been used for the purchase of arms.

Many of the able-bodied were shortly employed there, especially in the construction of fortifications and others returned to Spain. In time, the French Government made all male foreigners eligible for service in the army. By July the population of the concentration camps had fallen to about 200,000. Russia assimilated an uncertain number of Spanish Communists and their families. Two hundred Republican leaders, including Casado and Menéndez, were accepted in Britain.

*   *   *

The Spanish Civil War exceeded in ferocity most wars between nations. Yet the losses were less than had been generally feared. The total number of deaths caused by the war seems to have been approximately 600,000. Of these about 100,000 may be supposed to have died by murder or summary execution. Perhaps as many as 220,000 died of disease or malnutrition directly attributable to the war. About 320,000 probably died in action.[1]

The cost of the war, including both internal and external expenditures, was named later by the Nationalists at 30,000 million pesetas (£3,000 million in 1938 money). The chief cost was in labour, due on the one hand to the deaths and permanent disabilities caused, and on the other to the exile of 340,000 persons at the end of the war. Nationalist authorities estimated that approximately 4,250 million pesetas' worth of damage had been done to real property during the course of the war. Since this was supposed to be damage caused only by the Republicans, it is probably an under-estimation. 150 churches were totally destroyed and 4,850 damaged, of which 1,850 were more than half destroyed. 183 towns were so badly damaged that General Franco 'adopted' them – his Government, that is, undertook to pay the cost of restoration. About 250,000 houses were so badly ruined as to be uninhabitable. This probably does not take into account another 250,000 which were partially damaged.[2]

As for industry, the factories of Bilbao and Barcelona emerged from the war almost intact. The irrigation works around Valencia remained untouched. While Spain lost a third of her livestock and much of her farm machinery, farmland and farm buildings suffered less than might have been expected – far less, say, than

[1] See Appendix II for calculation of this figure.
[2] Report of the *Dirección General de Regiones Devastadas*, quoted Hamilton 21–2.

the fields of northern France in the First World War. The transport system suffered approximately 325,000,000 pesetas worth of damage. The railways lost 61% of their passenger cars, 22% of their freight cars, and 27% of their locomotives. Lorries were scarce but roads were in good condition. Stocks of raw materials and of food were very low. The outbreak of the Second World War in September 1939, six months after the end of the Spanish War, prevented Spain from making up these losses from abroad. The situation was worsened by a long succession of droughts. Consequently the years immediately following the war (especially 1941–2) were years of great privation for the majority of the Spanish people.

There was also the proscription. Every crime alleged to have been committed in the Republican zone of Spain was investigated. A Republican mayor would stand little chance if it were known that murders had been committed in his village; and in which village could this not be said? Ten men, for instance, were shot for their part in the massacre of the Model Prison in August 1936. Nearly all officers of the Republican Army were shot if captured. On the other hand, the rank and file were generally released. Others who had played a civil *rôle* in the Republic were condemned to varying terms of imprisonment up to 30 years. This sentence was often in practice revised. It would seem that twenty-one years after the end of the war there are no political prisoners who have been there consistently since 1939.

The number of the Republican rank and file executed for various crimes after the war, from church-burning to merely serving the Republic administratively, was estimated by a British journalist,[1] unfortunately captured in Madrid, at 100,000 by the end of 1939. Ciano, visiting Franco in July 1939, reported 200,000 persons in prison, with 'trials going on every day at a speed which I would almost call summary . . . There are still a great number of shootings. In Madrid alone between 200 and 250 a day, in Barcelona 150, in Seville 80'.[2] But Rodríguez Vega, Secretary-General of the UGT, who cleverly managed to escape from Spain in late 1939, estimated that the tribunals were passing death sentences at the rate of 1,000 a month. This, amounting to about 9,000 in 1939, would seem a more probable figure.

[1] Mr A. V. Phillips of the *News Chronicle*.
[2] *Ciano, Diplomatic Papers*, 293–4. For a dazzlingly brilliant impression of Madrid in this first summer of victory, see Georges Conchon's novel *La Corrida de la Victoire*.

But the victors showed no charity whatever. Rodríguez Vega later estimated that two million persons had passed through the prisons and concentration camps of Nationalist Spain by 1942. Many were sentenced to thirty years' imprisonment, many more to ten years, more still to shorter periods. Thousands suffered loss of employment or other deprivation. Besteiro died in Carmona Prison of untended tuberculosis in 1940. There were 241,000 persons in the squalid, damp and overcrowded prisons in 1942. Those who were disabled in the war on the Nationalist side received a small pension. Those disabled on the Republican side received nothing.

The end of the Civil War closed an epoch in Spanish history. Nearly all the main actors of the past turbulent half century were either dead or in exile. Many institutions and ideals had been swept away. The liberals and the Catholic politicians of the Republic had been pushed unceremoniously to the side even before the start of the war. Now the great working-class parties of Spain had also been overwhelmed, along with all their wild, generous and violent dreams. The Basque and Catalan Separatist leaders were separated by exile from their own dearly loved regions, as well as from Castile. And what deaths there had been among the victors! Who could forget the thirteen murdered bishops at the head of the army of seven thousand ecclesiastical ghosts. The philanderer Sanjurjo, the conspirator Mola, the brilliant Calvo Sotelo, José Antonio Primo de Rivera with all his charm, Onésimo Redondo, the Fascist from Valladolid, Ledesma, with his Hitlerian quiff – all had died, and had died violently. None of the vanquished parties in the Civil War had suffered such a toll of deaths among their leaders as the Falange – unless the poets, among whom the slaughter had also been terrible, are reckoned a party: for the great God-fearing humanist Unamuno was dead of grief in Salamanca; García Lorca lay in an unknown grave near Granada; Machado had died among the sand dunes of Argelés; Miguel Hernández was shortly to die in Alicante gaol. And beyond all these deaths of celebrated men there rose the mass spectre of those many thousands of warriors, known and unknown, who too had died, nearly all giving their lives – with less reluctance than in most wars – for causes which, on both sides, they had come to believe were noble.

Yet the causes themselves were almost all dead by 1939. The

three great quarrels which had led to the war had spent themselves, being transmuted in the strife from passionate conflicts between irreconcilable extremes into opportunistic battles for victory, or survival, at all costs. If liberalism and Freemasonry had been exorcised, the Church appeared almost prostrate before the Falange. But the social aspirations of the Falange had vanished almost as completely as had Communism, Anarchism and Socialism. The defeat of Basque and Catalan Separatism did not mean that the Monarchists or Carlists were in a position to impose their views. Upon the heaped skulls of all these ideals, one dispassionate, duller, greyer man survived triumphant, as Octavius survived the civil wars in Rome. Caesar and Pompey, Brutus and Antony, Cato and Cicero – all, with all their genius, lacked the minor talent of being able to survive. Francisco Franco was the Octavius of Spain.

His achievements in the Civil War were considerable. As supreme commander of the Nationalist forces his duties were throughout strategic and political, never tactical – though he was often at the front. He had no opportunities to show himself (or risk his reputation) as a field commander. His task was to decide in what region a new offensive should be, to be certain that an offensive did not begin till everything was ready, to halt a counterattack (as at Brunete) when it had accomplished its task. German officers serving with Franco, such as von Thoma, found him old-fashioned. But in his caution, patience and puritanism he resembled von Thoma's future conqueror at El Alamein – Lord Montgomery. When Mussolini, through his envoy, complained that the Nationalists were too slow in achieving victory, Franco answered: 'Franco does not make war on Spain. He liberates Spain. I cannot destroy a single enemy, nor towns, nor any part of the countryside, nor industries, nor centres of production. For that reason, I cannot hurry. If I were in a hurry, I should be conducting myself like a foreigner. Give me aircraft, give me ammunition, give me tanks and artillery and your diplomatic support, and I shall be grateful. But do not make me hasten because that would mean killing a large number of Spaniards.'[1] Was this true? General Franco has not always seemed the most humane of modern statesmen; and it would be difficult to argue that at any time he could have won the war faster even by a specially bloody campaign. But no doubt this was how the

[1] Cantalupo, 234.

Generalissimo rationalised his incomprehensible delays; it is certain that in battle Franco (unlike some of his Generals) was always reluctant to waste the lives of his men. Unlike von Thoma, Franco had no interest in military innovations *per se*. His achievements were not only in the sphere of generalship, where he was effectively served by a contrasting group of subordinates, among whom (chiefly because of their common experience in Morocco when they were young men together) he inspired an unquestioning loyalty. General Franco's greatest military success was in fact political. He was politically successful because he treated politics as a department of military science. Political leaders were to General Franco merely divisional commanders. Their views and aspirations were merely items among other stores of war material. He established himself as the political leader of the most passionately concerned country in the world by a contempt for political feelings. As a result, he was never in any real political danger at any time during the Civil War.

The political synthesis which he achieved among his followers was the chief factor in giving him ultimate victory. No doubt he was greatly assisted in providing some sort of theoretical basis for this homogeneity by Ramón Serrano Suñer. And this was itself the source of the propaganda which made it possible to mobilise five hundred thousand men with reasonable efficiency. But it was Franco's own calm (proverbially typical of his native Galicia) which first obtained for him the leadership of the Nationalists long before Serrano Suñer had escaped from a Republican prison, and then enabled him to maintain himself. There were almost as many possible fissures in the Nationalist side as there were among the Republicans. The delay in obtaining victory, and the incessant disappointments, gave many chances for the solidarity of the Nationalists to collapse. Doubtless agreement between Falange, Church, Monarchists, Carlists and Army was made easier by a certain class desperation, a greater knowledge of the really disastrous consequences of defeat than existed on the Republican side, perhaps by a greater cynicism which led these apparently disparate groups, like Franco himself, to believe that there were no political aims so important that victory might be jeopardised in obtaining them. But it was Franco who turned this desperation, this fear of defeat, and this cynicism into engines of war. Finally, even his enemies would not deny that Franco and his Foreign Minister Jordana (assisted by Nicolás Franco) carried out a supremely clever piece of diplomacy in ensuring adequate German and Italian aid without surrendering to the dictators of those countries much more than an admittedly large number of mining rights.

If this unity helped so much to the Nationalist victory, it is obvious that the disunity among the Republicans was a prime factor in their defeat. Of course, this disunity is the very fact which makes a study of the political anthropology of Republican Spain, particularly at the early stages, so peculiarly fascinating. As might be expected, nowhere were Republican voices more discordant than in attributing responsibility for the defeat. Some blamed the Communists for strangling the life out of the Republican cause by their own quest for power. Some argued that though many Spanish Communists sincerely sought victory as passionately as they said they did, Stalin was afraid of the consequences of a Republican victory, and, from a certain stage, discreetly did what he could to ensure its defeat. The Anarchists still believe that the war would have been won if a complete proletarian revolution had been carried out in its first days. Some attributed their loss of the war to the policy of non-intervention pursued by Britain, the USA and France. Others bluntly argued that German and Italian intervention was the only reason for General Franco's victory.

What is the truth of those matters? Undoubtedly the Republic was terribly hampered by the disputes between the parties who supported it. One excuse might be that all the parties felt so strongly about their own policies that defeat itself seemed preferable to a surrender of the purity of their individual views. It would perhaps be more truthful to say that no one was able to forge a real unity out of the Republican warring tribes as Franco and Serrano Suñer were able to do among the Nationalists. Dr Negrín did his best. But such a policy inevitably meant making great use of the already able and powerful Spanish Communist party. The non-intervention policy of the Western democracies further forced Negrín to a most dangerous reliance on the Soviet Union and the Comintern. It would have been mad, indeed inconceivable, not to make full use of the fighting qualities of the Communists. But this itself took Negrín into what was – as can be seen more plainly a generation later – an impossible position.

Finally there remains the controversial question of foreign intervention. The total quantity of foreign aid to Spain is estimated

in Appendix III. But figures are not all. It was the timing rather
than the amount of aid which made the supreme difference in the
Spanish War. There were five occasions when the arrival of
foreign aid was most critical. First, the supply of transport aircraft
by Germany and Italy in July 1936 enabled Franco to lift the Army
of Africa across the Straits of Gibraltar. To say simply that the
Nationalists would have lost the war had it not been for this aid
would beg too many questions. But the war would certainly have
taken a quite different course if the Army of Africa had not
reached the mainland so fast. This aid had a far greater effect than
the simultaneous purchase of aircraft by the Republic from
France. It was a really decisive moment. The second crucial
occasion was in November 1936, when the Russian assistance to
the Republic, the arrival of the International Brigades and the
whole organised support of international Communism probably
saved Madrid. Here the critical time was not the start of November, when the people of Madrid themselves certainly held the
Army of Africa for a while, but later on, in the battles of the
University City and along the Corunna Road. Thirdly, the heavy
supplies sent by Mussolini and Hitler early in 1937 probably prevented a collapse of Nationalist *morale* when Generals Mola,
Varela and Orgaz successively failed to capture the capital.
Fourthly, French aid, and the opening of the French frontier to
Russian and Comintern aid, staved off defeat for the Republic in
the spring of 1938 after the success of the Nationalists' Aragón
campaign. Finally, and most important, if Franco had not exchanged so many mining rights for German arms[1] in the autumn
of 1938 he could not have launched the brilliantly successful
Catalan campaign at Christmas of that year. Had it not been for
this, his army would have been as badly provided after the battles
of the Ebro as was the Republican Army. In that case, a compromise peace might, despite all suggestions to the contrary, have
eventually been inevitable.

The final campaign was decisive. The price was German participation in all the important iron ore projects in Spain. In return
for this rich prize, Germany committed enough war material to
Spain to tip the balance finally towards the Nationalists. This was
a reversal of Germany's policy towards Spain in the earlier part of
the war. The German Government had in fact decided that the
fears which she had entertained earlier of any spread of the war in

Spain into 'a European conflagration' were groundless, however flagrant a breach she might commit of the Non-Intervention Pact. For, since the Munich settlement, it seemed that Britain (and France) would never go to war, over Spain or over anything else. This impression was confirmed by the immediate implementation in November 1938 of the Anglo-Italian Agreement. The German Government was also encouraged to think that it could act with impunity towards Spain by the noticeable cooling of Soviet interest in Spain in the autumn of 1938, and indeed by various gestures, especially after Munich, of the Soviet Government towards Germany herself. But, until Munich, German policy had been to refuse to commit enough forces or war material to Spain to secure the triumph of their Nationalist *protégés*. The Germans had believed that such a commitment would inevitably have risked the expansion of the Spanish War into a European war. Indeed, Germany and Russia shared throughout most of the Civil War a strong disinclination to risk a general war breaking out over Spain. It is possible that, at the start of the Civil War, Stalin may have entertained, as one of his many schemes, the hope that France and Britain might become embroiled on the side of the Republic, and Germany and Italy on that of the Nationalists – so that Russia could remain the neutral arbiter of all the destinies of Europe.[1] But once Russia became committed to the Republic in October 1936, any general war resulting from the Spanish conflict would implicate her also. So henceforward Stalin followed a policy similar to that of Hitler: prevention of his *protégé's* defeat, without ensuring their victory. For to ensure a Republican victory would mean the commitment of troops and material on a scale which would surely risk general war.

Thus all the first four occasions described as being moments when intervention was decisive were defensive moments, when the interventionist powers took steps to prevent the defeat of one side or the other. This was one reason why the war lasted for so long. Hitler and Stalin both found various reasons to justify to themselves the continuance of the war in this way. They could continue to test military (and political) techniques. For each of them, victory in the Civil War might bring as many difficult questions as defeat. If the Civil War continued, such questions could be postponed. Mussolini, who above all sought grandeur in Spain, was naturally dissatisfied. He committed as many troops as

[1] See above, page 216 fn.

he could spare from his other activities. If either Germany or
Russia had sent as many men to Spain as he did – 50,000 –
a European war would probably have followed quickly. But
50,000 Italian troops were not enough to win the war in Spain
for Franco. Nor were they enough to expand the war into a
general conflict.

Non-intervention was as important as intervention. Had the
Republic been able to purchase arms from, say Britain, the USA
and France then the war would certainly have taken a different
course – as different, that is, as if Franco had not been so
materially helped by Germany just before the crucial Catalan
campaign. The British Government was throughout the real inspiration of non-intervention, even though the idea of a pact was
first suggested by Léon Blum. It was Britain who kept up the pact
and insisted that France generally did the same, even when it was
clear that it was being broken by Germany, Italy and Russia. Had
it not been for Britain, France and probably the USA would have
permitted the Republic to buy arms freely. It was, after all, a complaint by Ambassador Joseph Kennedy from London that caused
the State Department to go back on its decision to do away with
the Embargo Act in May 1938.[1] The French Governments of this
time were too fearful of Germany to risk a breach with Britain.
And, as the head of the Quai d'Orsay, Alexis Léger, pointed out, a
breach would have been inevitable if the French Popular Front
Government had really become embroiled on the side of its
ideological comrades in Spain. British policy was meantime dictated simply by a determination at all costs to prevent a general war
from developing out of the Civil War. This policy was followed
with equal resolution by Mr Baldwin's Government, as by Mr
Chamberlain's, by Eden as Foreign Secretary as by Lord Halifax.
Certainly, at the beginning, this was a perfectly reasonable policy.
But when it was clear that the pact was being disregarded, it was
very cynical to insist on its maintenance. This cynicism brought the
British Government as little credit as it did advantage. A denunciation of non-intervention might certainly have hastened a general
war, for the Republic might have immediately become more formidable militarily. Germany and Italy would then have been
tempted to send more help to Franco, but for the negative purpose of preventing him from losing. The dangers of such an arms
race are obvious. Non-intervention, like the Munich settlement at

[1] See above, page 536.

the expense of the Czechoslovak Republic, must therefore have delayed general war – at the expense, to some extent at least, of the Spanish Republic. But this delay, like Munich, was undoubtedly caused by a certain craven indolence on the part of the British Government which did not profit them at all. A general war which broke out over Spain in 1936, 1937 or 1938 would have been fought in circumstances more favourable for the Western democracies than that which came in 1939 over Poland. One alternative to the 'farce of non-intervention', was, of course (as it was to Munich, to the re-occupation of the Rhineland and to German re-armament), to stand firm and denounce the breach of the agreements. This policy had at least a possibility of upsetting the dictator without a war being needed. But this firmness did not exist. The bloody battles in Spain were thus partially decided by the commodity of the proposals and counter-proposals in the Non-Intervention Committee a thousand miles away.

Those foreign countries who became implicated in the war in Spain acquired from it many experiences in the art of war. Von Thoma, commander of the German tank unit which fought for the Nationalists, described the conflict as the 'European Aldershot'. The Italians also knew what lessons could be drawn from their Spanish experience, though not how to profit by them. Léon Blum, justifying, at his trial at Riom in 1942, the despatch of French aircraft to Spain, spoke similarly of the Spanish War as a 'test for French aviation material'. In general, however, the French drew the wrong lessons from the war in Spain. They even believed a German *émigré* writer, Helmuth Klotz, who, after a few weeks in Spain, wrote in his *Leçons Militaires de la Guerre d'Espagne* that the tank had been mastered by the anti-tank gun. As a result, the French General Staff entirely ignored the concept of mechanised warfare which had been tested in Spain. This was greatly to their disadvantage when Guderian's Panzer divisions streamed across their Northern plains in 1940. The Russians drew similarly false conclusions from their Spanish experience. General Pavlov told Stalin that the Spanish War had proved that tank formations could not play an independent operational rôle.[1] He may perhaps have given this advice to escape being branded as an admirer of the theories of the disgraced Marshal Tukhachevsky who had placed great faith in such formations. Anyway the whole enormous Russian tank force was in 1939 distributed as an infantry support

[1] Liddell Hart, *Soviet Army*, 316–17.

force. The success of German tanks in Poland and France led to a change back to Tukhachevsky's system, but this came too late for the opening of the Russo-German war in 1941. On the other hand, the Communist civilian leaders in Spain such as Togliatti and Gerö gained valuable experience which was to be put to good use in the years after the World War in East Europe. Both the Italian and Yugoslav Communists also found their time in Spain of inestimable help in the partisan fighting in their own countries in 1944–5. Even the British learned something. The *Illustrated London News* showed the way with an examination of the effects of the air raids in Barcelona entitled a 'Study in Human Vivisection'. Fred Copeman, ex-commander of the British Battalion of the International Brigade, found himself within a few months of the end of the war in Spain lecturing to the Royal Family at Windsor on air raid precautions.[1] The medical assistance to the Republic brought many advances of military and civilian surgery and general therapy. Of these, the most outstanding were the remarkable developments in the technique of blood transfusion inspired by the Canadian Dr Norman Bethune.

The general implications of the Spanish Civil War in the rest of the world cannot, however, be measured in such precise and military ways. It was, for the Western world at least, a most passionate war. The very uncertainties of the leading democratic Governments naturally exacerbated the feelings of citizens of those countries who concerned themselves in the conflict. For intensity of emotion, the Second World War seemed less of an event than the Spanish War. The latter appeared a 'just war', as civil wars do to intellectuals, since they lack the apparent vulgarity of national conflicts. The Spanish War looked, at least at first, when all the parties of the Left seemed to be co-operating, the great moment of hope for an entire generation angry at the apparent cynicism, indolence and hypocrisy of an older generation with whom they were out of sympathy. It was also a conflict small enough to be comprehensible to individuals. As a result, many polemics, much argument and several masterpieces sprang out

---

[1] Certain mistakes nevertheless crept into the calculations of the British Government in respect of the likely effects of an aerial attack on London deduced from the raids on Barcelona in March 1938. The officials worked out that 72 casualties might be caused by one ton of bombs. Later, however, in all the raids on Barcelona, an average of 3.5 persons were reported killed. This new casualty ratio was not apparently substituted in the British Home Office plans for the earlier and more drastic figures. Titmuss, 13–14.

of it. The struggle gave birth to a burst of creative engergy in many countries (as well as in Spain on both sides of the trenches), which can plausibly be argued as comparable in quality to anything produced in the Second World War. The few real masterpieces that were produced will survive as monuments to those who died.

EPILOGUE

This is not the place to describe what General Franco did with his victory. *Caudillo* and head of state, he still rules according to no theory of government save his own brand of compromise, developed during the Civil War, between Falange, Church and Monarchists. At one time or another, each of these groups has been in the ascendant or in decline. As ever, Franco treats them as cavalierly as he did the Moroccan chiefs of his youth.

Spain has been officially a Monarchy since 1947, but Don Juan still waits in the wings at Estoril for the call, for which he optimistically never gives up hope. (His father, King Alfonso XIII, died in Rome in 1941.) Of Franco's old supporters, Serrano Suñer dominated the Spanish scene during the World War, until, in 1942, it seemed probable that the Axis would lose. Now he lives still in Madrid, where there are also to be found, free but without responsibility such men of the past as Manuel Hedilla and Gil Robles. The former's life imprisonment ended in 1939, after which he worked as a dock hand in Majorca. Most of the political leaders since the Civil War have been new men, to whom the war and the peace brought the opportunity for advancement.

Some of the leading Generals of the Civil War were used by Franco as Ministers or in other posts. Varela, for example, eventually achieved his ambition of becoming Minister of War. Yagüe was for a time Air Minister. Both he and Asensio also served as High Commissioner of Morocco. Queipo de Llano secured no prizes at all from the victory. The Monarchists, such as Kindelán, suffered general deprivation after a feud between Don Juan and Franco in 1944. Most of the first rank of Generals – Dávila and Orgaz, Varela, Queipo, Saliquet – are dead, though others, like Aranda, live in retirement. García Valiño is today Captain General of the Madrid region, Alonso Vega, Minister of the Interior, and Asensio, Head of the Military Household. Muñoz Grandes is a 'Captain-General' and is expected to act as Franco's successor if another General should be called for.

The outbreak of the World War in September (following the political shock to the Nationalists of the Soviet-German Pact in

618

August) meant that the Germans had less to offer Spain commercially. As English Conservatives had prophesied, Franco turned to Britain for a loan for reconstruction. And, partly from poverty but more so from policy, Spain never entered the war by the side of Hitler, who was moved to declare 'that all his aid to Franco was an absolute gift'. Goethe defined genius as knowing where to stop. Even his worst enemies would not deny that Franco's achievement in keeping Spain out of the war was a remarkable one. This is the most obvious way in which Franco differs from the popular image of the imperialist, expansionist Fascist dictator. Hitler and Franco eventually met at Hendaye in 1940. Franco, insisting on his after luncheon siesta, kept the Fuehrer waiting half an hour – an unprecedented event. And Hitler later said that he found Franco so unyielding that he would prefer to have three or four teeth out than have another such interview.[1] Later, however, when Germany attacked Russia, the 'Blue Division' of Spanish Falangist volunteers (47,000 in all)[2] under General Muñoz Grandes, fought by the side of the Germans. Throughout the early part of the war, Nationalist Spain supplied Germany with submarine bases, monitoring services, war material and even air bases.[3] The agency into which HISMA, ROWAK and the Montaña project had been grouped together, SOFINDUS (*Sociedad Financiera Industrial Ltda.*), continued to control German-Spanish economic relations.

As for the defeated, history, as W. H. Auden prophesied, has said alas, but has given 'neither help nor pardon'. The leaders have passed their twenty years of exile quarrelling over their phantom power, and over the financial assets remaining to them. Negrín died in 1956 in Paris leaving in his will the documents relating to the Spanish gold to General Franco. In 1945, he had resigned as Prime Minister, in the hope of uniting all the exiles. Martínez Barrio then assumed the post of President of the Republic, which he held until his death in 1961. Prieto died in Mexico in 1962.[4] Álvarez del Vayo, still an optimist, was expelled from the Spanish Socialist party for his over-close friendship with the Communists. Largo Caballero died a broken man in Paris in 1946, after some years in a German concentration camp. He was luckier than Companys and Zugazagoitia, who were handed over to General Franco by Marshal Pétain during the Vichy *régime*. They were

---

[1] Schmidt, 193.   [2] *UN Security Council Report on Spain*, 76.
[3] *loc. cit.*   [4] *Informaciones* (Madrid), Feb. 13, 1962.

both executed. So was the Anarchist ex-Minister Peiró and several other lesser leaders. Azaña died in 1940 in Aquitaine. The Bishop of Montauban gave him extreme unction. The old anti-clerical thus returned in the end to the faith which he had so much attacked. Of the Republican Generals, Miaja died in New York, and Rojo returned to live in Spain in 1958. Others live on in South America or in Mexico. Alberto Bayo, of the Majorcan expedition of 1936, lived on to train Fidel Castro's first followers in guerilla warfare in Mexico and later to be regarded as the only General in Socialist Cuba. The Anarchists have maintained a flourishing organisation among the *émigrés* in southern France. Federica Montseny has for a long time been their moving spirit. García Oliver is in Mexico.

The leaders of the Spanish Communist party are now La Pasionaria, Antón, Lister and Modesto. Uribe, out of favour in Moscow, is in Prague. Díaz died mysteriously in Russia in 1942, probably murdered. Checa died in Mexico. Jesús Hernández left the party to form a 'Titoist' Communist group of his own. His autobiography was sufficiently malicious about his old comrades to be published in Nationalist Spain. El Campesino quarrelled with the rigid discipline with which he was required to conduct himself in Russia. After appalling adventures he escaped *via* Persia. The British handed him back to the Russians. After working as the latrine attendant of Vorkuta concentration camp, he escaped once more. Today he is in Brussels allegedly forming an army to invade Spain. Of the Basque leaders, Aguirre died in 1960 to be succeeded as President of the Basque Government in exile by Leizaola.

All the Republicans were disappointed when, at the end of the World War, Britain and America did not turn their arms against General Franco. Those Spanish exiles in France who fought with the French *maquis* against the Germans, attempted to stage a return to Spain by guerilla warfare, between 1945 and 1947, but without success.

The leading Germans and Italians who befriended the Nationalists – Hitler and Ribbentrop, Canaris and Goering, Mussolini and Ciano – have all of course vanished. Of their followers, Stohrer remained as Ambassador till dismissed by Ribbentrop in 1942 for failing to prevent the fall of Serrano Suñer. Faupel and his wife committed suicide in 1945 as the Russians entered Berlin. Among the Generals, Sperrle, Volkmann, von Thoma and Richthofen all fought with distinction in the Second World War – as well as most of their men. Galland, who flew over 300 sorties in his Messerschmitt with the Condor Legion, became, with Mölders who succeeded him in his Spanish posting, the most daring and well-known German pilot in the battles for Britain and France. Sperrle, the architect of Guernica, directed attacks on Rotterdam and Coventry. Warlimont became renowned, with Keitel and Jodl, as one of the German officers most loyal to Hitler and was accordingly sentenced to 18 years' imprisonment in 1949 as a minor war criminal – though he was released from Landsberg in 1957.

Among the Italians who fought in Spain, General Roatta served as Mussolini's Chief of Staff for a while, was disgraced and mysteriously vanished while awaiting trial as a war criminal; he is today in Madrid. Gambara was disgraced – partly because he told an officers' mess in Libya that he hoped to live long enough to command an Italian army marching on Berlin. He died in 1962. Bastico died a Marshal in Cyrenaica. Berti lived to be nicknamed 'the sly murderer' by his Egyptian and British opponents in 1941. Bergonzoli's defeat at Guadalajara was repeated in Cyrenaica. Count Grandi, having helped to overthrow his master, still lives, a business-man in Buenos Aires.

Among the Russians and foreign Communists who played so great a part in the Spanish War, the fate of Stalin, Litvinov and Molotov is too well known to be mentioned. The fates of most of the Russian Generals and officials are correspondingly unknown. Berzin, Stashevsky, Antonov-Ovseenko and Kol'tsov were all purged between 1937 and 1938 – and Berzin, Kol'tsov and Antonov have now been rehabilitated. Their deaths were regretted as a mistake, in passing, by Khrushchev in his speech denouncing Stalin in February 1956 at the 20th Party Congress of the Communist Party of the Soviet Union.[1] The tank General Pavlov was shot by Stalin in 1941 when he had lost his army in the first weeks of the German advance. General 'Stern' (Grigorovitch) commanded an army in the Far East. Marshals Malinovsky, Nedelin, Konev and Rokossovsky, ex-Spanish veterans, all enjoy a precarious eminence in Khrushchev's Russia.[2] But General

[1] 'Very grievous consequences, especially in reference to the beginning of the war, followed Stalin's annihilation of many military commanders and political workers during 1937–41 . . . during this time the cadre of leaders who had gained military experience in Spain and in the Far East was almost completely liquidated.' (Wolfe, 174.)

[2] Nedelin has since died in an air crash.

Etingon, who began his career as a director of sabotage and terrorism in Spain, was apparently shot with his then chief, Beria, in 1953. Orlov lives apparently as a respected U.S. citizen. General Kritvitsky (or Ghinsburg), that much-quoted witness of Communist espionage in the twenties and thirties, was found mysteriously shot in the Hotel Bellevue, Washington, on February 10, 1941.

In the late 1940s all those Communists from East Europe who had fought in Spain came under the cloud of Stalin's suspicion. The Hungarian Foreign Secretary, Laszlo Rajk, who had been Commissar of the Rakosi Battalion in the XIIIth International Brigade, 'confessed' at his trial in 1949 that he went to Spain on behalf of the secret police of Admiral Horthy 'with a double purpose: to find out the names of those in Rakosi Battalion . . . and on the other . . . to bring about a reduction of the military efficiency of the Rakosi Battalion. I should add that I also carried on Trotskyist propaganda in the Rakosi Battalion'.[1] After Rajk's execution, many veterans of the Spanish Civil War in Eastern European countries were arrested and many were shot. After the death of Stalin in 1953 these old 'volunteers for liberty' were, however, partially rehabilitated. La Pasionaria was even permitted, in the November 1953 issue of the Russian review *Questions of History*, to refer to the International Brigades in glowing terms. Today, it is again safe to speak with pride in East Europe of having fought in Spain. And such men are again to be found in important positions. Mehmet Shehn is still president of the Albanian Government. Raiko Damianov, vice-president of the Bulgarian Government, is an ex-member of the Dabrowsky Battalion. Twenty-four Yugoslavs who fought in Spain are today Generals in the Yugoslav Army. Most of them distinguished themselves in the partisan war under Tito, the organiser of the 'secret railway' to Spain. General Walter, under his real name as Świerczewski, was Minister of Defence in Poland between 1945 and 1947, when he was murdered allegedly by anti-Communist partisans. Togliatti and Luigo Longo (the latter having led the partisans in North Italy in 1943–4) still rule the Italian Communist party. Giuseppe de Vittorio was Secretary-General of the CGT in Italy till his death in 1958. Vidali (Carlos Contreras) is the leader of the Communists in Trieste. Codovilla (Medina) has returned to Buenos Aires. Pacciardi, of the Garibaldi Battalion, is the leader of the Italian Republican party and served as Defence Minister in the coalition Cabinets of de Gasperi.

[1] *Laszlo Rajk and his Accomplices before the People's Court*, 6.

Nenni is still leader of the Italian Socialists. Gerö, the Hungarian of many aliases who dominated the purge in Catalonia, became deputy premier of Hungary and later Khrushchev's tool in the Hungarian revolution of 1956. The present (1960) President of Hungary, Munič, is a Spanish veteran. Stepanov, the Bulgarian, is dead. Thorez is still the leader of the Communists in France. Marty was expelled at last from the Communist party before he died in 1955. Malraux is Minister of Culture under de Gaulle. Among the Germans, Ludwig Renn lives in Berlin and Hans Kahle died as police chief of Mecklenberg in 1952. Others of their comrades of the XIth Brigade, such as Franz Dahlem, are in fluctuating positions in and out of power in East Germany.

Of the surviving American members of the International Brigade, 600 fought in the Second World War. These men were, however, already suspect in the eyes of the administration. It was not until late in the war, therefore, that they were permitted to go abroad.[1] After the war, connection with the Spanish cause came to be regarded as subversive. The Abraham Lincoln Battalion itself was declared so in 1946, after their last reunion had been addressed by General 'Walter'.[2]

Unlike the veterans from the continent of Europe, few of the Anglo-Saxon ex-combatants in Spain have gained high official positions in their own lands. The only British Member of Parliament who fought in Spain is Mr Robert Edwards, once of the POUM Battalion in Aragón. Some of his colleagues, however, may be found in important positions in the trades union movement. Will Paynter, the present Communist General-Secretary of the National Union of Mineworkers for example, was British Commissar at the base at Albacete. The British Communist party administration, like that of most Western Communist parties, has not changed much with the years. Mr Harry Pollitt is dead, but Mr Peter Kerrigan can be found still in the big building with the frosted glass windows in King Street, Covent Garden. The last commander of the British Battalion, Sam Wild, lives still in Manchester. Of his predecessors, Alexander is in King Street; and Fred Copeman left the Communist party early in 1939. Later, he joined in turn the Roman Catholic Church, the Labour party and the Moral Re-armament Association. Jock Cunningham, after finding his undoubted military qualities rejected by the British

---

[1] *Volunteer for Liberty*. Introduction to bound edition of files, 3.
[2] See Taylor, 113–15.

Army in the World War because of his rebellious past, wandered for many years over the face of Britain as a casual labourer.

Now, after twenty years, Spain enjoys a prosperity greater than it did before the Civil War. The death rate has decreased and the country enjoys a *per capita* increase of real income of about 25%, although that of agricultural and industrial workers may not be much more than 6%. But freedom of speech is limited. No political parties are permitted – save for the Falange as organised in April 1937. Many linger in prison for criticism of the régime. The Nationalist authorities continue to believe that these measures are essential if the explosion of another civil conflict is to be avoided. In some areas, poverty remains a horror and a reproach to all who see it. Spain thus remains in travail.

But who can doubt that one day the Spanish people will attain the lasting happiness that they deserve? Who, that is, can doubt that one day they will pay heed to the advice of Manuel Azaña who, with all his shortcomings and weaknesses, once closed a speech, at the height of the Civil War, by saying: 'When the torch passes to other hands, to other men, to other generations, let them remember, if they ever feel their blood boil and the Spanish temper is once more infuriated with intolerance, hatred and destruction, let them think of the dead, and listen to their lesson: the lesson of those who have bravely fallen in battle, generously fighting for a great ideal, and who now, protected by their maternal soil, feel no hate or rancour, and who send us, with the sparkling of their light, tranquil and remote as that of a star, the message of the eternal Fatherland which says to all its sons: Peace, Pity and Pardon.'[1]

[1] Manuel Azaña at Barcelona, July 18, 1938.

THE ECONOMICS OF SPAIN FROM 1925-6 UP TILL THE OUTBREAK OF WAR

These tables show how the political troubles of the Republic were exacerbated by the fluctuating economic circumstances. The figures derive from the League of Nations annual statistical survey, 1936.

	(1) MAIZE		(2) RICE		(3) WHEAT	
	Area[1]	Production[2]	Area[1]	Production[2]	Area[1]	Production[2]
1925 1926 1927 1928 1929	428	5962	49	3063	4332	39,784
1930						
1931		6703		2662		36,585
1932		6931		3182		50,134
1933	432	6604	47	2951		37,622
1934	434	7878	46	2936	4608	50,849
1935	440	7335	47	2920	4554	42,997
1936	—	—	—	—	4358	33,065

	(4) SUGAR CANE	(5) WINE	(6) OLIVE OIL
	Production	Production (*million hectolitres*)	Production
1925		—	—
1926	92	15·4	2301[2]
1927	99	27·6	6656
1928	116	21·5	1914

KEY

[1] Thousand hectares (one hectare = 2·471 acres).

[2] Thousand quintals (one metric quintal = a weight of 100 kilograms, approximately 220 lbs).

(4) SUGAR CANE		(5) WINE	(6) OLIVE OIL
1929	134	24·3	6601
1930	169	17·7	1149
1931	176	18·6	3511
1932	175	20·6	3488
1933	157	19·2	3102
1934	184	21·2	3130
1935	198	16·0	4398
1936	180		

	(7) WOOL Production (1000 *metric tons*)	(8) SILK	
		Raw	Artificial
1925			112[2]
1926	38·6		
1927	38·1	83	143
1928	38·1		502
1929	37·6		900
1930	36·3		1523
1931	34·9	44	1639
1932	35·4	42	2160
1933	35·4	38	2295
1934	33·1	30	2526
1935	29·9	34	2722

	(9) SALT Production (1000 *metric tons*)	(10) COAL Production (1000 *metric tons*)
1925		
1926		
1927	979	6563
1928	983	6371
1929	1079	7108
1930	1038	7120
1931	889	7091
1932	959	6854
1933	929	5999
1934	762	5932
1935		7017

	(11) COKE		(12) ELECTRICITY
	Ovens	Gasworks	
	Production		(*million*
	(1000 *metric tons*)		*kWh*)
1926	832 (combined)		1708
1927	714	161	1849
1928	681	204	2370
1929	768	216	2433
1930	676	233	2609
1931	503	248	2681
1932	369	243	2795
1933	427	248	3066
1934	486	250	3198
1935			—

	(13) MANGANESE	(14) PYRITES	(15) LEAD ORE
	(1000 *metric tons*)	(1000 *metric tons*)	(1000 *metric tons*)
1926	44·9	3655	216
1927	36·9	3611	196
1928	13·7	3625	177
1929	17·9	3867	181
1930	16·8	3417	164
1931	17·9	2594	151
1932	2·6	2125	137
1933	2·8	2219	115
1934	3·8	2072	102
1935	1·3	2286	104

	(16) LEAD	(17) ZINC ORE	(18) ZINC
	(1000 *metric tons*)	(1000 *metric tons*)	(1000 *metric tons*)
1926	149		16
1927	144	132	17
1928	131	122	14
1929	143	145	12
1930	123	160	11

	(16) LEAD	(17) ZINC ORE	(18) ZINC
1931	110	112	10
1932	105	92	10
1933	88	95	9
1934	72	79	8
1935	63	83	8
1936	—	—	8

	(19) QUICKSILVER (metric tons)	(20) SILVER (metric tons)	(21) POTASH (1000 metric tons)
1926	1594		
1927	2493	95	1263
1928	2195	79	1518
1929	2476	83	1691
1930	663	88	1788
1931	682	96	1609
1932	816	105	1078
1933	676	91	871
1934	1096	56	1026
1935	1226	45	1389

	(22) TUNGSTEN (metric tons)	(23) IRON ORE (1000 metric tons)	(24) PIG IRON (1000 metric tons)
1926	74	3191	489
1927	102	4972	593
1928	125	5785	563
1929	153	6559	753
1930	152	5525	622
1931	81	3190	479
1932	25	1760	301
1933	26	1815	339
1934	30	2094	372
1935	—	2633	356

	(25) STEEL (1000 metric tons)	(26) COPPER ORE (1000 metric tons)	(27) COPPER (1000 metric tons)
1926	668	49·5	23·9
1927	671	50·7	28·7
1928	777	54·2	27·8
1929	1003	63·7	28·5
1930	925	58·4	23·0
1931	645	54·0	25·7
1932	532	35·0	15·6
1933	507	44·0	17·3
1934	647	30·0	13·8
1935	580	30·0	10·8

	(28) NEW VESSELS LAUNCHED	(29) MOVEMENT OF SHIPPING (Entry) (million tons)	(Clear)
1926	26		
1927	23		
1928	12		
1929	37	18	27
1930	25	18	28
1931	48	17	23
1932	11	16	23
1933	18	15	23
1934	18	15	23
1935	3	16	22

	(30) IMPORT-EXPORT (Special Trade) (metric tons)		(31) IMPORT-EXPORT (Merchandise) (million pesetas)	
1926	4127	7088	2148	1605
1927	5602	10285	2576	1887
1928	6634	11432	3004	2118
1929	7131	11533	2737	2108
1930	5862	9955	2447	2300
1931	4809	6693	1176	961

(30) IMPORT-EXPORT		(31) IMPORT-EXPORT	
1932	5133	5180	975	738
1933	4105	6159	835	669
1934	4892	6587	855	611
1935	5048	6364	878	583

<table>
<tr><td></td><td colspan="1">(32)
VALUE OF PESETA
(as % of gold
parity 1929)</td><td colspan="2">(33)
INDEX NO. OF SHARES
AND INDUSTRIAL PRODUCTION
(100 = 1929)</td></tr>
<tr><td></td><td></td><td>SHARES</td><td>PRODUCTION</td></tr>
<tr><td>1929</td><td>100</td><td></td><td></td></tr>
<tr><td>1930</td><td>79·5</td><td></td><td>98·6</td></tr>
<tr><td>1931</td><td>65·0</td><td>84·4</td><td>93·2</td></tr>
<tr><td>1932</td><td>54·8</td><td>65·1</td><td>88·4</td></tr>
<tr><td>1933</td><td>56·8</td><td>56·0</td><td>84·4</td></tr>
<tr><td>1934</td><td>55·3</td><td>57·6</td><td>85·5</td></tr>
<tr><td>1935</td><td>55·3</td><td>63·1[1]</td><td>86·9</td></tr>
<tr><td></td><td></td><td>65·7 (1936 Jan.)</td><td>89·0</td></tr>
<tr><td></td><td></td><td>64·9   Feb.</td><td>87·2</td></tr>
<tr><td></td><td></td><td>60·9   March</td><td>76·9</td></tr>
<tr><td></td><td></td><td>59·9   April</td><td>—</td></tr>
<tr><td></td><td></td><td>58·6   May</td><td>—</td></tr>
<tr><td></td><td></td><td>58·1   June</td><td>—</td></tr>
<tr><td></td><td></td><td>57·8   July</td><td>—</td></tr>
</table>

(34)
SAVINGS BANK DEPOSITS
(at end of each year)

	POST OFFICE	SAVINGS BANK
	(*million pesetas but note change of value of peseta, Table* 32)	
1928	239	1608
1929	252	1703
1930	265	1882
1931	278	2014
1932	298	2158
1933	318	2320
1934	338	2778
1935	370	—

[1] Highest number during the Republic = November 1935, when it was 67·3.

THE CASUALTIES OF THE WAR

The number of deaths in the Civil War is customarily held to be one million. This terrible round figure suits both victors and vanquished. The former can argue that they saved Spain from atheism and Communism at the cost of a million dead. The latter can allege that General Franco climbed to power over a million corpses. The figure was first named in a Nationalist press release in 1940. No one has ever revealed how it was arrived at.

There are several reasons for doubting the authenticity of this round number. When it was first put forward, the victors still estimated the numbers of assassinated on the Republican side at three or four hundred thousand. That calculation even appears in the monumental *Enciclopedia Universal Ilustrada* in its volume on the Civil War, published in 1943.[1] Now, however, the calculation for those killed in that way has sunk to about 86,000.

No estimate even purporting to be accurate, on the other hand, has been made in respect of Nationalist executions. I have suggested earlier that the figures named by Ramón Sender, the novelist, and Antonio Bahamonde, Public Relations Officer to Queipo de Llano, are undoubtedly exaggerated.[2] Here again there is fluctuation even in Republicans' estimates of partially complete figures: as earlier stated, the Bishop of Vitoria named a figure for arbitrary deaths in all the Basque provinces (7,000) which had previously been quoted for Navarre alone.[3] It is my considered belief that the total number of Nationalist 'atrocities' – by which I understand any shooting outside the battle line – is unlikely to have been greater than 40,000.

Similarly fluctuating estimates are apparent in respect of losses in the field. But recently an unofficial Nationalist estimate

---

[1] *Suplemento Anual*, 1936–9, Segunda Parte 1554.
[2] See above, page 168–9.
[3] A new and apparently reliable source used by the Basque historian Iturralde gives a figure of 1,600 executions in Valladolid – where the Nationalists were for a long time thought to have killed most indiscriminately – in place of 9,000 quoted by the Madrid Council of Lawyers in 1937. (Iturralde, Vol II, 109.)

has named their own fatal losses in action as being in the region of 110,000 men. No comparable estimates have been made of Republican deaths in action. It was hard in the early days to distinguish between those killed in what is conventionally known as 'battle' and those who were half-murdered in street fights. There are, furthermore, some important discrepancies in this field in published accounts. For instance, Manuel Aznar, in his semi-official *Historia Militar de la Guerra de España*, estimated that Republican total casualties in the biggest and bloodiest battle of the war, that of the Ebro, amounted to 97,000; of these 19,563 were prisoners, the same number believed to be killed, 17,000 fatally wounded and 41,000 less gravely wounded.[1] But the German Ambassador, Stohrer, reported to Berlin that his military advisers believed that the statement that the Republic was supposed to have lost 75,000 men (*sic*) was too high.[2] A cautious analysis of the announcements made of fatal losses at the time, checked against facts which have since become available, suggest that a rough figure of 175,000 for Republicans killed in action would probably not be an exaggeration.

The civilian deaths in aerial bombardment in the Republican zone was estimated in mid-1938 as being about 12,000. Perhaps another 2,000 were killed between then and the end of the war. Comparable figures in Nationalist territory probably did not rise above 1,000. Other civilian deaths (e.g. in aerial bombardment) might raise the total number of civilian deaths to 25,000.

All these figures would suggest that the total number of violent deaths in the Civil War was about 410,000.

Some estimate ought also to be made of the number of deaths from malnutrition, starvation or disease directly attributable to the war. But such figures as exist are unreliable or incomplete. Furthermore, deaths from these causes extended many years after the war – at least as long as political prisoners languished in Spanish gaols. It would be difficult, for example, to exclude Dr Julián Besteiro from the lists of those who died in consequence of the war, though he finally succumbed to tubercular meningitis in Carmona prison in 1940. It is hard to believe that the figures for deaths in this category could be less than 200,000.

Even so, the total figures of approximately 600,000 deaths due to the war is markedly lower than the customarily accepted figure.

[1] Aznar, 784
[2] *GD*, 796.

Spain can only in fact be said to have lost a million out of their population if the total number of exiles are included among the death lists.[1]

[1] An attempt to estimate the number of deaths in the Civil War from population figures has met with failure. The fact that the population of Spain increased during the thirties from 23,563,867 in 1930 to 25,877,971 in 1940 can be discounted by the continuing high birth rate in Spain. The only obvious impact made by the Civil War upon the population figures of Spain would seem to be the decrease of the populations of the Catalan and Aragonese provinces due to the great exodus from Catalonia in early 1939.

FOREIGN INTERVENTION IN THE SPANISH WAR

The total amount of foreign aid to the two sides in the war is difficult to calculate exactly. German aid to Franco amounted to over 500 million reichsmarks of war material (i.e. £43 million by 1939 exchange).[1] Of this, 88 million was used on salaries and expenses, for which they did not ask the Spaniards to pay; 124 million was used on direct deliveries to Spain; and 354 million on the Condor Legion.[2] The Germans apparently lost 300 lives in Spain.[3] The strength of the Germans in Spain reached about 10,000 at its maximum in the autumn of 1936. 14,000 veterans attended the Condor Legion parade in Berlin in May 1939. The total number of Germans who helped the Nationalists probably reached 16,000. But many of these were civilians and instructors. The Condor Legion always numbered about 6,000 men. This was accompanied by thirty anti-tank companies. Colonel von Thoma, who commanded the tank corps, told the Americans in 1945 that he took part in 192 tank engagements in the war.[4] No detailed figures have been found naming the number and character of the material sent to Spain by Germany.

The Italian forces in Spain at their maximum, in mid-1937, numbered about 50,000. Higher figures were given at the time because the units of Spaniards led by Italian officers and NCOs were estimated as if all-Italian. The death-roll of Italians in Spain was about 6,000. Italian aid to the Nationalists was named by the semi-official Stefani News Agency in 1941 and its figures may be accepted as approximately accurate. Thus Italy may be supposed to have sent 763 aircraft to Spain, 141 aircraft motors, 1,672 tons of bombs, 9,250,000 rounds of ammunition, 1,930 cannon, 10,135 automatic guns, 240,747 small arms, 7,514,537 rounds of artillery ammunition and 7,663 motor vehicles.[5] According to the Italian press in 1939, Italian pilots flew 135,265 hours in the war, participated in 5,318 air raids, hit 224 ships and engaged in 266 aerial combats in which they brought down 903 aeroplanes. These

---

[1] $4·64 = £1.   [2] GD, 892.   [3] Aznar, 862.
[4] Liddell Hart, The Other Side of the Hill, 126.   [5] New York Times, 28.2.41.

statistics, except perhaps the last, seem likely to be correct. 5,699 officers and men and 312 civilians of the Italian Air Force were engaged at different times. 91 Italian warships and submarines also took part in the Civil War. The latter are said to have sunk 72,800 tons of shipping. This is probably not an underestimate.[1] Ciano named Franco's debt to Italy in 1940 as 14 billion lire.[2] However, in 1941 Italy despatched a bill for $7\frac{1}{2}$ billion lire. (The sterling equivalent in 1939 was £80 million.) This corresponds more closely with other estimates made during the course of the war.

Portuguese aid cannot be exactly calculated, but about 20,000 Portuguese 'volunteers' fought in the so-called Legion de Viriato; about 8,000 were killed.[3] Six hundred Irishmen fought for the Nationalists under 'General' O'Duffy. Their losses were negligible. No Americans fought for the Nationalists.[4] Not more than a dozen British subjects appear to have done so. Of these, most were at least half Irish.[5] A group of right-wing Frenchmen fought for the Nationalists, serving in the Legion as the Jeanne d'Arc Bandera, while a White Russian company served with the *Requetés*. The Nationalists were also supported by a small number of semi-Fascists from Eastern European countries.

On October 27, 1936, Russia announced that the total amount of money raised 'by Russian workers' for Spain since the outbreak of the Civil War was 47,395,318 roubles. No more such announcements and probably no more such contributions were made. It is not clear whether Russia regarded these particular sums as a gift or a loan to the Republic. The day after this last announcement, the Russian Government's war material was used in battle for the first time. In 1956 the Soviet Government claimed that the Republic owed them 50 million dollars over and above the monetary gold reserve worth £63 million despatched to them in 1936; this was not far from the figure of 120 million dollars named

[1] Figures in Álvarez del Vayo, *Freedom's Battle*, 65.   [2] To Hitler.   [3] Hodgson, 70.
[4] The only American I have discovered to have fought with the Nationalists was the pilot Patriarca, shot down over Republican territory in October 1936.
[5] Those were: Captains Fitzpatrick and Nangle, ex-regular British officers who served with Castejón's column in the Legion, and later transferred to the O'Duffy Brigade. Rupert Belville, who fought with the Falangists in Jerez at the time of the rising; Peter Kemp, previously an undergraduate contemporary of Cornford at Trinity College, Cambridge, who fought first with the Carlists under Rada, later with the Legion, being wounded on the Ebro front just before the start of the great battle there; Patrick Campbell (not the writer), who fought with the Carlists in the Bilbao campaign; and two other unnamed Englishmen who fought in Andalusia.

in 1939 by Louis Fischer as owing to Russia. (Sterling equivalent of 50 million dollars in 1956 and 120 million dollars in 1939 being about £18 million). No Republican estimate of the cost of aid from abroad has been made available. But Louis Fischer[1] says that the gold in Russia was used to finance all the Republican arms purchases in all countries, the bills being paid through Soviet banks in London and Paris. The figure of £81 million (£63 million and £18 million) may be therefore regarded as a very approximate estimate of the total amount of Russian and Comintern aid.

The quantity of the Comintern's supply of arms to the Republic is impossible to estimate precisely. The headquarters of General Franco in October 1938 calculated, from material captured and other sources, that from July 1936 until July 1938 there had come across the French frontier 198 cannon, 200 tanks, 3,247 machine guns, 4,000 trucks, 47 artillery units, 4,565 tons of munitions, 9,579 vehicles of various kinds and 14,889 tons of fuel. These supplies came chiefly from Russia, Czechoslovakia and America. This figure is certain not to be an underestimate. Part of these supplies came directly from the French Government, which also supplied about 200 aircraft directly to the Government of the Republic.[2] This may be regarded as chiefly Comintern aid -- though if Louis Fischer's account that all Republican arms' purchase was paid for through Russia is correct, the difference between Comintern and non-Comintern aid cannot be regarded as so important.

As for Soviet aid by sea, the only report which even purports to be comprehensive is the analysis made by the German Military *Attaché*, Ankara.[3] This analysis is itself incomplete however, firstly because it does not deal with any shipments after March 1938 -- and it is certain that some did arrive after that date; secondly, because it is not clear whether the separate documents of which the report consists, should be considered as following on each other, or whether the two documents refer to two sets of activities quite separate from each other. However, the report can be considered as a general indication of the extent of aid received by the Republic by sea during 1936-8.

The tabulation of information, given on pages 640-43, is of the two reports of the German Military *Attaché*.

[1] *Op. cit.*, 346.   [2] *The International Brigades*, 33.
[3] The following derives from Mr D. C. Watt's analysis in the *Slavonic and East European Review* of June 1960, already quoted.

The total number of foreigners who fought in the International Brigade was about 40,000, though the Brigades never exceeded 18,000 at any one time.[1] Probably another 5,000 men fought at one time or another in other units of the Republican armies, chiefly in Catalonia. The largest national group of volunteers were the 10,000 French, of whom 3,000 were killed.[2] Germany and Austria together contributed about 5,000, of whom 2,000 died.[3] Italy came next with 3,350.[4] The United States contributed about 2,800. Of these, about 900 were killed.[5] There were about 2,000 British volunteers, of whom over 500 were killed and 1,200 wounded.[6] There were about 1,000 Canadian volunteers, 1,200 Yugoslavs,[7] 1,000 Hungarians, and 1,000 Scandinavians. The other 5,000 volunteers came from what was claimed to be fifty-three nations.[8] Perhaps 3,000 members of the Brigades were Jewish in origin.[9] The official Soviet History of the Second World War names the strength of Soviet 'volunteers' as 557, comprising 23 military advisers, 49 instructors, 29 gunners, 141 pilots, 107 tank-crews, 29 naval personnel, 73 interpreters, and 106 technicians, signal troopers and doctors.[10] In addition, probably over 20,000 other foreigners served the Republic at one time or another, either in Medical Services or in other auxiliary units.

The Mexican Government sent about two million dollars' worth of military aid to the Republic. The State Department calculated that over two million dollars' worth of aid had been

[1] Wintringham, 37; Rolfe, 8. The figures were greatly exaggerated at the time, to give an impression that the whole Republican Army had been taken over by the Brigades. The Spanish Foreign Ministry's pamphlet, *The International Brigades* (published 1952), though presenting a great deal of interesting material, maintains this exaggeration with an estimate of 125,000.

[2] *L'Epopée de l'Espagne*. This booklet names the number of French members of the Brigades as 8,500. But one of its authors has told me that he distrusted the sources of his information. Others give a figure of 15,000 for French participants.

[3] Kantorowicz, *Spanisches Tagebuch*, 15.

[4] Ferrara (268–9) names the figure 3,354, of whom 1,819 were Communists.

[5] Rolfe, 7.

[6] Rust, 210. Mr Neal Wood, however, says that there were 2,762 British volunteers, 1,762 wounded and 543 killed (Neal Wood, 56). He may be right, but no one else would give such exact figures.

[7] Zilliacus, 102. Dedijer, 108, gives the Yugoslav figure as 1,500 volunteers, 300 wounded 'almost half killed' and 350 interned in France after the collapse of Catalonia.

[8] This figure has been given to me by Mr Alec Digges of the International Brigades Association.

[9] *Epopée d'Espagne*.

[10] *Istoriya Velikoi Olecheshennoi voing Sovetskoyo Soyuza 1941–45*, Vol. 1, pp. 112–13.

collected by 26 American organisations of whom they approved as *bona fide* relief bodies.

These figures do not give a full picture of the foreign aid to Spain, since both sides bought wherever they could from private firms abroad. Certain American war material was found among Republican arms captured by the Nationalists. The State Department, however, concluded that nearly all of this had been exported earlier than the arms embargo. No American arms were found with the Nationalist forces. Certain American war material did, however, find its way to Republican Spain *via* the Soviet Union and Mexico.

THE INTERNATIONAL BRIGADES[1]

BRIGADES	BATTALIONS	Principal initial composition
XI (formed October 1936) (Hans Beimler)	I Edgar André	German
	II Commune de Paris (later transferred to the XIVth Brigade)	French-Belg.
	III Dabrowsky (later transferred to XIIth, 150th and XIIIth Brigades)	Pole Hungarian Yugoslav
XII (formed November 1936) (Garibaldi)	I Thaelmann (transferred to XIth)	German
	II Garibaldi	Italian
	III André Marty (Franco-Belge) (transferred to 150th, XIIth and XIVth)	French-Belg.
XIII (formed December 1936) (Dabrowsky)	I Louise Michel (transferred to XIVth)	French-Belg.
	II Tchapiaev (transferred to 129th Brigade)	Balkans
	III Henri Vuillemin (transferred to XIVth)	French
	IV Mickiewicz, Palafox	Poles

[1] *L'Epopée d'Espagne* (2nd edition), 249.

XIV (formed December 1936) (Marseillaise)	I Nine nations Battalion (transferred to Commune de Paris)	
	II Domingo Germinal (mostly Spanish Anarchist youth)	
	III Henri Barbusse	French
	IV Pierre Brachet	,,
XV (formed February 1937)	I Dimitrov (transferred to 129th and then XIIIth)	Yugoslav
	II British	British
	III Lincoln, Washington Mackenzie-Papineau	US Canadian
	IV Sixth of February (transferred to XIVth)	French
150th (formed June–July 1937)	I Rakosi	Hungarian
	II (transferred to XIIIth)	
	III	
129th	I Mazaryk (attached to 45th Division)	Czechoslavak
	II Dajakovich	Bulgarian
	III Dimitrov	Yugoslav Albanian
(in the 86th Brigade)	An international Battalion commanded by Col Morandi.	

SOVIET AID TO SPAIN, AS REPORTED BY THE GERMAN MILITARY ATTACHE

Date	Nation	Aircraft	Guns	AA guns	Tanks	Trucks	CARGO		
							War material (tons)	Ammunition (tons)	Miscellaneous
1936 September	3 Soviet	—	—	—	—	—	500	1000	—
October	16 Soviet 1 Spain	25 —	66 —	— —	58 —	240 —	2150 —	4850 —	3414 tons petrol 450 tons clothing 100 tons medical stores
Total	20								
November	2 Soviet 4 Spain 1 UK	24 — —	40 — —	— — —	147 — —	— — —	5700 — —	6850 — —	100 officers — —
Total	7								
December	2 Soviet 3 Spain 1 Mexico	— — —	57 — —	— — —	34 — —	35 — —	5500 — —	— — —	75 tons medical stores — —
Total	6								

1937									
January	3 Soviet 5 Spain – 8	6 —	35 —	— —	12 —	— —	3150 —	3250 —	— —
Total									
February	10 Spain	12	210	—	135	100	10,750	1800	100 rifle-machine guns 750 men
March	8 Spain	48	180	—	165	75	10,200	725	500 howitzers 50 tons medical stores
April	5 Spain	26	40	—	75	55	5000	1000	100 tons medical stores
May	14 Spain	27	—	—	—	120	11,300	2950	
June	11 Spain	30	40	12	37	150	5650	4550	
July	6 Spain	14	15	15	42	20	2450	1250	70 aircraft officers
August	4 Spain 1 France – 5	16 —	20 —	— —	26 —	— —	2300 —	900 —	—
Total									
September		—	—	—	—	—	—	—	—
October	1 Soviet	6	—	—	—	—	1700	—	—
November	2 UK	—	—	—	—	—	1000	—	—

						CARGO			
Date	Nation	Aircraft	Guns	AA Guns	Tanks	Trucks	War material (tons)	Ammunition (tons)	Miscellaneous
December	2 UK	—	—	—	—	27	—	—	920 officers and men 3414 tons petrol 450 tons clothing 325 tons medical stores 100 rifle-machine guns 500 howitzers
Total September 1936–December 1937	27 Soviet 71 Spain 5 UK 1 France 1 Mexico ___ 105	234	703	27	731	822	67,350	29,125	
1938 January	3 Soviet 12 UK 7 Greek 1 US	4 — — —	— — —	— — —	— — —	92 — —	1850 — —	— — —	15,400 tons petrol 7200 tons crude oil 4650 tons lubricants
February	2 Soviet 8 Greek 9 UK	4 — —	— — —	— — —	— — —	427 — —	— — —	— — —	6120 tons crude oil 187 tractors
March	2 Soviet 13 UK 2 Greek	—	—	—	—	45	—	—	9235 tons petrol 18,958 tons crude oil (Throughout this period, large quantities of manganese, ammonia, pitch, asbestos, asphalt, and corn)

Total January–March 1938	7 Soviet 34 UK 17 Greek 1 US — 59	8	—	—	—	564	1850	—	28,049 tons petrol 32,278 tons crude oil 4650 tons lubricants 187 tractors
Grand Total September 1936–March 1938	34 Soviet 39 UK 71 Spain 17 Greek 1 Mexico 1 France 1 US — 164	242	703	27	731	1386	69,200	29,125	920 officers and men 28,049 tons petrol 450 tons clothing 325 tons medical stores 100 rifle-machine guns 500 howitzers 32,278 tons crude oil 4650 tons lubricants 187 tractors

SELECTED BIBLIOGRAPHY

This comprises a list of the more important books, pamphlets, etc., on the Spanish Civil War, together with other material used in the construction of this book; but it is not to be regarded as a complete bibliography of everything written about the war and its immediate origins. Nor is it a complete list of all books I have consulted.

Sources referred to in the footnotes are indicated by an asterisk.

I DOCUMENTS

Carlist Archives (Seville). A mass of letters, memoranda, etc., together with posters, pamphlets, newspapers; the most important of the documents in this collection are: documents relating to the negotiations between the Carlist Communion and General Mola before the rising of July 18, 1936; documents relating to the exile of Manuel Fal Conde in December 1936; to the negotiations between the Falange and Carlists in February 1937; and a series of notes for a life of Prince François Xavier of Bourbon Parma, the Carlist Regent.

Communist International, VIIth Congress of. Abridged stenographic report of the Proceedings (Moscow 1936).

Declarations des Gouvernements Européens au Sujet des Affaires d'Espagne. (Summary of documents, in typescript, in the Rockefeller Library of the Palais des Nations, Geneva.)

Diario de Sesiones de las Cortes Españoles. (Complete collection in Library of the Cortes, Madrid.)

Documents Diplomatiques concernant la Guerre de Liberation d'Espagne (Burgos 1938).

Evénements Survenus en France 1933-1945, Les. [Rapport fait au nom de la Commission de l'Assemblée Nationale.] Témoignages. Vol. 1 (Paris 1951).

General Cause, The. Mass Lawsuit brought by the Spanish Nationalist Government [Preliminary Report] (English translation; Madrid 1953).

German Foreign Policy, Documents on. Series D (1937-1945) (Vol. III, Germany and the Spanish Civil War 1936-1939) (London 1951).

International Military Tribunal. The Trial of the Major War Criminals. Nuremberg 1947-9. 37 vols.

*League of Nations. Official Journal 1936-39.

PADELFORD, N. J., International Law and Diplomacy in the Spanish Civil Strife (Cambridge, Mass. and New York 1939).

*Parliamentary Debates: *House of Commons* 1936–9. *House of Lords* ibid.
**Report of the Sub-Committee on the Spanish Question.* (UN Security Council. New York 1946.)
Spanish (Nationalist) Government (*Ministerio de Gobernación*). *Dictamen de la Comisión sobre Ilegitimad de Poderes Actuantes en 18 de Julio de 1936* (Madrid 1939).
See also Section IV; *General Cause* (above); Estado Mayor (LATER ACCOUNTS); *International Brigades, The* (LATER ACCOUNTS).
Spanish (Republican) Government. *Documents de 'La No-Intervention'* (Madrid 1936); **Documentos 'Ocupados a las Unidades Italianas en la Acción de Guadalajara* (Valencia 1937); *Le Livre blanc de l' Intervention Italienne en Espagne* (Paris 1937).
*United States Government. *The Foreign Relations of the United States* (State Department Papers, USD) Vol. 2 1936; vol. 1 1937; vol. 1 1938; vol. 2 1939 (Washington 1952–4).

II LEADING MEMOIRS

(Autobiographies, etc., of persons who played a determining rôle in the events described.)

ABAD DE SANTILLÁN, DIEGO, **Por qué Perdimos la Guerra* (Buenos Aires 1940); *La Revolución y la Guerra de España* (Buenos Aires 1938).
AGUIRRE Y LECUBE, JOSÉ ANTONIO DE, **De Guernica a Nueva York Pasando por Berlín* (Buenos Aires 1944).
ALCALÁ-ZAMORA Y TORRES, NICETO, *Un Viaje Azaroso desde Francia a la Argentina* (Buenos Aires 1942).
ALONSO GONZÁLEZ, BRUNO, *La Flota Republicana y la Guerra Civil en España* (Mexico 1944).
ÁLVAREZ DEL VAYO, JULIO, **Freedom's Battle* (London 1940); **The Last Optimist* (London 1950).
ANSALDO, JUAN ANTONIO, **¿Para Que?* (Buenos Aires 1951) (French edition: *Mémoires d'un Monarchiste Espagnol* (Monaco 1953).
ARAQUISTAIN QUEVEDO, LUIS, **El Comunismo Y La Guerra de España* (Carmaux 1939); *Mis Tratos con los Comunistas* (Toulouse 1939).
AZAÑA Y DÍAZ, MANUEL, *Memorias Intimas (edited by Joaquín Arrarás, Madrid 1939); *La Velada en Benicarló* (Buenos Aires 1939); *Mi Rebelión en Barcelona* (Bilbao 1935).
AZCÁRATE Y FLOREZ, PABLO, *Memoirs (MSS.).
BONNET, GEORGES, *De Washington au Quai d'Orsay* (Geneva 1946).
BOWERS, CLAUDE, **My Mission to Spain* (New York 1954).
CAMPESINO, EL. See González, Valentín.
CANTALUPO, ROBERTO, *Fu La Spagna (Milan 1948).
CASADO, COLONEL SEGISMUNDO, **The Last Days of Madrid* (tr. Rupert Croft-Cooke) (London 1939).

CHURCHILL, WINSTON, *The Second World War*, Vol. I: *The Gathering Storm* (London 1948).

CIANO, COUNT GALEAZZO, *Diplomatic Papers* (edited Malcolm Muggeridge) (London 1948); *Diary 1937–38* (edited Malcolm Muggeridge) (London 1952); *Diary 1939–43* (edited Malcolm Muggeridge) (London 1947).

COT, PIERRE, *The Triumph of Treason* [tr.] (New York 1944).

Epistolario Negrín y Prieto (Paris 1939).

FEILING, KEITH, *The Life of Neville Chamberlain* (London 1946).

GALLAND, GENERAL ADOLF, *The First and the Last* [tr.] (Preface by Douglas Bader) (London 1955).

GAMELIN, GENERAL GEORGES, *Servir* (3 vols.) (Paris 1946–7).

GAMIR ULÍBARRI, GENERAL, *De Mis Memorias* (Paris 1939).

GARCÍA PRADAS, JOSÉ, *Cómo termino la Guerra de España* (Buenos Aires 1940). See also Section IV.

GARCÍA-VALIÑO Y MARCÉN, GENERAL RAFAEL, *Guerra de Liberación Española. Campañas de Aragón y Maestrazgo* (Madrid 1949).

GONZÁLEZ, VALENTÍN (El Campesino), * Listen Comrades!* (London 1952); *Comunista en España y anti-Stalinista en Rusia* (Mexico 1953).

GORKIN, JULIÁN (Julián Gómez), *Cannibales Políticos: Hitler y Stalin en España* (Mexico 1941).

GROSSI, MANUEL, *La Insurrección de Asturias* (Valencia 1935).

HERNÁNDEZ TOMÁS, JESÚS, *Yo fui un Ministro de Stalin* (Mexico 1953) ([French tr.] *La Grande Trahison*, Paris 1953). See also Section VI.

HODGSON, SIR ROBERT, *Spain Resurgent* (London 1953).

HULL, CORDELL, *Memoirs* (New York 1948).

IRIBARREN, JOSÉ MARÍA, *El General Mola* (Madrid 1945).

KINDELÁN Y DUANY, GENERAL ALFREDO, *Mis Cuadernos de Guerra* (Madrid 1945).

KRIVITSKY, GENERAL WALTER G., *I was Stalin's Agent* (London 1939).

LARGO CABALLERO, FRANCISCO, *Mis Recuerdos: Cartas a un Amigo* (Mexico 1954).

LERROUX, ALEJANDRO, *La Pequeña Historia* (Buenos Aires 1945).

LIZARZA IRIBARREN, ANTONIO, *Memorias de la Conspiración. Cómo se preparo en Navara la Cruzada 1931–6* (Pamplona 1953).

MARTÍN BLÁZQUEZ, JOSÉ, *I Helped to Build an Army* (with an Introduction by Franz Borkenau) (London 1939).

MOLA Y VIDAL, GENERAL EMILIO, *Obras Completas* (Valladolid 1940).

MUGICA, DR MATEO (Bishop of Vitoria), *Imperativos de mi Conciencia* (s.d.).

NENNI, PIETRO, *Spagna* (Milan 1958) (French tr. *La Guerre d'Espagne*, Paris 1959).

OSSORIO Y GALLARDO, ÁNGEL, *La España de mi Vida. Autobiografía* (Buenos Aires 1941). See also Section VI.

PAUL-BONCOUR, J., *Entre Deux Guerres* 1935–40 (Paris 1946).

PRADERA, VÍCTOR, *Un Estado Nuevo* (Pamplona 1934).

PRIETO, INDALECIO, *Cómo y por qué Salí del Ministerio de Defensa Nacional* (Paris 1939); *Yo y Moscú* (Collection of Prieto's writings, including the previous entry) (Madrid 1955).

PRIMO DE RIVERA, JOSÉ ANTONIO, *Obras Completas* (Madrid 1954).

'RENN, LUDWIG,' *Der Spanische Krieg* (Berlin 1955).

RIBBENTROP, JOACHIM VON, *Memoirs* (London 1954).

ROJO, GENERAL VICENTE, *¡Alerte los Pueblos!* (Buenos Aires 1939); *¡España Heroica!* (Buenos Aires 1942).

SERRANO SUÑER, RAMÓN, *Entre Hendaye y Gibraltar* (Madrid 1947); (French tr. Geneva 1947).

ZUGAZAGOITIA, JULIÁN, *Historia de la Guerra de España* (Buenos Aires 1940).

III OTHER MEMOIRS

(Accounts by eyewitnesses, etc.)

ABERRIGOYEN, FR IÑAKI DE, *Sept Mois et Sept Jours dans L'Espagne de Franco* (Paris 1938).

ACIER, MARCEL, *From Spanish Trenches* (London 1937).

ALCALÁ-GALIANO, ÁLVARO (Marqués de Castel Bravo), *La Caida de un Trono* (Madrid 1932) (English tr. *The fall of a Throne*, London 1933).

'ANDRÉS DE PALMA', *Mallorca en la Guerra contra el Marxismo* (Palma de Mallorca 1936).

ARMILLAS GARCÍA, LUIS (with MANUEL MONTELLA MUÑOZ), *Rutas Gloriosas* (Cádiz 1939).

ARMIÑÁN ODRIOZOLA, L. DE, *Por los Caminos de Guerra* (Madrid 1939).

ARSENIO DE IZARGA Y OJEMBARRENA, G., *Los Presos de Madrid* (Madrid 1940).

AVILÉS G., *Tribunales Rojos vistos por un Abogado Defensor* (Barcelona 1939).

BAHAMONDE Y SÁNCHEZ DE CASTRO, ANTONIO, *Memoirs of a Spanish Nationalist* (London 1939).

BAJATIERRA, MAURO, *Cronicas del Frente de Madrid* (Barcelona 1937).

BALBONTÍN, JOSÉ ANTONIO, *La España de mi Experiencia* (Mexico 1952).

BALK, THEODOR (editor), *La Quatorzième* (Madrid 1937).

BARAIBAR, CARLOS DE, *La Guerra de España en el Plano Internacional* (Barcelona 1937).

BARBERÁ SABORIDO, M., *Impresiones de un Año* (Barcelona 1937).

BAREA, ARTURO, *The Clash* (London 1946).

BARBIER, *Un frac de Nessus* (Paris 1950).

BASALDUA, PEDRO DE, *En España sale el Sole* (Buenos Aires 1938).

BAUER, EDDY, *Rouge et Or* (Neuchâtel 1939).

BELL, QUENTIN, [editor] * *Julian Bell: Essays, Poems and Letters* (Foreword by J. M. Keynes) (London 1938).

BENAVIDES, M. D., *El Ultimo Pirata del Mediterraneo* (Barcelona 1934); *La Revolución Fue Así* (Barcelona 1935).

BERNANOS, GEORGES, *Les Grands Cimetières sous la Lune* (Paris 1938).

BERTRÁN GÜELL, FELIPE, *Momentos Interesantes de la Historia de España en este Siglo: Preparación y Desarollo del Alzamiento Nacional* (Valladolid 1939). *Rutas de la Victoria* (Barcelona 1939). See also Section VI.

BERTÁN Y MUSITU, J., *Experiencias de los Servicios de Información del Nordeste de España* (Madrid 1940).

BESSIE, ALVAH, *Men in Battle* (New York 1939).

BEUMELBERG, WERNER, *Kampf um Spanien: Die Geschichte der Legion Condor* (Berlin 1939).

BLEY, W., *Das Buch der Spanienflieger* (Leipzig 1939).

BLOCH, J. R., *Espagne, Espagne!* (Paris 1936).

BOCINOS VILLAVERDE, A., *Cuando la Dominación Rojo* (Mieres 1938).

BORKENAU, FRANZ, *The Spanish Cockpit* (London 1937). See also Section VII.

BOUTHELIER, ANTONIO (with Jose López Mora), *Ocho Días. La Revolución Comunista en Madrid March 5-13 1939* (Madrid 1940).

BRASA, J., *'España y la Legión'* (Valladolid 1937).

BRERETON, G., *Inside Spain* (London 1938).

BUSTAMENTE Y QUIJANO, R., *A Bordo del 'Alfonso Pérez'. Escenas del Cautiverio Rojo en Santander* (Madrid 1940).

CABALLERO DE RONTE, V., *Santander Roja* (Palencia 1936).

CABINILLAS, A., *Hacia la España Eterna* (Buenos Aires 1938).

CAMIN MEANA, A., *España a Hierro y Fuego* (Mexico 1938).

CAMPOAMOR, CLARA, *La Révolution Espagnole vue par une Républicaine* (Paris 1937). See also Section VI.

CARASA TORRE, F., *Presos de los Rojos-Separatistas* (San Sebastian 1937).

CARDONA, MARÍA DE, *Terreur à Madrid* (Paris 1937).

CARDOZO, H. G., *March of a Nation* (London 1937).

CARRILLO, WENCESLAO, *El Ultimo Episodio de la Guerra Civil Española* (Toulouse 1939).

CASARES, F., *Argentina, España 1936-37* (Buenos Aires 1937).

CASARIEGO FERNÁNDEZ, J. E., *Flor de Hidalgos* (Pamplona 1937).

CASTILLO, J. DE, *La Justicia Revolucionaria en España* (Barcelona 1937).

CASTRO ALBARRÁN, A. DE, *Este es el Cortejo. Héroes y Martires de la Cruzada Española* (Salamanca 1938).

CASTRO DELGADO, ENRIQUE, *La Vida Secreta de la Komintern* (Madrid 1950); *Hombres made in Moscú* (Mexico 1960).

CAVERO Y CAVERO, F., *Con la Segunda Bandera en el Frente de Aragón* (Saragossa 1937).

CHAMINADE, M., *Feux Croisés sur l'Espagne* (Paris 1939).

CHAMSON, ANDRÉ, *Rien qu'un Témoignage* (Paris 1938).

CÍA NAVASCUÉS, POLICARPO, *Memorias del Tercio de Montejurra* (Pamplona 1941).

CIMORRA, C., *Frente Andaluz* (Seville 1937).

CIRRE, JIMÉNEZ, J., *De Espejo a Madrid* (Granada 1938).

Clergé Basque, Le (Paris 1938).

CLERISSEL, H. C., *Espagne '36–'37* (Paris 1937).

CLOUD, Y., *The Basque children in England* (London 1937).

COCKBURN, CLAUD, *In Time of Trouble* (London 1956). See also 'Pitcairn, Frank' below.

COLÁS LAGUÍA, E., *Gesta Herioca* (Saragossa 1936).

COLMEGNA, HECTOR, *Diario de un Medico Argentina en la Guerra de España* (Madrid s.d.).

CONZE, E., *Spain To-day* (London 1936).

COPADO, FR BERNABÉ (S.J.),, *Con la Columna de Redondo* (Seville 1937).

COPEMAN, FRED, *Reason in Revolt* (London 1948).

'CÓRDOBA, JUAN DE', *Estampas y Reportajes de Retaguardia* (Seville 1939).

CORDONIÉ CANELLA, RAFAEL, *Madrid bajo el Marxismo* (Avila 1939).

CORNFORD, JOHN. See Sloan.

COSSÍO, FRANCISCO DE, *Guerra de Salvación* (Valladolid 1937).

COWLES, VIRGINIA, *Looking for Trouble* (London 1941).

COX, GEOFFREY, *Defence of Madrid* (London 1937).

CUESTA, T., *De la Muerte a la Vida. Veinte Meses de una Vida Insignificante en el Infierno Rojo* (Burgos 1939).

CUETA, COLONEL JUAN, *Mi Segunda Vuelta* (Bilbao 1937).

Dabrowsrwacy (Collection) (Warsaw 1956).

D'ARCANGUES, PIERRE, *Le Destin de l'Espagne* (Paris 1938).

DELAPRÉE, LOUIS, *Mort en Espagne* (Paris 1937).

DESCHAMPS, B., *La Vérité sur Guadalajara* (Paris 1938).

Deutsche Kampfen in Spanien (Berlin 1939).

DE WET, O., *Cardboard Crucifix* (London 1938).

DIEGO, CAPTAIN DE (with LIEUT. QUINTANA and LIEUT. ROYO), *Belchite: Rapsodía Incompleta* (Barcelona 1939).

DOMENECH PUIG, R., *Diario de Campaña de un Requeté* (Barcelona 1959).

DOMÍNGUEZ, EDMUNDO, *Los Vencedores de Negrín* (Mexico 1940).

DUVAL, GENERAL MAURICE, *Les Leçons de la Guerre d'Espagne* (preface by General Weygand) (Paris 1938); *Les Espagnols et la Guerre d'Espagne* (Paris 1939).

'EL PRESO 831', *Del Madrid Rojo: Ultimas Días de la Cárcel Modelo* (Cádiz 1937).

ELSTOB, PETER, *Spanish Prisoner* (London 1939).

ESTEBÁN VILARO, JOSÉ, *El Ocaso de los Dioses Rojas* (Barcelona 1939).

EVERARD, C., *Luftkampf über Spanien* (Berlin 1937).

FALCÓN, CESAR, *Madrid* (Madrid 1939).

FALGARIROLLES, A., *La Milicienne* (Paris 1938).

FARMBOROUGH, FLORENCE, *Life and People in Nationalist Spain* (London 1938).

'FARRÈRE, C.', *Visite aux Espagnoles: Hiver 1937* (Paris 1937).

FERNÁNDEZ ARIAS, ADELARDO, *La Agonía de Madrid 1936–37* (Saragossa 1938).

'FONTERIZ, LUIS', **Red Terror in Madrid* (London 1937).

FOX, RALPH, **A Writer in Arms* (Ed. by John Lehmann and C. Day Lewis) (London 1937).

FRASER, J. A., *Spain's Pilgrimage of Grace* (Glasgow 1937).

FUEHRING, H. H., *Wir Funken für Franco* (Gütersloh 1939).

FUEMBUERRA, EDUARDO, *Guerra en Aragón* (Saragossa 1938).

GARCÍA ALONSO, E., *España Roja* (Barcelona 1939), **Mi Dos Meses en Prisión de Málaga* (Seville 1936).

GARCÍA MERCADAL, J., *Tres Reductos* (Saragossa 1938); *Frente y Retaguardia* (Saragossa 1937). See also Section VI.

GARCÍA-MORATO, JOAQUÍN, *Guerra en el Aire* (Prologue by General Franco) (2nd edition Madrid 1954).

GARRACHÓN CUESTA, A., *De África a Cádiz y de Cádiz a la España Imperial* (Cádiz 1938).

GARRATT, G. T., **Mussolini's Roman Empire* (London 1938).

GAY, FRANCISCO, *Dans les Flammes et dans le Sang* (Paris 1937).

GERAHTY, CECIL,**The Road to Madrid* (London 1937). See also Foss and Gerahty (Section V).

GILLAIN, NICK, **Le Mercenaire* (Lille 1937).

GODED, MANUEL, *Un Faccioso Cien por Cien* (Saragossa 1938).

GODDEN, GERTRUDE M., *Communist Operations in Spain* (London 1936) *Conflict in Spain* (London 1937).

GOERING, H. L. W., *Ich Muss dabei Sein!* (Berlin 1936).

COLLONET, ANGEL (with JOSÉ MORALES LÓPEZ), *Rojo y Azul en Granada* (Granada 1937); *Sangre y Fuego, Malaga* (Granada 1937).

GÓMEZ ACEBO, J., *La Vida en las Cárceles de Euzkadi* (Zarauz 1938).

GÓMEZ BAJUELO, GIL, *Málaga bajo el Dominio Rojo* (Cádiz 1937).

GÓMEZ MÁLAGA, JUAN, *Estampas Tragicas de Madrid* (Avila 1936).

GÓMEZ MANGADA, A., *España Sangra* (Barcelona 1938).

GONZÁLEZ OLIVEROS, W., *Falange y Requeté* (Valladolid 1937).

GRACÍA, V., *Aragón, Baluarte de España* (Saragossa 1938).

GREENE, H., *Secret Agent in Spain* (London 1938).

GRIEG, J. N. B., *Spansk Sommer* (Oslo 1937).

GUEST, CARMEL HADEN, **David Guest: A Scientist fights for Freedom* (London 1938).

GUTIÉRREZ, RICARDO (with JOAQUÍN GONZÁLEZ PASTOR), *Anecdotario de la Gesta Española* (Valladolid 1939). See also Section VI.

GUZMÁN DE ALFARACHE, J., *¡18 de Julio! Historia del Alzamiento Glorioso de Sevilla* (Seville 1937).

GUZMÁN, EDUARDO DE, *Madrid Rojo y Negro* (Buenos Aires 1939).

HANIGHEN, FRANK C., [Ed.] *Nothing but Danger* (London 1940).

HOYOS, COUNT M. S., *Pedros y Pablos* (Munich 1939).

In Spain with the International Brigade: A Personal Narrative (London 1938).

ITURBURU, C., *España bajo el Mando del Pueblo* (Buenos Aires 1938).

JEAN, ANDRÉ, *Transformation Économique en Catalogne* (Barcelona 1936).

JOHNSTONE, N., *Hotel in Flight* (London 1939).

JORDAN, P., *There is no Return* (London 1938).

JOUVE, MARGUERITE, *Vu en Espagne* (Paris 1937).

JUANÉS, JUAN, *Por qué Fuimos a la Guerra* (Avila 1937).

KAMINSKI, H. E., *Ceux de Barcelone* (Paris 1937).

KANTOROWICZ, A. [Ed.] *Chapaiev* (Madrid 1938). See also Section VI.

KNICKERBOCKER, H. R., *The Siege of the Alcazar* (New York, 1936).

KNOBLAUGH, H. E., *Correspondent in Spain* (London 1937).

KOEHLER, C., *Kriegsfreiwilliger 1937* (Leipzig 1939).

KOEHLER, HERMANN, *Inside the Gestapo* [tr.] (London 1940).

KOESTLER, ARTHUR, *Spanish Testament* (London 1937). See also Section VII.

KOL'TSOV, MICHAEL, *Ispanskij Dnevnik* (New Edition, Moscow 1957).

LA CADENA Y LAGUNA, R., *Entre Rojos y Azules* (Saragossa 1939).

LANDAU, KATIA, *Le Stalinisme en Espagne* (Paris 1938).

LLADO I FIGUERES, J. M., *El 19 de Juliol a Barcelona* (Barcelona 1938).

LANGDON-DAVIES, JOHN, *Behind the Spanish Barricades* (London 1936).

LAST, JEF, *The Spanish Tragedy* (London 1939).

LENT, A., *Wir Kämpften für Spanien* (Oldenburg 1939).

LINDBAECK, LISE, *Bataljon Thaelmann* (Oslo 1938); *Internationella Brigaden* (Stockholm 1939).

LLUCH Y VALLS, FRANCISCO, *Mi Diario entre los Mártires* (Granada 1937).

LOEWEL, R., *À la Recherche de Torquemada* (Paris 1938).

LÓPEZ CHACÓN, RAFAEL, *Por qué Hice las Chekas de Barcelona* (Madrid 1940).

LÓPEZ DE MEDRANO, L., *986 Días en el Infierno* (Madrid 1939).

Lo que han hecho en Galicia. Episodios del Terror Blanco en los Provincias Gallegas contados por quienes los han Vivido (Paris 1938).

LOUZÓN, R., *La Contra-Revolución en España* (Madrid 1943).

LOW, MARY (and JUAN BREA), *Red Spanish Notebook* (London 1937).

LUNN, SIR ARNOLD, *Spanish Rehearsal* (London 1937).

MACHADO, ANTONIO, *Madrid 1936–37* (Madrid 1937).

McCULLAGH, FRANCIS, *In Franco's Spain* (London 1937).

MCKEE, SEUMAS, *I was a Franco Soldier (London 1938).

McNEILL-MOSS, G., *The Epic of the Alcazar (London 1939); *The Legend of Badajoz (London 1937).

MADEM, GINA,* The Jews fighting for Freedom (New York 1938).

MARTÍNEZ ABAD, JULIO, *¡¡17 de Julio!! La Guarnición de Melilla, inicia la Salvación de España (Melilla 1937).

MARTÍNEZ LEAL, ALFREDO, *El Asedio del Alcázar de Toledo (Toledo 1937).

MARTINI, M., La Bataglia dell'Ebro (Paris 1939).

MATTHEWS, HERBERT, *Two Wars and More to Come (New York 1938). See also Section VI.

MEDIO, JUSTO, Three Pictures of the Spanish Civil War (London 1937).

MERIN, P., Spain between Death and Birth (London 1938).

MIRAVITTLES, JAIME, *Catalanes en Madrid (Barcelona 1938).

MITCHELL, SIR PETER CHALMERS, *My House in Málaga (London 1938).

MITCHELL, MAIRIN, Storm over Spain (London 1937).

MONTALBÁN, V. (and C. DOMI), Realidades Presentes. Aspectas de la Guerra Civil Española (Saragossa 1937).

MONTEON DE LLUVIA, ANTONIO EMILIO, Apendice a Catorce Meses de Legislación Revolucionaria (Valencia 1938).

MONTÁN, LUIS, Episodios de la Guerra Civil (Valladolid 1937-8).

MORALES, M., La Guerra Civil en Guipúzcoa (Valladolid 1937).

MORENO GONZÁLEZ, REMIGO, ¡Yo Acuso! Ciento Treinta Tres Días al Servicio del Gobierno de Madrid (Tangier 1938).

MORENO DÁVILA, JULIO, Frente a Madrid (Granada 1937).

MURO ZEGRI, D., *La Epopeya del Alcázar (Valladolid 1937).

NICHOLSON, H., Death in the Morning (London 1937).

O'BRIEN, KATE, Farewell Spain (London 1937).

O'DONNELL, PEADAR, Salud! (London 1937).

O'DUFFY, E., *Crusade in Spain (Dublin 1938).

OLIVEIRA, MAURICIO, La Tragedía Española en el Mar (Cádiz 1937).

OLLIVIER, MARCEL, Les Journées sanglantes de Barcelona (Paris 1937).

ORLOV, ALEXANDER, *The Secret History of Stalin's Crimes (New York 1953).

ORTIZ DE VILLAJOS, L., De Sevilla a Madrid (Granada 1937).

ORWELL, GEORGE, *Homage to Catalonia (London 1938).

PAGÉS GUIX, LUIS, *La Traición de los Franco (Privately printed Madrid ? 1939).

PALAU GARI, J., Treinta Dos Meses de Esclavitud en la Que Fué Zona Roja de España (Barcelona 1939).

PAUL, E. H., The Life and Death of a Spanish Town (London 1937).

PEIRÓ, J., Perull a la Retarguardia (Mataró 1936). See also Section VI.

PÉLLETIER, JEAN, Seis Meses en las Prisones de Franco (Valencia 1937).

PÉMAN, JOSÉ MARÍA, *De la Entrada en Madrid: Historia de Tres Días* (Madrid 1939); See also Section VI.

PERALTA, C., *El Comunismo en España* (Madrid 1940).

PÉREZ DE OLAGUER, ANTONIO, *Piedras Vivas, Arengas y Cronicas de Guerra* (Cádiz 1937); *El Terror Rojo en Andalucía* (Burgos 1938); *El Terror Rojo en Cataluña* (Burgos 1937); *Los de Siempre* (Burgos 1937); *Lágrimas y Sonrisas* (Burgos 1938).

PÉREZ FERRERO, M., *Drapeau de France* (Paris 1938).

PÉREZ MADRIGAL, JOAQUÍN, *Tipos y Sombras de la Tragedia* (Avila 1937); *Augurios, Estallido y Episodios de la Guerra Civil* (Avila 1938).

PÉREZ SOLIS, OSCAR, **Sitio y Defensa de Oviedo* (Valladolid 1938).

'PITCAIRN, FRANK' (Claud Cockburn), *Reporter in Spain* (London 1936). See also Cockburn above.

PORTELA, A., *En las Trincheras de España* (Cádiz 1937).

PRIETO, CARLOS (Charles Duff), *Spanish Front* (London 1936).

PROUDHOMMEAUX, A. & D., *Catalogne 1936–37* (Paris 1937).

PUENTE, JOSÉ VICENTE, *Madrid Recobrado* (Madrid 1939).

PUIG MORA, E., *La Tragedía Roja en Barcelona: Memorias de un Evadido* (Saragossa 1938).

QUINTANA, L., *Mallorca Siempre Española* (Cádiz 1938).

RASI, GUISEPPE, *L'Inferno Spagnolo* (Milan 1937).

RAYNAUD, JEAN, *L'Espagne Rouge* (Paris 1937).

REPARAZ, GONZALO DE, *Diario de Nuestra Guerra* (Barcelona 1937).

REPARAZ Y TRESGALLO DE SOUZA, CAPTAIN, *Desde el Cuartel General de Miaja al Sanctuario de la Virgen de la Cabeza* (Valladolid 1937).

RIESENSFELD, J., *Dancer in Madrid* (New York 1938).

RODRÍGUEZ DEL CASTILLO, J., *Vida y Muerte en las Cárceles Rojas* (Tudela 1939).

ROGERS, F. T., *Spain; A Tragic Journey* (New York 1937).

ROLFE, EDWIN, **The Lincoln Battalion* (New York 1939).

ROMERO-MARCHENT, JOAQUÍN, *Soy un Fugitivo* (Valladolid 1937).

ROMILLY, ESMOND, **Boadilla* (London 1937).

RUIZ ALBENIZ, VICTOR ('El Tebib Arrumi') **Crónicas* (Madrid 1939).

RUIZ VILAPLANA, ANTONIO, **Burgos Justice [Doy Fé*, tr. by W. Horsfall Carter] (London 1939).

RUST, WILLIAM, **Britons in Spain* (London 1939).

SÁINZ DE LOS TERREROS, RAMÓN, *Horas Criticas. Cómo se Desarollo el Movimiento Revolucionario en la Frontera de Bidasoa* (Burgos 1937).

SARABRIA, F., *Madrid bajo las Hordas* (Avila 1938).

SÁNCHEZ DEL ARCO, MANUEL. **El Sur de España en la Reconquista de Madrid* (Seville 1937); *Horas y Figuras de la Guerra en España* (Madrid 1939).

SÁNCHEZ Y RUEDA, E., *De Sigüenza a Madrid Pasando por Guadalajara. Apuntes para la Historia de la Horda Roja* (Sigüenza 1939).

SANZ Y DÍAZ, JOSÉ, **Por las Rochas del Tajo* (Valladolid 1938).

SAUVAGE, MARCEL, *La Corrida* (Paris 1938).

'SENCOURT, ROBERT', *Spain's Ordeal* (London 1938).

SENDER, RAMÓN, *The War in Spain* [tr. by Sir Peter Chalmers Mitchell] (London 1937). See also NOVELS.

SHEEAN, VINCENT, *Not Peace but a Sword* (New York 1939); *The Eleventh Hour* (London 1939).

SLOAN, PAT, *John Cornford: A Memoir* (London 1938).

SOMMERFIELD, JOHN, *Volunteer in Spain* (London 1937).

SOUCHY, AUGUSTINE, *The Tragic Week in Barcelona* (London 1937); *Colectivaciones. La Obra Colectiva de la Revolución Española* (Barcelona 1937); *Entre los Campesinos de Aragón, el Comunismo Libertario en las Comarcas Liberadas* (Valencia 1937).

STACKELBERG, C. G. VON, *Legion Condor. Deutsche Freiwillige in Spanien* (Berlin 1939).

STRONG, ANNA LOUISE, *Spain in Arms* (New York 1937).

TANGYE, NIGEL, *Red, White and Spain* (London 1937).

TENNANT, ELEONORA, *Spanish Journey* (London 1936).

TERY, SIMONE, *Front de la Liberté* (Paris 1938).

THARAUD, JEAN ET JEROME, *Cruelle Espagne* (Paris 1937).

TIMMERMANS, R., *Heroes of the Alcazar* (Prefaced by F. Yeats Brown) (London 1937).

TINKER, F. G., *Some Still Live* (London 1938).

TOMALIN, MILES, *Diaries* (unpublished).

TONI RUIZ, FR. TEODORO (SJ), *La Lección de Navarra* (Burgos 1938).

TRANSEHE, H. VON, *Ein Balte als Freiwilliger in Spanien* (Riga 1937).

VALLS, F. L. F., *Mi Diario entre los Mártires* (Málaga 1937).

WALL, BERNARD, *Spain of the Spaniards* (London 1938).

WATSON, K. S., *Single to Spain* (New York 1937).

WINTRINGHAM, T., *English Captain* (London 1939).

WOOLSEY, GAMEL, *Death's Other Kingdom* (Preface by J. C. Powys) (London 1939).

WORSLEY, T. C., *Behind the Battle* (London 1939).

WULLSCHLEGER, MAX [ed.] *Schweizer Kämpfen in Spanien* (Zurich 1939); *Les Volontaires Suisses en Espagne* (Basle 1939).

IV LEADING CONTEMPORARY PAMPHLETS AND POLEMICS, ETC.

ALCOLÉA, RAYMOND, *Le Christ chez Franco* (Paris 1938).

American Democracy v. the Spanish Hierarchy (New York 1937).

Apelación a la Conciencia Universal sobre el Caso de España (Saragossa 1937).

A Qui la Victoire? (Paris 1937).

ARAUZ DE ROBLES, JOSÉ MARÍA, *Plan (Obra Nacional Corporativa)* (Burgos 1937).

ARARRÁS IRIBARREN, JOAQUÍN (and L. JORDANA DE POZAS), *Sitio del Alcazar de Toledo* (Seville 1937). See also Sections V and VI.

ASENSIO TORRADO, GENERAL JOSÉ, *Mobilación Integral. Algunos de sus Aspectos* (Barcelona 1938); **El General Asensio: su Lealtad a la República* (Barcelona 1938).

*Authors take Sides (London 1937).

AZPILIKOETA, DR DE, *Le Problème Basque* (Paris 1938).

BARDOUX, JACQUES, *Le Chaos Espagnol: Eviterons-nous la Contagion?* (Paris 1937); *Stalin contre l'Europe* (Paris 1939).

BARRISTER, A., **I Accuse France* (London 1937).

BARTLETT, V., *I Accuse* (London 1937).

BASTOS ANSART, FRANCISCO, *El Evangelio del Honor Militar* (Valladolid 1938).

Bataille de l'Ebre, La (Paris 1939).

BAYLE, FR C., **¿Qué Pasa en España?* (Salamanca 1937).

BERNERI, CAMILLO, *Mussolini a la Conquête des Baleares* (Paris 1938); *Guerre de Classe en Espagne* (Paris 1938).

BERRYER, **Red Justice* (London 1937).

Bishop of Chelmsford Refuted, The (London 1938).

BLYTHE, H., *Spain over Britain* (London 1937).

BRINTON, H., *Christianity and Spain* (London 1938).

BROCKWAY, FENNER, *The Truth about Barcelona* (London 1937).

BROWDER, EARL (with BILL LAWRENCE), *Next Steps to Win the War in Spain* (New York 1938).

Buts Militaires de l'Allemagne et de l'Italie dans la Guerre de l'Espagne, Les (Comité Mondial contre la Guerre et le Fascisme) (Paris 1938).

CARRERA, B., *L'Europe Aveugle devant l'Espagne Martyre* (Paris 1939).

CASTILLEJO, J., *Education and Revolution in Spain* (London 1937).

CASTRO ALBARRÁN, A. DE, *Guerra Santa* (Burgos 1938).

Christ or Franco? An Answer to the Spanish Episcopate (London 1937).

Cobla Catalunya, La. (Barcelona 1938).

*Collective Letter of the Spanish Bishops on the War in Spain, The (London 1937).

*Communist Atrocities in Southern Spain, The (Preliminary, Second and Third Reports, tr. into English with preface by Arthur Bryant; London 1936–7; Fourth and Fifth Reports in Spanish, Burgos 1937).

CONFEDERACIÓN NACIONAL DEL TRABAJO: *19 Julio 1936* (Barcelona 1936).

COSSÍO, FRANCISCO DE, *500 Fotos de la Guerra* (Valladolid 1937). See also Section V.

*De Companys a Prieto. Documentos sobre les Industrias de Guerra de Cataluña (Buenos Aires 1939).

*De Julio a Julio (By GARCÍA OLIVER, etc.) (Barcelona 1937).

DEL BARCO, GUSTAVO, *Los Forjadores de la Nueva España* (Sánchez Rodrigo 1938).

DÍAZ, JOSÉ, *Lessons of the Spanish War 1936–9* (London 1940).

DIMITROV, GEORGI, *The United Front* (New York 1938).

DINGLE, REGINALD,` *Russia's work in Spain* (London 1936); *'Democracy' in Spain* (London 1938).

Documentos que publica el Ilustrisimo Cabildo de Vitoria y que afectán al Movimiento Nacional (Vitoria 1937).

Drame du Pays Basque, Le (Paris 1938).

DURAN JORDÁ, DR FREDERICK, *The Service of Blood Transfusion at the Front* (Barcelona 1937).

DZELEPY, E. N., *The Spanish Plot* (Preface by 'Pertinax') (London 1937).

Education in Republican Spain (London 1938).

EHRENBURG, ILYA, *Estampas de España* (Madrid 1937).

El Mundo Católico y la Carta Colectiva del Episcopado Español (Burgos 1938).

Epopeya de Africa, La (Ceuta 1938).

'ERCOLI, M.' (Palmiro Togliatti) *The Spanish Revolution* (New York 1936).

FAURE, E., *Méditations Catastrophiques* (Paris 1937).

FIDALGO CARASA, P., *A Young Mother in Franco's Prisons* (London 1937).

FISCHER, LOUIS, *Why Spain Fights On* (London 1938). See also Section VII.

FRANCO, GENERAL FRANCISCO, *Palabras* (Burgos 1938).

FULLER, MAJOR-GENERAL J. F. C., *The Conquest of Red Spain* (London 1937).

Fundamiento de la Nueva España (Salamanca 1938).

GANNES, HARRY, *How the Soviet Union helps Spain* (New York 1936) (with THEODORE REPARD); *Spain in Revolt* (London 1936).

GARCERÁN, RAFAEL, *La Falange Espagnole de Fevrier 1936 jusqu'au Gouvernement National* (San Sebastián 1938).

GARCÍA PRADAS, JOSÉ, *Antifascismo Proletario* (Madrid 1938).

GAY, FRANCISCO, *Dans les Flammes et dans le Sang* (Paris 1937).

GIMÉNEZ CABALLERO, E., *Genio de España* (Saragossa 1938).

GIMENO RIERA, J., *Aspectos de la Retaguardia* (? Seville 1937).

GREAVES, H. R. G. and D. THOMSON, *The Truth about Spain* (London 1938).

GWYNNE, H. A., *Controversy on Spain between H. A. Gwynne and A. Ramos Oliveira* (London 1937).

HELSBY, CYRIL, *Air Raid Structures and ARP in Barcelona To-day* (London 1939).

HEMINGWAY, ERNEST, *The Spanish War* (Printed in 'Fact' July 1938). See also Section VII.

HÉRICOURT, PIERRE, *Pourquoi Franco Vaincra* (Paris 1936); *Pourquoi*

Mentir? (Paris 1937); *Les Soviets et la France, fournisseurs de la Révolution Espagnole* (Paris 1938). *Pourquoi Franco a vaincu* (Paris 1939).

'HISPANICUS', *Foreign Intervention in Spain* (Vol. I) (London 1937).

How Mussolini Provoked the Spanish War (London 1938).

IBARRURI, DOLORES, *Speeches* (London 1939).

INGE, DEAN W. R., *Dean Inge Indicts the Red Government of Spain* (London 1938).

JERROLD, DOUGLAS, *Issues in Spain* (London 1937); *Spain: Impressions* (London 1937). See also Section VII.

JOHNSON, DR HEWLETT, *Report of a Recent Religious Delegation to Spain* (London 1937).

JOUBERT, VICE ADMIRAL, *La Guerre d'Espagne et le Catholicisme* (Paris 1937).

KLOTZ, HELMUTH, *Les Leçons Militaires de la Guerre d'Espagne* (Paris 1937).

La Justice du Frente Popular en Espagne (Par 3 Deputés au Cortes) (Paris 1937).

LA SOUCHERE, H. DE, *Guerre et Religion* (Paris 1938).

LINDLEY, F., *Tragedy of Spain* (London 1937).

Livre de la Quinzième Brigade, Le (Madrid 1937).

LLOYD GEORGE, DAVID, *Spain and Britain* (London 1937).

L'Oeuvre culturelle des Gouvernments de Gauche à la Generalitat de Catalogne (Barcelona 1937).

LOWENSTEIN, PRINCE H. M. F. L. ZU, *A Catholic in Republican Spain* (London 1937).

LOVEDAY, A., *British Trade Interests in Spain* (London 1937).

LUNN, SIR ARNOLD, *The Unpopular Front* (London 1937).

MCGOVERN, J., *Why the Bishops back Franco* (London 1936).

MALPARTE, CURZIO, *Viva la Muerte!* [Special number of *Prospettive*] (Paris 1939).

MANNING, MRS LEAH, *What I saw in Spain* (London 1935).

MARAÑÓN, GREGORIO, *Liberalism and Communism* (London 1937).

MARDONES ZABALANDIKOETZEA, F. G. DE, *Les Ouvriers Chrétiens sous le Gouvernement de Franco* (Paris 1938).

MARET, FRANÇOIS, *Les Grands Chantiers au Soleil* (Paris 1938).

MARITAIN, JACQUES, *Rebeldes Españoles no Hacen una 'Guerra Santa'* (Paris 1937).

MARIVAULT, LUCIEN, *El Requeté* (Paris 1937); *Glaieul Noir* (Paris 1938).

MARTÍNEZ, JUAN DE LA CRUZ, *¿Cruzada o Rebelión?* (Saragossa 1937).

MARTY, ANDRÉ, *España: Bastión Avanzada de la Libertad* (Barcelona 1938); *Volontaires d'Espagne. Douze Mois Sublimes* (Paris 1938).

MATHIEU, A. C., *Non, ce n'est pas Franco qui a Commencé* (Paris 1939).

Mediation en l'Espagne? (Paris 1938).

Medical Aid Unit, Story of the British (London 1936).

MENÉNDEZ REIGADA, FR IGNACIO, *La Guerra Nacional Española ante la Moral y el Derecho (Bilbao 1937); Catecismo Patriótico Español (Salamanca s.d.).

Milagro de Augustín Tellería, El (Seville 1937).

MINLOS, BRUNO ROBERTOVIC, Paysans de l'Espagne en Lutte (Paris 1937)

MIQUALARENA, JACINTO, Cómo Fui Ejecutado en Madrid (Avila 1937). See also Section VIII.

MIRO, J., Un Hombre: Durruti (Barcelona 1937).

MUGUETA, J., Los Valores de la Raza (San Sebastián 1938).

MUGUETA, DR M. (Canon of Ciudad Real), Ellos y Nosotros: al Mundo Catolico-y al Mundo Civilizado (Pamplona 1937).

Nazi Conspiracy in Spain, The (London 1936).

NEHRU, JAWĀHIR-LĀL, Spain! Why? (London 1937).

NOEL-BAKER, P. J., Franco bombs British Seamen (London 1938).

NORIEGA, F. M., Fal Conde y el Requeté (Burgos 1937).

OLMEDO, F. G., El Sentido de la Guerra Española (Bilbao 1938).

ORIZANA, G. (and JOSÉ MANUEL MONTÍN LIÉBANA), El Movimiento Nacional (Valladolid s.d.).

PÉREZ MADRIGAL, J., Aqui es la Emisora de la Flota Republicana (Madrid 1939).

PÉREZ OLIVARES, ROGELIO, ¡España en la Cruz! (Avila 1937).

POLLITT, HARRY, Arms for Spain (London 1936).

PONCINS, LÉON, Histoire Secrète de la Révolution Espagnole (Paris 1937).

Portugal ante la Guerra Civil en España (Lisbon 1939).

Poster Art in War (Barcelona 1938).

PRIESTLEY, J. B. (and REBECCA WEST), Spain and Us (London 1937).

'RABASSEIRE, HENRI', Espagne, Creuset Politique (Paris 1938).

Redondo, Onésimo. Collection of articles (Valladolid 1937).

Report on a visit of M.P.s (London 1937).

*Revolution d'Octobre en Espagne, La (Madrid 1935).

REY CARRERA, J., El Resurgir de España previsto por Nuestros Grandes Pensadores Donoso, Balmes etc. (San Sebastián 1938).

'RIEGER, MAX', *Espionnage en Espagne (Preface by José Bergamín) (Paris 1938).

'RIENZI', ¡Guerra! (Valladolid s.d.).

RIOTTE, JEAN, Arriba Espana! (Paris 1937).

ROBERT, P., Avec les Camarades Espagnols (Paris 1936); Spain Calling! Their Fight is our Fight (Paris 1937).

RODRÍGUEZ, T., Nueva Conquista de España (Valladolid 1937).

Romancero General de la Guerra en España (Madrid 1937).

ROSSELLI, CARLOS, Oggi en Spagna, Domani en Italia (Paris 1938).

Rothüch über Spanien, Das (Berlin 1937).

ROTVAND, GEORGES, Franco et la Nouvelle Espagne (Paris 1938).

RUBIO, N. M., Le Littoral Catalan dans un Conflit Mediterranéen (Montrouge 1937).

RUIZ GONZÁLBEZ, F., *Yo he creido en Franco* (Paris 1937).

ST. AULAIRE, COMTE DE, *La Renaissance de l'Espagne* (Paris 1938).

SALAZAR OLIVEIRA, DR, *L'Alliance Anglaise et la Guerre d'Espagne* (Lisbon, 1937).

SAROLEA, CHARLES, *Daylight on Spain. The Answer to the Duchess of Atholl* (London 1938).

SEMPRÚN GUERREA, JOSÉ MARÍA DE, *A Catholic looks at Spain* (London 1937).

SIMON, O. K., *Hitler en Espagne* (Paris 1938).

SOLAS GARCÍA, J., *La Nación en la Filosofía de la Revolución Española* (Madrid 1940).

'SORIA, GEORGE', **Trotskyism in the Service of Franco* (London 1938).

Spain Assailed (London 1937).

SPANISH NATIONALIST GOVERNMENT, **Guernica:* Report of the Commission of Enquiry (London 1937).

STEWART, MARGARET, **Reform under Fire* (London 1939).

STUDENT DELEGATION TO SPAIN, A (PHILIP TOYNBEE, GILLES MARTINET, etc.) *Spanish Gold* (London 1937).

TOLEDO, ANGEL DE, *Le Jour Pointe en Espagne* (Liege 1937).

TORRE ENCISO, C. (with D. MURO ZEGRI). *La Marcha sobre Barcelona* (Barcelona 1939).

TORRES, MANUEL, *L'Oeuvre Social du Nouvel Etat Espagnole* (Paris 1938).

TRADES UNION CONGRESS, *The Spanish Problem* (Speeches) (London 1936).

URRUTIA, FEDERICO DE, *El Nacionalsindicalismo es Así* (Seville 1938).

VILAR COSTA, FR J., **Montserrat. Glosas a la Carta Colectiva de los Obispos Españoles* (Barcelona 1938).

VILLARÍN, JORGE, *Guerra en España contra el Judaismo Bolchenique* (Cádiz 1937).

We Saw in Spain. Articles by C. R. ATTLEE, ELLEN WILKINSON, PHILIP NOEL-BAKER, JOHN DUGDALE (London 1937).

YSURDIAGA LORCA, FERMÍN, *Discursio al Silencio y voz de la Falange* (Salamanca 1937).

ZWINGELSTEIN, ANDRÉ, *Au Pays de la Terreur Rouge* (Paris 1937).

ZYROMSKI, J., *Ouvrez la Frontière!* (Paris 1936).

V CONTEMPORARY ACCOUNTS

ALCANTARA, JUAN MANUEL, *Historia Privada de la Revolución Española* (Buenos Aires 1938).

ALMAGRO SAN MARTÍN, M. DE, *La Guerra Civile Española* (Buenos Aires 1937).

ARALAR, J. DE, *La Rebelión Militar Española y el Pueblo Vasco* (Buenos Aires 1937).

ARRARÁS IRIBARREN, JOAQUÍN, *Franco (London 1937). See also Sections IV and VI.

ATHOLL, KATHERINE DUCHESS OF, *Searchlight on Spain (London 1938).

BELFORTE, GENERAL FRANCISCO, La Guerra Civile en Spagna, 4 vols. (Milan 1938–9); La Desintegradine dello Stati (Rome 1939).

BERNÁRDEZ ROMERO, B., Calvo Sotelo: Destellas y Sombra de su Obra (Vigo 1937).

BOLLATI, A. (and G. DEL BONO). La Guerra di Spagna, 2 vols. (Turin 1937–9).

BRASILLACH, ROBERT (with MAURICE BARDÈCHE), *Histoire de la Guerre d'Espagne (Paris 1939); (with HENRI MASSIS), Les Cadets de l'Alcazar (Paris 1936) and Le Siege de l'Alcazar (Paris 1939).

CARRERAS, LUIS, *The Glory of Martyred Spain [tr.] (London 1939).

DEL BURGO, J., Requetés en Navarra antes del Alzamiento (San Sebastián 1939).

(ESTELRICH, JUAN), *La Persécution Religieuse en Espagne [tr.] (with a verse preface by Paul Claudel) (Paris 1937).

FOSS, WILLIAM and (CECIL GERAHTY), *The Spanish Arena (Preface by the Duke of Alba) (London 1938).

GARCÍA MERCADAL, JOSÉ, Aire, Tierra y Mar (Saragossa 1936). See also Section III.

JELLINEK, FRANK, *The Civil War in Spain (London 1938).

MONTERO DÍAZ, SANTIAGO, La Política Social en la Zona Marxista (Bilbao 1938).

MOURE-MARIÑO, L., Galicia en la Guerra (Madrid 1939).

OUDARD, GEORGES, *Chemises Noires, Brunes, Vertes en Espagne (Paris 1938).

QUERO MOLARES, J., La Política de 'No-Intervention' (Barcelona 1937).

SAHARENO, JOSÉ, Villa Cisneros (Valencia 1937).

SIEBERER, A., Espagne contre Espagne (Geneva 1937).

STEER, G. L., *The Tree of Gernika (London 1938).

SUÑER Y ORDÓÑEZ, ENRIQUE, Los Intelectuales y la Tragedia Española (San Sebastián 1937).

TAXONERA, LUCIANO DE, 10 Agosto 1932 (Madrid 1933).

TORYHO, JACINTO, La Independencia de España (Barcelona 1938).

WHITE, F., War in Spain (London 1937).

VI LATER ACCOUNTS

ABSHAGEN, KARL, *Canaris [tr.] (London 1956).

ACEDO COLUNGA, GENERAL FELIPE, *José Calvo Sotelo (Barcelona 1959).

ALBERT DESPUJOL, C. DE, La Gran Tragedia de España (Madrid 1940).

ALCÁZAR DE VELASCO, ANGEL, *Serrano Suñer en la Falange* (Barcelona 1941).

'ARACELI, G.', *Valencia 1936* (Valencia 1939).

ARACIL, ANTONIO, *Dolor y Triunfo. Héroes y Mártires en Pueblos de Andalucía* (Barcelona 1944).

ARRARÁS IRIBARREN, JOAQUÍN, *Historia de la Segunda República Española*, Vol. I (Madrid 1956). See also Sections IV and V.

AUNÓS, E., *Calvo Sotelo y la Política de su Tiempo* (Madrid 1941).

AZNAR, MANUEL, *Historia Militar de la Guerra de España (1936-1939)* (Madrid 1940); *Guerra y Victoria de España* (Madrid 1942). *The Alcázar will not Surrender* (New York 1957).

BAKER, CARLOS, *Hemingway: the Writer as an Artist* (Princeton 1952).

BECCARI, GILBERTO, *Scrittori di Guerra Spagnoli* (Milan 1941).

BENDINER, ROBERT, *The Riddle of the State Department* (New York 1943).

BERTRÁN GÜELL, F., *Caudillo, Profetas y Soldados* (Madrid 1939).

BOMATI PÉREZ, LUIS, *Cautivas de Orihuela* (Orihuela 1952).

Bojovaljisme ve Španělsku (Prague 1956).

BRAVO MARTÍNEZ, FRANCISCO, *Historia de la Falange Española de las JONS* (Madrid 1940); *Jose Antonio. El Hombre, el Jefe, el Camarada* (Madrid 1940).

BUCKLEY, H., *Life and Death of the Spanish Republic* (London 1940).

CABALLÉ Y CLOS, TOMÁS *Barcelona Roja* (Barcelona 1939).

CACHO ZABALZA, A., *La Unión Militar Española* (Alicante 1940).

CAMPOAMOR, C. (with F. FERNÁNDEZ CASTILLEJO), *Heroismo Criollo. La Marina Argentina en la Drama Español* (Buenos Aires 1939).

CASARES, F., *Azaña y Ellos. Cincuenta Semblanzas Rojas* (Granada 1939).

CASTILLO, JOSÉ DE (and SANTIAGO ÁLVAREZ), *Barcelona: Objetivo Cubierto* (Barcelona 1958).

CID LENO, RICARDO (with LUIS MORENO NIETO), *Mártires de Toledo* (Toledo 1942).

COLES, S. F. H., *Franco* (London 1943).

COLODNY, ROBERT, *The Struggle for Madrid: The Central Epic of the Spanish Conflict (1936-37)* (New York 1958).

CONILL MATARÓ, A., *Codo: de mi Diario de Campaña* (Barcelona 1954).

Cruzada Española, Historia de la, Literary director: Joaquín Arrarás. Artistic director: Carlos Saenz de Tejada. Delegate of the State: Ciriaco Pérez Bustamente. 35 volumes. (Madrid 1939-43.)

CUESTA MONERO, GENERAL JOSÉ (with ANTONIO OLMEDO), *General Queipo de Llano* (Barcelona 1957).

CULE, C. P., *Cymro ar Grwdyr* (Llandysul 1941).

DEDIJER, VLADIMIR, *Tito Speaks* (London 1953).

DEL ALAMO, LUCIO, *El Ultimo Muerte de la Guerra de España* (Bilbao 1944).

DE SILVA, GENERAL CARLOS, *Millán Astray* (Barcelona 1956).

DÍAZ, G., *Cómo Llego la Falange al Poder. Análisis de un Proceso Contrarrevolucionario* (Buenos Aires 1940).

DÍAZ DOIN, G., *El Pensamiento Político de Azaña* (Buenos Aires 1943).

DUNDAS, LAWRENCE, *Behind the Spanish Mask* (New York 1943).

DUPRÉ, HENRI, *La Légion Tricolore en Espagne* (Paris 1942).

ECHEANDÍA, JOSÉ, *La Persecución Roja en el País Vasco* (Barcelona 1946).

L'Épopée de l'Espagne: Brigades Internationales 1936-38 (Compiled by L'Amicale des Anciens Volontaires Français en Espagne Républicaine. Paris 1956).

ESPERABÉ DE ARTEAGA, ENRIQUE, *La Guerra de Reconquista Española que ha salvado a Europa.* (Madrid 1940).

ESTADO MAYOR CENTRAL DEL EJERCITIO (of the Spanish Nationalist Government: Servicio Histórico Militar) *Historia de la Guerra de Liberación*, Vol. I (Madrid 1945).

ESTEBÁN INFANTES, GENERAL, *General Sanjurjo* (Barcelona 1957).

ESCH, P. A. M. VAN DER, *Prelude to War. The International Repercussions of the Spanish Civil War* (The Hague 1951).

FEIS, HERBERT, *The Spanish Story* (New York 1948).

FERNÁNDEZ DE CASTRO, RAFAEL, *Hacia las Rutas de una Nueva España. De Cómo se Preparó y Porqué Hubo de Comienzar en Melilla, la Santa Cruzada Nacional.* (Melilla 1940).

FERNSWORTH, LAWRENCE, *Spain's Struggle for Freedom* (Boston, Mass. 1958).

FOLTZ, CHARLES, *The Masquerade in Spain* (Boston 1948).

FONTANA, JOSÉ MARÍA DE, *Los Catalanes en la Guerra de España* (Madrid 1951).

FUENTES, A., *El Crucero 'Canarias' Proa a la Victoria* (Madrid 1940).

FUEYO TUÑON, A DEL, *Heroes de la Epopeya: El Obispo de Teruel* (Barcelona 1941).

GALÍNDEZ, JESÚS DE, *Los Vascos en el Madrid sitiado* (Buenos Aires 1948).

GALINDO HERRERO, SANTIAGO, *El 98 de los que fueron a la Guerra* (Madrid 1954); *Historia de los Partidos Monárquicos bajo la Segunda República* (Madrid 1954).

GALINSOGA, LUIS DE (with GENERAL FRANCO SALGADO), *Centinela del Occidente* (Semblanza Biográfica de Francisco Franco) (Barcelona 1956).

GARCÍA, JOSÉ, *Ispaniya Narodnogo Fronta* (Moscow 1957).

GAROSCI, ALDO, *Gli Intellettuali e la Guerra di Spagna* (Rome 1959).

GAY DE MONTELLÁ, R., *Atalayas de Mallorca. La Guerra en el Mar Latino* (Barcelona 1940).

GOMÁ, COLONEL JOSÉ, *La Guerra en el Aire* (Barcelona 1958).

GÓMEZ OLIVEROS, MAJOR B. (with help of General Moscardó), *General Moscardó* (Barcelona 1955).

GONZÁLEZ BUENO, JESÚS, *Paz en Guerra* (Cádiz 1944).

GORDON, SYDNEY (with TED ALLAN), *The Scalpel, The Sword* (Life of Dr Norman Bethune) (London 1954).

GRANDI, BLASCO, *Togliatti en España* (Madrid 1954).

GRIFUL, ISIDORO, *A los Veinte Años de Aquello* (Barcelona 1956).

GUADIOLA, A., *Barcelona en Poder del Soviet* (Barcelona 1939).

GUTIÉRREZ-RAVÉ, JOSÉ, *Las Cortes Errantes del Frente Popular* (Madrid 1953); *Diccionario Histórico de la Guerra de Liberación de España* (Vol. I only appeared) (Madrid 1943); *Los Meses* (Santander 1939).

HALDANE, CHARLOTTE, *Truth Will Out* (London 1949).

HAMILTON, THOMAS J., *Appeasement's Child* (London 1943).

HENRÍQUEZ CAUBÍN, JULIÁN, *La Batalla del Ebro* (Mexico 1944).

HERNÁNDEZ TOMÁS, JESÚS, *Negro y Rojo* (Mexico 1946).

HIGUERA Y VELÁZQUEZ, A. G. DE LA (with L. MOLINS CORREA), *Historia de la Revolución Española* (Cádiz 1940).

HUGHES, EMMET, *Report from Spain* (New York 1947).

HUIDOBRO PARDO, L., *Memorias de un Finlandés (Del Madrid Rojo)* (Madrid 1939).

INGLÉS, M., *Bajo las Garras del SIM* (Barcelona 1940).

International Brigades, The (Pamphlet issued by the Spanish Nationalist Government, Madrid 1953).

IRIBARREN, M., *Una Perspectiva Histórica de la Guerra en España* (Madrid 1941).

'ITURRALDE, JUAN DE', *El Catolicismo y la Cruzada de Franco*, vol. i (Bayonne 1956); vol. ii (Bayonne 1960).

JATO, DAVID, *La Rebelión de los Estudiantes* (Madrid 1953).

JAVIER MARINAS, GENERAL FRANCISCO, *General Varela* (Barcelona 1956).

JOANIQUET, AURELI, *Calvo Sotelo* (Barcelona 1939).

JULIO TÉLLEZ, EDUARDO, *Historia del Movimento Libertador de España en la Provincia Gaditana* (Cádiz 1944).

JUNOD, M., *Warrior without Weapons* [tr. from French] (London 1951).

KANTOROWICZ, ALFRED, *Spanisches Tagebüch* (Berlin 1949). See also Section III.

KEMP, PETER, *Mine were of Trouble* (London 1957).

KERSHNER, H., *Quaker Service in Modern War* (New York 1950).

KORTA, ADAM (with M. HOPMAN), *Karol Swierczewski* (Warsaw 1956).

LÁCIS, R., *Viva República* (Riga 1957).

LACRUZ, FRANCISCO, *El Alzamiento, la Revolución y el Terror en Barcelona* (Barcelona 1943).

LEVINE, ISAAC DON, *The Mind of an Assassin* (London 1960).

'LIZARRA, A. DE' (Andrés María de Irujo), *Los Vascos y la República Española* (Buenos Aires 1944).

LIZÓN GADEA, ADOLFO, *Brigadas Internacionales en España* (Madrid 1940).

LOJENDIO, LUIS MARÍA DE, *Operaciones Militares de la Guerra de España 1936–39 (Prologue by Col. Antonio Barroso) (Madrid 1940).

LONGO, LUIGI, Le Brigate Internationali in Spagna (Rome 1956).

LÓPEZ FERNÁNDEZ, A., *Defensa de Madrid (Mexico 1948).

LÓPEZ MUÑIZ, COLONEL, *La Batalla de Madrid (Madrid 1943).

MAIZ, B. FÉLIX, *Alzamiento en Espana (Pamplona 1952).

MARTÍN, CLAUDE, *Franco: Soldat et Chef d'Etat (Paris 1959).

MARTÍNEZ BARRIO, DIEGO, Orígenes del Frente Popular Español (Buenos Aires 1943).

MASLARIĆ, BOŽIDAR, Moskva, Madrid, Moskva. Sécanja (Zagreb 1952).

MATTHEWS, HERBERT, The Education of a Correspondent (New York 1946); *The Yoke and the Arrows (New York 1957). See also Section III.

MAURRAS, CHARLES, *Vers l'Espagne de Franco (Paris 1943).

MIGUEL, FLORIMUNDO DE, Una Cuña en Zona Roja (Barcelona 1956).

MILLÁN ASTRAY, PILAR, Cautivas. 32 Meses en las Prisiones Rojas (Valencia 1940).

MITFORD, JESSICA, Hons and Rebels (London 1960).

MORA, CONSTANCIA DE LA, *In Place of Splendour (London 1940).

MORENO, ADMIRAL A., La Guerra en el Mar (Barcelona 1956).

MOSCARDÓ, J., Diario del Alcázar (Madrid 1943).

NADAL, JOAQUÍN MARÍA DE, Seis Años con Don Francisco Cambó (Barcelona 1957).

NELSON, STEVE, The Volunteers (New York 1953).

NICKERSON, HOFFMAN, The Armed Horde (New York 1940).

NONELL BRU, S., Los Requetés Catalanes del Tercio de Nuestra Señora de Montserrat (Barcelona 1956).

NÚÑEZ MONGADO, AURELIO, Los Sucesos de España vistos por un Diplomatico (Buenos Aires 1941).

OSSORIO Y GALLARDO, Á., La Guerra de España y los Católicos (Buenos Aires 1942). See also Sections II and VII.

OYARZABAL DE PALENCIA, ISABEL, Smouldering Freedom (New York 1945); I must have Liberty (New York 1940).

PABÓN, J., Cambó (Barcelona 1952).

PACCIARDI, R., *Il Battaglione Garibaldi (Lugano 1948).

'PEIRATS, J.', *La CNT en la Revolución Española (3 vols.) (Toulouse 1951–3).

PEIRÓ, J., Problemas y Cintarazos (Rennes 1946).

PEMÁN, JOSÉ MARÍA, *Un Soldado en la Historia: Vida del Capitán-General Varela (Madrid 1954). See also Section IV.

PÉREZ SALAS, COLONEL JESÚS, Guerra en España (Mexico 1947).

PÉREZ DE URBEL, FR JUSTO, Los Mártires de la Iglesia (Barcelona 1956).

PITT-RIVERS, JULIAN, *People of the Sierra (London 1954).

PLENN, A., Wind in the Olive Trees (New York 1946).

PRIETO, TOMAS, *Soldados en España* (Madrid 1946).

QUEIPO DE LLANO, R., *De la Cheka de Atadell a la Prisión de Alacuas* (Valladolid 1939).

RAMÓN LACA, J. DE, *Bajo la Ferula de Queipo* (Seville 1939).

REDONDO, GENERAL LUIS (with MAJOR JUAN DE ZAVALA), **El Requeté* (Barcelona 1957).

REGLER, GUSTAV, **The Owl of Minerva* (London 1959). See also NOVELS.

REGUENGO, V., *Guerra sin Frentes* (Madrid 1954).

REY STALLE, A., *Laureado de Sangre* (Madrid 1954).

RICHARDS, V., **Lessons of the Spanish Revolution* (London 1953).

RISCO, A., *La Epopeya del Alcázar de Toledo* (San Sebastián 1941).

RODRÍGUEZ MARÍN, F., *En un Lugar de la Mancha. Divigaciones de un Ochentón Evacuado de Madrid* (Madrid 1939).

ROLDÁN, M., *Las Colectivizaciones en Cataluña* (Barcelona 1940).

ROMANO, JULIO, *Sanjurjo* (Madrid 1940).

ROMANONES, COUNT, *Y Sucedió Así* (Madrid 1947).

ROUGERON, C., *Les Enseignments Aériens de la Guerre d'Espagne* (Paris 1940).

ROUSSEAU, CHARLES, *La Politique de la Non-Intervention* (Paris 1939).

SABATER, M., *Estampas del Cautiverio Rojo* (Barcelona 1940).

SAN JUAN DE PIEDRAS ALBAS, MARQUÉS DE, *Héroes y Mártires de la Aristocracia Española* (prologue by Antonio Goicoechea) (Madrid 1945).

SALAS VIU, V., *Las Primeras Jornadas y Otras Narraciones de la Guerra Española* (Santiago de Chile 1940).

SALTER, CEDRIC, *Try-out in Spain* (New York 1943).

SALVO MIQUEL, FRANCISCO, *Francisco Franco* (Barcelona 1959).

SEVILLA ANDRÉS, DIEGO, *Historia Politica de la Zona Roja* (Madrid 1954).

SOLAS GARCÍA, J., *La Nación en la Filosofía de la Revolución Española* (Madrid 1940).

SOMOZA SILVA, LAZARO, **El General Miaja* (Mexico 1944).

SZINDA, GUSTAV, *Die XI Brigade* (Berlin 1956).

TAYLOR, F. JAY, **The United States and the Spanish Civil War* (New York 1956).

TARAZONA, FRANCISCO, *Sangre en el Cielo* (Mexico 1958).

Témoignages Complementaires pour l'Histoire de l'Espagne, La Guerre entre 1936-39 (Madrid 1953).

TEMPLEWOOD, LORD (Sir Samuel Hoare), *Ambassador on Special Mission* (London 1946).

THOMPSON, SIR GEOFFREY, *Front Line Diplomat* (London 1959).

TOYNBEE, ARNOLD (with V. M. BOULTER and KATHERINE DUFF), **Survey of International Affairs 1937: vol. ii; and 1938 vol. i* (Oxford 1938 and 1948).

VALDESOTO, F. DE, *Francisco Franco* (Madrid 1943).

VANSITTART, LORD, *The Mist Procession* (London 1958).

VEGAS LATAPIÉ, E., *El Pensamiento Politico de Calvo Sotelo* (Madrid 1941).

VIGÓN, GENERAL JORGE, *General Mola* (Barcelona 1957).

VILA SELMA, JOSÉ, *Tres Ensayos Sobre la Literatura y Nuestra Guerra* (Madrid 1956).

VILLEGAS, GENERAL JOSÉ DÍAZ DE, *La Guerra de Liberación* (Barcelona 1957).

VILLALBA DIÉGUEZ, FERNANDO, *Diario de Guerra* (Madrid 1956).

WEIZSÄCKER, ERNST VON, *Memoirs* (London 1951).

XIMÉNEZ DE SANDOVAL, FELIPE, *José Antonio* (Biografía Apasionada) (Prologue by Ramón Serrano Suñer) (Barcelona 1941).

VII GENERAL WORKS

ABSHAGEN, DR KARL, *Canaris* [Eng. tr.] (London 1956).

ALBA, VICTOR, *Histoire des Républiques Espagnoles* (Vincennes 1948).

ALEXANDER, R. J., *Communism in Latin America* (New Brunswick 1957).

BORKENAU, FRANZ, *The Communist International* (London 1938); *European Communism* (London 1953). See also Section III.

BRENAN, GERALD, *The Spanish Labyrinth* (Cambridge 1943); *The Face of Spain* (London 1950).

CATTELL, DAVID C., *Communism and the Spanish Civil War* (Berkeley 1955); *Soviet Diplomacy and the Spanish Civil War* (Berkeley 1957).

CHAMBERS, WHITTAKER, *Witness* (New York 1952).

CHASE, ALLEN, *Falange: The Axis Secret Army in the Americas* (New York 1943).

COLVIN, IAN, *Chief of Intelligence* (London 1954).

COMÍN COLOMBER, E., *Historia Secreta de la Segunda República*, 2 vols. (Madrid 1954); *La República en Exilio* (Madrid 1957) *Historia del Anarquismo Español*, 2 vols. (Barcelona 1956).

CONNOLLY, CYRIL, *The Condemned Playground: Essays 1927–1944* (London 1945); [ed.] *The Golden Horizon* (London 1953).

CREAC'H. JEAN, *Le Coeur et l'Epée* (Paris 1958).

CRAIG, GORDON (and Felix Gilbert) [ed.] *The Diplomats* (Boston 1953).

DÁVILA, SANCHO (with JULIÁN PEMARTÍN), *Hacia la Historia de la Falange: Primera Contribución de Sevilla* (Jerez 1938).

EINAUDI, M., *Communism in Western Europe* (Ithaca, N.Y. 1951).

FERNÁNDEZ ALMAGRO, MELCHOR, *Historia de la Republica Española* [1931–6] (Madrid 1940).

FERRARA, MARCELLA AND MAURICIO, *Palmiro Togliatti* [fr. tr.] (Paris 1955).

FERRER, MELCHOR, *Documentos de Don Alfonso Carlos (Madrid 1950).

FISCHER, LOUIS, * Men and Politics (London 1941).

FISCHER, RUTH, *Stalin and German Communism (Oxford, 1949).

GARCÍA VENERO, MAXIMILIANO, Historia de las Internacionales en España, Vol. I, 1868–1914 Vol. II, 1914–36 Vol. III, 1936–9 (Madrid 1957).

GA 'HOFF, R., *How Russia Makes War (London 1954).

GRAVES, ROBERT (with ALAN HODGE),* The Long Weekend (London 1940).

HALPERIN, E., * The Triumphant Heretic (Life of Tito) (London 1958).

HENDERSON, SIR NEVILE, Failure of a Mission (London 1941).

*Hitler's Tabletalk 1941–43 [With an Introduction by H. R. Trevor Roper] (London 1953).

HOBSBAWM, ERIC, *Primitive Rebels (Manchester 1959).

JERROLD, DOUGLAS, *Georgian Adventure (London 1937).

JOLL, JAMES, Intellectuals in Politics (London 1960).

KOESTLER, ARTHUR, * The Invisible Writing (London 1954).

LEHMANN, JOHN, * The Whispering Gallery (London 1955).

LEVAL, GASTON, *Né Franco né Stalin: La Collettività Anarchiche Spagnole nella Lotta contro Franco e la Reazione Staliniana (Milan 1955).

LIDDELL HART, CAPTAIN B., * The Other Side of the Hill (London 1948); [ed.] * The Soviet Army (London 1956).

LOVEDAY, A., World War in Spain (London 1939); Spain 1923–1948 (London s.d.).

MADARIAGA, SALVADOR DE, *Spain (2nd Edition, London 1942).

MAURÍN, JOAQUÍN, *Hacia la Segunda Revolución (Barcelona 1935) French translation: Révolution et Contre-Révolution en Espagne (Paris 1937). See also Revolution and Counter Revolution in Spain (New York 1938).

MENDIZÁBAL VILLALBA, ALFREDO, The Martyrdom of Spain [tr.] (Preface by Jacques Maritain) (London 1938).

MENÉNDEZ PIDAL, R., [tr. with introduction by Walter Starkie] * The Spaniards in their History (London 1950).

MIKSCHE, F. O., *Blitzkrieg (London 1941).

MONELLI, PAOLO, * Mussolini. An Intimate Life (London 1953).

MUGGERIDGE, MALCOLM, The Thirties (London 1940).

ORTEGA Y GASSET, JOSÉ MARÍA, España Invertebrada (Madrid 1922) [Eng. Tr.] Spain Invertebrate (London 1937).

OSSORIO Y GALLARDO, ANGEL, Vida y sacrificio de Luis Companys (Buenos Aires 1944).

PATTEE, RICHARD, This is Spain (Milwaukee 1951).

PEERS, E. ALISON, * The Spanish Tragedy (London 1936); Catalonia Infelix (London 1937); *Spain in Eclipse (London 1943).

'PERTINAX', Les Fossoyeurs: Défaite Militaire de la France (Paris 1946).

PINI, G. and SUSMEL, D., * Mussolini (4 Vols.) (Florence 1953–5).

PLÁ, JOSÉ, *Historia de la Segunda República Española [4 Vols.] (Barcelona 1940).

RAMA, CARLOS M., La Crisis Española del Siglo XX (Mexico-Buenos Aires 1960).

RAMOS OLIVEIRA, A., *Politics, Economics and Men of Modern Spain 1808–1946 (London 1946).

RUMBOLD, RICHARD, The Winged Life. A Portrait of Antoine de Saint-Exupery, Poet and Airman (London 1953).

SCHAPIRO, LEONARD, *The Communist Party of the Soviet Union (London 1960).

SCHMIDT, PAUL, *Hitler's Interpreter [tr. and abridged] (London 1952).

SMITH, LOIS ELWYN, Mexico and the Spanish Republicans (University of California Publications in Political Science, Berkeley 1955).

SPENDER, STEPHEN, *World within World (London 1951). (With John Lehmann) [ed.] Poems for Spain (London 1939).

TAMARO, ATTILIO, *Venti Anni di Storia (Rome 1952–3).

TITMUSS, R., *Problems of Social Policy (History of World War II) (London 1950).

TOMLIN, E. W. F., Simone Weil (Cambridge 1954).

TOYNBEE, PHILIP, *Friends Apart (London 1954).

TREND, J. B., *The Origins of Modern Spain (Cambridge 1934).

WOOD, NEAL, *Communism and British Intellectuals (London 1959).

WOOLF, BERTRAM D., *Khruschev and Stalin's Ghost (New York 1957).

VIII NOVELS, ETC.

(A short selection)

BREDEL, W., Rencontre sur l'Ebre [tr.] (Paris 1950).

BOTELLA PASTOR, V., Así Cayeron los Dados (Mexico 1959); Por qué callaron las Campañas (Mexico 1953).

CONCHON, GEORGES, *La Corrida de la Victoire (Paris 1960).

FERNÁNDEZ DE LA REGUERA, RICARDO, Cuerpo a Tierra (Barcelona 1954).

GIRONELLA, JOSÉ MARÍA, Los Cipreses Creen en Dios (Barcelona 1953).

HEMINGWAY, ERNEST, *For Whom the Bell Tolls (New York 1940); The Fifth Column (and other plays) (London 1938); The Spanish Earth (film commentary with John Das Passos, Lilian Hellman, etc.) (Cleveland 1938). See also Section IV.

KESTEN, HERMANN, Les Enfants de Guernica (Preface by Thomas Mann) [tr.] (Paris 1952).

LUCAS PHILLIPS, C. E., The Spanish Pimpernel (London 1960).

MALRAUX, ANDRÉ, *L'Espoir (Paris 1937); [English tr.] Days of Hope (London 1938); Man's Hope (New York 1938).

MIQUALARENA, JACINTO, El Otro Mundo (Burgos 1938).

NORMAN, JAMES, The Fell of Dark (London 1960).

REGLER, GUSTAV, * *The Great Crusade*. Introduction by Ernest Hemingway, tr. by Whittaker Chambers (London 1940). See also Section VI.

SARTRE, JEAN-PAUL, *Le Mur* (Paris 1939).

SENDER, RAMÓN, **Seven Red Sundays* [English tr.] (London 1936). See also Section IV.

SINCLAIR, UPTON, *¡No Pasaran!* (Privately printed New York 1937).

TERY, SIMONE, *La Porte du Soleil* (Paris 1939).

IX ENCYCLOPEDIAS

The most useful are:

Enciclopedia Universal Ilustrada (Bilbao)
Diccionario Enciclopedia Uteha (Mexico)

X NEWSPAPERS AND PERIODICALS

The most complete collection of newspapers for the Spanish War is that in the Hemeroteca Municipal in Madrid. This possesses newspapers published in both the Nationalist and in the Republican zones, including files of nearly all the newspapers and periodicals of the International Brigades. The Newspaper Library at the Royal Institute of International Affairs, Chatham House, St James's Square, London, SW1, holds a useful collection of selected cuttings from English and other non-Spanish papers of the time.

INDEX

Abad de Santillán, Diego, 568 fn
ABC, Monarchist newspaper, 38, 39, 40, 64, 119, 214
ABC de Sevilla, Seville edition of the above, 174 fn, 416 fn
Abd-el-Krim (*b.* 1882), 82
Abercrombie, Lascelles (1881–1938), 222 fn
Abraham-Lincoln Battalion, 377, 380, 392 fn, 460, 461, 464, 465, 472, 473, 519 fn, 557, 623. *See also* International Brigades
Abyssinia, 209 fn, 220, 226, 233, 283, 308, 475, 501, 531
    and International Brigades, 377
Acción Católica, 66
Acción Española, 40, 87, 414
Acción Popular, 66
Acción Republicana, 66
Acosta, Bert, 339
Action Française (party), 214, 523
Action Française, L' (newspaper), 451, 488 fn
Adams, Vyvyan (1900–51), 584
Addison, Christopher, later 1st Viscount Addison (1869–1951), 315 fn
Adelante (POUM newspaper), 431
Adler, Fritz (1879–1960), 459 fn
Admiral Antequera (Republican destroyer), 518
Admiral Scheer (German battleship), 317
Agadir, 144 fn
Agrarian Law, 51, 53, 57, 75, 89, 92
Agrarian party, 66, 90, 93
Agrarian Reform, Institute of, 51, 103, 367
Agricultural Loans, Committee of, 486
agriculture, 49–52, 382
Aguado Martínez, Major Virgilio, 243
Aguirre y Lecube, José Antonio (1904–60), 56, 195, 290, 345, 404, 406, 446, 470, 483, 551, 552, 577, 620
aid to Spain, 225, 235, 236, 257–60, 263, 279, 305, 315, 611–12. *See also* under different countries

Aiguadé Miro, Artemio (1889–1946), 426, 428
Aiguadé Miro, Jaime (1882–1943), 435, 529, 550, 551
Air Force, 39, 119 fn, 156, 206, 209
    Nationalist, 401
    Republican, 478, 489, 599, 600
Air France, 580
air-raids, 265, 317, 326, 329, 403, 419, 420, 421, 422, 440, 480, 513, 523, 527, 616. *See also* Barcelona
Aitken, George (*b.* 1894), 239 fn, 376, 378, 390 fn, 460 fn, 463, 465, 472. *See also* Basque provinces
Álava, 54, 77, 148, 168, 169, 344, 401
Alba, 17th Duke of (Jacebo Stuart Fitzjames y Falcó) (1878–1953), 329, 487, 488, 524 fn, 554, 585 fn
Albacete, 51, 151, 164, 204, 299, 300, 301, 303, 304, 337, 342, 377, 494, 534, 577, 602, 623
Albaicín, El, 159
Aibania, 277, 509, 603 fn
Albatross (German patrol ship), 440
Alberti, Rafael (*b.* 1902), 496
Albertía, Mt, 403
Albiñana y Sanz, Dr José María (1883–1936), 63, 268
Albornoz y Liminiana, Álvaro de (1879–1954), 23, 27 fn
Alcalá de Henares, 23, 24, 157, 242, 383, 594, 596
Alcalá Zamora, Niceto (1877–1949), 36, 45, 47, 76, 78, 88, 89, 90, 92, 93, 103, 104, 107
Alcañiz, 521, 545 fn
Alcantarilla, 301
Alcázar, The (Toledo), 156–7, 203–4, 255, 265, 277, 280, 282, 283, 284, 287, 320, 383, 423
Alcázar de San Juan, 174
Alcorcón, 317
Alcubierre, 525
Aldasoro, Ramón María de, 345
Aleubierre, Sierra de, 237
Alexander, A. V. (later Viscount Alexander of Hillsborough) (*b.* 1885), 411

ned in Bilbao, 369; 373; resign from Generalitat, 405; 419; and Barcelona riots, 424–8; and Communists, 429 fn; support Largo Caballero, 431–2; eclipse of, 434; refuse to join Negrín's Cabinet, 435; 443, 446; criticise Republican Government, 489; and Communists, 491; join Communists against Prieto, 527; agree to support Negrín, 529; in Republican Army, 550 fn; and decline of, 567; escape to France, 572–3; support plotters against Negrín and Communists, 586; and defeat of Republicans, 611; and exile in France, 620. *See also* CNT, FAI

Andalusia, 6, 16, 26 fn, 31, 38, 42, 49, 50, 51, 56, 75 fn, 135, 136, 141, 151, 152, 164, 170 fn, 181, 193, 204, 252, 265, 273, 281, 356, 372, 570, 602

André, Edgar (1894–1936), 324

André Marty Battalion, 326, 375, 376. *See also* International Brigades

Andújar, 194, 348, 422

Anfuso, Filippo (*b.* 1901), 333, 371, 486, 509

Angell, Sir Norman (*b.* 1872), 393

Anglo-Italian 'Gentleman's Agreement, 337 fn

Anglo-Italian Mediterranean Agreement, 530–1, 553, 555, 561, 613

Annemasse, 459

Ansaldo, Major Juan Antonio, 63, 117 fn, 162, 485

anticlericalism, 22, 56, 67, 78

Anti-Comintern Pact, 332, 503

Anti-Fascist Militias Committee, 158, 187, 190, 192, 236, 288

Anti-Fascist Revolutionary Alliance, 145

Antón, Francisco, 492, 620

Antonov-Ovseenko, Vladimir Alexeivich (1884–193?), 262, 363, 425, 453, 455, 621

Anual, defeat of, 15

Aosta, Amadeo, Duke of (1898–1942), 383

Aosta, Duke of, *see* Amadeo I

Aragón, 16, 150, 191, 209, 273, 276, 280, 288, 300, 324, 327, 351, 363, 364, 381, 382, 443, 504, 533 fn

Catalan offensive in 1936, 179 fn, 189, 205, 237, 240, 242

Republican offensive in 1937, 472–5, 478–9, 480

Nationalist offensive in 1938, 519, 522, 524, 542, 612

Aragon, Louis (*b.* 1897), 326

Arana-Goiri, Sabino (1865–1903), 55

Aranda (Burgos), 165

Aranda Mata, Colonel (later General) Antonio (*b.* 1888), 148, 151, 161, 254, 282, 479, 480, 507, 511, 514, 515, 519, 521, 524, 525, 530, 533, 541, 618

Aranguren Roldán, General José (1875–1939), 145, 268

Araquistain Quevedo, Luis (1886–1959), 68, 105, 107, 270, 318, 365 fn, 382 fn, 435, 509, 605

Arauz de Robles, José María, 412 fn

Areilza y Rodas, José María (later Conde de Motrico) (*b.* 1909), 603

Arenaldo, 49

Arenas de San Pedro, 276

Arganda, 376, 379

Argelès, 576

Argentina, 232, 605

Arias, General, 547, 549

Arin, Joaquín, Archpriest of Mondragón, 484

Aristimuño, Father José, 484

Armentía, Colonel, 591

Armstrong Company, 210

Army, the, 6; and possible revolt, 7–8; and role in Carlist Wars, 12–13; and campaign against the Riff, 15–16, 24; and the Republic, 39; and role in political life, 57–60; and Azaña's measures, 58; and conscription, 59; and Moroccan Wars, 59; dissatisfaction in, 59–60, 95; and Franco, 100 fn; and Azaña, 103, 110, 111; and Franco, 117; and rebellion, 129, 141; and Freemasonry, 139 fn; and the PSUC, 190, 209

Nationalist, 229, 291, 483, 488, 610

Republican, 365, 381, 382, 491–3, 504, 507, 575, 576, 589, 599, 600, 607

Army of Africa, the (Nationalist), 59, 109, 117, 119, 120, 138, 144, 151, 153, 162, 204, 205, 206, 244, 248,

148, 150–2, 159–60; loyal in Barcelona, 145–7; confined to barracks, 157; at Pozoblanco, 164; and García Lorca's death, 169; in Andalusia, 193; in Simancas barracks, 196; at Albacete, 204; numbers, 205; desert to Nationalists, 243–3; meeting at Badajoz, 246; in the Alcázar, 280; reorganised in Basque provinces, 290; in Santa María de la Cabeza, 307, 347, 422

Civil Service, 185

Claret y Clara, Ven. Antonio María (1807–70), 13

Claridad, 99, 105, 140, 373

Claudel, Paul (1868–1955), 173, 449

Clerk, Sir George (1874–1951), 219, 258

Clive, Lewis (1911–1938), 547

Clive, Lt.-General Sir Sidney (*b.* 1874), 270 fn.

CNT, see *Confederación Nacional del Trabajo*

Cocinas de Hermandad ('Brotherhood Kitchens'), 356

Cockburn, Claud (*b.* 1904), 523 fn.

Codo, 473

Codovilla, Vittorio (known as 'Medina' in Spain), 72, 105 fn, 215, 217, 363, 404, 442, 453, 454, 622

Cogulludo, 384

Cohen, Nat, 239

collectivisation, of restaurants in Madrid, 186; of farms, 187, 193; differences over, 192; 308, 363, 366, 367, 382, 424, 532

Collins, Norman (*b.* 1907), 222 fn

Colodny, Robert G., 315 fn

colonies, Spanish, 12, 22, 32, 33, 152, 164 fn, 235 fn

Colvin, Ian, 228 fn

Comert, Pierre (*b.* 1880), 522

Comintern (3rd Communist International), 71; agents in Spain, 72; differences with Spanish Communists, 73; VIIth Congress of, 90–1; relations with Díaz, 99 fn; 105 fn, 167, 184; relations with PSUC, 189; first reactions to war, 214–16, 232; and aid to Spain, 262–3, 295; and protests against breaches of non-intervention, 279;

294; and International Brigades, 298; and aid to Spain, 305; and aid from USA, 338; propaganda department at work, 523; 557; and Casado, 594; 611–12; aid estimated, 637

Comité International de l'Aide au Peuple Espagnol, 232

Commune de Paris Battalion, 276, 324, 346, 349. See also International Brigades

Communist Party, Spanish; and La Pasionaria, 8; founded, 26; and Freemasonry, 28; characteristics and origin of, 71–3; and Asturias, 80–1; and Popular Front, 90–1; and February elections, 93; members and numbers, 99 fn; and Largo Caballero, 107; 108 fn; and murder of Calvo Sotelo, 122; and atrocities, 179; in Madrid, 185; in Barcelona (*see also Partido Socialista Unificado de Cataluña*), 190; in Valencia, 192; in Gaén and Almería, 193; in Asturias, 196; and Soviet Government, 214–17; Mussolini's obsession with, 226–7; and Fifth Regiment, 241–2; and blackout, 256; and Giral, 267; joins Largo Caballero's Government, 269–70; and Basque Government, 290; and commissars, 292; and aid to Spain, 297, 308–9; in Madrid, 315 fn, 319–20, 333; 344; and attraction for regular officers, 346; and position in Republic, 360–2; and Republican Army, 364–6; and fall of Asensio Torrado, 373; and Anarchists, 381; and Socialists, 382; idea of unification with Socialists, 382 fn; meeting of executive, 404–5; in May Riots, 424–9; and attack on Largo Caballero, 430–1; and fall of Largo Caballero, 432–3; and Negrín, 433–4; and CNT, 436; and Almería incident, 442; and destruction of POUM, 452–3; and central control, 489; and new ideas of unification with Socialists, 491; demand new elections, 492; and SIM, 493; and International Brigades, 494;

demands more aid from Germany, 556; and battle of Ebro, 557; and Chetwode Commission, 559; gives Ciano present, 561; murder plot, 565; mounts new attack, 566; and future reprisals, 568; and belligerent rights, 569; English poll against, 574; and the Monarchy, 580; and decree *re* subversive activities, 581; demands unconditional surrender, 583; recognition by foreign Governments, 583-4, 585; his terms to Republic, 586; failure of Negrín's negotiations with, 587; peace terms to Casado, 598-600; and Pétain 604; and reprisals, 606-7; his rôle in war, 609-10; his future rôle, 618-19; meets Hitler, 619; and foreign aid, 635-7

Franco y Bahamonde, Nicolás (*b.* 1891), brother of General Franco, 231, 275, 286, 287, 291, 413, 415, 468, 487, 610

Franco y Bahamonde, Ramón (1896-1938), brother of General Franco, 83, 108 fn

Franco-Belgian (Sixth of February) Battalion (XIVth), 377, 461, 547.
See also International Brigades

Franco-Spanish Morrocan Agreement of 1912, 340

Franco-Spanish Treaty, 1935, 224

François Xavier of Bourbon-Parma, Prince (*b.* 1889), 76 fn, 101 fn, 126, 287, 416, 483

François-Poncet, André (*b.* 1887), 257, 259, 260, 336, 340, 441

Franklin, Sidney, 387

Freemasonry, its rôle and position in Spain, 27-8; in the Spanish Army, 59; Molas's antipathy to, 102; and rising in Morocco, 132; in the Army, 139 fn; persecution by Nationalists, 165; and the Church, 209; 358, 609

Frente Rojo, 515, 518

'Friends of Durruti', 427, 428

Fritsch, General Werner von (1880-1939), 230

Frusci, General, 509

Fry, Lieutenant Harold, 378

Fuat Baban (merchant), 295

FUE, *see Federación Universitaria Española*

Fuenteovejuna, 48

Fuentes del Ebro, 473-5

Funk, Colonel C. von ('Colonel Strunk'), 274

'Furies', the, 171

Gaeta, Mt, 549

Gaikins, 404, 434, 455

'Gal', Colonel (later General), 376, 378, 379 fn, 380, 390 fn, 460, 463, 465, 621

Galán Rodríguez, Captain Fermín (1899-1930), 18

Galán Rodríguez, Captain (later Colonel) Francisco, 201, 589, 591, 592

Galarza y Gogo, Angel, 430, 432

Galarza, Colonel Valentín (Nationalist officer), 129

Galera, General, 547, 549, 560

Galerna, Colonel, 473

Galerna (Nationalist armed trawler), 407, 411

Galicia, 4, 6 fn, 49, 51, 56, 82, 149, 395, 610

Gallegan Autonomists, 4, 97
    Nationalist, 45

Gallacher, William (*b.* 1881), 559 fn, 584

Galland, Adolf (later General) (*b.* 1912), 230, 421, 480, 525 fn, 620

Gallegan Autonomists, *see under* Galicia

Gallegan Nationalists, *see under* Galicia

Gallego (river), 478

'Gallo, El', *see* Longo, Luigi

Gambara, Colonel (later General) Gastone (*b.* 1885), 530, 561, 569, 572, 573, 581, 601, 602, 604, 621

Gamelin, General Maurice (1872-1958), 522

Gamir Ulíbarri, General Mariano, 443, 446

Gandesa, 527, 528, 547, 548, 549, 572

Gandia, 152, 602

Garabitas, Mt, Madrid, 322, 326, 329

Garcerán Sanchez, Rafael, 412 fn, 414, 415

García Aldave, General, 160

García Atadell, 176-7, 179

García Birlán, 568 fn

Macdonnel, A. G. (1895–1941), 222 fn

MacGowan, Sir Harry, *see* Imperial Chemical Industries

MacGregor (British ship), 411

Machado, Antonio (1875–1939), 23 fn, 496, 576, 608

Machado y Morales, General Gerardo (1871–1939), 122

Macía y Llusa, Colonel Francisco (1859–1933), 28–9, 53, 76

Mackenzie-Papineau Battalion, 473. *See also* International Brigades

Maclean, Donald (*b.* 1913), 220 fn

MacLeish, Archibald (*b.* 1892), 392 fn

MacNeice, Louis (*b.* 1907), 222 fn

MacNeil-Moss, Major G., 247 fn

McReynolds, Representative (Samuel Davis), 338

Madariaga y Rojo, Salvador de (*b.* 1886), 23 fn, 68 fn, 95, 97 fn, 99 fn, 209 fn, 334, 496, 551 fn

Madrid; and end of monarchy, 18, 21; Socialist strength at, 25; and Sanjurjo's rising, 63; and Communists, 71; 99 fn; and telephone strike, 74; and 1934 rising, 78–9; 87 fn; and February elections, 92, 96–7; and Falange, 102; shooting in, 118, 120; Anarchist headquarters in, 125; and 1936 rising, 126–7, 129, 135, 136–8; and arms for workers, 144; and fighting, 153–6; 159, 161, 164, 167; and Government, 171 fn, 172, 173 fn; atrocities in 176–7; 184–5; revolution in, 186–7; and Communists, 190; and battles of Sierra, 198–201; 240; and diplomatic corps, 220 fn; front at, 242; bombing of, 255–6; 263 fn, 265 fn; 267; 272; Army of the North at, 282; 291, 292; defence of, 307, 308–11, 315 fn, 316; battle of, 317–30; stalemate at, 344–6; winter battles at, 350–1; Anarchist-Communist quarrels at, 362, 365; and Nationalist plans, 399; 424, 430, 452–3, 464, 489; Writers' Congress at, 495–6; 497 fn; and food situation in 567; Casado *coup* at, 586–93; new

civil war in, 596–8; Casado leaves, 598; fall of, 602; 612

Alcalá, Calle, 38, 39, 40, 60, 592

Architecture, School of, 327

Ateneo Club, 27

Cancer, Institute of, 328

Casa de Campo, 157, 180, 319, 322, 324, 325, 327, 430, 597, 601

Castellana, Paseo de la, 104, 106, 596, 597

Clinical Hospital, 328, 601

Don Juan Barracks, 319

East Cemetery, 104, 124, 126

El Pardo, 156, 174, 353

España, Plaza de, 155, 319, 328

Florida Hotel, 325, 389, 495

Fundación del Amo, 319

Gaylord's Hotel, 262

Gran Vía, 319, 324

Gran Vía Hotel, 325

Hygiene and Cancer, Institutes of, 328

Independencia, Plaza de, 597

Liria, Palacio, 329

Manuel Becerra, Plaza, 597

Military Hospital, 326

Model Prison, 103, 156, 177, 224, 268, 319, 321, 328, 413, 607

Moncloa, Plaza de la, 328

Montaña Barracks, 153, 154, 155, 203 fn, 268, 319, 322

National Palace, *see* Royal Palace

North Station, 127

Nuestra Señor del Amparo, Convent of, 174

Palace Hotel, 106, 185

Philosophy and Letters, Hall of, 327, 328

Pontejos Barracks, 121, 122, 379

Prado, the, 3, 329 fn, 577, 604

Princesa, Calle de la, 328

Puerta del Sol, 3, 121, 140, 142, 156, 157, 595, 597

Radio Madrid, 106, 135, 140, 143, 146, 315, 322, 325

Retiro Park, 596

Rosales, Paseo de, 319

Royal Palace, 9, 107, 140, 157, 178, 319

San Ramou (suburb), 31

Santa Cristina Hospital, 328

Segovia Bridge, 322

Sol, Puerta del, 595

Telefónica, 329

ing of Permanent Committee of
Cortes in Paris, 605; after the
war, 620; and the International
Brigades, 622
Battalion, 241. *See also* militia
Patrols Committee, Barcelona, 405
Paul-Boncour, Joseph (*b.* 1873), 522
'Paulito', *see* Konev
Pavlov, General, 138, 305, 316, 346,
350, 386, 387, 615
Paynter, William (*b.* 1903), 623
Peace Ballot, 221
peace negotiations, 335, 496–7, 518,
526, 527, 529, 535, 551–2, 554–5,
569, 583, 587, 590, 593
Pearson, Drew (*b.* 1897), 536
'*Pecosa, La*', 174
Pedregal, Manuel, 104
Pedrero García, Angel, 177 fn, 591
Peiró, Father Francisco, 31
Peiró, Juan (1887–1942), 44, 318, 619
Pemán y Pemartín, José María
(*b.* 1898), 39
Peña y Boef, Alfonso (*b.* 1889), 512
Peñarredonda, Colonel Pedro, 545,
547
Peñarroya, 210, 430
Peninsular News Service, 233
Peñon de Veléz de la Gomera, 59 fn
'People's Army', *see* Army, Re-
publican
Perea, Major (later Colonel), 241,
570
Pérez, 592
Pérez de Ayala, Ramón (*b.* 1881),
17, 353
Pérez Farras, Major, 200, 205
Perpignan, 225
Perth, 16th Earl of (Sir Eric Drum-
mond) (1876–1951), 227, 514, 530,
538, 540, 561, 562, 573
Pestaña, Angel, 44 fn
Pétain, Marshal Henri (1856–1951),
357, 604, 619
Petit Parisien, Le, 353 fn
Phillips, A. V., 607 fn
Phipps, Sir Eric, 463 fn
Piatakov, Grigorii Leonidovick, 363
fn, 382
Picasso, Pablo Ruiz (*b.* 1881), 421
Picosa, Mt, 560
Pikoketa, 249
pilots, 224, 270, 422
American, 339

French, 224, 226
German, 230, 231, 235, 259. *See
also* Condor Legion
Italian, 226, 259, 337, 561
Russian, 337, 368
Pina, 237, 238, 525
Pindoque bridge, Jarama, 375, 376
Pinell, 560
Pingarrón, Mt, 374, 378, 380
Pinilla, Colonel, 196, 354
Pitman, Senator Key (1872–1940),
338
Pius XI, Pope (Aquiles Ratti) (1857–
1939), 17, 34, 36, 37, 67; attitude
to Republicans, 281; attitude to
Nationalists, 358; and the Basques,
358, 406; and Guernica, 420;
and murdered priests, 449; and
Basque priest, 451; 467; and truce,
570
Pius XII, Pope, *see* Pacelli, Eugenio
Pizzardo, Mgr Guiseppe (later Cardi-
nal), (*b.* 1877), 90 fn, 420 fn
Plymouth, Ivor, 2nd Earl of (1889–
1943), 279 fn, 284, 291, 292, 310,
331, 334, 335, 421, 463, 464, 509,
514
Poe, Edgar Allan, 526
Poland, 258, 277, 296, 395, 536, 557,
615
in International Brigades, 324,
328, 379 fn, 465
political prisoners, 267–8, 269, 290,
321, 356, 357, 368, 369, 573, 607
Pollard, Major Hugh, 119
Pollard, Miss, 119
Pollensa, Bay of, 279
Pollitt, Harry (1890–1960), 335 fn,
348 fn, 508, 519 fn, 623
Polo, Carmen, 82
Ponte y Manso de Zuniga, General
Muguel (1882–1952), 39, 58, 96,
150, 151, 180, 231, 240, 473
Ponteferrada, 161
Popolo d'Italia, 456
Popular Front, Spanish, 72, 90, 91,
92, 93, 94, 96, 97, 100, 103–4,
105 fn, 107, 111, 119, 132, 138,
139, 143, 150, 152, 160, 161, 162,
165, 166, 169 fn, 171, 174 fn,
176, 186, 197, 199, 213, 269, 300,
304, 320, 342, 390 fn, 491
French, 123, 214, 219, 295 fn,
579 fn

ABOUT THE AUTHOR

Hugh Thomas was born in Windsor, England, in 1933. He took a first in History at Queen's College, Cambridge, and spent a year at the Sorbonne. He was in the Foreign Office from 1954–1956 and in 1957 was lecturer in politics at the Royal Military Academy, Sandhurst. Mr Thomas, who has had two novels published in England, started work on this book in the summer of 1957. Of his research he says: 'I have consulted nearly a thousand books or pamphlets in Spanish, English, French, German and Italian. I have also consulted many newspapers in the same languages. I have had access to a certain amount of unpublished material, including diaries, and special papers. I have visited all the main battlefields in Spain itself and in most cases carefully worked over the development of the battles. This I have done both in battles in the countryside and in towns. I have studied during the preparation of the book in the libraries of Madrid, Barcelona, Paris, London and Cambridge.' Hugh Thomas at present lives in London.

COLOPHON BOOKS ON EUROPEAN HISTORY